Decade o

Malaya and the Stru ... us

1936–194

Decade of Change

Malaya and the Straits Settlements
1936–1945

Bryan C. Cooper

Graham Brash, Singapore

Email: 106347.2433@COMPUSERVE.COM
or BRYAN_COOPER_3

First published in 2001 by
Graham Brash (Pte) Ltd., Singapore
Mailing Address:
Jurong Point Post Office
P.O. Box 884
Singapore 916430

Email: oses@pacific.net.sg
Web Site: www.grahambrash.com

ISBN: 981-218-062-1

Cover design by Xuan Studio
Typeset by Semantic Graphics, Singapore
Printed in Singapore by Seng Lee Press Pte Ltd

CONTENTS

PREFACE

My book project was started in 1982. After four years of research, writing began in 1986 and was completed in mid-1992. Editing and re-editing for various reasons has been a protracted exercise, extending up to the present time.

Interest in my subject arose by courtesy of Her Britannic Majesty's government when I was posted to Singapore and Malaya in 1958 where I passed the next three years with the British army in Malaya at a place called Kenya Camp, some seventeen miles south of Kota Tinggi and eighteen miles north of Singapore.

This was a fascinating introduction to what became a long career. For the ensuing 34 years I had the good fortune to live in Malaysia, where I was fully involved with, and I hope contributed to, the rubber, oil palm, cocoa, coconut and tea plantation industries which form such a vitally important contribution to Malaysia's success in the 20th century.

Spending so much time in a country essentially foreign to my origins and birth undoubtedly implies a willingness to do so. I came to love the country and its multi-racial vibrant people and admired its many achievements. Living there, and always being made welcome, also made me want to enquire into the country's past, particularly that awesome period of turmoil when devastating events and outside influences over-ran this lovely land of natural abundance and relative calm. For the duration of the 1941–1945 Pacific war of foreign giants, peace-loving people paid the price and suffered. This is part of the chronicle I have endeavoured to relate — I trust with sufficient detail and accuracy, and without intent to offer offence. History might sometimes offend later generations but the greater offence is not relating it in truthfulness and thereby not learning from it.

Diversity has a maturing influence. With the decline of Imperialism, Malaya's post-war destiny developed the nation into its present status with dignity. I have not touched on the frightful twelve-year period of the Emergency that embroiled the country from mid-1948, as this has been written about by various accomplished authors.

Decade of Change is my contribution to the country in which it was a pleasure to spend many years.

B.C Cooper
Storrington
January 2001

ACKNOWLEDGEMENTS

I would like to thank my wife Maria for typing much of my research notes and my daughter Charlottee for her assistance during vacations in draft proof reading. Also I would like to thank Miss Hon Phaik Im who as my secretary in Plantations Agencies Sdn Bhd from 1988 to 1992, in addition to her heavy work load, also draft proof read and corrected spelling errors.

I would like to thank Mr Lam Chee Thye, the Manager of the Fima bookshop in Penang, for introducing me to Mrs Choo Campbell, owner of Graham Brash Publishers Pte Ltd, in May 1985. My thanks to Choo and Donald Campbell for their patience and encouragement during the ensuing six and a half years that it took me to complete the book. Editing has spanned several years. I am greatly indebted to my friend Mrs Edith Jeffery for all her patience and the vast number of corrections and improvements she made to the final text.

There are many other people who have helped me in one form or another, and if I have omitted any in the passage of time, it is entirely unintentional and I apologise. I would like to thank Mr Lim Kok Jin and Abdul Rahim bin Che Din at the Penang Museum for their initial research assistance; Miss Tang Wan Fong, Mrs Chang Siew Lai, Cik Fawzia Dawood (Assistant Librarian, Reference and Information Division) and Miss Yvonne Rasen at the library of Universiti Sains Malaysia in Penang for their help during the times I spent in that library and for subsequent information provided. Mohd Zailani bin Zakaria, the Chief Librarian at the Penang Public Library at the Dewan Sri Penang, was always considerate to my requests to search through old newspapers and documents about Penang. His knowledge of Penang was greatly appreciated. I also thank Dr Jagjit Singh Sidhu, PhD (Lon), Dip Law (Lon), Barrister at Law (Greys Inn), for his interest and assistance in providing me with useful research material.

Mr Ian Danson (Second Secretary Information, British High Commission in Kuala Lumpur) provided names and addresses of people from whom further research material was sought. Thanks to R.J. Tolley, Managing Director of Datuk Keramat Holding Bhd in 1985, for introducing me to Tuan Haji Yahaya bin Harun. Dr Alice Prochaska, Assistant Keeper Search Department and the staff of the Public Records Office, Kew, London, assisted in locating research documents. Also Miss Jane Carmichael, Keeper of the Department of Photographs at the Imperial War Museum, helped by sending requested photographs for inclusion in this work. The Manager of the Downing Street branch of the Hongkong and Shanghai Banking Corporation and the Controller, Group Archives of that bank in Hong Kong are thanked for their search of the archives and for sending me copies of letters written by their Manager in Penang, Mr N. De P. Fuzzey, on 16th December 1941.

I would like to thank Colonel Ariffin Rosli of HQ 2nd Division, Penang for permission to take photographs of some military buildings of historical interest in Penang, and Major Harbans Singh who accompanied me on such missions. Also Mr Tan Sau Hock for his introduction to Mr Law Joo Keun with whom an interesting interview was arranged. A special mention of appreciation is recorded of the late Sjovald Cunyngham-Brown, author of *The Traders* and *Crowded Hour*, for his moral support and interest.

My thanks also to all contributors of personal letters from people who were in Penang or Malaya during the 1940s, including: Messrs J. Childs, R.M. Skinner, S.R. Pettitt, P. Daintry, S.D. Lewis, E.W. Molesworth, G.R. Pitcher, Capt A.L. McLeod, Commissioner F.W. Harvey, Colonel C.H. James (Retd) and Mr R. Laird who, in addition to his letters, also provided some coastal photographs of Penang. I thank Miss S. Cowen of *The Daily Express* Readers' Letters Department for providing articles by war correspondent O.D. Gallagher, and Mr C. Seaton, the Librarian of *The Spectator* for sending two copies of the 'Letter to the Editor' columns on reports of Japanese camp conditions. I am also grateful to the Lady Orchid Photo Studio at Pulau Tikus, Penang for their professional assistance in photographing and printing the various material I presented to them.

I also wish to thank all persons who kindly allowed me to interview them, including: Sister Xaverine, Dr Arnold Warltier, Mr Hugh Watts, Mr Pothera Sreedharan, Mr Law Joo Keun, Mrs Lily Cordea De Seira, the Very Reverend Father I.I. Aloysius, Brother Anthony McNamara and Mr Heah Joo Seang.

None of the sources I have listed are responsible for any errors of fact or omissions. For these I am responsible, and any views expressed in this book are my own.

Storrington
January 2001

ABBREVIATIONS

AA	Ack-Ack (Anti-aircraft).
ABDACOM	American, British, Dutch and Australian Command.
AEBUS	Anti-Enemy Backing Up Society.
AFC	Air Force Cross.
AJUF	Anti-Japanese United Forces (Chinese communist groups operating behind Japanese lines in Malaya. Originally called MPAJA.)
AMS	Askar Melayu Setia (Loyal Malay Army).
ARP	Air Raid Precautions.
BBC	British Broadcasting Corporation.
BMA	British Military Administration.
CB	Companion, Order of the Bath.
CCP	Chinese Communist Party.
CBE	Commander, Order of the British Empire.
C-in-C	Commander-in-Chief.
CIAM	Central Indian Association of Malaya.
CID	Criminal Investigation Department.
CMG	Companion, Order of Saint Michael and Saint George.
CO	Colonial Office, London.
C of A	Council of Action.
DCCAO	Deputy Chief Civil Affairs Officer.
DO	District Officer (Civil servant in charge of an administrative district).
DPP	Deputy Public Prosecutor.
DSC	Distinguished Service Cross.
DSO	Distinguished Service Order.
E & O	Eastern and Oriental (Hotel).
EWA	Eurasian Welfare Association.
FFEPOW	Federation of Far East Prisoners of War.
FIPG	Free India Provisional Government.

FMS	The Federated Malay States, 1896–1942 (Perak, Selangor, Negeri Sembilan and Pahang).
GCVO	Knight/Dame. Grand Cross, Royal Victorian Order.
GEACS	Greater East Asia Co-Prosperity Sphere.
GHQ	General Headquarters.
GLU	General Labour Union.
GOC	General Officer Commanding.
HMS	His Majesty's Steamship.
HQ	Headquarters.
IGHQ	Imperial General Headquarters.
IIL	Indian Independence League.
INA	Indian National Army.
INC	Indian National Congress.
INCP	Indian National Congress Party.
JMA	Japanese Military Administration.
KCB	Knight Commander, Order of the Bath.
KRIS	Kesatuan Rakyat Indonesia Semenanjung (Union of Special People).
KMT	Kuomintang (Chinese Nationalist Party).
KMM	Kesatuan Melayu Muda (Young Malay Union).
MAS	Medical Auxillary Service.
MB	Menteri Besar.
MBC	Malayan Broadcasting Corporation.
MCS	Malayan Civil Service (Consisted, up to 1942, of three language streams: Malay, Chinese and Indian. Chinese language officers served in the Chinese Protectorate. Indian language officers served in the Labour Department).
MC	Military Cross.
MCP	Malayan Communist Party.
MCYC	Malayan Communist Youth Corps.
MGLU	Malayan General Labour Union.
MMA	Malayan Military Administration.
MOCAJMS	Malayan Overseas Chinese Anti-Japanese Mobilisation Society.

MPAJA	Malayan People's Anti-Japanese Army (Renamed AJUF towards the end of the war).
MPAJASCA	Malayan People's Anti-Japanese Army Ex-Service Comrades Association.
MPAJU	Malayan People's Anti-Japanese Union.
MP	Military Police.
MWA	Malay Welfare Association.
OBE	Order of the British Empire.
OCA	Overseas Chinese Association.
OCAJA	Overseas Chinese Anti-Japanese Army.
OCBC	Overseas Chinese Banking Corporation Ltd.
OCPD	Officer Commanding Police District.
ODO	Outdoor Officer.
PMS	Persatuan Melayu Selangor.
PNI	Partai Nasionalis Indonesia.
POL	Petrol, Oil and Lubricants.
POW	Prisoner of War.
PPC	Peace Preservation Committee.
PSC	Penang Service Committee.
PWD	Public Works Department.
P & PW	Penang and Province Wellesley.
RAF	Royal Air Force.
RAMC	Royal Army Medical Corps.
RIN	Royal Indian Army.
RN	Royal Navy.
RNVR	Royal Naval Volunteer Reserves.
SACSEA	Supreme Allied Commander South East Asia (Lord Louis Mountbatten).
SEAC	South East Asia Command.
SMYC	San Min Chu Yi Youth Corps.
SOS	Save Our Souls.
STS	Special Training School.
SSVS	Straits Settlements Volunteer Forces.
SS	Straits Settlements (A British Crown Colony comprising Singapore, Penang and Malacca, 1867–1942).
TB	Tuberculosis.

UMS	Unfederated Malay States (Perlis, Kedah, Trengganu and Kelantan, 1909–1942; Johore 1910–1942).
US	United States (of America).
USSR	Union of Soviet Socialist Republics.
VD	Volunteer Officers' Decoration; Venereal Disease.
YMCA	Young Men's Christian Association.

GLOSSARY OF TERMS

Malay	English
Amah	Children's nurse.
Asli	Original
Ayer	Water, liquid.
Baba	Straits-born Chinese.
Bahang	Glowing hot.
Bahasa	Language.
Bangsa	Race, nationality.
Batu	Rock (hence Batu Ferringhi — Foreigner's Rock), stone, jewel, measure of distance (one mile).
Bayan	Parroquet.
Besar	Large, great (hence, 'tuan besar' — great gentleman).
Bukit	Hill (as in Bukit Timah).
Bunga	Flower.
Chawangan	Branch (office).
Gunong	Mountain.
Haji	Honorific; title for one who has made the pilgrimage to Mecca.
Hidup	Alive.
Hitam	Black.
Jaga	Watchman of business premises, warehouse or residence (usually Sikh).
Jalan	Road, path.
Jati	Genuine, real, original.
Kampong	Village, group of rustic dwellings.
Kapitan China	Head of Chinese community (der. Portuguese).
Kati (Katty)	Unit of weight of 16 tahil, equivalent to 1.33 lbs (English measure).
Kesatuan	Union, association.
Ketua	Oldest person, chief, leader.

Kuala	River mouth (hence, Kuala Lumpur — muddy estuary).
Kuching	Cat.
Lebar	Wide.
Lebuh	Street, main road.
Lembaga	Board.
Lepas	Loosed, freed.
Lumpur	Mud.
Majlis	Council.
Mata	Eye.
Maung	Disgusting smell.
Melayu	Malay.
Menteri	Minister.
Menteri Besar	Chief minister of a Malay state.
Muda	Young.
Negeri	State.
Orang	Person, people.
Orang Asli	Aborigine.
Padi	Rice.
Pagar	Fence.
Pahat	Chisel.
Paya	Swamp.
Pemuda	Youth.
Pena	Pen.
Penghulu	Leader; head of administrative unit within a district, i.e. parish.
Persatuan	Federation, association, society.
Picul	100 kati.
Pulau	Island.
Raya	Great.
Sahabat	Friend, follower.
Saudara	Brother, sister, relative, comrade.
Sembilan	Nine.
Setia	Loyal, true (country).
Sungei	River (hence, Sungei Siput).
Tahil	Unit of weight equivalent to 1.33 oz or 37.8 gm.

Tanjong	Headland.
Telok	Bay.
Tikus	Rat.
Timbalan	Vice, deputy.
Tuan	A Malay form of addressing superiors, equivalent to 'sir'.
Ugama	Religion.
Utusan	Mail, correspond.
Warta	News.
Watanian	Fatherland, related to mother country.

Japanese	**English**
Bakayaru	Fool.
Banzai	The 'cheer' word in Japanese; literally, 'may the era live for ten thousand years'.
Bunka Eiga Gekijio	Government Propaganda Unit.
Bushido	Literally, 'the way of the Samurai'; the principles of loyalty and honour followed by the samurai.
Butai	A Japanese Army company.
Dai Toa Senso	War of Great East Asia.
Giyu Gun	Volunteer Army, comprised mostly of Malays, Indians and a few Chinese.
Giyu Tai	Volunteer Corps (as above).
Gunseikan	Governor.
Hakko Ichiu	Universal brotherhood of man.
Heiho	Regular army auxillary attached to a military establishment; liable for active service — mostly Malays and Indonesians.
Heika	Literally, 'Lord'; equivalent of 'Majesty'.
Jikeidan	Self Defence Corps.
Kaigan Setsu	Empire Day.
Kaisha	A big Japanese business concern.
Kame	Tortoise (political police).
Kamikaze	Divine wind.
Katakana	Japanese alphabet.

Kempeitai	Military Police (Japanese secret police).
Kikisui	Floating chrysanthenum.
Kinrohositai	Volunteer Serivce Unit.
Koa Kunrenjo	Youth leadership training school.
Kogyo Gakko	Trade school.
Kumiai	Syndicate, association, or guild.
Meiji	Posthumous name for Emperor who reigned from 1867 to 1912.
Nippon-go	The Japanese language.
Nomu Kacho	Agricultural chief.
Rei	Bow.
Sangikai	State council.
Seicho	State or provincial government concerned only with civil affairs.
Seicho Dobokuka	State technical training school.
Seishin	The Japanese concept of spiritual strength and the ultimate in courage and devotion to country and Emperor.
Shi	City.
Shikan Gakkos	Teacher training schools.
Shimbun	Newspaper.
Shinto	Literally, 'the way of the gods'.
Sho Cho	District police officer.
Shokoka	Commerce school.
Shu Saikan	State lottery.
Somubocho	Director General.
Syonan	Singapore.
Syurei	State order.
Tenno	Literally, 'Son of Heaven'; reigning emperor (either male or female).
Tenno-Heika	His Imperial Majesty the Emperor.
Tokubetsu	Government.
Tonarigumi	Neighbourhood Association.

Chinese	**English**
Ho Pi Tui	Reservist, volunteer.

Kee Tong	Medium.
Towkay	Head of family; a complimentary form of salutation used only when addressing a Chinese.

Hindustani	**English**
Azad Hind Fauz	Free India Army.
Chalo	On to; advance to.
Chit	Note; signed bill.
Jai Hind	Long live.
Mahatma	Great soul.
Shalid	Martyr.
Swaraj	Independence.

CHRONOLOGY

1902: Anglo-Japanese Alliance

This Alliance arose out of mutual British/Japanese concern over Russian interests in Manchuria threatening Britain's China interests and Japan's in Korea. It was a diplomatic triumph for Japan, permitting her as an ally to purchase high quality military equipment. It enabled Britain to withdraw forces from the Far East and elsewhere to strengthen her position closer to home.

1904–5: Russo-Japanese War

On 10th February 1904 Japan declared war on Russia after diplomatic negotiations failed to achieve Russian troop withdrawal from Manchuria. On 13th April the Russian fleet was defeated outside Port Arthur, which was not overrun on land until January 1905, with substantial casualties and losses to both sides. The war ended in May 1905 after Admiral Togo had decimated the Russian Baltic Fleet in the Tsushima Straits. Japan's resources were strained to their limit to achieve this stunning psychological victory which placed her firmly in control of Korea, embarrassing the Tsarist regime and enhancing her prestige as the first Asian nation to defeat a major European power.

1907: Fourth Hague Convention

The Convention established principles regarding the humane treatment of captives and the entitlement of all captured troops and non-combatants to prisoner of war status. It stipulated permissible work undertaken by POWs, standards of living and food, maintenance of records, and access for relief organisations such as the Red Cross. Japan was bound by the regulations established at the Convention.

1914–18: Japan and Britain, Allies in World War I

Japan was determined to extend her influence in Asia and the Pacific, and the war in Europe in 1914 provided a good opportunity to do this.

By declaring war on Germany she gained a foothold in China, annexing German leaseholds and concessions. Britain was criticised by Australia and New Zealand for allowing Japan to seize Pacific island territory from Germany as this posed a threat to Australia's north coast. The war stimulated the growth of Japan's navy, which by 1919 comprised 2 million tons, with 57 major shipyards producing more tonnage.

1919: Treaty of Versailles

The Treaty confirmed Japanese territorial gains obtained in the 1914–18 war, making Japan the dominant power in Asia and the Western Pacific. At the Paris Peace Conference the Chinese delegation, strongly supported by the United States, tried to redress Sino-Japanese differences arising from these territorial gains, but was not successful. Although the Conference did not recognise the validity of Japan's annexation of German leaseholds in China, or her 21 Demands on China, Japan remained in *de facto* control of the areas. The Treaty fostered some of the grievances which culminated in the outbreak of World War II.

1921: Abrogation of Anglo-Japanese Alliance

Britain's decision to decline renewing the Anglo-Japanese Alliance was looked on by Japan as an insult. Prompted by signs of Japan's expansionist plans in the Pacific, and pressure from the United States to limit Japan's naval power, a four-power pact to which England, France, Japan and the US were signatories replaced the Anglo-Japanese Alliance.

November 1921 — February 1922: Washington Conference on Naval Limitation

This Treaty was signed by Britain, France, Japan and the US on 6th February 1922. The Western victors of World War I aimed to limit Japan's naval expansion. It was viewed by voters and the growing militarist regime in Japan as an insult and an attempt to relegate Japan to an inferior power status. Three major topics were included in the Conference's agenda:

a) To find a system which would guarantee a stable balance of power in East Asia.
b) To limit naval arms.
c) To solve the China and Shantung problem.

By 13th December 1921 a four-power pact was agreed whereby the power balance in East Asia was ratified. Japan was successful in imposing restrictions on new naval base construction so that the US agreed not to build any in the Philippines, Aleutian Islands and Guam. Britain agreed similarly in respect of Hong Kong and also in any position east of 110 degrees longitude, except in Canada, Australia and New Zealand. In exchange Japan undertook not to construct bases on various islands, including Formosa, or the previous German territories she had gained in the 1914–18 war. She was forced to maintain a fleet only three-fifths the size of the British and US fleets. The 3:5:5: ratio still gave Japan naval dominance in the Western Pacific and along the China coast, but was not to her liking. She regarded these restrictions as insulting and an attempt by Western powers to deny her equal world status. It compelled her to concentrate on Asian affairs.

The Treaty remained valid until 1936, and from the date it was signed Anglo-Japanese relations grew increasingly strained. It was effective in checking the armaments race, but also resulted in the decision to construct the Singapore Naval Base, located at 100 degrees longitude.

1924: The United States Immigration Act

This Act discriminated against Asiatics, making them unacceptable as immigrants into the US. It produced an outburst of Japanese indignation. Japan seethed while nursing her hurt pride, viewing the Act as unjustified discrimination. By 1924 Japan was convinced that she was a victim of Anglo-American conspiracy.

August 1928: The Kellog-Briand Pact

By the terms of this Pact Britain, France, Germany, Italy, Japan and the United States agreed to renounce aggressive war.

1928: The Pact of Paris

Sixty-three signatories, with Japan one of them, agreed to this Pact which effectively moved to outlaw war except for reasons of self defence.

1929: The Tanaka Memorial

Baron Tanaka was Prime Minister of Japan from 1927 to 1929. In July 1929 he presented his 'notorious blueprint of invasion' to the Emperor, to solve Japan's economic woes and provide living space for her population, growing at 700,000 yearly. The blueprint was a plan for the Yamata Race (Japanese) to over-run half the world in the next generation – China first, followed by South East Asia, India, Australasia, the Middle East, Europe and then the rest of the world. When information on the Tanaka Memorial leaked out the Japanese government quickly and officially branded it a forgery.

1929: The Geneva Convention

Japan's representative signed the Convention but it was not formally ratified before Japan went to war in December 1941. The Convention required all signatories to treat future prisoners of war humanely and employ only fit POWs in work that would maintain them 'in a good state of physical and mental health'. Age, sex and physical aptitudes of individuals had to be considered when jobs were allocated. It was recognised that it was a POW's duty to try to escape, which Japan regarded as a crime punishable by death.

Realising her blunder in signing the Pact of Paris, Japan stood firmly against the Geneva Convention, arguing it would allow bombing raids from greater distances as pilots with insufficient fuel for their return could rely on bailing out to the safety of POW camps on completing their mission. In 1931 Japan circumvented the Geneva Convention by calling her offensive in China an 'Incident' and not taking prisoners.

Japan's youth were steeped in the ideology that dying for Emperor and country was a great honour. Surrender was ignominious. In 1942

Britain and the US, along with other powers, notified Japan that they would observe all the provisions of the Convention and requested her to reciprocate. The Foreign Minister, Togo, gave a formal assurance that Japan would apply the terms of the Convention, so that in the eyes of the Allies she was morally bound by it. Little or no attempt however was made to carry this out.

1930: The London Naval Conference and Treaty

Signatories were Britain, France, Italy, Japan and the United States in another effort to limit the naval arms race. Britain and the US were desperate to reduce defence costs during the Depression and preached a policy of disarmament. Their call to Japan for an extension of the 3:5:5 limitations to include non-capital ships was welcomed by the Japanese government headed by Premier Yuko Hamaguchi, who was prepared to reduce appropriations to the Imperial Navy. Hamaguchi forced the Treaty's ratification in the Japanese Privy Council, but was bitterly opposed by the Chief of Staff of the Imperial Navy and all senior officers. The Chief of Staff resigned, and in November 1930 militants attempted to assassinate Hamaguchi. Several month later he died from his wounds. The militants aspired to parity with Britain and the US. Fixing Japan's cruiser quota to an arbitrary fraction of the British and American quota was utterly obnoxious to them.

By the terms of the Treaty no new battleships could be built before 1937, and limitations were also agreed in respect of submarines, cruisers and destroyers. Article 22 dealt with aggressive action against merchant ships and catered for the safety of passengers and crews. It was deemed insufficient to put them in lifeboats unless land was nearby, or another ship could take them on board. The Treaty was allowed to expire on 31st December 1936.

September 1931: The Mukden 'Incident'

An outcome of the Russo-Japanese War was Japan's takeover of the South Manchuria Railroad Company which passed through Mukden from Port Arthur to Harbin. The world-wide slump in 1929 led to massive poverty and unemployment in Japan, causing a change of attitudes in the country. In March 1931 when the Chinese wanted to construct a new railroad parallel to the lines of the South Manchuria Railroad Company, Japan regarded it as an act of economic warfare, especially as she was settling substantial Japanese and Korean immigrants on land adjacent to the railroad and assisting them with generous loans.

In the summer of 1931 a Japanese captain was mysteriously shot by Chinese troops near Mukden. On the night of September 18th, following investigations of a small explosion in the area which slightly damaged a railway line in the city, a Japanese patrol, on the pretext of self-defence, engaged a small Chinese force at Mukden. The following morning units from Japan's Kwantung army occupied Mukden and neighbouring areas. There is adequate evidence that the Mukden 'Incident' was allowed, on a flimsy pretext, to develop into a full-scale invasion of Manchuria and was carefully planned by officers of the General Staff, along with their counterparts in the Kwantung army and members of the Cherry Society, to set up a satellite state for Japan. The conquest was completed by January 1932 when hostilities in Manchuria ended, but the *de facto* war between Japan and China continued. After Mukden the Japanese and Chinese were sworn enemies. It was the third invasion of the Chinese mainland by the Japanese, who deliberately ignored signed treaties of non-aggression, referring to the invasion as a mere 'incident'. The Japanese government was not consulted by the army prior to the attack, and protests from the League of Nations were defied.

February 1933: Japan decides to leave the League of Nations

Following China's appeal to the League of Nations over Japan's aggression in Manchuria and China, an investigative commission was appointed by the League, under the Earl of Lytton. The commission's report was submitted in September 1932. The investigation was agreed to by the Japanese government which had publicly denied China's charges of aggression. The Lytton Report conceded that Japan had important interests to protect and was likely provoked. It was forthright, however, in accusing Japan of aggression and called for voluntary withdrawal from all areas occupied by force. Japan denounced the Lytton Report and when the League of Nations expressed strong disapproval of her actions, she announced her intention of leaving the League in February 1933. Japan's representative, Yosuke Matsuoka, denounced the League's criticism as 'rude' and in his final address condemned 'certain people in Europe and America' for seeking 'to crucify Japan . . . in the 20th century'. Japan's exit from the League of Nations strengthened the opinions of militarists and additional funds were granted to modernise her army.

1934: Disarmament Conference in London

When Japan gave notice of her intention to quit the Washington Conference Treaty, due for renewal in 1936, a disarmament conference was held in London at which Britain, Japan and the United States participated. Proposals were made for an all-round reduction in naval armaments, but no agreement was reached and Japan withdrew from the conference. After negotiations failed work on the naval base in Singapore was speeded up as Japan could now blatantly expand her navy. By 1935 Japan was secretly building a naval and air base on Saipan Island, only 200 miles from the American island of Guam. Foreign travel restrictions to any of these island groups was enforced from 1933 to maintain secrecy.

December 1934: Japan abrogates the Washington Naval Treaty

The limitations of the Washington Naval Treaty irked the designers and builders of the Japanese navy. By 1934 they had told the Chief of Naval Staff that any further improvement in the quality of the fleet's material could only be achieved by ignoring these limitations. Naval officers were better educated than their army counterparts, and throughout the 1930s they grew more determined to force a showdown with Britain, Holland and the US with their enticing Far Eastern possessions. Japans two-year notice of withdrawal from the Washington Treaty indicated the first signs of internal dissent between the military and civil factions in the Japanese government. Worked immediately began to design more powerful battleships than those of Britain and the US.

July 1937: The China Incident

Protesting 'Red' lawlessness in China and attacks on the property of Japanese traders, Japanese troops opened fire on Chinese units at the Marco Polo Bridge near Peking, killing 2,700 men, women and children. Japanese commanders needed little excuse to renew hostilities against the Chinese, and the relatively minor Marco Polo Bridge incident provided it. By the end of July 1937 Peking and Tientsin were under Japanese control. Despite generous offers of settlement by Japan, Chiang Kai-Shek resolved to fight. By the beginning of September 150,000 troops of Japan's Kwantung army were involved in a full scale invasion.

The Chinese resisted fiercely in the battles for Shanghai and Nanking, but both fell by the end of the year. The Japanese incurred very heavy casualties and retaliated, particularly in Nanking, by going on a rampage of death, destruction, pillage and rape. The 'Rape of Nanking' — justified as a military necessity — involved the slaughter of 200,000 Chinese civilians and prisoners of war in the first six weeks of Japanese occupation. It was condemned as one of the most appalling crimes in modern times.

When Japan invaded China the Chinese in Singapore and Malaya organised a boycott of Japanese goods, throwing them into the streets and making a bonfire of them. On 7th July, the Double Seventh, labour organisations in Malaya connected with the Anti-Enemy Backing-Up Society (ABS), took direct action against those dealing in Japanese goods.

December 1937: Sinking of the US gunboat *Panay*

The sinking, by deliberate dive bombing on 12th December 1937, of the US gunboat *Panay*, stationed in the Yangtse River to protect American lives and property, was seen as evidence of continuing lack of restraint by Japanese forces. Despite clear American markings, two deaths and 48 casualties were caused. Japan hastily assured an outraged Washington that the incident had been a regrettable mistake and agreed to make indemnity payments.

26th February 1936: Insurrection by Army Officers

More than 1,500 men and young junior officers rampaged through the streets of Tokyo and seized all government buildings. Numerous political scandals during the previous decade led to the uprising which was prompted by the belief that the nation's problems were caused by corrupt politicians. Many junior officers, sons of poor farmers, had first-hand knowledge of the misery of the common people. They distrusted politicians and their senior officers and embarked on a course of intimidation, blackmail and assassination.

The loathed Finance Minister, Korekiyo Takahashi, was shot by rampaging 'killer officers', as were other ministers and senior officers. Another victim was the moderate intellectual and gentle former Prime Minister, Viscount Makoto Saito, who, with his wife, the evening prior to his assassination had dined with Joseph C. Grew, the US ambassador to Japan. An attempt was also made to murder the newly installed Prime Minister, Admiral Keisuka Okada who, it was thought, was trying to restrain the army's ambitions to extend into North China and Manchuria. The killings were halted abruptly after four days on orders of the Emperor and a number of ringleaders were quickly court-martialled and executed.

November 1936: Anti-Comintern Pact

Japan and Germany had designs on Russia. Part of Japan's preparations for war was to ally herself to Germany by the Anti-Comintern Pact, into which Italy was inveigled in 1937. Secret clauses made it obvious that the aim of the Pact was to threaten the USSR from both west and east. The Pact was not arranged by normal diplomatic means, but mostly by the Japanese Military Attaché in Berlin, with the Japanese Ambassador excluded from the discussions. Japan did not aim for a formal alliance with Germany at this stage as she did not want to be implicated in any future European war. The Pact provided some security to Japan against the possibility of Russian intervention under limited circumstances, plus a pledge against the spread of Communism. By strengthening her ties with Germany, Japan hoped it would have the effect of distracting Britain from Asian affairs.

15th February 1938: Opening of Naval Base at Singapore

The completion of the Naval Base in Singapore attracted world-wide attention. The project, started in 1922 following the abrogation of the Anglo-Japanese Alliance in 1921, was considered an essential measure to protect the British Empire's Far Eastern interests. Constructed on an immense scale and taking 16 years to complete, the Base cost £63 million. It was capable of sheltering an entire fleet and had two 50,000 ton dry docks, one of which was built in England in 1928 and towed out to Singapore. The siting of defences was primarily to protect the Base from amphibious attack. The defences comprised five massive 15″ naval guns, six 9.2″ guns and eighteen 6″ guns, plus secondary armament. The Naval Base was formally opened by Sir Shenton Thomas, accompanied by Lady Thomas, on 15th February 1938, precisely four years to the day before it was destroyed by the British prior to surrendering Singapore to the Japanese.

1938: Russian Forces Defeat Kwantung Army

The Kwantung army received a 'bloody nose' following their attack on USSR border forces. Emperor Hirohito, strongly critical of the action, forbade any further activities. His instructions were disregarded however and Japanese forces received another beating at Nomonham.

20th February 1938

Hitler announced German recognition of the State of Manchuko. Relations between Japan and the Western powers continued to deteriorate. The United States placed an embargo on the export of aircraft and all war materials to Japan.

March 1938: Germany Annexes Austria

Contravening the Treaty of Versailles, German troops crossed Austria's border on 12th March 1938. On the 13th Austria was proclaimed a province of the German Reich. In Vienna more than 70,000 people were arrested.

May 1938

Major-General W.G.S. Dobbie, General Officer Commanding Malaya, wrote, 'It is an attack from the Northward that I regard as the greatest potential to the Fortress. . . . The jungle is not, in most places, impassable for the infantry.'

23rd August 1939

The German-Soviet Non-Aggression Pact was signed, thereby discrediting the policies of Baron Hiranuma's cabinet. He resigned, stating that the the world situation had become 'too complicated to be understood'. The German-Soviet Pact ignored the defensive alliance and assurances given by Germany to Japan in the Anti-Comintern Pact of November 1936, enabling Russia to act as she wished in Manchuria.

1st–3rd September 1939

At 0445 hours on 1st September German forces invaded Poland without any declaration of war. Britain and France demanded an immediate withdrawal and the British army was mobilised. Young children from London were evacuated for fear of air attacks. On 2nd September frantic talks continued in London and Paris as German forces consolidated their positions, crossing the River Warta and completely dislocating Polish communications. Mussolini again reiterated Italy's neutrality and called for a peace conference.

The British parliament was opposed to Prime Minister Chamberlain's passive line and an ultimatum was presented to Germany which expired at 1100 hours on 3rd September. At 1115 hours Chamberlain broadcast to the nation that Great Britain was at war with Germany. Australia, New Zealand and France also declared war.

10th May 1940

Winston S. Churchill, First Lord of the Admiralty, succeeded Neville Chamberlain as British Prime Minister, following the disastrous Norwegian campaign. He also took over the post of Minister of Defence on 11th May 1940.

11th June 1940

Italy declared war with Great Britain and France.

June 1940

Following the outbreak of war in Europe in September 1939, the Compulsory Service (Volunteer Forces) Ordinance in Malaya and Singapore was passed compelling every male British subject to be called up for service in the Volunteer Forces, or into any other additional force that might be created for defence. A local defence corps — based on similar lines to the Home Guard in Britain — was formed in July 1940, and service was compulsory for all British subjects of pure European descent between the ages of 41 and 55 and any British subject between 18 and 41 years of age who had been granted postponement certificates in respect of the Volunteer Forces.

July 1940

A document prepared by C.A. Vieland, the first civilian Defence Secretary for Malaya appointed in 1938, about the economic importance but insignificant defence value of Singapore never became an official paper as he was asked by the Acting Governor, S.W. Jones, not to submit it.

In Japan the Yonai government resigned. Prince Fuminaro Konoye formed a pro-Axis government, having been put into power by the militarist factions. General Hideki Tojo was appointed to the Konoye cabinet as Minister of War.

27th September 1940

Japan signed the Tripartite Pact with Germany and Italy in which promises were made that each would declare war on any party that entered into a state of war against any of the three signatories. This agreement did not affect either Germany's or Japan's relations with the USSR.

16th–19th October 1940

Following discussions between the two countries, the Dutch East Indies agreed to supply Japan with 40% of her total oil requirement for the next six months. Britain attempted to block this agreement.

March–April 1941

In March the Japanese Minister of Foreign Affairs, Yosuke Matsuoka, gave emphatic assurances to the American Ambassador in Moscow that under no circumstances would Japan attack Singapore, or any American, British or Dutch possessions, and that Japan had no territorial ambitions.

Matsuoka subsequently initiated discussions with the Soviets that culminated in the five year Russo-Japanese Neutrality Agreement in April 1941. This turned out to be a bad joke on 22nd June 1941 when Germany invaded Russia.

16th–18th July 1941

In Japan a new cabinet was formed under Prince Konoye in a move to oust Matsuoka. Vice-Admiral Toyoda was appointed Minister of Foreign Affairs.

26th July 1941

Japanese assets were frozen by Great Britain, the Dutch East Indies and America. Overnight Japan was deprived of her entire oil supplies.

28th July 1941

Japan invaded Indo-China.

July–August 1941

The Japanese Ambassador to the United States, Admiral Kishisaburo Nomura, a moderate favourably inclined towards the US, gave assurances that Japan would evacuate Indo-China in return for renewed trade relations with the US.

16th October 1941

Emperor Hirohito summoned Hideki Tojo, the former Minister for War in the Konoye cabinet, to become Prime Minister and to form a cabinet. Tojo was promoted to General and on 18th October he named his new cabinet.

1st December 1941

A State of Emergency was declared in Malaya and Volunteers were called up. Rear Admiral Sir Tom Phillips was appointed Commander-in-Chief of the Eastern Fleet.

7th December 1941

Seven hundred Japanese national were arrested in Britain. Japan launched air attacks on US naval, military and air bases in Hawaii, including Pearl Harbour.

Other attacks were made on Manila, Shanghai, Malaya, Siam and Hong Kong. On the night of the 7th–8th the Japanese landed in Siam and North East Malaya. They also bombed Singapore.

PART ONE: ROAD TO WAR

CHAPTER ONE: PRIDE AND PREJUDICE

1:1 Build-Up of Resentment and Power

In 1900, General Katsuro Taro, when he was Governor General of Taiwan, drew up initial plans for Japan to invade and occupy Malaya, the Dutch East Indies and the Philippines. General Taro's plans were shelved until 1942 when, following Japan's series of quick military successes, they were revitalised and considerably expanded. The new concept ambitiously included the Middle East, South America, half of Mexico, Peru and Chile, parts of Canada and America, and all the Pacific islands, including Australia.

Rapid modernisation during the latter part of the 19th century had turned Japan into a powerful nation with a fast expanding population and ever growing needs. Her industrialisation programme had also become increasingly dependent upon imports of various natural raw materials, including iron, timber and rubber.

At the conclusion of the 19th century Japan and Russia were the main rivals for power in the Far East. Each competed with the other over Korea and Manchuria, both of which were nominally subjected to China, who was too weak to have much influence over them. In order to prevent Russian expansion into Korea, Japan declared war on China in 1895, and again, in 1904, to prevent Russian expansion into Manchuria, Japan declared war against Russia herself. In both conflicts Japan was successful. In the first, she gained the island of Taiwan (Formosa); and in the second conflict, in addition to securing enormous prestige by being the first Asian country to defeat a major European power, she gained Korea, as well as a strong influence in Manchuria. Japan was particularly attracted to Manchuria on account of two essential raw materials there that she required — coal and iron. Manchuria could also usefully serve as a settlement area for Japan's surplus and increasing population.

After China was seemingly unified under Chiang Kai-shek in 1927–8, Japan became aware that action might be taken against her interests to try and eject her from Manchuria, where the Chinese government had already encouraged many Chinese to emigrate. To forestall China in this, Japan decided to adopt her own path of ambitious aggression.

She had emerged from the 1914–18 war as a powerful country. While Europe had been locked in battle, Japan had gained significant advances in trade, and at the conclusion of the war had also gained territorial control over previous German possessions in the Far East. In 1921, therefore, Japan held a position of naval and military dominance in the East.

Although America and Japan had differing motivations towards China, their respective naval strengths augured a potential clash between them. In 1915 an American protest had prevented Japan from gaining control over China, and this had caused her to seethe with frustration. The main purpose, therefore, of the 1921–2 international conference held at Washington was to attempt to ratify the race for power in the Far East. The Nine Power Treaty signed in 1922, which sought to guarantee China's integrity, intensified Japan's grievances and the limitations imposed on her navy by the Treaty of Washington in 1921–2, which effectively restricted Japan's naval expansion plans, were all viewed as denying her the right to engage in colonial expansion.

Between 1921 and 1924 a series of further humiliations added insult to injury. Britain's polite refusal in July 1921 to renew her Alliance with Japan, which had been in operation since 1902, was taken as an insult. Britain's building of the Singapore Naval Base — intended as a check on the Japanese — was looked upon by them instead as a challenge. American legislation restricting Japanese immigration in 1924 virtually banned their entry into America and added further fuel to their burning indignation. The openly racist immigration policies adopted by Western countries during the 1920s and 1930s were bitterly resented. It seemed to the Japanese that every Western nation was granted the right to settle their people where they wished to do so, but this was being denied to them on account of their colour.

Britain became increasingly anxious about Japan's build-up in territory and power, following the conclusion of the 1914–18 war, but was in no position to oppose her. With Russian and German political and military presence having been eliminated from Eastern power-politics, Britain was therefore very anxious that the whole Far East question, as far as Japan was concerned, should be reviewed. After the First World War, Anglo-Japanese economic and naval rivalries increased, along with the growth of the Japanese navy. Japan at this early time started to see in Britain a potential enemy, or at least a rival. Britain, however, was desperate at this juncture to avoid any build-up towards war and Japan, finding herself in a position of power for the first time, behaved obdurately.

By 1924 Japan seethed under the obsession that she had become a victim of an Anglo-American conspiracy. Her national pride was fervent. She was sensitive to criticism, particularly from outsiders, and viewed the immigration restrictions into the United States as demotion to the same category as other Asian countries. This was an insult! Having gained world power status, following her involvement in the 1914–1918 war, in which she had fought as Britain's ally, Japan considered that she deserved rightful recognition and treatment, appropriate to her newly-gained status. In the 1930s Britain's support of Nationalist China therefore caused a further deterioration in relationships with Japan.

During the Depression years of the 1930s, when economic crisis engulfed the world, Japan was particularly hard hit. Arising from this, a growing discontent was exploited by the militarists to further their expansionary aims. Being almost totally dependent on outside sources for their essential raw materials made the Japanese increasingly wary of any foreign actions, and particularly of any restrictions, which they always chose to interpret as not being to their best interests.

Anti-Western feelings increased in Japan as she publicised her aspirations of territorial expansion and her concept of a new 'Co-Prosperity Sphere'. These aimed at Japanese military and economic domination throughout South East Asia.

When youth in Japan looked increasingly towards the West for entertainment and fashion, it was not surprising that this should give rise to grave annoyance particularly among militarists and also within the more conservative circles of Japanese society. American commercial influence was regarded as a defilement of ancient Japanese virtues.

New dance halls were condemned and attempts were made to force codes of restraint and austerity upon the young. Selected popular songs were banned in tea houses and cabarets, being considered too erotic and not in keeping with the dignity required of the 'Yamato' race.

Japan's motives for wanting Malaya were varied and involved economic, diplomatic and military considerations. Malaya's abundant sources of tin and rubber — Britain's top US dollar earner — were vital for her intended war effort.

Britain's attitude towards the Sino-Japanese War, her noted diplomatic weakness at Munich in September 1938, closely followed by Japan's capture of Canton — giving her control of China's main ports — all strengthened the Japanese militarists' popularity and arguments.

Japan waited for what she considered to be the ideal time before striking. The Germans had conquered France and the Japanese had entered French Indo-China. Holland had been over-run by the Germans and could do little to offer protection to the Dutch East Indies, where rubber, oil and tin were readily available. Britain was fully committed, defending herself against the German U-boat blockade, and defending the Suez Canal from capture by Italian and German armies in North Africa. Japan knew at that juncture that Britain could do little to effectively increase protection for Malaya and Burma. After defeating the Russians in 1904–5, Japan had always been fearful of a Russian revenge, but, late in 1941 Russia was fully deployed in defending herself against the Germans, and Japan realised that she was no longer a danger to her. One threat, and only one threat remained. The United States! Japan weighed the odds and decided to act, striking a telling blow on 8th December 1941 against the important American naval base at Pearl Harbour.

1:2 Rise of Militarism

Japan's triumph over Russia in 1904–05 so enhanced the prestige of the army that the Japanese believed it to be invincible. In contrast, the civil government at that time was smeared with scandal and accusations of corruption. Intense idealism brought about an explosive situation which was accentuated by increasing poverty at home and the militarists' lust for power abroad.

Although Japan was fast becoming an advanced industrial nation the heart of Japanese society remained feudal and the warrior was still regarded with special respect. Military influence, therefore, became immense. In combination with the ruling classes' power and the concept of the Emperor's divinity, it was not difficult to cultivate a patriotic, bitterly anti-foreign fervour, the underlying aim of which was to achieve ultimate Japanese domination over China and all of South East Asia. From the 1930s the military's increase in power was nurtured by threats and assassinations. This was climaxed in March 1931 when prominent opponents of the army in Tokyo were assassinated, in order to purge Hirohito of influences that might make him unsympathetic to the Army's intentions.

Political parties in Japan and their financial supporters were discredited when economic collapse caused by the Depression was accompanied by impoverishment of the peasantry. As national fervour mounted and relations with China deteriorated, extreme nationalist pro-military elements came into positions of power. Alarmed prominent businessmen voiced their indignation against the army's arrogance and the course they appeared bent on following. Other businessmen, despite misgivings that such a course of action would not be to Japan's best national interests, were prepared to go along with the new regime's policies.

By 1936, following a decade of anguish, of economic distress, abortive coups and assassinations, the military was the predominant influence in the government. It was to the militarists that the people turned for salvation and the enhancement of national pride.

In addition to their considerable powers, leaders of the military also had direct access to the Emperor. They resented the restrictions that the civil government attempted to impose on them and distrusted the party government system. If they so desired, military leaders were empowered to thwart civil government's activities.

Ultra-nationalists, who were opposed to big business and political parties alike, exploited the situation, causing economic turmoil and political confusion. It was junior officers in the military who were the main force behind the ultra-nationalists, and coming as they did from mostly rural backgrounds, they were ignorant in economic and political expertise. They distrusted the parliamentary system in general and also viewed their senior officers with suspicion.

In 1936 the assassination of many of the military's opponents in Tokyo was condemned by the Emperor, but the rift between government and army continued to widen. The former sought prosperity through peace; the latter sought it through conquest. War fever was fuelled by the Japanese army's activities in China and by the repeated references of General Hideki Tojo — then Chief of Staff to the Kwantung Army in Manchuria — to the threat from Russia. Although statements such as these conflicted with the government's policy, the military's strength was such that Tojo could not be suppressed.

Japan's blatant aggression in 1937–8 was not approved by everyone in the country. Some critics warned that it would lead to war with Britain and the United States, but reactions to this from the militarists were violent. Assassination of critics intensified, and adherence to the military's philosophy became obligatory. Japan became increasingly distant from other democracies and moved ever closer to the Axis camp. In Britain there was strong criticism of Japan's commercial activities as well as her militancy.

When Japan occupied Indo-China and announced a joint Protectorate with Vichy France in July 1941, the United States, Britain and the Netherlands retaliated by freezing Japanese assets and imposing an oil embargo. Although the cabinet of Prince Konoye professed willingness to negotiate and even to withdraw from Indo-China, the United States refused to attend any meeting unless Japan made prior concessions. On the other hand, the Japanese army had warned that any demand for troop withdrawal from China would be unacceptable to them. Thus, even before the oil embargo, war seemed inevitable.

1:3 Necessities for Survival and Expansion

Many people in Japan were poverty stricken in the early 1930s. Over 50 per cent of Japan's population were peasants and fishermen who earned less than 20 per cent of the total national income. The mountainous, tiny Japanese home islands were overcrowded, with a total population of 80 million people, and this was increasing at almost one million every year. With 2,900 people per square mile of usable farmland, Japan was the most crowded country in the world.

With such a huge population concentrated on a few islands Japan had manifold economic problems. Food imports were essential to avoid starvation. Exports of industrial products could only be made from raw materials, which the Japanese did not possess. Lacking oil, Japan was obliged to ask continually for trade concessions from Western powers. In retrospect it could well be surmised that war might have been averted had Japan softened her demands and had Western countries given her a more conciliatory hearing in the earlier stages. As it happened, however, with the militarists gaining power and the civil government's credibility disintegrating, war became inevitable — a war which, it was believed, would secure economic advantages for Japan.

The economic difficulties that plagued Japan in the 1930s paved the militarists' climb to power. They believed that the solution lay in an expansionist military policy. Japan's overpopulation and land shortage caused hardship to rural and city workers alike. She had to increase food imports, but had no money to pay for them. The world-wide depression in the 1930s caused many countries to adopt protectionist policies against Japan, thereby hampering her industrial growth. Finding more land to live on, and on which to produce more food, became a matter of sheer survival.

Japan managed to double her industrial output in the 1930s despite the economic and physical restrictions that she had to contend with. This creditable achievement, however, also intensified her oil shortage problems, especially as 80 per cent of her oil requirements came from the United States and another 10 per cent from the Dutch East Indies. It was during this period of fast industrial expansion that another expansion occurred which did not pass unnoticed amongst Western powers: Japan's allocation of funds towards military and naval expenditure soared from under 30 per cent of her national budget to over 70 per cent. By the latter part of the 1930s both army and navy chiefs realised that in order to sustain their hold over politicians and people alike, they needed new and convincing victories.

Japan's strategy against China was dual-purpose: to secure the latter's oil for Japan's own use, and to deprive China of the supplies she needed, thereby putting an end to her resistance. By 1939, however, Japan had made little progress in her attempts to conquer the inland areas of China. As this struggle was prolonged she grew increasingly aware of her vulnerability in respect of raw materials. Supplies of oil, rubber, tin and iron had become increasingly difficult to obtain owing to various restrictions imposed by producing countries, who were sympathetic to China. Japan was only able to produce 10 per cent of her own oil requirements, and it was oil that she needed for her navy to survive. Japan's aggressive intentions to achieve leading power status were therefore frustrated by her not having supplies of oil, rubber or tin readily at her disposal. Covetous Japanese eyes espied these rich prizes, which appeared, almost foolhardily, to be completely undefended and just for the taking in Malaya and the Dutch East Indies.

When Holland fell to the Germans in May 1940 and France collapsed one month later, it was thought by many that Britain was also on the brink of defeat. The chiefs of staff in London reportedly took some comfort from Japan's apparent vulnerability to economic pressure — since there was little they could spare in the way of reinforcements to Malaya. They estimated in August 1940 that even if Japan should capture the Dutch East Indies, a rigorous British and American embargo on raw materials would bring about her commercial ruin in just over a year. They underestimated the Japanese: in September 1940, as a prelude to later conquests and to secure for herself essential oil supplies, Japan attacked northern Indo-China.

Throughout her subsequent campaigns in Malaya, Burma, the Philippines and the Dutch East Indies, Japan never relinquished her original intention of isolating China from those sources of raw materials on which depended her continued ability to resist attack. Japan's other intention was to obtain these resources for use by her own massive war machine.

1:4 Divine Mission Concept

Japanese children were brought up to believe in Japan's glorious mission. Supremacy of country, and its expansion and advancement, were drummed into children's minds day and night, the aim being to make these ideals their sole interests. Shintoism, the national religion, was turned into worship of country. Children grew up believing that they had to sacrifice their lives gladly for the Emperor and motherland.

World domination was the guiding theme underlying the activities of the Greater Japan Young Men's Society. The Japanese were primed to see themselves as a master race and one that was destined to bring to an end the white man's tyrannical oppression, firstly over peoples in Southeast Asia and then in other countries throughout the world.

When Germany was repulsed at the gates of Moscow and the United States assembled a massive war machine, Japan realised that any subsequent German defeat and departure from world prominence would cast the die on her own ambitions of world domination. Many Japanese were already convinced of Japan's divine mission to lead Asia into a new era of economic expansion and prosperity. Many also considered that Japan had an unequivocal right to Asia's riches, which up to that time had mostly been in the hands of Britain, Holland and France.

1:5 Diplomatic Estrangement

As early as 1927, Tenaka, then the Japanese Premier, announced that Japan must first conquer China before she could conquer the world. From the outset of the China Incident in July 1937, and particularly following the fall of Nanking on 7th December that year, no doubts could have remained in the minds of Western nations regarding Japan's decisiveness of purpose and the depths of barbarity to which she was prepared to sink in order to achieve her expansionary goals. During the month that followed Nanking's capitulation, 100,000 victory-incensed Japanese soldiers ran amok, torturing and murdering over 200,000 surrendered Chinese soldiers and civilians and raping some 20,000 women. The Japanese army's lack of restraint, in what became referred to as the 'Rape of Nanking' sent shockwaves throughout countries of the civilised world.

Intrigue and diplomacy proceeded along inevitable courses, and the manoeuverings that resulted steadily brought about a deterioration in Japan's relationships with Allied countries. In November 1936 the Anti-Comintern Pact, which contained secret clauses, was concluded by Japan and Germany. Although not a formal alliance — as Japan did not want to be drawn into any future European war — its formation aimed to strengthen Germany's position against the Soviets and also to distract Britain from affairs in Asia.

In July 1940 Japan gained a brief success in closing the Burma Road route into China. This, however, only served to strain relationships further, as did Japan's conclusion of lengthy negotiations with the Vichy government and subsequent occupation of northern Indo-China in September 1940.

The Tripartite Pact, signed also in September 1940 with Germany and Italy, was directly aimed against the United States. Then, in blatant contradiction of the Anti-Comintern Pact's secret intent, signed four and a half years previously, Japan entered into a five-year Neutrality Agreement with the Soviet Union in April 1941.

When France capitulated in June 1940, Japan's expansionist designs suddenly came to life. Her nurtured bitterness against Britain and the United States escalated with each German victory in Europe. Japan saw in them an opportunity to disrupt finally British and American aid to China, and to seize a monopoly over Southeast Asia's rich natural resources.

Thus, war in Europe provided Japan with the chance to further her expansionist policies. An ultimatum to representatives of the Vichy government in July 1941 resulted in the declaration of a Joint Protectorate over the entire colony of Indo-China. On 28th July Japanese forces began to occupy bases in Southern Indo-China, from which aggressive moves against Malaya, the Philippines and the Dutch East Indies could be launched later. The United States' subsequent freezing of Japan's assets and refusal to hold proposed conciliatory discussions led to the resignation of Prime Minister Prince Funimaro Konoye's government on 16th October 1941. Significantly, he was expeditiously replaced by General Hideki Tojo, the Minister for War.

CHAPTER TWO: PRIME POSTING

2:1 Pre-War Treasure House

By 1937 Malaya's promises of wealth to immigrant workers were such that 89 per cent of Indian males who were new arrivals had come of their own accord and were not directly recruited into the country. Malaya — unlike other colonised countries in Southeast Asia at that time — had taken some effective steps towards improving workers' conditions of employment and renumeration. Indentured 'coolie' labour[1] had long been abolished in 1910, and in 1922 the penal sanctions system for labour offences[2] had been discontinued.

Indian labour traditionally needed considerable government assistance, whereas the Chinese neither required nor welcomed it. Guilds represented labourers from both communities up to 1940 but in 1946 all this was changed when Britain's recently-elected and peace-euphoric Labour government actively encouraged the introduction of legislation which legalised the organisation of trade unions in the country and even went to the extent of assisting workers to operate them.

Before 1941 the Labour Code[3] had introduced legislation which forbade the Truck System[4] payments in kind. The Code also established regulations governing maternity allowances, leave for women, payment of hospital fees for employees and their families, provision of nurseries for infants under three years of age, and schools for children under ten. A minimum wage rate was introduced at a level calculated to enable Tamil workers to finance a trip back to their homeland once every three years.

Not only was Malaya an attractive country for immigrant workers, but in 1939 it was also Britain's treasure house for accumulating foreign exchange. In that year, for example, Malayan exports to the United States were 25 times the value of imports from America. Priority was given by the Governor, Sir Shenton Thomas, and his administration to the production of essential war materials — rubber and tin — which were also economically vital to Britain. The Governor's well-meaning, albeit tardy, attempts to impose a gentle form of income tax were vigorously opposed by businessmen in general, who looked upon problems related to raising finances for defence purposes as being solely the military's concern. It was not for them — engaged in the all-important task of making more money — to condone it.

In 1941, approximately half of Malaya's rubber trees were owned by smallholders farming less than 100 acres each. The Chinese owned one-third of the tin mines and other large industries such as pineapple plantations and canning factories. Europeans either owned or managed large rubber and oil-palm plantations, tin mines, a variety of substantial commercial houses, and the prominent Straits Steamship Company.

2:2 The Social Scene

By 1927 Britain's administration in Malaya had brought about some remarkably good results, particularly in Penang. Turning an undeveloped and somewhat barbarous country into a prosperous place where a multi-racial population lived in relative harmony was a fine achievement. There were, however, certain concerns in which justifiable criticism continued to be expressed by the public, and one of these was education — or the lack of it. Another criticism was that the British kept aloof and made no determined attempt to intermix with the country's subject races or understand their problems. Instead, there was an ever-present overdose of pomp and ceremony, which provided the outward trappings of colonial rule. Despite the white tuan's predominance being gradually eroded, little thought was given to the possibility of a new order emerging — that there might come a time when just being white would not automatically bestow with it immunity from having one's decisions questioned.

In 1927 there was apparent racial harmony in Malaya, particularly in Penang. Pulau Penang (Betul-nut Island) derived its early Malay name from the Areca palm. Its 108 square miles are topped by a range of lofty forested hills, the slopes of which extend to the sea except in the south of the island, which is flat. When Captain Francis Light first landed in 1786 and took possession of the island in the

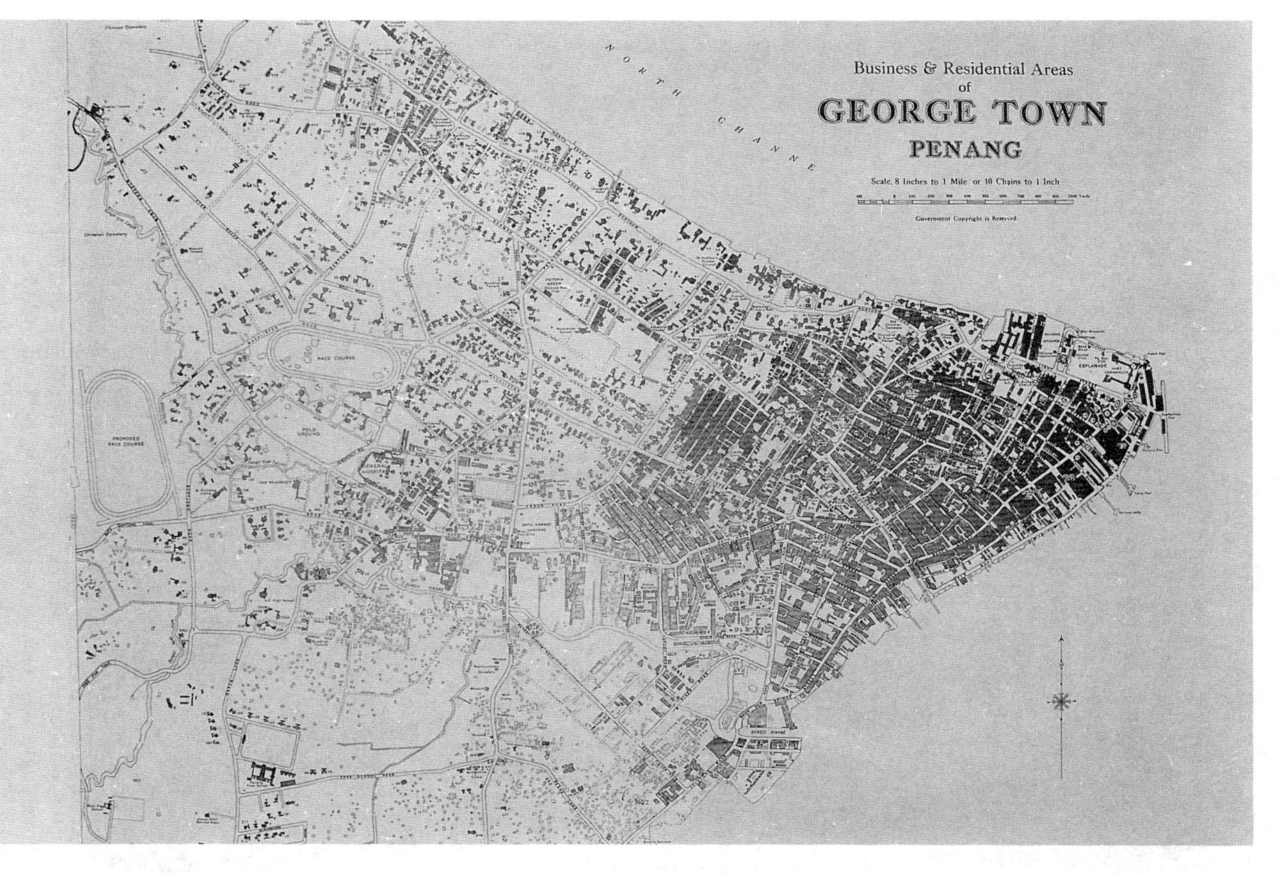

Business and residential areas of George Town, Penang. (Photo credit: 'Penang Through Old Picture Postcards', Penang Museum, Phoenix Press, Penang.)

Bronze statue (without sword and scabbard) of Francis Light (1740–1794), founder of Penang in 1786. The memorial was commissioned in 1936 by the Municipal Council of Penang to commemorate the 150th anniversary of the settlement's founding and was completed in 1939 when it was ceremonially unveiled by the Governor, Sir Shenton Thomas.

Grave of Francis Light at the Protestant Cemetery in Northam Road — renamed Jalan Sultan Ahmad Shah. The grave was last restored in October 1894.

The Penang Chinese community's memorial to Queen Victoria, unveiled by Governor Sir Cecil Clementi in 1930. The statue was concealed during the Japanese occupation by a four-sided sign-board made for the Propaganda Bureau Broadcasting Station Dai Nippon, and the four shields emblazoned with Union Jacks under the memorial's lions were instead adorned with the Rising Sun emblem.

The Clock Tower, on the former Fort Road, was presented to Penang by Mr Cheah Chen Eok to commemorate Queen Victoria's Diamond Jubilee in 1897. Its 60 foot height represented the 60 years of her reign.

Runnymede Hotel on Northam Road, Penang.

Municipal Offices near the Esplanade, Penang.

Eastern and Oriental Hotel, Penang, showing the Victory Annex, constructed in 1922. (Photo credit: 'Penang. The City and Suburbs in the Early Twentieth Century', Georgetown Printers, 1986.)

Foundation stone to commemorate the start of construction of the Turf Club on its new 230 acre site at Batu Gantung. The course was opened in 1939.

Founder's stone for the Salvation Army in Penang. Capt Harvey (Commissioner decd) refused to evacuate from Penang in December 1941 and was interned by the Japanese.

Coastal scene from the 11th mile beach along the north coast road near Batu Ferringhi (Foreigner's Rock). In the background is Kedah Peak. (Photo credit: Mr R. Laird.)

Raffles Hotel in Singapore. (Photo credit: Raffles Hotel, Singapore.)

name of the East India Company, he christened the new settlement the Prince of Wales Island in honour of the heir apparent, who was later to become King George IV.

A Municipal Commission administered Penang, the commissioners of which, more often than not, had little to discuss and few resolutions to pass. What in-council decisions were made were invariably accepted without comment. Public utilities were well maintained and almost 90 per cent of houses within Penang's small municipal limits were supplied with generated electricity. Electric buses and tramcars plied along local town routes, and outlying areas were serviced by old cars converted into private buses. Most people were not dissatisfied with Penang's pre-war administration, although political agitators in Kuala Lumpur and Singapore found more causes for criticism. In Penang as well as Malacca agitators made scant headway.

White men enjoyed vast and amazing privileges in Malaya in the 1930s and this was most prominent in the exclusiveness of their clubs. Such was the sacrosanctity of clubs that in 1934 when Mr S. Saravanamuttu, then the respected editor of the *Straits Echo*, wanted to hold a meeting of Malayan newspaper editors, this was not permitted in the Singapore Club because he was a coloured person.

The Penang Club, founded in 1859, was an all-male preserve, the only exception being an attached women's annex, referred to as the 'hen roost'. This senior club in Southeast Asia was the domain of the 'tuan besars' and admission was taboo to junior executives. The Sultan of Kedah was the club's patron — his ancestor having leased Penang island to the British in 1786 — and was automatically eligible for membership, as were recognised Asian community leaders. Segregation embalmed social circles, particularly in club life, in which other Asians did not attempt to mix. The club, for many British officers in the Malayan Civil Service (MCS) and the various military services, as well as for executives in commercial firms, was the centre of their social life. The British Raj reigned supreme in Malaya, albeit paternalistically, despite the beginnings of Malayanisation. Junior executives in Penang joined the cricket and swimming clubs, the latter being strictly reserved for Europeans.

Inflexible invitation rituals prevailed and new arrivals were expected to leave their visiting cards. Once credentials had been satisfied, invitations to cocktails or dinner followed and this continued *ad infinitum* as relationships developed. Marriages – a mother's prerogative – were contrived with a delicacy and dedication that racehorse breeders would have envied.

Few Europeans carried cash on their persons as most things could be signed for through a 'chit' system. An array of Chinese domestics, cooks and amahs made entertainment at home easy even on short notice. Within Penang's small community it was not unusual to accept a friend's invitation to dinner, and to eat it at a table adorned with one's own cutlery and crockery, which were being used to make good the host's shortfall in these.

Social separatism featured prominently among the European population and was especially noticeable between club members and non-members. Membership minimised social variations within the European community and higher living standards contributed towards the social divisions which continued to prevail between Europeans and Asians. One's occupation and even the company for which one worked determined one's social status within the European community. The 'nicest' people were said to work with Boustead's and the Asiatic Petroleum Company, whereas many Scottish planters went to Guthrie's, which was a traditional Scottish company. Europeans who worked for large retail stores, including John Little, Robinson's and Whiteaway, were looked upon as being tradesmen and were therefore slotted in lower down the social ladder. Separatism was not limited to social status, but was obvious along the lines of one's race, language and culture as well. British policy only admitted Asians very slowly into higher positions in government service, and those places were restricted to Malays. Such a policy had the effect of thwarting any improvement in social relations between colonial masters and subject peoples.

Male social life in the 1930s featured, amongst other diversions, the newly originated cabarets. Several of these were opened in Singapore, Penang and Kuala Lumpur. The main attraction at these cabarets were the dance hostesses or 'taxi girls', who were mostly young, nubile Chinese intermixed with some Eurasians. Taxi girls levied 10 cents for each dance from a book of tickets that had to be purchased in advance. They, in turn, were paid according to the number of tickets that they collected during the night. Although sexual relations with Asian women were scorned publicly, in private they were tolerated. Marriage was out of the question, however, as it resulted in job forfeiture. Some Europeans — planters in particular — took up with Japanese mistresses whom they had freed from their indentures with brothel keepers. Some of these mistresses were discarded after a few years but others lived with the same man for 20 years or more. A few unions formed before World War I were only broken off when the Japanese living in Malaya were interned at the outbreak of the Pacific War.

By the late 1930s Malaya had become a wealthy, happy and generally loyal land, thanks to civilian private enterprise and sound government administration. Living standards were generally high, and money was easily earned and just as easily spent. The diverse Asian community, many of whose members were well trained in business matters, was endowed with rich and varied cultures. Inter-community relations were generally cordial and there was little racial friction. The country's five-million population was made up of two million each of Malays and Chinese, and 700,000 Indians, with the remainder being Eurasians. The European 'tuan' — 30,000 in total — were then perceived to be an invincible entity, it being believed by both British and Asians alike that this status would never be changed.

The British were expert administrators and, although they may not have given the Asians the best of everything, they did rule the country well. The civil service was efficient and the law-enforcing body effective. Rival factions in the strife-torn tin mining areas of Perak and Selangor had been brought to heel, as had many pirates in the seas around Malaya. Roads and railways had been built and taxes actually reached treasury coffers and were spent on public services.

In Penang, mosquitoes had almost been exterminated by 1936 and by 1938 the use of mosquito nets was largely discontinued. Deaths from malaria were down to 25 people a year by 1939, compared to 103 people ten years earlier. In 1936, to commemorate the hundred and fiftieth anniversary of the founding of the Straits Settlements, it was agreed that a memorial should be erected to the founder of Penang, Captain Francis Light. This, however, took several years to complete and was only unveiled by the Governor of the Straits Settlements, Sir Shenton Thomas, at Fort Cornwallis in 1939. In his eulogy to Francis Light, Sir Shenton described him as an empire builder possessing 'vision, courage and determination'.

Malaya's year-long debilitating temperatures, averaging over 90 degrees Fahrenheit, disinclined people to hurry, particularly at mid-day. However, the cool, fresh air at hill stations in various parts of the peninsula and in Penang offered temporary respite. Work usually started in the relative cool of the early morning and finished around five o'clock. Large old bungalows on the outskirts of town — surrounded by spacious, well-tended gardens — were designed to provide sufficient space to enable the constantly hot, sticky air to circulate freely within them. Macalister Road — George Town's longest road, named after Colonel Norman Macalister, the Governor of Penang in early 1810 — was dotted along its tree-lined length with stately buildings, most of which were occupied by prominent British government officials.

The Sarkie brothers' Eastern and Oriental Hotel (the E & O) and its rival, the Runnymede Hotel, were popular pre-war social haunts in Penang, particularly at weekends, when planters came into town from Perak and Kedah to enjoy their sundowner rituals of sipping cocktails whilst relaxing in easy chairs on the long lawns. Arshak Sarkie was often to be seen waltzing around the E & O's ballroom, balancing a whiskey soda on his head, and on Sunday evenings an orchestra attracted large crowds by giving garden concerts. Following the great slump, dozens of planters' and tin miners' debts were 'overlooked' by this Armenian benefactor, who even provided some of these men and their families with passages home to Britain.

The Runnymede Hotel in its heyday was one of Penang's leading hotels, being described in *Seaports of the Far East* as 'charmingly situated in two acres of grounds at the edge of the sea'. The original building, put up in 1901 by Stamford Raffles for his wife, had been destroyed by fire. In 1938 the Runnymede bought over its long-standing and then-ailing rival, the E & O, for a bargain price of Straits $120,954 — estimated to be $333,000 less than its book price. The Runnymede itself was requisitioned by the British navy in 1940, and never again operated as a hotel, although in 1941 it was temporarily used as a transit hostel for Europeans fleeing from the advancing Japanese.

Early evenings in Penang were particularly pleasant, with the Botanical Gardens offering a peaceful respite after the heat of the day and the frustrations of office routines. There were many delightful places for weekend and holiday picnics, and the island's charm was enhanced by an abundance of cheap food and fruit, and a sea in which one could safely bathe.

Pre-war Malaya was an attractive posting for women who were lured by its equable climate, social opportunities and acquiescent natives renowned for their anxiety to serve. Wives of planters and tin miners — the self-assumed 'white masters of the Peninsula' — were intermixed with wives of civil engineers, surveyors, fire chiefs, customs officers and policemen. Career women followed, all essential to the colonial system — governesses, school teachers, missionaries, secretaries, ladies' companions and nurses. As rumours of war increased and military strengths were expanded, nurses, particularly, grew in numbers and importance. Native women were inseparable from this intricate set-up. Amahs, cooks, laundresses, maids and personal attendants became part of a colonial establishment that had been nurtured down the years and cultivated to a high degree. Robinson's — the Harrod's of Singapore — formed part of the women's daytime lives in Singapore, as did Raffles Hotel by night.

Overdressing was all the vogue in those pre-war days, and dress standards were regarded as important. Europeans wore mostly white or khaki drill suits, and hats were popular in the hot tropical sun. Even school boys wore hats, although they had no official uniforms.

Pre-war education facilities in Penang were not extensive. More boys than girls attended school as the education of girls was not greatly encouraged. The Christian Brothers had their large St Xavier's School, with a feeder school at Pulau Tikus. As there were few other boys' schools on the island, inter-school competitions were mostly held between St Xavier's, the Methodist Anglo-Chinese School and the Penang Free School, which was located next to the Cathedral of the Assumption in Farquhar Street. The Penang Free School building, which was partially destroyed during the war, was used after 1945 as the State Museum, while the school itself was shifted out of town to its present location in Green Lane.

In 1939 Pulau Tikus was a lonely, cobra-infested village, mostly populated by Eurasians. The modern-day residential areas of Green Lane and Ayer Hitam were then well-established coconut estates, and swamps and padi fields stretched over to Bayan Lepas. Although Penang had a sizable European community, the out-of-town population was sparse, and from Northam Road to Batu Ferringi the beaches were mostly deserted. Heavy loads were carried up Penang Hill by hand, and people thought little of walking down the 2600-foot slope for a swim at Batu Ferringi. There was little motorised transport on the island and on Sundays fleets of rickshaws would be lined up outside churches. Government officers in South Kedah took advantage of their Thursday half-day and Friday holiday to come to Penang, where many spent their evenings at the Wembley dance hall, which was Penang's only pre-war nightclub.

Before 1941 it was not done for European women to shop in the fascinating Asian streets of the city. Neither could they visit the teeming Chinese quarters or those areas where Indians re-enacted intact 'the sights, sounds and smells of Calcutta or Bombay'. By 1941, however, social changes were afoot and some of the rigid, restraining barriers between Europeans and Asians were being relaxed. These changes provided new, exhilarating experiences, as European women could now visit Chinatown without being socially scorned. The forbidden-city tag on these areas was later palled by conditions in internment camps, where women in rags could only reminisce about such luxuries as tailors speedily transforming glossy fashion-magazine photographs into enviable garments, or how it had been possible to have hand-fashioned shoes individually made, simply by placing a foot on a piece of paper around which the contour would be drawn.

The benevolence of British rule paradoxically nurtured in some recipients feelings of resentment and was interpreted as exploitation. Despite their booming industries, British tin and rubber magnates kept pre-war wages down. Britain's plural-society policy in Malaya condoned the staunch anti-Japanese stance of the Chinese, but in 1941 most Malays felt no animosity towards the Japanese. Some of them at first even welcomed the prospect of a change in colonial masters, seeing it as a means of ending Chinese political and economic encroachment.

Malaya's vast riches — rubber plantations, tin mines, packed warehouses, oil refineries, machinery, and enormous shipping and maritime facilities in Singapore — fell easy prey to the Japanese. They also inherited all the trappings and a remarkable bric-a-brac of the British imperial lifestyle, with its colonial bungalows, nurtured cricket pitches and tennis courts, swimming pools and club houses. It is not surprising that those who brought a New Order to Malaya's 'freed' subject races should have felt particularly exalted by their achievement. They won so much, so easily!

2:3 Multi-Racial Innuendos

The 1921 population census of the Malay Peninsula, including Singapore, revealed for the first time that Malays were no longer in the majority. This trend continued, as subsequent census results revealed.

Malay Peninsula Including Singapore
Main Racial Groups in Census Returns (in 000s)

	1921		1931		1947	
	Total	%	Total	%	Total	%
Malays	1,630	49.0	1,930	44.4	2,540	43.4
Chinese	1,180	35.5	1,710	39.3	2,620	44.8
Indians	470	14.1	620	14.3	610	10.4
Others	46	1.4	88	2.0	79	1.4
Total	3,326	100.0	4,348	100.0	5,849	100.0

By the 1940s the trend had been extended to the Federation of Malaya, excluding Singapore. Although Malays continued to be the single largest race, in total they equalled only 49.1 per cent, as the following figures for that period show:

Malay Peninsula Excluding Singapore
Main Racial Groups (in 000s)
Source: *Conflict and Violence in Singapore and Malaya* by R. Clutterbuck, p.33

Race	Total	%
Malays	2,600	49.1
Chinese	2,040	38.5
Indians*	578	10.9
Europeans	12	0.2
Others	70	1.3
Total	5,300	100.0

* includes Pakistanis, Sikhs, Sri Lankans

Pre-war livelihoods of Malays, Chinese and Indians complemented each other, although the respective races adhered to their own languages, social customs and religious beliefs. There was little reason in pre-war Malaya for the different races to interfere with one another. The Chinese, mostly town dwellers, were pioneers of numerous business ventures, all of which had a common aim — profit. The Indians were generally employed to develop rubber estates, railways and roads. The Chinese and Indians, therefore, provided most of the labour for the basic industries in the country. The Malays usually continued, as they had previously, to be proficient fishermen or proprietor-subsistence farmers, involved in most of the rice-growing, and favoured residing in rural areas.

In 1931, 2,877 Malays, 84 Indians and only 322 Chinese had land under rice cultivation in the Straits Settlements. At that time there were 9,159 Malay fishermen, compared with 6092 Chinese and 335 Indians. By 1937, there were 3.3 million acres being cultivated with rubber, of which 61 per cent were Asian- and European-owned estates larger than 100 acres, the balance being individually worked smallholdings.

Chinese and Malays lived in a state of relative harmony prior to 1939. Many from each community depended on the other in an economic state of equilibrium. The Malays promised to sell their future crops or sea-catches to the Chinese, who gave them advances in kind against the eventual proceeds that they would earn. These advances helped the Malays during protracted inter-crop periods, or seasons of inclement weather, to which they were annually exposed.

Disruption of this mutually beneficial arrangement arose when the British administration, through a proposal originating from the Colonial Office, attempted a well-intended introduction of a Co-operative scheme. Not only was this scheme unsuccessful, it also served to spread distrust between the two communities. The Malays began to look upon the Chinese middle-men's profits as vast and disproportionate to the efforts that the latter put in, and sought by participation in the Co-operative scheme to end their economic imbalance with the Chinese. They gave little thought to the years of friendly association which both races had built up at village level, an association based on trust, in which the Chinese had cheerfully undertaken the risk of financing Malays during their non-earning seasons. When the Co-operative scheme commenced, Malay fishermen received comparatively enormous sums for their catches. However, when the monsoons prevented them from putting to sea, they found themselves without any income. Previously, all they had had to do was to go to their Chinese fish-buyer and obtain from him what they needed against their next catch. When they tried to do the same with the Co-operative, no advances were available. The Malays then tried to revert to the Chinese businessmen, but found that the traditional feelings of goodwill and mutual interdependence had been dissipated.

By 1937 total Chinese investments in Malaya were estimated to be £40 million, compared with foreign investments of £90.9 million. In 1941 a clear indication of the wealth of the Malayan Chinese was their remittance of £12.8 million to China, for the China Relief Fund.

1. A system whereby labourers, mostly from India but also from China, were imported and contracted to work on rubber plantations and tin mines. They were bound by the indenture under which they were hired.
2. A method of enforcing labour laws by exacting punishment in a monetary form. This was a cruel method of punishment for cheaply-paid indentured labourers as it kept them in a state of permanent indebtedness that prolonged their bondage.
3. Regulations that stipulated through extensive experience the minimum terms of employ-

ment and basic amenities for workers, in order to safeguard their interests and prevent abuse.

4. The selling of necessities to labourers by their employers. Wages paid in kind or by other means, in lieu of money. A type of enforced barter system whereby wages for human toil were given in the form of issues of rice, salt, sugar and other essential foodstuffs. The system was introduced because of the isolated locations of newly-opened mines and plantations, and was subject to much abuse.

CHAPTER THREE: VOICE OF DISSENSION

3:1 Pre-War Chinese Immigration Trends

Although the first Chinese came to Malaya in the sixth century, their immigration patterns remained erratic until the 1870s when Britain intervened in the Peninsula, after which there was an influx of Chinese immigrants. They were quick to realise that a peaceful administrative climate was to their own economic advantage. They were particularly attracted by the country's general stability and potential for prosperity, despite there being unresolved racial problems and intermittent internecine fighting with the Malays. Early Chinese immigrants were content to leave the British and their Malay underlings to govern the country, provided that they themselves could prosper. Connections with China were not severed and thousands continued to send money back to relatives there in order to finance shiploads of newcomers, who swarmed the Malayan shores every year.

Those Chinese who emigrated from China to Malaya and other parts of Southeast Asia were tough and resourceful people. Discontented with their life in China, they sought self-improvement in other countries. Those who flooded into Malaya were given full encouragement by the British, who approved of their adventurous spirit and resourcefulness. The more prosperous among them favoured a colonial form of government, realising that this would maintain a level of law and order in which they could flourish. The peasantry, however, remained apolitical. They continued to live apart in the remoter areas of the country, avoiding all contact with authority as their forefathers had done in China.

Movements of the Chinese, both into and out of Malaya, were numerous in the 1920s and 1930s, so much so that on 1st April 1933 the Federated Malay States enacted an Immigration Restriction Ordinance which was similar to one that had been passed in the Straits Settlements in 1928.[1] Unemployment had become acute following the

Depression of 1929, which made it necessary to introduce stricter immigration controls. In the Straits Settlements a quota system was started and in the Malay States entry of immigrants virtually stopped. The effectiveness of the measures taken is clearly seen in figures for 1932, when almost 283,000 Chinese left Malaya, compared to only 33,000 who arrived. Arrivals in the mid-1930s, particularly after Japan invaded China, were mostly confined to family members of Chinese who were already in the country. As the Chinese community became more permanently established, their eagerness to become landowners increased. But although large numbers continued to arrive, departures were almost as many: for example, in 1939, there were 116,000 arrivals against 106,000 departures.

Two-thirds of the Chinese in pre-war Malaya had been born in China and, as mentioned previously, many of them continued to remit money to their own native districts. As more Chinese women arrived, remittances to the homeland declined. The presence of more women, however, tended to upset the somewhat tenuous balance that existed between the various clans and ethnic groups as competition for their favours grew.

Up till 1941, therefore, only about one-third of the Chinese in Malaya had actually been born in the country. The immigrant remainder still had every intention of returning to China once their fortunes were made. In June 1941 the Chinese in Penang comprised 67.5 per cent of the total estimated population on the island.

Penang Population Figures by Race as at 30 June 1941

Race	Total	%
Chinese	166,974	67.5
Malays	41,853	16.9
Indians	31,916	12.9
Eurasians	2,374	1.0
Europeans	2,464	1.0
Others	1,879	0.7
Total	247,460	100.0

Of their own volition they led a separate existence, but within the framework of British administration, and in Penang continued to name streets in a manner which bore no resemblance to the official names given to them.

Between 1921 and 1941, throughout the Federated and Unfederated Malay States as well as the Straits Settlements, the Chinese population increased from 35 per cent to 43 per cent. By 1941 Malays, on the other hand, totalled only 41 per cent throughout these areas.

3:2 Chinese Secret Societies and Social Problems

In China, secret societies existed in simple form as early as AD 300. In the seventeenth century, an organisation known as the Hung (Flood) League was set up by monks of the Shoa Lin Monastery in Fukien. Circumstances caused this society to oppose the Manchu (Ching) Dynasty and its members endeavoured to overthrow the foreign Manchu rulers in China. Malayan Chinese secret societies are generally considered to have been derived from this Hung League, known otherwise as the Thian Ti Hui (The Heaven and Earth League). Most of the centuries-old secret societies in China were originally self-help or benevolent religious associations. Only later did they assume political and anti-dynastic characteristics, eventually degenerating into criminal organisations.

Among the first societies to be established in Malaya and the Straits Settlements were some that were akin to the modern concepts of trade unions, Freemasons and mutual benefit clubs. They were secret in nature and took care of newly arrived settlers, fitting them into the prevailing social and political structures of the country. Newly arrived immigrants were given loans and put in touch with prospective employers, but coming as they did from diverse parts of China, speaking different dialects and having different customs, not everyone joined the same society. This resulted in the development of competing groups within the original Triad Society, which gradually separated and became rival entities. Cantonese mostly joined the Ghee Hin, or the Virtuous (or Patriotic) Prosperity Society, whereas Hakkas joined the Hai San society. All immigrants were forced to join one or other of these societies, and unswerving allegiance was expected of them. In this manner society leaders amassed considerable powers. This was especially so with their appointment by the government as 'Kapitans China'. By 1880 the Chinese community was governed largely through these societies and more notice was taken of society regulations than of the laws of the country. As competition for power increased, the mutual-aid aspect of societies slowly declined and activities veered more towards the criminal. With Singapore and Penang becoming increasingly prosperous, secret societies came into more open conflict with one another over who should control the various legal and illegal activities in both places.

Chinese social life in Malaya was therefore virtually controlled by the vice-like grip of the Triad Societies, until British administration started to exert some controlling influence. By the 1930s the once-mighty Triads, who a hundred years previously had plotted to set fire to George Town, had been reduced to little more than a few bands of street hooligans who extracted protection money from brothels and shopkeepers and occasionally resorted to street fights over boundaries of protection areas.

By 1941 most of these societies had degenerated into illegal, criminal organisations which controlled the underworld in Singapore and the large towns in Malaya. They resorted to extortion, assault and murder for a price. They imposed protection rackets on shopkeepers and controlled prostitutes, drugs and gambling dens in their own areas. They had become a vicious menace and were a far cry from their earlier counterparts, and from the purpose of their origin.

In 1931 in the Federated Malay States there were only 436 Chinese females to every 1,000 Chinese males. This imbalance caused an increase in trafficking in women and girls in the 1930s, and also led to prostitution becoming widespread and more difficult to control. With the convergence of large numbers of immigrants of different races, customs, religions and traditions, all living under unstable conditions, the need to implement controls became increasingly acute. In the 1930s, therefore, in both the Straits Settlements and the Malay States, entry restrictions were placed on known prostitutes and brothels were banned. As a result, the cabaret emerged as a popular form of entertainment at that time. Professional dancers were employed on fixed salaries assessed on their popularity, and also received part of the proceeds arising from the sale of dance tickets. Although cabarets were socially censured they provided many girls with a means of livelihood and prevented some of them from becoming prostitutes. No doubt some dancing girls were prostitutes, but many did manage to lead respectable lives.

From the outset of British rule in Penang and Singapore, various administrators had expressed misgivings concerning the adverse effects of opium smoking on the health of the Chinese. But as sales of opium had always provided the Straits Settlements with a ready source of revenue, it was not until the turn of the century that effective action was taken to investigate the extent of damage to health from opium-smoking. By the end of 1941, however, efforts were being made to stamp out opium-smoking and known smokers were registered and rationed. As these people died, the number of addicts gradually decreased. Although attractive profits from smuggling opium hampered reform, the government's policy at that time was to replace taxes on opium eventually with other sources of revenue, for which objective an Opium Revenue Displacement Guarantee Fund was set up. By 1943 the British government, in absentia, had decided upon a total ban on opium-smoking in Malaya.

3:3 Pre-War Chinese Political Developments

After the 1911 Revolution, events in China drew the political aspirations of the Chinese there closer to those of their counterparts in Malaya. Long-established secret societies in Malaya were infiltrated by Kuomintang Nationalists (KMT), and later by their off-shoots, who had been recruited into the Communist Party. Although most Straits-born Chinese, and those in the Malay States, devoted themselves to business, the arousal of China-oriented political consciousness deepened the already-existent rifts among the various immigrant Chinese clans in the country. British administration during the 1920s and 1930s, therefore, enforced strict curtailment of these militant political factions. However, Masonic orders and community organisations, established for educational, commercial or for social reasons, were permitted to operate without restrictions. China-oriented nationalism and politics took precedence over colonial-oriented politics among the

Chinese in Malaya, until the British took over the control and administration of the country. It was only after this that the Chinese made an attempt to participate in it.

In the 1920s Kuomintang propaganda in Malaya was openly anti-British, and aimed at stimulating China-oriented nationalism among the Chinese in the country. The KMT's activities were considered subversive and were therefore suppressed in 1925. In 1930 the Party was banned, whereby political factions were driven underground but were not suppressed. During the first quarter of the 20th century, as both Chinese politics and education reflected what was happening in China, it was not until 1924 that communist activities first became noticeable in Malaya. Arising from the 1927 communist and KMT split in China, nationalist Chinese propaganda in Malaya was reduced. The KMT's triumph in China resulted in China-oriented nationalism becoming paramount in the minds of most Chinese in Malaya after 1927. Later, in the 1930s, however, when the Chinese communists challenged the KMT's authority, they increasingly appealed to the Malayan Chinese, whose objectives at that time included making a stand against Imperialism. A further decline in support for the KMT occurred in 1931 when Japan threatened aggression against China. Thus, the KMT/Communist Party split in China caused political rivalries amongst the Chinese in Malaya, where both factions competed for support. The outcome of this was that for a time both these factions became less effective than the old KMT Party had been by itself.

Chinese political parties in Malaya remained as underground organisations, even after the KMT under Chiang Kai-Shek became the legitimate government in China, as the British administration in Malaya refused to permit branches of foreign political parties to operate openly in the country. As Japan's threat to China increased, so the KMT and the communists played down their staunch nationalistic aims. Although by 1936 the communists had gained sufficient influence within trade unions in Malaya to organise strikes, China needed allies. After the Sino-Japanese War commenced in 1937, therefore, Chinese nationalistic fervour was almost exclusively directed against the Japanese. Boycotts of Japanese goods were organised and trade with Japan was discontinued. In the 1930s, although events in China had taken the edge off Chinese political activity in Malaya, Chinese political groups were still sufficiently active to arouse apprehension among the Sultans and those who administered the country. Stricter controls over Chinese immigration and education were therefore introduced.

The San Min Chu Yi (SMCY),[2] an off-shoot of the KMT, was initiated by President Chiang Kai-Shek in China in 1938 and was first introduced into Malaya shortly before the war, as a means of checking the rapidly growing influence of the communists. The SMCY's objectives were to train young men in a 'New Life Movement' and to extend their support to the local government administration in Malaya. The training given imbued Chinese youths with patriotic fervour. It upheld strong, even violent, Chinese nationalism, so that both the KMT and the SMCY, rather than the communists, had the essence pre-war to become the real menace to any subsequent proposals for Malaya's independence within the framework of the British Empire. The non-recognition of the KMT in Malaya required that the SMCY's headquarters remain underground, and during the subsequent Japanese occupation the organisation disappeared completely for a time. It re-emerged only after the war when the KMT was revived, following the visit of a Chinese consul from China.

Pre-war Chinese community leaders in Malaya were mainly guild, association or clan officials, as well as representatives of English-educated professionals in state legislative councils and various voluntary community organisations. These officials were further subdivided into two groups: those who had been born and educated in China, who were mostly businessmen, and those who were Straits-born and English-educated. Most of the businessmen, or 'towkays', as they were referred to, had considerable wealth and were of high social standing, whilst those originating from the English-educated group had political influence. After Japan's invasion of northern China in 1937, both these groups became involved in anti-Japanese activities and gave financial support to Britain's war efforts in Europe and elsewhere.

It was not unusual for the Babas, the Straits-born Chinese, to remain aloof from new immigrants and to look down on them. Some Babas proudly held claim to being British subjects, and immigrants from China were barred from joining clubs frequented by Straits-born

Chinese. The Babas carefully preserved the outward signs of their Chinese origin, including the 'queue' — a badge of servitude —, the conical hats, mandarin costumes and thick soled shoes. Their claim to superiority was similar to that of other aristocracies, one of priority through earlier arrival. Although inter-marriage was a frequent occurrence, the progeny of these matches were invariably brought up in the ways of their Chinese fathers, even though their mothers were Malays or half-castes.

Most of the leadership of permanently domiciled Chinese in Malaya came from the English-educated Straits Chinese. Although they were small in numbers they were amongst the wealthiest and best educated of all races in the country and were also ardently pro-British. During the early 1930s, a combination of circumstances arose that made them become fearful for their future as they envisaged becoming socially and politically isolated on account of various policies that were being adopted. The British 'pro-Malay' attitude, which favoured Malays for employment in subordinate government posts, was seen as being contrary to the best interests of the domiciled Chinese. The sharp repressive measures taken by the British against those elements of the Chinese community who had expressed anti-British sentiments following the KMT/communist split in mainland China, were also viewed with increasing alarm by them as they did not want to become associated with any repercussions that surrounded these anti-British activities. In the Straits Settlement's Federal and Legislative Council, Chinese representatives attacked Britain's decentralisation and pro-Malay policies and urged that non-Malays should be included in the Malayan Civil Service (MCS). Various claims for equal rights and privileges were voiced, sometimes in abrasive terms, particularly by a Mr Lim Ching Yan when addressing the Penang Chinese Association.

> 'Who said this is a Malay country? Our forefathers came here and worked hard as coolies — weren't ashamed to become coolies — and they didn't send their money back to China. They married and spent their money here, and in this way the Government was able to open up the country from jungle to civilisation. We've become inseparable from this country. It's ours, our country.'[3]

Many Chinese in pre-war Malaya either joined secret societies or affiliated themselves to one or other of the China-based political parties: Chiang Kai-Shek's Nationalist Kuomintang government, which was recognised by Britain and America; or the Chinese Communist Party based in Yenan, which was not accorded such recognition. Both these factions, however, fielded armies against the Japanese when they invaded China in 1937.

Of striking significance in the years between the two World Wars was the absence of any substantial challenge to British political rule in Malaya. Throughout this period intense political activity among the Chinese was mostly concentrated on events that were taking place in China. Many Chinese in Malaya were not interested in Malaya-oriented politics, and some actively gave support to Britain's rule in Malaya. The strength and organisation of the British administration throughout this period were also sufficient to suppress effectively any Chinese individual or organisation whose activities were considered subversive to their authority.

In the 1930s both the communist and KMT factions opposed Britain's lawful administration of Malaya, to such an extent that some of their leaders were either imprisoned or deported for sedition. The communists were the more active and effective of the two factions and held greater appeal to the young, radically-minded Chinese peasant masses in Malaya. In contrast, the more conservative and wealthy Straits-born Chinese inclined towards the KMT, having identified themselves commercially, for generations, with Europeans and with the general affluence that had made Malaya so important to Britain's pre-war economy. When hostilities with Japan commenced in late 1941, it was ironic that it was these troublesome political elements that were belatedly recognised by the British, and themselves alike, as being the logical factions from which co-operation with the government against the common enemy could be obtained.

3:4 Education and Implications

The Chinese have always had an enormous respect for academic learning.

Pre-war Chinese schools in Malaya were nothing more than transplanted little Chinas. The education policy that was adhered to in these schools was merely an extension of the national educational system in China, the policy of which had been formulated in the 19th and early 20th centuries.

Education for the Chinese in Malaya was unassisted, which required them to finance and build their own schools, and to recruit teachers from China. This resulted in a curriculum being followed which inculcated Chinese patriotism as well as providing a subtle platform for nurturing anti-British ideas. Textbooks were exclusively China-oriented. No reference was made to Malaya's culture, geography, history, or to the intricate make-up of the country's multi-racial population, from which arose socio-economic administrative ramifications. When registration and some control over Chinese schools and teachers was introduced, they were vehemently opposed.

In 1939 out of 268,000 pupils attending all types of educational institutions in the Straits Settlements and the Federated States, approximately 204,000 were by this time in government-aided or maintained institutions. Despite there being few facilities and a scarcity of teachers, the Chinese in Malaya continued to educate their children to the best of their ability.

3:5 Boycott and Anti-Japanese Riots

In 1932, following Japan's seizure of Manchuria, the Chinese merchant community throughout the Malay States, and particularly in Penang and Singapore, revealed openly and vividly their anti-Japanese sentiments. Chinese merchants organised trade boycotts and harassed customers at Japanese shops, with the seemingly apparent condolence of the police. Some Japanese, including a few children, were even killed on sight. One victim of the November 1932 outbreak of violence — an eight year old girl — was the sister of Tani Yutaka, who nurtured his hatred and years later organised and led a group of revenge-seeking Malay and Thai gangsters.

When Japan declared war on China in 1937, Chinese traders again organised a rigid boycott against the sale of Japanese goods in Penang and throughout Malaya. In 1938, also in Penang, anti-Japanese riots broke out. Japanese goods, particularly soya beans, were flung into the streets, where bonfires were made of them. These anti-Japanese activities continued, in various forms, until Japan invaded Malaya in December 1941.

The organisers behind these boycotts of Japanese trade were invariably local committee members of the China Relief Fund and leaders of the China National Salvation Movement. The boycotts were well organised and effective. Many who participated in them did not succumb to the crude blackmail and propaganda tactics to which the Japanese resorted in order to stifle commercial opposition.

3:6 China Relief Fund

The overseas, or China-born, Chinese formed the largest non-Malay ethnic group in Malaya. Most of them lived in urban centres and participated prominently in the economic sector of the country. In the 1920s the overseas Chinese became politically active. The emphasis of their action, in the 1930s, veered towards a staunch China-oriented nationalism, in opposition to Japan's aggression in mainland China. When the China National Salvation Movement was formed, the overseas Chinese were the more dedicated anti-Japanese elements within its ranks.

When Japan invaded China in 1937, the government in Malaya became enmeshed in a politically explosive situation. The Chinese in Malaya strove to consolidate support for their motherland, and in doing so made a determined effort to embarrass the Japanese in commerce. In addition to trade boycotts, massive sums of money were remitted by the Chinese from Malaya and elsewhere to finance armed resistance against Japanese aggression in China. Britain was therefore faced with a diplomatic dilemma. Being at peace with Japan, at this juncture, she was obliged to suppress any anti-Japanese acts which originated in territories under British control. Although recognising this obligation, the government in Malaya was also sufficiently sympathetic towards the plight of the Chinese to extend their moral support, and was therefore as lenient as political expediency would allow. No obstructions were imposed on the remittance of vast sums of money from the Chinese in Malaya to China on behalf of the China Relief Fund, the purpose of which, it was fully known, was to help finance the resistance against Japanese aggression there.

The Straits-born Chinese gave donations under various guises of compulsion. Their financial contribution, therefore, was considerably less than that of the China-born or overseas Chinese.

1. A law that imposed a quota system on immigration, for which a new departent, the Immigration Department, was created. Prior to this, the police had been exclusively responsible for attending to aliens.
2. *The Masked Comrades. A Study of the Communist United Front in Malaya 1945–8* by Cheah Boon Kheng, p.33. Sun Min Chu Yi (SMCY) means the Three People's Principles — Nationalism, Democracy and Socialism — of Dr Sun Yat Sen, the founder of the Republic of China.
3. *Origins of Malay Nationalism* by W.R. Roff, p.209. (Taken from p.182 of the *Journal Al-Ikhwan*, 5 February 1931.)

CHAPTER FOUR: CHANGING PATTERNS

4:1 Pre-War Malay Rulers and Aristocracy

Before 1941 Malay rulers had little control over the affairs of state to which they affixed their seal. Care was taken, however, to offer them a sense of participation by consulting them on matters directly affecting their State as a whole, and in particular with regard to those appertaining to their Malay subjects. British authority was invariably accepted, therefore, with polite indifference by Malays who simultaneously continued to revere their sultans. In contrast, the aboriginal inhabitants of Malaya (Orang Asli) — not seriously considered an indigenous racial entity — refused to acknowledge the sovereignty of the sultans.

Britain, by treaty, was required to protect the interests of the Malays. By 1921, however, arising from Britain's 19th century colonial policy, which allowed unrestricted immigration of Chinese and Indians for working the mines and rubber plantations, the indigenous Malays had been outnumbered. Contrary to previous opinion, the 1931 census also revealed that one-third of the Chinese in the country, and a quarter of the Indians, were no longer transients. Having been born in Malaya, they regarded the country as a place for permanent settlement. Malay rulers, therefore, actively opposed any further unrestricted immigration into their States.

British colonial administration always recognised the sultans' religious authority within their states. They were regarded as being supreme rulers as well as religious heads. As chairman of advisory councils they had powers to appoint and dispense titles and honours among the aristocracy, and were generally looked upon as being benevolent rulers of the faithful. The British, through their resident advisors, assumed almost complete control over matters of government and decisions regarding foreign affairs and defence. However, by retaining much of the Malay trappings, British policy aimed at maintaining for the rulers their semblance of position as rulers. Younger generations of aristocracy were drawn into the elite Malayan Civil Service (MCS) through which Britain governed the country and into which preference was given to the employment of Malays. Selected Malays were therefore able to play an active political role, which helped preserve the rulers' positions, as well as other traditional institutions. British policy until 1941 aimed at preserving Malay society behind the protection of British administration. The Malay aristocracy enjoyed a relatively high social status, receiving incomes from fixed allowances, and pensions from the Colonial administrative system. All that was to change suddenly after February 1942, when the country came under the Japanese occupational military administration and control.

4:2 British Pre-War Policies towards Malays

From the outset of British rule in Malaya the government's frequently declared public policy was one that protected Malay reserve lands and preserved the Malay peasants' way of life. A large majority of the working Malay population in the 1930s was still the traditional class of peasant farmers, who were either directly or indirectly associated with the cultivation of wet rice.

Before the war, British policy in Malaya was based on practical cost advantages. It was a tactful policy in that it made use of a long-established Malay leadership organisation in areas of local administration. The appointment of village headmen, 'penghulu', was exploited, as it was found that this position provided an adequate incentive to nurture and satisfy Malay aspirations for involvement in local government.

There were many within the Malay community who did not deny that they had been receivers of favours from the British. This, however, did not stop others among them from having their own various complaints about the administrative establishment, and the extent of their permitted involvement in it. As early as 1924, during a visit to London, the Sultan of Perak complained to Sir Edward Gent that his State Council had neither any real power nor any work to do, and that the Malays employed in government service received lower pay than their European counterparts. He was of the opinion that this wage differentiation made Malay government employees vulnerable to bribes, and forced many of them to become dependent upon the none-too-tender mercies of Indian money lenders. His Highness regarded the commercial monopolies of the Chinese as a menace. He also considered that his own authority was insufficient in comparison with the authority enjoyed by fellow rulers in the Unfederated States, where British officers only advised them, and did not manipulate them as levers of power behind a facade of rule. Ten years later, the Sultan of Selangor similarly expressed annoyance that the British Resident, not being content with running the State completely, had also interfered in matters appertaining to the royal succession.

Malays really had little cause to disapprove of the pre-war British administrative system, from which they derived various benefits. Malay rulers under the system became increasingly wealthy and enjoyed lives of ease and respect. The British ensured a 'Malayophile' policy over Malay reserve lands, and also afforded and safeguarded for well-educated and elite Malays a privileged, albeit limited, access into the Malayan Civil Service (MCS).

British Residents in the Federated Malay States exercised direct control over every aspect of government, for which the final recourse to authority was the Governor of the Straits Settlements. Whilst ensuring that this system prevailed, a subtle outward appearance of upholding independent Malay initiative was also preserved. The respective rulers presided over their State Council meetings, but other than this, genuine participation by Malays was restricted. The Resident's obligation went only as far as 'accepting advice' that he chose to request of the rulers. Other Malay officials were dependent upon the allowances they were given by their appointments to various councils, although the majority of them remained unfamiliar with the diverse issues involved in administrative, judicial and fiscal decision making.

During Sir Cecil Clementi's tenure in office as Governor of the Straits Settlements from 1930–33, matters came to a head. Although Clementi's decentralisation proposals were agreed to in principle by Sir Edward Gent, when he visited Malaya in 1932 to investigate their feasibility, they met with opposition from other renowned quarters. Sir Frank Swettenham vigorously and publicly opposed the proposals as did other highly placed government officials. Businessmen in Malaya also rejected them, and in doing so earned for themselves a scathing rebuke from Sir Edward Gent, who described them as being 'emotional, reactionary and closed minded'.[1]

It was not uncommon for non-Malays to interpret the good manners of Malays as a sign of weakness and inferiority. The custom of addressing the white man as 'master' or 'tuan' was accepted by many pre-war Europeans as their right; they viewed themselves as self-nominated inheritors of the title and the 'masters' of the Malays.

Some of the more adept and discerning British administrators, however, were skilled in placating the character conflict that arose within many Malays. They realised just how far they could go, so that the British administrative takeover of the country was marred with only a few unpleasant incidents. Even the deluge of immigrants, who effectively displaced the Malays, did not seem to arouse much political and racial opposition to pre-war British control, although it was the British who were directly responsible for bringing foreign immigrants into the country in the first place.

British administrators generally liked the Malays as a people, although they had a low opinion of their ability to govern themselves. As the threat of war loomed, many Malays appeared to become almost pathetically bewildered by the prospect. Although numerous Malays assisted the British in any way they could, there were factions who gave cause for justifiable concern that they would in due course offer similar help to the Japanese. Many Malays became demoralised with fear. As the tide of events in late 1941 and early 1942 cast the dye on Britain's fate throughout the length and breadth of the Malay Peninsula, it became increasingly evident that it had been Britain's benevolence towards the Malays in general, and her protective administrative policy in particular, that had effectively 'stamped out their inherent fighting spirit',[2] at a time when so little could be done to help them.

4:3 Educational Influences

In the early part of the 20th century there were three main educational influences in Malaya, which tended to divide the Malay community into factions with conflicting aspirations.

One of these influences was Arab-oriented. Teachings from Islam motivated a small group of religio-social reformists. Through the English educational system a second, slightly larger, group emerged, from which were drawn the pro-British administrators, as well as those who were employed as subordinate staff in a variety of government service departments. The third group comprised teachers and journalists who formed a more politically radical Malay-educated intelligentsia that came from the vernacular school system, and were noted for their Malay-cum-Indonesian orientation. This group, as well as the religious reformists, were unable to achieve any degree of organisation or popular support at grass root levels.

Pre-war education in Malaya did not develop much beyond the primary school level. Although the British encouraged a national type of education and permitted an assortment of language mediums and curricula, some Malay schools functioned only as places where literacy was increased, and did not develop a curriculum oriented to either regional or national topics. The English-type schools produced semi-educated, potential white collar workers, many of whom had apparently more allegiance to Britain, and the myth that surrounded the mother country, rather than to their own country of birth.

The effect of Islam on Malays was total. The Koran was taught in all village schools. Malays absorbed the Arabic language and culture which introduced drastic alterations to their life-styles. The adaptation of Arabic script by Malay scholars increased literacy levels, and drew students closer to the philosophy and sciences of the Middle East. Most of the cultural and educational changes resulting from Islam's influence were more concentrated among people living in town areas. When religious schools were expanded and established in the rural areas, teachers tended to limit the instruction they provided only to religious matters.

During Britain's pre-war colonial administration of Malaya, not only were the Malays backward economically, but they also fell behind educationally. Although there were more Malays than non-Malays attending schools during this period, the majority of these students only went to primary vernacular schools. This was a free form of education for the Malays, but the curriculum that was adhered to did not help them to become assimilated into an ever increasingly modern society. The majority of Malays felt no need to be assimilated. Following tradition, they expected to remain in their villages, leading poverty-stricken lives like their forefathers.

In contrast, the relatively well-off non-Malays profited more by the introduction of secondary education by the British, and many non-Malay students went on to achieve as high standards of education as their parents' wealth would permit. Not all non-Malays were wealthy, and many of them could not afford a good education. However, those who did so were sufficient in numbers to have an adverse effect on the overall educational standards of the Malays, who fell behind in this respect.

In the 1930s Malay women were discouraged from pursuing higher forms of education. The Malay Women's Reform Movement set only limited goals, which included some improvement in female education facilities as well as an increase in social and occupational freedom. Pre-war Malaya was almost devoid of women's movements, except for those formed by small elite groups of English-school graduates and teachers. The majority of Malay women lived in seclusion and were even prohibited from appearing in public. Despite the social and educational restrictions imposed on Malay women, many were more industrious and shrewd than their male counterparts. The purchase of gold and jewellery was seen by many women as a sensible means to accumulate wealth, rather than to squander money on less tangible luxuries.

4:4 New Leadership Groups

The decision to admit a few suitably qualified Malays into the Malayan Civil Service (MCS) was made in 1921. During the decade that followed ten posts only were created, and all those who were selected for these were confined to applicants from the traditional elite class of Malays. The creation of these opportunities gave rise to the emergence of a new English-educated leadership group among the Malays, who were influenced by western ideas of government and social organisation. They derived their authority in part from an inherited social status within the Malay community, as well as from their new association within the ramifications of British colonialism.

By the early 1930s individuals in this small but growing group of English-educated government servants were particularly conscious of the competition to their positions from non-Malays. They turned to the British to safeguard their interests, whilst the modernisation of Malay society slowly proceeded on its way. Heading this group were the administrators, who were mostly from the aristocracy, and had been educated at the Malay College. Next were a few Malay officials in the customs, police, agricultural and co-operative departments, who had either been promoted through special schemes for Malay recruitment and training, or had also progressed by way of the Malay College. Below this group were those who had taken up either clerical or semi-technical occupations. In 1931 all the people within the three categories of this group totalled probably less than 1,500.

During the early decades of the 20th century there were three new elite groups within Malay society contending with each other. Each in its own way refused to accept some aspects of colonial traditionalism, and had varying aspirations towards speedy political and social change. The Arabic-educated religious reformists founded their ideological origins on the Islamic renaissance that took place in Egypt and Turkey around the end of the 19th century. The radical Malay intelligentsia, strongly influenced by the Indonesian nationalist movement, looked towards freeing Malaya from colonial rule, and towards a political unification with Indonesia, under the guise of a Greater Malaysia Raya. Drawn from mostly the peasant classes, members of this group often had a confused and naive political ideology, but they did manage to attract privately some of the traditional Malay elite and the new English-educated bourgeoisie. The third group contending for position and political influence came from the traditional elite themselves, amongst whom were the English-educated administrators and government servants.

4:5 Economic Anxiety and Inequality

The web of economic hardship caused by the Great Depression in the early 1930s enveloped all classes of society in Malaya. The peasant land-owning and agriculturally-oriented Malays were also enmeshed within the resultant financial turmoil, their debts increasing both during and after this period. As has been mentioned, their problems stemmed from their being dependent on seasonal crops, which made it necessary for them to resort to other means of financing during the non-cropping seasons. This they did by obtaining advances in cash and kind from Chinese shop-keepers and rice millers, as well as mortgaging their land, mostly to Indian chettiars. In 1933, of the 2,300 rubber estates of 100 acres or more, only 59 were owned by Malays. On larger rubber estates during this period, Malays were also in a significant minority. Only about 7,400 Malays lived on these, compared to 37,900 Chinese and 203,000 Indians. As incomes decreased in line with the decline in rubber and other commodity prices, so widespread land-oriented indebtedness increased. Even smallholdings within Malay reservations were mortgaged or sold, to an extent which caused serious anxiety among British and Malays alike.

Disputes between Malays over land ownership often became emotional issues. Acrimonious legal wrangles and the money expended to obtain a court ruling sometimes greatly exceeded the value of the land under dispute. Peasant Malays were generally unsound businessmen and many of them seemed unable to comprehend the potential and capacity of money. They seemed to be incapable of planning alternative ways of acquiring money, other than by selling what they directly produced, or by performing tasks requiring manual labour. Interest on loans, however small that might be, was interpreted as usury. This was a religious consideration, and therefore played a significant role in blocking Malay involvement and advancement in enterprises related to money-lending and banking. A Muslim could borrow money, but his religion forbade him to lend it for profit.

Another cause for concern among Malays, in the late 1920s and 1930s, arose from increasing Chinese demands for equal rights and privileges along with the Malays. They agitated for a larger share in the administrative cake and for more opportunities to obtain employment in government service. The tide of harmonious inter-racial feelings began to ebb when domiciled Chinese altered their outlook and chose to regard Malaya as their home, not simply as a temporary abode for making enough money to enable them to return to China.

Many Malays sought, by adherence to their traditional forms of education, a means of safeguarding their cultural and personal identity. Their anxiety increased as they began to realise that, in a fast modernising world, their role had been transformed into an apparently subordinate and inferior one, compared with that of the other races in the country. The Malays' social and political position compared unfavourably with that of the British, and their economic position with that of the Chinese. They were even in a culturally inferior position to the other ethnic groups in the country. Although this caused widespread uneasiness, before the war the Malays were unable to find an agreeable solution to their dilemma.

They grew increasingly anxious over their economic subservience to the Chinese, particularly when inflammatory Chinese claims, similar to those made by Mr Lim Ching Yan to the Penang Chinese Association (see Chapter 3:3), were made. Claims that the country belonged equally to the Chinese as it did to the Malays provoked an explosive reaction.

4:6 Political Developments prior to 1941

British rule in Malaya was never really welcomed by the Malays. From the onset they staged a series of token revolts against it, the last of which was in 1928. The British made treaties with the respective state rulers, by which they were required to extend their advice and protection on all matters affecting the states, except on those appertaining to the Islamic religion and Malay customs, which remained at the sole discretion and prerogative of the state rulers. The treaties, particularly in the Federated Malay States, gave the British an almost unfettered mandate, and from this there later arose much justifiable criticism of British policy concerning immigration, which had allowed the Chinese to gain economic dominance throughout the Federated Malay States of Perak, Selangor, Pahang and Negeri Sembilan. This, the Malays viewed, was not in accordance with the spirit of the treaties that had been made ostensibly to protect their interests. The subsequent discontent of the Malays over their lack of participation in — and share of — the economic cake led to an awakening of political consciousness among them, and then to the gradual development of a nationalist movement. An impact was also made on the Malays by the Middle East Islamic Reformist Movement, which Britain regarded as a threat to the country's stability. Another threat was the influence of Indonesian communist refugees in Malaya between 1928–30, who stimulated enrolment into Soekarno's Partai Nasionalis Indonesia (PNI), following their abortive attempt in 1926–7 to overthrow the Dutch. In 1938 it was this group that joined up with other radical Malay graduates to form the Young Malay Union (Kesatuan Melayu Muda, KMM), the immediate aim of which was to achieve independence. In 1941 only KMM followers were seriously thinking and planning towards this.

A variety of influences during the late 1920s and throughout the 1930s coincided to mollify and divert the ermerging impetus towards nationalistic unity. The diverse economic, cultural and educational backgrounds of the majority races in the country were disincentives towards political unification, and produced a variable approach towards any nationalism. Similarly, the overall and relative prosperity enjoyed by people, apart from those hardships caused by the post World War I trade depressions and again in the early 1930s, dulled the urgency of nationalism. The movement of immigrant races, both in and out of Malaya until 1931, meant that there was a high proportion of immigrants who regarded the country only as a temporary home, and did not wish to become politically or administratively involved in it. Another important delaying influence was the opportunity presented by the British to intelligent, educated Malays to take up appointments in high-level positions in government service. By making such opportunities available to the Malay elite, within the existing regime, the British astutely averted mounting feelings of discontent among potential political leaders.

Although the political consciousness of the Malays had been awakened in the late 1930s, Malay nationalism had scarcely come into being before the commencement of World War II in 1939. It was also felt that continued British protection was required to contain the rapid growth of the Chinese community. The policy of decentralistion in the 1930s not only gave more clout to state autonomy but also extended preference to the Malay aristocracy. This meant that the intelligentsia within evolving Malay nationalist movements looked upon themselves not only as the vehicles of preservation of an inherited culture, but also as insufficiently strong entities to stand alone. During this period the aristocratic Malays dominated the political scene, and more often than not professed loyalty towards the British. Thus, although racial tension in the years between the two World Wars was negligible, it was noticeable in the political manoeuvrings of the Malays that they wished to protect their interests in relation to those of the Chinese, rather than to aspire towards the end of British rule.

Before 1941 no single race had an absolute majority in Malaya. The agglomeration comprising the four Federated Malay States (Perak, Pahang, Selangor and Negri Sembilan), the five Unfederated Malay States (Perlis, Kedah, Kelantan, Trengganu and Johore) and the three Straits Settlements (Penang, Malacca and Singapore) meant that there was hardly any nation, and no unified nationalism. As mentioned earlier, each race had different customs, educational outlooks and political aspirations. The Chinese and Indians were oriented towards the culture and politics of their own homelands, and became involved in national activities that opposed Western imperial dominance in them. Social, occupational and religious divisions within the main races in Malaya, and even within the Malay community itself, were such that the development of any unified approach to politics was continually being frustrated. The Malay peasantry never gave its support to any nationalistic movement. They seemed content to be guided by their aristocratic leaders and by British District Officers. Britain's pre-war policy clearly emphasised that Malaya was the country of the Malays. Even so, Malay organisations such as the Kaum Muda and the Young Malay Union (Kesatuan Melayu Muda – KMM) were at first politically motivated by events in Egypt, Indonesia and Turkey and were not inclined to view each other as competitors.

The Malays were at the bottom of the economic ladder in British Malaya. The Chinese, having amassed wealth, education and experience, held the strongest economic position. They were also better able to adapt to changing circumstances and to seize new opportunities. As Malay political influence began to assert itself, Malay newspapers started demanding an end to uncontrolled immigration and urged that Malays be given economic parity with the other races in the country. The situation augured future problems, when the Malays commenced to voice their opinion that the Indians and Chinese were parasites of British colonialism, which in turn was sucking the wealth out of the country. Thus, while Malay self-consciousness and assertiveness increased, economic pressures remained in the background, as did the controversy of decentralisation and threatened alien encroachment on Malay rights.

Three attempts were made between 1934 and 1941 to create large-scale, pan-Malay organisations, aimed at providing the Malays with the means of running their own affairs. Each organisation was established by one or other of the new elite groups, but none of them was able to gain any significant mass support.

Although, prior to 1941, there were no large political groups vying for independence in Malaya, individual Malays were affected by nationalistic ideals which were already stirring in other parts of Asia. Western-type education, and the emphasis this placed on values such as patriotism, democracy and political freedom, had a stimulating effect, and pre-war British administrators in Malaya were not unsympathetic to thoughts of nationalism within the confines of the colonial regime. However, in the absence of any strong political party with a nationalist platform, there was no sense of urgency. Also, the political and administrative divisions throughout the country did not encourage unity, as no less than eleven different governments had to become involved before any agreement could be reached. Only the Straits Settlements were under direct British rule. The different states, or groups of states, that formed the Federated Malay States (FMS) and the Unfederated Malay States (UFMS), had various and differing treaty relationships with Britain. In the FMS, British administration was strongly entrenched, whereas in the UFMS a considerable measure of independence was still retained, and any suggestion to reduce this was viewed with grave suspicion.

In contrast to the politically active Chinese, whose energies were directed mostly to the Kuomintang rather than the illegal Malayan Communist Party, or the Indians, whose sympathies and nationalistic aspirations were channelled away from Malaya by the Congress Party in India, the loyalty of the Malays in 1941 was oriented firmly towards their own sultans and respective states.

The British pre-war policy of isolating communities from one another reduced social changes and conflict. This policy also acted as a deterrent to nationalism, preventing the emergence of a unilateral view-point and a united nationalist movement. When resentment was sufficiently strong, the Malays were as capable of a change of political heart as any others. Before World War II, however, most of them were politically inactive and disinterested. They did not appear to care what happened in their country, and instead of showing resentment against the British, they were full of praise for them. The Malay masses considered politics none of their concern, and confirmed this by not dabbling in it.

At the outset of the Japanese occupation the bulk of Malays, and especially those who had Pan-Malay ideals involving links with Indonesia, were not particularly hostile towards their new masters. During the early part of the occupation, Malay co-operation was significant. The occupation emphasised the depth of communal differences, and by its end had exposed underlying pre-war tensions and anxieties which later exploded into open and lasting conflict. The occupation also had an important political impact on the Malays. It acted as a catalyst in the emergence and development of a new ideology for Malay nationalism.

4:7 Brotherhood of Pen Pals (Sahabat Pena)

The *Saudara* was a Penang based newspaper published twice weekly by religious reformists. In March 1934 the newspaper introduced a new feature for its younger readers, in addition to its regular reportings and editorials. Part of the paper was set aside for young journalists to voice their opinions on a wide range of topics, especially those that were of immediate interest to the Malays. From this small beginning there emerged the first, and one of the largest pan-Malay organisations.

The Brotherhood of Pen Pals (Sahabat Pena) movement attracted large numbers of writers and members, and provided them with a politically safe outlet for Malay anxieties and insecurities. The loyalty of Malays to their language was emphasised in its columns, from which a lasting slogan arose: 'Long live the language; long live the nation!' (Hidup bahasa; hidup bangsa!) The slogan was taken up a decade later by the post-war nationalist movement, which championed the country's cause for independence.

In 1935 Sahabat Pena's membership was just over 2,000. By the latter part of 1937 it had reached almost 10,000. The increased size of the organisation introduced tensions, and in late 1937 an open rift developed. Malay writers turned away from cultural topics and instead diverted their attention to overt political interests. A decline in the membership of Sahabat Pena followed this change of direction, and by 1940 numbers had fallen to about 3,000.

4:8 Young Malay Union (Kesatuan Melayu Muda – KMM)

While Sahabat Pena's popularity was waning between 1938 and 1940, some English-educated Malays of the elite bureaucracy, and two other groups of radical Malay intelligentsia, were active in trying to form basic political organisations. There was no pre-war agreement, however, between Islamic traditionalists and reformers. Other educated people, including school teachers, and many from the peasant classes, were influenced by Indonesian anti-colonialists and wanted Malaya to draw closer to Indonesia. This faction never gained the mass support of the Malay middle classes and administrators, on account of their expressed opposition to the Malay royalty.

On 6th August 1939, in Kuala Lumpur, the Pan-Malayan Malay Association held its first conference. This event was a major step along the path towards attaining Malay national solidarity, and also realised the early efforts of Malay nationalism. A second conference was held in Singapore on Christmas day 1940, but due to the subsequent outbreak of war, a third one had to be cancelled.

By the end of 1941, therefore, the Malays were broadly divided into two political groupings. The first, a right-leaning entity, was led by upper class, English-educated Malays and was often referred to as the 'Malay College Group'. It was this group that mainly sponsored the conference of Pan-Malayan Malay Associations, and whose principles were based on Malaya for the Malays. The other faction was left-leaning and originated from Malay-educated radical intelligentsia, who were more often than not graduates from the Sultan Idris Training College at Tanjong Malim. Their demands included political freedom for all oppressed people in Malaya. The leader of this leftist group was Ibrahim bin Haji Yaacob.

Ibrahim was born in 1911 in the Temerloh district of Pahang. He joined the Sultan Idris Training College in 1929, where he became associated with refugee political leaders who had fled Indonesia, following the failure there of the 1926–7 communist-led revolution. Arising from his meetings with these Indonesians, Ibrahim's interest in politics was stimulated and, emulating their example, he took up an anti-colonial political stance. In 1937 Ibrahim bin Haji Yaacob, along with Ishak Haji Mohammed and others whose sympathies were Indonesia-oriented, formed the Young Malay Union, otherwise called the Kesatuan Melayu Muda (KMM). Between 1938 and 1941 the leadership of the small pseudo-political KMM was influenced by Seokarno's policy of non-cooperation in Indonesia. In 1939 KMM leaders and Malay-educated intellectuals within the organisation commenced propaganda attacks against British policies and what they considered to be colonial neglect of Malay welfare. These activities brought them under the surveillance of British Special Branch officers and resulted in their being distrusted by the majority of the Malays. The KMM was considered a threat to the British government's position and interests in Malaya, and in 1940 the leaders were arrested.

The KMM's aim was to seek independence for Malaya within the framework of a Greater Indonesia. It worked towards promoting the nationalistic feelings of the lower classes, and professed no loyalty towards the British or the Sultans. It wanted wider union with Indonesia and through this, independence for Malaya. The KMM's ideology required that all Malays in one region should regard themselves as being one race, speaking one language and belonging to one nation. It wanted to develop a wider sphere of loyalty, outside those bounded by ethnic origin and geographical limitations. Such new ideas were distrusted by many Malays in the country, especially as Malay states were still pre-occupied with their individual state autonomy. Not only did the KMM want to liberate Malaya from British rule, but it also aspired to rid the country of titled and propertied Malays, who were considered the tools of the British. Although the KMM's ideology appealed to a minority of educated Malay intellectuals, it was not sufficiently well thought out to attract the masses and to succeed. The KMM's attempted conflict with British administration prior to the Japanese invasion marked a change in Malay sentiments.

It revealed a growing desire to break from the bondage which the Malays had hitherto accepted. However, when subsequent Japanese victories in 1942 negated geographical boundaries, the KMM was unable to make positive use of this opportunity.

The KMM's size was unknown in December 1940 as no constitution, manifesto or list of officers had been published. Among its leading members were: Ibrahim bin Haji Yaacob as President, Onan bin Haji Sirag (Ibrahim's brother-in-law) as Vice President, Abdul Karim Rashid as Secretary and Haji Othman bin Abdullah as Treasurer. Although the KMM meant different things to different people, its leaders called unanimously for the alleged exploitation of Malays to be stopped, and the creation of nationalist feelings through a closer cultural association with Indonesia. Ibrahim admitted that the KMM wanted to throw off the 'foreign colonial yoke and create a free Malaya'.[3] He condemned colonialism and the 'assumptions of innate superiority shown by many British in Malaya'.[4] However, these views were voiced mainly in private and did not figure prominently in the KMM's political activities. Thus, the KMM under Ibrahim Yaacob's leadership utterly failed to obtain the support of the masses, although it did meet with some success in training a nucleus of Malay left-wing politicians, who later became instrumental in more than one radical Malay political movement.

Prior to the outbreak of hostilities between Japan and Britain the KMM contributed significantly towards a resurgence of Malay nationalism. In its anxiety to topple British colonial power, the KMM was drawn towards the Japanese, and into espionage activities aimed at assisting Japan with preparations for her planned invasion of Malaya. The KMM alleged that the support given to the Japanese was conditional on financial payment and promises of independence being considered. The latter included assurances that Malay sovereignty, religion and custom would be safeguarded, as would the respect of Malay women and property. The Japanese later denied that they had given any such political promises, but they did allocate a sum of $18,000, which was paid to Ibrahim bin Haji Yaacob for the purchase of the *Warta Melayu* newspaper. This he purchased from its Arab proprietors in August 1941, and used as a subtle organ in which to promote Japanese propaganda. Ibrahim and his colleagues were charged with fifth column activities under wartime defence regulations, and became some of the first occupants of the newly completed Changi jail in Singapore. They remained there until they were released by the Japanese in February 1942, when the British took their place.

The KMM made little attempt before the war to conceal its hostility towards British policies and operated openly as a legal political organisation. Early in December 1941 Ibrahim bin Haji Yaacob, as the President of the KMM, issued an order for the KMM to cooperate with invading Japanese forces. However, on 7th and 8th December 1941 British Special Branch officers raided the offices of the *Warta Melayu*, and arrested approximately 150 pro-Japanese KMM leaders and members who were holding a meeting there. These arrests reduced the co-operation that the KMM was able to extend to the Japanese during the initial stages of their invasion. KMM members and officials who managed to avoid being arrested later acted as guides and interpreters for the Japanese, thereby assisting their advance down the peninsula, in the face of the British retreat.

The KMM failed to attain a wide following before the war and lacked the support of the traditional ruling classes. Because of its fifth column activities, which were inspired by the Japanese Consul General in Singapore, Malay motivations were viewed with distrust by the British until the closing stages of the war.

4:9 State Associations (Persatuan Persatuan Negeri)

The aims of individual state associations (Persatuan Persatuan Negeri) were directed at safeguarding the automony of respective states and the political rights of Malays. The associations were started in the peninsular states in early 1938, in addition to those that had already been established in Singapore, which had branch offices in Malacca and Penang. Representations were made to government by state associations on a variety of topics. These mostly took the form of special pleas for continued Malay privileges. The associations were not anti-colonial by nature, neither were they particularly nationalistic. Not only were they 'unswervingly loyal'[5] to the British, particularly after the outbreak of war in Europe in September 1939, but they were also loyal to their state rulers and to the traditional form of Malay establishment.

Leading pre-war spokesmen for the Malays and prominent in state associations were the English-educated lawyers and those civil servants who had connections with Royalty. Being traditional in their outlook, they opposed the administration's hitherto uncontrolled immigration policy, as they did the KMM's manoeuvrings for an united Indo-Malaya, which was an anathema to them.

In August 1939 a National Congress of Malay State Associations was held in Kuala Lumpur. The purpose of this Congress was to propose ways and means by which the efforts of the Malays, and those of state associations, could be strengthened. In Penang there were two associations at that time, and both wanted to send representatives to the Congress. The Singapore Malay Union — Penang Branch (Kesatuan Melayu Singapore — Chawangan Pulau Pinang) was the one that was invited to attend, as this branch was claimed to be truly Malay in nature (Melayu Jati). The second branch, the Penang Malay Association (Persatuan Melayu Pulau Pinang), was comprised largely of Jawi members, and for this reason was not invited to attend. The dispute that arose over this selection was to later become the cause of continued repercussions between both these associations.

On 10th September 1939 the Selangor Malay Association announced its official and full backing of Britain, and resolved to remain unruffled by war rumours. This support also extended to the concept of preparing for Malaya's own territorial safety, and constant prayers were offered for Britain's speedy victory over Germany. The Association requested that priority should be given to the enlistment of Malays into the Volunteer Infantry Corps and that three additional Malay Regiments should be raised. They further proposed that one or two small battleships should be purchased and Malays trained to serve on them. All Malays in government service were called upon to contribute generously to the Lady Thomas Patriotic War Fund, which was organised by the wife of Sir Shenton Thomas, the Governor of the Straits Settlements, on the day following the outbreak of war between Great Britain and Germany.

A second Congress of State Associations was held in Singapore on 25–26th December 1940. This was attended by 41 delegates. After two days of intensive discussions, only five out of a total of 17 resolutions had been passed, all of which were of a conservative, pro-Western bias. The Selangor State Association's delegates proposed that a Spitfire Fund should be established, in order to purchase aircraft for Britain's war effort. Another resolution urged that English education should be made more readily available to the Malays.

Despite talks of unity and attaining common strength, agreement over a proposal to amalgamate Malay state associations into a single national entity completely failed. This most important question continued to elude solution. After the second Congress had been closed, Onn bin Jaafar, who had attended as a special guest, declared,

> 'The Malays as a people have not yet fallen and with the creation of the Malay Associations I believe they can regain the political and civil rights which have slipped from them.'[6]

When, five years later, the Malayan Union proposals threatened the continued existence of traditional Malay establishments, the Malays turned as one to their state associations and to the leadership that had been generated through them.

Support for Malay state association movements in the 1930s arose from the increasing anxieties among English-educated Malays in government employment that specific Malay interests could be lost by default to locally domiciled aliens. Although the associations were loyal to their separate state structures, and to the British colonial system of rule, they no doubt at this early stage envisaged a time when Malaya might be in a position to declare her independence. They did not, however, envisage one Malay Association for the whole country, but foresaw that with the coming of independence, the sultans and their states would remain intact as an 'enduring symbol of Malay political authority and cultural identity'.[7]

4:10 Malay Vernacular Press

After the *Utusan Melayu* ceased publication in 1922, following a financially crippling libel suit, the *Lembaga Melayu* was the only daily Malay newspaper in circulation until it stopped publication in 1931.

The *Lembaga Melayu*, although controlled by the English-language press, was 'edited by a "loyalist" Malay in the confidence of the government'.[8] The paper voiced for many urban, middle-class Malays, and British officials alike, progressive but moderate Malay opinions.

A new era of Malay journalism dawned following the demise of the *Lembaga Melayu*, and in 1930 the *Warta Malaya* became the first of many independent Malay dailies. Between 1920 and 1930, 34 new vernacular newspapers and periodicals mushroomed in Malaya, 11 of which were published in Penang. Only three were published in Singapore, with the remaining 20 being published throughout the other peninsular states. Rather than Singapore, Penang at this time became renowned and re-established as a centre that extended its support to journalistic religious reform.

During the 1930s a total of 81 Malay-language newspapers and periodicals flooded into print all over the country. In 1935 and 1936 alone, 25 new Malay-language newspapers and magazines appeared. Malay journalism revolved around a few select metropolitan daily newspapers, the most influential of which were the *Warta Malaya* between 1930 and 1941, the *Majlis* between 1931 and 1941, the *Lembaga* between 1935 and 1941, and the *Utusan Melayu* from 1939 to 1941.

The *Warta Malaya* newspaper was originally published in Singapore in January 1930. For the first four years of its existence it was edited by Onn bin Ja'afar, a recalcitrant and somewhat outspoken son of the Mentri Besar of Johore. The *Warta Malaya* was a pro-Malay publication rather than an anti-Colonial one. Although its editorials were highly critical of Britain's implementation of policies, it also sought to obtain the promotion of more Malays to senior administrative posts within government service, rather than to oust the British completely. Onn gave up the editorship of the *Warta Malaya* at the end of 1933, and in 1935 started another daily newspaper, the *Lembaga*. The editorial policy of the *Lembaga* followed closely to that of the *Warta Malaya*, although it concentrated more on affairs appertaining to the State of Johore, rather than to those of a more national nature.

The *Majlis* was based in Kuala Lumpur and was edited by Abdul Rahim Kajai from 1931 to 1935. This newspaper championed many questions that were agitating the Malays. In particular, it highlighted Malay opinion and suspicions concerning other Asian races in the country, and the extent that they were being 'permitted to usurp the rights of the Malays in their own land'.[9] The paper's editorials were adamant that Britain, whether she liked it or not, was under a solemn obligation to give first preference to upholding Malay interests. In 1938 Ibrahim bin Haji Yaacob became the assistant editor of the *Majlis* and also in that year, in conjunction with other people of similar radical political opinion, he formed the KMM, which was the first left-wing Malay political organisation in the country. In November 1939, when the *Majlis* started to publish dailies, Ibrahim became its third editor. He held the post until late in 1941, when he purchased, with Japanese money, the *Warta Malaya* newspaper, which he then used on behalf of the Japanese to publish propaganda and anti-British articles.

The first issue of the *Utusan Melayu* appeared on 29th May 1939. The paper was presented to its readers as being a purely Malay enterprise. In political matters, however, the *Utusan Melayu* was most careful, to the extent of being timid, in what it published. By 1941, having overcome a bitter struggle for survival against competition from the *Warta Malaya* and the *Lembaga*, the *Utusan* was quite firmly established, with a daily circulation of 1,800 copies.

The *Warta Malaya, Lembaga* and the *Majlis* were financed, and thereby controlled, by non-Malays. Even so these newspapers were able to provide an increasingly important forum and outlet for the Malay intelligentsia, in literary and editorial aspects of Malay-language journalism.

1. *British Rule in Malaya 1942–57* by Robert Heussler, Ch.4, p.89.
2. *The Jungle is Neutral* by F. Spencer Chapman, Ch.2, p.24.
3. *The Origins of Malay Nationalism* by W.R. Roff, Ch.7, p.232. (Refer to *Nusa dan Bangsa Malaju*, p.59–60, and *Sekitar Malaya Merdeka*, p.21.)
4. Ibid, p.233.
5. Ibid, p.240.
6. Ibid, p.247.
7. Ibid, 'Retrospect', p.256.
8. Ibid, Ch.5, p.161.
9. Ibid, p.171.

CHAPTER FIVE: IDENTITY DILEMMA

5:1 Pre-War Politics – Effects on Indians in Malaya

Nationalism was embedded into the hearts of the Indian masses during the 19th century rule of the British Raj in India. Twenty years of constitutional progress by the Indian Movement of Emancipation ended in 1906, and was followed by a prolonged period of aggressive, revolutionary activities that lasted until 1919. The politically inflammatory years between 1920 and 1941 were influenced considerably by Mohandas Karamchand (Mahatma) Gandhi's doctrines of non-cooperation and civil non-violent disobedience against the British government of India, which in late 1942 yet again culminated in his arrest.

When Subhas Chandra Bose, a Bengali revolutionary and a political refugee in Berlin, was manoeuvred into resigning his position and bid for leadership in the Indian National Congress Party (INCP), he founded and became the leader of an extremist 'Forward Bloc' element within the ranks of the INCP, which developed into the nationalist movement's militant wing. By doing this, Bose came into direct opposition with the conservative leadership of the INCP, and with Mahatma Gandhi, over the question of using force against the British. Following Bose's attendance at an 'Anti-Compromise Conference' in March 1940 and his ever increasingly violent anti-British speeches, he was arrested on 2nd July 1940 on charges of sedition. Within six months, however, and just prior to his trial, Bose disappeared from Calcutta, and by devious routes eventually was flown from Moscow to Berlin, where he arrived on 28th March 1941.

Although the British government's authority in India had been under constant threat, British rule in Malaya, in the years prior to the outbreak of World War II, was not challanged by the Indian community. The Indians who lived either in the Straits Settlements, or in the Federated or Unfederated Malay States, were mostly concerned with nationalistic issues in their own homeland. In Malaya, their interest was generally limited to matters such as working conditions on estates, opportunities for employment in government departments and regulations related to citizenship rights.

Although pre-war migration of Indians into Malaya had been high, they did not fare well economically. They were the major source of cheap manual labour in the country and their low economic status was regarded with disdain by both Malays and Chinese alike. This attitude increased the cultural and social gulf that already divided the various races in the country and added to the antagonisms that were building up between them.

The great majority of pre-war Indians in Malaya were Tamil labourers from the Madras Presidency. They invariably worked on rubber estates, the railways, or in the public works department. Most of them did not hold any strong attachment for Malaya and usually opted to return to their native Madras after working for a few years. Second generation Tamils were employed mostly as clerks, school masters and overseers. Many Indians were divided in their loyalty, but at this time more were interested in the politics of their homeland and India's struggle for independence. However, many Punjabis and Sihks did enlist into the Malayan police force, in which they became valuable members.

The pre-war Indian population in Malaya was also divided into two segments of origin, the India-born and the Malaya-born. The former experienced a conflict of loyalties and supported either the National Congress Party in India or other political organisations which were rallying Indians to the call for independence.

The Central Indian Association of Malaya (CIAM) came into being after a visit to Malaya by Nehru in 1937. The main pre-war political activities of CIAM revolved around giving evidence to the Shastri Commission in 1937, which investigated working conditions of Indian labour, mobilising Indian middle and working class people, and supporting the 1941 Klang strikes. The upper echelons of leadership within the CIAM were mainly professional men who failed to identify themselves with the interests of Indian workers. They looked on Indian labourers with contempt, and although they were well aware of their plight, they took no particular interest in them, neither did they attempt to organise them. For the most part, CIAM leaders were not Tamils, and therefore any progress that could have been made was thwarted or averted on account of a language barrier. Because of this, Indian labourers remainded unorganised until world events overtook them in 1941, when many flocked to join the ranks of the Indian Independence League (IIL) and the Indian National Army (INA). Ironically, some of the leaders in the IIL in Malaya came from the pre-war CIAM, and they provided some continuity among the leaders of the Indian community.

The Japanese branch of the IIL was organised in October 1937 with Rash Behari Bose — a pro-German terrorist who had fled to Japan in 1916 — as its President. Bose was recognised as a leader of Indian nationalists and refugees in Japan, and formed the Japan branch of the IIL for the express purpose of spreading anti-British propaganda, in the promotion of India's struggle for independence.

CHAPTER SIX: SLY ADVANCES

6:1 Military Espionage before 1941

The spying activities of Japan in the late 1920s and throughout the 1930s were notorious in their extent, and in the open manner in which they were carried out. Throughout countries in the Far East, and particularly in the Malay Peninsula, copious notes were prepared on a variety of subjects. Included prominently among these were details concerning static military defences, jungle tracks, the movement of warships, the construction and condition of airfields, road and rail communications throughout the country and the habits and irregularities in the behaviour of some planters in the remoter parts of the country. The activities of Japanese agents and spies, many of whom had posed for a long time in various guises of business and trade, were mostly allowed to continue unchecked during much of this period, arising from political and economic expediency, and the 'cricket' code of ethics to which British peace-time administrators seemed to be addicted. The frequent complaints made by senior officers in the armed forces, regarding irregular and suspicious movements of Japanese nationals were to no avail. They fell on the deaf ears of a trade-oriented civil administration.

In October 1936 Colonel F. Hayley Bell was sent out to Singapore by the War Office in London, as a defence security officer. Bell's task was to attend to matters related to military intelligence, as opposed to those of a civil nature, which came under the jurisdiction of the Governor of the Straits Settlement and his staff. With the co-operation of British Intelligence in the Far East, and the Chief Inspector of Police, Bell began to investigate the extent and methods of Japanese espionage in Malaya and Singapore. During two and a half years of exhaustive investigations Colonel Bell and his team discovered extensive evidence of Japanese espionage systems, and from the invaluable evidence that was adduced they were able to make an accurate assessment of what, in due course, proved to be a future reality. Bell's perceptive and valuable report was so unpopular and so disturbed the civil administration in Malaya, which viewed trade profits as more important than security, that, astoundingly, they were able to instigate the disbandment of Colonel Bell's excellent organisation and his recall to Britain in May 1939.

Lieut Colonel Masanobu Tsuji — a brilliant, pushy and mysterious man — earned considerable distinction at the Staff College in 1934, and then as a tutor to Prince Mikasa, the youngest brother of Emperor Hirohito. Tsuji was assigned to set up the Taiwan Army Research Section, Unit 82, which was based in Formosa. The responsibilities of this unit included the collation of all intelligence information gathered from Japan's vast network of agents throughout South-East Asia. Lieut Colonel Tsuji was responsible for much of the planning of Japan's 'stunning campaigns' in her conquest of Malaya, Singapore and the Philippines.

Under Tsuji's capable organisation, the small team of Unit 82 made detailed studies of the numerous reports submitted by overseas agents, staff and sympathisers alike, since 1934. These covered a wide range of aspects concerning living conditions in Malaya and Singapore, and circumstances that could have an effect on the fighting efficiency of ground troops operating there. Hygiene, diet, sanitation and tropical medical care requirements, along with communications, clothing and transport, were some of the subjects that were all carefully examined. Unit 82 members became the most knowledgeable group of people in the world on the subject of tropical jungle warfare. They gathered a wide variety of information, including marching conditions in the tropical heat, the preservation of weapons and vehicles in the jungle and in salt water, and the best way to live off the country's natural resources. They assumed victory and made psychological studies of the best methods of administering occupied territories.

The detailed information which was studied revealed clearly that the back door to Singapore was virtually unguarded, and that the Royal Air Force (RAF) were far weaker than the British had made them out to be. The strength and weaknesses of British forces in the theatre were accurately ascertained, and the benefits that each Japanese division would derive by being accompanied from the outset by an engineer regiment were appreciated. It was realised that the presence of engineers would be invaluable to the progress of advancing ground troops, and would facilitate the repair of any or all of the 250 bridges which were known to exist along the road from Siam to Singapore. The tardy progress in constructing the Singapore Naval Base was common knowledge to the Japanese high command, as was Britain's fateful decision in 1937, at the Imperial Conference in London, to leave Singapore as a 'base without ships'.

By 1938 Japan's policy-makers believed that they were destined to rule the world. Their propaganda spread Japanese culture throughout Asia and, under the guise of the Great Asia Society, professed their goal as freedom for Asians from the yoke of Western influence. They preached racial, religious and cultural freedom, and 'Asia for the Asiatics' was taken up as their slogan. Western influence was anathema to the Japanese mind. Their interpretation of Pan-Asianism demanded the expulsion of everything Western, and Japanese propaganda reeked of anti-white sentiments.

On 10th September 1940 Colonel T. Tanikawa, the planning chief of Japan's Imperial Army HQ in Tokyo, arrived in Singapore. He was accompanied by Major Kunitake, who later became a staff officer with General Yamashita's 25th Army. Both officers arrived unceremoniously and in plain clothes, their purpose being to inspect discreetly the east and west coastlines of the Malay Peninsula. Before doing so, they toured Singapore and passed the Tengah Air Base that was still under construction. On returning to Singapore on 13th September, Colonel Tanikawa was already convinced that a direct sea-borne attack against the island would be impossible. It was his confirmed opinion that the best way to attack and conquer the 'island bastion' was by coming through the Malayan peninsula, and then across the unprotected Johore Straits to the north of the island. This information was duly passed to Lieut Colonel Tsuji, who was to become General Yamashita's chief planner of the future campaign.

The fact-finding coastal mission of Tanikawa and Kunitake had been assisted by Mr Mamoru Shinozake, who at that time was on the staff of the Japanese Embassy in Singapore. Shinozake was naïvely unaware that Singapore Special Branch officers had maintained a silent watch over his movements, and were well informed regarding his spying activities and attempts to coerce British navy and military personnel. He was later arrested and charged with collecting information that might be useful to a foreign power, and was sentenced to three and a half years of imprisonment with hard labour by the Singapore Supreme Court. Shinozake remained confined in Changi prison, in Singapore, until he was released on the evening of 15th February 1942, when the island was surrendered.

The pre-war independence aspirations of countries throughout South-East Asia were also made use of by Japan, with a view to weakening Britain's influence in the area. The Japanese indulged in political warfare, using this as a tool, without openly professing their own interests and intentions. Japan's outward and apparent sympathetic support for liberation movements was used as a means to further her own expansionary aims.

Malaya had been for years one of Japan's targets. With that ultimate goal in mind, numerous resident sleeper agents had been infiltrated into the country. Outwardly, these people appeared to be harmless, respectable businessmen, but they reported to Japan any important military details that became available to them. At the start of hostilities in December 1941, only some of the more well known Japanese agents in Singapore were rounded up. Others managed to evade arrest. Many of those who were caught had been long-standing businessmen, or had been in service trades such as photography and hairdressing, with easy access to information from unsuspecting, well-known customers. By the time the arrests were made these agents had completed their work well, and had pointed out defence weaknesses, troop numbers and quality, and shortages of aircraft and equipment. In February 1941, ten months before the attack on Malaya commenced, such was the extent of Japan's detailed knowledge of the country that Colonel Tsuji's Unit 82 was able to produce 40,000 copies of a book entitled 'Read This Alone and the War Can Be Won'. In this publication, soldiers were told exactly what conditions to expect in the tropical Malayan jungles, and how they could overcome the various problems which they would encounter there.

In Colonel Tsuji's plans for the invasion of Malaya and Singapore he formulated a time-table which allocated less than 100 days for the conquest of both. Similarly, he allocated less than 60 days to capture Manila, and less than 130 days to over-run Java.

6:2 Manipulations and Commercial Intrigue before 1941

Japan's commercial penetration into Malaya commenced during World War I. After 1918, when peace was resumed, the Japanese set about purchasing tracts of undeveloped agricultural land as well as established rubber estates. Most of these areas were carefully selected with pre-conceived intent and were later found to be in locations of strategic importance. In the two decades that followed the end of the 1914–18 Great War, Japanese trading enterprises expanded throughout the country. Most of them operated under a veneer of respectability which concealed their malignant aims.

During the 1930s Japanese nationals were prominent in every city and major town in Malaya, especially in Johore and Singapore. Their activities were people and strategy oriented, and spanned a wide cross-section of the community. Their ranks included businessmen, bankers, shipping agents, photographers, sundry traders, barbers, brothel-house keepers, sailors, restaurant owners and taxidermists. All had a single common denominator — a proximity to the general public from whom information could be obtained. Subsequent good use was made of the accurately drawn maps of rubber estates, roads, rivers and jungle paths that were prepared by these agents, many of whom had been living in Malaya for numerous years. In addition, there were also Japanese nationals who owned rubber plantations and mines. One Japanese company owned an iron mine in Trengganu, from where iron ore was exported in Japanese ships. In south Johore particularly, the Japanese owned a large number of strategically placed plantations, most of which, it was later discovered, were near important geographical features, either cross-roads, mouths of rivers, railway lines or major promontories. Many Japanese managers and supervisors in commerce and business had previous military experience, and most of them were well qualified to become involved in some form of spying, including arranging for fifth column activities. It was not uncommon to find that a plantation manager was in effect a Japanese naval commander, and that his senior Japanese staff were all naval officers.

In the autumn of 1931, subsequent to the Manchurian incident, the Chinese organised their first boycott of Japanese goods. This lasted until mid-1932. As China was Japan's chief trade opponent at that time, the Japanese retaliated to the boycott by resorting to dubious trading methods. A highly organised distribution network of low cost goods was developed, and prices were effectively undercut, particularly in the textile industry. Established quotas for cotton and rayon items were purposely evaded. With complete disregard for commercial integrity, Japanese goods were repacked under foreign trade marks to disguise the fact that they were being imported back into Malaya at cut-throat prices. By 1933, by various and illegal means, the flow of Japanese products into Malaya had increased to a substantial 13.6% of Malaya's total imports. Every endeavour was made by the Japanese to take full advantage of trade situations which would enable them to increase their knowledge of the country. In 1933, while working to salvage the *Jemchug*, a Russian cruiser which was sunk in Penang harbour early during the First World War, Japanese salvage experts took advantage of the opportunity to photograph the harbour and to determine the depth of its available anchorages.

By 1937, when the China Incident occurred, Japan's commercial position in Malaya was strong. Japanese propaganda was also intensified, with the aim of convincing others that Japan wanted to seek a lasting peace in the Pacific. The Penang Chinese were singled out for attention, because they had organised another trade boycott against Japanese goods and were also remitting several million dollars monthly to China, to help finance the resistance there against Japanese aggression. Japanese agents threatened those who supported China with reprisals against their relatives who were still living there, and with the confiscation of their property. Various means were used to bring pressure on those Chinese in Malaya who were giving financial and moral support to China, in the event that their anti-Japanese sentiments remained unabated. By using weapons of bribery and blackmail, Malaya was turned into a political battlefield. Chinese patriotic organisations were infiltrated in order to hamper their progress, and eventually to crush them. Thirty thousand dollars was given to a Japanese firm, for the express purpose of taking counteraction to offset the effects of the Chinese trade boycott, and to offer assistance to Indian merchants through the Indian Chamber of Commerce.

Rumour mongering was a powerful propaganda tool. Whispering campaigns aimed at stimulating racial prejudices and fomenting distrust of the established government. Unease was cultivated among both the civil population and the armed forces. Such was the effect of rumour mongering that by the end of 1939 it was feared that because of dissatisifaction in some of the garrisons in Malaya, they could not be relied upon to defend the country. A typical example was the rumour regarding a purported mutiny by 2,000 men of the Punjab Regiment, who had reportedly refused to go to Hong Kong. The rumour claimed that the mutineers had been landed at Penang, following the killing of an officer. Favourite topics for propaganda were stories of rifts between officers and men, and clashes between Indian, British and Australian troops. The molestation of Malay and Chinese women was another favoured topic, all the rumours being designed to increase the public's suspicions and prejudices.

In March 1941 Hideo Naito, a distinguished Japanese author, travelled extensively throughout the Malay Peninsula and also visited Penang. Naito made particular note of Penang's potential as a tourist and commercial centre, based on an assumption that the island would soon be occupied by the Japanese. He also identified some Malay school masters as potential fifth columnists.

Although Japanese trade declined in Malaya during the pre-war years, its nucleus and organisation was retained and was used as a means to gather political intelligence and to disseminate propaganda. Reactivating it was, therefore, not a difficult task. In 1941, in anticipation of future aggression in the region, and despite the boycott effects by the Chinese, a sudden flurry of activity occurred. The Japanese owned and controlled a Singapore-based newspaper, the *Herald*, referred to facetiously as the 'Voice of Japan'. It was permitted to continue printing until the bombing of Singapore commenced. Its editor, a Welshman named Jones, filled the paper's leading articles with his own weird mixture of Shintoism and socialism.

CHAPTER SEVEN: CRACKS IN THE ARMOUR

7:1 The 'Thin Red Line' — Benevolent Misconception

Britain encouraged a plural society in Malaya, as a communal mixture was deemed to be the best to serve her interests as she set about opening up the country. The British policy of encouraging the Malays to remain in relative rural isolation in their kampongs was designed to keep them ignorant of urban politics, and conveniently complemented the lack of interest shown by most Chinese and Indians in this respect. Only comparatively few people within the three major ethnic groups in the country were politically involved during the 1920s and 1930s. The majority, in all classes of society, including estate workers and shop owners, were apathetic towards the politics of Malaya and of their original homelands.

Britain's policy was one of divide and rule. The social isolationism of each ethnic group, and their political separatism, served her purpose well. Notwithstanding her policy of uncontrolled immigration, which by 1931 had resulted in the Chinese and Indians outnumbering the Malays, Britain continued to preserve the Malay religion and culture and to safeguard the legal position of the sultans. British administrators regarded the Malays as the country's indigenous people and accepted the responsibility to safeguard their welfare and ensure their enhancement. In 1936 Sir Shenton Thomas, Governor of the Straits Settlements and High Commissioner of the FMS and the UFMS, still strongly adhered to the British view that the Chinese were a transient labour force, despite the findings of the 1931 population census figures being to the contrary. It was his opinion that no one other than a native of the country, or an Englishman, should hold high administrative office, and he considered it dangerous to infer that there was among the Chinese any tendency towards permanent settlement. This view was also extended to the Indians, although the 1931 census again had clearly revealed that 20% of their total had been born in Malaya.

The advantages arising to the British from this stand were apparent, especially as the Peninsular States remained constitutionally and juridically autonomous Malay monarchies. It was anticipated that there would have been considerable opposition had any attempt been made to change the citizenship status of the Chinese and Indians. Britain's role as arbitrator of Malaya's plural society was to maintain and preserve the various communities' distinctions. This role was given added credibility by the political disinterest of the Chinese and, to a lesser extent, the Indians. Provided they were able to make money, and were allowed to follow their own religion and educational methods, the British authorities were able to avoid the troublesome responsibility of attempting to integrate them within the Malay community sector.

Outwardly, the British continued to look after the special interests of the Malay ruling classes. Non-Malays were excluded from positions of political authority as well as from senior administrative posts. At subordinate levels, however, the position was vastly different. By 1920, Indians and Chinese, both immigrants and the locally-born, were admitted into service with government departments, where they formed the majority of junior clerical and technical workers.

Notwithstanding policy distinctions of an ethnic origin, the welfare of the Chinese was by no means ignored. The Chinese Protectorate of the Malayan Civil Service (MCS), established in 1877, held a unique position in pioneer Malaya, and in the history of British colonial administration. Its purpose was to train officers to speak Chinese so that they could deal with the diverse important social problems of the Chinese, which included the control and suppression of secret societies and the well-being of immigrants. The protection of girls and women also came under the umbrella of the Protectorate, which eventually evolved as an essential contact between the Chinese community and the government. Not only was the head of the Chinese Protectorate the advisor to the government in political matters affecting the Chinese, but he was also designated the Registrar of Societies, and in this capacity his staff visited places where Chinese worked to ensure enforcement of the provisions of the Labour Code.

In 1934, a combined appointment of Secretary for Chinese Malaya was created.

Suppression of female trafficking was another responsibility of the Protectorate and the 'Protector' was gazetted as such under the Women and Girls' Protection Ordinance. Every Chinese girl and woman who arrived in the country was inspected, to ascertain whether or not she was a victim of the trafficking system.

The Chinese Protectorate touched the Chinese community at every level. Not only did it report on social aspects of their activities, but it became an essential pulse regulator which enabled the government to maintain up-to-date information concerning secret societies, political groups, social and educational bodies. The Protectorate, along with the Police and Courts, issued licences, enforced laws, controlled immigration and inspected all sorts of businesses, from boarding-houses to brothels, from orphanages and other charitable institutions to opium dens. It functioned as a bridge between the government and the Chinese community, and provided some guarantee of communal peace.

Conflicts of interests were bound to occur occasionally, particularly when certain Chinese customs conflicted with the interests of the community as a whole, or of the Malays specifically. In the 1930s, as some Chinese became more vocal politically, government interference in their activities increased, with the wide and general support of the community as a whole. A large degree of goodwill was generated among the Chinese community, particularly after the formation of the Chinese Protectorate. Although much of this was to be eroded by Britain's defeat at the hands of the Japanese, and the attempt after the war to make Malaya an independent communist state, among many ordinary non-politically oriented Chinese there still remained strong memories of previous goodwill.

British protocol, on which rule in Malaya was based, required that Europeans should live to a certain elevated standard to gain and retain the respect of the Asian population. Such was the importance of maintaining prestige that during the pre-war years, when planters enjoyed great prosperity and standards of living far above those of senior government servants, the latter successfully appealed to the Colonial Office for salary increases to enable them to match the lifestyle of the planters. Similarly, to maintain British prestige, both during and after the Great Depression, the government supported out-of-work Europeans and even provided some of them with passages back to England to avoid the embarrassment of their being seen as destitute. Similar reasoning motivated the decision to replace European train drivers in Malaya with Eurasians and Asians, just as soon as this could be implemented.

Throughout the existence of the Malayan Civil Service, a policy of outright rule over Malaya was followed. The Straits Settlements being a crown colony, the Governor's control was absolute. His knowledge of local affairs invariably enabled him to persuade his London superiors on policy matters. In both the Federated and Unfederated Malay States the Governor presided as High Commissioner, and was senior to all Residents, Advisors and lesser officials. The 200 officers of the MCS, about 20 of whom, by the 1930s, were Malays, had pervasive powers in a government that was 'authoritarian and benevolent'.[1] The post of Resident Councillor in Penang was one of the most senior in the Straits Settlements Civil Service, being next to that of Colonial Secretary. During Mr A. M. Goodman's tenure as Resident Councillor from 1934 to 1940, his earlier position as Head of Chinese Affairs enabled him to make good use of his expert knowledge to deal firmly but fairly with the Chinese community.

Prior to 1941 the MCS operated efficiently and the country was generally content and prosperous. There appeared to be little need for nationalism, and Britain's contribution towards health and education had been impressive. Most of the pre-war MCS officers knew little about Chinese or Indian affairs, being mainly proficient in Malay. Many of them, therefore, reached positions of considerable power without having any real interest in the aspirations or lives of half of the population in the country.

When Japan attacked Malaya, administrative changes were quick and startling. Soldiers were suddenly placed in command and civil servants were made painfully aware that they were no longer in charge as they had been before. Many MCS officers joined regular or volunteer military units, and for those in the most northern states of the country their change of role and loss of authority were traumatic and instant. Those working further south recalled that in some instances they

> 'lived for days or weeks in a twilight world of administration that was normal in most respects, though punctuated by bombings, rumours, frantic messages and constant turmoil'.[2]

The military disaster of 1941–2 was to signal the end of Britain's domination in the area and brought home vividly to the Malays, Chinese and Indians alike, Britain's inability to defend the country.

7:2 Financial Zealousness

Between 1919 and 1941 Malaya's population of 5.5 million voluntarily contributed £32 million towards Britain's imperial defence requirements. A large proportion of this total — £20 million — was consumed by the long drawn out project to construct the Naval Base in 'Fortress' Singapore. Following the outbreak of war with Germany in September 1939, and before Malaya was attacked in December 1941, special War Loan funds were raised in the Straits Settlements and the Federated Malay States, which by June 1941 had totalled £8.7 million. In addition, large sums were also voluntarily subscribed by the public towards the purchase of aircraft, and for a variety of war relief organisations.

During the first year of the war in Europe, total contributions from the Straits Settlements' War Fund and from the Federated and Unfederated States amounted to £3.75 million. Of this, in excess of £700,000 was raised through the Straits Settlements' War fund for the purchase of bombers, and towards the operational costs of a Straits Settlements' Squadron, which subsequently fought gallantly against the Luftwaft in Europe. All nationalities and classes of people gave generously to the various war funds that were arranged, and between September 1939 and December 1941, a total of £17 million was received, in addition to the substantial tax proceeds that were derived from the export of rubber and tin. Contributions from Malaya totaled more than two-thirds of all the contributions that were made from Britain's entire Colonial Empire.

When war broke out with Germany in September 1939, Malaya was allotted specific and important financial functions, and her rich material resources were made ungrudgingly available for Britain's war cause. The production of as much rubber and tin as possible became the 'order of the day', and these commodities went a long way towards provisioning Britain's war machine, as well as enabling her to obtain essential United States Dollars to finance her massive requirements. Malaya, therefore, was Britain's dollar arsenal. All available manpower was required to be fully used towards this goal, and British citizens of European descent were refused exit permits, even though their reason for wanting to leave Malaya was to volunteer to join one of the armed forces. Their continued services in Malaya, where they could bolster tin and rubber production, were considered to be more valuable than whatever contribution they could otherwise make by joining up.

On the day following the outbreak of war in Europe, Lady Thomas, the wife of Sir Shenton Thomas, the Governor of the Straits Settlements and High Commissioner to the FMS and UFMS, encouraged the organisation of a committee of wives from all races employed in government service, to establish the Malaya Patriotic War Fund. Every community enthusiastically supported this 'Lady Thomas' Fund and by January 1940 contributions had reached £100,000. The Chinese, in particular, were generous in their support, with even rickshaw-pullers contributing up to $1,000. The Fund's committee worked tirelessly, arranging for clothing to be made for members of the armed forces and organising various entertainments to raise funds. Thousands of dollars were raised to provide British troops with comfort, and for the relief of distressed British persons anywhere in the world. The Chinese were by far the largest subscribers to this fund, from which it was possible to send to the British Red Cross £375,000 for the aid of distressed Londoners. Some criticised the generous hospitality and entertainment for officers and men of the armed forces who were on short periods of leave in towns. Although the purpose behind the entertainment was to raise money, critics voiced their disapproval of what they considered to be 'good-time binges' at a time when danger loomed around the corner.

At a meeting of the Selangor Malay Association (Persatuan Melayu Selangor — PMS), on 10th September 1939, unanimous support for Britain was resolved, through thick and thin, in her conflict against Germany. The Selangor Malays further resolved to give wholehearted support towards making preparations for the safety of Malaya, and proposed various ways in which the Malay community could participate in this. It was also agreed that Malays should be asked to contribute to the Malaya Patriotic War Fund, although it was realised that the total that could be

> 'raised in Malaya was bound to be small in relation to the vast sums required in Britain for war expenditure'.[3]

However, it was felt that

> 'this gift will make them [the British people] understand that we at the other side of the British Empire are not forgetting them'.[4]

7:3 Cumbersome Constitutions — Administrative Hotchpotch

Sir Cecil Clementi, in his new capacity as Governor of the Straits Settlements and High Commissioner to the Federated Malay States and the Unfederated Malay States, realised in 1931 that some kind of closer association between the FMS, the UFMS and the Straits Settlements, would be needed eventually. As independent entities they were all too small to survive financially in the 20th century, and the Malay Peninsula was, equally, too small a country for so many independent governments to function effectively and efficiently. Continuance of the existing system would lead to unnecessary expenses, inefficiency and duplication of effort and purpose. Clementi also was firmly of the opinion that Malay rulers of each state should agree to uniform policies, especially in respect of immigration into their states. Preliminary figures of the 1931 Malay Peninsula and Singapore population census showed, for the first time, that immigrant races outnumbered the indigenous Malay population in the country. The census revealed only 1.93 million Malays, as opposed to 2.33 million Chinese and Indians. A common policy on immigration applicable to all States within the Malay Peninsula and in the Straits Settlements was therefore fast becoming necessary, in Clementi's opinion, as increasing numbers of Chinese were becoming permanent residents in the country.

Each of the four states within the FMS had its own legislature, although the Federal Government's administrative system was common to all of them. This was headed and co-ordinated by a Chief Secretary, who was an official of the British Colonial Office. He answered to the High Commissioner who, also being the Governor of the Straits Settlements, was based in Singapore. The High Commissioner presided at Federal Legislative Council meetings, and the four FMS shared a common civil service and police force, as well as customs and immigration departments. Most appointments of senior government administrative officials were held by officers who had been seconded to the Malayan Civil Service (MCS) from the British Colonial Office (CO). The handful of Malays who were employed in the MCS were all promoted from its local counterpart, the Malay Administrative Service.

The UFMS of Johore, Kedah, Perlis, Kelantan and Trengganu depended less on Britain for administrators. Each state had its own civil service and most heads of departments were Malays. Each state also had its own police force, customs and immigration departments and volunteer forces. Johore was the only State in the country which also had its own small, regular militia (Timbalan Setia Negeri).

Clementi's proposals were aimed at amending the constitution of the Federated States and making them constitutionally as similar as possible to the Unfederated States. In proposing to do this, he hoped that the latter would not object to the closer association that would result from his proposals. Contrary to Clementi's wishes, the rulers of the Unfederated States staunchly resisted him. They had no intention of relinquishing any of the powers they possessed. Neither did they intend to submit to having their autocracy restricted, as had the rulers in the Federated States. Clementi hoped that by increasing the powers of rulers in the Federated States, he would be able to overcome any objections that might be made.

The famous Clementi decentralisation speech was given during the Rulers' Conference at Sri Menanti in 1932. He urged that there should be only one Federation in a small country like Malaya and pointed out that the prevailing cumbersome divisions were not far short of being ridiculous administrative fragmentations. The rulers of the UFMS immediately opposed Clementi's proposals. They had no desire to be reduced to the mere figure-heads which they considered the FMS rulers to be, for in those States the administration was actually in the hands of British Residents. In the UFMS British Advisors only functioned as such, and power still ostensibly rested in the hands of the rulers and their state councils. They did not agree to relinquish any part of their individual state autonomy.

The Clementi proposals for the FMS envisaged a form of Federal control under a Federal Secretary in respect of central services, such as railways, immigration and customs. Other departments were to be the responsibility of individual states, among whom two-fifths of available revenue would be divided, and whose councils would be enlarged and given some legislative powers. Clementi envisaged the four Residents becoming more like Advisors, as in the five Unfederated States.

Heads of commercial establishments in the FMS strongly challenged Clementi's proposals, fearing that their profits would suffer if the central government's powers were reduced. They also foresaw that the prerogatives of planting and mining companies might be jeopardised if increased power was given to Malay rulers. The *Straits Times*' response was an editorial in which the Clementi proposals were criticised as being tantamount to reversing the country's clock of progress. The Chinese, by now a more settled community, also were vigorously opposed to the plans. With investment by the Chinese in the FMS having been greatly increased, many schools had been established by them which were entirely outside the sphere of government control. The Chinese were also suspicious that any weakening of Federal Government influence would bring them increasingly under the control of the Malay-dominated state governments. In addition to such opposition within the FMS, various factions in the UFMS of Johore and Kedah regarded any British move with suspicion, especially one that they deemed might reduce the constitutional standing of their states to that of the FMS. Although the UFMS were quite content to obtain British assistance, they did not want British control. In addition to this confrontation from both the Federated and

Unfederated Malay States, Singapore also staunchly resisted Clementi's designs for a Customs' Union which was regarded as heralding a threat against the free port status of the Colony.

An investigation in 1932 by the Colonial Under Secretary, Sir Samual Wilson, concluded that centralization was probably best for the country economically, but that political decentralisation was still essential. Britain's form of indirect rule was required to ensure that the Malays were not over-run by Western ideology or by immigrant communities. A cardinal factor in Britain's policy should be to ensure the continuity of the Malay rulers' authority, position and prestige. A compromise was finally recommended, whereby a gradual process of decentralisation was agreed upon. The transfer to state control of various central government departments was to be made over a period of four years. Among these were included the departments for agriculture, education, medicine, forestry, mining and public works. State governments were to receive an annual block grant from the Federal Government, which in effect provided them with less financial independence than was originally intended by Clementi. The process of change was also slower than he had envisaged. State councils in the FMS were enlarged and strengthened. Automatically, the number of Malays appointed into the Malayan Civil Service was increased. A separate civil service was also established in the Straits Settlements, in response to a long-standing request by the Chinese, and because rulers of Malay states would not agree to an interchange of personnel if it involved the employment of Chinese administrative officers in their states. By 1939, when war seemed imminent, only the first stages of decentralisation in Peninsular Malaya had been concluded.

When war broke out in December 1941, the constitutional hotchpotch in Peninsular Malaya had by no means been resolved. Unification of the conglomerate states throughout the country appeared to be as distant as it had ever been, and they still continued to be separated into the four Federated States, the five Unfederated States and the three Straits Settlements inclusive of Singapore. The prevailing opinion among some senior administrators was that unity among the Malay states could only be achieved if the type of Federation that had been established in 1896 was relinquished. Then it might be possible to devise some scheme which would subsequently bring the FMS and

UFMS into closer association with each other. Proposals such as these, however, had found no favour in the UFMS, as they were in the enviable position in 1941, under the prevailing constitutional terms, of having the best of both worlds.

The Malayan constitutional set-up in 1941 was indeed complex. The three widely separated entities that comprised the Straits Settlements, ie Penang, Malacca and Singapore, being a British colony, were all governed from Singapore and were subjected to the authority of the Colonial Office in London. The FMS of Perak, Pahang, Negeri Sembilan and Selangor, located in the centre of the Peninsula, were dependent on considerable British administration, the core of which was based in Kuala Lumpur. The UFMS, comprising Perlis, Kedah, Trengganu and Kelantan to the north – over which Siam formerly claimed suzerainty – had separate treaties with Britain, which provided for a selection of 'British Advisors' and a relatively small number of other British officials. Similarly, the remaining Unfederated State of Johore, at the southern end of the Peninsula, had enjoyed a close association with Britain from the time that Singapore was founded, whilst still being able to maintain a considerable degree of independence and Malay control.

There were, therefore, inherited administrative headaches within Sir Shenton Thomas' realm of authority. As Governor of the Straits Settlements he was also the High Commissioner for both the Federated and Unfederated States, and often had to deal with eleven separate governing bodies before any agreement, which might affect the country as a whole, could be activated. Although in many respects each of the four states in the FMS were self-governing, a Federal Government in Kuala Lumpur administered their overall policy. In contrast, in the Unfederated States of Johore, Trennganu, Kelantan, Kedah and Perlis, there was in each an 'autocratic sultan' and a British advisor. Sir Shenton, also by courtesy, held the rank of Commander-in-Chief, which in effect had no more military authority than did the King of England in similar circumstances.

The British presence in Malaya formed a buffer between the Malays and the fast increasing immigrant Chinese and Indians. Social and administrative contact between the three races was kept to a minimum, and immigrant community problems remained outside the purview of Malay officialdom. These were attended to by British Protectors on behalf of the Chinese and by Agents for the Indians. Arising from social segregation, language and cultural difficulties, immigrants came to understand little regarding Malay characteristics and behaviour. Improved health standards, with accompanying prospects for longer life, were responsible for immigrant population increases during the 1930s, as was Malaya's attractive and growing economy. Epidemics of cholera, smallpox, typhoid, dysentery and malaria had previously taken a heavy toll, as had a high infant mortality rate. The Chinese, as the largest racial immigrant group in 1931, were mostly shopkeepers, merchants, estate owners, as well as labourers in mines and plantations. They were not particularly attracted to padi planting, although they took an active role in the fishing industry, both as fishermen and middlemen. The 1930 Immigration Ordinance's quota system, which was aimed directly at restricting the entry of Chinese males, placed little or no restrictions on the immigration of Chinese women and children, and contributed to further increases in their numbers.

The British made no pretence that they regarded the Malays as the definite people of the country, although in the Straits Settlements British rule proceeded without reference to them, as they were in no constitutional position to protest otherwise. Elsewhere in the Peninsula, the British ruled through Malays, who in turn had no choice but to obey them. Within the treaties concluded with each ruler, there were degrees of convenient hypocrisy, whereby they had to 'accept the advice of British Advisors when (that) advice was offered'.[5] This enabled the British to do exactly as they pleased, even to the extent of removing rulers and tampering with the laws of succession. Notwithstanding this one-sided autocratic benevolence, the British only ruled Malaya through the Malays, and through no one else. Only a few non-Malays were included into the FMS's Advisory Legislative Councils. They were allotted only slight responsibilities and were therefore no more than convenient tools through which the British were able to assuage their conscience.

As tensions increased in the Far East, to a level threatening hostility, Sir Archibald Clark Kerr, the British Ambassador to China, proposed that a man of considerable standing should be selected to head an organisation capable of co-ordinating civil activities throughout the area, in the event that communications with civil authorities in London were interrupted. The Right Honourable Alfred Duff Cooper, one time Secretary of State for War, First Lord of the Admiralty and Minister of Information, was selected to go to the Far East and investigate this proposal. He arrived in Singapore in September 1941 as the Prime Minister's roving advisor, with a mandate to visit all British territories from India to Australia. His task was to submit a report on the state of readiness of each area, in the event that hostilities broke out in the Far East. As Chancellor of the Duchy of Lancaster, Cooper also held Cabinet rank.

On 29th September 1941 Cooper called for a conference in Singapore, which was attended by Governor Sir Shenton Thomas, Air Chief Marshall Sir Robert Brooke-Popham the Supreme Head of Far East Command, Sir Geoffrey Layton the Commander in Chief – China Station, Sir Archibald Clark Kerr, Sir Josiah Crosby the Minister to Siam and Sir Earle Page the British High Commissioner to Australia. Amazingly, this meeting concluded that Japan would be unlikely to risk an attack against Malaya during the North-East Monsoon, as she was concentrating considerable forces for an attack against Russia. It was also assumed that Japan did not wish to be involved in a war with Britain, the Netherlands and the United States at the same time. These conclusions, despite all warning signs to the contrary, were not submitted by Duff Cooper until one month had elapsed, and his report did not reach London until 24th November 1941. Although Cooper's belated submission was critical, and emphasised the need for improved central co-ordination, no corrective action was taken by the War Cabinet in London by the time that hostilities commenced on 8th December 1941.

7:4 Social Insouciances

The social climate in Malaya was little altered as a result of the outbreak of war in Europe in September 1939. Shops and stores continued to overflow with food and medical supplies. In the white tuans' clubs alcoholic drinks were plentifully available. The air-freighted daily supply of fresh salmon and strawberries continued unabated, as did the ritual of decorating half-shuttered rooms with bowls of roses and orchids. There was no thought of curtailing street lighting, which functioned normally as many people pursued their favoured pastimes.

On the night of 29th November 1941 'Return to Unit' notices were flashed on cinema screens in Singapore and in other towns throughout Malaya. A stage of second degree readiness was ordered, with Volunteer Forces being mobilised, following a warning that talks in Washington had broken down, and that the Japanese might decide to embark on an invasion of Siam, the Philippines and the Dutch East Indies. These early indications did little to abate the 'gay, luxurious social life' which continued in Singapore in the form of a variety of sporting activities by day and the theatre, dinner, dancing and cocktail parties by night.

When Australian troops first arrived in Singapore they were snubbed by many British residents there and omitted from the white tuans' clubs. Except at the highest levels, there was little social mixing between the races, but many Australians did get on well with the Malays. When subsequent war reversals dissipated all pre-war social fetishisms, some people professed the need to excuse their earlier attitudes by explaining that it had been hard to get to know the Australians, as they invariably hung around houses of ill repute.

The *Sunday Tribune*, on 7th December 1941, advised the public of Malaya, in most guarded terms, to stay at home. Those who had left home were told to return immediately, as the railways would soon be needed for military purposes. The *Tribune's* lead article of that day reported that Japanese transport ships, with accompanying protective vessels, had been sighted off Cambodia Point, some 300 miles north-east of the Malayan coastline. Sir Robert Brooke-Popham, albeit the Supreme Head of Far East Command, considered that it was 'most improper to print such alarmist news at a time like the present'.[6] Ill-informed as he was, he expressed in public the not untypical opinion that 'the position (was) not half so serious'[7] as the *Tribune* made it out to be.

1. *British Rule in Malaya 1942–57* by Robert Heussler, Ch.2, p.15.
2. Ibid, p.16.

3. *The Origins of Malay Nationalism* by W.R. Roff, Ch.7, p.241.
4. *Utusan Melayu* (10th November 1939), cited in *Soenaron*, 'Malay Nationalism, 1900–1945', p.16.
5. *The Malay Dilemma* by Mahathir bin Mohamad, Ch.8, p.129.
6. *In Seventy Days. The Story of Malaya* by E.M. Glover, Ch.5, p.72.
7. Ibid, p.72.

CHAPTER EIGHT: IRREVERSIBLE TRENDS

8:1 Collision Course

As early as 1902, Britain recognised that Japan would become a significant, contentious power and made an alliance with her. This was soon verified when in 1904 Japan gained enormous prestige by her victory over Russia, being the first Asian country to defeat a major European power. During the 1914–8 World War, Britain and Japan fought as allies and at the conclusion of this Japan was given charge over ex-German territories in the Far East. However, four years later, in 1922, the Anglo-Japanese Alliance of twenty years' duration came to an end.

The Naval Limitations Treaty — signed on 6th February 1922, after several months of discussions between leading naval powers — was predetermined to remain in force for a period of 14 years. It prescribed limitations on participating members concerning the number of battleships that they were permitted to build, and required that these be maintained within a ratio 3:5:5 by Japan, the United States and Great Britain respectively. Japan argued that the terms of the Treaty were unfair to her, and that Britain and the United States had been favoured by the allocated ratios. This line of reasoning was claimed, irregardless of the extended and distant areas that both Britain and the United States had to defend. Japan, within the context of the Treaty, still remained the most powerful naval nation in the Far East, and particularly so as she was able to concentrate her fleets in one area. In addition to fleet size control, the Treaty also required that the United States would not construct any new naval bases or fortifications in the Philippines, the Aleutian Islands and in Guam. Britain similarly agreed that she would not arm Hong Kong, or any of her other possessions East of 110 degrees longitude, with the exception of Canada, Australia and New Zealand. In turn, the Japanese also agreed that they would not establish naval bases in Formosa, or in any of the ex-German territories over which they had been made trustee.

Relations between Britain and Japan became increasingly strained after the Naval Limitations Treaty. This was further exacerbated when in 1923 the British Conservative government authorised the commencement of construction at the Singapore Naval Base, to be situated, ironically, a few degrees west of 110 degrees longitude, and for which an initial sum of £1.3 million was allocated. When a Labour Government was returned to power in 1924, orders were sent to stop all work on the base, and an allocation of £12,500 was granted to cover the cost of demolition works. The Governor at that time – Sir Lawrence Guillemard – instead chose to ignore these instructions and continued with the anti-malarial works that were then already in progress. Work was officially resumed on the base shortly afterwards, when the Conservatives were returned to power, and in 1929 when the next Labour Government was elected, the project was too far advanced to be abandoned.

Both Britain and the United States were desperate to cut their defence spending during the Depression and began to preach disarmament. Realising that actions such as this could well be seized upon as an opportunity by Japan to strengthen her naval forces, the London Naval Treaty was signed in 1930, to which Japan was forced to become a signatory. This, in effect, imposed upon her much resented restrictions.

In December 1934 Japan gave notice of her intention of no longer being a member of the Washington Naval Treaty when it next came up for review in 1936. Arising from this decision, a Disarmament Conference was held in London in 1934, and was attended by Great Britain, the United States and Japan. Japan declined to agree to any all-round reduction in naval armaments and withdrew from the conference without any agreement being reached. The way was now open for Japan to expand her navy, and to build naval and air bases just as she pleased. Britain in turn, following the failure of these discussions, decided to speed up work on the Singapore Naval Base. At the outbreak of hostilities in 1941, the Base, having cost £63 million, was completed and ready for use. But, it contained no fleet. Neither was there one available for it!

8:2 Devious Diplomacy

The Earl of Lytton Commission was appointed in mid-1932, following an appeal by China to the League of Nations, to investigate circumstances surrounding the Mukden Incident on the South Manchurian Railway, and any justification that Japan may have had for her invasion and conquest of Manchuria in early 1932. The subsequent report, published in early 1933, expressed strong disapproval of Japan's actions, although it did concede that she had considerable important interests to protect there. Japan nevertheless was branded as the aggressor. Disregarding the validity of this publicly expressed criticism, Japan considered that she had been insulted. Her resentment over this censure provided her with sufficient excuse to withdraw from the League of Nations, from which she resigned in March 1933. Yosuke Matsuoka, the Japanese delegate to the League of Nations in 1932–33, stated in his final address to the League,

> 'What guarantee is there? . . . Certain people in Europe and America are seeking to crucify Japan here and now in the twentieth century.'[1]

Japan's departure from the League of Nations had far-reaching internal political repercussions. The more militant sections within the government used it as a means to strengthen their credibility and further their designs for later expansionist aggression. In November 1936 Japan and Germany concluded the Anti-Comintern Pact, to which Italy later became a signatory. This nominally defensive pact inextricably linked Japan's fate to that of Nazi Germany and Fascist Italy, and made clear to the world Japan's aggressive inclinations. In 1937, therefore, Japan was ranked second in importance to Germany as a future enemy of Britain.

Secret clauses in the Anti-Comintern Pact aspired to intimidate the eastern and western frontiers of the Soviet Union, and to condone the subsequent use of Indo-China as a spring-board from which to escalate Japan's bellicose intentions towards Britain's Far Eastern domains. As mentioned in Chapter 5:1, Japan at this stage did not want to become involved in Germany's threatened European war, so she decided, contrary to what had recently been agreed, to await the outcome of further negotiations with the United States, and then to determine whether or not there were sufficient inducements to keep her out of any European conflict. The Pact, however, loosely provided some basis on which a subsequent military alliance could be made.

From July 1937, resulting from an incident at the Marco Polo Bridge, fighting between Japanese and Chinese forces escalated throughout northern China. The Japanese quickly gained control of Peking and Tientsin, and by December 1937 they had captured and sacked Nanking. When Chiang Kai-shek repeatedly rejected surrender terms, many moderates in Japanese political circles were prepared to negotiate for peace as the war had become a heavy economic burden. The Japanese Army General Staff also wanted to divert their forces to prepare for war against the Soviet Union. Notwithstanding some further heavy losses in early 1938, Japan was able to convince Hitler of an impending certain victory in China. In the spring of that year, von Ribbentrop, the German Foreign Minister, proposed the formation of a general military alliance with Japan, which was now much sought after by the military elements within the Japanese government.

Much of the preliminary discussions and groundwork towards the first draft of an agreement were concluded by von Ribbentrop and Colonel Oshima, the Japanese Military Attaché in Berlin, without the knowledge of Shigenori Togo who was the Japanese Ambassador to Germany at that time. Togo — a vigorous anti-militarist and proponent of peace — was replaced by Oshima as Japan's Ambassador to Germany, which meant that the army held for the first time a post which had always previously been assigned to a professional diplomat. Oshima, with enhanced powers, returned to Germany in the spring of 1939, where he set about promoting Japan's desire for a Tripartite Military Alliance with Germany and Italy. Discussions revealed that Germany also favoured a military alliance, but one that would be directed against both the Soviet Union and Western powers, a concept which had already been openly supported when the new Hiranuma cabinet was formed in January 1939. Emperor Hirohito was opposed to this concept and wanted a treaty that would be solely directed against the Soviet Union, and not one that might lead Japan into a state of war should conflict occur in Europe. A deadlock arose. Throughout April to June 1939 Prime Minister Hiranuma, War Minister Itagaki and the Army opposed the Emperor, who was supported by his Foreign Secretary and the Navy. A direct approach to Hitler and Mussolini by Prime Minister Hiranuma also failed to resolve the deadlock.

By August 1939 war in Europe was inevitable. With Japan, at this stage, hesitating to make any firm commitment, von Ribbentrop issued a warning that Germany might feel obliged to come to some individual arrangement with the Soviet Union, if Japan did not decide quickly. In the face of this threat War Minister Itagaki renewed his efforts to persuade the Japanese cabinet to assent to an offensive and defensive general alliance with Germany and Italy.

It was at this point that a crushing political blow completely discredited the Japanese cabinet. On 23rd August 1939 the Berlin-Moscow Non-Aggression Pact was signed. The Japanese were shocked, and the cabinet was forced to resign. Japan considered herself ill-treated by Germany, especially as relations between Japan and the Soviet Union had been soured by localised hostilities over the boundaries between the newly-created states of Manchukuo and Outer Mongolia.

On 23rd September 1940, after a long period of negotiation with the Vichy government in France, Japanese forces entered the northern part of French Indo-China. Four days later Japan concluded the Tripartite Pact with Germany and Italy, which gave assurances that each signatory would declare war on any other party that engaged in war against one of the three. An Imperial Rescript hailed the Pact as an instrument of peace, although this opinion was not shared by Marquis Koicho Kido, the Lord Privy Seal. Kido realised that the war in China must now be quickly brought to an end, as sooner or later Japan would have to reckon with the United States of America and Great Britain. The Tripartite Pact did not publicly or officially affect either Germany's or Japan's relationships with the Soviet Union, although only one day prior to signing the agreement, Japan's Foreign Minister Matsuoka had given to Germany a clandestine assurance that Japan would come to Germany's aid in the event of a Soviet German war. The signatories hoped that the Pact would discourage the United States from participating in the war in Europe, or indulging in a more positive role in the Far East.

Matsuoka, Japan's Foreign Minister in 1940–1, played an active, instrumental role in the negotiations which preceded the signing of the Tripartite Pact. He was a firm believer in Germany's ultimate victory, despite having been brought up by a Methodist family in Portland, Oregon. He held a degree in Law from the University of Oregon and was described as being a 'dynamic and erratic genius' as well as a 'talkative chauvinist'.[2] Masuoka strongly mistrusted both the United States and Britain, and had no doubt that Europe's destiny was to come under Germany's control. He anticipated, with Germany's control of Europe, an opportunity for Japan to seize from the colonies of defeated European powers their vast riches and resources of raw materials in the Far East.

Britain and her overseas domains were clearly, therefore, Japan's targets in becoming party to the Tripartite Pact. Germany and Italy agreed to recognise Japan's leadership in establishing a new order in East Asia, and in the ideology of Hakko Ichiu, which aimed to bring the 'eight corners of the world under the aegis of the Japanese Imperial House'.[3] In return for this, Japan recognised and accepted the leadership of Germany and Italy in establishing a new order in Europe. Although mutual military assistance had been pledged within the terms of the Pact, Japan wanted further assurances and, by a secret exchange of letters, reserved the right to act with freedom of decision in the event that any one of the signatories was attacked by a power 'at present not involved in the European war or the Sino-Japanese conflict'.[4] Japan's military leaders anticipated that the Tripartite Pact would influence Britain and the United States to relinquish their support of China, who in turn would then be compelled to accept Japan's settlement terms in respect of the China Incident. Admiral Mitsumasa Yonai, the Navy Minister, however, was opposed to the Pact and considered that such an agreement would inevitably lead Japan into a war with both Britain and the United States.

In mid-October 1940 successful oil supply discussions were held by Japan and the Dutch East Indies authorities, despite an attempt by Britain to block negotiations. An agreement of six months duration was arrived at, whereby 40% of the Dutch East Indies' oil production would be supplied to Japan. On 13th November further agreements were concluded with main oil producing companies in the Dutch East Indies who agreed to provide Japan with 1,800,000 tons of oil annually.

Japan betimes realised that the United States had not been intimidated by the Tripartite Pact, and in February 1941 Admiral Nomura Kishisaburo — a moderate — was sent to the USA as Japan's new ambassador. Nomura was favourably disposed towards the USA, and in early March began a series of long-drawn talks with Secretary of State Cordell Hull, which lasted until the summer. While these negotiations were proceeding, the Japanese Foreign Office was busy preparing a tentative plan of seizures in the southern regions, which provided for the occupation of Singapore, Malaya and the Dutch East Indies, on the presumption that this would all still be possible without becoming involved in a war with the United States and Great Britain. In the event that hostilities were unavoidable, an escalation contingency was planned to provide for the Philippines, Guam and other American Pacific possessions to be seized.

Meanwhile, in April 1941 Foreign Minister Matsuoka, with single-handed initiative, concluded on behalf of Japan a Neutrality Pact with the Soviet Union. The April 13th conclusion of a five year friendship treaty with the Soviet Union was a complete diplomatic volte-face by the Japanese only seven months after they had concluded the Tripartite Pact with Italy and Germany, and ostensibly swept aside any question of war between Japan and the Soviet Union. Japan in 1941, irregardless of her alliance with Germany, did not want war with the Soviet Union, as such a war would require her to keep her fighter planes at home bases rather than send them to accompany bombers to Indo-China, north Malaya and Siam.

The five year Neutrality Pact with the Soviet Union was, therefore, an historical reversal in the relationship of the two countries, and had been negotiated almost single-handedly in Moscow by Matsuoka, on his return from a visit to Europe. Although the pact gave a degree of security to Japan along her vulnerable Manchurian flank, the Japanese cabinet were outraged by Matsuoka's individualism, and resigned en masse expressly to discredit him and to secure his removal from office. When, on 22nd June 1941, Hitler launched a surprise invasion of the Soviet Union, Japanese leaders, who had no advanced knowledge of this, were aghast and placed in a quandary. The invasion was a blow to their pride!

At a liaison conference between the Japanese cabinet and Imperial Headquarters on 25th June, it was decided to disregard completely the two month old Neutrality Pact with the Soviet Union, and to extend military and material aid to Germany, without declaring open warfare on the Russians. Japan's perfidy in these events cannot be doubted. Matsuoka had assured Hitler, just two weeks before he signed the Neutrality Pact with the Soviet Union, that Japan would be a 'loyal ally' in any German Russian war. Again, when he returned to Tokyo, he assured the German Ambassador that Japan '. . . by force of necessity' would attack the Soviet Union at Germany's side in the event of a conflict between them. When the time came, however, Japan held back. Instead, she fed military intelligence concerning Soviet forces' movements and concentrations to Germany, and although still avoiding open aggression, by concentrating a large army in Manchuria, Japan succeeded in pinning down many Soviet Divisions along her eastern frontiers. These actions were in complete defiance of Japan's obligations under Article 2 of the recently concluded Neutrality Pact with the Soviet Union, which required that neutrality should be maintained by both contracting parties.

Deceptive diplomacy became increasingly the mode in early 1941. American and British interference in China was blamed, and was used by Nomura in his explanation to the United States for Japan's enforced participation in the Tripartite Pact. In offering this excuse, Nomura omitted to reveal that Japan had already decided to deprive the United States of friendly Pacific bases by attacking Singapore, and that on 24th February 1941, 40,000 Japanese troops had already sailed to occupy southern French Indo-China in order to construct air and naval bases near Siagon and at Camranh Bay. Matsuoka's emphatic denial, to the American Ambassador in Moscow, that Japan had any territorial ambitions in the Far East was contradicted a few days later in Berlin, when he told Hitler that his assurance had been given solely to mislead the Americans and the British, until Japan was ready to attack Singapore.

Although the moderates in Japan still sought to avoid war with either Britain or the United States, the militarists were swept along by

Germany's boasts that Britain would soon be defeated. When France and Holland fell, and with Great Britain fully committed to a life and death struggle for survival, the militarists foresaw a golden opportunity to seize without opposition the territories of French Indo-China, the coveted oil-producing Dutch East Indies, and then Malaya. They felt invulnerable. The Tripartite and Neutrality Pacts boosted their contentions, and they were now poised more than ever to risk total war in order to command the riches of oil, rubber and tin in South East Asia, that were needed so desperately to keep their naval and military forces in action.

Discussions between Foreign Secretary Cordell Hull and Ambassador Nomura commenced on 28th May 1941. No sooner had they started than one hundred Japanese planes bombed Chungking, and destroyed American property there. Also, the Japanese navy initiated training exercises for their proposed future attack on Pearl Harbour. By June 1941 Japan had completed her occupation of Indo-China, and her forces were poised to strike southwards, not only at the British in Malaya, but also at the Americans in the Philippines and the Dutch in the East Indies.

Diplomatic negotiations between the United States and Japan continued throughout June to August 1941, without any satisfactory conclusions being reached. On 6th August the Konoye government proposed some concessions in China and Indo-China, in the hope that the United States would ameliorate their freeze on Japanese assets. When these proposals were rejected the Japanese further suggested that Prime Minister Konoye and President Roosevelt should meet, to discuss the issues at stake. In the wake of these moves, Admiral Nomura continued his negotiations with Cordell Hull, in an attempt to stave off any further trade restrictions that the Americans might be considering.

Prime Minister Konoye resigned on 16th October 1941 and was replaced by War Minister Lieut General Hideki Tojo. On 18th October, following the announcement of Tojo's new war cabinet, the Counsellor of the Japanese Embassy in Washington, Mr Wakasugi, informed Cordell Hull that the Japanese government desired to resume peace negotiations. Hull, however, persuaded President Roosevelt to maintain a firm and uncompromising stand towards this Japanese approach and to insist, as a prelude to any discussions, on their withdrawal from the Tripartite Pact, and from French Indo-China.

On 17th November 1941 Tojo outlined Japan's foreign policy to the Diet as being one that still sought peace in East Asia. He reaffirmed that Japan was doing her utmost towards a peaceful diplomatic settlement for the Far East although her 'legitimate efforts at self defence' were viewed with suspicion by Britain, the United States and the Netherlands East Indies, who regarded them as being aggressive. Tojo emphasised that third powers should refrain from obstructing Japan's successful conclusion of the China affair, and that the government viewed any 'economic blockade between non-belligerent countries' as being 'a measure little less hostile than armed warfare'.[5] Despite these pronouncements of innocent intent, when Tojo addressed officials at the War and Home Ministries on 20th October 1941, he emphatically declared that the Japanese Empire stood at the cross-roads of its rise or fall, and on the next day, in contradiction of newly pronounced peacemaking overtures, the Diet voted in favour of a 4,315,000,000 Yen military budget, equivalent to £223,000,000.

On 5th November 1941 the Japanese Foreign Office's official newspaper in Tokyo further stipulated what they required the United States to do, 'or face the alternative', and demanded that

> 'Japan's Co-Prosperity Sphere must be acknowledged and Manchuko, China, Indo-China, Thailand, the Netherlands East Indies and other States and Protectorates must be allowed to establish their own political and economic relations without any interference of any kind.'[6]

This threw down the gauntlet, and the United States was given until 25th November to comply with Japan's wishes. Assurances were required that no more aid would be provided to China, neither would American or British forces be increased in the Far East. Failure to agree left little doubt as to what the article inferred — a clear intent by Japan to declare war!

At an address to the American Society in London, on 20th November 1941, Mr Anthony Eden, the British Foreign Minister, confirmed Britain's complete confidence in the ability of US spokesmen in discussions with the Japanese. The subsequent results of these negotiations were an American ten-point settlement proposal, issued on 26th November 1941, which fell far short of Japan's demands. These required Japan to evacuate China and Indo-China completely, as well as to abandon her Manchurian puppet empire. Not unsurprisingly, the terms were rejected, and at a conference on 4th December, in the Emperor's presence, it was decided that hostilities would commence on 7th December. The United States were fully aware that there was little or no hope of agreement with Japan, having in late 1940 broken the Japanese diplomatic code which enabled them to decipher incoming and outgoing secret Embassy messages.

Saburo Kurusu was sent as a special envoy to Washington and opened discussions with Cordell Hull on 1st December 1941, in an attempt to allay American suspicions and break the deadlock in negotiations which now cast the dye of imminent war between the two countries. Ten days prior to Kurusu's departure to Washington, secret orders had already confirmed Japan's intention to mount simultaneous attacks on Pearl Harbour, Malaya, Hong Kong and the Philippines, on 8th December 1941, in the event that Kurusu's negotiations failed. When it was realised that no headway was being made, Japan's attack instructions were put into effect whilst both Kurusu and Nomura were still engaged in their negotiations.

The fourteenth part of Japan's final message to the United States, which specifically broke off relations between them, only reached Washington on the morning of 7th December 1941. The Japanese Embassy in Washington was ordered to deliver Japan's main message at 1 p.m. Washington time, which approximately coincided with dawn at Pearl Harbour. Delays and transmission errors resulted in the message arriving too late at the Pearl Harbour headquarters, and by the time the US and British Ambassadors in Tokyo were presented with the declarations of war, the attacks on Pearl Harbour, Singapore and on the north-eastern coast of the Malay Peninsula had already commenced.

8:3 Frozen Assets — Consequences

The United States became increasingly suspicious of Japan's aims, arising from her precipitation of and extended participation in the

China Incident. However, direct political involvement was still avoided, provided that the economic interests of the US, and their long-established rights in China, were being safeguarded. When, by Japan's actions, which included repeated attacks against American and British personnel and property in China throughout 1937 and 1938, it became clear that this would no longer be the case, the United States' attitudes hardened. An embargo was placed on exporting aircraft and all other war materials to Japan, and in July 1939 the United States terminated its thirty year old Commercial Treaty with her.

The expansionary ambitions of Japan in South-East Asia gave rise to serious concern among political leaders in the United States, following the outbreak of war in Europe, and they decided that a more forceful policy of restraint should be imposed upon her. The American Secretary of State, Cordell Hull, therefore refused to negotiate in 1939 the renewal of the 1911 Commercial Treaty between Japan and the United States, unless Japan completely changed her attitude towards American interests in China. Japan's Ambassador in Washington, Admiral Nomura, attempted to compromise and made promises to the effect that Japan would not seek any further territorial advancements in South-East Asia, and would also evacuate Indo-China as soon as a satisfactory settlement of the China Incident had been achieved, provided that the United States would renew trade relations. By terminating the Commercial Treaty with Japan, the United States achieved an absolute freedom of choice, either to limit or completely cut off exports to Japan, depending upon what the situation warranted. Perhaps, at that time, the United States did not fully appreciate that her actions would bring about the ultimate decline in relationships, and convince Japan that her only recourse was aggression.

On 17th July 1940 Prince Fumimaro Konoye was appointed to head a new Cabinet in which there were 'a number of supporters of a more aggressive policy'.[7] By September of that year, these aggressive elements had sufficiently negotiated with and intimidated the Vichy French authorities to impose upon them a force of 6,000 troops, to be stationed in military bases in Indo-China for the express purpose of denying aid to China by that route. In response to this the United

States instigated a series of commercial retaliatory measures, which culminated on 26th September 1940 in the form of an embargo on the sale or export of all high-grade scrap iron, aviation gasoline, ore scrap metal and steel, all of which were essential war munitions and imposed serious limitations upon Japan's heavy industries. This was further extended at the end of December 1940, when an export-licensing system was implemented, whereby iron ore, pig iron and many other important iron and steel items became restricted. This action again was aimed directly at Japan and had considerable adverse effects on her economy. However, none hit her harder than the freezing of her assets on 26th July 1941.

By the end of July 1941 Japan's occupation of Indo-China had been completed. Her forces were now poised to strike southwards at the British in Malaya, the Americans in the Philippines as well as the Dutch in the East-Indies.

On 24th July the United States demanded that Japanese troops should be withdrawn from Indo-China which, it was proposed, should be regarded as a neutral country. When Japan ignored Roosevelt's proposals to this effect, harsh retaliatory measures were activated. On 26th July Japanese assets in both the United States and Great Britain were frozen, and an immediate embargo was placed on the supply of oil. Similar action was taken on the 28th by the refugee Dutch government in London, who also cancelled all oil arrangements that had been previously made between the Dutch East-Indies and Japan. Japan retaliated on the 28th by freezing US assets in Japan and then on the 29th similar action was taken against Dutch assets. These moves brought almost 75% of Japan's foreign trade to a standstill and also cut her off from 88% of her total oil supplies. President Roosevelt tightened the screws still further on 1st August by forbidding the export of oil and aviation fuel from the United States, except to Britain, the British Empire and to countries of the Western Hemisphere. Japan was hit particularly hard by this decision, and was now left only with her strictly limited stocks, and her trading options with occupied French Indo-China, Manchuria and Thailand. All oil, essential for the survival of the Imperial Japanese Navy, had been denied to her.

It was a stranglehold. She had to decide quickly! Either she had to alter her foreign policy, or go to war in order to obtain by force the oil that she required from the Dutch East-Indies. Serious consideration was given, therefore, to the disastrous effects that trade embargoes would impose. Realising also that by the conquest of Malaya, 80% of the world's rubber output and 66% of the world's tin would become available to her, recourse to aggression was decided upon if the embargoes could not be lifted. Resulting from this serious worsening in relations, most of the 1,000 British and 300 Indian residents in Japan were warned by the British Embassy at the end of August 1941 that they should leave the country.

It was not Roosevelt's intention to force Japan into an irredeemable corner by these measures. But, in effect, he did just this, particularly as his intentions were not made clear either to the Japanese or to his subordinates, who were charged with the responsibility of implementing them. During the time that Roosevelt was preoccupied with Churchill at secret meetings, all of Japan's applications for supplies of gasoline and oil were rejected by government officials. By the time that Roosevelt became aware of this, it was too late to alter course. Consternation erupted in Tokyo over the action taken by the United States, which effectively cut Japan off from all her vital supplies of oil and other raw materials, and reduced the potential of her resources to a level that was insufficient to support her war machinery for two years. The Navy estimated that oil was sufficient only for 18 months' operational service.

By the autumn of 1941, therefore, Japan was left with four options. Either she could accept the terms dictated by Roosevelt and face the shame that abandonment of her expansionist ploys would imply, or she could ignore Roosevelt's terms and wait for her factories and military machine to falter and come to a grinding standstill. Another course of action open to her was to negotiate a settlement with the United States whereby the embargoes would be lifted. The fourth choice, if she was unable to persuade her opponents to alter their stance, was to advance southwards and seize Malaya and the Dutch East Indies, from which she could avail herself of the raw materials that were so desperately required. The latter action left little doubt that this would certainly mean war with Great Britain and the United States.

Japan attempted to follow a public course of diplomatic reconciliation, at the same time as she feverishly prepared for aggression. On 6th August 1941 the Konoye government made proposals to the United States offering some concessions to their previous stand in China and Indo-China, in return for an ending of the freeze on Japanese assets. When this was rejected by the United States, a proposal was made by the Japanese requesting that Premier Konoye and President Roosevelt should hold a meeting, with the purpose of trying to resolve the deadlock and the issues at stake between them. In response to this, on 17th August 1941, the United States issued a formal warning to Japan on the lines discussed and agreed by Churchill and Roosevelt at their recently concluded meetings at Placentia Bay. This was followed up on 3rd September, when the Japanese were informed that their proposed Konoye/Roosevelt meeting had not been agreed to. Diplomats in Washington continued to talk appeasement until hostilities started, whilst General Tojo, Japan's new Prime Minister, was dead set on a course for war.

By freezing Japan's assets, the United States, Great Britain and the Dutch East-Indies effectively brought all commercial transactions between them and Japan to an end, which severely affected every aspect of Japan's industry and war preparations. Stockpiles that had been built up for over a decade would now have to be used. Admiral Yamamoto referred to the embargo as

> 'the final outrage of breaking off economic relations'.[8]

Colonel Mabuchi, the Chief of the Army Press Section at Imperial Headquarters, in a broadcast on 2nd September 1941, further denounced the actions of the ABCD (Australian, British, Chinese and Dutch) powers. He accused them of 'strangling' Japan's economy and said that the embargo would have to

> 'be broken, "by diplomacy if possible, by force if necessary"'.[9]

Freezing Japan's assets and depriving her of raw materials were condemned as 'unpardonable crimes', and Churchill's reference to Japan being the aggressor in Indo-China was an

> 'inexcusable insult which could "not be tolerated" against the Japanese soldiers fighting a "holy war"'.[10]

Captain Hiraide, the head of naval intelligence at Imperial headquarters, declared on 16th October that

> 'US-Japanese relations were "approaching a parting of the ways" and that the Imperial Navy had "prepared for the worst" and was "itching for action".'[11]

On 3rd September 1941, having been informed of Roosevelt's rejection of the proposal to meet Premier Konoye, a decision was made. If Japan's diplomats were unable to persuade the United States to lift the crippling embargoes by the first week of November, Japan would then finalise her preparations to launch attacks on the Pacific territories of the United States, Great Britain and the Netherlands.

The final stiff ten-point note that the US Foreign Secretary, Cordell Hull, sent to Japan on 26/27th November 1941 required, among other things, that Japan should leave China and Indo-China, and that recognition should be afforded to the Chinese Nationalist Government. In return for this, the United States gave an assurance that she would be prepared to negotiate new trade and raw materials' agreements with Japan. The Japanese government regarded Hull's note, however, as a pre-determined insult.

8:4 Political Manoeuvring in Japan

The lives of Japanese ministers and leaders were frequently threatened throughout the 1930s, and were tenuously linked to the whims of a growing anarchy that prevailed within Japan's ruling classes. In May 1930 a group of young army officers assassinated Prime Minister Inukai, on account of his advocating support of the terms of the London Treaty, which the militants had hoped would give Japan some form of military parity with Great Britain and the United States.

The Japanese constitution always provided for the posts of army and navy ministers, in any government, to be filled by serving officers, which effectively jeopardised the continued existence of a government that opposed any course of action favoured by the military. The Mukden Incident in September 1931 was a case in point, where the army did not convey its intentions to, or consult with the government, which was then left with no other alternative but to go along with the army's action.

Blackmail and assassination were used as tools against ministers, admirals and generals alike if they were suspected of not being whole-heartedly in favour of the army's policy. By 1936 the independent power of the military was made even more clear when in February of that year more than 1,000 young Japanese officers staged an almost successful insurrection, in a far-reaching plot to overthrow the government and seize power. An attempt was made to murder the Prime Minister, and two ministers, including the Finance Minister, were assassinated. Kantaro Suzuki, a known anti-militarist, who was later to play an important part in Japan's destiny, was another of the prime targets of this attempted coup. Although senior politicians managed to regain control after several days of confusion, and trials and executions were afterwards enacted, the militants' message was all too clear.

The signing of the Soviet-German Non-Aggression Pact, on 23–24th August 1939, heralded the downfall and discredit of the Hiranuma cabinet. On 23rd September 1939, just 23 days after Great Britain had declared that a state of war existed between her and Germany, General Abe was summoned by the Emperor to form a new cabinet, in which Admiral Nomura was appointed Foreign Minister. This government was instructed to pursue a policy of co-operation with Great Britain and the United States, and some conciliatory steps were taken to try and improve relations. When these were not reciprocated and embargo restrictions were increased by the United States, the position of the more militant factions was strengthened. They continued with their efforts to reinforce Japan's solidarity with the Axis powers, aided and abetted by Germany's encouragement for Japan to expand territorially in South-East Asia, where glittering prizes were available to her for the taking. General Abe's chances of success were indeed remote, particularly as any government that renounced Japan's establishment of a new order in China could not expect a long tenure in office.

On 14th January 1940 General Abe resigned, along with his cabinet. Admiral Mitsumasa Yonai was selected to form a new government, but by 16th July Yonai had also resigned, owing to pressure from the militarists, and on account of his non-intervention policy in the European war, and Germany's victory-inspired diplomatic rebuff of Japan's overtures to form an alliance with her.

A new cabinet was formed by Prince Fumimaro Konoye – a military nominee – on 17th July, in which Yosuke Matsuoka became the new and influential Foreign Minister. By bringing Konoye into power, the leaders of the militarist factions could at last become the undisputed rulers of Japan, and those political groups who were opposed to their policies would be suitably suppressed. The most important, amongst a number of supporters of a more aggressive policy in the cabinet, was General Hideki Tojo, who was appointed Minister of War, a nomination that was made by the army's General Staff.

On 16th July 1941 Prince Konoye dissolved his cabinet and resigned with the express intention of removing the increasingly unpopular, albeit dynamically aggressive, Matsuoka as Foreign Minister. Matsuoka had been urging the abandonment of the recently negotiated Neutrality Agreement with the Soviet Union, in which he had taken a major part, in favour of Japan joining forces with the Germans who had attacked the USSR on 22nd June 1941. Matsuoka's admiration for Hitler was well known and other Japanese leaders, who did not wish to plunge headlong into the European conflict, decided that if Matsuoka was removed from office there would be a better opportunity of coming to an amicable settlement with the United States over Japan's serious oil supply problems. On 18th July Konoye therefore formed a new cabinet with Baron Hiranuma as the Deputy Prime Minister and Admiral Toyoda as the Foreign Minister.

Konoye dined with the American Ambassador in Tokyo, on 6th September 1941, when he acknowledged responsibility for the deterioration in relationships that had developed between their two countries. He also accepted four principles, as a basis on which to start improving relations again, put to him by the American Secretary of State, Cordell Hull. These required that Japan should respect all nations' sovereignty and territorial integrity and should not interfere in the internal affairs of any country. Japan was required also to recognise equality of commercial opportunities for all countries and to uphold the Pacific status quo, which should not be disturbed other than by peaceful changes.

Internal differences of opinion in respect of national policy and Konoye's inability to accept the awesome responsibility for plunging the nation into a titanic war, resulted in the resignation en bloc of Prince Konoye's third cabinet on 16th October 1941.

On 17th October, in accordance with advice given by elder statesmen and Marquis Kido, the Lord Keeper of the Privy Seal and a leading proponent of aggressive war, the Emperor called upon Lieut General Hideki Tojo, the former War Minister in Konoye's cabinet, to form a new cabinet. Tojo took for himself the offices of Prime Minister, Home Affairs Minister and War Minister and nominated Shigenori Togo, who was a vigorous anti-militarist and advocate of peaceful negotiation, as his Foreign Minister. Although four of the ministers selected to serve in Tojo's cabinet had previously been in the Konoye cabinet, the official Japanese News Agency, Domei, described the new cabinet as 'vested with powers to direct the nation towards peace or war'.[12] The *Japan Times-Advertiser*, 'the mouthpiece of the Japanese Foreign Office', viewed the selection of 'a professional soldier as Premier of Japan' as being 'a logical one at a time when Japan was "imperilled by the encirclement of hostile powers"'.[13] Tojo addressed officials of the War and Home Ministries in Tokyo on 20th October 1941, and emphasised 'his conviction that "the Japanese Empire (stood) at the cross-roads of its rise or fall"'.[14] With the replacement of Prince Konoye's government by one led by Lieut General Hideki Tojo, the final phase of Japan's road to war had begun.

Tojo's diminutive stature as a youth pre-conditioned him in his early days to condemn everything that was pleasurable. After completing staff college he served as a military attaché in Switzerland and Germany, and in 1934 was given command of a brigade. In 1935 he was promoted to Major-General and was posted to Manchuria where he took command of the Kempeitai, the Japanese Military Police. Tojo had been closely associated with the military political factions in Japan since 1936 when he was Chief of Staff of the Kwantang Army. It was he who made plans to attack the Soviet Union and for Japan's extension of military operations in China. Tojo discontinued active military command when he became Vice-Minister of War in early 1938, and in July 1940 he was given the office of Minister of War. Tojo did not succeed Prince Konoye as Prime Minister because he was considered the best man for the post, but on account of his fanatical outlook which coincided with the whims of the military at that time. Nicknamed 'the Razor', in his ill-fitting uniform, with his fierce moustache and glinting eye-glasses, his appearance veered towards the ludicrous.

Tojo's forceful 'forward policy' was favoured by the Japanese press who regarded his cabinet as being a 'War Cabinet'.[15] They also pursued an extremely intransigent attitude towards the United States and other democratic powers in the Pacific, to the extent that the Domei Agency on 2nd November 1941, declared that an armed clash in the Pacific was inevitable unless American economic pressure on Japan was reduced. The *Japan Times-Advertiser*, on 4th November, published a seven-point plan that had to be accepted by the United States if peace in the Pacific was to be maintained. Aid to China should be stopped, and China was to be left free to deal directly with Japan concerning the ending of hostilities between them, which the United States was required to encourage her to do. The United States was required to acknowledge Japan's concept of a Co-Prosperity Sphere in East Asia and to recognise the puppet state of Manchukuo. Japan's frozen assets had to be released, a new trade treaty between the United States and Japan had to be negotiated, and all trade restrictions were to be removed.

On 10th November Mr Okinori Kata, the Finance Minister, reiterated that Japan's aim was to 'force Britain and the US to retreat from East Asia'.[16] In contrast to this, Mr Shigenori Togo, the Foreign Minister, stated in more placatory terms nine days later that 'Japan harboured no territorial designs on her neighbours',[17] whereas Mr Toshio Shimada, a former Minister of Agriculture, declared that 'the cancer in the Pacific lies in the minds of arrogant American leaders'. He continued that it was the 'responsibility of Japan "to remove this cancer by wielding the big knife"'[18] in what Japan considered to be a holy war.

Clearly, Tojo's task was to initiate the war in the Pacific, which he directed until 1944, and for the conduct of which he was completely responsible. He was a hard-working authoritarian who organised a regime indistinguishable from a military dictatorship.

8:5 Intentions of War

Japan was involved in a series of expansionist military activities ten years before she declared war on Great Britain and the United States. In 1931 Manchuria was invaded, following the staging of an incident between Japanese and Chinese officials at Mukden. The express intention of this invasion was to forestall China's increasing influence over the country, and the Incident served Japan as a ready-made excuse by which she hoped to justify her activities to other nations in the world. Japan expelled the Chinese administration from Manchuria and set up a puppet goverment. Manchuria was renamed Manchukuo, and in early 1932 a Puppet Emperor was installed, being a descendant of the Manchu emperors. Officers of the Army General Staff, the Kwantung Army, Cherry Society members and others were involved in planning the Mukden Incident which, in effect, was Japan's third invasion of the Chinese mainland, and concerning which the government was not consulted.

Following Japan's resignation from the League of Nations in March 1933, and as the militarists gained increasing political dominance, so the lust for territorial expansion was inflamed both by 'imagined insults' as well as from economic necessity arising from the effects of the world Depression. Japan's war preparations continued unabated. By 1935, only 200 miles from the United States' base of Guam, the secret construction of a naval air base, on Saipan island in the Marianas, had been well advanced. In 1936 Toto Ishimaru wrote a book entitled *Japan Must Fight Britain*, in which he clearly inferred that Singapore would become a battlefield, and to which no one in Britain appeared to take cognizance. In February 1936 a group of young officers and other extremists mutinied against what they considered to be the government's imposition of restraint on the army's ambitions and ventures in north China and Manchuria. Some ministers were assassinated, including the Finance Minister, before the mutiny was brought under control.

By 1937 the Manchurian conquest was insufficient to satisfy the appetite of militant expansionist factions within the Japanese government. In China, also by this time, the two main rival political factions — the Nationalist Kuomintang and the Communists — had emerged in the form of a united front for the express purpose of opposing the common and external aggressor, Japan. To forestall intended Chinese retaliatory action, in July 1937, following a clash at the Marco Polo Bridge, the Japanese Kwantung Army invaded North China. As coastal areas were quickly overrun the Kuomintang was forced into the interior where a new capital at Chungking was established. This location was not an easy one to attack, but neither was it readily accessible to supply routes from the outside world. The Kuomintang therefore became cut off from their supply routes via Hong Kong. When Britain and the United States continued to send supplies to the Kuomintang, by means of the Burma Road, Japan greatly resented this outside interference, which enabled the Kuomintang forces to continue with their resistance. What at the outset General Tojo, the Chief of Staff of the Kwantung Army, had assumed would be only a minor affair, by the middle of 1937 had turned into an irrevocable and expensive commitment by Japan to the conquest of China.

After the commencement of the China Incident in mid-1937, the United States' policy towards Japan took on a firmer but albeit condescending approach. Although American public opinion was firmly in favour of China, the American government at this stage of events did not either openly oppose or condone Japan's actions, as it was not prepared to risk war with Japan over the China issue. When, in December 1937, the US gunboat *Panay* was deliberately sunk in the Yangtze River by Japanese bombers, American indignation rose in momentary anger. This subsided when Japan apologised profusely and agreed to pay the cost of damages, whereupon the incident was quickly overlooked. This compliant attitude of the United States would have been interpreted as one of weakness by the Japanese, and only served to emphasise to them an American reluctance to be drawn into an escalation of events. Frequent attacks, however, against British and American citizens and property in China left scant doubt that, far from making any effort to ameliorate her fast deterioriating relationships with western powers, Japan seemed intent on exacerbating them.

In January 1938 Germany's opposition to Japan's activities against China was officially withdrawn. In return, Germany was promised some economic participation in Japan's intended 'New China', where the Japanese army was by now anxious to bring the war to a quick and successful conclusion. Despite a beating given to the Kwantung Army by Russia's border forces in 1938, nothing could dispel the militarists' ego. This was such that even the Emperor's command, not to become involved in any future similar escapades with Russian forces, was disobeyed, and between May to August 1939 the Japanese took another beating at Nomonhan, where 11,000 men out of a total force of 15,000 were lost.

The fall of France in June 1940 linked Japan's destiny to that of Germany and Italy, and cast shadows of increasing uncertainty over Britain's Far Eastern tenures. On 18th July, in response to Japanese pressure, the British government closed the Burma Road, through which supplies were being provided to Chiang Kai-shek's Chinese Nationalists. The closure had little material effect, as the monsoon had just started. On 18th October 1940, when the road was reopened and with the onset of better weather, supplies to Chiang Kai-shek's forces were again resumed.

As a result of an Imperial Conference decision on 2nd July 1941, an ultimatum was presented to representatives of the Vichy government on the 19th, demanding that Japan be given bases in southern Indo-China. The ultimatum made use of Japan's earlier self-imposed mediation over a Japanese-devised dispute between France and Siam, whereupon she now insisted that troops, planes and warships should be stationed in strategic parts of French Indo-China, in order to ensure the preservation of good order, and to protect a recently negotiated trade agreement. The French Vichy Government, helpless after the collapse of France, unsuccessfully appealed to the Germans and the United States for help. However, on 21st July 1941, they acceded feebly to Japan's ultimatum and signed an agreement. Vichy France by this agreement was ostensibly allowed to retain sovereignty and civil government control in Indo-China, but in exchange for this they were obliged to admit 50,000 Japanese troops in occupation there. Japanese troops commenced landing on 28th July, and on the next day Vichy France announced her further agreement to hand over eight aerodromes to Japan. The tiny garrison put up bitter resistance for 72 hours, although the occupation was reported in Japan to have been completed 'peacefully'. Over a decisive period of only three days, Japanese warships took control of the Camranh Bay Naval Base and a Japanese convoy arrived at Saigon harbour, where the occupation forces were disembarked. Tokyo officially reported that only 50,000 troops had been landed, but British intelligence reckoned that the total was nearer to 200,000, and that all of them were fully trained shock troops and not trainees or reservists. By this occupation of southern French Indo-China, Japan had gained a major naval base less than 700 miles from Singapore and a series of air bases within 600 miles. She now had an ideal spring-board for the further expansion that she was planning. The great port of Saigon harboured Japanese warships, which also cruised at will in the Gulf of Siam. Japan's Ambassador to Indo-China, Mr Yoshizawa, arriving at Haiphong, described his mission as one that would reinforce the 'political and economic ties between Japan and Indo-China'.[19] With the setting up of a consultative council, ostensibly to 'assist' the Governor-General, Admiral Decoux, this virtually reduced Indo-China to the status of a Japanese colony and completely set aside all remaining French influence there.

Between April and September 1941 Japan's oil stocks shrank by 25%. When her assets also were frozen towards the end of July, Japan was forced to face up to reality. Either she must make war against Britain and the United States to secure her needs, or she had to abandon her expansionist plans. In October 1941 the decision was made. It now remained a matter of waiting for the right time to commence an offensive. On 6th September, influenced by military pressures, an Imperial Conference decided that the declining oil stocks necessitated concluding war preparations by mid-October. War games were finalised at the Naval War College in Tokyo in September, and a detailed time schedule was drawn up for the occupation of Malaya, the Philippines, Hong Kong and Java. Ammunition and armament production was increased, a workers' mobilisation plan was put into operation, enormous quantities of occupational currency were printed, and by 1st November the final plans were completed.

General Tojo, on 15th November 1941, in his capacity as Minister of War, declared that Japanese forces, which were stationed in vast areas in East Asia, from Manchukuo to Indo-China, were making '"heroic efforts" to destroy the Chungking Government and to establish the "Greater East Asia Co-Prosperity Sphere."'[20] Great progress was being made to secure vital raw materials such as coal, iron ore, salt and cotton, to offset the effects of trade embargoes imposed by Britain and the United States. Assistance of 'third powers' and Marshall Chiang Kai-shek's 'wealth of manpower' were still threats to Japan's bid to establish the Co-Prosperity Sphere. In Tokyo, on 30th November, at a mass meeting to celebrate the first anniversary of the treaty with the Nanking government, General Tojo declared that, in order to construct the Greater East Asia Co-Prosperity Sphere, Japan would, if necessary, 'proceed over the corpses of our comrades' in order to 'purge East Asia . . . of Great Britain and the United States' who were trying to 'exploit the 1,000,000,000 people of East Asia to satisfy their greed'.[21]

Events moved precipitously during November 1941, following the finalisation of Japan's plans. On the 16th, four hundred and fifty Japanese nationals were evacuated from different parts of Malaya and departed on the Japanese *SS Asama Maru*. On the 18th, eleven Japanese submarines left home bases on scouting missions and took up stations off Hawaii, and another nine vessels sailed towards Hawaii from Kwajalein. On the 19th, four Japanese cruisers arrived at Saigon. Although the actual decision to go to war was made on 25th November 1941, Admiral Yamamoto, the Commander-in-Chief of the Japanese Combined Fleet, was ordered to cancel the proposed attack on Pearl Harbour in the event that negotiations with Washington were successful at the last moment. On the 26th, the Japanese Carrier Force commenced moving eastwards across the Pacific towards Pearl Harbour, and on the following day the United States issued a 'war warning' to all her overseas commanders. Also on the 26th, all US citizens in China and Hong Kong were ordered to leave immediately, and on the next day the first detachment of US Marines in China left Shanghai bound for Manila.

On 29th November 1941, at a government liaison conference, it was decided that the final terms contained in the United States' stiff ten-point note of the 26th were unacceptable. Japan therefore felt obliged to go to war. On 1st December, this decision was confirmed at an Imperial Conference attended by Emperor Hirohito. Contrary to custom, which only required the Emperor's silent approbation of his ministers' deliberations at such meetings, Hirohito astounded those present by reading a poem that his grandfather, Emperor Mutsohito, had composed:

> 'Though I consider the surrounding seas as my brother,
> Why is it that the waves should rise so high?'[22]

Japanese naval forces were reported to be on the move, on 30th November, by British units based in Borneo, and further reports of military movements during the next few days caused an increase in tension throughout Malaya and the Dutch East Indies. On 4th December a report was made by the Chinese Army headquarters in Chungking that forty Japanese warships, including aircraft carriers, had been sighted in Camranh Bay, and that hasty activities to construct air bases had been observed in western Indo-China, near the Gulf of Siam. Also on the 4th, approximately 450 British subjects left Shanghai by steamer, and in Hong Kong the Governor gave authority to the Hong Kong and Shanghai Banking Co-operation to move their headquarters out of the colony to London for safety reasons. On the 5th, in Melbourne, it was officially reported that Japanese navy and military forces had been observed moving southwards, and on the next day President Roosevelt sent a personal appeal for peace to Emperor Hirohito. This was both misunderstood and resented by the Japanese, who considered it grossly improper that the burden of such decisions should be inflicted upon the Emperor. Although Tokyo received the appeal by the afternoon of the 7th, it was not decoded and taken to the Foreign Minister, Mr Shigenori Togo, until 12.15 a.m. on the 8th. The American Ambassador, Mr Grew, was informed that Togo would personally hand the message to the Emperor, but by the time that this was done it was already 10.30 a.m. on 7th December in the United States and the Pacific War had already started. The headlines of the Sunday edition of the *Malay Tribune* on 7th December 1941 ominiously stated, '27 Japanese Transports Sighted Off Cambodia Point', reported to be steaming west, either towards the coast of Malaya or southern Siam. People were told not to travel, and those on holiday were advised to return home.

The Japanese commenced transmitting their final message to the US government, late on December 6th, United States time. The first 13 parts of the message were intercepted and quickly translated by the US code breaking service. There could be little doubt that their meaning was a declaration of war.

Notwithstanding American interception of Japanese diplomatic telegrams, and an expectation that hostilities would be commenced any time after the end of November 1941, when Japan did strike, the Americans were caught utterly unprepared. They had expected Singapore to be Japan's foremost target. Japan had twice previously opened hostilities against other countries without prior declaration of war. December 7th 1941 was the third occasion!

There can be no doubt that the Japanese gained considerable advantages by their surprise attack on Pearl Harbour. It also ranked as a major factor towards their eventual defeat. They virtually crippled the US Pacific Fleet, which gave them some short-term security in subsequent actions in the south-west Pacific. Their success was only partial, however. The US aircraft carriers — their prime targets and the future nemesis of Japan's reversals later — were missed. Also, oil tanks and other important installations were not destroyed. The attack, coming apparently before any declaration of war, aroused violent disgust and indignation and united the American people to President Roosevelt's call to arms. It was not Japan's intention to act outside the bounds of legality, although she had planned to gain maximum possible benefit from the element of surprise. Japanese verbosity accounted for their undoing. Their final 5,000 word note to the Americans took so long to decode, that it was not ready for delivery by their Ambassador until 1400 hours Washington time — 35 minutes after the air attacks on Pearl Harbour had been launched.

The attack on Pearl Harbour — brilliantly conceived by Admiral Isoroku Yamamoto — aimed at total surprise. A striking force of 360 aircraft made a roundabout approach, and attacked before sunrise. The effect was shattering. At 0755 hours local time, ahead of the declaration of war, the main base of the US Pacific Fleet at Pearl Harbour came under a shattering attack, and in little over one hour the Japanese had gained control of the Pacific Ocean.

Some scholars refer to Japan's war as a fifteen year war dating from 1931 and the Manchurian Incident. They put the blame squarely upon the militarist-capitalist clique who, they consider, led the Japanese people astray. Right-wing nationals, however, choose to date the war from December 1941 when Japan attacked Pearl Harbour and invaded other territories in South-East Asia. They refer to it as being a war of Greater East Asia, a term often used by wartime propagandists to justify Japan's invasion. Those holding to this point of view seek as an alibi for Japan's actions, the supposed freeing of fellow Asians from Western colonial oppression. The misery inflicted on millions of people throughout South-East Asia, during 1942 to 1945, gives scant support to this line of argument.

8:6 Declaration of War

At meetings between Prime Minister Winston Churchill and President Roosevelt at Placentia Bay in Newfoundland, between 9–12th August 1941, it was agreed that strong warnings would be sent to the Japanese in respect of their aggression in French Indo-China. It was also agreed that, in the event that Japan attacked British or Dutch possessions in Malaya or in the Dutch East Indies, the United States would almost certainly enter the war. Three months later, on 10th November 1941, Churchill in a public speech reiterated the understanding reached at Placentia Bay and gave an assurance to the United States that should she 'become involved in a war with Japan, a British declaration of war will follow within the hour'.[23]

In Washington, news of the attack on Pearl Harbour was announced whilst peace negotiations at the State Department with Mr Cordell Hull were still being pursued by Admiral Nomura and Mr Kurusu. Hull was disgusted by Japan's obvious duplicity and indignantly declared that he had never seen a document 'more crowded with infamous falsehoods and distortions'[24] in all his years of public service. President Roosevelt immediately ordered full mobilisation throughout the country and in an address to a joint session of Congress, at 12.30 p.m. local time on the 8th, he described 7th December as 'a date which will live in infamy', when 'the United States of America was suddenly and deliberately attacked by naval and air forces of the Empire of Japan'.[25]

He reiterated firmly that, irrespective of '. . . how long it may take us to overcome this premeditated invasion, the American people in their righteous might will win through to absolute victory'. He continued,

> 'We . . . will make it very certain that this form of treachery shall never again endanger us. Hostilities exist. There is no blinking at the fact that our people, our territory, and our interests are in grave danger. With confidence in our armed forces, with the unbounded determination of the people, we will gain the inevitable triumph, so help us God.
>
> I ask that the Congress declare that since the unprovoked and cowardly attack by Japan on Sunday, Dec. 7, 1941, a state of war has existed between the United States and the Japanese Empire.'[26]

The President's request to Congress was passed without any debate in the Senate by an absolute majority of 82 votes. In the House, it was passed by 388 votes to one, the only dissenting vote coming from Mrs Jeannette Rankin, a Republican pacifist, who had voted against war with Germany in 1917. The attack on Pearl Harbour, and other areas in the Far East, gave rise to instant national unity. All impending strikes were immediately called off and the rush to join up, from all parts of the country, exceeded that of 1917. Roosevelt did not reveal that Pearl Harbour had been a completely surprise target, and that he had thought that Japan's prime target was to be Singapore.

Winston Churchill's first emotions were close to elation. For months he had bargained and begged with President Roosevelt and now, by their own actions, the Japanese had brought the United States into the war. The simultaneous attacks on Malaya and Hong Kong were momentarily dwarfed in comparison to what had happened at Pearl Harbour, and by the profound implications that this outrage would subsequently have on the entire course of the war. By mid-morning of the 8th, the American presence in Singapore was visibly evident, as one or two small American flags mysteriously fluttered in the windows of Chinese shops.

At 3.30 p.m. on 8th December, Churchill addressed the House of Commons and made the following statement:

'As soon as I heard last night that Japan had attacked the United States I felt it necessary that Parliament should be immediately summoned . . .

With the full approval of the nation and the Empire I pledged the word of Great Britain about a month ago that should the United States be involved in war with Japan the British declaration of war would follow within the hour. I therefore spoke to President Roosevelt on the Atlantic telephone last night with a view to arranging the timing of our respective declarations. The President told me that he would this morning send a message to Congress which, of course, can alone make a declaration of war on behalf of the United States, and I then assured him that we would follow immediately.

However, it soon appeared that British territory in Malaya had also been the object of Japanese attack, and later on it was announced from Tokyo that the Japanese High Command — not the Imperial Japanese Government — had declared that a state of war existed with Great Britain and the United States. That being so, there was no need to wait for the declaration by Congress. American time is very nearly six hours behind ours. The Cabinet therefore, which met at 12.30 to-day, authorised an immediate declaration of war upon Japan. Instructions were sent to H.M. Ambassador at Tokyo and a communication was dispatched to the Japanese Chargé d'Affaires at 1 o'clock to-day to this effect:

"On the evening of Dec. 7 H.M. Government in the United Kingdom learned that Japanese forces, without previous warning either in the form of a declaration of war or of an ultimatum with a conditional declaration of war, had attempted a landing on the coast of Malaya and bombed Singapore and Hong Kong.

In view of these wanton acts of unprovoked aggression, committed in flagrant violation of international law, and particularly of Article 1 on the Third Hague Convention relative to the opening of hostilities, of which both Japan and the United Kingdom are parties, H.M. Ambassador has been instructed to inform the Imperial Japanese Government in the name of H.M. Government in the United Kingdom that a state of war exists between the two countries."'[27]

Just before hostilities started Churchill had sent a message to the Siamese Prime Minister urging, 'If you are attacked defend yourself.'[28] Churchill confirmed that any attack on Siam would be of extreme interest to Great Britain, who would regard such an attack as 'an attack on ourselves'.[29] In Churchill's address he referred to the 'characteristic Japanese treachery' that was 'employed against the United States'. The Japanese envoys had been ordered to prolong their peace mission negotiations as a cover-up for the surprise attack that was 'made before a declaration of war could be delivered'.[30]

The Labour Party expressed complete support for Churchill's declaration and called for 'unceasing toil from the workers' of the country. Sir Percy Harris (Liberal) called for 'solidarity and a redoubling of our efforts in this struggle between civilisation and barbarism'.[31] In a broadcast to the nation on the evening of 8th December 1941, Mr Churchill appealed to workers in war industries to make 'greater efforts for increased output, especially of tanks and above all, aircraft'.[32]

Across the world, nations were united in abhorrence of Japan's treachery. The Canadian declaration of war was issued on 8th December, retrospective from the 7th, following an emergency Cabinet meeting. Canadian forces were ordered to 'engage the enemy where ever he may be found'.[33] New Zealand similarly declared war on Japan on 9th December, and Mr Peter Frazer, the Prime Minister, spoke of the danger which threatened New Zealand and concluded that 'the people of Britain have set us a noble example; we will live up to it come what may'.[34] India declared war on Japan on 8th December, and a round-up of Japanese nationals was commenced. South Africa followed suit on the 9th. The Governor of Burma, Sir Reginald Dorman-Smith, declared on 7th December,

> 'We will fight till we win. We will fight in our hills, on our plains, in our towns and villages.'[35]

On 8th December Sir Robert Brook-Popham issued an order of the day declaring that 'Malaya was ready to resist any aggression'.[36] With China's declaration of war on the 9th, their Ambassador in London, Dr Wellington Koo, declared, 'It will be a war to a finish, but it will be Japan's finish.'[37] Also on 8th December, the Netherlands and the Netherlands East-Indies declared war on Japan and simultaneously rounded up 2,000 Japanese residents, as well as some Chinese who had been suspected of nurturing pro-Japanese tendencies. Diplomatic relations with Japan were broken off by Belgium, Egypt and Iraq on 8th December, with Greece following suit one day later. Czechoslovakia and Poland declared war on 9th and 12th December respectively.

Free France intimated her readiness to cooperate, and declared war on December 8th, following which 1,100 Japanese nationals were arrested in New Caledonia. Other countries, including Costa Rica, the Dominican Republic, Guatemala, Haiti, Honduras, Nicaragua, Panama and Salvador also declared war on Japan, and the Argentine Government decreed that it would not consider the United States to be a 'belligerent nation' in the ensuing conflict. Colombia and Mexico broke off relations with Japan on 9th December, with Mexico sending strong troop reinforcements to her Pacific coast. President Vargas of Brazil declared Brazil's unanimous 'solidarity with the United States'.[38]

Churchill's feelings on 12th December, when he embarked for the United States on the battleship *Duke of York*, were next to exaltation. America's entry into the war had made a reality of his long-hoped-for invincible coalition against the Axis powers. Churchill later wrote,

> '. . . to have the US at our side was to me the greatest joy. Hitler's fate was sealed. Mussolini's fate was sealed. As for the Japanese, they would be ground to powder.'[39]

In Emperor Hirohito's imperial rescript to the Japanese nation various reasons were given for Japan's declaration of war against the United States and the British Empire. The Emperor referred to Japan's 'far-sighted policy' which aimed to 'cultivate friendship' among nations in common prosperity. He said that China had failed 'to comprehend' Japan's 'true intentions' and had recklessly courted trouble and 'disturbed the peace in East Asia', as had the 'inordinate ambition' of Britain and the United States, whose purpose was to dominate the affairs of the region. He accused Britain and the United States of obstructing 'by every means' Japan's right to 'peaceful commerce', by 'direct severance of economic relations', which had menaced 'gravely the existence' of the Japanese Empire.[40]

He continued,

> 'Patiently have we waited and long have we endured in the hope that our Government might retrieve the situation in peace. But our adversaries, showing not the least spirit of conciliation, have unduly delayed a settlement, and in the meantime they have intensified economic and political pressure to compel our Empire to submission thereby.

This trend of affairs would, if left unchecked, not only nullify our Empire's efforts of many years for the sake of the stabilisation of East Asia, but also endanger the very existence of our nation. The situation being such as it is, our Empire, for its existence and self-defence, has no other recourse but to appeal to arms and to crush every obstacle in its path.

Hallowed spirits of our imperial ancestors guarding us from above, we rely upon the loyalty and courage of our subjects in our confident expectation that the task bequeathed by our fore-fathers will be carried forward.'[41]

In a broadcast to the American nation on 9th December 1941, President Roosevelt referred to 'the sudden criminal attacks perpetrated by the Japanese in the Pacific' as being the 'climax to a decade of international immorality'. He likened Japan's course in the past ten years as being parallel to that of 'Hitler and Mussolini in Europe and Africa' and made special mention of Japan's invasion on Manchukuo without warning in 1931. Italy similarly had invaded Ethiopia in 1935, as had Hitler occupied Austria in 1938.

'In 1939 Hitler invaded Czechoslovakia, without warning. Later in 1939 Hitler invaded Poland, without warning. In 1940 Hitler invaded Norway, Denmark, Holland, Belgium and Luxembourg, without warning. In 1940 Italy attacked France and later Greece, without warning. In 1941, Axis powers attacked Yugoslavia and Greece and dominated the Balkans, without warning. In 1941 Hitler invaded Russia, without warning. And now Japan has attacked Malaya and Thailand, and the United States, without warning.'[42]

Within a short time of war being declared, many Japanese civilians in Singapore, including Mr Okamoto, the last Consul General, were interned at Changi prison. Those who had already been convicted for various offences were sent to the Outram Road prison.

1. *Japan Against the World 1941–2041. The 100 Year War for Supremacy* by Russell Braddon, ch.1, p.23.
2. *Japan. The Years of Triumph* by Louis Allen, p.106.
3. Ibid, p.106.
4. *Allies of a Kind. The US, Britain and the War Against Japan 1941–45* by Christopher Thorne, Ch.2, p.52.
5. *Keesing's Contemporary Archives. November 22–29, 1941*, p.4897.

Chapter Eight

6. *The Fall of Singapore* by Frank Owen, Ch.2, p.29.
7. *The Almanac of World War II* edited by Brigadier Peter Young, Chronology p.67.
8. *Japan Against the World 1941–2041. The One Hundred Year War for Supremacy* by Russell Braddon, Ch.20, p.287.
9. *Keesing's Contemporary Archives. October 18–25, 1941*, p.4843.
10. Ibid, p.4843.
11. Ibid, p.4843.
12. Ibid, p.4843.
13. Ibid, p.4843.
14. Ibid, p.4875.
15. Ibid, p.4843.
16. Ibid, p.4875.
17. Ibid, *November 22–29, 1941*, p.4897.
18. Ibid, p.4897.
19. Ibid, *November 5–15, 1941*, p.4876.
20. Ibid, *November 22–29, 1941*, p.4897.
21. Ibid, *December 6–13, 1941*, p.4921.
22. *Sons of Heaven. A Portrait of the Japanese Monarchy* by Jerrold M. Packard, Ch.9, p.288.
23. *The Almanac of World War II* edited by Brigadier Peter Young. Chronology, p.126.
24. *Keesing's Contemporary Archives. December 6–13, 1941*, p.4921.

25–38. Ibid, pp.4921–4924.

39. *Eagle Against the Sun: The American War with Japan* by Ronald H. Spector. Ch.6, p.123. (Taken from *The Second World War, Vol.2* by Winston Churchill.)
40. *Keesing's Contemporary Archives. December 6–13, 1941*, p.4923.
41. Ibid, p.4923.
42. Ibid, p.4925.

PART TWO: DEFEAT

CHAPTER NINE: IMPOSSIBLE REALITY

9:1 Storm Clouds Develop

The decision, in 1921, to build a Naval Base 'Fortress' in Singapore, was deliberated at length, in the belief that any possible future attack on Singapore, or Peninsula Malaya, could only be mounted from the sea. The view that the Royal Navy (RN), in conjunction with the Royal Air Force (RAF), would be capable of protecting the area from Japan, situated some 3,000 miles away, and that any hostile shipping in the Gulf of Siam and the South China Sea would be suitably dealt with by these forces, was paramount in all early defence planning for Singapore. Heavy guns were to be established on the island to prevent any enemy warships from coming within range of the proposed 'bastion'. It was calculated that relief to Singapore would be possible within 90 days, and this contingency remained until 1939. The outbreak of war in Europe, and Britain's commitments there and in North Africa, compelled a change of plan, and in 1940 the Chiefs of Staff lengthened the 'Relief Period' to 180 days. Strategists were therefore put under unavoidable duress long before the commencement of the Malayan campaign.

Work on the Naval Base was slow prior to 1933, owing to insufficient funds being allocated, and because Sydney, in New South Wales, Australia, was being considered as a possible alternative. Any such change would have been fallacious and irresponsible, with Malaya exporting a third of the world's rubber, and 60% of the world's total tin production, and with Singapore being situated at the nodal point of the communication route between Europe and the riches of East Asia. Since 1922 the Naval Base had been publicised as playing an essential role in the protection of the British Empire's Far Eastern interests, and its completion in 1938 attracted world-wide attention. Although the Naval Base was ready, it had no ships, and after 1939, when war broke out in Europe, there was no longer any possibility of significant naval forces coming, as these were fully committed in the Atlantic Ocean against the Germans. When the 'Relief Period' was increased to six months, proposals were made to stock essential food supplies for a similar period. When hostilities broke out, however, no provisions on such a scale had been implemented.

Sir Shenton Thomas, the Governor of the Straits Settlements, officially performed the opening ceremony of the Naval Base on 15th February 1938. What had taken sixteen years in the making, at a cost of £63 million, was – ironically and unknown to anyone at that date – to be surrendered to the Japanese precisely four years later, to the very day. Malaya, despite protestations to the contrary, was totally unprepared for war.

Inter-service quarrels, in connection with defence strategy for Singapore and the Malay Peninsula, were so bitter by 1929 that there was virtually no co-operation between the service heads of the various armed forces in the region. The navy and army argued for the use of heavy, fixed armaments to repel any sea-borne attack, whereas the air force considered aircraft would be better suited for this purpose, claiming that any enemy attack would be eliminated before it came within range of the defensive big guns. The army and navy won. The army was also insistent that no enemy could advance by land down the Malay Peninsula from the north, despite more than one British general sending reports to Whitehall, which clearly held that this course of action was not only possible, but was also tactically sound. The RAF view was totally different, and from as early as 1936 the RAF commenced constructing airfields up-country, which infuriated army commanders, especially as these were sited without sufficient consultation on how best to defend them. The army's view-point having been accepted as official tactical policy, nothing was done about the controversial and enlightened reports which were submitted to Whitehall in 1937. Perhaps they were purposely overlooked in order to 'teach the RAF a lesson'.[1]

The defence of Malaya had always been viewed historically as a naval matter, and strategists had never envisaged the awesome possibility of having to fight simultaneously Germany, Italy and Japan. In August 1940, however, it was realised that the available fleet strength for the defence of Singapore would always be inadequate until such time as Germany and Italy had been defeated. It was also realised that it was no longer sufficient to give priority to defending Singapore alone, and that all of Malaya had to be considered. In the absence of a fleet, air and land forces therefore had to become the defensive mainstays.

Evidence of Japan's intention to invade Malaya, which had been openly debated and rehearsed in the form of trial sea-borne landings and jungle missions, was known to British Intelligence sources for more than ten years before it actually happened. In the 1930s there was ample documentation of Japan's supreme plan to conquer South-East Asia, which was supported by her massive increase in political and propaganda activities. In 1937 Japan ranked as Britain's number two potential enemy, and in February 1939 the Chiefs of Staff made a new tactical appreciation, based on the assumption that war might well be possible against the combined forces of Germany, Italy and Japan. Japan's plans to construct another sixteen capital warships was also known by the British by mid-1940 and when, by the end of that year, Japan's diplomatic code was broken by the United States' Intelligence Service, further detailed inside information also became more readily available.

Although by mid-April 1940 there was adequate evidence to confirm that war with Japan was more than a probability, the official view was still held in Malaya that it was improbable. It was generally, and erroneously, thought that there was little to fear from the Japanese, and their military prowess was considered as being of little consequence. In Malaya at that time the armed forces were thin on the ground, and there were no sizable ships at the Singapore Naval Base. Most of the ships that were available to the Commander-in-Chief China Squadron had either been deployed for convoy protection or were assisting to maintain communications in the Indian Ocean. There were no fighter planes in the theatre, and the less than one hundred first-line aircraft were mostly obsolescent. General L.V. Bond, the General Officer Commanding (GOC), had only one infantry brigade of five regular battalions (three British, one Indian and one Malay), plus the local territorial volunteer forces.

British Cabinet papers, released in January 1970 under the 30 year secrecy rule, revealed that wishful thinking had played a considerable part in the defence preparation of Singapore, particularly by the Admiralty, during the period referred to as 'the phoney war', which lasted until the Spring of 1940. Winston Churchill, as the First Lord of the Admiralty, circulated on 11th December 1939 a Cabinet paper which stated:

> 'Singapore is a fortress armed with five 15-inch guns and garrisoned by nearly 20,000 men. It could only be taken after a siege by an enemy of at least 50,000 . . . It is not considered possible that the Japanese, who are a prudent people and reserve their strength for the command of the Yellow Sea and China, in which they are fully occupied, would embark on such a mad enterprise.'[2]

Only after Singapore was lost did Churchill admit that he had never been made aware of the true situation.

Chamberlain's government had realised in late 1939 that Britain's Far Eastern Dominions would only be held, in the event of hostilities with Japan, with the aid and participation of the United States. This realisation of weakness on Britain's behalf was never revealed to those countries that were potentially to be directly involved in such a conflict, and no doubt Chamberlain considered this evasion of the truth to be justified.

Winston Churchill replaced Chamberlain as Prime Minister on 10th May 1940, the day on which Hitler invaded the Low Countries and France, and Italy declared war on France and Great Britain. The British were forced to evacuate France at Dunkirk on 1st June 1940, shortly after which France collapsed. Britain now stood alone to face Hitler in Europe. German control extended virtually to all the central and western areas, except for Switzerland and the Iberian Peninsula. These events significantly affected the Far Eastern political scene, and posed threats to British interests there, with French Indo-China having become a Vichy France satellite, and Siam's neutrality being suspect. It was correctly assumed that Japan would regard this combination of events as presenting her with an ideal opportunity to become the 'ruler' over the South-West Pacific. On 8th August the War Cabinet met and considered the Far East war strategy. The Chiefs of Staff acknowledged that the total defence of Malaya was now necessary, and that the existing numbers of ground forces and first-line aircraft were well below the minimum required. On 4th September 1940, they told Churchill of their intention to send the 7th Australian Division and two infantry brigades to Malaya, but this was disallowed. Churchill still regarded the fleet as being the major defensive arm of Singapore, and any policy that envisaged defending the whole of the Malay Peninsula as having no merit.

On 10th September Churchill wrote to General Sir Hastings Ismay, the Deputy Secretary (Military) to the War Cabinet, that he could not entertain 'the idea of trying to defend the Malay Peninsula', which was seen by some policy makers as being indefensible. He regarded the threat of a Japanese attack on Singapore as being remote, and that '... nothing could be more foolish from their point of view ...'[3] Three months later Churchill still held to this opinion when, on 15th December 1940, he declared to the Secretary of State for the Dominions:

> 'I do not view the situation in the Far East as immediately dangerous. I do not wish to commit myself to any serious dispersion of our forces in the Malay Peninsula and Singapore.'[4]

Necessity — that dictator to decision makers — begets misjudgements. On 8th December 1940, one year to the day before Japan opened hostilities in the Far East, Churchill confided in writing to President Roosevelt:

> 'Japan is thrusting southward ... thus bringing them within a comparatively short distance of Singapore and the Dutch East Indies.'[5]

On 15th February 1941, on what, one year hence, was to be an infamous day in British military history, Churchill again communicated his misgivings to Roosevelt that Japan's actions could indicate their '... intention to make war on us, or do something that would force us to make war on them in the next few weeks'.[6] These intermittent flashes of clairvoyance are surprisingly contradicted by a minute dictated to the Chief of the Chiefs of Staff on February 13th 1941, in which Churchill maintained that the 'political situation in that area did not at that time warrant the maintenance there of large forces'.[7]

Even as late as October 1941 Churchill remained doubtful, and on the 20th he told the Cabinet Defence Committee that he did not anticipate 'an attack in force on Malaya',[8] and would not accept the imminent threat to Singapore, nor the Chiefs of Staffs' strategy for defending it. Although the Cabinet had approved the recommendation to increase the complement of first-line aircraft up to 336, Churchill still maintained that in any attack 'the prime defence . . . is the fleet',[9] and that Singapore should have a strong local garrison in addition to the 'general potentialities of sea power'.[10] Churchill appeared to be satisfied that Japan's efforts would be concentrated against the China trade routes, and this conviction lulled his subordinates within the government against taking more energetic safeguards to offset the impending threat.

Despite information on Japan's intent to deceive Britain, the Right Honourable Alfred Duff Cooper — Churchill's protégé on a mission of enquiry — concluded, at a conference in Singapore on 29th September 1941, that the threat to the Singapore Naval Base was exaggerated. Cooper considered that the Japanese were concentrating their troops against Russia, and that any attempt at an east-coast monsoon landing in Malaya would therefore be remote. Delusion had been inculcated at such high levels that even Churchill was deceived, and four days before Pearl Harbour was attacked, he was still describing Japan's hostilities as a remote contingency. Against the Admiralty's wishes, and 'through a process of illogical reasoning',[11] the *Prince of Wales* and *Repulse* were authorised to show the flag in the Far East, which was deemed to be sufficient to call Japan's bluff. Their arrival in Singapore on 2nd December 1941, with four escorting destroyers, was proudly announced over the radio to all who cared to listen. Sent at the personal insistence of Churchill, British power in the Far East was then described as being more invincible than ever. Their presence stirred the hearts of many, although, sadly, not sufficiently to ignite renewed efforts to improve Singapore's sorely overlooked civil defences. It was assumed that the Japanese would be intimidated, but instead they chose to call Churchill's bluff. Churchill later wrote:

> 'I confess . . . the whole Japanese menace lay in a sinister twilight, compared with our other needs. If . . . Japanese aggression drew in America, I would be content to have it. On this I rested . . .'[12]

Lieutenant-General Arthur Ernest Percival, CB, DSO, OBE, MC, was born in 1887. In July 1941 he was appointed the General Officer Commanding Malaya, and was given only three days' notice in which to fly out to Singapore. Percival had been General Dobbie's Chief of Staff in Malaya from 1936–8 and was well aware of weaknesses in Malaya's defensive arrangements. He soon realised, on his arrival in mid 1941, that little had been done in the interim to rectify earlier shortcomings, since priority of necessity had been given to the European and home fronts.

Percival found badly sited airfields, sticking out like sore thumbs in the surrounding countryside, manned with insufficient, obsolescent aircraft, far below the total that had been recommended and promised. Defensive works, proposed four years earlier in his own reports to General Dobbie, were still only completed on paper. The armed forces were understrength and no tanks had been made available throughout the Peninsula. Percival did not even have a military aircraft available for his own use.

Although 566 first-line aircraft and five divisions, comprising 48 infantry battalions, had been estimated as necessary for the defence of Malaya and Singapore, and had been asked for by Percival, when hostilities commenced on 8th December 1941 there were only 141 mostly obsolescent planes, with no dive-bombers or torpedo bombers, and only three weak divisions of land forces: the 8th Australian and the 9th and 11th Indian Divisions, comprising 32 battalions, without tanks. At sea there were no light naval craft that could patrol and defend Malaya's long coastline. The local defence forces, formed too late in 1940, were also ill-equipped for the tasks demanded of them. The fleet — such as it was in Singapore — was soon to be crippled by the sinking of the *Prince of Wales* and *Repulse*, as was the United States Pacific Fleet by the attack on Pearl Harbour, which Britain's strategists had always looked upon as being a deterrent against Japan.

General Percival's initiative was curtailed from the moment of his arrival in Singapore by Treasury financial controls, as were those of

RAF Commanders through the Air Ministry. Although the Empire had been at war since 1939, there was hardly any relaxation in the Treasury's detailed control, which denied the army any financial initiative to quickly implement urgent defensive measures.

Air Chief Marshal Sir Robert Brooke-Popham, GCVO, KCB, CMG, DSO, AFC — a highly distinguished officer — was retired from the RAF in 1937, when he became the Governor of Kenya. He was reinstated on the active list in 1939, and in October 1940, when he was 63 years old, he was appointed as the Commander-in-Chief Far East. He was selected for this position for professional military reasons, and because he was considered to be the best choice to smooth ruffled brows and secure co-operation and goodwill between the armed forces and the Governor, as well as with the MCS and the civilian community in general. Although Brooke-Popham was given the title C-in-C Far East, and was a man of seniority, able to dominate other personalities, he did not enjoy ultimate command, and had no control over the Royal Navy. In Singapore, in effect, there were two Commanders-in-Chief, which was ridiculous, as each was 'responsible to a different authority in London'.[13] The navy, however, maintained control over the Combined Intelligence Bureau. Although some writers have been strongly critical of his lack of direction and decision, Brooke-Popham had been given an almost impossible task and had only a small staff of seven officers with which to do it.

In retrospect, his contribution can be seen in the light of opinions that he expressed at that critical time. In an interview on 3rd December 1941 he maintained, 'There are clear indications that Japan does not know which way to turn. Tojo is scratching his head.'[14] He confessed that his most urgent concern as C-in-C was over the shortage of aircraft, but at the same time, he considered that

> 'We can get on alright with Buffaloes out here, but they haven't got the speed for England. Let England have the super-Spitfires and the hyper-Tornadoes, Buffaloes are quite good enough for Malaya.'[15]

This he said in the full realisation that Japan had a powerful force of long-range bombers stationed in south French Indo-China, and seven days later the *Prince of Wales* and *Repulse* went up the east coast of Malaya to their doom, without any fighter protection.

The Combined Intelligence Bureau was an organisation that did much to play down the deadly fighting efficiency of the Japanese and in doing so gave allied forces an utterly false and inaccurate sense of security. Claiming that Japanese pilots were incapable of flying in the dark, intelligence officers discounted the necessity of manning Air Raid Precaution (ARP) stations at night. Others lectured that the Japanese were 'small, myopic, ill-equipped, frightened of the dark and anyway physically repulsive'.[16] How little these 'experts' knew! Most of what was told about the Japanese was couched in fiction, and although someone must have known the truth — that many Japanese were 'tall, strong, splendidly equipped, conspicuously unbespectacled, and very nearly beautiful'[17] — intelligence experts and politicians alike decided to lie about it. When Colonel Ward lectured on the 'magnificent fighting qualities and the intensive jungle training of the Japanese troops',[18] he was criticised for his defeatist views and never asked to lecture again. Government radio aimed at keeping up morale. While the media over-estimated Malaya's defensive strength it also derided the capabilities of Japanese pilots and troops. Although most military authorities considered an east coast sea landing during the north-east monsoon as impractical, many old hands in Malaya fully realised that during the monsoon it was not uncommon to have periods of complete calm for five or six days at a time. It is little wonder that, with such counsel, the 'fortress' of Singapore, with its magnificent and expensive Naval Base, was doomed, even before hostilities commenced.

From the outset, the government in Malaya set an example of indifference. People were discouraged from believing that Malaya would ever be involved in war. The myth of implied security lulled the thoughts of most 'white tuans', whose relatively comfortable lifestyles were further reassured by the arrival of the *Prince of Wales* and the *Repulse* at the 'Empire's mightiest Naval Base'.[19] The RAF constantly droned overhead. Thousands of troops throughout the Peninsula and in Singapore braggingly spoiled for a fight. Most Europeans had scant regard for the Japanese, as their experience of them had been limited to seeing them only as barbers, photographers, restaurant owners and brothel keepers. For many civilians it was an exaggerated 'make believe period', and 'no one could be whipped into a state of anxiety when there were hardly any shelters in the streets'.[20] Even as late as 7th December 1941, Chamberlain-type Munich reassurances were still being made by politicians and military leaders alike.

Incredibly, with every indication pointing towards Japan's intention to attack Malaya, her assault troops still waded ashore with the benefit of surprise. Japan's four carefully synchronised invasions were timed to within a few hours of each other. Considerable local variations in time were caused by the international dateline, but by using Tokyo time as a standard, Malaya was the first to be attacked at 2.15 a.m. on 8th December, after which came Pearl Harbour at 3.25 a.m., with the landings at Singora at 4 a.m., and Hong Kong at 8.30 a.m. When these times were localised to the various Pacific areas the attack on Pearl Harbour commenced at 7.55 a.m. on 7th December and that on Malaya at 12.45 a.m. on the 8th. This local time difference, though significant in its various areas, was in fact only one hour and ten minutes apart.

9:2 Defensive Appreciations Disregarded

Field-Marshall Sir John Greer Dill, the Director of Military Operations and Intelligence at the War Office in 1936, and formerly the Commandant of the Staff College at Camberly, considered A.E. Percival 'to be the best of all the distinguished staff and students at the College'.[21] It was Dill who recommended Percival for a place at the elite Imperial Defence College, where he spent 1935, and was afterwards promoted to full Colonel. Dill also favoured Percival as Chief General Staff Officer in Malaya Command in 1936, when that command had just been taken over by Major-General W.G.S. (later Lieut-General Sir William) Dobbie. Percival toured the Malayan mainland extensively and found that most of the British there were disinterested in defensive matters, being completely engrossed in their lucrative tin and rubber businesses.

Dobbie was impressed by the performance of Japanese troops in China. In 1937 he asked Percival to prepare a review of the defences of Malaya from a Japanese point of view. On his own initiative, Percival elaborated this into an appreciation, forecasting the most likely methods the Japanese would use if they decided to attack Malaya and Singapore. Percival's appreciation was based on observations made of Japanese troops practising in combined operations on the China coast, and in the firm conviction that it would be Japan's intention to seize airfields in southern Siam and northern Malaya, to stage any assault on Singapore. The possibility of a 'back-door' approach in attacking Singapore was emphasised. This took into consideration the ninety-day Relief Period, on which the defensive strategy for Malaya and Singapore had been formulated. His view was also that it would be possible for the Japanese to make landings on the eastern coast of Malaya during the north-east monsoon, which normally occurred between November and February every year. Percival envisaged that likely sites for these landings would be at Singora and Patani in southern Siam, and at Kota Bahru in north Malaya, and that any landings during this period would more than likely be assisted by low cloud, causing bad visibility and rendering counter air reconnaissance more difficult.

Dobbie supported Percival's appreciation, basing this on the view that an invasion might well take place before a British fleet could reach Singapore. When Percival left Singapore in July 1938, Dobbie sent a warning to the War Office, following up Percival's November 1937 report, to the effect that he regarded the threat of an attack on Singapore from the north as being an imminent danger. He further reiterated that such an attack could be carried out during the north-east monsoon and that the jungle was in most places passable for infantry. The Committee of Imperial Defence acted on this warning, agreeing to keep an Indian battalion stationed at Taiping in Malaya, which was due to return to India in early 1939. Little other attention was paid by the War Office to Dobbie's reports and only after repeated requests had been made was an extra £60,000 sent to Malaya Command for the purpose of constructing machine gun placements in Penang, in southern Johore, and on the southern end of Singapore island. As a result of Dobbie's persistence and his reports, he was relieved of his command.

It was due to both Percival's and Dobbie's foresight that later commanders, including Lieut-General L.V. Bond, at last realised that it would be insufficient to defend the Singapore Naval Base alone and that the defence of the whole of Malaya, with its long and vunerable coastline, was essential. It has been a contentious issue among historians as to whether or not the jungle was passable. Three-quarters of the country was covered by jungle, and like a smoke-screen it shielded any attacking force, which was able to appear and disappear at will. In April 1940, when Lieut-General Bond succeeded Dobbie, he concurred with the view that the Japanese would launch an attack from south Siam, and that the main defensive tactic should be to prevent the enemy from making any landing, for which an effective naval and air force striking contingent was needed.

President Roosevelt's personal advisor, Mr Harry Hopkins, in July 1940 expressed the view that greater priority should be given to Singapore's defences, as opposed to 'trying to do too much in the Middle East'.[22] Churchill was unswayed by such arguments, particularly as Britain at that time was still essentially fighting alone. It was understandable, therefore, that commitments and dire priorities in the North African and European theatres of war should have absorbed both men and machines, and that the inadequate defensive preparations for Malaya were a result of Churchill's insistence on giving priority to those areas. As it turned out, the premature offensive in North Africa was a fiasco, and Churchill later frankly confessed that the entire Japanese menace had seemed, at that stage, to be in a 'sinister twilight'. This degree of mental unpreparedness in those who one might have expected to be better informed is more difficult to understand and accept, and by one historian was likened to the 'mental blindness of the Europeans in India before the Mutiny'.[23]

In May 1941 Field-Marshall Sir John Greer Dill, the Chief of the Imperial Staff, submitted a paper to Churchill in which he also argued that the security of Singapore should come before that of Egypt, and that the defences there were 'still considerably below standard'.[24] Churchill was upset by these views, which opposed his plan to take the offensive against Rommel. Churchill was convinced that should Japan enter the war, the United States would come in on Britain's side and that 'Japan would not be likely to besiege Singapore at the outset, as this would be . . . dangerous to her'.[25] He seriously miscalculated the dangers threatening Singapore.

The official history of the fall of Singapore subsequently substantiated Dobbie's opinions. Japan's official account of the war also confirmed that the north-east monsoon period had been specifically chosen, as it would give them the added advantage of surprise.

It was to Percival's credit that he anticipated brilliantly the plan eventually adopted by the Japanese. Percival's appreciation of the Malayan problem made a good impression on Dill, and was instrumental in his promotion over his contemporaries, and in his selection for the post of General Officer Commanding in Malaya in July 1941. It was indeed unfortunate for Percival that Dill did not live through the subsequent disaster, as he would have been the best person to have recounted just how hopeless a task the Malayan command was.

9:3 Other Priorities and Misjudgements

Japan's interest in Malaya was increasingly apparent from 1923. Throughout the 1930s her designs for future territorial expansion loomed menacingly. By 1937 the British Chiefs of Staff regarded Japan as second only to Germany as a possible enemy. They also rated Singapore, along with Britain, as the keystones on which the British Commonwealth would survive. Hong Kong, although of importance, was not considered as vital, and only to be defended for as long as this should prove possible. A revision of these opinions was made in early 1939, and although similar conclusions were drawn, the security of the Mediterranean was placed before that of the Far East. The Relief Period was lengthened from 90 to 180 days, following Britain's declaration of war with Germany on 3rd September 1939.

When France collapsed and Italy entered the war in June 1940, a further review of defence policies for the Far East acknowledged that Hong Kong was indefensible and recommended that the four battalion garrison be withdrawn. Despite Churchill's acceptance of this view, nothing was done and, one year later, when the Canadian government offered to strengthen the reinforcement of the Hong Kong garrison, this was accepted. On 27th October 1941 two Canadian battalions sailed for Hong Kong, to increase subsequently the vain sacrifice on its surrender by almost fifty percent.

France's collapse resulted in other startling implications. Japan was presented with the opportunity to isolate China and to seize naval and air bases in Indo-China. On 20th July 1941 the Petain government conceded that Japan could make a military mission into Indo-China, which provided her with a big naval base only 750 miles from Singapore and airfields within 300 miles of the Malayan coast at Kota Bahru, rendering both Singapore and Malaya open to subsequent attack from the rear.

While the French fleet contained the Italian navy in the Mediterranean, British warships were released to patrol in Far Eastern waters. Britain's first priority now became the building up of her own defences and of those in the Mediterranean area. The British fleet had to be kept closer to home to ensure the security of Great Britain, as in 1940 and 1941 there was still the dire threat of a direct German invasion. Modern aircraft and warships could no longer be spared or sent to the Far East theatre, which might never become involved in war. This line of thinking was nurtured, until as late as November 1941, by many responsible people in Whitehall, who at least hoped that the Far East would not be drawn into open conflict, in the misconception that Japan had over-extended herself in China.

There were many others who doubted this line of argument, and considered it likely that the Japanese would open up an offensive against Britain's interests in the Far East, particularly as Britain stood alone in Europe at that time and was fighting for survival. With air reinforcements and any sizeable complement of modern warships being unavailable for Malaya's defence, this responsibility was divested entirely in the army. Japan was therefore presented with an opportunity too good to overlook, especially when Germany declared war, on 22nd June 1941, against the traditional enemy, Russia.

Decisions were not easily made, necessitating profound and exacting heart-searching. Egypt, with the Suez Canal, and other Middle East countries were considered to be of more importance than Malaya, and Singapore was classified as a lower priority to Cairo. These precedences were to be upheld, unless imminent attack against Australia and New Zealand was threatened. Churchill, therefore, resigned himself to 'pay whatever forfeits were exacted in Malaya'.[26]

The *Malayan Gazette's* editorial on Friday 16th December 1941 simultaneously condoned and condemned Britain's strategic policies. Their short-sightedness was criticised, but at the same time it was conceded that the main British fleet had to stay in home waters while Europe was in such a turmoil.

> 'How can the British main fleet leave home waters when events in Europe are in such a state? . . . In Malaya the defences are weak and troops scarce; there are no . . . battleships, aircraft carriers, no cruisers, submarines.'[27]

Although the great Naval Base at Singapore had been opened by Governor Sir Shenton Thomas on 15th February 1938, the political situation, and then the war in Europe, precluded any chance of the navy coming to the Far East. Ships were desperately needed to defend the British Isles. The long feared possibility — simultaneous war in Europe and the Far East — had now become nightmare reality. Had Japan struck earlier it would have been more to her advantage, as by December 1941 Britain's worst days in Europe were coming to an end. A British Far Eastern Fleet of seven battleships, one aircraft carrier, ten cruisers and twenty four destroyers were under construction and the Japanese, fully aware that these would be ready by February 1942, commenced their attack in December 1941.

The British government persisted with the policy of avoiding war with Japan for as long as possible. Although in early August 1941 the Commander-in-Chief Far East, Air Chief-Marshall Sir Robert Brooke-Popham, GCVO, KCB, CMG, DSO, AFC, sent details of 'Operation Matador' to the Chiefs of Staff in London, which proposed an advance into southern Siam to occupy the Patani/Singora area, the British government refused to initiate any action that could be interpreted as a violation of Siam's neutral territory. Britain was anxious not to be viewed as an aggressor, which might jeopardize the long-hoped for support from the United States.

Britain's reluctance to be the first to impinge on Siam's territory was further influenced by previous assurances from the Siamese Premier that Siam would make a stand to slow down any Japanese advance, and would resist to the last man. The resistance of Siamese forces only lasted for five and a quarter hours, so her subsequent easy submission came as a shock, resulting in the dislocation of time-tables for the 'Matador' and 'Krohcol' plans of the British High Command. The Siamese army's resistance against Japanese landings was brief and ineffective and made their former assurances seem little more than hypocrisy. There was never any real intention, or attempt, to effect a determined resistance to Japan's attack.

Siam subsequently announced that permission had been granted to Japanese troops to pass through her territory, having received assurances from Japan that her integrity and sovereignty would be respected. By the evening of 8th December Japanese troops had been allowed to enter Bangkok. Despite this, on 10th December Siam still announced that she did not consider herself at war with Britain, but four days later Japan and Siam signed a ten year Treaty of Alliance.

When Admiral Sir Tom Phillips received a confirmatory message that the United States would regard any Japanese invasion of Malaya, Burma, the Dutch East Indies or Siam as a hostile act, and had requested the Royal Navy to attack any Japanese ships steering west or south across the Gulf of Siam, it was already too late. The Admiralty's message reached Phillips at 2.18 a.m. Singapore time on 8th December, three minutes after the Japanese had commenced their attack on Kota Bahru.

9:4 Civil Government's Omissions

When Sir Shenton Thomas was initially offered the most important appointment in the Colonial Service, as Governor and Commander-in-Chief of the Straits Settlements and High Commissioner of the Malay States, he at first was not interested in taking up the position. It was a cumbersome and complex appointment, requiring him to hold three posts simultaneously.

He was, firstly, the Governor and Commander-in-Chief of the four Straits Settlements, which were a Crown Colony, with Penang — ceded to Great Britain in 1786 — being the oldest part.

Secondly, he was High Commissioner to the ten individually ruled Malay States, which had been formed into two separate groupings. One of these was the Federated Malay States (FMS), of Perak, Selangor, Negeri Sembilan and Pahang. Their capital was at Kuala Lumpur, and a Federal Budget controlled their main sources of revenue and expenditure. Each State had its own parliament, comprising both Leglislative and Executive Councils, and a British Resident, who controlled a series of administrative departments, all of which were the ultimate responsibility of the High Commissioner. In the Unfederated Malay States (UFMS) of Johore, Trengganu, Kedah, Kelantan and Perlis a different administrative and political set-up was established. A British Advisor, not a Resident, offered advice when necessary on domestic affairs, couched frequently in terms of persuasion. Ostensibly, Britain maintained control over foreign affairs and defence only. In the UFMS the High Commissioner's powers were limited, as no direct order could be given to any Malay Ruler. Although the States were protected, they were not British Crown possessions. Sovereignty remained with the Malay Rulers and was not invested in the British Crown.

The third facet of this complex appointment was as Agent for British North Borneo and Sarawak, an area covering 80,000 square miles, with a total population of over half a million people. As Agent, Sir Shenton was required to keep London informed of the political, social, economic and financial developments affecting this vast area, although he had no authority over it. The geographical size involved by these tripartite responsibilities was such that it necessitated the establishment and running of four official residences. The one in Penang, aptly captioned 'Bel Retiro', was scenically located in pleasant coolness at the summit of Penang Hill.

Before Sir Shenton first set foot in Penang on 9th November 1934, the *Straits Times* pre-emptively reported on 16th July that he was a man of considerable administrative ability and tact, and had been singled out for very considerable advancement. It was anticipated that he would be capable of soothing the ruffled feelings which Sir Cecil Clementi, his predecessor, had created by

> 'his unwise discrimination against the Chinese population of Malaya, who bitterly resented their exclusion from plans for rice cultivation and educational grants'.[28]

On arrival in Penang, and in his first address to the Penang Legislative Council, Sir Shenton made a good impression, reassuring them:

> 'I am prepared to listen to anyone who may feel able to offer me useful advice, and I hope he will not wait for me to ask for it. I shall take no decision without first inviting the views of all parties interested.'[29]

Sir Shenton firmly believed that the factual possession of a country by expatriates amounted only to 'trusteeship, not to ownership' and that Malaya 'and the products of its soil belonged to the indigenous races'.[30]

Be that as it may, Sir Shenton's initial popularity waned during his first years in office, on account of his cautious and tight financial policies, which gave rise to successive years of financial surpluses, gaining him increasing popularity with the Colonial Office in London, but not in Malaya. During his initial two years, various inherited problems had to be resolved. Prominent among these were Clementi's aborted decentralisation strategy, and the question of which of the Sultan of Selangor's three sons should be selected to succeed him.

Monsieur A. Glineur, a businessman, resident in Singapore at that time, held grave reservations, contrary to the good press originally extended to Sir Shenton, and regarded him as being 'the first Whitehall-type Governor, and a yes man!'[31] He considered Sir Shenton did not know how best to deal with the indigenous population of Singapore and Malaya, basing this opinion on what had previously occurred in Nigeria. Others chose to regard Sir Shenton as

> 'an admirable man, determined to do his very best for the people under his charge, completely dedicated to a public service, not a prig in any way, but a strong and upright character with a deep sense of duty'.[32]

His achievement was to organise an honest and efficient peace-time administration which was run economically.

In 1939 Sir Shenton, as only titular Commander-in-Chief Malaya, had no executive control over the armed forces. His civil government's attitude towards the proposed military defence of Singapore and Malaya clearly indicated his underestimation of the gravity and urgency of the diplomatic situation, as well as his failure to appreciate the enormous temptation represented by Malaya's riches to the economically impoverished Japanese. Such attitudes placed an increasing strain on subsequent relations between the civil and military authorities, especially after war in Europe began in September 1939, when the Defence Committee in Singapore was expanded to a War Committee, and when the Governor was appointed Chairman.

Sir Shenton's chairmanship of War Committee meetings was hampered by vacillation. He appeared incapable of enforcing the means to prepare Malaya against invasion. Included on the War Committee were the heads of the three fighting services, along with senior civil government departmental officers, and Mr C.A. Vlieland, who was the first civilian Defence Secretary for Malaya, appointed by Sir Shenton in December 1938. Vlieland had served in the MCS for 26 years, and was an efficient officer with good knowledge of the country. He also held strong opinions regarding the strategic value of the Singapore base, and the need for all of Malaya to be defended.

On 18th October 1939 Sir Shenton was requested in a personal letter from Malcolm MacDonald, the Secretary of State, to remain in his post in Malaya, notwithstanding his pending retirement. MacDonald expressed his complete confidence in Sir Shenton's ability to handle the many difficult economic and political problems likely to arise during wartime. Sir Shenton agreed to stay for as long as required. The *Times* in London reported that he would 'continue to hold office for the duration of the war, provided that his health permits'.[33]

Press coverage in praise of Sir Shenton was at this time by no means unanimous. By 1939 the *Tribune* held powerful editorial sway in Malaya. By virtue of this paper's large Asiatic following its views were compelling the government's attention, particularly those expressing favour for fuller Asian control in government affairs, and disapproval of a system whereby the Governor, as head of the Executive and Legislative Councils, could nominate unofficial members who were to serve within them. Sir Shenton readily accepted the *Tribune's* attempts to promote Britain's war effort, but did not welcome, in the process, what he considered to be criticism by its Asian directors.

In January 1940 Sir Shenton requested a period of not less than six months home leave, commencing in April, although considerably more was due to him. He was 61 years old and, apart from one short leave, had served for six years, since 1934, in Malaya's hot, humid and debilitating climate. With the benefit of hindsight it is easy to criticise him for his request for leave at this juncture, but it would be improper to accuse him of being slack when the facts, as then known, are taken into account.

In March 1940 the war was still confined to Europe and the immediate safety of Great Britain was the prime concern. The Foreign Office strongly supported Sir Shenton's view that nothing should divert Malaya's potentially huge economic contribution to Britain's overall war effort, and considered 'it to be our duty to give absolute priority to the claims of industry'.[34] Japan's internal political crisis and weak economic position, as a result of the war with China, were thought to put her in no position to embark upon further ventures, or to launch a campaign of aggression against distant British bases. The Foreign Office supported this view that the threat to Singapore was remote, and that 'war with Japan was possible though improbable'.[35]

The *Tribune* begged to differ with these views and its editorials criticised the Governor for not having foregone his leave, although he remained in England for only three months. They were not mollified by the proffered explanation that he could have had 'equally important work to do ... in London'[36], which he did not reach until late June 1940. On 1st August Sir Shenton personally, and resolutely, put his case for increasing the RAF's strength in Malaya to the Joint Planning Sub-Committee of the War Cabinet. In the latter part of September he commenced the tedious return trip to Malaya, via Lisbon to Canada and then across the Pacific to Australia, not reaching Singapore until 5th December.

During the seven and a half months that Sir Shenton was away, Stanley W. Jones, the Colonial Secretary, stood in as the Acting Governor. He had enormous responsibilities which, day and night, he tackled single-handedly, undertaking a job which should have been shared by many. Having to comply with officially accepted peace-time procedures meant that things moved only with laborious slowness.

In early 1941 the *Tribune* advocated that defensive measures should be intensified against possible future air raids. Their proposals included all generally accepted safety measures, which had already been adopted in other countries. They were told not to be alarmists!

The white population in Malaya and Singapore enjoyed an easy and protected lifestyle and showed little interest in the war in Europe. It provided them with a topically invocatory subject to discuss at the breakfast table over their newspapers. War rumours were far away. No one thought that anyone would want to fight over Malaya. The gradual build-up of military forces, along with small quantities of equipment in that area, were insufficient to cause panic, and did not unduly alarm civilians. They viewed these as being unlikely to ruffle their lifestyles. Newly arrived soldiers, sailors and airmen disembarked in 'something of a holiday mood'[37] and, being ignorant of local social protocol, some of them proceeded to behave quite scandalously. The misconduct of a few members of the Australian contingents, in particular, cast aside colonial social conventions to such an extent that many among them were treated, not without some amusement, as socially undesirable.

The popularly expounded myth concerning the state of readiness of the Singapore Naval Base, with its massive 15-inch guns, clouded logic and reasoning over crucial defensive issues, diverting attention from the reality that omissions in these invoked. European residents of Malaya, noted Brigadier C.N. Barclay, even after the commencement of war in Europe, appeared to be 'mentally sitting in a corner with their eyes shut and their fingers in their ears, waiting for it to go away'.[38] Anyone who hinted that war with Japan was more than a remote possibility was branded as an alarmist. When defence exercises were suggested, despite causing little inconvenience, resentment flared. Rubber plantations were looked on as if they were located on sacred ground and defensive works, including the construction of weapon ranges, were objected to as being costly, damaging and troublesome. While the Japanese expended maximum effort in preparation, the pattern of British social life went on unabated, with its regular office hours, rounds of golf, horse racing and cricket. An air of complacency prevailed in Singapore as late as September 1941. Visitors noted an underlying determination among government officials that war would not engulf them. Two American newspaper correspondents reported that an extremely confused state of organisation pervaded Singapore.

Despite the depredations of war in Europe and North Africa between 1939 and 1941, life in Malaya continued to be fully enjoyed, and richly lived by those who had long grown accustomed to this.

There was a willing response to a variety of war charity appeals, but in many cases this did not entail any sacrifice. The rubber and tin industries were booming, with fantastic company profits, from which individuals in turn benefited. Rubber and tin made pre-war Malaya the richest part of Britain's Colonial Empire, and not only were they essential to the war industries, but their production also directly brought in enormous quantities of urgently needed American Dollars. During the twelve months following the outbreak of war with Germany, US$97 million had been accounted by the Bank of England through the nett sales of Malayan foreign exchange. By 31st July 1941 this had exceeded US$135 million.

Both Europe and the United States urgently clamoured for raw materials. In Malaya, with three million acres of rubber and a capacity to produce half the world's tin requirements, there was a desperate race to fill the holds of ships, and to many people this was the only thing that really concerned them. In 1939 and 1940, therefore, two contrasting and urgent mandates were given to Malaya by Whitehall, and these resulted in conflicting priorities. The armed forces were told to prepare for possible war against Japan, while Sir Shenton and his civil servants were expected to ensure maximum rubber and tin outputs. Malaya was Britain's best potential dollar earner and maximisation of rubber and tin production was essential to Britain's continued successful administration of the country. Human resources were diverted to attain these goals as opposed to being made available for improving the country's defences. British executives were refused permission to leave their civil employment, and to return home to volunteer for service in the armed forces. It was made categorically clear to them that foreign currency was vital to Britain's war efforts and that nothing compared in importance with producing rubber, tin and oil, which were all vital war supplies.

Such being the priorities ordered by Whitehall, little or no attempt was made to create a substantial military force out of the indigenous population, and the civil authorities in turn showed scant interest in defence problems, or in the training of civilians at short notice. Some thought that arming the local population might divert commercial power from the British, and transfer it to the Chinese. Englishmen of draft age, who were involved in trying to increase the country's productivity, were relatively few in numbers and most of them either joined the Volunteer Forces or the belatedly organised Civil Defence Services, from which only diminutive, positive, defensive strength could be expected.

There have been various accounts claiming that the English in Malaya were unaware of the increasing peril around them. Nothing could have been further from the truth. Although business was booming everywhere, and an atmosphere of prosperity prevailed, most people realised the impending dangers, but there was no point in bemoaning them. Those who wanted to return to Great Britain to enlist were told to get on as normal with their jobs in Malaya, and if their services were wanted they would be called up. A morose reaction to such a directive would not help matters, as circumstances were out of the individual's control. Many considered their best course of action was to put on a cheerful face and to counteract, as well as they could, any tendency to spread panicky rumours. There were numerous people from all nationalities who were anxious to participate in any defensive measures the authorities deemed necessary, provided these were suitably explained to them. In this respect it was clear leadership that was lacking.

Mr F.D. Bisseker — the General Manager of the Penang Tin Smelting Company — was elected in 1940 by the Penang commercial community as their representative on the Straits Settlements Legislative Council. He was to become the senior unofficial elected member. His frequent criticisms of the government's unsatisfactory preparations for war made him unpopular with Sir Shenton and with senior MCS officers. The *Straits Times* in Singapore, and the *Straits Echo and Times* in Penang, invariably published and endorsed Mr Bisseker's criticisms, which also gained some public assent.

A lengthy speech by Mr Bisseker in the Legislative Council was reported by the *Straits Times* on 27th August 1940. He made many constructive suggestions, cautioning against

> 'the continuance of subversive elements, . . . (as) the danger had not passed "because labour troubles had ceased momentarily"; the lack of Government propaganda despite its immense value on public opinion; . . . Government "aloftness" on war questions; . . . no war economy campaign; failure to make

> the most of Malayan mineral and vegetable products other than tin and rubber; no effort at encouraging maximum Malayan financial contribution to the war; the taxation muddle; corruption; no public enthusiasm for the war effort; lack of sterness and determination (in officials and non-officials) to prepare to fight; (and) the stupid jealousies of peace-time'.[39]

Both the *Straits Times* in Singapore, and *the Straits Echo and Times* in Penang, covered another of Mr Bisseker's speeches in the Legislative Council on 7th November 1940, in which he defended freedom of speech and public debate. He drew attention to

> 'war taxation problems with suggested remedies; the necessity for more Government support and encouragement to passive defence (later called Civil Defence) personnel; the shortage of their equipment; divided responsibility at many points as between Government, Municipality and Chief Medical Officer; . . . and the suggestion that the Secretary of Defence should tour more to see the shortages in Civil Defence for himself'.[40]

The Colonial Secretary, Mr Stanley W. Jones, the overburdened Acting Governor at that time during Sir Shenton's leave, strongly resented this last suggestion.

A proclamation declaring a State of Emergency was signed by Sir Shenton on 1st December 1941. The Straits Settlements Volunteer Forces along with the Malayan Royal Naval Volunteer Reserves (RNVR), and the Volunteer Air Force were mobilised, and a warning 'Albert' (meaning 'Watch Out for Hostile Aircraft) was issued. London announced that Rear-Admiral Sir Tom Phillips had been appointed the C-in-C Eastern Fleet, commanding ships and naval establishments of the China Station. By 6th December all leave for naval personnel in Singapore had been cancelled, and all army and RAF personnel had been recalled to barracks.

Civil servants failed to foresee, or plan for, the eventuality that northern Malaya might fall into enemy hands following the outbreak of war. Contingency plans had not been formulated in the event that any territory was lost, and the human element was ignored. A network for distributing rice stocks throughout the country had not been set up, neither had facilities for feeding and housing evacuees. The likelihood of essential labour deserting under threat of bombing had not even been envisaged, and similarly it was not perceived that 'many of those in the voluntary civil defence services would leave their posts in order to look after their families'.[41] No thought was given to 'evacuation of areas threatened by the enemy; for example, were Europeans and Asians to be treated on a basis of equality?'[42] This in due course became a real bone of contention after the evacuation of Penang. These, plus various other problems that subsequently arose, were left to be partially resolved on an ad hoc basis, assuming 'the inherent capability of the British to improvise'[43] when they are in a fix. Various District Commissioners, and officers of the Public Works Department (PWD), FMS Railways, and the Post and Telegraph Services had to resort to their own initiative, and it was their spontaneity that filled the administrative void at local levels, diverting many potential disasters. Credit must also be given to these officials for the manner in which they 'kept the civil administration in being in various States of Malaya under circumstances of the greatest difficulty'.[44]

Although reports of the first Japanese landings on the north-east coast of Malaya, in the early hours of 8th December 1941, were not taken seriously by many people, they heralded in effect what was to be 'the beginning of the end of a way of life that had matured . . . across the span of one hundred and fifty years'.[45] During succeeding days, however, panicky rumours rapidly spread of threatened encirclement due to more landings south of Kuantan, and as no reassurance to the contrary was forthcoming from the Resident Commissioner for Kuala Trengganu, civilians were advised to evacuate southwards. Thus, picnic and beach-party acquaintances became embroiled in an extraordinarily arduous cross-country trek, that 'would have been daunting to professional explorers, let alone lady violin teachers and colonial civil servants'.[46] After five days of trekking they reached the north-south railway line, where a train appeared as if by some pre-ordained force, but still the 'dirty and disreputable-looking band of escapers were actually asked to pay their fares to Kuala Lumpur'.[47] When Sir Shenton was informed that the Japanese had landed in the north, he is reported to have said, 'I trust you'll chase the little men off',[48] reflecting the attitude of many Europeans who looked upon the Japanese as being a band of 'unruly Asiatics'.[49]

When Singapore was first bombed every street light was still glowing. The island was unaccustomed to black-outs, having only had two previous practices, and the Civil Defence organisation was still controlled by the civil administration, who had no real co-ordination with the armed services. The few bombs that were initially dropped on Singapore were insufficient to shake people out of their inertia and easy manner of living. Hotels and clubs continued to be patronised, as they had been previously, and no restrictions were placed on their use. Had the civil government followed a strong course of action at this critical juncture, and an emergency been fully enforced and publicised, it would have shown the indigenous races how seriously those in command considered conditions to be.

After one week of hostilities, news censorship concerning set-backs in the north was such that people living in Singapore did so under an aura of illusion. Newspapers reported actions on the North African and Russian fronts in detail, and these were given precedence over the rigidly censored, and much clamoured for, local news. Official communiqués were released but were highlighted with meaningless platitudes on the lines of 'strategic withdrawals' and 'falling back to prepared positions'. A study of advertisements in these same newspapers, announcing the closure until further notice of various branches of the Hongkong and Shanghai Bank, were a more accurate assessment of the progress that the Japanese were making. With the Japanese over-running the four northern Unfederated Malay States of Perlis, Kedah, Kelantan and Trengganu, an extremely serious situation developed for Sir Shenton. The Rulers of other States, not yet affected, would be quick to realise that the British government was unable to guarantee the protection of their territories, as their diplomatic treaties required.

By mid-December 1941 various measures were proposed by Sir Shenton to bolster civil defence. Included among these was instant trial without jury for treason or fifth column activities, which on conviction carried the death penalty. This was also extended to incidents involving looting. People who showed lights during air raids were liable to be shot, as were those who did not halt when challenged to do so by a sentry. Towards the end of December, when the civil government found that it was no longer confident of maintaining law and order in Singapore, martial law was imposed. It was thought this would hardly affect the civilian population.

Although considerable apathy existed among civilians in Singapore, there had not been any significant internal disorder. It was unfortunate, therefore, that Sir Shenton's broadcast, which was intended to reassure the public, linked the imposing of martial law to fifth column activities, despite these having been minimal up to that time. Many uneasy suspicions were aroused that fifth column activities had been more than previously publicly admitted. General Percival was not in favour of introducing martial law, as its implementation and policing increased the strain on his already thinly spread armed forces.

Censorship of news since early December 1941 had prevented foreign correspondents, over a period of weeks, from reporting Singapore's lack of shelters and defences. Ironically, being a government department, the Malayan Broadcasting Corporation (MBC) eluded censorship and was the first to provide London with information of the 'grim way in which a million civilians were living and suffering – and how little had been done for them'.[50] Mr Tim Hudson caused a stir in a broadcast to the people of Singapore on 6th February 1942, when he criticised the government for their inactivity in providing adequate shelters for protection against Japanese bombing. Many tin miners, he pointed out, had specialised knowledge and had taken refuge on the island, but had not been asked to help. Response to this broadcast was immediate and violent. Unwittingly this broadcast informed people in Great Britain and the outside world of the terrible plight of civilians in Singapore, and how they had become the victims of wanton shelling and bombing, without any means of protection.

9:5 Military and Civil Planning Divergencies

Senior military commanders, from as early as 1925, could not agree on a co-ordinated defensive policy for Malaya. By 1929 there was 'virtually no co-operation between the services'.[51] The RAF reasoned that Malaya could be invaded from the north, and from as early as 1936 commenced constructing up-country airfields. The British Army chiefs officially refused to accept this contention, and accused the RAF of building airfields without prior consultation, and in locations where they could not defend them properly. The Navy's prescience that a Japanese assault would come from the sea made them rely on their 'useless guns — so much so that no-one ever gave any serious thought even to defending the north shores of Singapore island'.[52] It was only after September 1939 that the heads of the three armed services found an element of unity of opinion in excoriating the civil administration, especially over the sacrosanctity of rubber plantations, and their reluctance to release civilian labour to carry out military defence works.

When Major-General L.V. Bond arrived from London in August 1939 to replace General Dobbie as GOC Malaya, he held vastly different opinions from his predecessor on the paramount importance of the defence of Singapore, which 'did not permit him to concern himself with the peninsula'.[53] As C.A. Vlieland, the Defence Secretary for Malaya at that time, later recorded in his memoir, Bond 'clearly considered my functions should be strictly confined to "civil defence", and that defence policy and military strategy were no concern of mine, or even the Governor'.[54] This divergence of opinion between the civil and military authorities introduced embarrassing misunderstandings and hampered future planning for Malaya's defence, which could have been overcome if pride and personal prejudice had not been valued more than the security of the area. Bond, although an experienced professional army officer, remained aloof and tended to exercise control from an office chair, rather than studying problems in the field. He strongly opposed civilian members of the War Committee trying to give him advice, although his personal misconception of what was required imposed lamentable restrictions on the pre-war defence planning for the country. Although Bond was well aware of General Dobbie's conviction that Japan would attack from Siam and the north, despite the small forces at his disposal, he showed scant interest in defending the whole country, refusing to commit his forces to defend the RAF's new northern airfields near the east coast of Malaya and close to the Siamese frontier. In the light of the 'Relief Period' being subsequently increased to 180 days, however, Bond in a volte face submitted a reappraisal, on 13th April 1940, in which he acceded to the importance of using the RAF to the 'fullest possible extent'.[55]

Air Vice-Marshall J.T. Babbington, the Air Officer Commanding Far East, held the view that the defence of Malaya and the Singapore Naval Base could be realistically undertaken only by the RAF, in the absence of any significant fleet based at Singapore. He viewed the army's task as definitely including the defence of his northern airfields, which had been sited to enable his aircraft to operate at maximum range. Babbington failed to comprehend that the obsolete aircraft at his disposal were unable to undertake the enormous task expected of them.

In September 1939, when young European men wanted to leave Malaya to volunteer for service in the European war, Major-General Bond pressurised the government to introduce compulsory military service to supplement his inadequate forces with volunteers. Bond's request was duly granted, and the Volunteer Forces were mobilised in June 1940, which soon brought the civil and military authorities into open conflict in respect of the use of available European manpower. Mobilisation was designed to improve the efficiency of the Volunteer Forces, but this had to be achieved without jeopardy to the production of rubber and tin. On this occasion both Major-General Bond and Air Vice-Marshall Babbington shared similar opinions with Sir Shenton, and all felt that the Colonial Office had not fully comprehended that available European manpower in Malaya was insufficient to release men for duty with the volunteers, as well as provide the essential increases required within the Civil Administration and Civil Defence services.

A major requirement of any army is an unlimited supply of inexpensive and disciplined labour. In Malaya labour was scarce and expensive, arising from a conflict of interests between the needs of industry and those of the military. By the end of 1940 only two Indian Labour Companies had been made available to Major-General Bond, and when a third company was requested for the construction of defences on Penang, the War Office disagreed, on the grounds that this would interfere with India's programme for forming labour companies to be sent to the Middle East. 'Bond was told to make arrangements to use the large resources of local labour which . . . were available in Malaya, if and when a threat to Penang should arise.'[56]

Clashes over the availability of labour frustrated essential defence works and the construction of airfield and road fortifications leading from the north. Until August 1941 a considerable portion of many units' time was of necessity taken up on defence construction, as Malaya Command was denied the money for suitable civilian labour to be employed for this purpose. Military training programmes and junior officers' training were adversely affected by such deployments, and civil labour continued to be diverted for the production of more rubber and tin. Following Lieut-General Percival's arrival in May 1941, the War Office agreed that six local labour companies should be organised, to whom a daily wage of 45 cents should be paid. Percival soon realised that such a rate would not attract suitable people for his requirements, and this was further aggravated when the Labour Controller of Malaya advised against the recruitment, as he considered it would be detrimental to Civil Defence proposals and to industry. The Controller put forward a scheme recommending recruitment of labour at $1.10 per day, plus rations and accommodation. This was, however, turned down by the War Office, which refused to pay more than 45 cents per day. Percival then requested the Hong Kong government to raise three labour companies for Malaya, in an attempt to overcome his difficulties. Although agreement was quickly reached in October 1941, nothing was heard from the War Office, despite an urgent request for early approval. On 18th November Percival announced proposals to commence recruiting on the 24th, which brought an immediate response from the War Office. It refused to pay $2.75 per day for reliable, English-speaking Platoon Commanders, authorising a maximum of only $2. The only disciplined labour forces available to Percival, therefore, by early December 1941 were two Indian labour companies. After hostilities commenced, one Chinese labour company was raised locally in late December, and two more were formed during January 1942.

The restrictions under which Percival was forced to manage considerably reduced the preparation of essential defence works throughout the country. Had he been allowed a free hand to fix workers' rates of pay, much more could have been achieved with the help of the efficient Public Works Department (PWD), or through the Volunteer Forces. In many respects, it would also have been preferable to have taken advantage of European planters' and tin miners' intimate knowledge of the mentality of the Malayan labour force and local conditions. These experts should have been utilised to employ and organise the labour companies, rather than participate in volunteer force activities, for which they were inadequately equipped and trained.

British officers in the Malay States and Straits Settlements Volunteer Territorial Forces were ordered to remain with their units, where they carried out mostly regimental duties. Most of these officers were either plantation executives, tin miners, forestry officers, civil engineers or agents of mercantile houses and many among them had detailed knowledge of the country and its people, including knowledge of the tracks that traversed the jungle and mountain ranges. It was an error of judgement, and a failure in communication that throughout the Malayan campaign these people were not properly used. Only when it was too late was this mis-use of their expertise finally corrected. In 1939 Sir William A.C. Goode was a District Officer in Kelantan, having served in the MCS in a variety of posts since his arrival in Malaya. On being mobilised in 1941, he was called up and joined B Company of the 1st Battalion Straits Settlements Volunteer Force as a lance corporal, and spent most of his time during the remaining weeks of the campaign either on guard duty, or in digging trenches in ground which later had to be refilled. Only latterly was the wastefulness and absurdity of allocating such work to an expert in his own right realised, after which he was appointed to the post of Assistant Commissioner for Civil Defence.

Percival was emphatic that it was the failure of civilian labour that had a crippling effect on the British war effort in Malaya. For example, the crossroads at Gurun, in north Kedah, had previously been reconnoitered as a suitable defence site, but no preparatory works had been done, despite orders to use large numbers of civilians for this. Very few civilian workers arrived on the scene, and as soon as aggression commenced, the labour that had been assembled there disappeared. Similarly, in Penang, municipal workers left Georgetown for the relative safety of the hills as soon as bombing started. It happened also in hospitals, and equally disastrously on the Singapore docks, where ships had to be discharged and reloaded by military labour, who were diverted from more important tasks. Only labour in the railways, the post and telegraph, and survey departments did not bolt under threat of fire. Ruthless censorship bred confusion and insecurity. Truth was concealed from civilians and troops alike, who were instead fed with pompous and inaccurate pronouncements. Even when a situation of considerable urgency pended, it took Service Chiefs and the Civil Government ten days to reach accord on pay rates for desperately needed workers, despite Churchill's clarion call for action. Labour recruitment arguments went on for weeks at War Council meetings in Singapore, while Whitehall persisted in its refusal to sanction more attractive wages for crucially sought-after defence workers than those being offered to people in ordinary, menial civilian jobs. Only from 20th January 1942 did the Malayan government approve measures to conscript essential civilian labour, and by this time it was already too late. In subsequent contrast, the Japanese did not tolerate any shortage of labour. They used threats and abuse, and made it more than life itself was worth for labour to be withheld.

Mr F.D. Bisseker was appointed by Duff Cooper to the post of Deputy Director Civil Defence, under Brigadier Ivan Simson, and simultaneously held the position of Director of Labour and Transport in the Civil Defence organisation. Bisseker, as a severe critic of government at Legislative Council meetings, was disliked and distrusted by civil servants, from the Governor downwards, and none would willingly assist him, or anyone associated with him, in carrying out his duties in these appointments. Brigadier Simson was even placed under severe pressure by Sir Shenton and other senior civil servants to get rid of him. It was the opinion of Simson that, had British officers, who were on good terms with the Sultan of Johore, approached him with requests for labour, sufficient workers would have been made available to enable Bisseker to have operated in Johore effectively. Simson considered that Bisseker 'gave Trojan service and worked harder and with more loyalty in the public interest than most others in the Civil Defence organisation'.[57] Contrary to rumour, Bisseker only left Singapore on 13th February 1942, with reluctance, on Simson's direct order and with the Governor's agreement. He did not bolt the scene, as did many other civil servants and civilians who had responsibilities and appointments in the Civil Defence organisation.

9:6 Indigenous Races' Potential Under-Utilised

The indigenous races within Malaya were brought up to confidently entrust their security in the hypothetical roar of the British Lion, and did not realise that this aura of assimilated well-being was almost totally unfounded. It was generally believed that native participation in defence matters was little needed, and that British effort alone would be sufficient to propagate and safeguard national security for generations to come.

A divide and rule governmental strategy by the British expressly perpetuated colonial rule, and also provided to those administering the system the best of trade advantages. The mêlée of races within Malaya were conveniently segregated into distinctive employment sectors, and this segregation was even extended to the educational standards available for various components within the population. Arising from such pre-selection, therefore, it is hardly surprising that native participation in various defence activities was confined only to joining a hotch-potch of diminutive civil volunteer organisations, such as the Passive Air Defence Corps, Food Control Departments, the Red Cross Society, and the Auxiliary Medical, Fire and Transport Services, most of which were formed in 1940. Only a few hundred people were recruited into each of the various Malay States' and Straits Settlements' volunteer forces, and the only pre-war regular military force was one battalion of the Malay Regiment which was raised in 1933. A second battalion was formed in early 1941.

The British government never harnessed the loyalty and trust of the populace in Malaya as they could well have done, and the part played in this by the civil Malayan administration at that time leaves nothing to its credit. Thousands of people would have flocked to join up had they been encouraged and allowed to do so. What better potential jungle fighters were readily on hand than the Chinese, Eurasians, Indians and Malays, had they been properly equipped and trained. This is especially so as they would have been defending their own families and homes. When Japan attacked, the calamity was regarded by many Indians and Chinese with resigned bravery and stoicism. People were simply not conditioned for the eventuality or possibility of war, or to what extent this would implicate and overrun their lives. They took their cue from the country's leaders, many of whom in turn gave an impression of not seeming to worry about pending events. One of the contributing causes which culminated in the disaster of 15th February 1942 was inextricably exacerbated by the government's failure to appreciate the extent of many peoples' national spirit.

An insufficient call was made upon the indigenous races to participate in the defence of their own territory. Too much was left to the widely dispersed and largely under-strength British and Allied forces. Although it is easy to criticise with hindsight, at the time in question there was no advertised demand for recruitment and those in authority deemed that there was no need for it. The expense involved, no doubt, would have been considerable, and to achieve unity of action would have necessitated agreements being reached between the various State governments, making efforts towards unity very complicated to establish and administer. Had any British-sponsored plan been made to increase the armed forces of the Malay States, such action might well have been interpreted in some circles as being provocative.

It is indeed difficult to comprehend or condone the logic of the Malayan authorities in not utilising the full potential of the Malays and Chinese, who both had a large stake in their country, when this is contrasted to Winston Churchill's galvanisation of the entire population in the United Kingdom, to help fight, in one form of other, the war in Europe. Excuses for not doing so invariably revolve around there having been insufficient weapons available in the country with which to arm and train people, although this did not prevent people in Britain being made to use broom handles, as imitation weapons, to assist them with their training.

The authorities made a series of grave misjudgements which influenced the outcome of events in Malaya. Not only were the Chinese in general, and the Straits-born Chinese in particular, disregarded as possible allies in arms, but also the sympathy and co-operation of the Malays were not enlisted. No one appreciated that there were thousands of able-bodied people in Malaya who would have been willing to take up arms against the Japanese, had adequate encouragement, facilities and leadership been displayed to them.

Chinese patriotism should never have been doubted. From the 1920s the Chinese had donated generously to the Armistice Day Appeal for Lord Haig. Even road sweepers and rickshaw pullers had contributed whatever pittance they could afford in order to wear a poppy with pride. Following the China Incident of July 1937, the Chinese in Malaya had organised an efficient scheme for collecting massive financial aid for their motherland in her struggle against Japan. Despite such clear indications, the government in Malaya failed to acknowledge the extent of loyalty to Britain among the Chinese community. Had this loyalty been nurtured, even from as late as September 1939, this massive manpower potential might have been rallied later to harass and impede the Japanese while they were overrunning Malaya.

During the Malayan campaign, as it transpired, the Chinese did remain mostly co-operative, as did some Indians, but many Malays gave an impression of being generally apathetic towards what was happening. S. Cunyngham-Brown OBE, who first joined the MCS in 1929 and who, until his recent death, was a respected senior resident of Penang, clearly understood the Malays' lack of interest and did not blame them. As he saw it, '... two vast overseas giants ... were fighting their disgusting battles ... smashing and destroying everything'.[58] Although the Malays might have benefited from their involvement with the civilised West, they now 'realised with horror that they were about to pay for it ... so they stood by'.[59] 'The Indians became all-three-wise-monkeys-rolled-in-one; and saw nothing, heard nothing and said nothing – pulling the grass over their heads and lying doggo.'[60] Being a poorly represented minority, they should not be blamed for this approach as they were entrapped. For the Chinese, it was different. They were already committed as their mother country was at war with Japan. Reports of Japanese atrocities during this war made the Chinese in Malaya fearful, and many anticipated violent reprisals by Japanese frontline battle-crazed troops. The more courageous among them busied themselves by getting arms to go and fight the Japanese, and to die if necessary in the jungles.

It was the European and not the Asian who was defeated in the subsequent loss of Malaya. Britain's policy of not arming the locals served not only to delude them into a belief in British invincibility, but it also meant that no effective home guard was organised and 'apart from a few in the Armed Services' the majority did not consider 'it worthwhile to fight as one master replaced another'.[61] When the defeated colonial masters were marched off to internment, 'Asians slowly found that they could get along without the European after all'.[62]

Some recruitment measures were taken by the Malayan government, but these were insufficient. The Malay Regiment, created in the FMS in 1933, was expanded after war commenced but never exceeded 1,000 men. Various volunteer forces were formed in the Straits Settlements and in most of the Malay States, but, including the Johore Engineers, these did not exceed 2,000 men. Each State raised local Voluntary Defence Corps, but enlistment into these was confined to people who were ineligible for compulsory military service, being Europeans over 41 years of age, and European British Subjects between the ages of 18 and 55. In all these organisations, the total never exceeded 10,000 men and women. The Asian population in Malaya was, therefore, never really given sufficient opportunity to defend their way of life and were never adequately prepared for war.

9:7 Japan Underestimated

Japan had infiltrated an active and elaborate network of spies and agents throughout Malaya and other countries in South-East Asia long before the outbreak of hostilities in the area.

Among these were included specially trained Javanese and Sumatrans, as well as a variety of fifth columnists, who worked covertly against British and Dutch interests in the region on behalf of the Japanese.

Hundreds of Japanese were also employed throughout the length of the Malay Peninsula and particularly in South Johore and Singapore. Many who worked as fishermen were able to gain an intimate knowledge of the Malayan coastline, and others as village shopkeepers combined into their various services the useful, albeit clandestine, sideline of developing films. Japanese barbers were numerous and through their trait of trade they amassed and passed many useful snippets of gossip. Those whose trade was to repair bicycles collected knowledge on the whereabouts of all the bicycles in their neighbourhoods, which was later put to good advantage. Japanese tourists and businessmen were avid upcountry travellers on the pretext of photographing game. In this manner they became well acquainted with highways, jungle paths, harbours, rivers, airports and all other strategic places, which were accurately mapped and subsequently passed on to Tokyo. Employees working on Japanese-owned estates surreptitiously stockpiled bricks, girders and tree trunks, which they carefully concealed near many of the 250 bridges that had to be crossed along the main trunk road down the peninsula from the Siamese border to Singapore.

By the time that the Japanese commenced their attacks on Malaya they were fully aware that previously earmarked tanks, artillery and aircraft for the country had been diverted to the Middle-East and Russia. They also knew that air defences depended on outdated and mostly obsolescent aircraft.

The British intelligence organisation in Singapore was fully aware of Japan's spying activities for many years before hostilities commenced. Being able to decode and intercept Japan's messages, they did not disrupt their operations, considering that the information so gained would be a worthwhile asset to them in the eventuality of war. When this occurred, however, many known Japanese agents managed to evade capture, and just disappeared into thin air. Much of Japan's spying was orchestrated without any undue attempt at concealment, under the very noses of numerous Europeans who were equally well dispersed throughout the country. Few among these became sufficiently diverted from their gracious life-styles to be aware or suspicious of what was really going on around them.

Japanese troops were assisted by fifth columnists, who led them through jungles and plantations, enabling them to outflank the retreating British forces. The Japanese cause was further abetted by these elements spreading rumours of rape and violence in towns and villages, which effectively frightened people, and fomented alarm and disorganisation.

The Japanese recognised the diverse commitment within the various races and the scant concern of some people as to who ruled the country. They were able to exploit the lack of national consciousness and the absence of a home front. It was relatively easy for Japanese to disguise themselves as Malay or Chinese farmers, and in this manner to cause disruptions by freely mingling with the population.

Contrasting opinions concerning Japan's intentions and capabilities undermined British defence strategy and preparations. There was an influentual element that never quite believed that Japan would dare to commence hostilities. From the outset, followers of this concept underestimated Japanese strengths, initiative and capabilities. Although Japan's resourcefulness and power were appreciated by many who considered that it would be tantamount to madness to underestimate them, senior commanders in Singapore diverted little of their time and effort to make a purposeful study of their potential enemy, and the majority of them grossly underrated the Japanese soldiers' fighting abilities and their scope for courage and endurance. This led to entirely inaccurate intelligence reports being fed to British and Allied forces. Whereas it was acknowledged that the mixed force of Allied troops were disgruntled and disunited, it came as a subsequent shock to find out that the Japanese were tough, loyal and strictly disciplined soldiers, who were capable of adapting to various climates and terrains, and that they also possessed an alarmingly scant fear of dying.

Inaccurate propaganda misinformed British and Indian troops in defence lectures and did much harm by failing to prepare them psychologically for what they had to face eventually. Whether it was spread in an unwitting attempt to play down Allied weaknesses, or was just a result of apathetic intelligence work, intelligence officers frequently and blandly portrayed their ignorance in the most childish manner. Japanese troops were described as being diminutive, short-sighted and frightened of the dark. Furthermore, it was reported that they reacted poorly when surprised, were not jungle trained and were equipped only with rifles left over from their 1905 war. Junior officers were reportedly lacking in initiative and unit training. Troops in the 18th Division were quite cheerfully told that Japanese pilots were inexpert at night flying, as 'slant-eyed people were unable to fly',[63] and if they could, their obsolete planes and poor vision rendered them incapable of dive bombing. On account of Japanese being short-sighted, they could not shoot straight and were physically unable to close one eye.

Contrary to the eloquent, albeit fanciful, inaccuracies that were fed to unsuspecting British and Allied troops, as it turned out, Japanese forces were better prepared and equipped to cope in tropical climatic conditions, where British, Indian and Australian troops were at a constant disadvantage. Japanese soldiers easily adapted to feeding in Malaya, as rice was their staple diet and they could live easily off the land. Being strictly disciplined and inculcated with a willingness to die, they carried out orders to the letter. Some of their tactical manoeuvres were fearless to a point of madness. Although the Japanese might not have been the best soldiers in the world at that time, they were tough, fierce fighters and their attributes more than offset many of their shortcomings. Australian troops were not misinformed about the Japanese, and were told that they were well trained and equipped, with considerable limits of physical endurance. Furthermore, they were acknowledged as being ruthless, skilled in duplicity and capable of moving cross-country at speed.

The Japanese had several distinct advantages over the Allies. They had a clear, well rehearsed plan to follow and they were prepared and determined to conclude it successfully. As they deployed well guided, fit and highly trained troops, underestimating them caused the downfall of many civil and military leaders at that time. Many such leaders argued that Japan, following four years of war in China, should be near economic collapse. Nothing could have been more erroneously conceived. General Percival was one person who did not underestimate them. He realised that in the entire force that he was hurriedly and belatedly given to command '. . . there was a serious lack of experienced leaders, the effect of which was accentuated by the inexperience of the troops.'[64]

Japan's 'Hakko Ichiu' ideology — the world under one roof of Imperial Japanese domination — was relegated to nothing more than jingoistic fantasy in Western diplomatic circles. As a result, observers of Far Eastern affairs underestimated Japan's strength. The disastrous defeats in Malaya in Singapore, although a legacy of this miscalculation and Allied unreadiness, bore subsequent witness to the justifiable credit that Japanese militarists deserved, as they effectively proved themselves capable of planning precise strategic military actions and executing them accurately.

Much time had been obviously devoted to prepare Japan's detailed plans for the invasion of Malaya and Singapore, and her whirlwind success was an 'unthinkable swift victory ... and in military terms was an exercise of textbook neatness'.[65] The smaller but more mobile Japanese force engaged a considerably larger army and turned its strength into weakness. The Western world was dumbfounded by Japan's speed and efficiency, and as the end of 1941 lapsed into the early months of 1942, the 'white tuan' in South-East Asia was confronted with a series of embarrassments. Japan's surprise attack against Pearl Harbour had already given her unopposed superiority of the Pacific Ocean, and Siam's duplicity had completely disrupted any time-table that the British High Command had to halt Japanese advances down the Malay Peninsula. The shock sinking of the *Prince of Wales* and *Repulse* had numbed the British in Malaya so much that morale had started to flounder. Japan's air superiority was unquestionable from the outset and it was realised only too well that Malaya's air defences depended on outdated, obsolescent planes.

Contrary to what British and Indian troops in Malaya were informed through ill-advised intelligence sources, the Japanese army, by December 1941, totalled over one million in strength. It was organised into 90 Divisions, 51 of which were on active service, and 11 out of these were used for the various theatres in the south-west Pacific. Their navy had been modernised and was made up of 10 battleships, including the giant *Yamato* of 64,000 tons, 10 aircraft carriers, 36 cruisers, of which 18 were armed with 8-inch guns, 113 destroyers, 63 submarines and an assortment of 13 gunboats and other ancillary craft. Comparative naval strengths in the Pacific in December 1941 are summarised in the table[66] on p.159.

Far from having 'aircraft made from old kettles and kitchen utensils',[67] the Japanese army and navy together fielded 2,340 first-line aircraft, of which 1,540 were initially committed. These compared with only 307 operational aircraft that could be mustered by the United States in the Philippines, along with 158 mostly obsolescent

	Cap'al Ships	Aircraft Carriers	Heavy Cruisers	Light Cruisers	Destroyers	Sub-marines
British Empire	2	—	1	7	13	—
USA	9	3	13	11	80	56
Netherlands	—	—	—	3	7	13
France	—	—	—	1	—	—
Allied Total	11	3	14	22	100	69
Japan	10	10	18	18	113	63

British planes in Malaya and Singapore and another 144 from the Dutch in their territories. The Japanese Zero fighter was a fast, light plane with superb manoeuvrability and when it was 'flown with flair and dedication . . . it could out-do anything else in the air'[68] at that time. Despite ready accessibility to this information, various defence reviews consistently underrated the skills and efficiency of the Japanese. Churchill hoped that Britain could stabilise the volatile situation in the Far East and put his trust in a token show of strength. The Joint Planning Staff in London and Air Chief Marshall Sir Robert Brooke-Popham, the C-in-C Far East, likened Japan's air force capabilities to those of the Italians, while the Royal Navy miscalculated the strength of Japan's Imperial Navy to be about 80% of its own.

In December 1941 Japan had ten divisions amassed in Indo-China and these were supported by 670 planes. British and Allied military forces stationed throughout the length of the Malay Peninsula and in Singapore at that time comprised two and a half under-strengthed divisions, which were not jungle trained. These were supported by an air strength of 158 inferior planes. General Yamashita's three-division 25th Army comprised the physically and technically superb Imperial Guards, along with the 5th and 18th Divisions, supported by the 3rd Tank Group, which fielded 80 medium and 100 light tanks, and had a combat strength of 70,000. Out of this force only 17,000 combat troops, with another 9,000 support troops, were landed during the initial stages of the campaign as sea transports were insufficient to carry more across the Gulf of Siam. Although the British had numerical superiority on paper, without tanks and with outdated and fewer airplanes they were outclassed and outmanoeuvered from the start. Japan had originally planned to use five divisions for her attack on Malaya and Singapore, but when the extent of Allied weaknesses was subsequently realised, General Yamashita decided to reduce his strength to only three divisions.

The Japanese enjoyed a variety of advantages over British and Allied forces in Malaya. Their racially homogeneous forces were unaffected by command or language difficulties, and were thoroughly experienced in jungle warfare. They were equipped with and supported by modern weapons, and had been well trained with previous combat experience together. They had faith in their commanders and in their support units, and did not have to resort to distant bases across vast oceans. In addition to the experience gained in 1937 in coastal invasion landings, the forces that were earmarked for the attack on Malaya had also participated in two other thorough rehearsals, from which useful knowledge and experience were derived. The first of these was in February 1941, when training invasions of Kyushu in Japan were carried out from Formosa, 1,000 miles away, over a period of two weeks. More intensive and detailed manoeuvres were practised when an invasion from the mainland was mounted on Hainan.

The keynote of Japan's unorthodox tactics was speed and more speed, even at night, and fatigue was discounted. The daring swiftness of the Japanese Imperial Guards bewildered cut-off retreating Allied troops. Small groups of Guards worked with dazzling efficiency and never hesitated to strike first, with single-minded speed, which flung whole regiments into an exhausting and endless retreat. Japanese troops were well co-ordinated and seemed to know exactly where they were going. Their ability to overcome obstacles, in conjunction with bold use of tanks, kept retreating troops constantly off balance, and by infiltration — the basis of their tactics — they exploited every opportunity. Individuals and small parties who became separated from the main thrust looked for something to shoot at, and did just that as soon as they found it. They used loudly exploding Chinese fire-crackers in pretence that attacks were being made in force, and then they cunningly slipped through defenders' flanks. They did not favour close-in bayonet fighting; the tommy gun was their favourite weapon. For the Japanese, infiltration was greatly simplified as they were able to don Chinese coolie or Malay peasants' attire and in this guise could mix relatively freely with the local populace. Although Japanese soldiers had never fought in the Malayan jungles before, they quickly adapted to becoming remarkable jungle fighters. Using a combination of 'reckless frontal attacks with skilful flanking movements from the sea and through supposedly impassable jungle',[69] they overran retreating British and Commonwealth troops who totalled almost twice their number.

The early capture of Penang afforded the Japanese a telling advantage, as it enabled them to make use of various undamaged boats that had been left gift wrapped at Penang Harbour when the island was hurriedly evacuated. With these they were able to ferry their troops down the west coast of the peninsula and land them behind British defensive positions. Such cunningly devised strategic movements against semi-trained and tired troops, whose morale had been shaken by the realisation that they had been misinformed about their enemies' deftness, mobility and prowess, had quick and telling results. General Percival's intended delaying tactics were nullified as retreating British forces came to realise and fear that such Japanese actions could effectively cut them off.

The impenetrability of Malaya's green mythical defensive blanket should not have lulled those at GHQ in 1941, had they taken the trouble to make a study of exercise records of two years previously when men of the British-Indian Army, in full battle order, had carried mortars through it. The retreating defenders, however, functioned from the outset under severe limitations, with no tanks to spear-head any thrust, and only a few outdated aircraft to provide essential overhead protection. The advantage of initiative and surprise always fell to the Japanese. Unlike them, the disorientated British and Australian troops in particular did not adapt easily to rubber plantations and jungle. Night noises, dripping vegetation, leeches, razor sharp remnants of decomposing stumps, roots embedded in decaying vegetation, and dank smelling mud clamping a vice-like grip on legs, all heightened the awe-inspiring semi-gloom and characteristic limited visibility of the jungle and constantly evoked fears among exhausted and bewildered troops that the enemy could be anywhere and everywhere.

Excellent roads had been constructed by the British in Malaya and these, in conjunction with cheap Japanese bicycles, some of which folded up, were used in devastating combination by the Japanese infantry:

> With 'absolutely no precautions, (they) squeaked and rattled down Malaya's trunk road in hot pursuit of those who staggered southward on foot, their motor transport long since shot up at road blocks, or bogged down in rubber'.[70]

Few seasoned British troops were prepared for the blinding rain, as they blundered southwards under the burden of their heavy equipment, fighting brave rearguard actions against swarms of bicycle-riding Japanese who scampered through tracks in rubber plantations.

Many Japanese troops searched roadside kampongs for food and bicycles as they made their way south. With their varied equipment slung over their bicycles, they rode three and four abreast in groups of up to fifty, and talked and laughed,

> 'just as if they were going to a football match. They seemed to have no standard uniform or equipment and were travelling as light as they possibly could',[71]

with some of them even wearing football jerseys. The greatest variety was seen in their head apparel which included

> 'a few tin hats, topees of all shapes, wide-brimmed planters' hats or ordinary felt hats, high-peaked jockey hats, little caps with eye shades, or even a piece of cloth tied around the head and hanging down behind'.[72]

They lived off the land, collecting rice, vegetables and chickens as they passed, and rain did not seem to deter them, as they all were able to produce an efficient mackintosh cape with a hood, which appeared to be their only item of standard equipment. When Spencer Chapman first saw the Japanese he

> 'was astonished by their extraordinary resemblance to current caricatures of them – little evil blustering bespectacled popinjays with huge ears, projecting front teeth, toothbrush moustaches, wearing high-peaked jockey caps and untidy uniforms'.[73]

In contrast British soldiers were 'equipped like Christmas trees ... so that they could hardly walk, much less fight'.[74]

Japanese air superiority was decisive in the Malayan campaign. In addition to their having considerably more planes, they also had planes of superior quality. This enabled the Japanese to pound retreating Allied troops off the roads in daylight at will and also to cover all attempted troop movements. It also allowed them to make unchecked landings and establish shore bases with relative ease. Out of a total of 1,540 first-line army aircraft only 700 were used for the initial attacks in the Pacific. These were reinforced by 480 naval aircraft as well as 360 that had been used for the Pearl Harbour attack.

The Japanese Navy's Mitsubishi A6M Zero fighter, which was fitted with auxiliary fuel tanks to increase its range, could boast of a top speed of 325 m.p.h., and completely outclassed the Brewster Buffalow, which was slow in comparison and had limited climbing abilities. The Japanese torpedo bomber equally outclassed the obsolete Vickers Wilderbeest torpedo bomber, with its maximum speed of 110 m.p.h., which was aptly nicknamed 'the flying coffin'. The Japanese long-range bomber was similarly far superior to its British counterpart, the Blenheim. If this was not sufficient, the Royal Air Force entered the fray without any dive bombers, transporter planes or photo reconnaisance planes and also with a serious shortage of spare parts and trained pilots.

The lethargy of pre-war Allied administration compounded the imbalance of physical power, that might well have been ameliorated had they taken more cognisance and advantage of a report concerning the capture of a Japanese Zero fighter which was shot down over China in May 1941. Full details of this fighter's armament and tank capacity, along with a very accurate assessment of its performance capabilities, were passed over to Singapore on 26th July, but 'faulty organisation at HQ Air Command ... resulted in this valuable report remaining unsifted ... and in no action being taken upon it'.[75]

9:8 The 'Fortress' That Never Was

Singapore's defence strategy revolved around a seaborne attack only, as the jungles and swamps throughout Malaya were considered to be in themselves adequate deterrents against any large scale land invasion. Ever-ready British naval forces were to be on hand to thwart any attempt to make major landings on the Peninsula. When war in Europe commenced in September 1939, it was generally thought that Malayan coastal defensive arrangements were adequate and that the Naval Base was almost ready. Few in authority questioned the concept of the Fortress's impregnability, which in turn overshadowed reports concerning insufficient troops, and relegated in importance the concept of sending early reinforcements, which had been the topic of previous deliberations. Recommendations for building defensive positions in south Johore had been suspended, owing to lack of funds, and although a few new aircraft squadrons did arrive, the first-line complement of these, that were available in the country, were pitifully few. When the Admiralty transferred major units from the China Squadron for convoy duties in the Indian Ocean, Britain's naval forces were also considerably weakened in the area.

In 1937 at an Imperial Conference in London, Britain decided to keep her fleet in European waters, unless necessity dictated otherwise, which destined Singapore to become a shipless base. Despite this, it was still considered that the key to defence in Southeast Asia was a fortified naval base, and Singapore was often, albeit dramatically, referred to as being the Gibraltar of the East. From the spring of 1940 onwards Britain urged the United States to send some of her naval forces to Singapore, but this was not agreed to as the United States had doubts regarding Singapore's strategic value, especially as it was in their opinion inadequately garrisoned, and was also within range of Japanese aircraft from Indo-China. The dockyards also lacked spare parts, machinery tools and the personnel to carry out major repairs to large warships. The Singapore Naval Base, therefore, contributed more to the economy of the region than it did to defence. Thousands of people were employed during its prolonged period of construction and also for its upkeep. What defensive arrangements were incorporated into the Base, in effect did more harm than good, as prominent politicians were led to believe that the island was impregnable. The Japanese, on the other hand, were well informed of 'Fortress' Singapore's defensive weaknesses, and they regarded the potency of its naval contingent as being negligible.

Mr C.A. Vlieland, appointed in December 1938 as the first civilian Defence Secretary for Malaya, was one of the officials who realised that Malaya's dense jungles would not form an adequately secure defensive barrier for Singapore in the event of any overland invasion originating from the north. Contrary to all previous official conceptions, Vlieland equally held the opinion that Singapore had no significant strategic value but still remained a valuable prize to the Japanese on account of its economic importance. Thus, he argued that Japan would never conceive a plan which involved a direct attack against Singapore from the sea, and provided that the whole of the Malay Peninsula was suitably defended, there should be little need for concern. Such views were supported by Sir Shenton Thomas and were apparently well received by Whitehall in 1938. As it became apparent to both army and air commanders that the defence of the Singapore Naval Base did involve that also of the whole of the Malay Peninsula, an afterthought garrison was quickly established in Penang, and hurried preparations were made to establish a line of resistance at Jitra, both of which were incomplete by the time the Japanese initiated their attack on 8th December 1941.

The appearance of strength, therefore, was false. As mentioned previously, the RAF had insufficient and mostly obsolescent planes and there were virtually no ships and certainly no tanks. The original anti-aircraft defence scheme for Malaya only covered Singapore island and part of Johore, although the War Office, as early as 1936, had given approval for anti-aircraft defences to be emplaced in Penang. Last but not least, there were insufficient men to defend Malaya's long and vulnerable coastline, in addition to the numerous airfields and other known defensive locations.

Singapore's defences were concentrated on the southern part of the island in anticipation of a seaborne assault, and some senior commanders as a matter of policy were opposed to the building of additional defences, which they considered could be bad for morale. Omissions were made as much for this reason as for the more popularised justifications such as shortage of time, or restrictions on finances, materials, labour or even ideas. Singapore's northern coastline was undefended except for a few strands of barbed wire and some searchlights, as the authorities did not wish to frighten people by erecting additional defences, which might give the impression that it was possible for the enemy to get that far south.

Brigadier Ivan Simson's attempts to improve the defences, in his capacity as Controller of Civil Defence Malaya, were largely balked by General Percival, who appeared to be adamantly opposed to such measures. Simson was correctly and mostly concerned with what he considered to be the defensive inadequacies along the northern shores of Singapore island that faced the southern shoreline of Johore. At a secret Boxing Day meeting at Flag Staff House, Percival's residence, Simson passionately and implicitly set forth his proposals for improving the defences of the island's northern shoreline which he considered would become the main killing areas. To his utter dismay, Percival stubbornly refused to agree with his plans, despite by this time his complete realisation that the Japanese were better trained and equipped than his own partially trained and considerably dispirited troops, and that they were riding in the wake of a spate of unbroken victories.

Their meeting was a very long and friendly one, but Percival did not give any reasons for his adamant stand. It was indeed incredible at this juncture of a campaign that was obviously heading for ultimate disaster that any General Officer commanding it could have believed that '. . .defences of the sort you want to throw up are bad for the morale of troops and civilians'.[76]

On 31st December 1941 Simson was told to report immediately to the Rt Hon Duff Cooper at the War Council room in Singapore. In the absence of, and without prior consultation with, both the Governor, Sir Shenton Thomas, and General Percival, Simson was instructed by Duff Cooper to take over the full responsibilities of Controller of Civil Defence. At Cooper's request Simson prepared a list outlining what he considered to be the ten most important requirements for defence improvements. This was subsequently sent to Churchill, and was also revealed to General Wavell. Wavell demanded of Simson full details of every obstacle that had frustrated his progress, and then called for Percival to accompany him on an inspection of the island's defences. Despite Wavell's apparent displeasure over the lack of suitable defensive preparations along Singapore's northern coastline, Percival in explanation firmly held to his argument, as he had with Simson, that the suggested preparations would have had a bad effect on morale.

Wavell telegrammed Churchill on 19th January 1942, and bluntly informed him that 'little or nothing was done to construct defences on the North side of the island . . .',[77] as all plans had been based on repulsing an attack from the sea. Although Churchill was staggered by this revelation and admitted later that he 'ought to have been told and I ought to have asked',[78] he personally cabled Wavell and left no doubts that he expected

> 'every inch of ground to be defended, every scrap of material or defences to be blown to pieces to prevent capture by the enemy, and no question of surrender to be entertained until after protracted fighting among the ruins of Singapore city'.[79]

These expostulations, although designed no doubt to strengthen failing resolve, proved to be neither practical nor well founded, and had they been implicitly adhered to, would have invited wholesale slaughter and massive loss of civilian life.

Churchill's instructions to Wavell contained, in unchanged written form, Brigadier Simson's ten defensive priorities which Duff Cooper had previously requested and had forwarded to Churchill. Percival was, therefore, directly instructed to implement them, and in the third week of January 1942, a basic plan for the island's defence was issued. A more detailed plan was compiled by the 28th, by which time it was obviously too late for significant construction works to be carried out, and by this late hour there was no civil labour willingly available to do them.

The majority of Singapore's static defences were located in the two areas which the Japanese never attacked. These included a variety of concrete pillboxes, anti-boat and anti-tank obstacles, gun posts, land mines and barbed wire fences and traps. The north and the west of the island, where the Japanese did attack, were left almost without defences. This inconceivable lack of planning arose because the southern shoreline defences from Changi to the Naval Base were built pre-war, when a sea-borne invasion was considered to be most likely. By the time the Japanese were poised to assault Singapore,

> 'sites for forward defended localities and for reserves had been selected. Artillery observation posts and gun positions had been reconnoitered and selected. Locations of formation headquarters had been fixed and communications arranged . . .'[80]

True as Percival's claims may be, very little actual digging or building had been done, and owing to the island's geography, there was a shortage of troops with which to effectively man the whole area.

News bulletins given out by the Malayan Broadcasting Corporation referred to 'standing firm' and 'strategic defeats', but it was obvious that retreating troops were in a shambles. Continuous retreats generated a sense of bewilderment. Indian soldiers in the British Indian army were disheartened by withdrawal, and their faith in the might of the British Raj was shaken. The Naval Base was evacuated without a fight, even before retreating troops had crossed the Causeway. At the very time in its destiny when its whole purpose and existence was to be tested, it was found to be valueless and impotent. One demoralised British anti-aircraft gunner from Penang voiced many soldiers' sentiments about the Malayan campaign. He said, 'As far as I'm concerned, the Japs can have bloody Malaya.'[81]

9:9 Disunited, We Endeavour

When the relief period for Singapore was increased to 180 days, following the outbreak of war in Europe in September 1939, Lieut-General Sir Lionel Bond, the General Officer Commanding Malaya, submitted in April 1940 a new defence appreciation. In this he emphasised that Malaya's northern frontier would have to be held for a longer period than was previously envisaged, and possibly against a considerably larger force. Bond estimated that to fulfil this new and protracted role, Malaya Command would need four infantry Divisions and two tank regiments.

On 16th October 1940 the three service commanders in Singapore (Vice-Admiral Layton, Lieut-General Bond, and Air Vice-Marshall Babbington) submitted their first joint tactical appreciation to the Chiefs of Staff in London. They precisely defined the Airforce's role in Malaya as being the repulsion at sea of any enemy invasion force, as well as its destruction should any landings be attempted. The Army's role was identified as being the close-up defence of naval and air bases, as well as to defeat any Japanese forces that succeeded in landing. The requirement for first-line aircraft was increased to 556 planes, in addition to which it was estimated that 176 heavy and 100 light anti-aircraft guns would be needed, along with 186 searchlights. Three flotillas of motor torpedo boats were also considered to be essential, so that enemy forces could be prevented from moving down the coast by sea. Had such personnel and materials been provided, Percival's task would have been made considerably easier. The highest military minds in Malaya at that time regarded these requirements as being the minimum to ensure that the defence of Malaya and Singapore could be secured. They were also firmly of the opinion that without them a Japanese invasion could not be defeated.

When Lieut-General Percival took over Malaya Command in May 1941, it comprised three major groupings. The 3rd Indian Corps, under Lieut-General Sir Lewis Heath, was responsible for the northern States of Malaya, including Penang island, and had its HQ situated in Kuala Lumpur. Within Heath's northern sub-area, Major-General Murray-Lyon commanded the 11th Indian Division, in addition to which there were another two brigade groups that formed part of the 9th Indian Division. The 15th Brigade was located at Sungei Patani in southern Kedah and the 6th Brigade, less one battalion, was posted in northern Kedah at Tanjong Pau. These troops were deployed to defend various northern aerodromes. One infantry brigade was held in reserve in the Ipoh area, in readiness to join up with the 11th Division should this be required. Brigadier C.A. Lyon commanded the under-equipped and so-called Penang 'garrision' comprising one infantry battalion, one FMS Volunteer battalion, two 6-inch batteries with searchlights, as well as a company of Royal Engineers and other administrative units. Major-General Gordon Bennett commanded one division, less one brigade group of Australian forces, as well as the Johore military forces. His area of responsibility included everything in the States of Johore and Malacca, except for Singapore's anti-aircraft defences, which were located in the south-east corner of Johore. Singapore 'Fortress' was commanded by Major-General F. Keith Simmons, with its two fixed defence fire commands, one at

Changi and the other at Faber. Fortress units included several companies of Royal Engineers, with the defence of selected targets on Singapore island coming under the responsibility of Brigadier A.W.G. Wildey, who was in command of anti-aircraft defences. Most of these guns were a static type with very limited ranges. Command reserve was the 12th Indian Infantry Brigade Group, commanded by Brigadier A.C. Paris, which was to be held in readiness for operations anywhere throughout the country.

The administrative tasks of the 11th Division were formidable. In addition to training and setting up their own hutted camps, they were also required to site and establish buildings for hospitals. Camps throughout Malaya were initially located in rubber plantations, in order to find cover, but these localities proved to be strange environments for uninitiated and newly arrived troops. Such was the significance of the spread of a complaint nicknamed 'rubberitis' among many of the men, who suffered from symptoms of lassitude, depression and loss of appetite, that in the autumn of 1941 new locations for camps in more open terrain had to be found.

By December 1941 the total strength of Allied armed forces in Malaya Command was more than 88,000, of which 15,000 were administrative and non-combatant personnel. A large majority of these forces were crowded into Singapore. There was a total of 32 battalions, many of which were under-strengthed and only partially trained, and 10 field artillery regiments, all hastily assembled, in a hotchpotch combination of 19,000 British, 15,000 Australian, 37,000 Indian and 17,000 locally enlisted Malayan recruits. Not only were the British soldiers, who had been sent to Malaya Command, untrained in jungle fighting and ill-equipped for tropical conditions, but there were also insufficient troops to enable Percival to start an offensive, even had he had available the other means of doing so. London considered Malaya to be a low priority and had consistently refused urgent requests for materials, as these were needed for other more desperate theatres of war. Therefore, there was not one solitary tank up or down the length of the Malay Peninsula, neither was there one in Singapore. There was also a desperate shortage of artillery, communications equipment and even of spare parts. All that was available was a small number of Rolls Royce armoured cars that were manned by Argyll and Sutherland Highlanders. Some of these vehicles were still decorated by bullet holes from previous engagements in Palestine, and most of them could be likened to museum pieces, having been used in the Middle East during the 1914–18 war. Only one in six of these armoured cars carried a heavy machine gun, which, it was proudly acclaimed, could be dismounted in two minutes should the cars have to be abandoned.

Many civilians in Malaya really thought that the country had been adequately prepared, but when the Japanese attack started, the reality of this misconception was quickly and starkly communicated to the civilian population, whose courage failed them. People fled from towns and villages to what they hoped would be the relative safety of the countryside, ahead of the advancing Japanese hoards. The *Malayan Gazette* in its editorial on 16th December 1941, the last for forty-five months, sought refuge and respite by bitterly criticising the establishment which, in its opinion, was miserably faltering.

> 'People in Penang are still stunned by the sudden invasion of the Japanese and are still shocked by the desertion of the British. Has Britain really deserted us? Why are the troops being evacuated from the island to leave us to fend for ourselves? . . . Also a question in the minds of many, especially the Chinese for some time, is a nagging fear of coming under Japanese rule. What will happen to the people of Penang, when the Japanese learn that many of them have been giving aid and money to the nationalists in China who are Japan's enemies. Will they be punished or even tortured? In Malaya the defences are weak and troops scarce. . . . Besides, some of the British staff are inefficient. We grant that they are courageous soldiers and fighters, but the snag is they are not up-to-date men! They fought with distinction in the First World War. . . . They may be good in their way but they've had little practical training in the many years prior to the outbreak of war. . . . All in all, due to bad planning and bad strategy, lack of co-operation and numerous blunders made, it may not seem such a surprise in Penang being taken and the possible fall of Malaya.'[82]

Before Percival's arrival in Malaya, on 14th May 1941, he had not commanded anything larger than a battalion in action. He was still an acting Lieut-General, and Heath, who had recent experience in Divisional command, was senior to him. Relationships were strained between them on account of this, as they were to become between

Percival and the Australian commander, Major-General Gordon Bennett, between whom a number of clashes occurred. Discord among high ranking officers was not infrequent and Admiral Layton on occasions made open fun of Sir Robert Brook-Popham, referring to him as 'Old Pop-off'.

One of the flaws which plagued Percival's forces was their heterogeneity. They were not an homogeneous, united fighting force. The British, Indians and Australians continually complained about each other and were disunited in spirit. Good officers who had already been taken for the Middle East and European theatres of war were, instead of being suitably replaced, made up by precipitous promotions within units. Discontent, therefore, was rampant and was accompanied by invariable arguing and jockeying over priorities and seniority. The Indian regiments lacked seasoned officers and non-commissioned officers, and their ranks included large numbers of inexperienced, young soldiers. They were also inter-mixed with Indian State Forces, whose training and morale were inferior to that of the British Indian Army units. Officers in the British Indian Army looked down on their British army counterparts, who in turn regarded them as being their social inferiors. The different rates of officers' pay in the Indian and British armies heightened the sense of general discontent between them, and increased administration difficulties to such an extent that it was difficult, if not impossible, to ask individuals to accept transfers. Command headquarters was therefore denied the services of the best available officers, which in retrospect could have been easily overcome at little additional cost to the Treasury had someone had the foresight to realise the benefits that making an exception would have meant to Malaya Command at this crucial juncture.

Percival's conglomeration of forces had among them, therefore, a variety of customs, languages, eating requirements, pay structures, religions and habits. The Malay Regiment, raised in 1933, and subsequently expanded for war purposes, fought gallantly against insurmountable odds, but in virtual isolation from the Malay civilian population, from whom no help was expected or forthcoming. The local Malay territorial forces were in contrast poorly trained and armed. A large majority of the British Indian Army units, although from regiments with fine traditions, were severely devoid of senior experienced British and Indian officers, owing to the fast expansion and pressing needs of the Middle East. British Indian Army units, which totalled two and a half million troops throughout all theatres, contained a varied assortment of races, including Gurkhas, Sikhs, Punjabis, Jats, Garhwalis, Baluchis, Dogras and Hyderabidas. Many of these were volunteers, who had been attracted to the colours because of pay, food and clothing, which by Indian standards were good. Many also volunteered because in India a soldier's profession was looked upon as being honourable. With such precipitous expansion in the British Indian Army, at a pace that exceeded the availability of efficient Indian junior leaders, junior and inexperienced wartime commissioned British officers, who were unfamiliar with their mens' mentality and language, were promoted as stopgap measures. The efficiency of such Indian units, therefore, became almost entirely divested in a small group of regular Indian officers, and rapidly declined as they were either killed or wounded. This miscellany of impractically equipped and under-trained forces, were consequently no match for Lieut-General Tomoyuki Yamashita's three divisions which were reputed to be the best in the whole Japanese Imperial Army.

The discipline, physical fitness and level of training among units of Malaya Command varied enormously. Some British units had been stationed in the Far East for as long as six years, in the arduous tropical climate, and had grown accustomed to the East's slower living conditions. However, the 22nd Australian Brigade was probably better equipped than most for jungle warfare, having been in Malaya for only 11 months when hostilities commenced. In contrast to this, newly raised Indian formations as well as British battalions from China and many of the Australians, on arrival in Malaya were found to be only partially trained and had no previous jungle warfare experience. A British private soldier lost accidently in the Malayan jungle was estimated to have a life expectancy of only a few months, whereas a more intelligent, average non-commissioned officer might last for a year or even longer. The jungle to them was a fearful, hostile place which was filled with 'a host of half-imagined nameless terrors'.[83]

Troop training to a great extent had been neglected, and the inexperience of most Allied soldiers in Malaya Command cannot be denied. Other than for official inspections, sports and drills, men watched films, went dancing, and made friends with swarms of Malay children, who frequently cadged their cigarettes and not infrequently offered them their sisters. Australians were invariably nicknamed Joe. Training instructions issued by Command headquarters were founded on European type 1914–18 warfare strategies, rather than being adapted to 1941 Malayan conditions. A military training directorate issued by General Headquarters in India in 1940 had simply been shelved at Command Headquarters, and no action for various reasons had been taken on it. Whereas there is little evidence to indicate that the failure by under-trained and outclassed troops was a decisive factor in the rapid collapse of Malaya, there is ample evidence of

> 'unimaginative leadership, both military and civil. . . . The people in Malaya, especially in Singapore, both military and civil, lived in a fool's paradise. The policy of the government and the fighting services was "Don't worry, it may never happen".'[84]

Senior commanders gave insufficient attention to preparing inexperienced and untrained troops, and by doing so they invited maximum casualties on them, whilst inflicting minimum casualties on the enemy. Notwithstanding this, there were memorable exceptions, and the 2nd Battalion Argyll and Sutherland Highlanders fought magnificently throughout the campaign, under the leadership of Lieut-Colonel I. Stewart, who was later promoted to Brigadier.

A considerable number of hastily sent, partially trained reinforcements arrived in Malaya during the latter part of 1941 and in January 1942. Inefficient training depots in Australia turned out poorly trained men who posed more of a problem to the already overstretched and diminished forces in Malaya, rather than being an asset to them.

> 'When a large batch of reinforcements reached Malaya in October 1941 the best any unit could say about them was that their training had been bad and the men were not well disciplined.'[85]

Some of the Australian troops, who arrived on 23rd January, had not received extensive training and some of them had never even fired a rifle. It is not surprising that unit commanders confronted with ill-trained troops such as these found them to be sadly lacking in aggressive spirit. In an article published in the British *Daily Mail* on 15th November 1957, General Gordon Bennett wrote:

> '1,900 untrained Australian troops arrived in Malaya in January 1942, a few weeks before the fall of Singapore. Some of them had never fired a rifle. Some of them were recruited in Martin Place, Sydney, on the Friday and put on a boat for Malaya the following week.'[86]

The first British reinforcements, the 45th Indian Infantry Brigade Group and a Pioneer Battalion, disembarked in Singapore on 23rd January 1942. They were sent as reinforcements, but Percival found them to be 'very young, unseasoned and untrained'.[87] They were sent to Malacca a few days after arriving where their fate was sealed in bloody hand to hand fighting at Muar with crack assault troops of the Imperial Japanese Army. Their sister brigade, the 44th Indian Infantry Brigade, also comprised equally inexperienced and raw recruits. General Percival said on their arrival:

> 'I dared not send it into action . . ., so I decided to retain it on Singapore island in the hope that it would get a chance of some training and also be able to work on the defences.'[88]

The ill-fated 53rd Brigade Group of the 18th British Division, comprising 'nine battalions of magnificient fighting men, all territorials from famous East Anglia Regiments,'[89] only disembarked at Singapore on 29th January 1942. None of them had been trained in jungle fighting, having been diverted from their original Middle East destination while still at sea. Very few had ever been abroad, and almost none of them had ever seen service in the tropics. They arrived without transport, without supporting guns and without adequate maintenance facilities, as these were all following in a separate and slower convoy. When the 6th Heavy and 35th Light British Anti-Aircraft Regiments, and the 85th Anti-Tank Regiments arrived, they also did so without their guns!

It was indeed incredible that such mistakes could have been made, and that such ill-suited and under-equipped reinforcements could have been sent to an already battle-scarred and weary army in

Malaya, and within only ten days of Churchill's specific warning to Wavell about useless mouths. For the hapless individuals concerned, it would have been better if the convoys delivering them to the humiliation and tribulation of three and a half years of cruel incarceration, had never arrived in Singapore, but had instead been diverted elsewhere.

9:10 RAF's Pre-Destination

Sir Shenton Thomas' request to London in January 1940, to increase the striking power and size of the RAF in Malaya, fell on deaf ears. He realised that as the RAF's role in the country's defence would be crucial, and in the absence of a significant naval force at Singapore, they would need more aircraft to enable them to carry out their commitment. Successful defence of Singapore involved defending all of Malaya, including the vital northern airfields from which planes could be launched. The Air Ministry at that time was fully extended in building up the RAF's strength to counteract the immediate threat posed by the Luftwaft, and Malaya's needs were allocated a very poor third placing compared to the priorities in Europe and the Middle East. An imminent threat to Malaya at that time was considered as improbable, and her future defenders were told to make do with the resources already at their disposal, and to improve the Volunteer Forces' effectiveness, without interfering with the production of tin and rubber. It was even intimated that some aircraft already in the area might be withdrawn to other locations, rather than additional aircraft being provided in the foreseeable future.

In early 1940 Major-General Lionel V. Bond, the General Officer Commanding Malaya, realised that defensive requirements had been dramatically altered when Japan gained control of South China and of Hainan island. He wanted the RAF to take over the main defensive role, and recommended that they should be made totally answerable for detecting and destroying any enemy expeditionary force at sea, and in the event of this failing, to prevent the Japanese from setting up bases within striking distance of the Malayan airfields. Despite Bond's memorandum to this effect, and the Overseas Defence Committee's general acceptance of Bond's views, they still decided that the overall situation in other theatres at that time took precedence, and outweighed any need to send further reinforcements to Malaya.

In August 1940 the British Chiefs of Staff recognised the need to expand the RAF's presence in Malaya from their 88 mostly obsolete aircraft, up to a minimum of 336 first-line planes, which they anticipated could be provided before the end of 1941. Only two months later, at a General Defence Conference attended by representatives from all over the Far East, a further upward revision of the minimum establishment was endorsed, altering it to 566 first-line planes, plus additional ground forces. Despite all Whitehall promises, and notwithstanding all previous establishment proposals, 'the RAF could only call on a shop-soiled, bedraggled assortment of 141 operational aircraft'[90] when Japan commenced her attack in December 1941. Lack of fighter power was the RAF's greatest weakness, and what obsolescent planes there were, had to operate out of dubiously located airfields that had been developed for civil purposes. Against Japan's 670 modern aircraft, this was an invitation to certain defeat.

When Air Chief Marshall Sir Robert Brooke-Popham GCVO, KCB, CMG, DSO, AFC ostensibly took over as C-in-C Far East in November 1940, he lost no time in preparing airfields throughout the country. Of the 22 airfields that were constructed, 15 had only grass surfaces which were unsuited to the rainy tropics. The northern airfields also were uncamouflaged and stood out starkly against the surrounding countryside when viewed from the air. Communication between airfields was both inadequate and unreliable, as outdated ground to air, limited range radio sets broke down with frustrating frequency. All airfields were also insufficiently equipped with anti-aircraft fire-power, and only the Tengah Base, of the four airfields on Singapore island, was completed by the day that war commenced, being solely due to the efforts of officers and men who laid 400 yards of metalled paving during the immediate twenty-four hours before Japan started her attack.

The siting of northern airfields remained a topic of bitter contention. They had been constructed with insufficient co-ordination between air force and army officers, and were located in places where defending them against strong enemy land forces was nigh impossible. The army's criticism was justified in that they were located to suit the air force's requirements, and had been constructed regardless of costs in endeavouring to defend them. Air Vice-Marshall J.T. Babbington demanded, however, that the army should garrison the northern airfields, realising that the successful defence of Malaya would be impossible if the RAF lost air superiority. When this quickly happened, all airfields fell easy prey to Japanese attacks, and were equally quickly abandoned to them, some with large quantities of stores left intact.

Operational aircraft in Malaya Command comprised 17 American designed long-range Lockheed Hudsons, 34 Bristol Blenheim light bombers, 24 Vickers Wilderbeste torpedo bombers, 60 Brewster F2A-1 Buffalows; 10 Bristol Blenheim night fighters; 3 Catalina flying boats; 4 archaic-looking, dangerously obsolete, fabric-covered Fairey Swordfish, with a top speed of 139 mph, and 5 Sharks. There were no reserves for these aircraft, for which there was also a serious shortage of spare parts. Few of the available pilots had experience in flying fighter aircraft in tropical conditions, and their obsolescent crates were incapable of supporting the few operational bombers that were on hand. Percival therefore had none of the aircraft that he required for effective close supporting action and for transportation purposes. Despite such a precarious situation, Air Marshall C.W. Pulford, the Air Officer Commanding the Far East, on 19th October 1941 expressed his opinion that the RAF was ready. He considered that the Brewster Buffalows would not find it difficult to deal with Japan's best A6M Zero fighters, regardless of their inferior speed and climbing ability, and that the purpose-built long-range Lockheed Hudson heavy bombers were equal to Japan's best range of Mitsubishi bombers.

On 9th December half a sortie of Blenheim bombers, flying without fighter escort to attack Singora, were lost when they came up against 30 Japanese fighters. A second raid, scheduled to leave Butterworth at 5 p.m. that evening, was devastated by scorching machine-gun fire before they could leave the ground. Only one plane escaped damage and flew off alone to Singora to press home an attack. The pilot, Squadron Leader A.S.K. Scarff, was mortally wounded, but managed to crash land safely at Alor Star without harm to his crew. Scarff died in hospital and was posthumously awarded the Victoria Cross for his bravery.

By Wednesday 10th December, just two days into battle, the RAF had only 50 fit planes remaining for operations, and were outnumbered by almost thirteen to one. Most of these aircraft had already been withdrawn from Malaya and were concentrated in Singapore. Insufficient fighter protection was available to enable daylight bombing raids on Japanese troops to be continued, and Dutch reinforcement pilots from Java, who were untrained for night bombing, had already been flown back there.

Despite Japan's mastery of the air, British pilots disregarded the odds and took up their crates to give battle. Air domination invariably meant that the Japanese knew the whereabouts of defenders and were able to surprise them. The retreating Allies therefore came under constant daylight attack as they tried to take up new defensive positions, and with the occupation of Penang the Japanese obtained complete air superiority over northern and central Malaya.

Insufficient ground ack-ack defences and an ineffective air-raid warning system meant that planes were caught time and time again on the ground, either being refuelled or reloaded. There was little that pilots could do, other than helplessly huddle in shelters or slit trenches and watch as many of their planes were destroyed. As British losses increased, General MacArthur was urgently asked for assistance, but with his bomber force in equal smouldering disarray on Clark Field in the Philippines, there was nothing that he could do. An urgent request for immediate reinforcements was sent to London, but time was fast running out and was something that the Allies had precious little to squander. Airfield evacuations were hurriedly carried out, and at Kuantan and Sungei Patani large stocks of valuable POL and stores were left, gift wrapped, for the enemy. Scorched earth operations required delicate timing as precipitous actions gave rise to undue alarm. Petrol and oil, therefore, were ordered to be run to waste, rather than torched, and buildings were ordered only to be smashed.

9:11 Naval Dilemma

Churchill gambled on a show of strength and bluff being adequate deterrents to discourage Japan from embarking on an act of aggression that would put her in open conflict with the combined mights of Great Britain, the United States and Russia. Thus, Z Force, which boasted 'the smallest number of the best ships'[91] comprising the 36,000 ton battleship the *Prince of Wales*, the 32,000 ton battle cruiser the *Repulse*, along with four escorting destroyers, the *Electra, Empress, Vampire* and *Tenedos*, arrived without aircraft carrier cover, and amid much publicity, at Singapore's Keppel Harbour on 2nd December 1941. The *Prince of Wales*, one of Britain's newest battle ships, had a speed potential of 29 knots and, with her 15-inch guns, had a reputation of being unsinkable. The reconditioned *Repulse*, originally built in 1915, also had 15-inch guns and was capable of reaching 28 knots. The original intention was to provide Z Force with suitable air support but the aircraft carrier *Indomitable*, to whom this duty was allotted, ran aground at Jamaica, just before sailing for Far Eastern waters. Sir Shenton Thomas had been completely surprised to learn that the arrival of Z Force was little more than a bluff, and as such was equally sure that the Japanese were aware of its shortcomings.

Japan's complex master plan required the dispersal of forces and ships over an area enveloping thousands of square miles. Their initial success, therefore, exceeded the most optimistic hopes of their Imperial General Headquarters, and during the first few days of war, British naval power in the Far East, as well as that of the United States in the Pacific, was sufficiently crippled so that throughout the Indian and Pacific Oceans control of the seas was lost.

Admiral Sir Tom Phillips, the C-in-C Eastern Fleet, fully realised what dangers were involved by taking Z Force into action without adequate fighter aircraft protection, but could not condone the Royal Navy remaining inactive in such an emergency. Although his chances of success were less than half, Phillips considered that the gamble was essential, to try and halt the Japanese invasion and to scotch their landings at Kota Bahru. At 5.35 p.m. on 8th December, Phillips' six-ship Z Force sailed north out of Singapore, watched by several hundred people. O.D. Gallagher, the *Daily Express* war correspondent, who was on *HMS Repulse*, wondered whether mingling in the crowd 'there were any Japanese agents among them with access to small portable radio transmitters'[92], as did General Percival who believed that messages were transmitted by enemy wireless from Singapore throughout the campaign.

Before departing, Phillips asked Air Vice-Marshall Pulford for three types of air support from aircraft stationed in Singapore. Firstly, he wanted reconnaissance flights up to a distance of 100 miles north of Z Force from dawn on the 9th; secondly, further reconnaissance flights up to and beyond Singora from the 10th, in a 10 mile swath from the coastline; and thirdly, he wanted fighter protection off Singora from dawn on the 10th, as the northern Malayan airfields had already become untenable, and others in mid-Malaya were being devastated by enemy bombing. The last demand was an impossible one, as the combat time left to the short-range Buffalow fighters, operating out of distant Singapore, would be severely curtailed, owing to refuelling requirements.

By sunset on 9th December Phillips realised that, in the improved visibility following a rain-storm, his force had been spotted and altered his course southwards towards Singapore. The War Room was not informed of this change of course and only received news, at 11 a.m. on the 10th, that Phillips' force was off Kuantan, through a pilot from an aircraft from the *Prince of Wales* that had landed at Penang. Phillips took Z Force to investigate a report from the Indian Garrison Commander at Kuantan that the Japanese were landing there. It was only on arrival that it was discovered that this was false, arising from the failure to investigate the detonation of mines in a padi field, which was subsequently attributed to water buffaloes. Phillips' unannounced diversion towards Kuantan denied him air escort from 11 Brewster Buffalows of No 453 Fighter Squadron, which on the 10th morning were standing by for that very purpose at Sembawang in Singapore.

Z Force was sighted near Kuantan just before dawn on 10th December. Pilots of Japan's elite 22nd Air Flotilla hurriedly exchanged bombs for torpedoes and commenced a blistering attack against Z Force at 11.30 a.m. Malayan time. 34 high level bombers put in a prolonged and intensive attack from 17,000 feet, followed by 51 torpedo bombers which attacked with daring determination from all directions and with remarkable accuracy. In their first assault, a bomb crashed through *Repulse's* funnel, blowing up the ammunition magazine and setting her on fire. The *Prince of Wales* soon lay helpless, listing to port with her screws and steering gear destroyed. Escorting ships continued to give protective fire to the *Prince of Wales*, and in doing so neglected their own defence, but, as more torpedoes struck, she turned slowly over to port and her stern went under. When Phillips realised that the *Prince of Wales* was defenceless, he ordered all crew who were not urgently needed to go up on deck, so that when the abandon ship order was given many were in a position to jump into the sea and save themselves. Not a single member of the *Repulse's* crew was released from duty, as she was in action to the last. Her guns fired non-stop throughout all attacks on her, and were still firing when the third torpedo struck. As she listed irreversibly to starboard, one of her port multiple-Lewis guns still continued to fire.

> 'It was only after the third torpedo shook the ship that the loud-speakers sounded throughout the ship. "All hands on Deck! Prepare to abandon ship. God be with you."'[93]

The *Repulse* went down at 12.30 p.m., followed by the *Prince of Wales* at 1.20 p.m. Most of the men who were killed came from the *Repulse*.

Captain W.G. Tennant's emergency signal reached the Operations' Room at Singapore at 12.12 p.m. on the 10th. Only seven minutes later, 11 Buffalows took off for the scene of action, arriving just after the *Prince of Wales* had sunk, to find 'the sea covered with men and wreckage'.[94] Out of a total crew complement of 2,921 from both ships, 2,081 were rescued by destroyers and subsequently taken to Singapore. Admiral Sir Tom Phillips was reported missing along with Captain J.C. Leech, the Captain of the *Prince of Wales*. The Commander of *HMS Repulse*, Captain W.G. Tennant, was among those to be rescued.

Japanese planes withdrew and did not try to interfere as destroyers picked up survivors. Later, making necessity resemble chivalrous virtue, they flew over the watery grave and one pilot dropped a message to the destroyers saying, 'We have completed our task ... Carry on.'[95] Two wreaths were dropped in a tribute to a worthy foe, which could well be viewed as an act of brash bravado from pilots who were already desperately short on fuel and ammunition, and who were unable to push home any further attack. Japanese pilots' skill and daring were emphasised in Captain Tennant's report, in which he stated:

> 'The enemy attacks were without doubt magnificently carried out and pressed well home . . . I observed only one torpedo bomber who apparently had cold feet and fired his torpedoes at a distance of at least two miles from the ship.'[96]

Winston Churchill announced the loss of *HMS Prince of Wales* and *HMS Repulse* in the House of Commons on 10th December 1941. The sinkings shocked the nation and many wept on hearing the news. Perky Perkins recalled 'the utter depression which fell on us at the time when these two great ships were sunk'.[97] It had a stupefying effect on morale. People in Singapore were stultified, and many saw it as being 'the beginning of the end. When the news reached Raffles Hotel, the famous verandah emptied as though the last waltz had just been played.'[98] People could not believe what had happened, and the nerves of some cracked. In Malaya, a panic exodus towards Singapore began, and as leading European company executives evacuated, so disorganisation became manifest within the civil administration.

> 'This shattering blow was worth a division of troops to the Japanese and it showed us that we were up against something after all. I cannot over-emphasise the effect of this news on all of us. We couldn't believe it — such a thing was quite unbelievable. The Japanese surely couldn't have done that to our crack ships — but they had, they had, and our morale dropped and dropped.'[99]

The loss of the *Prince of Wales* and *Repulse* was a fateful stroke that helped to seal the destiny of Malaya and Singapore. It also proved Churchill and the Admiralty Heads as being incorrect in thinking that battleships were invulnerable to air attack. The sinkings exploded the long-held myth of the invincibility of battleships!

9:12 Shenton Thomas Versus Duff Cooper

Duff Cooper arrived in Singapore on 9th September 1941, with a mandate to study methods of improving the co-ordination between British territories from India to Australia, and to report on their state of readiness for war. Cooper, a close friend of Churchill, was an astute man who intensely disliked routine work. Although he was capable of making splendid speeches, he had not been particularly successful in his previous appointment as Minister of Information in London. It did not take long for Cooper to discover ineptitudes of function duplications in Singapore involving two senior officials, who lived happily together in the same bungalow and pooled their information which was then sent to their respective Whitehall departments — the Ministry of Economic Welfare and the Ministry of Information. Within three days of Japan attacking Malaya, Cooper was elevated by Churchill to the position of 'Resident Minister for Far Eastern Affairs with Cabinet rank'.[100] He was given the authority to settle emergencies on the spot, on the understanding that he did not

> 'impair the existing responsibilities of the Commanders-in-Chief or government representatives, who would still deal directly with their departments in Whitehall'.[101]

Initial relations between Cooper and the Governor, Sir Shenton Thomas, were adequately cordial, although the former's appointment to the Far East had not been particularly welcomed. Sir Shenton considered that the Far East was 'being landed with a failure'.[102] Cooper's aggressive personality at the daily War Council meetings, over which he presided, made Sir Shenton quickly distrust him, as did the commanders of the three armed services, who disliked a politico instructing them how to carry out their jobs. Cooper's claim that he was empowered to establish a clearing house to settle routine matters promptly was the cause for open disagreement between him and Sir Shenton, who never regarded Cooper's appointment as being vested with executive powers over the War Council, or over the course of the war.

Defeatist talk was introduced for the first time into the minutes of a War Council meeting on 13th December 1941, when Cooper expressed his doubts regarding the military's capability of defending Malaya successfully. Such an unsubstantiated opinion, made officially in this manner by a Cabinet Minister to Service Chiefs, was abhorrent to Sir Shenton. It served only to intensify the ill-effects arising out of their personality clash, and fomented an increasingly inconducive working atmosphere at subsequent War Council meetings. Cooper's behaviour warranted severe criticism, as he either egoistically chose to ignore Churchill's personal advice, which cautioned that 'the successful establishment of this (War Council) machinery depends largely on your handling of it in these critical days',[103] or he conveniently disregarded the limitations implied by the trust that had been placed in him. Instead, his handling of events caused needless upsets and bitterness between senior personalities, and the methods he used encouraged furtive recriminations and unwarranted actions that were founded on biased counsel. Such actions were both disruptive to the progress of war planning, as well as unfair.

Cooper's position gave him easy access to 'informed and responsible men and to mischievous axe-grinders alike'.[104] He listened to the latter, and especially to the Editor of the *Straits Times*, G.W. Seabridge, who was aggrieved by Sir Shenton's income tax proposals. Seabridge and F.D. Bisseker were volatile critics of Sir Shenton's handling of civil defence matters, and over the disciplinary action taken by the Chinese Protectorate against Chinese secret societies. By being openly critical in this manner they ingratiated themselves with Duff Cooper. He, in turn, used the information that they provided to scathingly criticise the MCS, implying that it was unable 'to deal with wartime conditions'.[105] Furthermore, he described Sir Shenton to Churchill as a person who

> 'could not adjust to new circumstances and was "the mouth piece of the last person he speaks to", while Jones [the Colonial Secretary] was "a sinister figure . . . defeatist . . . immensely detested in the Colony ".'[106]

By the end of December 1941 it was evident that Duff Cooper was winning the power tussle in the War Council and that Sir Shenton 'was being increasingly relegated to being a figure-head stripped of any power'.[107] This equally applied to Stanley W. Jones, for whom Cooper had worked up an active dislike.

At a meeting of the War Council on 30th December 1941, which Sir Shenton did not attend, Cooper authorised two new senior civil government appointments to take effect from 1st January 1942. Both were also promulgated in the War Council meeting's minutes. Claiming that civil defence systems were unsound, Cooper appointed Brigadier Simson as the Controller of Civil Defence, with F.D. Bisseker as his deputy. Bisseker was also appointed Director of Labour and Transport. What particularly angered Sir Shenton, on his return to Singapore on 31st December, was to learn that Cooper had boasted to some of his friends that he had 'put one over on the little man'.[108] In Sir Shenton's diary on that day his annoyance was evident when he wrote:

> 'Duff Cooper, being led by the nose by Bisseker and Seabridge . . .. DC has officially appointed Bisseker, and War Council has officially appointed Simson, all in my absence . . . though neither has authority to make any appointment under the civil government. I cannot agree to Bisseker; . . . Seabridge has written an article in the *Straits Times* . . . either I must give way to DC, or DC to me. . . . it is fearfully bad for morale . . .'[109]

Cooper's interference, particularly when the Governor was away from Singapore, was a categorical attempt to 'strip him of all responsibility for civil defence'[110] and revealed the near detestation that they had by this time for each other. Sir Shenton's dislike and distrust of Bisseker was well known, particularly on account of the latter's outspoken criticism of the Governor since 1939, and his prominent part in the 'European scuttle from Penang'.[111]

Simson's plenary powers, given by Duff Cooper over Singapore and the State of Johore, were promptly amended by Sir Shenton, who granted him 'full powers for civil defence on Singapore island only'.[112] These were also subjected to existing laws, with sole recourse being through the Malayan Legal Department. This move completely negated Cooper's objective for Simson, the success of which was dependent on speed. Simson was therefore effectively stripped of his plenary powers by having to refer any challenges to his proposals through the time-consuming legal department, which clearly revealed that Sir Shenton's and Duff Cooper's personal antagonism for each other had taken precedence over considerations for efficient defence preparations for Singapore and southern Malaya. With Cooper's plenary order in one hand, and the Governor's restrictive order in the other, Simson was left with no alternative but to follow a course 'whichever best suited my purpose . . . Mr Duff Cooper approved of my duplicity for the sake of speed in action.'[113]

Cooper's behaviour in surreptitiously canvassing men in the Governor's service, in an attempt to persuade Whitehall to recall Sir Shenton, was an unthinkable action by a person with his extent of historical understanding and experience, and exhibited an astonishing lack of procedure. Cooper did not realise that despite Sir Shenton's weaknesses and lack of dynamic personality, he was still generally liked and trusted by the Malay, Chinese and Indian community leaders and traders.

Sir Shenton's diary entry on 9th January 1942 claimed that Duff Cooper's departure would be

> 'hailed with shouts of joy! He is suspect by most people; partly for his broadcast reference to the evacuation of the "majority" of the population from Penang, (well knowing it could only refer to Europeans) and partly for the Simson-Bisseker-Seabridge racket. I shall see him out with a sigh of relief. A rotten judge of men, arrogant, obstinate, vain; how he could have crept into (Cabinet) office is beyond me.'[114]

Sir Shenton's optimism, in assuming that with Cooper's departure no more would be heard of him, was short-lived. On 16th January the Colonial Office ordered the immediate summary retirement of S.W. Jones, in response to two secret cypher telegrams that Cooper had sent personally to the Secretary of State for the Colonies. In the first, he criticised the civil authorities for lamentably failing 'to make adequate preparations for war'[115] and in the second, on 11th January, he said that 'there existed a widespread and profound lack of confidence in the administration',[116] and suggested that a state of siege should be declared and a military Governor appointed.

The outcome of such scathing criticism was the dismissal of Jones, who was a brilliant, forceful and popular career officer. His dismissal was used as a means to placate the government's critics, rather than replace the Governor, as Cooper had recommended. Sir Shenton was plainly aggrieved by this instruction, and on the 16th wrote in his diary:

> 'I was deprived of the services of my chief executive officer at a very critical time. . . . I told no one but Jones and Percival.'[117]

On the 20th Sir Shenton summoned the Executive Committee members of the War Council and informed them of Jones' departure and of the appointment of Hugh Frazer as his successor.

Sir Shenton cabled Churchill and the Secretary of State for the Colonies and denounced Jones' dismissal as being 'a gross injustice'.[118] He argued that Jones was highly regarded in the MCS, was a first-class Malay scholar, and was popular with the Chinese. He contended that both the Prime Minister and the Colonial Office had been misled. But, despite his protestations, Jones' dismissal was upheld.

The treatment of Jones was a dark and sinister excuse and he was seen as being a 'scapegoat for lapses in other quarters'.[119] Jones was naturally shocked, but he begged to be allowed to stay on in any capacity, in order to assist in what had to be done. His admirable behaviour during this stressful time was a true measure of his character, especially when it is compared with Bisseker's subsequent actions prior to and during the evacuation of Singapore.

During Duff Cooper's four months in Singapore, he seldom visited Malaya Command HQ, and his understanding of the army's functioning was negligible. Being influenced by people who had been longstanding critics of the government in Malaya, however, he made decisions that begot consequent confusion.

When Cooper left Singapore on 13th January 1942, he did so with 'an uncomfortable feeling that I was running away',[120] but also with the realisation that had he stayed, it would have been 'without any power or significance'.[121] There is little doubt that he was an intelligent man, but notwithstanding this, he completely failed to perceive the necessity for delicate political balancing in the Straits Settlements and in the Malay States. The vagueness of his commission blinded his approach to it, and the evaluations he made. In effect, it was a 'classic case of responsibility without power'.[122]

Sir Shenton considered that the acrimony that was built up between them during this short period arose from Cooper's magnification of the responsibilities that were entrusted to him by the Prime Minister. Clearly, there must have been more to it. Cooper's attempts to attain popularity by entertaining guests at dinner parties with his mimicry of Sir Shenton, as well as of Brooke-Popham and Percival, were unworthy, childish gestures that could only aggravate the other undesirable traits in his character, revealed when he surreptitiously canvassed the opinions of Sir Shenton's subordinates. This he undertook to the extent of even discussing the desirability of replacing Sir Shenton with the newly appointed Brigadier Simson. After Cooper returned to the United Kingdon he did not stop in his attempts to discredit Sir Shenton, and persisted by expounding his concern at being 'politically damaged by his association with the disaster in Singapore'.[123]

1. *Sinister Twilight (The Fall of Singapore)* by Noel Barber, ch.3, p.41.
2. *Percival and the Tragedy of Singapore* by Sir John Smyth VC, ch.3, p.54.
3. *Eastern Epic* by Compton Mackensie, ch.18, p.219.
4. *The Second World War* by Winston S. Churchill, vol.2, p.623, Appendix A.
5. *The Fall of Singapore* by Frank Owen, ch.1, p.22.
6. Ibid, p.22. (*The Second World War* by Winston Churchill, vol.2.)
7. *War Against Japan* by Maj-Gen S. Woodburn Kirby CB CMG CIE OBE MC, vol.1, ch.7, p.64.
8. *Allies of a Kind. The US, Britain and the War Against Japan 1941–45* by Christopher Thorne, ch.1, p.4, (ref. CAB 69/8).
9. *70 Days to Singapore* by Stanley L. Falk, ch.3, p.50.
10. *The Fall of Singapore* by Frank Owen, ch.3, p.40.
11. *Allies of a Kind. The US, Britain and the War Against Japan 1941–45* by Christopher Thorne, ch.1, p.4. (Ref. CAB 69/2.)
12. *The Second World War* by Winston S. Churchill, vol.3.
13. *Sinister Twilight (The Fall of Singapore)* by Noel Barber, ch.3, p.43.
14. *Retreat in the East* by O.D. Gallagher, ch.5, p.84.
15. Ibid, p.85.
16. *Japan Against the World 1941–2041. The 100 Year War for Supremacy* by Russell Braddon, ch.1, p.13.
17. Ibid, p.13.
18. *Sinister Twilight (The Fall of Singapore)* by Noel Barber, ch.3, p.43.
19. Ibid, ch.1, p.21.
20. Ibid, ch.1, p.22.
21. *Percival and the Tragedy of Singapore* by Sir John Smyth VC, ch.2, p.40.
22. *History of the Second World War* by Liddell Hart, ch.17, p.234.
23. *The History of Modern Malaya* by K.G. Tregonning, ch.13, p.273.
24. *History of the Second World War* by Liddell Hart, ch.17, p.241.
25. Ibid, ch.17, p.242.
26. *The Second World War* by Winston S. Churchill, vol.2, p.379.
27. Extract from the Editorial of the *Malayan Gazette* dated 16th December 1941, by courtesy of the Penang Museum.
28. *Shenton of Singapore, Governor and Prisoner of War* by Brian Montgomery, ch.4, p.47.
29. Ibid, p.47.
30. Ibid, ch.4, p.51.

31. Interview with Monsieur A. Glineur, February 1985, at Kampong Rajah, Cameron Highlands, Malaysia.
32. *Shenton of Singapore, Governor and Prisoner of War* by Brian Montgomery, ch.10, p.203.
33. Ibid, ch.5, p.64.
34. Ibid, ch.5, p.68.
35. Ibid, ch.5, p.69.
36. *In 70 Days. The Story of Malaya* by E.M. Glover, ch.2, p.40.
37. *Women Beyond the Wire* by Lavinia Warner and John Sandilands, ch.2, p.17.
38. *Out in the Mid-day Sun. Singapore 1941–1945* by Kate Caffrey, pt.1, p.29 (Ref. to General C.N. Barclay. *On Their Shoulders; Generalship in the Lean Years, 1939–1942, p.116–7).*
39. *Singapore. Too Little, Too Late* by Ivan Simson, ch.13, p.121.
40. Ibid, p.121.
41. *Singapore. The Chain of Disaster* by Major General S. Woodburn Kirby CB, DMG, CIE, OBE, MC, ch.18, p.188.
42. Ibid, p.188.
43. Ibid, p.188.
44. Ibid, p.188.
45. *Women Beyond the Wire* by Lavinia Warner and John Sandilands, ch.2, p.24.
46. Ibid, ch.2, p.25.
47. Ibid, ch.2, p.26.
48. Ibid, ch.3, p.27.
49. Ibid, ch.3, p.27.
50. *Sinister Twilight (The Fall of Singapore)* by Noel Barber, ch.7, p.137.
51. Ibid, ch.3, p.41.
52. Ibid, p.42.
53. *Shenton of Singapore. Governor and Prisoner of War* by Brian Montgomery, ch.5, p.67 (extract from C.A. Vlieland's *Memoir*).
54. Ibid, p.67.
55. Ibid, p.69.
56. *Singapore. The Chain of Disaster* by Major-General S. Woodburn Kirby CB, DMG, CIE, OBE, MC, ch.10, p.97–8.
57. *Too Little, Too Late* by Ivan Simson, ch.8, p.85.
58. *Tales from the South China Seas. Images of the British in South-East Asia in the Twentieth Century* edited by Charles Allen, ch.11, p.255 (refer *The Crowded Hour* by S. Cunyngham-Brown).
59. Ibid, p.255.
60. *The Crowded Hour* by S. Cunyngham-Brown OBE, ch.10, p.90.
61. *Malaysia* by K.G. Tregonning, ch.3, p.27.
62. Ibid, p.27.
63. *Out in the Mid-Day Sun, Singapore 1941–5* by Kate Caffrey, ch.2, p.52.
64. *The Fall of Singapore* by Frank Owen, ch.2, p.28,
65. *Women Beyond the Wire* by Lavinia Warner and John Sandilands, ch.1, p.11.
66. *History of the Second World War* by Liddell Hart, ch.16, p.217 (figures from *The War at Sea* by Roskill, vol.1, p.560).
67. *Out in the Mid-Day Sun. Singapore 1941–5* by Kate Caffrey, ch.2, p.52.
68. Ibid, p.53.
69. *Eagle Against the Sun. The American War with Japan* by Ronald H. Spector, p.128.

70. *Japan Against the World 1941–2041. The 100 Year War for Supremacy* by Russell Braddon, ch.5, p.84.
71. *The Jungle is Neutral* by F. Spencer Chapman DSO, ch.2, p.26.
72. Ibid, p.27.
73. Ibid, p.31.
74. *The Bitter End. The Fall of Singapore 1941–2* by Richard Holmes and Anthony Kemp, ch.6, p.117.
75. *The Fall of Singapore* by Frank Owen, ch.2, p.29.
76. *Sinister Twilight (The Fall of Singapore)* by Noel Barber, ch.4, p.66.
77. Ibid, ch.6, p.95 (refers to *War Memoirs* by Winston Churchill).
78. Ibid, ch.6. p.96.
79. Ibid, ch.6, p.96.
80. *The Fall of Singapore* by Frank Owen, ch.11, p.151.
81. *Tales from the South China Seas* edited by Charles Allllen, ch.11, p.254.
82. Extract from the Editorial of the *Malayan Gazette* dated 16th December 1941, by courtesy of the Director, Penang Museum.
83. *The Jungle is Neutral* by F. Spencer Chapman DSO, ch.6, p.115.
84. *Singapore. Too Little, Too Late* by Ivan Simson, ch.1, p.20.
85. *Percival and the Tragedy of Singapore* by Sir John Smyth VC, ch.5, p.89.
86. Ibid, p.88.
87. *The Fall of Singapore* by Frank Owen, ch.8, p.102.
88. Ibid, ch.10, p.139.
89. *Shenton of Singapore. Governor and Prisoner of War* by Brian Montgomery, ch.6, p.86.
90. *Sinister Twilight (The Fall of Singapore)* by Noel Barber, ch.2, p.40.
91. *History of the Second World War* by Liddell Hart, ch.17, p.235.
92. *The Fall of Singapore* by Frank Owen, ch.4, p.52.
93. *Retreat in the East* by O.D. Gallagher, ch.4, p.72.
94. *Percival and the Tragedy of Singapore* by Sir John Smyth VC, ch.8, p.122.
95. *Japan Against the World 1941–2041. The 100 Year War for Supremacy* by Russell Braddon, ch.20, p.288.
96. *The Fall of Singapore* by Frank Owen, ch.4, p.59.
97. *Tales from the South China Seas* edited by Charles Allen, ch.11, p.251.
98. *Sinister Twilight (The Fall of Singapore)* by Noel Barber, ch.3, p.51.
99. *The Way It Was* by Alex L. Archer, ch.10, p.79–80.
100. *Sinister Twilight (The Fall of Singapore)* by Noel Barber, ch.3, p.48.
101. Ibid. p.48.
102. *Shenton of Singapore. Governor and Prisoner of War* by Brian Montgomery, ch.5, p.77.
103. *Sinister Twilight. (The Fall of Singapore)* by Noel Barber, ch.3, p.50.
104. *British Rule in Malaya 1942–57* by Robert Heussler, ch.2, p.25.
105. Ibid, p.26. (Refer DC to PM 18/12/1941. PREM 1951A/12.)
106. Ibid, p.26.
107. *Sinister Twilight (The Fall of Singapore)* by Noel Barber, ch.4, p.61.
108. Ibid, ch.4, p.68.
109. *Shenton of Singapore. Governor and Prisoner of War* by Brian Montgomery, ch.6, p.105.
110. Ibid, ch.6, p.106.
111. Ibid, ch.6, p.106.
112. *Sinister Twilight. (The Fall of Singapore)* by Noel Barber, ch.4, p.69.
113. *Singapore. Too Little Too Late* by Ivan Simson, ch.8, p.82.

Chapter Nine

114. *Shenton of Singapore. Governor and Prisoner of War* by Brian Montgomery, ch.7, p.109.
115. Ibid, ch.7, p.113.
116. Ibid, ch.7, p.114.
117. Ibid, ch.7, p.117.
118. Ibid, ch.7, p.119.
119. *British Rule in Malaya 1942–57* by Robert Heussler, ch.2, p.27.
120. *Sinister Twilight (The Fall of Singapore)* by Noel Barber, ch.5, p.80.
121. Ibid, p.80.
122. *Shenton of Singapore. Governor and Prisoner of War* by Brian Montgomery, ch.6, p.97.
123. Ibid, ch.7, p.115. (Refers to *Old Men Forget* by Duff Cooper, p.310.)

CHAPTER TEN: HIT AND RUN

10:1 Penang Garrison and Volunteer Forces

Throughout 1940 and into 1941 the standard of life in Malaya, and in Penang in particular, continued to be both comfortable and leisurely. The public was not unduly affected by the horrendous news briefs that emerged from Europe, and found it difficult to conceive that the war which had been raging there for one and half years was real.

The Europeans in Penang, especially the British, were so influenced by government instigated propaganda that they believed the Japanese would not be so foolhardy as to embark upon an attack of Malaya and, in doing so, tempt the wrath of Britain's might-of-arms. Chinese women, however, were equally certain that an attack by Japan was inevitable. When European and Chinese women met, as members of the Medical Auxiliary Service for regular weekly practices to make and sterilise bandages and dressings for the hospital, their discussions highlighted the basic differences in attitude between them in respect of the war reaching Malaya. The Chinese women knew to what extent people had suffered in China after the 1937 China Incident, and feared the sort of revenge the Japanese would exact against the Chinese, should Malaya be invaded. This would apply especially to any Chinese who took an active part in Malaya's defence.

> 'A question in the minds of many, especially the Chinese . . . a nagging fear of coming under Japanese rule. What will happen to the people of Penang, when the Japanese learn that many . . . have been giving aid and money to the Nationalists in China — Japan's enemies? Will they be punished or even tortured?'[1]

The Chinese in Malaya fully realised that the Japanese would consider them as the most hostile of any of their potential future subjects.

When Singapore was first bombed, around Raffles Square, at 4.45 a.m. on 8th December 1941, all the lights in the city were ablaze. The following morning, people in Penang, ignorant of these developments, went innocently about their daily routines. Only at 8 a.m., when the BBC transmitted through the Penang Wireless Station, was the news given out that Singapore had been bombed and that the Japanese had made landings on the east coast of Malaya, at Kota Bahru.

Penang held strategic importance, but could never truthfully be described as a fortress. Its port facilities, with their supply installations, gave it a military value, especially as substantial quantities of general stores and ammunition were held there. It boasted a good, secure anchorage from which the Royal Navy intended to operate warships, as well as using it as a convoy collecting port. It was also an important terminus for ocean-going cables which connected Malaya to both India and Ceylon.

The defence of Penang was, therefore, of considerable importance to the overall defence plan for Malaya, and a strategy to hold onto it should have been afforded greater priority. Once Penang was lost, the enemy would be provided with a base from which amphibious attacks could be launched anywhere along Malaya's undefended west coast, and any defences south of the island came under the danger of being outflanked. It was thought at one stage that the Japanese might attempt to overrun Penang in their initial assault and then use it as a base from which to launch further operations against Singapore. However, much of Penang's strategic significance evaporated once the Japanese had landed in southern Siam and on the east coast of northern Malaya. Only on account of its aerodrome and ocean cable terminus did its tactical value remain.

Despite assurances from 1936 that Penang was a fortress, the island was such in name only. At best, it was no more than a 'satellite fortress'. The Penang Garrison formed part of Lieut-General Sir Lewis Heath's 3rd Indian Corps, and in early December 1941 consisted of: Fortress HQ and Signals; 11 Coast Regiment Hong Kong/Singapore Royal Artillery, comprising 'two out-of-date batteries of 6-inch guns';[2] 36 Fortress Company Royal Engineers, who could have manned searchlights (had these arrived); one company of the 5/14th Punjab Regiment; the 3rd Battalion Penang and Province Wellesley SSVF, plus a mixed reinforcement camp and assortment of administrative units, including a labour battalion. In addition to this, Heath located one of his detached Indian infantry battalions there, not as part of the garrison but held in readiness to move to the mainland in the event that hostilities broke out. The garrison was supported by meagre fixed defences, an airfield that was undersized for military use, and there were no anti-aircraft guns on the island. Much of the equipment which had been ordered previously, with a view to making the island a self-contained fortress, had not arrived by December 1941.

The garrison was commanded by Brigadier C.A. Lyon — familiarly known as 'Tiger Lyon' — a veteran who had originally been commissioned during the Boer War. Lyon was recalled from retirement for this appointment, and had previously been an excellent commander as well as a fine sportsman. Being out of touch with changes in command requirements, Lyon opted for a decentralised method of control, and merely gave directions on policy matters. The garrison Staff Captain was Captain Malcolm Moffat, a natural soldier and an efficient officer. He had served during the 1914–1918 war and had then turned his hand to business, spending most of his career in Malaya.

Pre-war preparations for defending Penang island included: constructing beach obstacles; securing the airstrip against paratroop attack; strengthening vulnerable locations against acts of sabotage; implementing security and intelligence procedures; storing enormous stocks of rice and other essential foodstuffs; and arranging controls over imports and exports as well as for the distribution of petrol, oil and engineering supplies. The British army in 1935–6 also constructed a labyrinth of underground machine-gun nests and ammunition dumps among the lush hills of Teluk Tempayak, overlooking the south-east promontory of the island, which it took them almost two years to complete. The island, however, never contained sufficient troops for it to be directly defended.

High water-levels in congested George Town made the construction of underground shelters impossible. Similarly, as the building and financing of above-ground shelters also presented disproportionate difficulties to their calculated worthiness, municipal departments and commercial firms protected their buildings and employees as best they could, even if this meant relying on concrete roadside drains in the event of an emergency.

The island did have some sort of early warning system, but without the benefit of radar, this depended on the efficiency and keenness of individual observers and the communications systems available to them. None existed further north, although a scheme was hastily contrived, but without the necessary equipment, it was difficult to find and train suitable people. In December 1941, therefore, Penang island was inadequately defended and protected. It had no anti-aircraft defences, and equipment earmarked for this purpose had not yet arrived from Great Britain.

At that time the Penang and Province Wellesley Volunteer Corps was made up of two inadequately equipped infantry battalions of volunteer land forces. Whereas the minority European group within the population was very much implicated in these units, insufficient determined effort had been made, physically or mentally, to mobilise the local population for war. This, as it turned out, was a serious strategic error, particularly as many Chinese were naturally opposed to the Japanese and were only too willing to take up arms against them.

The two infantry battalions of volunteer forces in Penang were formed in late 1939, following the outbreak of war with Germany. They were raised to supplement the inadequate military presence in the country and were open to civilians of all races. From the outset, British male civilians were expected to join, and although there was no compulsion,

> 'the system and social set up was such that you would have been uncomfortable if you hadn't . . . Run by officers and sergeants seconded from the British army as staff instructors, these volunteer units provided opportunities for enjoyable and expense-free get-togethers that cut across many of the barriers of race and class . . . Training was never taken too seriously.'[3]

In June 1940 the Compulsory Service (Volunteer Force) Ordinance 1940 was promulgated in the Straits Settlements, by which the government was empowered to compel every British male subject between 18 and 55 years of age to enlist for service in the Volunteers, or in any additional force that might be formed to defend the country. By this ordinance the military authorities could require anyone to serve. Most affected was the small European community, making fewer Europeans available for other civil defence work.

With such a high percentage of Europeans holding key commercial posts, it was difficult for them to combine their employment responsibilities with afternoon drills each week, plus compulsory attendance at week-end camps. When training sessions in Penang were later increased, many executives had only the afternoons to attend to their civilian jobs, and were required to resume training in the evenings. Although government policy compelled Europeans to participate in the Volunteers,

> 'an indefinite impression always existed in Malaya that the Volunteer Force was not very seriously regarded by military authorities, despite the fact that the General Officer Commanding at any inspection never failed to assure the officers and men that he took the keenest interest in them and their public-spirited devotion, and to congratulate them upon their numbers and efficiency'.[4]

In February 1941 the Police Force (Military Service) Regulations required the police also to take part in military operations as additional military forces. In spite of keen interest shown by the Ex-Service Association of Malaya and every effort being 'made to stimulate voluntary recruitment in the non-European Volunteer units',[5] by 21st May 1941 the G.O.C. Malaya, Major-General W.G.C. Dobbie, expressed his continued disappointment that insufficient numbers had been recruited, particularly as additional troops could not be sent to Malaya as they were desperately needed in other theatres of war.

An Observer Corps, comprising men or women, was authorised in late August 1941, and on 19th September the Volunteer Ordinance was amended. This empowered the government to form a corps wholly or partly of women. When a State of Emergency was declared on 1st December, all Volunteer forces were mobilised by proclamation of the Governor, and subsequently 'went into action alongside regular forces'.[6] Only one Chinese company was formed in each of the Straits Settlements Volunteer Forces, and these each had a paper strength of 120 English-educated men.

A Volunteer Air Force was created in 1936, and in 1939 was reconstituted as the Malayan Volunteer Air Force. Equipment and personnel from various flying clubs throughout the country were used, and in 1941 the total force comprised 20 officers and 150 men, of whom only 50 were qualified pilots. A contingent of this was stationed on Penang.

In September 1939 the Penang unit of the Royal Naval Volunteer Reserve (constituted in 1934) totalled 30 European officers and 100 Malay ratings. One armed motor launch was also stationed at Penang and was used continuously for mine-sweeping and local observation patrols.

The original intention was to defend Penang. As military set-backs escalated on the mainland, the Far East War Council decided, on 14th December, that Penang's defensive policy had to be reviewed and would now revolve around the outcome of fighting on the mainland. Trying to hold both areas, and splitting available forces, would be unwise. Penang's main function of providing good fleet anchorage had been negated in the absence of any effective navy, and as Percival's forces were retreating southwards on the mainland, the original plan to spare troops to reinforce Penang was deemed to be no longer possible.

A new policy was devised requiring the evacuation of Penang with as much of the garrison as possible, rather than expose it to further air attacks against which there would be no defence. Penang's Resident Councillor, Mr L. Forbes, was told this and instructed that all preliminary arrangements for an evacuation had to be kept secret, to avoid causing alarm.

10:2 Passive Defence Services

Civil defence preparations got off to a slow start, as many people in Malaya could not believe that, in the twilight period that preceded war in the Far East, such precautions would become necessary. Their introduction was regarded as being contradictory to the country's priorities of producing maximum tin and rubber, especially at a time when the implied dangers of aggression seemed remote.

Passive Defence Services commenced first in the Straits Settlements and were later extended throughout all states in Malaya.

Although segments from all nationalities voluntarily participated in various aspects, their totals were insufficient, as was their equipment and training, to enable them to satisfy the demands that were later imposed on them. It was mostly the Chinese who joined the Passive Defence Services, and they were also predominant in other Miscellaneous War Services, as well as in Government offices and the armed services' support departments.

In addition to the Local Defence Corps, other Passive Defence Services included Air Raid Wardens, Medical Auxiliary Services, Auxiliary Fire Services and Rescue and Demolition Squads. The miscellaneous services included facilities for canteens, blood transfusions, censorship, telephone exchanges, government offices and Special War Services. The Penang Air Raid Wardens were called up on 6th December 1941, and on the 8th both the Passive Defence Services and the Local Defence Corps were mobilised. They worked with untiring heroism and against overwhelming odds, and their contribution towards humanity in many respects was remarkable.

Proposals for the formation of the Local Defence Corps were first considered in 1940, and it aimed at being the equivalent of the Home Guard in Great Britain. Section 16 of the Compulsory Service (Volunteer Force) Ordinance 1940 empowered the government to create additional forces, through which the Local Defence Corps Regulations 1940 were enacted in October of that year.

Initial eligibility for enrolment into the Local Defence Corps was restricted to three categories of Europeans:

(a) Male British subjects of pure European descent, between the ages of 41 and 55, with discretionary enrolment up to the age of 61.
(b) Male British subjects of pure European descent, between the ages of 18 and 41, who held postponement certificates in respect of the Volunteer Forces.
(c) Male British subjects and British protected persons, provided that they had been trained either in an armed force, or police or civil force, or under any other category that was acceptable to government.

Until February 1941, the local Defence Corps was exclusively European as the small European community was compelled to enrol in it. Non-Europeans were permitted freedom of choice until this time, after which admission procedures were relaxed to include non-European British subjects and British protected men over the age of 18. An establishment of 2,000 was agreed on 31st March, with provisions to increase this, provided that arms and equipment were available.

Local Defence Corps duties were:

(a) To assist to preserve local and internal security.
(b) To guard vulnerable areas, ie. power stations at Prai and Glugor, water works, bridges and possible parachute landing grounds.
(c) To supply mobile units in areas where danger from civil disturbances, or parachute landings might arise.

Corps members were required to serve anywhere in Malaya, and in a state of emergency could be temporarily placed under the command of a Chief Police Officer, or become part of the military forces. Full-time officers were appointed and training was carried out on five evenings weekly. Arms, equipment and uniforms were issued and a provision was made to pay compensation in respect of those who were either killed or injured in the course of carrying out their duties. People engaged in part-time duties were provided with allowances, but full-time members received pay.

Passive Defence preparations were first commenced in Penang during the second half of 1939, when European officers of the Police Force were seconded into full-time service with the Corps of Air Raid Wardens. It was not until February 1941, however, that a European from the Malayan Civil Services (MCS) was seconded on a full-time basis to the post of Director of Passive Services.

Many of the Air Raid Wardens who were recruited were young, well educated, English-speaking Chinese who were quickly given a course of instruction. The initial nucleus of recruits were mostly merchants, shopkeepers, school teachers, secretaries and clerks, whose weekly five-evening training periods included lectures on dealing with gas attacks, parades and route marches, as well as day and night exercises that were organised in conjunction with other Passive Defence Services. The Penang Corps of Air Raid Wardens was always an English-speaking body, and was proud to maintain this distinction.

Passive Defence activities were first introduced in Penang in January 1940. Sirens were put up in the streets and were tested every Saturday morning. Air raid warning regulations were issued and compulsory practices for 'Black Outs' and 'Brown Outs' were arranged. Light control regulations for railway stations, trains, ships and all kinds of vehicles were formulated, and in addition to this, house occupiers had to guarantee that sufficient fire watchers were available at their premises, to whom only a refreshment allowance was provided. All males between the ages of 16 and 55 were required to participate in this activity, and Air Raid Wardens were permitted to enter premises at any time, and to inspect them if they were authorised to do so by the Chief Air Raid Warden or any police officer. This was an unpopular but necessary ruling.

Penang had approximately 1,000 well trained Air Raid Wardens, of whom the majority were Chinese, with the exception of twelve Europeans, five Eurasians, nine Indians and one Malay. There were five divisions on the island, which were sub-divided into 80 posts, controlled from a central headquarters that was located in part of the main police building in Penang Road. The enthusiasm of both 'the officers and men was admirable'.[7] From 1st-16th December 1941, Air Raid Wardens were paid only $1.50 per day. Senior Deputy Wardens received $1.65 and Senior Wardens $1.80 per day. These low rates became the subsequent topic of controversy some four years and eight months later!

The Medical Auxiliary movement was initially started in Singapore during the latter part of 1939. It was predominantly a voluntary service for women, and European women in every town were informally requested by the Medical Department to offer their services at hospitals and first aid posts. The concept was formulated on the lines of St John's Ambulance Brigade teams, and was organised by medical officers on their return from Great Britain, where they had studied similar methods used there during the air raids of 1940. In February 1941 the Medical Auxiliary Service (MAS) officially came into being and thereafter 'constituted an integral part of the Medical Department'.[8] Similar training programmes and examinations to those in Great Britain were organised for members in Malaya, and included periods of working in hospitals and sometimes being present during operations. Instruction in English was initially given, but with increased recruitment of Eurasian and English-speaking Asiatic women, it soon became necessary to augment this by Chinese medical officers giving lessons in Chinese. The Ambulance Corps section of the MAS was mostly made up of English-speaking, non-European men, in charge of whom were a few European officers.

The MAS became a crucial arm of the Passive Defence Services. First aid posts were opened at the Penang General Hospital and in three different parts of the town, in which all races worked with enthusiasm. All posts were staffed by a trained medical officer and nurse, as well as by MAS members.

The actual number of European women who were involved in the MAS was unknown, but had it not been for their initiative it would undoubtedly never have been organised throughout Malaya. Communal cooperation prevailed, as all member races shared common work commitments. A special feeling of comradeship was generated among those women who were later forced to work under the most ghastly conditions. Following the European evacuation of Penang the Asian and Eurasian women of the MAS continued to care for the wounded splendidly.

With European men being required to enrol into the Volunteers and Defence Corps, openings for the employment of women were created in various new government departments that were formed as part of the defence preparation build-up, such as Food Control and Censorship. In the Penang Censor's office 25 European women were employed on a full-time basis, and many more than this worked on a part-time arrangement. Some even remained behind after the general evacuation for women, and assisted to destroy records and code books. They were duly evacuated, after completing their tasks along with the military forces.

> 'Very large numbers of European women were employed in other Government offices and at naval, military and air force headquarters, where they were teleprinters, typists, confidential secretaries, and entrusted with the secret cyphers.'[9]

European and Eurasian women took up employment with banks, and although they were untrained for these jobs, some of them turned out to be very efficient. A hostel was opened by the Rotary Club in Penang in which meals and accommodation were provided for 250 men.

The Government Telephone Exchange in Penang, on which both the civil and military authorities depended, continued to function without interruption, although 'during a bombing attack, private calls were not allowed, but every official call was put through immediately'.[10] On 11th December a previously arranged Shadow Exchange was run by Eurasian and Chinese girls by day and by men at night.

> 'One girl walked some miles in an air attack, and another left her bomb-damaged house to report for duty. One male operator spent the whole of every day in search for his evacuated family and came on duty for the night.'[11]

The telephone services were magnificent throughout the duration of bombing in Penang and only at 1 p.m. on the 16th, when the electric power station was destroyed by the military prior to their evacuation, did the exchange cease to function. Some telephone operators accepted a passage to Singapore and took up duties there. Others chose to stay in Penang with their parents and families.

Many people in Malaya and Penang realised what was in store, and were not bemused about their immediate prospects for the future. There was little that anyone could do 'about it except attend Air Raid Precaution exercises, Ambulance Corps drills, and be ready for active service with the Volunteer Forces which abounded everywhere'.[12] When the balloon did go up, many Volunteers and Passive Defence Service members lost their homes and possessions to the enemy because they chose to stay at their posts until the last moment. Many gave courageous and dedicated service as best they could under the most arduous physical conditions.

10:3 Fiery Baptism — The Bombing of George Town

From bases in southern Indo-China, General Sugawara's 3rd Air Group launched repeated attacks on Malaya's northern airfields at

Kota Bahru, Alor Star, Sungei Petani, Butterworth and Penang. While fighters either came in low to strafe their targets, or 'flew effective cover overhead, the bombers dropped mainly fragmentation and anti-personnel bombs, deadly against men and machines, but practically harmless to the runways',[13] which Sugawara intended to make good use of when they had been taken. The initial attacks against airfields left no doubt concerning the daring skill of Japanese pilots, and General Percival was quick to acknowledge this.

> 'The performance of the Japanese aircraft of all types and the accuracy of their high level bombing had come as an unpleasant surprise.'[14]

On Tuesday 9th December Japanese planes flew over George Town, without meeting any opposition, and then went on to bomb the aerodrome at Butterworth, causing considerable damage. Leaflets were dropped warning people to evacuate,

> 'as the Japanese were waging war solely against the "White Devils"'.[15]

The next afternoon large formations passed over George Town on their way to bomb Butterworth. Disregarding police warnings, and efforts by air raid wardens to keep people under cover, thousands of Asians rushed to congregate along the sea front, for a grandstand view of the dog-fight over the Mata Kuching aerodrome, and Butterworth being blitzed.

W.B. Patterson, the editor of the Penang edition of the *Tribune*, and an eye-witness of events that day reported:

> 'All-day long Jap planes have been flying over Penang, most of them at low altitude, but there has been no bombing on the island itself, although Butterworth seems to have been catching it pretty badly. I have not seen a British plane up all day and there seems to have been no anti-aircraft gun firing either. People are asking; "Where's the RAF?", and we're not having an easy job explaining where they are. Everybody's excited, running around like mad dogs, and the Municipal services are only just managing to keep going; the first bomb that drops will scatter the crowd and we'll see them no more. . . .I cannot . . . understand why the Japs didn't bomb us to blazes today. They had no opposition. Where the hell are our defenders?'[16]

On the next day, – the fateful 11th – twenty-seven bombers again flew over George Town at 11 a.m. Thousands of Malays, Chinese and Indians, with almost childish trust, rushed out for another blitz show. Similarly, on this occasion there was 'not a British fighter in the sky, nor the bark of a single AA gun'.[17] To the horror of the crowds, Butterworth was not the target that morning. It was George Town itself!

In immaculate formation the bombers, without fighter escort, 'leisurely and unopposed, as if at practice, rained death down on the city',[18] which suddenly burst into flames. Casualties were everywhere, cluttering the streets and lanes in their groaning agony. No government orders for public safety had been issued, and no air raid warnings had been sounded. Such laxity should have been impossible from administrators whose homeland had been embroiled in a bloody war for survival for almost two and a quarter years.

Large numbers of people were hit while they were still standing. As they gazed up, a silent rain of bombs descended. There was no time to run, and no shelters to run to. A shuddering roar of explosions erupted with deafening intensity, as if every bomb had struck simultaneously. A second attack, with machine gunning, came after a lapse of twenty minutes, followed by a brief respite, and then, half an hour later all twenty-seven planes again swooped in low, and for the third time ravaged the town. These first attacks against the China Town areas of George Town on 'bloody' Thursday aimed at terrorising the Chinese population. The tactic worked!

Bombing of towns panicked the civilian population. By using small calibre fragmentation bombs, and machine-gunning people in the streets, they 'caused the helter-skelter evacuation of towns and villages, turning them into deserted ghost habitats'.[19] Repeated bombing raids of George Town and its close surrounding areas resulted in extensive damage. Capsized ships cluttered the pier and streets were confettied with roof tiles, whilst the nauseous stench of dead bodies permeated through the rubble of collapsed buildings.

> 'Most of the bombs exploded in the thickly populated native sections of George Town and the planes followed this up by screeching down low and machine gunning the streets.'[20]

Extensive damage to buildings, plus numerous civilian casualties terrorised the urban Chinese population. As the planes droned away, the dead and wounded lay in the fetid mid-day heat, amidst a curtain of dust that rose from the rubble of devastated buildings. Chaos prevailed.

> 'Terribly mutilated bodies are lying about the streets all over the town and there is nobody to move them. The Municipal services as such just don't exist and . . . looters have got to work and there is absolutely no law and order. The native *mata-mata* (police) have fled into the country and the few European inspectors are having a devil of a time.'[21]

The main police station in Penang Road received a direct hit, killing many Sikh policemen. The Memorial Clock Tower was shaken out of its vertical position, and an estimated 1,100 houses were destroyed. The attacks set half the town on fire and severely damaged dock installations and the business areas. The main fire station in Beach Street was virtually demolished and the principal water mains were extensively damaged.

> '. . . the town and harbour soon became a bonfire. The nightly rains, however, prevented the fire from spreading very much and the residential and out-lying districts, where the population had taken refuge, were not affected.'[22]

Most of the police vanished during the raids and by the 11th evening many of the Malay and Indian policemen had deserted. Morale crumbled in the face of stark reality, which was a direct contradiction of the confident 'Order' of the previous day, that had emblazoned George Town's colourful streets and declared: 'We are ready; our preparations have been made and tested.'[23]

On Friday 12th December George Town again was heavily bombed. As many people had already fled the town to surrounding countryside areas, or had stayed indoors, there were fewer casualties. The harbour and fishing villages close to the town were bombed and ferry boats and launches were machine-gunned, with heavy casualties among crews and fishermen.

The civilian population was unable to adjust to the nightmare, and in the ensuing panic was afforded little chance of doing so. The

Municipal Health Department's plans for removing the dead completely collapsed, as burial and demolition squad labourers disappeared and deserted immediately after the first raids. Rapid putrefaction happens in the tropical heat requiring burial within twenty-four hours. With no one available to remove the hundreds of stinking dead bodies that were strewn along the streets of George Town, air raid wardens were given the awesome task. Rats scurried about in the deserted streets, feasting on human flesh, and in forty different parts of the town, fires raged simultaneously as 'the fire fighting facilities available were utterly insufficient to deal with even a quarter of the number of outbreaks,'[24] although scattered units persisted to operate stoically.

The Chief Sanitary Inspector, J.E. Miller, estimated the total casualties as being not less than 5,000, and most of these occurred on 11th December. His department's role in the Passive Defence Service was to dispose of dead bodies, but when labourers flatly refused to assist and deserted, his

> 'staff themselves undertook the gruesome task of moving and disposing of the hundreds of mutilated bodies that were the victims of the indiscriminate bombing and machine gunning of the town. This department dealt with 483 bodies between 11th and 16th December and hundreds still remained. I would estimate the total casualties, both dead and wounded as not less than 5,000.'[25]

Many among the native population in Malaya played the role of disinterested spectators. Exceptions to this were many Straits Settlements Chinese who functioned stoically and bravely. English-speaking Chinese air raid wardens toiled magnificently in the confused havoc of George Town and commandeered any available sort of lorry or car to ferry the wounded to hospital or to first aid posts. They filled the gap where regular drivers had fled and other Volunteers and Defence Corps personnel, who knew how to drive, were elsewhere on duty.

> 'In every kind of vehicle about 850 wounded were rushed to the First Aid Posts and to the hospital. The others apparently were taken to their houses by their friends. At the First Aid Posts women of all nationalities set to work to bandage the most hideous wounds . . . the congregation of vehicles

was controlled by Air Raid Wardens . . . the wounded were taken to beds or laid on the floor . . . the Matron inspired all the nurses and auxiliary staff.

At five operating tables, surgeons worked throughout the day and night.

About 200 of the wounded were in such a desperate condition that they died within a few hours . . . All the private practitioners came to render their services, and more surgeons and doctors arrived the next day by air from Kuala Lumpur and Singapore. The whole organisation, under the charge of Doctor L.W. Evans, the Chief Medical officer, was splendidly efficient.'[26]

Sir Shenton Thomas succinctly described George Town's plight in his diary on 13th December:

'More air raids on Penang . . . No-one to bury the dead; water mains burst; fire engines out of action and fires still burning. Looting because people could not buy food, all shops shut. I asked whether we were going to defend the place or leave it. Percival replied that we shall defend to the last, to the best of our ability. Decided that I should advise European women and children to leave and other Europeans who wanted to.'[27]

Phillis Liddelow, then fifteen years old, 'was sitting for her School Certificate in a hall in the town . . . and with the rest of the candidates she sat out the massacre beneath the flimsy protection of her desk'.[28] Following the bombing, she recalled 'being rushed through the streets, in which vivid flames lingered, back to the house'[29] where she and her twelve year old sister Doris were staying with their Scots-Irish godparents. Phillis's godfather shot his five fox terriers, not wanting them to end up in some Chinese cooking pot, then they 'hurried down to the harbour, past piles of dead on whom kerosene had been poured, before they were set alight'.[30]

On Saturday the 13th eight Brewster Buffaloes of 453 Fighter Squadron were flown up from Singapore and landed at Butterworth. When 27 unescorted Japanese bombers attacked on the 13th, they were less successful and five of them were shot down. On the 14th three separate attempts to attack Penang were thwarted by RAF fighters, and after a half-hearted attack was made on Monday 15th, no more occurred.

The civilian population had little choice left to them and many of them 'streamed out of the town seeking safety in the country-side, and particularly at the foot of Penang Hill'.[31] Many went to a hurriedly set-up evacuation camp run with a voluntary staff of helpers. The government started distributing free food on 14th December from their enormous warehouse stocks, by which time bread had fallen into short supply as bakers had also left the town. On the *Malayan Gazette's* last day of publication — Friday 16th December — a prophesy-of-doom editorial was the theme of its swan-song:

> 'Is this the last day of Penang? Will the morrow bring alien troops to our shores? We, the staff of the *Malayan Gazette*, know definitely, however, that this is the last day of the paper . . . Good Luck and bless you all.'[32]

In contrast, the *Straits Times* in Kuala Lumpur and Singapore was enforced to observe strict press censorship during George Town's blitz, to the extent that 'the only hope of restoring public morale and Asiatic confidence in the Government was to make a frank and full disclosure of the facts'.[33]

This was not done, and British newspapers during this period surprisingly gave more space to America's role in the Far East.

> 'Malaya, like a poor relation, was accorded little attention except when there was a real surprise and these were nasty, like the fall of Penang.'[34]

F.D. Bisseker said that Penang had been 'bombed into impotency', and the civil population had 'evaporated in the most amazing manner. There was looting, pollution, 'complete disruption', dirt, stink, debris, rats, blood, and 'innumerable horrors which cannot be mentioned'.[35]

During the raids, contact with the Resident Counsellor and his senior assistants was impossible. Those embroiled in voluntary defence functions were left to do

> 'the best they could according to the way they viewed matters and having regard to the circumstances in which they were placed. There were, therefore, as may be imagined, many well-intentioned people giving directly opposing orders.'[36]

Some civilians were told to evacuate quickly and to take only what they could personally carry. Others were told to stay put. No one appeared to know what to do.

In the opinion of Mr M. Saravanamuthu the 'much-vaunted British prestige'[37] suffered irreparable damage with the collapse of administrative and municipal services when George Town was bombed. He was scathingly critical of British officials' actions during this time, and when looting reached a rampant level whilst various heads of departments were still in Penang, he accused them of 'hiding in their holes or homes, in terror of the Japanese bombs'.[38] Mr Saravanamuthu chose to overlook that it was a minority of officials who attempted to shoulder overwhelming responsibilities in such a hopeless situation. He also conveniently overlooked the advantage taken by many among the local population, who were in turn abetted by the desertion of municipal workers and the police force. It was easier for him to be belatedly critical of the British!

A Service Committee, comprising responsible local men and some Japanese civilians released from gaol, welcomed the first detachment of occupation troops, who landed from sampans at the Railway Pier during the night of 19th December 1941. They established a temporary military government headquarters in the Eastern and Oriental (E & O) Hotel on the outskirts of the city, which by that time resembled a city of the dead!

One year later, on 19th December 1942, the *Penang Shimbun* published an article to coincide with the first anniversary of Japanese landings on Penang, in which the paper, with its flair for propaganda opportunism and slanted misrepresentation of facts, concluded:

> 'As the first bombs crashed on Penang, British officials gave self-government to mobs and lawlessness erupted.'[39]

10:4 A Lust for Looting

For a short span of time, when towns and villages were evacuated and before Japanese troops arrived to establish their rough ad hoc authority, Malaya disintegrated into a paradise for looters. In contrast to the severity reached in some parts of the country, although Penang was more heavily bombed in comparison to other inland towns, it only suffered 'a limited measure of looting and that occurred only in and around the damaged areas',[40] where it first broke out during the morning of Friday 11th December.

When looting started in George Town on the 11th, British officials and heads of departments were still controlling affairs in Penang, but neither the Resident Commissioner, Mr L. Forbes, nor the Chief of Police took action to introduce effective preventative counter-measures to curb the upsurge of panic and lawlessness at that crucial time. Opportunities for looting in the semi-deserted and damaged parts of town were abundant, and beyond the resistance of many among the poor. Merchandise strewn into the streets from partially demolished shops and warehouses was theirs simply for the taking!

Police desertion invited disastrous consequences. Had this possibility been anticipated and a contingency made for an Auxiliary Police Force, with a strong European component, looting might have been lessened or even prevented in Penang. This had not been possible under the circumstances, however, as most Europeans had been compelled to join the Volunteers. Few remained available even for the Local Defence Corps, and this also was stationed outside the town area.

During the five days that George Town was bombed, from 11th to 15th December 1941, many civilians who were not involved with Passive Defence activities left the town and headed either for the suburbs or to the rural areas where supplies of food were adequate. Had it not been for the outbreak of looting and lawlessness within the town, they could have continued to stay there.

Ideal conditions for looting existed, particularly when bombed houses and godowns gaped open invitingly to those on the streets. Panic and desperation thus led to increased disorder, and many otherwise quite honest people, on finding that their own possessions had been looted, also resorted to theft.

Looting of damaged areas in George Town started on a small scale shortly after the first bomb attacks occurred. Air raid wardens' attempts to stop this were mostly ineffective as it was difficult for them to distinguish potential looters from those people who wanted to remove their own possessions out of the town for safe keeping elsewhere. George Town also was never completely deserted. Some shop and store owners remained to protect their property, as did people without belongings, or with no relatives and friends to go to, as they had nothing to gain by running.

> 'There were also the ricksha-pullers, and bullock-carters, the jagas, the vagabonds, the pedlars and the beggars. These were the people who became the first looters.'[41]

Following the second day's raids a period of pandemonium, mob rule and more generalised looting broke out. The first targets were the food and provision stalls in the Chowrasta Market. Soon everything became fair game, from general goods and hardware provisions, to jewellery, watches, clothing, liquor and cigarettes. Government rice godowns, customs warehouses, and large European-owned godowns were broken into. Looters worked with scavenging-locust proficiency, both by day and night. Residential houses were emptied of clothes, crockery, silver and furniture. Even bathroom fittings fetched a price. Churches were defiled as looters ransacked them of their silver ornaments, hymn books, bibles and benches. 'ARP wardens arrested some policemen in uniform who were leading some looters,'[42] and other ex-policemen, who had deserted during the initial stages of the bombing, discarded their uniforms and were either foremost among the looters, or stood guard to drive off rival gangs. Clashes between looters erupted, resulting in some deaths as looters ransacked each others' caches.

After the evacuation of European civilians and British troops from Penang to the mainland, looting would have been far more serious had it not been for the efforts of those members of the Passive Defence Services and the Volunteer Forces who elected to stay back and tried to maintain order until the Japanese arrived. Many air raid wardens also assisted with civil administration duties as well as trying to stop looting by assuming responsibilities of a volunteer police force. Although these formations were temporarily shocked into disorganisation following the first bombing raids, they rallied promptly and attempted to keep order in the best manner that they could.

Before European Volunteers evacuated the island, Captain Pooley paraded his 'D' Company at the Telok Bahang Semi-Deployment Camp, and gave his men a choice, either to follow him and others onto the mainland in a bid to stop the Japanese advance, or to remain in Penang. Only two or three decided to leave and the majority who stayed back were instructed to try and maintain some semblance of law and order in George Town.

'E' Company of the 3rd Battalion P & PW Volunteer Forces commanded by Captain A.S. Willweber, along with 'D' Company, then entrusted to the Penang Magistrates, Mr Lim Cheong Ean and Mr Lim Koon Teck, took up volunteer police duties and endeavoured to stop the looting in the main shopping and harbour districts by cordoning off these areas. Preventing unauthorised access to these places was nigh impossible, especially to Campbell and Kimberly Streets, which were also residential areas where people lived above their shop houses.

> 'The volunteer police were empowered to stop anyone moving goods, question them and confiscate such goods if ownership could not be satisfactorily proved. All such confiscated goods were stored at the Francis Light School Hall and soon there were large collections of motley goods from bags of rice and cases of milk, to bales of cloth and packets of cosmetics.'[43]

Such confiscated goods could only be moved on the written authority of the Penang Service Committee Chairman.

To deter would-be looters, the town area was patrolled by night, and rural areas by day. When chaos erupted in Ayer Hitam, due to shopkeepers' refusal to open for business for fear of looters, 'D' Company's arrival there stabilised tensions and gradually business was resumed. With the introduction of rice rationing, the rice godowns at Kampong Bahru were guarded day and night and rice was distributed on a card system. Looting was almost brought under control throughout George Town within two days of the European evacuation, and the Volunteers, under the guidance of the Penang Service Committee, assisted to rally the spirit and discipline of the fearful population as they waited in trepidation for the Japanese to arrive.

As British troops retreated southwards, scorched earth measures, aimed at denying the Japanese, worked hand-in-hand with the upsurge of lawlessness, looting and recriminations that spread the length and breadth of the country. In some areas these were to become particularly rife.

> 'Chinese gangs were foremost in the looting and then in rioting and terrorism . . . They worked mostly under cover of night and wore masks or masqueraded as Japanese soldiers. Torture was often included among the means to force victims to reveal the whereabouts of their valuables. Punjabis and Pathans were a close second to the Chinese: the Malays were not far behind.'[44]

Isolated farms were favourite targets for roving gangs of Indian robbers. These were made up of ex-policemen and detectives, as well as deserters from the Volunteers, most of whom were armed. Various sorts of weapons, and masses of ammunition, had been left by the British as they retreated hastily and these were collected up by the roving gangs who used them to their own advantage. Initially, the gangs were formed to protect themselves and their womenfolk in the kampongs, but soon they turned their hands to more lucrative vengeance raids and resorted to pillage and murder.

It was a time when the poorer elements within society became rich, and the rich became impoverished. Manual workers ate and drank expensive foods and liquors, and equipped their hovels with fine pieces of furniture, carpets, ornaments and paintings. Abandoned vehicles of all types either disappeared or were gutted. Gangs of mechanics either stripped these of anything that had resale or barter value, or quickly made them roadworthy again if this was possible.

Frontline Japanese soldiers were vicious and greedy looters who robbed hundreds of people as they passed through towns and villages. Watches and bicycles caught their fancy in particular, and their cruel actions struck terror into the hearts of the people in their wake.

Following the surrender of Singapore, a quick turn about officially occurred and the activities of looters became short-lived, as was the period of terror that they had inspired. Harsh retributive measures were introduced by the Japanese to curb looting. Those who were caught at it, or in possession of stolen goods, were publicly and summarily executed. Their heads were displayed on pikes at crossroads in towns, as a gruesome introduction to a method of law enforcement that would prevail throughout the succeeding three and a half years.

10:5 Evacuation of Penang and Consequences

Percival ordered two evacuations from Penang. The first was secretly organised to be executed during the night of 13/14th December 1941, and catered for all the 'bouche inutiles', comprising 650 European women and children who were still on the island, together with those who were either sick or wounded from the Military Hospital.

Brigadier C.A. Lyon, the Penang Fortress Commander, and the Resident Commissioner of Penang, Mr Leslie Forbes, were instructed to implement this, and although many European women who had served in the MAS were compelled to comply, and did so with feelings of humiliation – on leaving their Asian counterparts behind to face the music – it was a military decision, carried out under strict secrecy, and one that could not be disobeyed.

In contrast to this well documented decision, however, a phoned telegram was sent to Leslie Forbes on 13th December by Sir Shenton Thomas, with instructions that

> 'European males should not, repeat not, be encouraged to leave, and to all who stay of whatever race I send my sincere thanks for their courage and determination and my sympathy in this time of trial'.[45]

Some doubt therefore revolved around the identity of the first evacuation authenticator, although it has since been agreed that the civil government had little to do with it. The authenticator's identity paled into insignificance in the light of the evacuation's calamitous effect, particularly when it was realised that scant consideration had been given to attempting any evacuation of Asian civilians, as this was deemed impossible on account of there being insufficient transport to implement it. In the ensuing confusion and panic, no list of names was compiled to keep check upon those Europeans who were evacuated, neither was one made in respect of the more important Asians. The Resident Commissioner never knew who stayed back or who left, and many who did proceed to Singapore did so in the general belief that they would soon be able to return to Penang.

The second evacuation was carried out during the night of 16/17th December, and regardless of its subsequent adverse repercussions and stultifying effects on public confidence throughout the country, it was effectively a military decision arising from enforced defence strategy alterations. In this, the European Volunteers and nearly all the male European civilians on the island, plus a few women who had stayed back after the first evacuation, along with some influential Asians, accompanied the military forces on their southbound flight towards Singapore. With events increasingly turning against Percival's forces, the impending isolation of Penang and its facilities had fast become obvious. Lieut-General Sir Lewis Heath, as Commander of the 3rd Indian Corps, was therefore given discretionary powers to withdraw the Penang Garrison, and with it as many essential military stores as time and transportation would allow. On the 15th Heath issued evacuation orders, amid typhoid and cholera alerts, which bestowed precious little time for essential demolition works to be concluded and concerning which no centralised plan had yet been evolved.

Little was published in newspapers at the time regarding the evacuation of Penang, but its fall was soon realised in Singapore, by the incoming stream of refugees and by Japanese broadcasts in English, using the Penang Radio Station.

A proliferation of exaggerated rumours concerning the brutal treatment of European civilians by Japanese forces nurtured increasing disquiet among Europeans in Penang, and understandably prompted some of them to seek respite through hasty evacuation. Although such recourse was understandable, the manner in which it was surreptitiously organised and implemented was reprehensible, and evoked contempt and scorn among those who were forced to remain.

Without warning, only European women and children were secretly ordered out of Penang despite a previous firm undertaking from the civil authorities in Singapore that no discrimination would prevail should an evacuation become necessary. Asian women who had worked ungrudgingly as equals in the MAS, and shared the appalling working conditions at the hospital and first aid stations, realised with disbelief that they had been left in the lurch when they awoke on the morning of the 14th, to find that they had been deserted by their European counterparts, who had run 'away like thieves in the night'.[46]

People acted hastily and in panic. Many among them later expressed feelings of shame for their behaviour and hurried departure and for leaving those who had depended on them to face an unknown destiny. This was especially so when it was subsequently realised that the evacuation of Asian civilians had been officially disregarded, on account of there being insufficient transport available to cater for such large numbers. Secrecy and haste dictated actions. One woman at

5 p.m. on the 13th knew nothing of the evacuation, and chose to disregard stories of it as being panic rumours. Later, having arrived home up Penang Hill, she was phoned and ordered to report to the pier by 7 p.m., leaving her time only to hastily pack a few things and take the train down again. Children were bundled into the arduous night-time flight, firstly by a railway ferry named *Violet* from Penang to Prai, and thence by rail to Singapore, dressed only in what they were wearing at that time. The ferries were manned by fifty survivors from the *Prince of Wales* and *Repulse* who had been sent to Penang to operate them, as native crews had vanished. The *Violet* was subsequently bombed and sunk with the loss of all on board. To numerous European women, including those with children, their evacuation came as a complete and humiliating surprise. This was especially so to those who had worked alongside their Asian colleagues in hospitals, first aid posts, government centres, offices and canteens. To them the concept of running away was distasteful.

On 13th December, barely five days after hostilities commenced, the Governor, Sir Shenton Thomas, made a radio appeal to people in Singapore to provide temporary shelter for a trainload of evacuees from Penang. Many of the women with small children who subsequently arrived on the 15th morning did so without luggage, and to add to their plight they had nowhere to stay. Some were lucky and were extended hospitality by complete strangers, who offered them the use their homes. Others were less fortunate and fell prey to the callous manipulations of get-rich-quick exploiters and fortune seekers, whose actions were dictated by greed and nurtured on the distress of the temporarily homeless. Despite Churchill's explicit instructions to divest the responsibility of supporting 'useless mouths' in a war zone, they continued to stream into the 'bastion' island.

Tales of Penang's disorganisation spread without respite with the arrival of the first evacuees in Singapore. Some women with children had managed to bring luggage with them, whereas others recounted how they had been brusquely denied from doing so on reaching the wharf, prior to embarkation for the mainland at the outset of their long and perilous journey. No food had been provided, and very little water, throughout the two-day nightmare train journey south, and in that brief span of time the image of an equitably-run colony, which had been meticulously nurtured by the British Colonial administration over the past 150 years, was dashed to pieces by the bungled evacuation arrangements. The administration was suddenly exposed as being incapable of reacting to changing circumstances of war, and far too many individuals elevated the importance of their personal safety and circumstances to the detriment of their given responsibilities and their duty towards people who had depended on them.

Every woman who was accompanied by a child was promptly taken and put on a steamer bound for Batavia. Those who arrived alone were also given no choice and were ordered to remain in Singapore. There was no appeal to these decisions. Many women, thus earmarked for Batavia, knew no one there and had hoped to be able to stay in Singapore a while, or be allowed to return to England. To ensure their compliance, the women and children were locked into railway carriages, through the windows of which they were given refreshments. Friends brought clothes for them, and at 10 a.m. on 15th December they were embarked on the SS *Nellore*, which sailed later that day for Batavia, and thence to Australia. Prior to leaving, these hapless evacuees, and earlier stalwarts of a fast dissipating era, were only allowed to send a pre-worded telegram to their husbands which starkly informed them that they were 'Leaving now for unknown destination.'[47]

Although five days of unprecedented death and devastation delivered a stunning blow to the morale of the Asian population in Penang, it was at the hands of their self-professed defenders that their morale was shaken to its very core. The stark and sudden realisation that Penang was at the total mercy of the Japanese and virtually defenceless from the outset, came as a shock in the face of earlier and frequently publicised placations to the contrary. The worthlessness of the no-discrimination guarantee was a profound revelation in duplicity, which was to have a long term effect on their confidence in the British, particularly after it was realised that the military commander of Penang had secretly ordered out all European women and children, plus some sick and wounded.

On 14th December Municipal Councillors of George Town warned the Fortress Commander, Brigadier C.A. Lyon, of the pending failure of civil administration which would likely result in the outbreak of cholera and typhoid epidemics, arising from the fouling of the water catchment area and the breakdown of sanitation and conservancy services. On the 15th at 11 a.m., Brigadier Lyon received orders to evacuate the garrison by sea during the night of 16/17th December. Acting on information that 11th Division had been forced to withdraw the previous day, to a position south of the Muda River, and that the RAF had abandoned Butterworth Airport, the small garrison of regular forces and volunteers which had already been depleted by most of the fighting troops having been sent to complement forces on the mainland, started to evacuate Penang at 11 p.m. on 16th December, amid heightened threats of pending outbreaks of cholera and typhoid.

Preparations to evacuate Penang island started on the 16th morning when the non-European members of the Straits Settlement Volunteer Force were mustered in the town and were given one of three choices. They could go home and throw away their uniforms, or they could enlist in an Emergency Civil Police Force under the command of selected Asian officers from the Volunteer Forces, or they could depart for Singapore with the European volunteers. Approximately 500 volunteered to take on the responsibilities of an Emergency Police Force in Penang, and following the conclusion of the evacuation, they tried to keep law and order as best they could in the town, until it was surrendered to the Japanese. It was not unnatural that the majority chose to remain on the island with their families, and only a handful of them elected to go to Singapore. This decision to stay soon became the epicentre surrounding racial discrimination allegations, although the official reasoning that Asians would suffer less by remaining in their homes in Penang, rather than crowding helter-skelter down into Singapore, was probably a correct assumption.

Civilians European males were told to report to the wharf at 5 p.m. and not to tell anyone about it so that the area would not become cluttered with Asians who also wanted to leave. Although no cars were permitted, some European mining officials took them, and as much luggage as they could, even to the extent of using up valuable ship space with their tennis rackets and golf clubs. Many evacuees, however, walked to the wharf. Montague Selfe, a Penang businessman, was refused entry into his bombed Beach Street office, from which he wanted to collect some business records and his wife's jewellery from the safe, by Indian troops who were under orders to shoot looters.

From 7 p.m. onwards, in a downpour of heavy rain, crowds of cars hustled for position around the pier. The alert was sounded, and for the first time at night the Japanese tried to bomb, but poor visibility fortunately blotted out their potential targets and another slaughter was averted. The Penang evacuation regrettably had the appearance of favouring Europeans and rich Asians. The poorer classes of Asians were 'left behind to face the music'.[48] Many Chinese, on realising that only Europeans were being evacuated, became resentful and bitter over the lack of organisation that had allowed this. Many Asians were refused permission to embark on those ferries that were operating and were left with no alternative other than to carry their pitiful few belongings and head for the countryside.

Evacuees were crowded onto ferries, which set out to steam down the increasingly hazardous west coast towards the sanctuary of Singapore. The Harbour Board ferries, *Bagan* and *Kulim*, were among the craft involved on this first leg of the final evacuation of Penang. They took the evacuees only as far as Port Swettenham. The *Kulim*, however, broke down off Pulau Rimau, and when all passengers and crew had been transferred to a Royal Navy mine sweeper, she was

> 'sunk by shell fire and the first shot fired went through the Commanding Officer's motor car which was lashed on deck. This caused a great cheer to come from the other ships.'[49]

The *Bagan*, commanded by Captain A.L. McLeod, ferried approximately 300 evacuees, and was 'loaded down to the gunwales with human cargo'.[50] Her departure was delayed for about two hours when she was forced to anchor and sit out a Sumatra, which suddenly blew in across the Malacca Straits. On arrival at the Shell Wharf at Port Swettenham, all evacuees and crews were entrained for the second part of their journey to Singapore.

Among those who did not evacuate from Penang with the other Europeans were Dr E.B. Evans, the Chief Medical Officer at the Penang General Hospital, Dr L.W. McKern and Captain F.W. Harvey, who was the officer in charge of the Salvation Army in Penang. A number of others also resisted being evacuated, especially among those who were working in the hospital and in the censor's office. Inspired by Dr Evans' stoicism, the European theatre sister from the General Hospital refused to leave, as did two Dutch nurses who volunteered to remain to care for the sick and injured. Other Europeans, including hospital nurses, had to go and were given no choice by the Resident Commissioner, who ordered them to do so. Eurasian and Chinese telephone girls were given a choice either to stay or leave. The Salvation Army officers elected to remain with their congregations, following the example set by Captain Fred Harvey.[51] Throughout Penang's crisis the General Hospital functioned without a break, due to the unfailing influence and determination of Dr Evans, and by his contrivance the medical staff were paid their December wages. Dr Evans was awarded an OBE after the war for his services, and even the Japanese, when they arrived on the island, appreciated his good works. Although he expressed his dire reservations, they allowed him to live in the hospital as an internee, so that he could continue working for the benefit of the sick. Dr McKern took refuge in his bungalow basement (the present Socfin bungalow) at Tanjong Bunga and remained hidden there by his servants for over two years. He secretly operated a radio and made transmissions to Allied forces, but was subsequently given away by his Malay driver and was executed by the Japanese.

Although Churchill was condemningly critical of the Penang evacuation, and the First Sea Lord scathingly sought in it a scapegoat when he acclaimed that 'the rot appears to have started there',[52] official strategy cannot be overlooked and that required maximum troop availability for Singapore's defence, which was considered second to none in importance at that time. It was wrong to blame the European women for the government's evacuation decision, as they were never consulted. Equally, it was wrong to blame the European men for following the orders to leave Penang along with the military forces.

Blame for such an evacuation cannot be expected to burden the conscience of individual Europeans who were merely obeying orders. F.H. Grummit, the proprietor of North Malayan Papers Limited, was sorry to have to leave Penang, as was Dr Fisher, the Senior Physician at the Penang General Hospital, who could not see why he should do so. If fault is to be apportioned then much of it should rest on the shoulders of those who were in charge. Dilution of such blame, as was later attempted, among people whose only fault had been to follow the orders given to them to participate in it, was unjust escapism. In fairness to those who were told to leave, and were criticised subsequently for doing so, many of them thought that the move would be only for a temporary period, and that their services were needed for the defence of all-important Singapore.

In the rush to condemn the European evacuation of Penang, there are some important and decisive factors which cannot be ignored. Although the order was dictated by military secrecy, and priority was given to Europeans, there were other launches and trains running for several days and these carried passengers free of charge if they were unable to afford the fare. Every Eurasian and Asian who reportedly wished to leave Penang island had an opportunity of doing so, and large numbers did avail themselves of this. Although broadcasts from Singapore made the non-European community in Penang quickly aware of the evacuation, they did not rush to the pier. Last but not least is the consideration that attempts to prolong the defence of Penang would have resulted in failure, and the annihilation of an already exhausted division of troops on the mainland following the Gurun defeat, as well as the probable wholesale slaughter of the civilian population that remained on the island. Evacuation at least averted these disasters.

The evacuation of European women and children on 13th December, along with hospital patients, was a shock to both those who were forced to depart, as well as to those who stayed. Some Europeans were ashamed of what they were forced into doing and felt that they had deserted people who depended on them. No choice was given, however, and launches ferried evacuees, under cover of darkness, to the mainland. It was the subsequent mention of the successful evacuation of Penang that left a bad taste in everyone's mouth, as this gave an impression that discrimination, in its ugliest guise, had been used against Asians and worse still that the British had reneged on their pledge to defend them.

The editorial of the *Malayan Gazette*, on December 16th, voiced an abandoned populace's stunned shock and disbelief in being entrapped by the violent events that had engulfed them.

> 'People in Penang are still stunned by the sudden invasion of the Japanese and are still shocked by the desertion of the British. Has Britain really deserted us? Then why have her troops been evacuated from the island? – to leave us to fend for ourselves?'[53]

In contradiction to the Order of the Day which had publicly proclaimed confidence, strong defences and sufficient weapons, when the war was barely one week old the invincible tuans departed, much to the distress of the native population who can be forgiven for thinking that their benefactors

> '"thought only of saving no skins but their own", leaving the natives to face the Japanese, "as if they didn't care a damn what happened to them".'[54]

The news that Penang had been lost took three days to reach London and caused little reaction there. In Singapore, however, the effect was far more evident, and portrayed the Japanese in a new and terrifying light, in contrast to previous British propaganda. On 22nd December Duff Cooper broadcast from Singapore an ill-worded and inaccurate account of what had happened, in which he prevaricated that due to Japanese successes,

> 'it had been necessary to evacuate many of the civilian population. We can only be thankful so many people have been safely removed (from Penang).'[55]

This official misrepresentation gave cause for much consternation throughout the country, particularly as Cooper failed to clarify that he had only referred to the European civilian population, and that Asians had been virtually ignored.

No doubt the renowned British political pomposity of that era condoned, in some circles, the disgracefully distorted picture that Cooper's broadcast conveyed, elevating the European evacuation of Penang to an accomplishment, while giving scant regard to those Asians who had been denied similar facilities. The damage was quickly done. An angry Sir Shenton Thomas was aghast that such an evacuation could have been described as a success by a Resident Minister, and attempted to restore some element of confidence among

Asian community leaders. Anticipating adverse reactions, and amid a rising furore of indignation among many Europeans, Sir Shenton hurriedly arranged a meeting with leading representatives of the Chinese, Indians and Malays in Singapore on the afternoon of 20th December, to offer them some reassurance in respect of future events, and to apologise to them for what had already transpired. Although Sir Shenton denied prior knowledge of the evacuation, the seeds of doubt had been sown and 'a wave of defeatism swept down to Singapore'[56] and attached itself to people in all walks of life.

Sir Shenton was equally concerned that the loss of Penang would adversely affect the opinion of Rulers in other States and of their people in general, and that the Malays would also soon realise that Great Britain was incapable of upholding her treaty commitments, just as the predominantly Chinese population in Penang now knew. Concern about adverse Chinese opinion was also shared by S.W. Jones, the Colonial Secretary, and A.B. Jordan, the Secretary of Chinese Affairs, both of whom volunteered to try and get through to Penang, which by now had been completely cut off by the advancing Japanese.

In an article written for the *Penang Gazette* on 9th September 1945, M. Saravanamuthu criticised the secretive evacuation as being 'a disgraceful betrayal of the general public of Penang'.[57] Others thought quite differently, however. Among these were Mr T.J. Rea, a former MCS officer, and his colleague Donald Chadwick, who was a chartered accountant in Penang and also an NCO in the Volunteers. Both of them took part in the evacuation and realised that as the island was indefensible, evacuation was the only sensible course of action to take under the circumstances.

The stampede from Penang was looked upon by some as being akin to a dirty trick by the British. Rumours of Asian women being chased off launches at bayonet point were circulated. When only European evacuees arrived at the Singapore Railway Station, to be welcomed by the Governor as if they were conquering heroes, many people were angered and interpreted this as substantiation of the rumours. It is not surprising that some Asians were not initially ill-disposed towards the Japanese, who were also quick to exploit what had transpired by propaganda broadcasts over the Penang

Broadcasting Station. Notwithstanding all criticism, hardly more could have been done during the short time available. Had thousands of Asians decided to leave, lack of transport would have made it impossible to take them to Singapore. Had they reached Singapore, then there would have been insufficient facilities and accommodation available for them there.

Various attempts were made to contact the Japanese High Command to inform them of the European evacuation and to request cessation of bombing. Penang's Resident Commissioner, Mr Leslie Forbes, prior to his departure wrote to the Japanese commander and requested him to afford good treatment to those people who remained behind. Mr M.J. Thorpe, the pre-war Municipal Engineer in Penang and also one of the founders of the Penang Wireless Society who established the Amateur Penang Radio Station ZHJ, made contact with the Japanese headquarters in north Malaya, and appealed to them to stop bombing Penang following the evacuation. Also, Japanese detainees at the Penang gaol were released as soon as the evacuation was concluded and one of them made his way to Fujiwara Kikan'a headquarters in Sungei Patani and advised them that the British had left the island. It was later learnt that Mr Ivan Allen, an apprentice jockey under the trainer George Macgill, went to Sungei Patani on the 18th, accompanied by a Japanese named Izumi who had been a pre-war barber in a saloon in Argyll Road. They also told the Japanese that the island had been evacuated.

Two days after the British had evacuated Penang Major Andrews of the 1/8th Punjab, along with 170 British and Indian other ranks, rowed across the channel from the mainland and landed on the island, under the impression that they would be able to reinforce the garrison there. On arrival, Major Andrews, accompanied by two of his officers, went to the General Hospital, from where they were directed to the Penang Service Committee's HQs. It was agreed that his men would be fed and housed at the large Penang residency, provided that by daylight they would all stay indoors and he would surrender his men to the Japanese when they arrived to occupy the island.

In addition to these various approaches it was decided by members of the Penang Service Committee that the British Union Jack should be hauled down, as an additional indication that the island had in effect capitulated to the Japanese. Although Mr M. Saravanamuthu was opposed to doing this, as Chairman of the Service Committee he was obliged to do so, and with the aid of Mr R.S. Gopal, who climbed up a rope ladder, the flag was brought down.

The 17th to the 19th of December were hectic days for members of the Penang Service Committee as they attempted to restore law and order in the town and on the island. They set up their headquarters at 10 Scott Road, the former residence of the Penang Municipal Engineer, Mr M.J. Thorpe, and held meetings there twice daily. At a meeting on Wednesday the 17th, arrangements were made with those Penang Volunteers who had remained on the island to be pressed immediately into service as a Voluntary Police Force for the purpose of maintaining law and order, guarding rice godowns, petrol dumps and water reservoirs. The Eurasian Volunteer Company, commanded by Captain A.S. Willwebber, set up their headquarters in the Francis Light School in Perak Road, and the Chinese Company, commanded jointly by Lim Cheong Ean and Lim Koon Teck, moved to Ayer Hitam to where many of the Chinese had fled for safety. The Service Committee published a daily bulletin in which they advised the public on ways in which they could cooperate with their ad hoc authority so that there would be some semblance of order until the Japanese took over. Such actions, it was later acknowledged, prevented Penang from being afflicted with the initial mass executions and atrocities that accompanied Japanese forces' arrival and occupation of other towns in Malaya.

Mr E.A. Stains, a pre-war Controller of Posts in Penang, and one of those Europeans who did not evacuate, praised Mr Saravanamuthu as being a driving force as the Chairman of the Penang Service Committee. Due to his dedication a threatened outbreak of typhoid and cholera was averted, rice and petrol stocks were safeguarded, law and order were preserved and the innumerable requirements of a city in distress were attented to. For three days Saravanamuthu issued instructions, urging the people of Penang to adhere to law and order until the Japanese arrived. On the 19th, when the Penang Wireless Station was made operable by connecting it to the hospital's auxiliary electricity plant, an appeal was sent to the Japanese:

> 'This is Penang calling. Penang calling the Japanese Headquarters in North Malaya. Penang has been evacuated by the British. There are no more troops or any defences whatsoever in Penang. Please refrain from bombing Penang.'[58]

The broadcast was transmitted in Japanese by one of the Japanese residents who had been released from the Penang gaol, and was repeated at half-hourly intervals until 4 p.m. on the 19th, when two companies of Japanese troops arrived on the island.

Japanese troops were confined to their billets for the first night of the occupation, which probably spared the population some of the horrors that can accompany the early stages of any military domination. On the 20th Mr Hiroyasu arrived and started to function as the Japanese Civil Administrator to Penang. The Service Committee was asked to continue temporarily, but to also arrange for separate committees to be formed for each of the four main communities. When these started to function on 23rd December 1941, the Penang Service Committee was disbanded.

10:6 Scorched Earth — Omissions; Implications

Scorched earth measures in Penang were ineffective and palpably clumsy. No detailed demolition plans were drawn up prior to the Japanese invasion, and two days were positively insufficient time in which to organise and carry out effective demolitions, especially with a depleted staff and without the assistance of civilian labour.

Despite the imposed restraints, Brigadier A.C. Lyon did manage to arrange for a considerable amount to be carried out at very short notice. Fixed defences, including the bunker sites dotted over the Batu Maung hills, as well as ammunition stocks in magazines were destroyed. Small weapons were withdrawn and petroleum and oil were run to waste. British Army engineers wrecked machinery at the Prai Power Station, and buildings and installations at the Civil Airport were severely damaged, as was much equipment and machinery belonging to civil organisations. The Eastern Smelting Company

Works were destroyed, and by wrecking telegraph instruments at Penlaga, the direct cable link with India and Great Britain was put out of action. Some serious omissions, however, did occur in the haste of events, and these had grave consequences. They also gave the enemy a tactical and moral advantage.

At least one oil installation was left intact, as were large quantities of tin, oil, petrol, and warehouses full of rubber, all raw materials that Japan desperately needed. Huge stores of rice and other foodstuffs were also left, plus 24 seaworthy motorised vessels. The Penang Broadcasting Station was not destroyed and an attempt to mine the southern channel was unsuccessful.

The defection of a large proportion of the native labour force during the bombing raids had a considerable adverse effect on the implementation of denial plan activities and made their completion, in the short time provided, almost impossible. Demolition activities were also severely frustrated as some of those in charge evacuated the scene more swiftly than they should have, in view of their position and responsibilities.

On 11th December Sir Shenton Thomas instructed Mr F.D. Bisseker, as Chairman of the Eastern Smelting Company, to remove all tin from the island, which was an impossible feat at that point in time. With a diminished labour force after the first bombings, not only was the physical removal of these stocks impossible, but there were not even enough workers to throw the stocks into the sea before the evacuation on the 16th occurred. A valuable present of tin was therefore left for the enemy, who took over 1,299 tons of refined tin in ingot form, plus another 1,700 tons in the form of alloy, slag or fume in the furnaces. Bisseker was highly critical of the incomplete demolition of tin smelting works in Penang, and after the war continued his pre-war criticism of the government. On 2nd September 1958 he wrote:

> '. . . there seemed to be some at the head of affairs who had no conception of what it meant to be at war. It amazed me that the Governor should go home on leave for a period of some months . . . leaving in charge as officer administering the government a man . . . who on one occasion . . . said publicly that the building of air raid shelters for the general public was too expensive.'[59]

Time constraints, combined with panicky haste and a reluctance to destroy private property, brought about a serious failure to scuttle an assortment of boats that cluttered the eastern section of Penang harbour. Among these were 24 self-propelled craft, several dozen junks, some sampans, tongkangs, other ferries and sailing craft and many crudely constructed barges and rafts that had been deserted by their native crews. Most of these were left intact, and many among them were of sufficient size to enable the Japanese to ferry their troops southwards along the coast, to mount repeated flanking attacks against Percival's retreating forces, thus contributing to the eventual fate of Malaya. The Penang boats, it was subsequently confirmed in a report from Singapore on 4th January 1942, were most useful supplements to the 40 or more craft that the Japanese had already used at the Singora and Patani landings, and had carried overland to the Alor Star river, where they were reassembled and relaunched.

The Penang Broadcasting Station, the most powerful in the Far East at that time, was surprisingly left undestroyed. Only its valves were put out of action and the Japanese were quickly able to reinstate them after taking over the island, and used the station to spread anti-British propaganda and to broadcast threatening messages to Singapore of their intention to bomb the city. Incredible as it may seem, no one was told to smash the radio transmitters and when Penang radio came on the air asking, 'Hullo Singapore. How do you like our bombing?', despondancy increased as morale waned.

Millions of dollars held by banks in Penang became spoils of war in the hands of the Japanese as soon as they arrived. Only one bank — the Hongkong and Shanghai Banking Cooperation — had the good sense to get money off the island, to the credit of their manager Mr N. De P. Fussey, who evacuated with $10 million in his bags and cases, which were thrown hurriedly into the back of his car. To escape to the mainland with this valuable cargo, however, he was forced to don a soldier's uniform. Thus some funds reached Singapore safely.

It was only after the fall of Penang, on 19th December 1941, that an official scorched earth policy was formulated for mainland Malaya. This was still left very much to the discretion of local commanders. It involved draining off or burning millions of gallons of petrol, and destroying stores of rubber as well as scuttling and sinking tin dredges. The policy involved massive wastage. The public were invariably allowed to help themselves, and in its wake it left a wave of squalor and destruction that stretched throughout the length of the country.

1. *Malayan Gazette*, part of editorial of last edition on Friday 16th December 1941.
2. *Who Dies Fighting* by Angus Rose, p.26.
3. *Tales from the South China Seas* edited by Charles Allen, ch.3, p.89.
4. *The Civil Defence of Malaya* by Sir George Maxwell KBE, CMG, Part 1, 'The Volunteers', p.12–13.
5. Ibid, p.17.
6. Ibid, Part 2, 'Action', p.37.
7. Ibid, Part 2, 'The Passive Defence Services', p.24.
8. Ibid, p.24.
9. Ibid, Part 2, 'Miscellaneous Services', p.33.
10. Ibid, Part 2, 'The Passive Defence Services', p.46.
11. Ibid, p.46.
12. *Crowded Hour* by Sjovald Cunyngham-Brown, ch.9, p.85.
13. *70 Days to Singapore* by Stanley L. Falk, ch.4, p.75.
14. *The Fall of Singapore* by Frank Owen, ch.3, p.38.
15. *The Civil Defence of Malaya* by Sir George Maxwell KBE, CMG, p.42.
16. *In 70 Days. The Story of Malaya* by E.M. Glover, ch.6, p.92.
17. *Sinister Twilight (The Fall of Singapore)* by Noel Barber, ch.3, p.54.
18. *Women Beyond the Wire* by Lavinia Warner and John Sandilands, ch.3, p.28.
19. *Malaya Upside Down* by Chin Chee Onn, ch.1, p.7,
20. *Out in the Mid-Day Sun. Singapore 1941–5* by Kate Caffrey, ch.3, p.79.
21. *In 70 Days. The Story of Malaya* by E.M. Glover, ch.7, p.105.
22. *The Sara Saga* by M. Saravanamuthu, ch.7, p.84.
23. *Sinister Twilight (The Fall of Singapore)* by Noel Barber, ch.3, p.54.
24. *In 70 Days. The Story of Malaya* by E.M. Glover, ch.8, p.111.
25. *Penang Past and Present, 1786–1963. A Historical Account of the City of George Town Since 1786*, p.81. (Refers to Annual Report 1946 by J.E. Miller, Chief Sanitary Inspector.)
26. *The Civil Defence of Malaya* by Sir George Maxwell KBE, CMG, p.43.
27. *Shenton of Singapore. Governor and Prisoner of War* by Brian Montgoery, ch.6, p.93.
28. *Women Beyond the Wire* by Lavinia Warner and John Sandilands, ch.3, p.28.
29. Ibid.
30. Ibid.
31. *The Civil Defence of Malaya* by Sir George Maxwell KBE, CMG, p.44.
32. *Malayan Gazette*, Friday 16th December 1941, extract from editorial comment.
33. *The Civil Defence of Malaya* by Sir George Maxwell KBE, CMG, p.76.
34. *Out in the Mid-Day Sun. Singapore 1941–5* by Kate Kaffrey, ch.5, p.102.
35. Ibid, ch.4, p.88.
36. *In 70 Days. The Story of Malaya* by E.M. Glover, ch.8, p.111.
37. *Sunday Gazette*, 9th September 1945, 'Penang's Nightmare' by M. Saravanamuthu (Managing Editor).

Hongkong & Shanghai Banking Corporation.

KUALA LUMPUR.

16th Dec 1941.

Dear Rab,

I have posted a letter to Cardiff ~~today~~ to day in the hope that he will hear some news of my whereabouts but I shall be surprised if he gets it as we have had no mail for almost a week.

I enclose a copy which will give you an idea of what we have done.

I propose to go to Singapore to morrow night with all the Secs as I hear it is hopeless to attempt to return to Penang; it was my intention to do so at once not that there was any work actually requiring tq two but to stand by with Cardiff. After 23 hours on the road with practically no food and my experiences in the last week I feel I cant take any more until the reaction has worn off, it is the immediate panic amongst the natives which is so big a strain. I trust you will understand.

I left with $445450 in Notes, which I shall probably hand over to this Office. $2051800 in Bearer Bonds, All Secs, Safe Custody packets except very large ones, the Securities Registers and the General Ledger Balance books I could get no more on the car and all my kit is in Penang still.

When we can get a few anti aircraft guns to defend our aerodromes we shall be able to hold our own but at present the Japs come and go as they like from what I have seen. Yours sincerely,

N. DE P. FUZZEY

Hongkong & Shanghai Banking Corpn K.L., letter dated 16.12.41 to 'Dear Rab' from N. de P. Fuzzey. (By courtesy of Group Archives, HSBC, Hongkong.)

BROUGHT FROM PENANG:

1. General Ledger Balance Book
2. The Securities Register (2)
3. Safe Custody Records Books with 41 Safe Custody packages
4. All securities with the exception of Title Deeds and their respective Insurance Policies.
5. All Bearer Bonds.
6. War Savings Certificates.
7. Travellers' Cheques in hand (Blank Forms)
8. "Take out" of Current Account Ledger balances of the 10th instant.
9. Warrants covering 655 tons of Refined Tin.
10. Sundry Files.
11. $761,410.- in Currency Notes.

LEFT IN PENANG.

All records other than the above together with:-

Cash	$162,849.08
Revenue Stamps in Hand	$ 710.34
Postage Stamps in Hand	$ 310.01.

List of securities taken from Penang to Singapore by Mr N. de P. Fuzzey. (By courtesy of Group Archives, HSBC, HK.)

COPY:

Kuala Lumpur,

Tuesday, 16/12/41.

Dear Cardiff,

I hope you received my wire which I sent off at 8.30 last night - Monday - saying arrived safely etc., I endeavoured to send you two messages en route but once on this side one enters an area of such great activity that it is hopeless to attempt anything which one might do under normal circumstances.

We arrived at the jetty and had to wait four hours before I got on the Ferry - that was a strain but we had no alarms.

We left at 11.55 p.m. and on getting over we motored until 3 a.m. when we reached Parit Buntar.

I sat on a chair and tried to sleep until 6.30 in a shack of sorts.

Just then the air raid warning went and I found myself under a building with the notes which I slept on - thanks to the Syce. All clear went after some Japs passed over, but, before long the alarm went again when I dumped the notes in an incinerator [for safety] and left the boxes in the car.

We eventually set off and every few minutes I realised we were getting closer to real war.

It was a "windy" situation. We stopped for breakfast at Kuala Kangsar where I felt very worried owing to the congestion of traffic.

We eventually entered Ipoh at 12.30 at the same time as a number of Jap planes. The second car ahead of me had been driven by a houseboy (in 2nd gear'') for miles, the poor lad was not fit to drive neither I understand did he have a license! He looked up at the Japs, failed to take a corner and crashed. We stopped to pull him out but by then they began to machine gun the roads and bombs fell although not actually near us. I took a header into a ditch and the Syce crawled behind a tree with the notes and a fire extinguisher. We survived all that and during the lull drove off in the car to a nearby house; there we unloaded all the securities and chucked them under a house which seemed the only thing to do with machine gun fire all round. After this show we drove on to the bank where I found Ralston shut in with many people. I understood from him Ipoh Office were not keen on taking over any more responsibilities under the circumstances and from what I saw in Ipoh I feel sure it will not be long before all the local shops and people run as they

Kuala Lumpur 16.12.41, letter to Cardiff from N. de P. Fuzzey.

did in Penang. I decided at once to drive on here and arrived at 6 p.m. it was a great relief to get all the things locked up. If I can advise you that to do at present it is for you all to send your cars to this side with as much as possible; I would not hesitate to buy a sampon in view of the rush there may be if the final getaway is left to the Local Authorities who did nothing to speak of from the beginning. Will you tell Carey not to sacrifice anything in order to save any of my things should you have to clear out. I have heard from all sides it is impossible to return just now and unless Rab has other plans I am going down to Singapore to-morrow with all our stuff. I shall have a certain amount to do with the papers in any case and I shall be of more use than trying to get through congested roads etc. I am feeling the strain a good deal today. My Syce was a grand fellow and on every occasion he did the right thing.

All good luck and I will carry on with any Penang business which crops up until I return or you get out and join us.

Yours,

(Sgd.) N. de P. Fuzzey.

To Cardiff from N. de P. Fuzzey (contd).

38. Ibid.
39. *Penang Shimbun*, 19th December 2602.
40. *Malaya Upside Down* by Chin Kee Onn, ch.3, p.17.
41. Ibid, ch.3, p.18.
42. *Sara Saga* by M. Saravanamuthu, ch.7, p.84.
43. Ibid, ch.7, p.88.
44. *The Chinese in Malaya* by Victor Purcell CMG, Ph.D., ch.7, p.247–8.
45. *Shenton of Singapore. Governor and Prisoner of War* by Brian Montgomery, ch.6, p.93.
46. *Sara Saga* by M. Saravanamuthu, ch.7, p.86.
47. *The Civil Defence of Malaya* — 'The Method of Evacuation. Penang (European Women and Children)' by Sir George Maxwell KBE, CMG, p.108.
48. *In 70 Days. The Story of Malaya* by E.M. Glover, ch.6, p.101.
49. Letter from Captain A.L. McLeod (retired) to the author in 1986.
50. Ibid.
51. Letter dated 18th November 1987 from Brigadier Arthur R. Harvey (retired) to the author, advising that Commissioner Fred Harvey, his brother, had died in March 1987, having been admitted to hospital on Boxing Day 1986.
52. *Penang Past and Present 1786–1963*. A Historical Account of the City of Georgetown since 1786, p.82.
53. Editorial comment in the *Malayan Gazette* on Friday 16th December 1941.
54. *Out in the Mid-Day Sun. Singapore 1941–5* by Kate Caffrey, ch.4, p.84.
55. *Sinister Twilight (The Fall of Singapore)* by Noel Barber, ch.3, p.55.
56. Ibid, ch.3, p.56.
57. *Sunday Gazette*, 9th September 1945 — 'Penang's Nightmare' by M. Saravanamuthu.
58. *Sara Saga* by M. Saravanamuthu, ch.7, p.92.
59. *Singapore. Too Little Too Late* by Ivan Simson, ch.13, p.124. (Extract from letter from Mr F.D. Bisseker to Mr I. Simson dated 2nd September 1958.)

CHAPTER ELEVEN: A DREAM ENDS

11:1 Retreat to the Bastion

Throughout December 1941 the quick succession of British withdrawals was startling. Jitra was lost after brief fighting, with heavy casualties, only four days into the war, and in this action the 15th Brigade was reduced to a quarter of its fighting strength. The 11th Indian Division was routed and was no longer fit to do battle without reorganisation and rest, but had to continue to withdraw and fight without respite as there were no other troops available to relieve them. Jitra was a major disaster for British forces in Malaya and one from which they never recovered. Front line defence preparations at Jitra were described by a visiting agent to one of the plantations in that vicinity as being 'just paltry'. He continued:

> 'If those are the main defences of Malaya, thank God we've got a navy.'[1]

The most serious consequence of this early reversal was the effect it had on morale, combined with the realisation that the

> 'Japanese mental approach was too brutal and professional for the more "civilised" British — who must always do "the right thing"'.[2]

When Major-General Murray-Lyon was forced to withdraw his men from the Gurun positions he did so with disastrous consequences. Some of his units, being unaware of the withdrawal, were still in position the following day and were then only able to leave in small groups and with the loss of much of their equipment.

Following the decision to abandon Penang there was no logical military argument in favour of trying to hold the Muda River line of defence. This was especially so as the Japanese were able to make use of a variety of boats and crafts that they had seized intact in the Penang harbour

> 'in which they crowded troops and set off to invade the mainland some forty or fifty miles down the coast. They crept inshore at dead of night in twenty different isolated places — most of them swamp lands — and before the allied defenders knew what had happened, the Japanese had established themselves in some force,'[3]

outflanking defending troops and cutting off their line of retreat. As soon as their presence was realised, they adeptly and speedily slipped away in various directions, but always pointedly heading eastwards and southwards. Encircling tactics were constantly used which stranded the static pillboxes and strong points that had been conventionally, and conveniently as far as the Japanese were concerned, constructed along the only main road leading south.

Wrong tactical decisions escalated in frequency and consequence as communications broke down and retreating troops were cut off and outflanked by the unrelenting invaders, who inflicted mounting casualties with their skillful enveloping tactics. When the first Japanese tanks arrived they were a complete surprise to the British who had none of their own in the country. As faulty strategy invited disastrous situations Churchill issued a cabled warning to Commanders in Malaya.

> 'Beware lest troops required for ultimate defence of Singapore Island and fortress are not used up or cut off in Malay peninsula. Nothing compares in importance with the fortress.'[4]

GHQ hesitancy had disastrous consequences and Brooke-Popham certainly underestimated the importance of speed and quick decision making.

Although the early disasters at Jitra were none of Major-General Murray-Lyon's making, by late December he was succeeded as commander of 11th Division by Brigadier A.C.M. Paris, of 12th Infantry Brigade. Murray-Lyon had run himself into the ground in trying to contain and shore up an impossible situation and Percival was correct to replace him. His precipitous and impromptu retirement from the service, however, was an iniquitous and unjust decision against an officer who had given his best under conditions for which he was not to blame. On 27th December Lieut-General Sir Henry Royds Pownall relieved Air Chief Marshall Sir Robert Brooke-Popham, as the Commander-in-Chief Far East. This appointment, previously agreed to by Churchill before the outbreak of war in the Far East, had been held up by the Chiefs of Staff, and was made largely on the insistence of Duff Cooper. Pownall was proficient in all aspects of the Japanese language, having spent his childhood in Japan, and was a good choice as successor to Brooke-Popham whose performance and opinions certainly warranted the criticism they attracted. However, Pownall's appointment was short-lived. At the Arcadia Conference, held in Washington between 22nd December 1941 and 7th January 1942, a Germany first strategy was confirmed. Of immediate concern also was the decision to establish a single unified command over the Pacific and South East Asia region. Thus, ABDACOM, representing American, British, Dutch and Australian Command, was conceived, with an operational area that encompassed Burma, Malaya, Singapore, the Dutch East Indies, Western New Guinea, North West Australia, and initially the Philippines. Although the successful defence of such an area was improbable, a principle of command unity was created and General Sir Archibald Wavell was chosen for its command. On 3rd January 1942 Wavell took over his newly established command which was given the immediate task of holding a line from Malaya through the Dutch East Indies to Borneo. Meanwhile, withdrawals in Malaya had continued unabated, with Ipoh being abandoned on 28th December, followed shortly by Kampar and then Slim River.

Japanese air attacks intensified as their new bases in Siam became operational, and as the defenders retreated southwards troop columns and convoys were heavily bombed. Damaged armoured cars and trucks littered the roadside, demoralising troops as they passed. Daylight driving was unsafe as the Japanese had complete air control and flew at will up and down the roads, bombing and machine gunning any vehicle that they saw. Every man in the 11th Division was by now suffering from sheer fatigue, but constant enemy air attacks prevented them from sleeping by day. By night either they had to move to or prepare new defensive positions. The stage was soon reached when

> '... the hard-pressed troops were falling back on one ill-prepared position after another, worn out, hungry, tired in the unceasing rain'.[5]

On 5th January, following new Japanese landings at the mouths of the Perak and Bernam Rivers, a build-up of pressure was reported in the Kuala Selangor area, with the objective of forcing an Allied withdrawal from the Perak front, which was only 70 miles north west of Kuala Lumpur. This was achieved on the following day. In Pahang after fierce fighting between Japanese and Australian units, the Kuantan aerodrome, along with considerable undestroyed supplies, was captured.

On 6th January Sir Shenton noted in his diary some advantages that the Japanese had compared to the disadvantages that consistently worked against Allied troops:

> 'They have the advantage of being rice eaters, and are much less dependent than we are on man-made communications. They enter the villages and live there, fed by the villagers (who can't refuse with a tommy gun at their stomachs). They then go out on guerrilla warfare. We on the other hand have gone in for mechanized transport to the nth degree; it is a fearfully cumbersome method and we have pinned our faith to the few roads. But the enemy uses the tracks and paths and cuts in behind us very much as he likes, particularly on bicycles . . . He can ride his bicycle on the excellent roads we have made! and replace them easily from the villages.'[6]

By 7th January Japanese infantry and tanks had broken the 11th Indian Division's defences at Kampong Slim and Trolak. At the conclusion of this decisive battle, the 11th Indian Division was devastated and had been practically wiped out. The battle of Slim River sealed the subsequent fate of both Malaya and Singapore.

General Wavell arrived in Singapore on 8th January and immediately ordered a tactical withdrawal to a position south of the Muar River, where he considered the next stand could be made. Using all available reinforcements, a defensive line was speedily prepared in Johore, but in doing so Kuala Lumpur was abandoned on the 11th, as was Tampin on the 13th. This decision presented the Japanese with unhindered access to the superior road system in Johore, and they were virtually unopposed as they progressed through the States of Selangor, Negeri Sembilan and Malacca. It also enabled them to deploy two divisions simultaneously, rendering ineffective the tough Australian defences at Gemas. By the time that the Muar River defensive positions were taken up, the 11th Division was no longer an effective fighting force.

Instead of reporting enemy advances truthfully, official press releases hid to a large extent the calamity of repeated Allied reversals, which were labelled either as tactical retreats or skillful delaying actions. Chinese tradesmen in Singapore were not bemused by what was happening, however, and as soon as the Muar positions had been lost the Asian grapevine swiftly spread its premonition, earmarking an end of a way of life. Overnight 'every Chinese shopkeeper abruptly terminated the age-old chit system'.[7] What clearer way had they of telling the British that they were done for. As increasingly severe bombing raids were launched against Singapore, Wavell authorised Percival to plan his ultimate retreat to the 'bastion', which Percival confirmed would now become a necessity within one week.

The 18th British Division (less its 53rd Brigade) was mostly made up of territorial units that had been recruited in East Anglia. On 29th October 1941 the Division left Gourock in Scotland on the Polish troop carrier *Sobieski*, destined for the Middle East. They arrived in Halifax, Nova Scotia on 8th November, and were transferred to a neutral American ship, the *USS Mount Vernon*, which set a south-bound course the next day towards Trinidad. Following Japan's attack on Pearl Harbour and America's entry into the war, the 18th Division's destination was hurriedly altered, and a rapid course was set for Mombassa, which was reached via Cape Town on Christmas day. The Division was landed at besieged Singapore on 29th January 1942, having journeyed for just on three months, and

> 'although fit, were naturally very soft. Very few of them had ever been abroad before, and almost none of them had been in the tropics. Absolutely none whatever had been trained in jungle fighting. They arrived without their transport, which was following in a slower convoy.'[8]

During their long travels these unsuspecting troops had been subjected to inaccurate and inept propaganda lectures and were told that the Japanese had no tanks or heavy artillery and that they had only a few antiquated planes. As the Japanese 'soldier was poorly fed, shoddily equipped and could not even close one eye when sighting a rifle,'[9] the uninitiated 18th Division thought themselves 'lucky indeed to be facing the armies of the Mikado rather than the Afrika Corps'.[10] How wrong they were! Arriving barely 17 days before the surrender of Singapore, they were destined to become POWs for an awesome three and a half years, which many never survived.

By 31st January the last Australian and British forces had withdrawn from the Malayan mainland onto Singapore island. The Argylls, Gurkhas, East Surreys, Leicesters, Manchesters and the Malayan and Australian forces along with the Hydrabads and Punjabis had fought every mile of the retreat down the Peninsula, and by the time the Argylls crossed the Causeway, with their piper playing them across, they had less than 100 men left. It took the Japanese just 54 days to conquer Malaya, with a loss of about 4,600 men, compared to 25,000 Allied losses, of whom many were Indians who had either chosen to become, or been coerced into becoming prisoners of war. From Jitra to Singapore was approximately 515 miles, which was covered at an average of 9.5 miles per day. Despite this arduous retreat, many who did reach Singapore were still able to subsequently make a stand and fight.

Rumours undermined morale and set a pattern of panic in motion. The Allies' powerful numerical superiority was negated and Japan's control in the air induced terror and 'a blind urge to be elsewhere'.[11] Churchill later accepted full blame for Japan having gained complete air control so early in the war, as he had insisted that a major part of the RAF, earmarked for Malaya, should be diverted to the Libyan theatre to stem Rommel's thrust towards the Suez Canal.

11:2 Belated Arrangements for Stay-Behind Parties

In December 1940 Colonel J.D. Dalley, a superintendent in the Special Branch of the Federated Malay States Police, and an authority on secret societies, presented a report entitled 'Jungle Ambush Patrols'. This report recommended the formation of a network of guerrilla-type stay-behind groups to be set up throughout Malaya, in the event that the country should be overrun. The objectives of such groups would be to disrupt enemy attempts at infiltration through the hills and jungle, to supply intelligence information about their activities, and to operate against enemy lines of communication. The groups would also form a nucleus for organised raiding parties which would be trained to sabotage the enemy's progress in any way they could, and to carry out subversive and propaganda activities behind their lines. Dalley's original concept envisaged setting up similar organisations that would link other countries in the Far East, should the need arise. His detailed plans were put to Sir Shenton Thomas, as the Commander-in-Chief Malaya, but were rejected in October 1941, without any alternative suggestions being made, although earlier in the year Lieut-Colonel J.M.L. Gavin RE had been allowed to start a small Irregular Warfare training school in Singapore. Dalley's subsequent efforts to recruit volunteers for this purpose from the police and civil service were also opposed.

In early 1941 the prospect of having to resort to guerrilla warfare was afforded little priority by the Malayan High Command, as many within this elite circle still reasoned in 1914–18 war terms They viewed Malaya's defence as being purely a matter for the military, and already well under control.

The establishment of such a scheme was categorically opposed on three counts. Firstly, it was argued, it would drain the availability of European manpower. Secondly, the employment of Asians in any proposal that conceded the possibility of an enemy over-running the country was highly objectionable to the British administration and military alike, as both considered that such an admission would have disastrous psychological effects on the indigenous population. Thirdly, under no circumstances could any scheme that involved the participation of members of the illegal Malayan Communist Party, or one that gave the Chinese recourse to arms be acceptable to the British at that juncture. This remained the official stand up until as late as 8th December 1941, when, in a complete volte-face, permission was given to train stay-behind parties. By then, however, it was far too late for the proposals to be implemented properly, and only last minute improvisation was possible.

For almost one year Sir Shenton had ignored Colonel Dalley's report, considering it an undesirable impracticality. The Governor failed to recognise or make use of the Chinese hatred for the Japanese, and the plausibility of arming them, even though many were members of the illegal Malayan Communist Party. He also held to the view that arming Asians would be bad for morale, despite the numerous clarion signs that Japan intended to invade Malaya. When he did belatedly authorise a stay-behind scheme, it was considerably less effective than it could have been, had the impending dangers been realised earlier. Only when the military situation in Malaya had seriously deteriorated and the fall of Singapore was imminently threatened was Dalforce belatedly formed. The force only totalled about 2,000 mostly Chinese men, but could have been ten times this size had it been permitted one year earlier.

In the last week of December 1941 an Overseas Chinese Mobilisation Committee, under the chairmanship of Mr Tan Kah Kee, a prominent Chinese Nationalist Party member, was organised. The committee's function was to raise recruits from the Chinese community, who were prepared to volunteer to assist in the defence of Malaya, and Tan Kah Kee worked closely with Colonel J.D. Dalley towards this purpose. The first armed Chinese force, nicknamed 'Dalco', was mostly made up of communist-inclined recruits who fought against the Japanese in Johore. The second group of Dalforce volunteers, totalling about 2,000, were scraped together by Colonel Dalley and Tan Kah Kee and came mostly from people released from gaol and from supporters of both the KMT and the communists. They were recruited from all classes of Chinese, including college teachers, undergraduates, rickshaw boys and labourers, many of whom had previously worked on various defence projects. They were poorly trained and equally poorly equipped, many of them being only erratically armed with anything they could lay their hands on, including crudely fashioned clubs and household knives. Under British officers, as an independent unit attached to the 3rd Indian Division, they stoically went into action for four days and courageously fought in the mangrove swamps outside Singapore, where they played an important part in the battle and inflicted severe casualties on the Japanese before the surrender. Many were killed in the fierce fighting, and they deservedly earned their nickname of 'Dalley's Desperadoes'. After the fall of Singapore, some of them managed to escape to the mainland jungles where they continued to operate behind the Japanese lines and became the heart of the Chinese-led resistance forces in Malaya. The Japanese neither forgot nor forgave them, and Lieut-General Tomoyuki Yamashita, the commander of the Japanese 25th Army and also referred to as the 'Tiger of Malaya', was infuriated by their determined participation in Singapore's defence. He decided that the Chinese community as a whole should be cauterized, and many of them who surrendered with the fall of Singapore were summarily executed.

The Malayan Communist Party's (MCP) pre-war strategy aimed at sabotaging Britain's war preparations. After Germany declared war on Russia, the MCP suspended their aggressive policy and offered their services to the British government. This gesture was initially rejected. Following the confirmation on 15th December that the British intended to release all leftist political prisoners, a secret back-street meeting was held on the 16th between Lai Tek, the Secretary General of the MCP and another Chinese, and Major F.S. Chapman who at that time was the Deputy Commander of the newly formed 101 Special Training School (101 STS) in Singapore, where instruction was given in guerrilla warfare and sabotage. After this meeting the MCP made a second offer to the British on 18th December which was accepted. At subsequent secret talks it was agreed that the MCP would provide a number of young Chinese as recruits for 101 STS, where they would be trained to become stay-behind parties, whose purpose would be to sabotage enemy communications and to make things generally awkward for them. It was clearly established from the outset that trainees would be used only as the British deemed necessary, but this victory in principle was considerably offset as the MCP was allowed to select those students who would receive training.

On 21st December training courses of 10 day duration were commenced. 165 recruits were rushed through a vigorous training programme and those who survived subsequently formed the nucleus of the Malayan Peoples Anti-Japanese Army (MPAJA). The original British plan envisaged providing a British officer to lead each stay-behind party, but this, however, did not materialise due to the swift of advance of Japanese forces, and the little time left to organise and implement things properly. Recruits were therefore sent to work very much on their own to various locations in Selangor, Negeri Sembilan and in north and south Johore. Sir Shenton's belated recognition that young and mostly pro-communist Chinese wanted to volunteer to fight against the Japanese, considerably undermined the results that were achieved. Had hundreds of strong, well organised Chinese stay-behind parties, commanded by British officers, been in position before Japan attacked Malaya, they could have undoubtedly frustrated and delayed the Japanese advance sufficiently to enable the British 18th Division and the 9th Australian Division (which only reached Java on its way to Malaya) to be put to some useful purpose.

Small groups of seven or eight young Chinese, all briefly trained in sabotage activities, were dispersed into the jungle from where they had some success in disrupting the communications and activities of Japanese troops. Maintaining contact with them presented a serious problem, as at that time there were no suitable lightweight wireless sets available in the Far East. Each party was equipped with a three month supply of ammunition, food and demolition equipment. In addition, they were also given seeds and gardening equipment to enable them to exist for up to one year in the jungle without resorting to help from Chinese villagers.

The extent of the stay-behind parties' success was realised only after the war had ended. During a 14-day period those parties that were accompanied by Spencer Chapman were credited with derailing 7 or 8 trains, disrupting railway lines in about 60 different places, severely damaging or destroying 15 bridges and 40 trucks, most of which were carrying Japanese troops. Chapman estimated that 500 to 1,500 Japanese were killed during this time and that their activities denied the enemy the full unhindered use of roads and the railway. 1,000 pounds of explosives, plus 100 grenades or home-made bombs were also used during this fortnight. With such results in so short a time, the justification of Asian stay-behind parties led by Europeans was indisputable.

The Japanese mounted savage reprisal raids following any sabotage action by stay-behind parties. These were directed against Chinese villagers in the immediate locality, irregardless of their innocence or whether they had given moral or material support to the stay-behind groups. People who were sufficiently brave to try and assist were increasingly badly treated, and were tortured and killed.

When news of Singapore's surrender was made known, Chapman realised the uselessness of continuing to aggravate the Japanese, as this would only invite various acts of retribution against anyone who assisted, or who even lived in the district where incidents were arranged. Chapman's first objective became to get out the country, so that he could assist with training a select force that would return in due course, on a much larger scale, when the time was right. Spare weapons and stores were to be handed over to Chinese stay-behind guerrillas, who would be instructed in their proper use if time allowed. It was also decided that a few Chinese, who were suitable to be trained as potential officers, should accompany the party when it sailed secretly for India.

11:3 Fall of Singapore and Evacuation

In the early hours of Monday 8th December 1941 Flight Lieut Harry Grumbar, the duty Filter Officer in Singapore, plotted 17 incoming aircraft and immediately telephoned this information to ARP Headquarters. He recalled being told by the staff on duty there that

> 'they were powerless to sound the air raid sirens because their Chief Warden was at the late night cinema . . . and only he had the keys that controlled the Alarm switch'.[12]

At 4 a.m. that morning Air Vice-Marshall C.W.H. Pulford telephoned Sir Shenton Thomas and tersely told him of approaching hostile aircraft. Within fifteen minutes of that call the first Japanese bombs crashed down on the brightly lit streets of Singapore city and on an unsuspecting population there. Thousands of bewildered Asians along with many hundred Europeans were shocked out of their sleep, and at first assumed that the noise was only another practice alert. This misconception was but temporary, however, and although it was not a large raid, and caused only slight damage to property, some bombs fell onto the thickly populated Chinese quarter of the city where 61 people were killed and another 133 were injured. The new

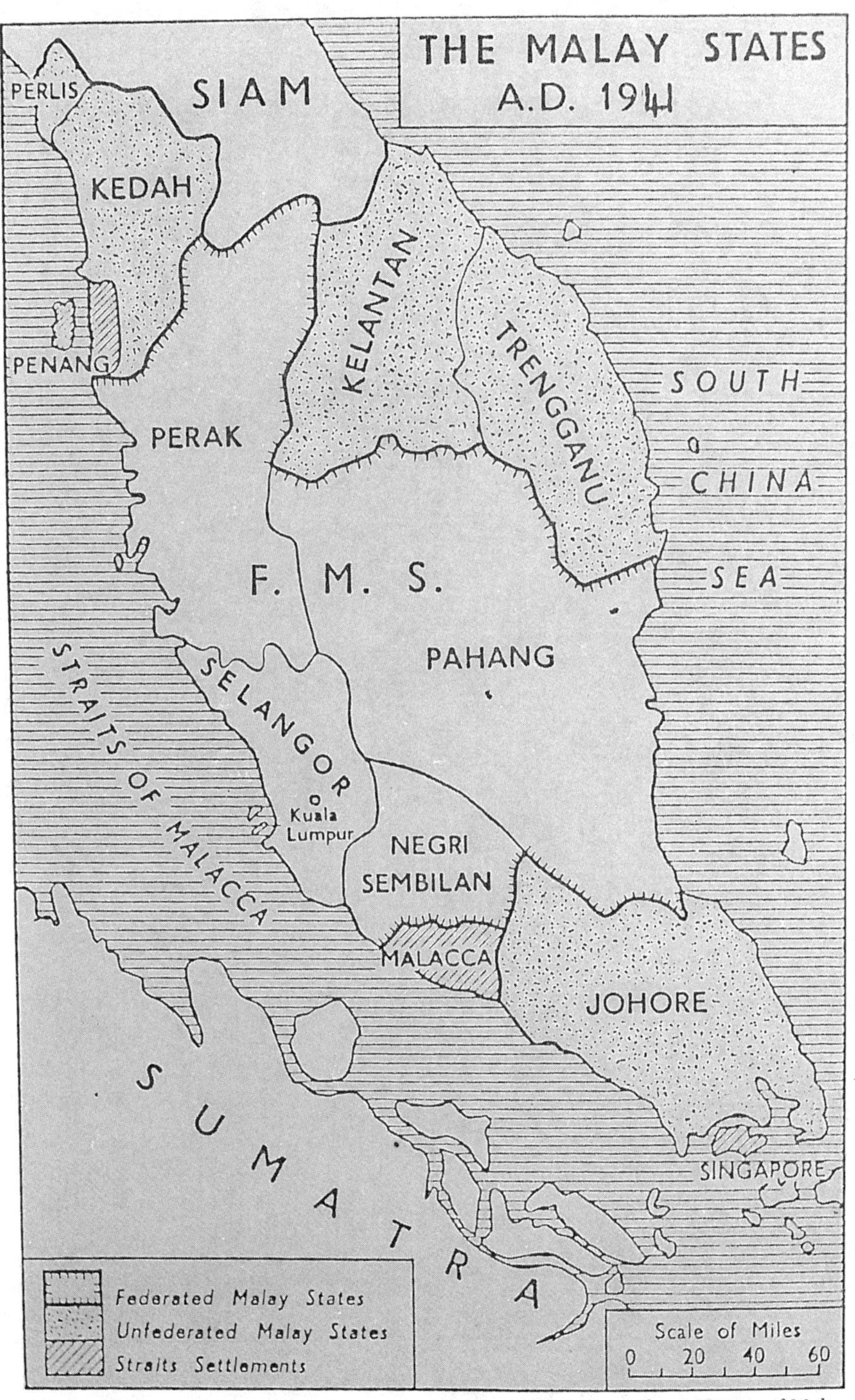

The Malay States (FMS, UMS and SS), 1941. (Photo credit: J. Kennedy, *A History of Malaya*, Macmillan, London, 1967.)

An example of the hurriedly constructed pill-box defences on Penang that were only installed in 1940.

In 1941 this building was used as the headquarters of the 3rd Bn SSVF.

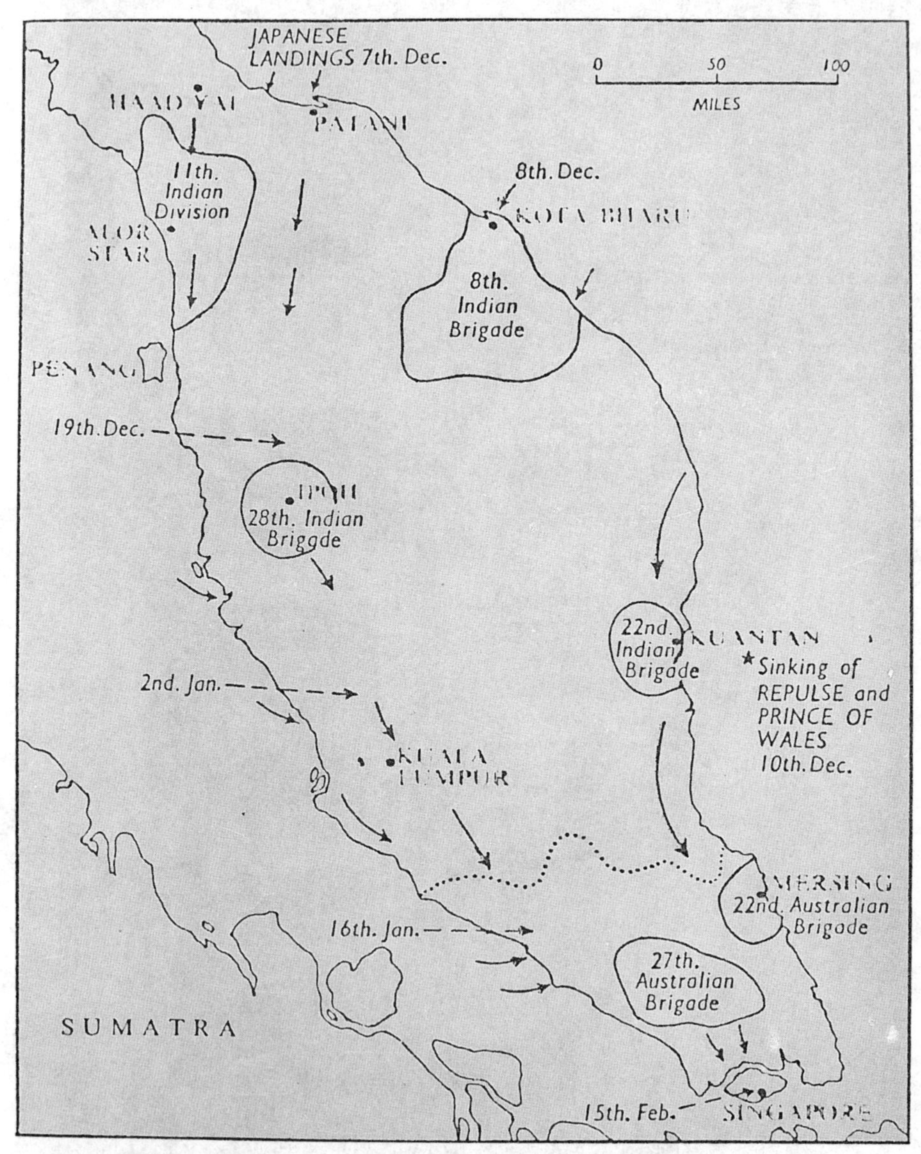

Japanese campaign in Malaya 1941–2. (Photo credit: N.J. Ryan, *The Making of Modern Malaysia*, Oxford University Press, 1968.)

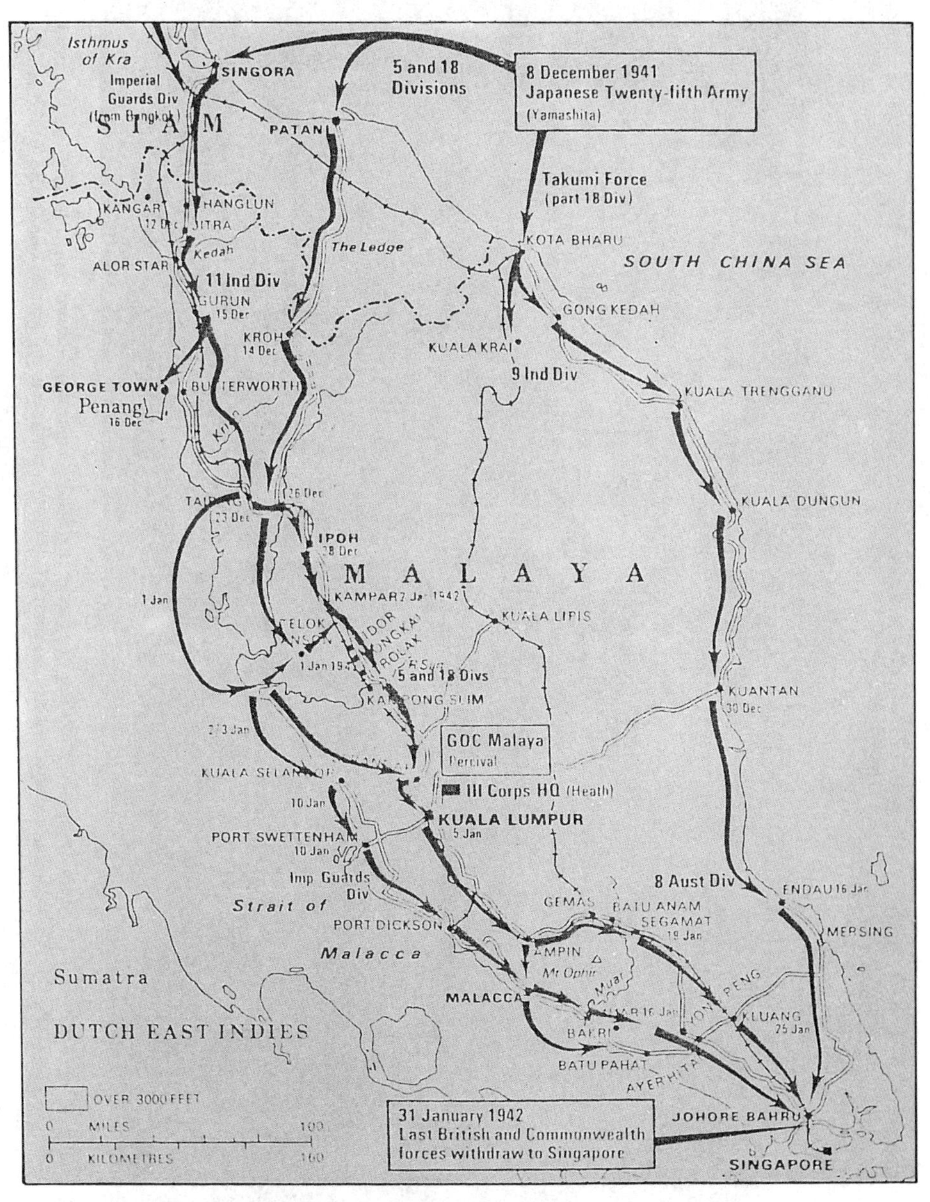

Japanese campaign in Malaya 1941–2. (Photo credit: Bison Books, England, 1984.)

Tower from which General Yamashita had a commanding view over the Straits separating Johore Bahru from Singapore, and from where he could see the Allied defence preparations and plan his final assault on Singapore. No one in the 'Fortress' thought of shelling and destroying this obvious vantage point.

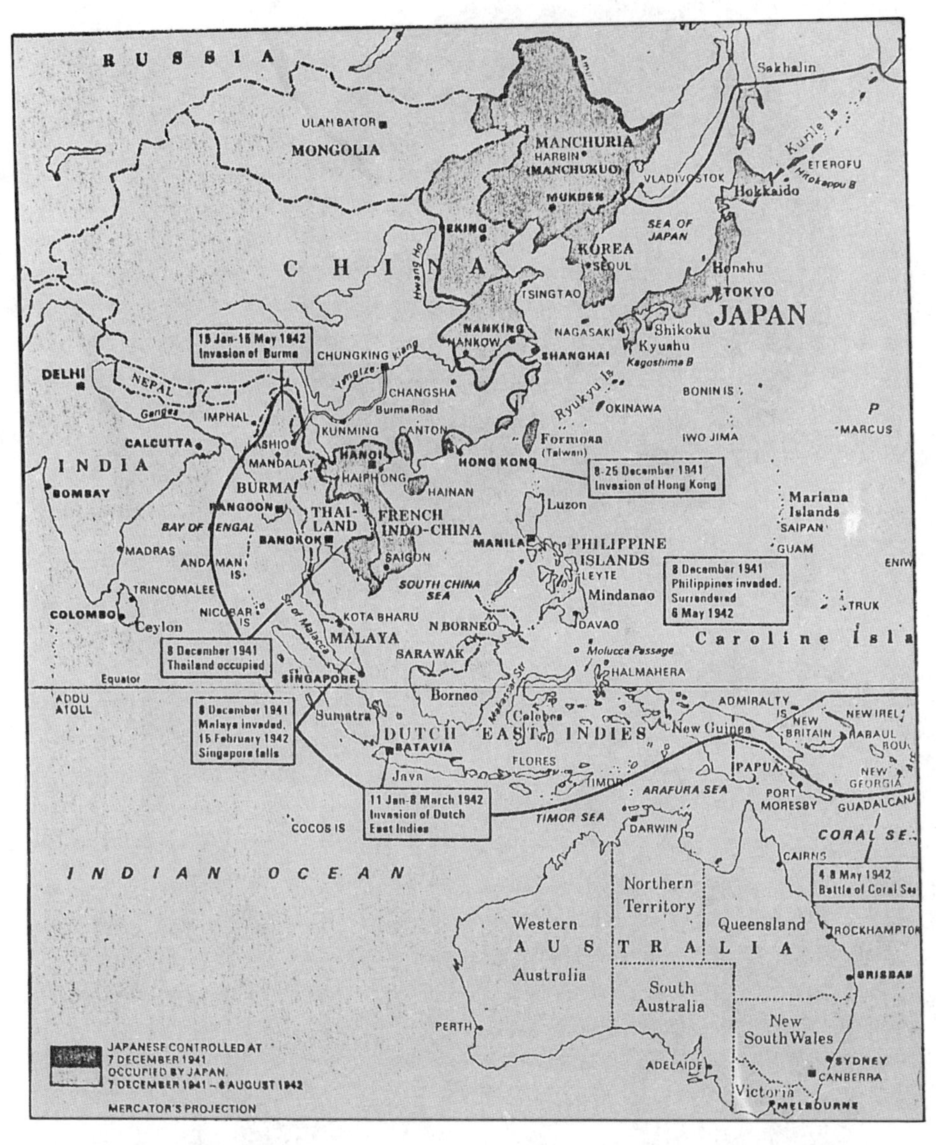

Japanese controlled areas from 7.12.41 to 6.8.42. (Photo credit: *Almanac of World War 2*, ed. Brig. Peter Young, Hamlyn, U.K., copyright Bison Books, 1981.)

Field Marshall Sir Archibald Wavell on his last visit to Singapore a few days before Percival was compelled to surrender the 'Fortress'.

Lieut-Gen. A.E. Percival CB, DSO, MC, GOC Malaya. (Photographs: British Official Crown copyright, Assoc. Press. *The Second World War* Vol.4, Amalgamated Press, London.)

Lieut-Gen. Gordon Bennett CB, DSO reviewing Australian troops in Kuala Lumpur. (Photograph, Paul Popper.)

H.E. Sir Shenton Thomas, Governor and C-in-C of the Straits Settlements and High Commissioner for the Malay States, and Lady Daisy Thomas. (By courtesy of *Shenton of Singapore, Governor and POW*, by Brian Montgomery.)

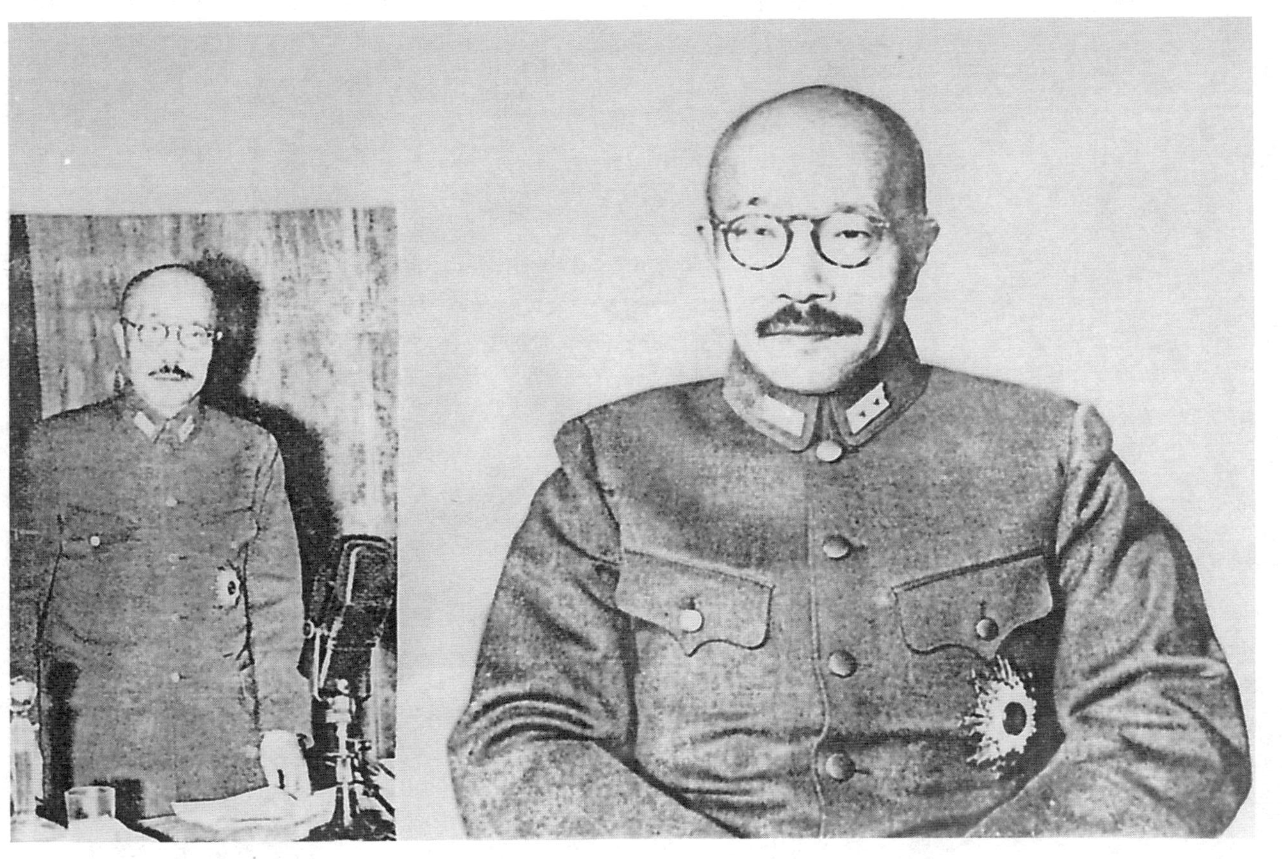

Lieut-Gen. Hideki Tojo, who became Premier, Home Minister and War Minister on 9.10.41. He entered the war with misgivings. (Photo: Wide World. *The Second Great War*, vol.4, Amalgamated Press, London.)

Col. Masanobu Tsuji, a flamboyant military character. Chief, Army Planning Staff and author of 'How To' manual entitled 'Read This Alone — And the War Can Be Won'. (Photo: *Sankai Shimbun*, 'The Rising Sun', 1977, Time-Life Books, USA.)

Lieut-Gen. Tomoyuki Yamashita (inset), a middle-aged, combat-hardened veteran, accompanied by staff officers & photographer on inspection after fall of Malaya. (Photo: Assoc. Press, Wide World, *The Second Great War*, vol.4.)

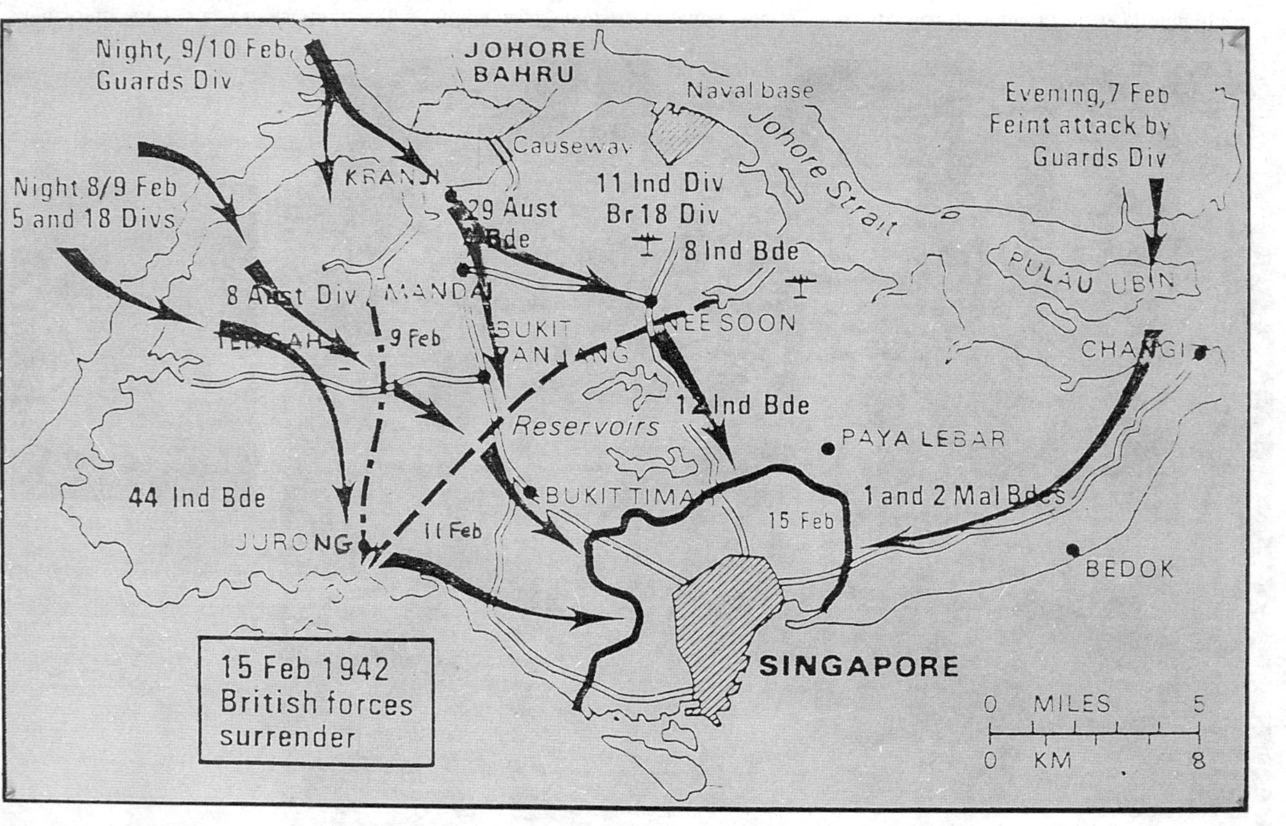

Map showing how Singapore was overwhelmed. (Photo: Bison Books, UK, 1984.)

Surrender of Singapore on 15.2.42. The white-flag party on its way to meet the Japanese C-in-C. (Photo: Assoc. Press, Keystone.)

Lieut-Gen. Yamashita interviews Lieut-Gen. Percival at moment of surrender of Singapore, 1900 hrs, 15.2.42. (Photo: Robert Hunt Library, Bison Books, UK, 1984.)

air-conditioned restaurant at Robinsons in Raffles Place sustained a direct hit, as did Police headquarters in New Bridge Road, but no damage was done to any of the military installations in the island.

By 18th December it had become evident that reversals on the mainland were escalating in quick succession, and a system of security registration was introduced in Singapore. A warning was issued to the public to be on guard against the possibility of the Japanese attempting parachute landings, and people were asked to help with the construction of trenches in pre-selected open spaces within and around the city limits. The island was declared a War Zone and the law courts were geared up to deal with any offenders who might subsequently be charged with either looting or treachery. The stark reality of war escalated as the wounded started to arrive, a red tide of agony flowing incessantly through every crowded room and corridor at the General Hospital.

Confusion prevailed in every exercise aimed at enhancing Singapore's defensive preparations. When the Deputy Municipal Engineer's department organised the digging of six-foot wide and three-foot deep trenches on many of the island's sports grounds, as a deterrent against Japanese attempts to land aircraft on them, another official insisted on changing their direction to make them less easy machine gun targets. Then yet another busy-body official required the removal of all soft earth left behind by making the change of direction, as he felt this would be ideal for parachutists to land on. These arduous alterations having all been done by hand, the health authorities then demanded that each trench should be half filled in, as their present depth provided ideal mosquito breeding grounds. Earth, therefore, that had only recently been taken away to satisfy the change of direction was again manually returned so that the depth of the trenches could be reduced.

On 28th December, as circumstances continued to worsen, Lady Daisy Shenton Thomas broadcast to the women of Malaya:

> 'Stick to your job, whatever it is, and whatever happens. Courage is very catching and even though we may be frightened inside, if we do not show it others will take heart. There is work for everyone, hospitals to be manned.

> The men need any rest they can get, and we can help by not bothering them with our worries.'[13]

In the light of such unselfish counsel it was shameful how some civilians clung to petty protocol and self-esteem and denied spontaneous co-operation with the armed forces. One such example arose when the secretary of the Singapore Golf Club refused to allow the army to use the area as a strong point, without first calling for a special committee meeting. In another instance an army officer was refused permission to fell some trees on the outskirts of the city to improve his line of fire, unless he could produce some written authority in support of his request to do so.

As weekly bulletins issued by the official services publicity office in Singapore heralded the arrival of reinforcements, a false impression of Singapore's impregnability was cabled by reporters to various parts of the world. The outside world was given to understand that Singapore, in particular, was receiving more attention than it justifiably deserved, but this was indeed not so.

On 19th January, '. . . the myth of Singapore was finally exploded for Churchill', who at last saw the island for what it really was – a 'grand illusion of the fortress that never was'.[14] Wavell also, on arrival in Singapore on the 20th, immediately realised the hopelessness of the situation and cabled Churchill in London:

> 'I warn you that I doubt whether island can be held for long once Johore is lost.'[15]

By 1st February tiny Singapore island's population had swelled to more than one million people. Added to these were another 85,000 tired and utterly demoralised troops, most of whom had experienced bitter weeks of continuous defeat, except for the uninitiated 18th British Division that had only disembarked on 31st January, two days before the Causeway linking Johore to Singapore had been partially ruptured in a final, parting gesture at the end of the flight down the Peninsula.

85,000 men were available to defend Singapore. Of these, 15,000 were administrative and non-combatants. Many among the remaining 70,000 men were in second-line combat units, and all were too thinly dispersed on the ground to defend Singapore effectively, especially as the enemy had decisive control over air and sea.

Percival's actual combatant forces were all in a pitiable state by the time they arrived in Singapore. They included the remnants of thirteen British, six Australian, seventeen Indian and two Malay Infantry battalions, along with what was left of two British and one Australian machine gun battalions, plus some supporting artillery and ack-ack guns. Six of the thirteen British battalions had recently landed and were untrained, unfit and unacclimatised. The seven others were all grossly understrength. Five of the six Australian battalions were made up with untrained reinforcements, some having sailed from Australia within two weeks of enlistment and many unfamiliar with small arms. The seventeen Indian battalions had borne the brunt of heavy fighting down the length of the Malayan Peninsula, and had suffered appalling losses. They were also desperately short of experienced line officers.

In contrast, Lieut-General Tomoyuki Yamashita's three fully trained and jungle experienced crack divisions — the Imperial Guards, the 5th and the 18th Divisions — were flush with success and had strong air, artillery and tank support.

Percival had a choice of two courses of action to defend Singapore. Either, he could try to stop the Japanese from landing in force on the island, or he could submit to this and hold back a 'strong centralised force to strike at the invaders in a decisive inland battle'.[16] Percival chose the first of these two options.

A dawn report of 8th January by a daring Australian patrol, that penetrated two miles into enemy territory, incredibly did not reach Percival until 3.30 p.m. that afternoon. This report clearly showed that the Japanese were building up massive troop concentrations opposite the Australian sector, which was positioned on the west of the Causeway. The report also intimated that the Japanese would launch a major offensive in this area, which was duly preluded by a fearful barrage and remorseless pounding of the Australians' positions. The Japanese bombardment of Singapore on the 8th was described as being as bad as that at Flanders in 1914. Poor communications and telephone failure hampered the defenders,

> 'causing some units to be shelled by their own guns. This was one reason the Australians who bore the brunt were unable to hold the attackers.'[17]

Only after a few infantry SOS signals flashed in the night sky, did some defending guns open up intermittently. Both Percival and the Australian Commander Major-General Gordon Bennett were not apparently unduly concerned over the bombardment's intensity as they both anticipated

> 'that it was the first of a number of days of softening, or that the enemy would switch the bombardment back next day to the Causeway and north-eastern shores of the island'.[18]

During the night of the 8/9th February, from 10.45 p.m. onwards, 13,000 Japanese troops were landed on Singapore in the sector held by the 2/20th Battalion of the 22nd Australian Brigade. They crossed the Johore Straits

> 'in special armoured landing-craft, each vessel carrying about forty men. [Others] breasted their way across the Strait (at this point a good half-mile wide), holding their rifles and ammunition above their heads. Quite a number had compasses strapped on their wrists . . . and had been thoroughly briefed, how to reach certain objectives — and people.'[19]

Within one hour positions had been sufficiently secured to enable them to send across, almost without interruption, as much of their supporting artillery, tanks and vehicles as their barges could carry. As only one section of the Causeway had been earlier breached near the Johore end by the British, Japanese sappers were able to make good the rupture within three hours. Shortly after daybreak another 10,000 men had been landed.

The Australian position, 500 yards from the shore, was heroically and stubbornly defended and held throughout the night, but with the coming of dawn, 'to Yamashita's astonishment . . . all resistance had melted away'.[20] Brigadier Maxwell was adamant that he had been given permission to withdraw his forces and Major-General Gordon Bennett was equally insistent that no such permission had been given. At dawn on the 10th, 'the causeway area had been abandoned and the road to Singapore lay open.'[21]

Wavell's order of the day emphasised the defenders' superiority in numbers and urged the destruction of those Japanese who had recently landed.

> 'It will be disgraceful if we yield our boasted fortress of Singapore to inferior enemy forces. There must be no thought of sparing the troops or civilian population . . . There must be no question or thought of surrender.'[22]

Wavell's mere mention of surrender implanted a lingering seed of doubt in everyone's mind. The wrong impression was imparted to people in Britain when several newspapers leaked these instructions, and chose to interpret the possibility of surrender as a result of lack of courage.

The evening that Wavell left Singapore for his Java HQ, he told Percival to fight to the end, with no question of surrender. By this time there were no aircraft left in Singapore and all remaining air force officers had been withdrawn from the island. Wavell did not hide his deep concern when he cabled to Churchill:

> 'Battle for Singapore is not going well. Japanese with their usual infiltration tactics are getting on much more rapidly than they should in the West of the island. I ordered Percival to stage counter-attack with all troops possible on that front. Morale of some troops is not good, and none is as high as I should like to see . . . I have given them most categorical orders that there is to be no thought of surrender, and that all troops are to continue fighting to the end.'[23]

On the 11th a final desperate counter attack attempt was beaten back with heavy losses, and a withdrawal to the city perimeter began.

The 1st Malay Brigade's stubborn defence against overwhelming opposition 'was a living and dying illustration of the folly of not having raised more such local forces before the war in which men could defend what was their homeland'.[24] Their courage was commendable and they held out until they were almost obliterated. In other areas of the island, Allied soldiers' morale was fast crumbling and many of them felt that if the 'brass hats in their arm chairs back home hadn't let them down',[25] then Singapore would not have been lost. It was difficult for them to condone or even understand that

Singapore's loss would be insignificant in comparison to the crucial stakes that were involved in Russia and North Africa.

* * * * * *

Singapore's pre-war daily consumption of water was more than 25,000,000 gallons, of which 10,000,000 gallons came by pipe-line from Gunong Pulai, 20 miles from Johore Bahru, which had already been cut by the Japanese. Three small storage reservoirs, in the MacRitchie catchment area on Singapore island itself, now had to provide what was needed. With harsh restrictions and careful rationing, they might have been able to last for a couple of months, but they had insufficient capacity to provide a long-term supply for a population that had doubled to over one million people, and also included many refugees from the mainland. No water rationing was ordered, despite the substantial restriction in supply, and even if the civil government had tried to implement rationing at this late stage, it would have been impossible to enforce as the damage caused to pipes by bombing was far greater than it was possible to repair. The shortage of water had by now, therefore, become a critical factor and as this intensified so did the threat of disease. This untenable situation should never be overlooked when Percival is criticised over his decision to surrender Singapore.

Sufficient food supplies had been previously built up in Singapore to enable the island to hold out for a six month siege. Both the two largest cinemas on the island, the Capitol and the Pavilion, together with other protected places, had been converted into food stores, in addition to which 9,000 cattle had been imported from Bali. The island had 125,000 pigs and sufficient milk as two large dairy herds, normally kept in Johore, had been relocated on the island late in January.

There was mounting concern over the shortage of available hospital accommodation for the constantly escalating numbers of sick and wounded, especially as some 10,000 had already been evacuated from the Malayan mainland to Singapore. British troops were crowded into the Alexandra Hospital and the Indians were crammed into the overflowing wards at the Tyersall Park Hospital. Temporary arrangements were made to ward the wounded in the Great Cathay building, as well as in schools, churches, clubs and service and government quarters. Civilian casualties had reached almost 2,000 daily, many of whom had been crushed under collapsed buildings, or had been burnt or blinded by flames and smoke in the hovels surrounding the blazing dockland areas.

Rumours circulated wildly around Singapore in the final days before the capitulation, prompted by a constant flow of propaganda broadcasts by the Japanese through the Penang radio station, spreading alarm about secret British army evacuations, desertions, and civil unrest. However, inter-mixed with such alarmist gossip during the last two weeks before the surrender, fragments of gaiety and romance lingered. With the Japanese poised for their final thrust on the city, Dan Hopkins's dance band still entertained at the Raffles Hotel, and would-be optimists continued to advertise reputable properties in the *Straits Times*, either for immediate occupation or for sale. No accurate assessment of civilian deaths in Singapore has ever been ascertained, but during some of the severe attacks,

> 'whole sections of Chinatown were obliterated and hundreds of bodies were never dug out. The hospitals and aid posts did try to keep some records, but even most of these were lost in the confusion following (the) surrender.'[26]

By 13th February Singapore had degenerated into a state of disorder. An ugly mood undermined the troops as groups of hungry stragglers wandered aimlessly without instructions or leaders through the streets, and deserters hid in cellars, or roamed in gangs intent on looting. Many of them, desperate with fatigue and unable to find their own units, turned to the YMCA for a place to sleep on the floor. Increases in desertion occurred, and ugly scenes erupted at the docks as armed deserters attempted to force women off evacuation launches. Others sneaked onto ships that were preparing to sail for Java or Sumatra or stole fishing boats at gunpoint. Morale sank among many, but others, like the briefly-trained Singapore Volunteer Corps, and the 1st Malaya Brigade, managed to retain some of their splendid fighting spirit.

* * * * * *

Shattered windows, rubble-littered streets, burst water mains, skeletons of burnt out vehicles and uprooted trees all starkly depicted the havoc caused by repeated bombing in and around the city centre. By 13th February it was not a question of whether or not the battle had been lost. By now it was a matter of time, and even Churchill 'no longer nursed illusions about the protracted defence of Singapore. The only question was how long.'[27] Astonishingly, Churchill cabled to Wavell and ordered that the fighting must be continued to the end. The newly arrived, semi-trained territorial 18th Division was exhorted to make a name for itself in history. Commanders and senior officers were ordered to die with their troops, as the honour of both the British Empire and the British Army was at stake. By now the Japanese had gained control of the strategic village of Bukit Timah, together with the vast stores of food and petrol that were located there. In various parts of the island, hand to hand fighting had already broken out and a Japanese aircraft flew overhead to drop a courteous invitation to surrender from General Yamashita.

Percival correctly requested Wavell at this juncture for wider discretionary powers, and recommended immediate capitulation. In an uncompromising reply, his request was denied and Wavell instructed him to 'continue to inflict maximum damage on the enemy, for as long as possible by house-to-house fighting if necessary'.[28] As circumstances deteriorated by the minute, and the failing supply of water took on critical significance, Percival's long-awaited wider discretionary powers were cabled to him:

> 'So long as you are in a position to inflict losses and damage to the enemy, and your troops are physically capable of doing so, you must fight on . . . When you are fully satisfied that this is no longer possible I give you discretion to cease resistance. Inform me of your intentions. Whatever happens I thank you and all your troops for gallant efforts of last few days.'[29]

By now Percival was convinced that continued resistance would be a wasteful and futile effort that would place intolerable burdens on the people. He believed that capitulation was the only humane course remaining open to him. He did not realise that the Japanese position had become dangerously over-extended, and that they were facing an acute shortage of ammunition. Lieut-Colonel Masanobu Tsuji, their Chief of Operations, later confessed that they were down to their last one hundred rounds for each gun and even less for their heavy ones. Yamashita, therefore, could ill-afford any delay in achieving the cessation of fighting, but Percival, being unaware of the weakened state of the Japanese forces by the time they had reached Singapore, fell victim to Yamashita's bluff and his demand for unconditional surrender on Sunday 15th February 1942.

At a hastily called conference that barely lasted twenty minutes, Percival reiterated Wavell's permission to capitulate. A letter was written to Yamashita, suggesting that both sides should observe a cease-fire at 4 p.m. on the 15th, to give them an opportunity to discuss capitulation terms. Yamashita rejected this proposal and flatly refused to order any cease-fire until Percival, and nobody but Percival, had signed a surrender document.

Yamashita went to some pains to ensure that the surrender would be historically degrading. He ordered Percival, accompanied by his staff officers, to walk with a Union Jack and a White Flag to the Ford Motor Works at Bukit Timah village, where negotiations were to be conducted. The names of many Japanese officers were chalked on the floor of the building, as privileged witnesses of the ceremony and of the imperialists' mortification. Yamashita expressed amazement that 100,000 allied forces surrendered to him, and in his book entitled *A Soldier Must Hang*, he states:

> 'My attack on Singapore was a bluff — a bluff that worked. I had 30,000 men and was outnumbered more than three to one. I knew if I had to fight long for Singapore, I would be beaten.'[30]

The news of the proposed surrender reverberated throughout the battlefield like an electric shock. After one hour of humiliating negotiations Percival was flatly told by Yamashita that 'The Japanese Army will consider nothing but unconditional surrender at 10 p.m. Nippon time.'[31] (8.30 p.m. Singapore time.) Percival, in a last request, attempted to procure some guarantee of security for the city, and for the welfare of troops under his command. He also requested protection for women, children and for British civilians, to which Yamashita gave his positive assurance. At 6.10 p.m., on Sunday 15th February 1942, one copy of the surrender document was signed and this was kept by Yamashita. At 8 p.m.

> 'a long wail from a siren sounded and pandemonium abruptly ended. The ensuing silence was uncanny. Soldiers with sunken eyes and battle-worn clothes straggled in. Said one Tommy, "Well it's over. I hope I'll be sent home soon. We'll settle accounts later." Poor boy, little did he know what was in store for him.'[32]

Some troops on hearing the news wanted to continue the fight rather than be captured, and some attempted to do so, resorting to their bayonets when they ran out of ammunition.

Instructions were subsequently issued for all troops to remain in their positions until further orders were released. All weapons, equipment, secret documents, ships and planes were required to be handed over intact. With the exception of 1,000 British troops, who were told to maintain order and prevent looting during that first night, all others were ordered to be immediately disarmed. Japanese soldiers were forbidden to enter the city until the following morning, and Percival was warned that any violation of the surrender terms would result in an immediate full-scale attack.

> 'Percival was quite right to have surrendered, for the disaster to the million Asians in the city, and to the troops, would have been very great had the surrender been delayed by even a few hours.'[33]

The last message to Wavell out of Singapore said:

> 'Owing to losses from enemy action, water, petrol, food and ammunition practically finished. Unable therefore to continue the fight any longer. All ranks have done their best and grateful for your help.'[34]

Yamashita's dramatic victory had taken him only 70 days to achieve, despite earlier Japanese estimation that the campaign would last for 100 days.

The loss of Malaya and Singapore was the worst defeat in British military history, and was directly responsible for bringing to an end a period of Western predominance throughout Asia, that had spanned more than 150 years. The loss of Fortress Singapore

> 'impinged remarkably little on the consciousness of the British people except of course in those families who had members serving in the Far East', as 'only 30,000 British servicemen died in the war against Japan, as compared to 235,000 in the war against Germany'.[35]

Actual Commonwealth battle casualties in the Malayan campaign were only 8,700, compared with 9,824 lost by the Japanese. In addition to this, however, 130,000 British and Allied troops were marched off following the surrender to become prisoners of war — fourteen times the total of Japanese casualties! Included with these figures are those losses reportedly suffered by the Indian Army in Malaya. These were subsequently calculated to total 41,900, of whom only 285 were killed, 708 were wounded and 2,047 were reported as missing. 38,860 were taken as prisoners of war. In addition to this, and not included in the figures, there were approximately 20,200 Indian troops not accounted for who possibly could also have been captured.

Had British and Allied forces been as well trained and equipped as the Japanese, and had they been prepared to fight in similar flexible small groups, the outcome to the campaign might well have been different. Had the British had a staff officer of similar brilliance and creativity to Lieut-Colonel Masanobu Tsuji, the outcome again could well have been different.

> 'It was allegedly Tsuji, however, who enabled Yamashita to bluff General Percival — a kindly man — into surrendering so prematurely . . . At a time when the defenders of Singapore had vast quantities of ammunition and food available to them, Yamashita's arsenal was almost empty. So Tsuji, it is said, employed once again the terror tactic that had earlier compelled the surrender . . . of Hong Kong's hapless garrison. The tactic was pitilessly and publicly to rape and murder . . .'[36]

On the 16th morning,

> 'a token "Triumph Parade" of 175 Japanese medium and light tanks was staged through the main streets while Rising Sun flags fluttered in the breeze from all public buildings'.[37]

The masses of victorious Japanese forces were not allowed to enter the city, which was 'spared the horrors of rape, murder and massacre which had disgraced the Japanese capture of Hong Kong'.[38]

* * * * * *

From October 1941 onwards, numerous large ships had sailed practically empty from Singapore as Sir Shenton had declined to order the compulsory evacuation of European and Asian women and children. Even as late as January 1942, many more women and children could have been saved from internment in prison camps had all the available liners been forced to sail with a full complement of passengers. Many among those who delayed their departure, or refused to leave when they could, did so out of conviction, nurses, for example, feeling that they had to stay longer to assist with the wounded. Nobody in authority wanted a repetition of the flight from Penang!

The plight of many refugees arriving in Singapore was appalling. Most of them were Chinese, who had fled the Japanese advance and by mid-January 1942, the half million population of Singapore had almost doubled. People arrived either on foot or on bicycles, clasping their meagre possessions, and huddled among the debris-strewn streets in make-shift shelters, only to run in mass hysteria with each fresh bombing raid. Singapore was also host to numerous Europeans who had come from Penang and other northern towns and who constantly bumped into old friends as they looked for safe places to stay. A.L. Archer, a rubber planter, recalled how he had left his estate and his workers:

> 'We just ran, leaving them to their fate. We left behind everything that we owned, all our personal belongings, our furniture, our wedding presents, everything . . . As we drove down the road I looked over my shoulder towards the bungalow — a small crowd was advancing on it and I realized that in a few minutes time all our belongings would be in the hands of our Tamil work-force.'[39]

An assurance had been given by Sir Shenton that there would be no organised departure of Europeans from Singapore, but that those women with children, regardless of nationality, who wanted to leave would be given equal facilities to do so. The government's scheme to stake the fares of people in financial hardship, and their instructions to shipping agents that women with children could also sign for their passages, were not made public, as it was felt that such information would have an adverse effect on the British image. This omission imposed a grave financial constraint on many of the poorer classes, who were unable to avail themselves of an opportunity to leave.

An evacuation committee was established to monitor applications from women with children, but many who should have left earlier could not make up their minds what to do. Many women felt that asking to leave was akin to running away.

> 'What they wanted in their hearts was to be ordered to go; what they needed was an official lead from the government, implementing a demand by Churchill that all "useless mouths" should be evacuated.'[40]

It was typical of the government's indecision that no lead was given and individuals were left to decide their own fate, as the *Narkunda* sailed safely to Australia half empty.

When the belated rush of civilian evacuees did occur, the dock areas were under heavy air attack and many of the large godowns were ablaze.

> 'It was every woman for herself. The police and the Army had long since given up any attempt to marshal the traffic . . . The roads leading to the three-mile dock area were often impassable — not only because of the congested stream of "useless mouths" on their way, at last and too late, to freedom, but because they clashed head-on with convoys of army lorries, racing to get the military stores away from the docks . . . so that ships could sail.'[41]

The final evacuation fleet from Singapore totalled 44 vessels, of which only a handful escaped being sunk or captured. Unaware of lurking danger, this assortment of ships sailed directly towards Admiral Ozawa's waiting fleet. Along with other ships, the *Vyner Brooke*, equipped for twelve passengers but loaded with 250, including the resourceful and happy-go-lucky Australian Army nurses, was ferociously attacked by six Japanese bombers on the 14th afternoon. Only three of the *Vyner Brooke's* lifeboats reached the water in a serviceable condition. The *Mata Hari*, having picked up survivors during the early hours of the 14th, fell squarely among the Japanese fleet on Sunday 15th February, and was forced to surrender. The *Giang Bee* was sunk within minutes of being viciously attacked by Japanese destroyers, with the loss of 200 people on board. Their deaths were unnecessary and an act of sheer callous brutality.

* * * * * *

Sir Shenton Thomas refused to meet the Japanese and never officially surrendered his office to them. He personally led the fifteen mile march of civilian internees to Changi, through the stiflingly hot, bomb-damaged streets that were strewn with litter, and along which Rising Sun flags fluttered listlessly in the fetid air. The Asian population took little notice of the bedraggled lines of civilians and soldiers as they passed by on their way to captivity. People just hurried past them, eyes averted and noses and mouths covered, in an attempt to shut out the nauseating stench of dead bloated bodies. At each cross-road Japanese sentries stood with fixed bayonets. When the women internees arrived at Changi, their undaunted spirit evoked soul-searching emotion.

> '. . . as we came in sight of the prison we all got into step, and, singing "There'll Always be an England" at the top of our voices, we marched through the high walls. The men, already there at the other side, cheered themselves hoarse.'[42]

11:4 Criticisms; Blame for Disaster

The rapid loss of Malaya and Singapore cannot be blamed entirely on those strategists at home, or the commanders and troops enmeshed in the fiasco; neither should blame be unfairly apportioned to those civilian officials who had the misfortune of circumstance to be associated with it. Blame lies squarely at the door of British statesmen throughout the 1930s, who failed in their duty to assemble a superior force in the right place at the right time.

Britain had favoured an Anglo-American alignment, instead of renewing her earlier Anglo-Japanese one. This, combined with her failure to transform the Singapore Naval Base into a strongly defended and garrisoned fortress, left Malaya's various riches an attractive and easy prey to Japan's militarist ambitions. Similarly the separatist policy, encouraged by the British in pre-war Malaya, cultivated weaknesses within the various races' attitudes towards the country, and as such warrants criticism, for it 'demanded a privileged position for Malays within the states and, more particularly, power and wealth for Malays of the aristocracy, whether they deserved it or not'.[43]

Britain was already vastly overstretched in respect of both men and equipment. Dunkirk had been only eighteen months previously, and the Battle of Britain had been gallantly fought and miraculously won. The Middle-East, of necessity, had been given priority for stores and men, on the premiss that there would be ample time for reinforcements to be sent to the Far-East even after Japan had gained access to southern Indo-China in the summer of 1941, which had brought her within striking distance of Malaya. Even at that juncture, however, strategists persisted in assuming that Siam would be willing and able to delay any Japanese advance through her territory.

The necessity to defend Great Britain at all costs can never be overlooked. Of equal importance was the guarantee of aid to Russia, as her defeat would enable Germany to mount a gigantic air and land-based attack against the British Isles. Far better, it was argued, to sacrifice British possessions in the Far East than let Russia be defeated, and to adopt a strategy aimed at crushing Nazi Germany first, before turning full attention to defeating Japan.

In the face of such decisions and events Percival realised that he could only demand the minimum requirements in both men and weapons, and that he was obliged to make the best with what he was given. He did not complain on this score, but did with good reason query the failure of the Chiefs of Staff to amend their Far Eastern strategy, as events inevitably changed and deteriorated. Both Air-Vice Marshall C.W. Pulford, the Air Officer Commanding Malaya, and Air-Chief Marshall Sir Robert Brook-Popham, the Commander-in-Chief Far East, were not responsible for the critical shortage of effective aircraft that were made available to Malaya, as both of them had repeatedly made representations for more reinforcements to the Chiefs of Staff in London. The Chiefs of Staff in London must have been fully aware that their mid-1941 promises of first-line aircraft could not be fulfilled. They should have told Percival, at the earliest possible juncture, so that he could have amended his pre-campaign strategy. The army in Malaya was left to face an impossible task and initially did so with both resolution and courage. Vastly superior numbers of Allied and British forces were overwhelmed, not by better armed and numerically stronger opponents, but by ingenious and simple infiltration tactics, executed by small determined groups who were able to cause panic in the defenders and the gradual loss of their fighting spirit.

Alfred Duff Cooper, the Chancellor of the Duchy of Lancaster – and a protégé of Churchill with Cabinet Minister standing – arrived in Singapore on 9th September 1941. During his brief and stormy stay, until he departed on 13th January 1942, his contributions to the overall performance of the campaign were negative and, catastrophically, achieved nothing but harm. Given his privileged position, Cooper could have quickly appraised Churchill of the desperate shortages that existed in the Far-East, had he seen fit to discuss such matters properly with those Commanders who were required to lead their troops into the battle. Tanks were available in the Middle-East – as the 7th Armoured Brigade was sent to Burma a few months later – but Malaya was denied them, even though a request for two tank regiments had been made as early as 1937 and again by Percival in May 1941, as soon as he arrived to take over the Command. Percival had realised long before the war commenced that the Japanese would use tanks, but what fighting commanders knew as being essential to their performance, and what their seniors considered essential, regrettably and inexplicably remained far apart. Instead of helping Duff Cooper chose to assume the role of character assassin.

He wrote derogatorily of Sir Shenton Thomas 'as being unable to adjust his mind to war conditions and as having lost his grip on the situation'.[44] He also criticised the Malayan Civil Service (MCS) as having 'failed lamentably in making adequate preparations for war',[45] and he faulted Lieut-General Percival's leadership capabilities. Cooper's companion in criticism was Major-General Gordon Bennett, the Australian commander, who censured the British old-school-tie method of command selection. Surprising indeed from a commander who shortly after this left his own troops, without appointing any replacement and without informing Percival of his intention to slip away from Singapore for his own safety, thereby avoiding the probability of becoming a prisoner of war for an extended period.

The Japanese had several initial advantages over British and Allied forces. They had a clearly devised and well-rehearsed plan that they were fully determined to carry out. They deployed fit, highly trained troops who were well led, and who could adjust easily to the climate and to the basic essentials of the country. Japanese troops had been action-hardened, their good morale constantly elevated by their early successes, in contrast to many among the defenders, whose morale sank along with the *Prince of Wales*. Japanese propaganda was also effective and prompted many defections among Indian soldiers from the ranks of the British Indian Army. Many of them were already confused by the proclamations of leaders in India who were against her entry into the war to fight the Axis powers, and the use of Indian soldiers in Malaya. Last but certainly not least, was the serious underestimation of the Japanese by many civil and military leaders at that time, who thought that after four years of war in China, Japan was on the verge of economic collapse. Nothing could have been further from the truth.

Years of indifference and negligence camouflaged the serious weaknesses in Britain's defensive strategy and planning for Malaya. If these are discounted and only those blunders dating from Percival's assumption of command are taken into consideration, the failures of individual commanders and various British authorities are only too evident. Mistakes were numerous and many of them were illogical. The selection that follows falls far short of being exhaustive but includes: the failure to construct proper defences in known strategic positions; denying troops realistic training opportunities in rubber plantations; out-dated training manuals; insufficient training and use of the Asian population to defend their homeland; shortage of troop equipment and transport; no modern aircraft; no fleet protection; no aircraft carriers; no tanks; inability to stop any attempted land attack anywhere in Malaya, let alone in Johore; the indecision over and failure of Operation Matador; the late arrival of troops at the Ledge; the sinking of the *Prince of Wales* and *Repulse* due to communication failure and no air protection; the lack of an orderly plan for scorched earth activities in Penang; the preference shown to Europeans in the scuttle from Penang; the late arrival of untrained, ill-prepared reinforcements; poor co-operation between the military and civil government; the failure of the radio and other means of communication; leakage of final-stand orders for Singapore's defence; the failure of searchlights and British artillery to go into effective action during the initial assault by Japanese troops on the island; the failure yet again of artillery to seek out and destroy General Yamashita's prominent, elevated five-storey advanced headquarters in the Palace of the Sultan of Johore, from where he had a bird's-eye view of Singapore island and of the Causeway; the indecisive rupture of this final link with the mainland; the breakdown of discipline among many troops in the days prior to the surrender; Percival's misconceived belief that he was outnumbered; Churchill's exhortations to fight to the end when this bore no relation to the facts; and last but certainly not least in importance, the continual stream of falsehoods that fed hope to civilians and troops alike. This did much to damage their morale, and made them the prey of rumour mongers. Had some of these, in any combination, been corrected or avoided in sufficient time, the outcome of the Malayan campaign might well have been different.

Many of the fighting men, who had withstood the exhausting endless retreat down the Malayan Peninsula, were particularly bitter. They blamed their officers for the disaster, and in similar manner junior officers blamed their senior officers. Individual commander's decisions, however, were not ultimately responsible for the disaster, as they had no power to alter or influence its outcome. Wavell blamed training deficiencies and a lack of toughness and fighting spirit, which he considered stemmed from Malaya's hot, humid and sleepy atmosphere which detracted from effective peace-time training and positive tactical planning. A lethargy had developed that was impossible to shake off during the lightning haste of defeat. Although it was acknowledged that Percival had raised the level and tempo of troop training in preparation for the war, he 'was unable to overcome the effects of years of inadequate preparation and the long-standing lack of close cooperation in Malaya between all concerned in its defence. Shackled by the accepted view that war with Japan was unlikely and with his hands tied by the retention of control of major expenditure in London, no commander could have accomplished much in this period.'[46]

Many of the British in Singapore were shocked by the capitulation. Some troops and units had scarcely seen any combat action and could not believe what was being proposed. John Forrester, with a unit of bren gun carriers,

'thought the man who'd brought the news about the surrender was some fifth columnist and somebody even suggested shooting him. We were particularly amazed and dumbfounded because . . . we had never actually seen a Japanese or fired a shot in anger. We had done nothing worthwhile to stop the capture of Singapore.'[47]

The unexpected defeat was criticised severely in both Australia and Great Britain. The Australians were now concerned at the prospect of having the Japanese practically at their doorstep and condemned British leadership and the poor training of the Indian soldiers. The Indians in turn blamed the British military and civil authorities, while the British poured condemnation on their own Commanders, on their Chiefs of Staff, and on the fibre and training of Australian troops. Churchill thought that keeping the Burma Road open would be strategically more important than holding Singapore, but was aghast at the outcome of this decision and the enormity of the defeat. The Australian Premier, Mr Curtin, angrily protested that he would regard any evacuation of Singapore 'as an inexcusable betrayal'[48] after all the assurances previously given.

The British were shocked by the Malayan fiasco, and Britain's Commonwealth partners felt betrayed. After Malaya and Burma fell an American diplomat was told by Nehru that

'there is a widespread belief in India that the British have no serious intention or capacity to resist the Japanese invasion'.[49]

Many people thought that Britain should not have surrendered Singapore so readily and that fighting should have been continued to the last. Churchill was of this opinion and attempted to cover up the home Government's failure to adequately provide for the war, by exhorting that

> '"the battle should be fought to the bitter end at all costs," and that commanders "should die with their troops" for "the honour of the British Empire"'.[50]

Orders to destroy everything of use to the enemy with

> '"no thought of saving the troops or sparing the population" . . . showed an extraordinary ignorance of psychology on the part of the authorities at home',[51]

and did nothing to improve the morale of the fighting men who by now had realised that they had been abandoned either to death or captivity. Further resistance would have invited greater destruction, hardship and disaster, especially for the Chinese civilian population. The disgrace of the surrender was that so many troops, civilians and resources were left stranded, caught in a trap, and thereafter had to languish and suffer in POW camps, where conditions in most cases became inhuman.

* * * * * *

Major-General Woodburn Kirby, author of the *Official History of the War Against Japan* which was published in 1957, labelled Air-Chief Marshall Sir Robert Brooke-Popham as being

> 'a man of great charm (who) had clearly passed his prime and was not forceful enough a personality to deal with this complicated and difficult situation'.[52]

As the Commander-in-Chief Far East, from November 1940 until 27th December 1941, Brooke-Popham was stranded in an untenable situation of position without power. Nevertheless, despite his 61 years of age and having been recalled out of retirement, he was strongly sanctioned for his lack of personal energy and professional determination as circumstances continued to deteriorate. He failed to achieve those goals expected of him and his incomprehension of events was all too clearly revealed in a Memorandum that he issued to his own staff officers in September 1941, in which he assured them:

> 'Until the latter part of February (1942) the danger of a Japanese offensive against Malaya will be less than it has been during the last six months . . . Our preparations should include a period of leave and recreation for as many individuals as possible so that they shall be on the top of their form by the early part of 1942.'[53]

When Brooke-Popham was confronted with a real emergency he dallied and failed to launch Operation Matador, for which he has been justifiably blamed.

* * * * * *

Sir Shenton Thomas voiced what many people devoutly held to be true when he said:

> 'It doesn't matter about us. It's the people I'm sorry for. It's their country — and somehow we've let them down.'[54]

Until his death on 15th February 1962, twenty years to the day when Singapore fell and at an age of 83, Sir Shenton never ceased in his attempts to defend the rubber planters in Malaya against the vindictive whiskey-swilling slurs made against them. He was equally embittered by criticisms made against his officers, and as early as 21st January 1942 he wrote in his diary:

> 'The behaviour "of the military" ever since the retreat began has been disgraceful . . . If Singapore falls it will be the army's fault; they have been incredibly inefficient.'[55]

By 9th February Sir Shenton had obvious grave misgivings, not only on the fighting men's performance but also in regard to the potential leadership capabilities of senior commanders in the field. A diary entry on that date confirms this.

> 'Australians are not fighting well. They had been heavily shelled and many had been found wandering about the roads. Not easy to proceed with denial schemes when we are given no progress reports. Absence of personality in the High Command most unfortunate. Percival doubtless good on paper but not a leader and his staff are all small men . . . RAF much worse – Pulford nice but no more . . . Heath is a tired man who has retreated 400 miles in a few weeks and no one had confidence in him. We need someone really big here.'[56]

In the *Official History of the War against Japan* by Maj-Gen. S. Woodburn Kirby grave accusations are made against the civil government's performance in Malaya and Singapore. Sir Shenton was particularly aggrieved by this and in a letter written on 1st November 1956, he objected to what had been recorded in that he felt

> 'obliged to point out that I was never consulted by the historians in the preparation of the original draft; nor, as far as I can trace, on any points arising out of my own commentary, nor in the preparation of the revised and final draft . . . I regard this as unfair to Malaya.'[57]

Two points annoyed Sir Shenton. The first was an incorrect assumption that the population of Singapore had not been warned of approaching Japanese bombers on 8th December 1941, 'because the ARP HQ was not manned'.[58] The ARP centre most certainly was manned, 'but the Alarm sirens could not have been sounded as the Chief Warden was at the cinema and had the control key with him'.[59] The second was the inference that no attempt had been made to black out the street lights of the city, to which Sir Shenton explained:

> 'A crash blackout was not possible in Singapore as much of the lighting was by gas which had to be put out by men going round to extinguish each light with a pole!'[60]

Air-Vice Marshall Pulford accused Sir Shenton of malignly influencing the conduct of the Malayan campaign, and especially blamed him for not diverting from Singapore the essential fighter aircraft cover needed by Z Force during those crucial two days. Sir Shenton flatly denied having been responsible for this decision.

Such public accusations may raise the suspicion that Sir Shenton was singled out as a scapegoat for other peoples' failings. After the war all his efforts to publish his own views, and to obtain a fair hearing concerning them, were disregarded.

* * * * * *

Percival first met Field-Marshall Sir John Dill when he was an instructor at the Camberly Staff College. Dill thought highly of Percival and duly wrote of him to the Director of Staff Duties at the War Office that:

> '. . . he is the best officer I have met for a long time.'[61]

In 1941 Dill, as the Chief of the Imperial Staff, promoted Percival to Lieut-General over the heads of all his contemporaries, and then recommended that he should be sent to Malaya as the General Officer Commanding. In doing this, Dill in effect signed the death warrant of Percival's subsequent career, and then himself died without being able to exonerate Percival from any of the criticism over subsequent events. Dill was responsible for appointing Percival and posting him to a position for which he was ill-suited. Although the loss of Singapore was a devastating psychological shock to the general public in Britain and to Britain's allies, it came as no real surprise to the British Chiefs of Staff. During the following three and a half years, when Percival was in internment, he was ignorant of the extent of the scornful criticism levied at him. This was so great that on his release from captivity he was immediately retired from the service. If Percival was such a military failure, Dill should have surely been blamed. There was probably no General in service who could have turned defeat into victory under the circumstances that existed in Malaya when Japan attacked. Percival had the misfortune to be the man on the spot. He was known to be a brilliant strategist, but lacked the leadership qualities to command troops in battle. He was by no means a dynamic commander and did not strive to infer that he was either by way of behaviour, deportment or manner of dress, but he was physically and morally courageous, and beneath his quiet exterior there was a core of steel. He was a highly qualified and professional soldier with many admirable qualities, and was utterly loyal to his superiors and subordinates alike.

The early reversals of the campaign both on land and at sea were stoically accepted by Percival who was not prone to belly-aching about past errors not of his making. Neither was it in his character to attempt to lay blame at the door of anyone for past mistakes. He was one commander who was loyal to his superiors.

After the war Percival wanted the facts, as he saw them, to be made public and he received an assurance from the War Minister that this would be allowed. Several sensation seeking, ill-informed authors wrote emotional and scurrilous attacks to discredit Percival in books during and after the war, and to a great extent his own account of events was discarded by the official historian. Percival was naturally considerably criticised for surrendering the largest ever number of British troops in the history of the British army. He faced the criticisms with considerable equanimity and took offence only when he thought that his troops had been unfairly criticised.

The remaining years of his life were dedicated to rehabilitating the men who had suffered defeat with him and who had become POWs. Those who had served under his command who survived the three and a half years of harsh treatment at Japanese hands, held him in whole-hearted affection. This was a great satisfaction to him and a lasting memorial to his character. Percival died a broken man at the age of seventy-nine in 1966, and despite much of the blame resting on his shoulders he fully deserves sympathy. Colonel A.M.L. Harrison CBE wrote of Percival:

> 'I was proud to count (him) as a friend. Particularly I admired him for his moral courage after the capitulation of Singapore, and for the way he devoted his great Christian qualities to doing all he could for the alleviation of his troops in captivity, to whose welfare he devoted himself after the war. In all this he proved himself a great and selfless leader to whom adversity was a spur. As a commander of what was inevitably a lost cause I consider he lacked the quality of ruthlessness. But the fall of Singapore was inevitable anyway.'[62]

Percival should certainly not be solely blamed as his involvement came at the end of two decades of misconceived planning and execution. Churchill had been forced into making some

> 'hard decisions about the allocation of scarce resources. The Middle-East got priority over South-East Asia, which never received adequate naval protection and armoured forces and where reinforcements of aircraft arrived too late'.[63]

Percival's strategy, however, failed to grasp any advantages and instead he only reacted to 'each successive Japanese onslaught in piecemeal fashion'.[64] His final mistake was to surrender Singapore when the Japanese were exhausted by their efforts, and were desperately short of ammunition.

* * * * * *

When Britain was fighting alone against Germany, civil and military leaders in Malaya should have shown greater initiative, and been allowed more authority to make use of it. Instead, they were handicapped by centralised control from London. To blame the disaster on a lack of trained men and modern equipment is nothing short of a convenient over-simplification that hides many cumulative errors in judgement and implementation. Both the civil government and the army in Malaya could have responded earlier and more positively to their material shortages and acted to ensure the safety of the area by other means, such as an intensive programme that involved jungle training for the available forces, and making fuller use of the indigenous population.

Japan was fully aware of Britain's weaknesses in Malaya and this knowledge enabled General Yamashita to assign only three divisions for his task, instead of the five that were originally intended. The defeat was quick and spectacular, with only 3,507 Japanese killed during the campaign — one for every forty Allied troops who surrendered.

On 26th March 1942 Churchill described the loss of Singapore as 'the greatest disaster to British arms which our history records'.[65]

What Churchill did not say was that the loss was due to a series of economic, international, military and political mistakes that had been made over a period of time, the culmination of which rapidly undermined events throughout the Far East, commencing from the fateful 8th December 1941. With the capitulation of Singapore, Japan was now free to raid at will throughout a vast area in the Far East. India, Ceylon, Australia and New Zealand were suddenly left stranded and open to attack, and with the overrunning of Burma, Java, Sumatra and the Philippines, Japan had gained possession of all the oil, rice, rubber and tin that she had hitherto lacked, and was poised to expand further.

Scapegoats are required following any military disaster. Obvious choices are always the commanders and their fighting troops. The official history implied that the British were out-generaled by the Japanese. Wavell knew that this was not so and that Percival's task had been an impossible one, but he found a scapegoat by implying that British troops had been a disgrace, by not being able to beat the Japanese whom they heavily outnumbered. Wavell chose to overlook the fact that many among those troops he condemned were only recent arrivals, and were untrained young soldiers who were given a task that was completely beyond their capabilities.

1. *Tales from the South China Seas* edited by Charles Allen, ch.11, p.248.
2. *Percival and the Tragedy of Singapore* by Sir John Smyth VC, ch.9, p.135.
3. *In 70 Days, The Story of Malaya* by E.M. Glover, ch.9, p.124.
4. *Sinister Twilight (The Fall of Singapore)* by Noel Barber, ch.3, p.53.
5. Ibid, ch.4, p.57.
6. *Shenton of Singapore. Governor and Prisoner of War* by Brian Montgomery, ch.7, p.111.
7. *Sinister Twilight (The Fall of Singapore)* by Noel Barber, ch.5, p.83.
8. *The Fall of Singapore* by Frank Owen, ch.8, p.112.
9. *Bamboo and Bushido* by A.G. Allbury, Prologue, p.10.
10. Ibid.
11. *Women Behind the Wire* by Lavinia Warner and John Sandilands, ch.3, p.27.
12. *Shenton of Singapore. Governor and Prisoner of War* by Brian Montgomery, ch.5, p.80. (Harry Grumbar to B. Montgomery.)
13. Ibid, ch.6, p.102–3.
14. *Sinister Twilight (The Fall of Singapore)* by Noel Barber, ch.6, p.95.
15. *Shenton of Singapore. Governor and Prisoner of War* by Brian Montgomery, ch.7, p.125.
16. *The Fall of Singapore* by Frank Owen, ch.11, p.152.
17. *British Rule in Malaya 1941–1957* by Robert Heussler, ch.2, p.30.

18. *Sinister Twilight (The Fall of Singapore)* by Noel Barber, ch.8, p.143. (Refers to *The War Against Japan*, Vol.1, by Major-General S. Woodburn Kirby.)
19. *The Fall of Singapore* by Frank Owen, ch.12, p.164.
20. *Sinister Twilight (The Fall of Singapore)* by Noel Barber, ch.8, p.176.
21. Ibid, ch.8, p.176.
22. Ibid, ch.8, p.178–9.
23. *The Fall of Singapore* by Frank Owen, ch.12, p.178.
24. *Sinister Twilight (The Fall of Singapore)* by Noel Barber, ch.9, p.203.
25. Ibid.
26. Ibid, ch.5, p.71.
27. Ibid, ch.8, p.177.
28. Ibid, ch.9, p.204.
29. Ibid, ch.10, p.222.
30. *Singapore. Too Little; Too Late* by Ivan Simson, ch.16, p.155. (Refers to 'A Soldier Must Hang' by Major-General Tomoyuki Yamashita.)
31. *Sinister Twilight (The Fall of Singapore)* by Noel Barber, ch.10, p.227.
32. *When Singapore Was Syonan-To* by N.I. Low, ch.1, p.2.
33. *Shenton of Singapore, Governor and Prisoner of War* by Brian Montgomery, ch.7, p.136. (Refers to *Official History of the War Against Japan*, Vol.1, The Loss of Singapore, The Cabinet Office, Historical Section [HMSO 1957].)
34. *Sinister Twilight (The Fall of Singapore)* by Noel Barber, ch.10, p.228.
35. *Allies of a Kind. The US, Britain and the War Against Japan. 1941–45* by Christopher Thorne, ch.5, p.155.
36. *Japan Against the World 1941–2041. The 100–Year War for Supremacy* by Russell Braddon, ch.3, p.54–5.
37. *The Fall of Singapore* by Frank Owen, ch.1, p.11.
38. *Ibid.*
39. *The Way It Was* by Alex L. Archer, ch.10, p.80.
40. *Sinister Twilight (The Fall of Singapore)* by Noel Barber, ch.5, p.87.
41. Ibid, ch.6, p.106.
42. *Shenton of Singapore. Governor and Prisoner of War* by Brian Montgomery, ch.8, p.149. (Refers to *Dear Phillip* by Freddy Bloom.)
43. *Allies of a Kind. The US, Britain and the War Against Japan 1941–45* by Christopher Thorne, ch.7, p.203. (Refers to CO865/1.)
44. Ibid, ch.7, p.203.
45. Ibid.
46. *Percival and the Tragedy of Singapore* by Sir John Smyth VC, ch.18, p.245.
47. *Tales from the South China Seas. Images of the British in South-East Asia in the Twentieth Century* edited by Charles Allen, ch.11, p.263.
48. *Sinister Twilight (The Fall of Singapore)* by Noel Barber, ch.6, p.98.
49. *Eagle Against the Sun: The American War With Japan* by Ronald H. Spector, ch.6, p.139.
50. *History of the Second World War* by B.H. Liddell Hart, ch.17, p.239.
51. Ibid.
52. *Shenton of Singapore. Governor and Prisoner of War* by Brian Montgomery, ch.10, p.192.
53. Ibid.
54. *Sinister Twilight (The Fall of Singapore)* by Noel Barber, ch.10, p.238.
55. *Shenton of Singapore. Governor and Prisoner of War* by Brian Montgomery, ch.7, p.124.
56. Ibid, ch.7, p.131.

57. Ibid, ch.9, p.185.
58. Ibid, ch.9, p.186.
59. Ibid.
60. Ibid, ch.9, p.187.
61. *Percival and the Tragedy of Singapore* by Sir John Smyth VC, ch.2, p.40.
62. Ibid, ch.18, p.261.
63. *British Rule in Malaya 1942–1957* by Robert Heussler, ch.2, p.12.
64. Ibid.
65. *Shenton of Singapore. Governor and Prisoner of War* by Brian Montgomery, ch.10, p.189.

PART THREE: OCCUPATION YEARS

CHAPTER TWELVE: MALAYAN MILITARY ADMINISTRATION (MMA) EFFECTS AND REPERCUSSIONS

12:1 Co-Prosperity and Hakko Ichiu

When invading the countries in Southeast Asia, Japan fully anticipated being able to exploit their increasing and respective nationalistic aspirations and desire for independence. By quickly occupying these vast regions, designated the Greater East Asia Co-Prosperity Sphere (GEACS), Japan hoped to remain in ultimate possession of most of them by subsequent peaceful negotiations with the countries from whom they had been snatched. Japan's benevolent propaganda slogans such as 'Asia for the Asians' and 'Japan is the Light of Asia' conjured up visions of improved economic and political leadership, along with the promised expulsion of outsiders, all to the benefit of the subjected peoples. The propaganda messages were carefully tailored to suit circumstances as they existed in the various countries that came under Japan's control: Burmese and Siamese were appealed to as fellow Buddhists; in Indonesia the Japanese condemned the infidel Dutch and their despised trading practices and gave support to Islam. Japan's promises of pending self-government were vague shadows under a morning sun, that would eventually evaporate into the dim obscurity of dusk.

On 16th February 1942 Tokyo radio broadcast:

> 'A new chapter in the history of our great and Imperishable Empire begins. From today Singapore becomes Syonan, the Illustrious Light of the South. Nippon is the Liberator of Asia and its Sacred Mission is the establishment of the Co-Prosperity Sphere, the establishment of the New Order, and the spreading of the doctrine of Hakko-Ichiu, the Universal Brotherhood of Man.'[1]

The Imperial Nipponese military administration declared that liberated Malaya had been resurrected and renamed Ma-Rai-Ee, from which Anglo-American culture would be purged and replaced by 'the fresh and invigorating air of Nippon culture and civilisation'.[2] This was to entail 'massacre, rape and the sorrows of a lifetime'.[3]

The GEACS was established within four months of the start of Japan's offensive in the region. In her original strategic plan Japan conceived the possibility of changing tack onto a defensive course at the conclusion of her successful offensive operations, but when this stage was reached she was reluctant to do so, for she

> '... feared that such a change might bring a gradual decline of fighting spirit, while giving their Western opponents, economically much stronger, a breathing space for recovery'.[4]

The concept of GEACS was an integral part of the 'Hakko Ichiu' (Universal Brotherhood of Man) ideology which to the Japanese was presented as a sacred mission to gather all corners of the earth under the one roof of Japanese Imperial domination. Euphuisms such as 'Asia for the Asians' promised the banishment of white races and their influence from liberated areas, and was a convenient ploy while Japan seized most of Asia and hoped to achieve her goals.

Hakko Ichiu aspired to replace all influences of Western culture with those of Japan, which entailed spiritual cleansing, Emperor worship, Nippon-go and Japanese culture. Subjected races were meant to be both physically and spiritually fit in order to be of useful service to the Japanese Empire, and the populations of conquered countries were expected to emulate the Imperial Japanese way of life. Oriental morality was encouraged rather than that of the Western world with its dependent fixation on materialism and all attitudes associated with this concept.

Nipponisation of the population was Japan's goal, and slogans to this effect were continually expounded and repeated like dogmatic rituals through the mass media and through the educational system. Constant propaganda heralded the benefits arising from the formation of the GEACS and of Hakko Ichiu which, it was claimed, would liberate Asians from all Anglo-American influence.

Early in the occupation the Japanese boasted considerably of

> 'the equality of all races in their much-vaunted brotherhood of New East Asia, [in which] if you met a Japanese – whether you were Chinese, Malay, or Tamil – you had to cover your face with both hands and bow down low before him'.[5]

The *Penang Shimbun* also repeatedly assured its readers that provided people made sacrifices and endured hardships, the rewards, once victory had been achieved, would be adequate.

The interpretation of 'Co-Prosperity' by the liberators of Ma-Rai-Ee was to squeeze every cent out of the Chinese community that they could, and to drain the country of its resources for Japan's material gain. Their propaganda soon rang hollowly in the ears of the thousands of enslaved Asians who were forced to work in native labour units, and even the Malays were not spared this fate, notwithstanding early preference being given to them. Many of them ended up on the Siam Death Railway, although they had initially been recruited to work in their own country.

India's position on the western perimeter of GEACS made Japan desirous to assist her in her aspirations for independence, for Japan perceived this circumstance would be to her advantage. In early 1942 General Hideki Tojo, the Japanese Prime Minister, declared that without India's liberation there could be 'no real mutual prosperity in Greater East Asia',[6] and in April he reiterated that 'it has been decided to strike a decisive blow against British power and military establishment in India'.[7] Between January and April 1942 Tojo repeatedly called upon Indians to take advantage of the war and rise up against British power. Japan tried hard in this manner to obtain the support of Indians. The reality, however, was that 'Tamil coolies were dying so fast' on the Siamese railway 'that large numbers were laid out for burial every day'.[8] Some of these unfortunates were buried alive, and others, mistakenly earmarked for burial, were summarily dispatched in the most vicious manner if they had any signs of life in them.

Japan's war of liberation, therefore, was one of many missed opportunities where, especially at the outset, there was a measure of initial goodwill among local nationalist elements. The Japanese had an uncanny knack of turning potential friends into enemies through their arrogance and brutal behaviour. Little or no attempt was made to practise the brotherhood that they preached, and whatever the sufferings of the people, the Japanese enjoyed the best of everything. Their administrative hypocrisy fomented silent contempt. The military police in many instances spoilt any good intentions by civil authorities, although some officials were able to recognise people's difficulties and there were occasions when Japanese women were able to prevent soldiers from beating people.

Elaborate celebrations were held to mark the anniversary of the declaration of the War of Great East Asia (Dai Toa Senso), and to commemorate the fall of Singapore. The public were ordered to attend these and everyone was required to bow to the Japanese Emperor (Tenno-Heika), and

> 'be harangued by the Japanese Governor, while community leaders made speeches expressing the loyalty and gratitude of the local people for the benevolent Nippon rule! One must admit that this benevolence was not altogether absent. Arrangements were made for importing rice and other foodstuffs from Burma and Siam; the Jeikaidan or Voluntary Police system was introduced, . . . and communications rapidly re-established throughout the country.'[9]

Some people had enthusiastically welcomed the Japanese on their arrival, but by the end of 1942 the majority of them were 'longingly awaiting the day of their release from Nippon bondage'.[10] Tokyo's liberation of Malaya subjected people to a worse form of bondage than had ever existed under the worst aspects of British pre-war administration. In three and a half years Japan generated more bitterness throughout Southeast Asia than her Western colonial predecessors had managed to cause over centuries. Japan had ample experience as an aggressor, but little as a coloniser.

12:2 The Malayan Military Administration (MMA)

The decision to set up a form of Military Administration for Malaya and Singapore was made on 20th November 1941, on the assumption that Japan would succeed in over-running the country and defeating the British. Thus, on 2nd March 1942, 15 days after Singapore was surrendered, the Japanese formed the Malayan Military Administration (MMA), which was to become an integrated centralised system of government ruling over both the Federated and Unfederated States as well as the three component parts of the Straits Settlements, for the next three years and five months.

The General Commanding the 7th Area Army, with his headquarters at Singapore, was the Director General (Somubucho) of the

MMA, which was organised into ten Provincial units, one for each State, under their respective Japanese Governors (Gunseikan). Some of the ten Governors were selected from bureaucrats in the powerful Ministry of the Interior, and others were chosen from a list of retired Generals. They replaced State Rulers as respective Heads of State, and combined their duties with those of the Rulers and the former pre-war British Advisers. The Governors sat as Chairmen of the State Regional Advisory Councils on which Malay Rulers were only allowed to sit as Vice-Chairmen from 1943 onwards. The Malay Rulers, however, were initially allowed to remain as nominal heads in their respective States, but in effect were demoted to positions of minor officials, with their authority severely diminished and restricted to matters relating to the Islamic religion. Singapore was renamed Syonan (Light of the South) and, because of its strategic and locational importance, was made into a special Municipality with its own Mayor.

The Japanese assumed direct control over the Straits Settlements. Existing forms of government were allowed to remain in the various Malay States, with their powers curtailed and subjected to the advice of Japanese political agents, in conjunction with the requirements of military commanders. The MMA fostered a corrupt and incompetent system of administration which imposed considerable hardships on the people in order to satisfy its aims. It was also open to numerous forms of bribery.

In contrast to Japan's brilliantly planned and executed military campaign, her subsequent administration of Malaya and Singapore was highlighted by a series of foolish mistakes. Although some senior Japanese administrators at State level appeared 'to have extracted more work from the Malay elite than the British'[11] before them, the majority, entrusted with large responsibilities, were unsuitable and incompetent. The MMA was a form of imperialistic rule. Its objectives were the military domination and exploitation of the people and natural resources of the occupied countries of Greater East Asia. Perhaps through naivety, but more likely through sheer haughtiness, the Japanese tried to achieve their administrative goals not by using trained and skilled administrators as they should have done, but by quickly substituting them with people whose previous vocations had been barbers, assistants in curio shops, sailors off junks, photographers and even brothel house keepers.

From the outset of the occupation the Japanese made it irrefutably clear that they regarded Malaya as a military stronghold which would be directly governed as a colony and as a permanent possession of the Japanese Empire. They considered any question of early independence for Malaya as unfeasible, citing the political backwardness of the indigenous peoples. In Burma, the Philippines and Indonesia a different policy was followed and some measure of self-government was gradually permitted, but in Malaya all planning for political control and

> 'the exploitation and distribution of its raw materials, and the use of local shipping were formulated as part of the larger Japanese plans for the Southern Regions'.[12]

The army dominated Malaya's administration, and only in late 1942, as a policy of integration within the Empire, did Tokyo instruct that the army would be required to

> 'consult with civilian agencies in Japan in choosing suitable technical personnel to emigrate to Malaya to work under the Military administration'.[13]

This form of administration continued until the second half of 1943, after which a change in policy started to emerge. A 'New Malai' concept was formulated in which all races were required to cooperate. The four northern States of the country — i.e. Kedah, Perlis, Kelantan and Trengganu — were ceded by treaty to Siam, and by way of appeasement for this deceit, the MMA announced the setting up of State Consultative Councils in October 1943, which were arranged on similar lines to the pre-war British Executive Councils for the Straits Settlements Colony and the Malay States. Members of State Councils were nominated either by the Mayor of Singapore or the Governor for each State, who were also appointed as the ex-officio Chairmen of the Councils. The Malay Ruler in each State was nominated as Vice-Chairman of his respective State Council. No other Japanese served on these Councils other than the Chairman and, following this administrative policy change, an increased number of Malayan officials were allowed to function in various administrative services, with preference being given to the promotion of Malays. State Consultative Councils had the potential to develop into a form of State government, but the Japanese only permitted them to function in an advisory and minor capacity. Even so, their initial support of Malays in particular, and of the Kesatuan Melayu Muda (KMM) and Indonesian Raya political factions encouraged a revival of Malay nationalism, which grew steadily during the years of occupation, to emerge openly after the conclusion of the war.

Many of the Japanese nationals who were imprisoned at the outbreak of war had lived in Penang, Singapore and most other parts of the Malay Peninsula, for anything between ten to thirty years. They were fluent in the various spoken languages of the country. When these people were released from prison, not only were they extremely useful to the Japanese forces as they sped southwards, but following the fall of Singapore many of them were automatically seconded into the military administration instead of being allowed to open their previous pre-war businesses. Many were placed in positions far above their intellectual capacity and social standing. This served to inflate their sense of power and increase their arrogance. Initially British POWs were told to continue to look after public utilities in Singapore, but as more qualified Japanese engineers and technicians arrived and took charge, the POWs were sent back to their places of internment.

As the Japanese community in the country grew, so did the number of companies that they operated. The leading capitalists who had financed Japan's militarists were all represented in Malaya and Singapore and to these select companies went the choice fruits of Japan's military conquests. Singapore soon became Japan's regional military supply base and as many Japanese firms opened up branches there so the number of Japanese entrepreneurs considerably increased. Accommodation had to be found for all these new arrivals. Some of them behaved decently, and correctly acquired the houses and factories that they wanted by leasing them from their rightful owners. Others just took what they wanted and misbehaved as it suited them. Control was strictly imposed over all Chinese, Indian and Malay businesses as the Japanese

> 'had only one use for Malaya, and that was to turn it into an arsenal for Japan. Malaya existed merely as a cog in the Japanese war machine and a supplier of war material. Its inhabitants were just cannon-fodder or field coolies to serve Jap designs.'[14]

The MMA mobilised and made use of every segment of Malayan society and economy in order to further their war efforts. People were forced to grow more food and to provide voluntary labour, as well as produce raw materials for Japan. The Japanese imposition was complete and extended beyond material things to the spirit of Seishin and the language of the conquerors.

Among the initial aims of the MMA were

> 'the restoration of the country's economy as far as possible to its pre-war level within the concept of the Greater East Asia Co-Prosperity Sphere; substitution of Japanese culture for western culture, as symbolised by bowing instead of shaking hands, and the extirpation of Communists'.[15]

Japan's policies included the calculated humiliation of Europeans by any means, and an attempt to stamp out all Western influence. The constant deluge of propaganda was designed to inflict lasting damage on British prestige in the region, and towards this end they removed any historical monument that testified to Britain's pre-war presence and achievements in the country, and replaced English in schools with the enforced learning of the Japanese language.

The Japanese home economy worsened, following a quick succession of military and naval setbacks which started with the Midway calamity in June 1942 and continued throughout 1943. As a result, the basic tasks confronting the MMA were altered. It was required

> 'to develop and export essential raw materials to Japan; and to produce and distribute consumer goods and foodstuffs within Malaya'.[16]

Japan's military administration was constantly restricted from attaining efficient management standards as there were insufficient trained personnel to cope with her vast and quickly conquered new empire. This was particularly noticeable in Malaya and Singapore where, alongside the numerous difficulties of wartime administration, the Japanese also inherited the unsolved organisational difficulties inherent in a long-established and complicated inter-racial community. It mattered little what they did, as any change suffered in comparison to pre-war conditions, and even greater social divisions were created.

> 'To anyone as cosmopolitan and sophisticated as an educated overseas Chinese it was inevitable that the Japanese would seem heartless, laughable and stupid by turns.'[17]

The MMA concentrated on exploiting the natural resources of Malaya for Japan's continued war effort, rather than trying to win over the hearts of the people. In pre-war days these same natural resources had been an important hard currency earner for Britain, and Japan now intended to exploit them fully for her own material gain. As an essential component in realising these goals, the Japanese made some effort to secure the initial support of the Malays by keeping those Malay administrators who had served under the British. The pre-war system of administration was continued to a certain extent, by retaining some administrative procedures and rules, but their spirit and interpretation were altered, so that District Officers merely became rubber-stamping condoners of decisions and policies already formulated for their districts by the Japanese. In law courts judges and magistrates had no option but to hand down predetermined verdicts. The pre-war system, which had cultivated a responsible administration that functioned with discretion, degenerated into one that was authoritarian in nature, in which no discussion was permitted. An outward show of courtesy towards the Rulers was proffered and as a form of appeasement attempts were made to gain some knowledge of the Malay language. In contrast to these superficial trappings, the single act of handing over Perlis, Kedah, Kelantan and Trengganu to Siam undermined any pretence of the good intentions claimed in MMA propaganda.

On 10th August 1943, the Domei news agency announced that the 'right has been restored to Malaya to determine its own future'.[18] The deceit in this statement became only too clear ten days later when the MMA signed away the four northern and predominantly

Malay populated states to Siam. The formal partitioning of Kelantan, Trengganu, Kedah and Perlis occurred on 18th October, in recognition of Siam's friendship and support during Japan's initial military undertaking against Malaya. Siamese officials never actively organised or administered these States and refused to deal with their Japanese counterparts. The Siamese maintained that they had been brought in only for the convenience of the Japanese army, and that the States had been transfered to them in name only.

> 'The Thais set up a military regime in each state . . . [but] in December 1943, the Thai authorities announced plans to turn over the administration of the four States to their respective Sultans, in direct variance from the Japanese practice in the rest of the peninsula.'[19]

Siamese military administrators continued to function only as advisors under this arrangement. The partitioning marked the commencement of Malay disillusionment, emphasising the insincerity of the MMA's rule over Malaya. It highlighted the MMA's insensitivity to the dominant Malay fear whereby, for the first time in the history of the country, the Chinese outnumbered the Malays in the country of their birthright. The attitude of Malays changed after the partitioning of these four northern states, and became one of silent disaffection. This was not lost on the Japanese, who began to appreciate the important role the Chinese could perform in assisting them to propagate their war economy. Therefore, in early 1944 the MMA began to show more consideration towards the communal interests of the Chinese.

The MMA's rough and ready tactics were inflicted on all towns in Malaya, but although obtaining essential supplies became increasingly more difficult, some essential services were reasonably well maintained in Penang.

> 'The water supply was very efficiently maintained by Mr H.C. Goh in what was afterwards described as "one of the worst bombed and devastated towns in Malaya". Sanitation too remained effective and public transport was maintained at a satisfactory level. The one thing the Japanese really approved of and cherished was the Hill Railway.'[20]

Much pre-war legislation had been enacted throughout the Straits Settlements and in all the Malay States to provide a form of protection for Chinese women and particularly young girls. This was mostly swept aside by the MMA and treated cynically by many of the Japanese during the occupation. The rapacious demands of Japanese soldiers and officials doomed all communities to the lowest level in living standards in the recorded history of the country. The MMA's occupational policies forced ever increasing numbers of girls and women into lives of prostitution as economic hardship increased, and as the pre-war protective machinery for both girls and women ceased to function. When the British returned to Malaya at the end of the war, moral, social and living conditions had deteriorated to a lower extent than ever before.

Britain's pre-war policy of racial segregation in Malaya had required a sensitive understanding of the component peoples, and a delicate balancing of their individual aspirations. This policy successfully reduced social conflicts among the races and generally promoted harmonious relationships in the country. During the occupation years the Japanese injected into Malayan society a new consciousness which resulted in mounting communalism and racial tension. These were so mishandled that they deteriorated into lasting conflicts. The MMA failed to develop a consistent ethnic policy and, while Asians were generally urged to take pride in their birthright, the hypocrisy and social arrogance of many Japanese nurtured inequality and a perceived policy of divide and rule. Cooperation was not encouraged by good example, but was demanded from all races, in order

> 'to build up a new system under which they took everything and gave very little in return. The new order brought neither justice nor equality, and the people were not contented. The Japanese violated their own declared policy of equality because of the methods used by the Japanese military.'[21]

Although racial stress, leading to subsequent conflict, was not deliberately fostered by the MMA, much of their policy certainly resulted in this. The Chinese were cruelly suppressed and victimised and sought respite and revenge in the formation of a Chinese dominated resistance movement. The Japanese, with their '"pro-Malay" policy, created an undercurrent of resentment and distrust among Chinese towards Malays'[22] that percolated throughout most levels of Chinese society. The competition that naturally existed for ever decreasing resources, and the political favours shown towards the Malays, exposed and intensified the disparity and uneasy feelings between the two communities. These had been held in check before the war, but now drove both on a direct collision course. While the Chinese were subjected to atrocities condoned under the MMA's method of administration, the Malays were able to secure for themselves an element of increased political leverage. When the Japanese eventually tried to make some amends and to treat the Chinese in a more favourable manner, their attempts were met with scant regard from the Chinese. Such small concessions could not make up for the many hardships they had already tolerated. The extent to which the Japanese misunderstood the need for delicately balancing sensitivities cannot be more expressly seen than in their misconceived encouragement of Chinese farmers and settlers to encroach into areas traditionally earmarked as Malay Reservation lands. The Malays saw this as a direct threat to their special position in the country, which they considered their birthright.

The Malays have been criticised for their mute acceptance of the MMA's rule, but this was in line with their previous tolerance of benevolent British rule prior to the occupation. The Chinese, in contrast, remained bitter enemies of the Japanese and regarded the Malays and their attitude as treacherous. The Malays were encouraged by the Japanese to 'regard the Chinese — and particularly the Communists — as immigrant bandits disrupting the Malay homeland'.[23] A ready-made formula for subsequent conflict between the two communities was smouldering.

12:3 Peace Preservation Committees (PPCs)

Prominent citizens in Penang enraged the Japanese chief of the Military Administration as none came forward to pay their respects, following his arrival on 19th December 1941. On 22nd December distinguished Chinese and other community leaders, who had fled the bombing and hidden in the relative safety of Penang Hill and Ayer

Hitam, were summoned with threats of punishment to attend a meeting with Japanese officials at Asdang House in Northam Road. These Chinese were told that they were enemies of Japan, that their property and lives no longer belonged to them, but that the latter might be spared if they fully cooperated with Japan's design to develop a Co-Prosperity Sphere. Community leaders were ordered to organise Peace Preservation Committees (PPCs) to replace the Penang Service Committee which was to be disbanded. The PPCs would be held responsible for the conduct of the communities they represented, and would also be required to act as a liaison between the Japanese administration and the people. The first meeting of these committees was held on 23rd December at the Runnymede Hotel, which the Japanese had turned into their military headquarters. Committee members were ordered to guarantee the collection and handing in of all weapons and ammunition in the island from their various communities. Failure to do so would result in summary execution.

On 2nd January 1942 General Manakai, displaying his arrogance and complete lack of understanding, convened another meeting of the Penang PPCs. Japanese attitudes, and the methods they adopted, were contrary to their propaganda claims that they would liberate the people of Southeast Asia, and invariably invited instant alienation. At this meeting people in Penang were told that they were British subjects, the enemies of Japan, and should be therefore arrested. Their life and property now depended on the goodwill of the Japanese military. Community leaders were threatened with imprisonment, confiscation of their property and even death if they did not positively assist the military authorities. They were also told not to grumble if food shortages should occur. They were expected to follow the good example set by the forces of Dai Nippon, who willingly went without food for several days in succession.

Following initial tribulations and threats, the PPCs were able to settle into an ad hoc sort of routine and for almost four months after the arrival of the Japanese in Penang, they had virtually a free hand to control the activities and welfare of their own communities. They arranged for sufficient foodstuffs to be made available, and set up provision stores which at first helped people considerably. Penang's transition from benevolent pre-war British rule to the often cruel, authoritative rule of the Japanese was quite smoothly effected by these measures, despite some corrupt PPC Chairmen and committee members personally benefiting. 'Protection Passes' were issued as a form of identification to many Chinese and these provided them with an element of respite from being molested by Japanese soldiers and sentries. The possession of these passes on several occasions saved human lives. Following the surrender of Singapore, nationals of Germany, Hungary, Italy, Southern Ireland and Switzerland, in addition to numerous Chinese, benefited from being given protection passes. These were liberally handed out by a Mr Shinozaki of the Foreign Affairs office, who countersigned all passes inscribed:

> 'The bearer of this pass is a good citizen. Please look after him and protect him, and let him go about his business without hindrance.'[24]

Protection cards were later issued to people in Singapore, not only for their personal safety, but also for the protection of their homes and personal belongings. PPCs initially assisted with the issue of travel documents for those wanting to go from Penang or Singapore to the mainland, or to travel to Sumatra, Burma or Siam. The issue of import and export permits was also arranged and helped businessmen to disperse the goods held in transit from the time the civil administration collapsed.

PPC members supported various charitable institutions in Penang, which included the Jubilee Home for the Deaf, the Dispersal Camp for evacuees, the St Nicholas Home for the Blind, as well as patients in the General Hospital. There were also instances when they acted as buffers between greedy Japanese soldiers and those vulnerable to abuse from fear of recrimination. When Japanese soldiers forcibly removed bicycles from people as they passed in the streets, arrangements were made for the military to obtain what they wanted from the stocks of various bicycle dealers. No dealer under this arrangement had his whole stock confiscated, and because of this many individuals escaped being deprived of their only means of transportation.

In April 1942 all PPCs were summarily dissolved. In Penang, as elsewhere, they were superceded by various organisations to represent the different races. The Chinese had the Overseas Chinese Association (OCA); the Malays, the Malay Welfare Association (MWA); the Indians, the Indian Independence League (IIL); and the Eurasians were represented by the Eurasian Welfare Association (EWA). During the PPC's brief and active tenure, their timely assistance saved hundreds, possibly thousands, of people from imprisonment, torture and even death. This was particularly so as the Japanese considered all office bearers in pre-war Legislative and Municipal Councils, secret society members, China Distress Relief Fund subscribers, Kuomintang members, and the communists as special threats to them, and therefore targets deserving their full wrath. Mr Heah Joo Seang — a local pre-war businessman and agent of a Japanese shipping line in Penang — was Chairman of the Chinese PPC in Penang. (His actions is this capacity, along with his pre-war trading activities, were targets of criticism, especially his dealings over rubber stock sales at the end of the war, which made him a millionaire overnight.)

Contrary to general opinion, most community leaders during the occupation were not Japanese quizzlings. Many of them, including Heah Joo Seang, were brave men. They were forced by the Japanese to remain community leaders, and acted as best they could under confused and dangerous circumstances.

12:4 MMA's Law Enforcement Methods

Individual Japanese in Malaya and the MMA were cruel in a most profound manner although in comparison with their Axis partners they were not necessarily worse. Their spontaneity and unpredictability were the most frightening aspects of their administration, as were their concepts of discipline and honour, which directly contradicted all previously practised methods of law enforcement and justice. An attitude that viewed all suspects as guilty — notwithstanding rules of evidence — in combination with the abolition of *habeas corpus* and any mechanism for bail, were terrifying aspects of their justice system, and were invariably subject to abuse for ill-conceived purposes.

A short period of lawlessness erupted throughout Malaya as Allied forces withdrew southwards and Singapore was surrendered. Lawless elements exploited the fears and weaknesses of a population suddenly bereft of all semblance of sanity, leadership and law enforcement. Looting and pillage were openly perpetrated in many towns and villages and before the police could be reorganised, many Chinese, joined by robbers and looters, flush with money from their ill-gotten gains, blatantly flaunted the law by gambling. When some form of order was restored by the MMA, gamblers were arrested and decrees promulgated to stop looting. Looters were required to surrender the goods they had plundered, or face the risk of being summarily executed. Harsh measures such as these were effective, and in the ensuing panic looters rushed to discard the material evidence of their greed by dumping their booty into mining pools and rivers, as well as in back lanes of towns, which were soon strewn with a variety of discarded items. In most parts of the country the first taste of Japanese methods of justice was

> 'the public execution of a few criminals in nearly every big town. The heads of victims were exhibited at public places. In Singapore, thousands of Chinese were massacred in cold blood on the beaches as real or imaginary anti-Japanese elements.'[25]

Malaya fell into a state of panic and chaos as the MMA resorted to executions as a means of re-establishing law and order. It was effective! There were, however, lapses in justice and terrifying inconsistencies — for example, in the treatment of the various races. When eight Chinese looters were caught in the Singapore dock area they were publicly beheaded with a samurai sword, and their heads displayed on poles as a warning to others. When seven looters — all Malays and Indians — committed a similar offence they were given only a caution and released. While the Chinese were invariably treated without mercy, the Malays and Indians were regarded by Japan from the outset of the occupation as potential partners in the Co-Prosperity Sphere. This practice of double standards was extended to the Japanese themselves, who often turned out to be bigger brigands and rogues than many of those living lawlessly, who had been forced into this form of temporary lifestyle out of sheer necessity. The lesser brigands had their heads chopped off as delinquents, while the exploits of the Japanese mostly went unpunished.

In early 1942 General Yamashita ordered the setting up of a military court system having jurisdiction over all political cases. These would be strictly judged according to military law. People lived in perpetual fear under this system and as disenchantment and hatred of the Japanese gradually increased during the occupation, so did the fervour and size of various resistance elements which gradually became better organised.

In order to maintain tighter control over the whereabouts of people, the police sub-divided townships into supervisory sections. A system of family registration was introduced, with every family being provided with a 'Peace-Living Certificate' on which births, deaths, marriages, plus any changes of address were recorded, and on which all journeys had to be reported. Under this system one person was nominated within a group, and made answerable for every group member's actions. The system was an inhumane instrument of control. On numerous occasions innocent people were made scapegoats as a matter of convenience and put to death for crimes of which they were entirely innocent.

The abolishment of *habeas corpus* gave the police a free hand to detain anyone on suspicion for an unlimited period. This invited many instances of abuse, with people being arrested as a result of personal grudges or jealousies. Lip service to British concepts of law only applied when the outcome did not conflict with the MMA's designs, or with Japanese laws. All Japanese in the country were a law unto themselves, and as such were able to do as they pleased without interference. The trials of the 'liberated' Asian majority were pre-judged, defence lawyers carefully ensuring that their arguments would not offend Japanese Deputy Public Prosecutors (DPPs). Despite blatant abuses of natural justice, there were some instances of exemplary behaviour, with certain judges trying to uphold justice.

On 1st February 1943 a law was promulgated imposing a mandatory death penalty for rioting, circulating seditious literature and for committing armed robbery and rape. The public were made aware of this decision only 19 days later when, with typical unpredictability, the *Penang Shimbun* announced that this law applied to offences committed prior to the published date. However, people confessing to their crimes and surrendering to the authorities, might have their penalties reduced or even remitted!

Various harmless peace-time pursuits were branded as political crimes and those suspected of committing them were immediately arrested, often tortured, and not infrequently put to death in a cruel, degrading manner. High on the list of activities considered criminal were owning or listening to a radio fitted with short wave tuning (only medium wave frequency was permitted), and discussion of any radio news. Many brave people ran the risk of being discovered or given away in order to listen to overseas news bulletins, to learn the truth about the war's progress. They had to keep alert for both Jeikaidan patrols, coerced into helping police the towns, and also for collaborators and informers whose underhand activities filled innocent and guilty alike with dread. The 'All India Radio' station was popular in Malaya and broadcast news twice daily. Despite fierce news censorship and a prolonged persistent drive by the Kempetai (Military Police) to wipe out short-wave listeners, quite a lot of people managed to conceal their radio sets and obtained a more accurate indication of world events and some truthful reporting on the progress of the war. All Japanese reporting was partial, even such momentous events as the dramatic fall of the Tojo and Koiso cabinets in July 1944 and April 1945 respectively. These were merely announced as measures further strengthening Japan's war efforts.

Numerous other activities judged politically sensitive were classified as crimes inviting immediate arrest and the added threat of being tortured and sentenced to death, irrespective of the circumstances under which crimes might or might not have been committed. High on this list was anything connected with secret societies, listening to or spreading rumours, voicing anti-Axis or anti-Japanese sentiments, possession of, or attempting to deal in, Allied currency, expressing dissatisfaction over the MMA's performance, including its inability to curb the runaway high cost of living, racketeering in essential goods, even making sarcastic comments about community leaders. Poking fun at the administration was a particularly sensitive issue and was strictly censured, since this conflicted directly with the egocentric and humourless nature of most Japanese officials.

The MMA also promulgated decrees ordering the destruction of all photographs of King George VI and Chiang Kai-Chek, and of the Union Jack. The censorship of everything in the English language led to the wanton destruction of thousands of tons of valuable books, in both private collections and libraries, many of them irreplaceable. Much of this loss stemmed from people acting in panic as rumours circulated of search parties hunting out collections and owners being subjected to harsh recriminatory measures.

A system dictated by fear predominated. People feared being suspected, feared offending others and inviting grudges. They feared for their attractive young relatives, feared other people's greed, feared informers, neighbours, being overheard, misunderstood, or disliked. Fear was the constant dominant accomplice in the MMA's method of dispatching justice and maintaining law and order. Innocent and guilty alike lived in this state of fear induced by the unpredictable whims of officials.

12:5 Royal Status and the Elite — Effects of the Occupation

On 10th December 1941 the Rulers of the Federated Malay States (FMS) of Perak, Pahang, Negeri Sembilan and Selangor were pressured 'to urge publicly that their subjects remain loyal to the British and resist the invading Japanese forces'.[26] Despite their public pronouncements, and the courageous actions of two battalions of the Malay Regiment, military intelligence reports 'told of how Malays working as Japanese fifth columnists had guided Japanese troops in their march south'[27] towards Singapore, and how some members of the KMM movement had assisted the Japanese Military Intelligence Agency (Fujiwara Kikan) by offering their services as guides and interpreters.

Within a relatively short space of time it was realised that Britain's defeat was imminent. It was therefore decided to try and persuade all the Rulers to leave the country for their own safety. As part of this exercise, on 18th December 1941 a British convoy attempted to take the elderly and infirm Ruler of Kedah to Penang. This failed and he was abducted in mid-journey by his son, Tungku Abdul Rahman Putra, who first took him to Kulim in South Kedah and then to Kampong Sidim, where he was well cared for and protected by villagers. The Tungku was adamant that his father's place was with his people. He appreciated the concern of the British for the Ruler's safety, and that they did not want him to fall into the unpredictable hands of the Japanese. All Rulers correctly and unanimously refused to leave the country 'on the ground that their duty required them to remain with the people'.[28]

The refusal by Rulers to leave Malaya, and the initial cooperation given by some Malays to the Japanese during their progress southwards and during the early stages of the occupation, heralded the dawn of a period during which British officials and the Colonial Office in London became disenchanted with the Malays. This lasted for the duration of the war. As Japan's ultimate defeat became an increasing reality, unease spread among the Malay ruling classes that following Japan's capitulation and on account of supposed Malay collaboration, Britain might abrogate the various pre-war treaties that had been favourable to the Malay Rulers. Also, it was apparent that the Japanese had given the Malays more favourable treatment than the other two majority races in the country. As it turned out, the Malays anticipated correctly, and as a sequel to Britain's distrust there emerged a form of post-war constitutional proposals, the essence of which would be to deprive the Rulers of much of their sovereignty.

For most of the occupation Malay Rulers' authority and status were restricted to that of minor officials, although their subjects continued to pay obeisance to them. To encourage the people's support for Japan's war effort, the MMA allowed Rulers to continue having autonomy in religious matters, but they were not recognised as sovereign heads of their States, as Japan intended to incorporate Malaya within her own Empire as a permanent possession. Rulers remained in their pre-war positions, but the MMA did not consult them on policy or administrative matters. There was a considerable decline in status compared to that previously enjoyed under the British. During the first year of the occupation Colonel Watanabe Watru, an executive officer in the MMA, was ill-disposed to everyone. He paid only lip service to the Rulers to induce them to offer their titles, lands and followers to his Imperial Majesty, and to set an example by swearing loyalty to the Japanese. Rulers' stipends were reduced, sometimes by as much as two-thirds, depending on their degree, or lack, of cooperation. Those who appeared un-cooperative were also treated coldly.

The Japanese had no coherent policy towards Islam in Malaya but, with the appointment of Kathis, the Rulers did lose part of their religious authority and perogative. The MMA did not attempt to make use of Islamic groups, or to establish any system of control over Islam through religious teachers or scholars, although the curtailment of the Rulers' political authority

> 'might have been welcomed by Islamic reformists, such as the Kaum Muda (modernist) group, and other non-conformist groups such as the Sufis whose activities were suppressed under British rule by the Sultans' Majlis Ugama (Religious Council), the bastion of orthodox religious authority'.[29]

In 1943, with Japan's military fortunes declining, the MMA altered its policies. They looked to the Rulers and to the Malay elite administrators as a source of leadership with their people. In January 1943 Rulers' honorific titles were once more recognised but their authority was still restricted to matters of religion. It was only in 1944 that Rulers were 'given back a great deal of their pre-war allowances and powers, but not their status as sovereign rulers'.[30] In 1944 Rulers also became the vice-chairmen of State Advisory Councils in their own States, and were supposedly advisors to Japanese Governors. They were afforded an outward show of increased power, subject to the overall authority of the Japanese, but their prestige had been considerably eroded by becoming mere figureheads of Japanese policy. The occupation was a revelation to the Rulers. For the first time their status depended on their courting favour with a foreign and ruling power of the time. Japanese appointees succeeded to the throne in several States during the occupation, and this gave rise to further misgivings and contention among the British at the end of the war.

Many of the traditional Malay elite, owing to their enforced predicament, attempted to foster closer relations with the people by assisting with community projects. They also tried to maintain their relationship with the Rulers as best they could within their drastically altered social standing. In doing so they were aware of the Rulers' loss of power compared to pre-war days, and that the protection they could offer had to a great extent evaporated. In some instances relationships between the Rulers and the Malay elite were less than cordial. As some of the latter were promoted to top civil service posts, some of them in turn developed a more fearful, pliable and cooperative stance towards the MMA, rather than attaching wholehearted allegiance to their Rulers.

Early in the occupation few alterations to pre-war administrative staffing were made but the position of Mentri Besar (MB) (Chief Minister) was discontinued. The employment of Malays was gradually more favourably regarded by the MMA, with those considered trustworthy permitted to become higher administrative officials, such as District Officers, Judges and Magistrates, OCPD's, Customs Superintendents, Medical Officers and Kaisha Executives. In the Straits Settlements during 1942 pre-war officials of all races continued to be employed.

The MMA's policies subscribed to promoting a large number of Malays at local government level, some of whom were put into the position of DOs. More work was demanded of these officials, along with Penghulus (Headmen) and Ketua Kampongs (Village Elders) than had previously been required by the British, especially when they were used 'to requisition rice, labour and volunteers for the Japanese war effort'.[31]

Before the war Malay DOs had considerable discretion and responsibility within the confines of their areas and the existing rules and enactments. When they sat as magistrates, their deliberations and decisions were subject to existing law and precedent, and should any review of their findings be required, this was carried out in accordance with standard procedures, and not subjected to British interference. During the occupation all this was altered, and State Council meetings became authoritarian, where the wishes of the MMA and its officials were merely rubber stamped. DOs did as they were told and made little effort to show any initiative or to consider what their communities really required. They merely abided by the guide-lines forced on them by the various Provincial headquarters.

Both the Malay and non-Malay public were exposed to the full venom of the MMA's demands as their policies were directed through DOs. These in turn were caught in the middle and threatened with arrest if their quotas were not attained. Although DOs were not hated as much as the rice policemen and the Malay Kempeitai informers, they did become natural targets for reprisals by MPAJA guerrillas, who later took the credit for executing collaborators and those DOs, Pengulus and Ketua Kampongs thought to have cooperated with the Japanese administration.

Malay administrative officers were employed by the MMA by the start of 1943. In these positions they were socially and economically relatively better off, compared to other Malays, as they were given additional rice rations and had access to government servants' cooperatives, where prices of goods were cheaper. Their employed status provided some protection against conscription as labourers and the all-too-frequent and unwelcome attention of the Kempeitai.

The Japanese sought to exploit Malay fear and resentment of the Chinese, and the pressures that their economic success was perceived to impose on Malay society. It mattered little to the Japanese that to achieve their goals they created almost inconceivable inefficiency by failing to allocate jobs to suitable people. In Sungei Patani in north Kedah, an English school teacher was put in charge of electricity supply, and Tungku Abdul Rahman, who subsequently became the country's first Prime Minister in 1957, was allocated the job of auditor, although he later stated, 'I did not see even a single account book.'[32]

The elite Malay administrators, fearing the Japanese, were prepared to undermine their social standing and to cooperate with them during the occupation. The Japanese gradually relied on their knowledge and advice, and as their trustworthiness increased they were generally better treated. The Malay elite were consequently forced to walk a dangerous tightrope, with their activities strictly controlled. They were impotent to function with any real authority. They invited the scorn of the masses as they performed the onerous duties required of them by the Japanese. Instead of receiving salaries, they were renumerated in kind with rice and other rations, plus some degree of protection against conscription. They were obliged to join some form of voluntary corps, and forced also to participate in 'grow-more-food' campaigns. Before the war the elite Malays had become urbanised, keeping themselves aloof and apart from kampong (village) life. Now they were forced to try to become closer to the people again, and in doing so they turned to manual labour and sundry trading. This was a levelling experience as for many it was the first time they had suffered the indignity of using a changcol. An antipathy to Japanese rule was nurtured among all classes of Malays with the erosion of administrators' white collar status, and the undermining of the elites' social standing. There was no alternative than to make the best terms possible with the Japanese and on occasion to appear to befriend them. However, there

> 'can be little doubt that the experience which the elite gained during the Japanese occupation strengthened their political self-confidence and enabled them to assert themselves forcefully when the British returned'.[33]

Many Malays at the start of the occupation bowed to Japanese control and cooperated with the MMA until they realised the rotten extent of their rule. The Malays initially were not particularly hostile to the Japanese and sought in their regime a means of 'relief from Chinese political and economic encroachment'.[34] It mattered little to many Malays who ruled the country, one colonial master being as unpalatable as another.

Many European officers in the MCS, who had served in the country for any length of time, fully realised early in the campaign that the hapless Malays would have to make their peace with the victors, whoever they might be. What else could they possibly do under the circumstances? Why should any blame be laid at the door of Malay MCS officers for continuing to serve under the Japanese, as they had the British before them, especially when it was the British government who had advised them to do just that? Who, also, would subsequently be justified in attaching blame to them for their actions, when their fellow 'European brother officers vanished over the hills with the retreating troops, leaving them to their own devices'?[35]

Disregarding these numerous mitigating circumstances, the Colonial Office in London became increasingly disturbed during the war over reports of

> 'Malay subservience to the Japanese . . . They were shocked by the pro-Japanese remarks of the Sultan of Johore, a swash-buckling type, notorious for his cavalier outbursts before the war.'[36]

Those MCS officers who previously knew him well comprehended and appreciated the Johore Ruler's colourful style. The CO's concern was understandable, especially with the Ruler's comments being reported alongside constant reports of Malay cooperation with the Japanese. The CO viewed with disapproval a seemingly voluntary visit to Japan by the son of the pre-war Mentri Besar of Kelantan, as they did the MMA's choice and confirmation of a successor for the Ruler of Kedah when the latter died. The CO therefore decided that it could not condone anything decided during Japan's administrative period until such decisions and actions could be closely examined after Japan's defeat.

Many Malays living in remote kampongs cared little who governed the country and, as they watched the Japanese drive the British out, were initially willing to abide by the orders of their new colonial masters. Japanese propaganda implied early independence for Malaya and the curtailment of economic domination by the Chinese. In both respects they were misled. Many innocent Malays in remoter areas suffered alongside other races when savage Japanese reprisal raids were carried out against suspected communists and Anti-Japanese elements. In the circumstances the Malays had no alternative but to comply with the demands of the Japanese. Malay disenchantment with Japan's autocratic form of colonial rule was endemic by the end of the occupation.

12:6 'Sook Ching' — Massacre of the Chinese

For decades the Chinese had despised the Japanese as the 'hated oppressors' of their homeland, and in a similar manner the Japanese regarded the Chinese above all as their enemies. With such long-standing bitterness between the two races it was not surprising, therefore, that the Chinese in Malaya were repeatedly singled out, by Japanese soldiers and civilians alike, and subjected to especially harsh and cruel treatment. It was this barbarism that branded them in Chinese eyes as savage and without compassion.

The communists among the Chinese were hated most of all by the Japanese and extirpating them became an obsession. As soon as Singapore fell, mopping-up operations of suspected communists, anti-Japanese elements and Dalforce volunteers were single-mindedly and remorselessly carried out. During this black period the Japanese, in their obsession to punish the Chinese, seemed to forget that their propaganda had represented them as being the liberators of Asia.

It was also during this purge that several of the Malayan Communist Party (MCP) officials were arrested and subsequently forced to become spies and informers, while many others were summarily put to death. One of the most important informers recruited was Lai Tek (alias Chang Hong alias Wong Kim Goek alias Wong Show Tong alias Mr Wright), the Secretary General of the MCP — a renowned agent for three powers — whose actions on behalf of the Japanese had devastating consequences.

In the initial two weeks of the occupation, and before the MMA was formed, the Japanese 25th Army was solely preoccupied with law enforcement. Their methods were brutally simple and effective.

> 'Offenders were shot and beheaded on the spot, their heads displayed on pikes at prominent points in the city, particularly marketplaces. The Kempeitai (Japanese military police), accompanied by local spies and informers, conducted house-to-house raids for stolen goods in selected areas. Anyone found hoarding . . . was hauled away to be shot. The campaign spread fear and panic among the local population, but was extremely effective in stopping looting and lawlessness.'[37]

The round-up of Chinese civilians was a terrifying feature of the occupation. The round-ups were savage, lacking in any compromise or understanding. These first oppressive contacts with people in Singapore and Malaya confirmed the arrogance and brutality of the Japanese, losing them whatever opportunity they might have had initially of winning the affection of the people that they tried to subjugate for the next three and a half years. Duplicity inter-mixed with this barbarism was manifest when they invited local Chinese in Singapore to come forward and admit they had helped the British. One hundred and sixty-eight of them unsuspectingly did so, and over the next two days they were taken by lorry to Changi beach where they were ordered to wade into the sea and massacred by concealed machine-guns.

The atrocities and massacres that occurred in Singapore were duplicated elsewhere in the country and in south Johore Chinese were slaughtered on a large scale. In Penang the Japanese fully intended to be avenged for the anti-Japanese riots that the Chinese traders had supported in 1938, and for the massive support that all classes of the Chinese community had given to the China Relief Fund.

The day following the capitulation of Singapore the decision was made to extirpate all undesirable elements within the Chinese community. Lieut-General Yamashita, the commander of the 25th Army, issued instructions to his four commanders, Nishimura, Matsui, Mutaguchi and Kawamura, to initiate Operation Clean-up, a plan conceived by his master tactician Lieut-Colonel Masanobu Tsuji. Tsuji wanted to eliminate all anti-Japanese elements, including those Chinese Dalforce volunteers who had tenaciously fought in Singapore's defence, contributors to the China Relief Fund, and any others who had participated in anti-Japanese organisations, before the 25th Army's intended move to Sumatra, when only caretaker defensive forces would remain on the island. The responsibility for implementing the operation was given to Colonel Satoru Oiishi, the commander of No. 2 Field Kempeitai Group, comprising mainly young soldiers from the rural districts of western Japan, many of them with only a basic level of education.

Operation Clean-up or 'Sook Ching' meant 'Purification by Elimination'. Arrangements for this were set in motion on the afternoon of 17th February when the Chinese community of Singapore was ordered to congregate at five specific assembly points around the city by noon on the 21st. They were told to bring their own water and food, and both sexes of all ages were required to attend. Sick and healthy alike were forced to encamp in back lanes and in any other available open spaces in the selected areas as best they could, without any protection from the heat of the sun or from the rain.

The five assembly points were located at the north end of Arab Street near to the Jalan Besar Stadium, near the junction of Clemenceau Avenue at the eastern end of River Valley Road, near the Tanjong Pagar Police Station, at a rubber factory near the junction of Geylang and Kallang Roads, and at an open area off the Paya Lebar Road.

Tens of thousands of Chinese, mostly between the ages of eighteen and fifty, were forced to assemble on the instructions issued by the

No. 2 Field Kempeitai Group. Those known to have criminal records or anti-Japanese feelings, along with some government employees, were immediately singled out and taken away for questioning, torture and for execution, as were those with tattoo marks on their bodies.

> 'Those who failed to apologise at once to the young Kempei for not being able to write their names in Chinese, or for having tattoo marks, were detained and later slaughtered.'[38]

Although the Japanese pretended that tattoo marks were an indication of membership of a secret society, this was only an excuse to single people out as they were fully aware that the Chinese practice of decorating the body with tattoos had no significant political meaning.

The people placed under immediate suspicion and also in the most danger were those known to have donated to the China Relief Fund, and this included the rich on the assumption that they had done so generously, and anyone who had been remotely involved in Dalforce. Other prime suspects were followers of the veteran community leader Mr Tan Kah Kee, volunteers and reserve corps members, government servants, justices of the peace, members of the previous legislative councils, and anyone with a knowledge of English as they were automatically classified as pro-British. School masters and high school students from Chinese schools, newspapermen, and natives from Hainan island, all of whom the Japanese considered communists, as well as any people resident in Singapore for less than five years were immediately suspects, as were all healthy looking youngsters and girls with short cropped hairstyles.

Screening of people continued until March 3rd, and many were taken away and never seen again. During the sorting out process in the densely populated areas, where no food or shelter from the sun was provided, hundreds suffered from heat stroke and some died of thirst. After four days, men over 60 and women and children were allowed to go home. The next day more people were allowed to go and

> 'were presented with a piece of paper, one-inch square, upon which was stamped the word "Examined" in Chinese. In days to come that slip was worth its weight in radium. It conferred a modicum of immunity on its possessor',[39]

especially at the numerous barricades erected at most major intersections. The identification parades were petrifying ordeals, with people forced to pass in single file in front of hooded reformed communists and assorted rogues, who had turned Japanese informers for their own gain. A nod from these 'hooded terrors' was sufficient, and a suspect would then be pounced on and taken either to the military police or garrison headquarters for questioning. Manhandling and slapping were common occurrences and 'many were taken away to satisfy the vengeance of their enemies among the informers'.[40] Thousands among those who were taken away were completely innocent people and the

> 'selection of the victims and the time, place and method of killing were all left to the discretion of the sector commanders . . . The massacres themselves, and they were many in number, were carried out under the supervision of the Kempeitai, the Hojo Kempei being employed to do the actual shooting under orders of a Kempeitai officer.'[41]

The massacre of Chinese in Singapore and Malaya, especially in south Johore was perpetrated in a vengeful spirit, as the Chinese had dared to give support to the British cause. One frightful aspect was that the killings were invariably

> 'preceded by the rape of their women and young girls whose male relatives or friends were then beheaded in the presence of their women by an executioner using a two-handed Samurai sword'.[42]

Following his release from Changi Prison, Mamoru Shinozaki — a senior official of the Syonan Tokubetsu Shi (Singapore City Government) — was critical of the 25th Army's behaviour after Singapore's surrender.

> 'The dreaded Kempeitai went round searching for young men, and girls, and dragged them into the open . . . Thousands of Chinese were huddled together, waiting for the execution that was their fate, particularly for any Chinese volunteers who had fought so tenaciously against the Japanese; 6,000 Chinese were thus murdered in what the Kempeitai called their operation clean up.'[43]

The death toll of the 'Sook Ching' bloodbath cannot be accurately ascertained. Various authoritative sources have estimated the numbers as anything between 6,000 to 40,000, and even figures released by the Japanese Kempeitai admitted that they were not less than 6,000. The screening was a shameful ruse and most victims were only given the opportunity to give their name and sometimes their address. The Japanese, in not untypical fasion, were so intent on wreaking vengeance on the Chinese that they threw away whatever slim chance there was that fair play and kindness at the onset of the occupation would have altered peoples' attitudes towards them. Instead, they sowed bitterness among all with whom they came in contact. Rather than face such fearful uncertainty, hundreds of young Chinese fled into the jungles to hide, with many of them subsequently joining the communist-led resistance movement, particularly the Malayan Peoples Anti-Japanese Army (MPAJA). The oppressive measures taken by the Japanese against the Chinese in Singapore, south Johore and Penang, as well as in other parts of the peninsula, brought dishonour to the brilliance of the Japanese military campaign in Malaya. They 'have remained an unerasable blemish on the honour of the Japanese army and a sorry event in Japanese history'.[44]

At first the Chinese in Penang were more fortunate than their counterparts in Singapore. Although some instances of rape, molestation and looting by Japanese troops were reported in the early stages of the occupation, the Chinese were not particularly singled out for acts of reprisal and vengeance. When some tough, quarrelsome China-war veterans — recruits from the Kyushu coal-mine district — committed atrocities in Penang, General Yamashita was so furious that he insisted on court-martialling them, much to the disapproval of Lieut Colonel Tsuji. During the first few days of Penang's occupation about 200 anti-Japanese suspects were rounded up at random in the Ayer Hitam district and were crowded into the Penang gaol. Most of these were Chinese youths later released when their families implored the assistance of community leaders, who in turn made representations to the Japanese, pledging their own lives and properties as guarantee for the youths' good behaviour.

Public executions, however, were a feature of the early days of the occupation in Penang. Some were carried out within the quadrangle of the Penang Road police headquarters, but many more died in this manner on the esplanade at Butterworth.

> 'The officer in charge of the Police garrison at Butterworth, Tadashi Suzuki, who was also in charge of all the police in Province Wellesley, gained quite a reputation for cutting heads off and earned the Tamil soubriquet of "Thalaivetty", ie headcutter.'[45]

The Kempeitai organised two main round-ups in Penang, the first one of which was in March/April 1942, and the second a few months later in October. Hundreds of people were incarcerated in Penang gaol for months on end without trial or hearing, as had already occurred in Singapore. This was done under the guise of eliminating suspected undesirable elements. Prominent citizens as well as alleged communists were arrested in their hundreds and many singled out, especially on 6th April, were

> 'the teachers and students of the Chung Ling High School, which was the foremost Chinese school in Penang. The Japanese suspected this institution of being a "Communist cell" . . . No English schools were allowed to function and the teachers were rendered jobless and, thereby embittered against the new regime, they refused to cooperate with the Japanese.'[46]

Private homes were raided and many people arrested were kept in gaol for three months or more. Some were never heard of again. Many innocent people were subjected to unspeakably cruel tortures during this period and the public lived under a constant threat. Their fears were heightened by frequent night arrests of the innocent and guilty alike. People lived in a state of mental agony, anticipating that knock on their door in the middle of the night when they might be taken away on the slightest pretext or suspicion. Sleeping fully dressed was a normal precaution as the arresting Kempeitais gave no chance for their victims to get dressed. Many of them were hauled away in a semi or completely naked condition.

Penang in some ways was more fortunate than other towns in the country as the presence of the Japanese Navy throughout the occupation had a salutary influence over the Japanese military. Although invariably the two did not see eye to eye, and on at least one occasion the naval authorities interceded to call off one of the planned round-ups, 700 Chinese, of whom 86 were women, were either beheaded, shot, tortured to death or killed by other means by the Japanese during their three year nine month tenure of Penang. Slaughter of innocent suspects was commonplace during the early months of the occupation, and many Chinese during that time disappeared suddenly and without further trace. Suspects were rounded up by the truckload during the March/April and October 1942 'Sook Chings', and many of these were taken to Tanjong Bunga under cover of night where they were mowed down on the beach by machine-guns. The names of all known victims were recorded in a register at the Penang China Relief Fund office, and at the conclusion of the war a monument was erected in 1946 at the road junction leading to Ayer Hitam and the Penang Hill railway, to commemorate their massacre.

The *modus operandi* of the Kempeitai was to subjugate the public to a reign of terror from the middle of March 1942, spreading to every town throughout the mainland. It lasted for the duration of the occupation. The Kempeitai concentrated first on so-called communists, and those Chinese who had supported the Chungking regime, thousands of whom were thrown into gaol, where many were tortured and died. The Eurasian community also received harsh retaliatory treatment as they were regarded as having pro-British sympathies.

The threat imposed by the Kempeitai was therefore not confined to one class or community alone. All people lived in fear of being reported to them and even the merest suggestion of this 'would strike terror into the hearts of the hardiest'.[47] People lived day by day. No one knew who would be arrested next. People avoided unguarded comments, criticising the Japanese administration or supporting the Allies, as this could lead to their immediate arrest and subsequent torture if it was reported to the Kempeitai. The occupation left a lasting legacy of distrust among those forced to endure it.

Between 1942 and 1945 many thousands of innocent civilians were murdered in territories occupied by the Japanese, often under circumstances of the utmost barbarity. In the rural districts of Malaya whole villages (kampongs) were sometimes rounded up and placed under strict quarantine on the slightest hint of their having communist sympathies. Whole populations in these villages were slaughtered, including children and babies.

The Japanese method of attending to a kampong suspected of collaboration was unpredictable in its extremes. Having concentrated the entire population into one house, they would be lectured, then either let free afterwards or tommy-gunned and bayonetted to death. No one escaped such treatment — neither old men, women or children — and in one incident in Perak over 100 Chinese were herded into an attap shed where they were burned to death. In another instance the 160 inhabitants of a Chinese kampong were loaded into lorries and taken away. The men were forced to dig a large trench, into which men, women and children were tommy-gunned to death.

By the spring of 1943, as Japan's war endeavour deteriorated, her policies towards the Chinese became generally less punitive and more conciliatory. The Japanese began to realise that they needed the cooperation of the Chinese to achieve their trade objectives and to sustain some form of economic self-sufficiency. Chinese representatives were appointed to consultative councils and an information office was established to foster better communications and relations between the Chinese people and the MMA. The Chinese publicly paid lip service to the MMA's change of policy, but in fact it was not successful. Considerable numbers of Chinese continued to collaborate with the MPAJA, which grew in numbers in the jungles, as well as enlisting greater sympathy and following in urban areas.

The MMA's favourable treatment of the Malays resulted in many Malay officials and policemen staying at their posts during the occupation. They argued that it was

> 'better for them to maintain some semblance of order in their own land rather than abandon it wholly to Japanese officials, but, because of the Japanese butchery of Chinese, the relations between Chinese and Malays, which had been good before the war, were ruined'.[48]

The outcome of this was appalling massacres of Malays by Chinese immediately following the surrender of the Japanese on 15th August 1945.

12:7 Extortion of Chinese — The $50 Million Gift

Every year since 7th July 1937 the Chinese in Malaya remembered with mass meetings and patriotic speeches the Double 7th commemorating the Marco Polo Bridge incident that had 'touched off Japan's undeclared war of aggression in China'.[49] Anti-Japanese feeling was widespread among the Chinese, and many prominent community leaders publicly spearheaded massive fund-raising campaigns to aid Nationalist China's struggle against the Japanese.

Before Singapore capitulated several prominent Chinese community leaders — known for their anti-Japanese sentiments and participation in raising donations for the China Relief Fund — fled the country in fear for their lives, seeking refuge elsewhere. Those who remained tried to hide from the Japanese and did not join the representatives of all other communities who went to Bukit Timah to welcome the victors and pay obeisance to them.

By the time they arrived in Singapore, the Japanese were resentful of the Chinese in Malaya, whom they denounced as tools of the British. They also bitterly resented the several billion dollars which Malayan Chinese had willingly donated to support Chiang Kai-Shek's nationalists. Japanese animosity was further heightened by reports of their own nationals being roughly treated and threatened by the Chinese during anti-Japanese demonstrations and trade boycotts before the outbreak of hostilities.

Lieut-General Tomoyuki Yamashita decided that the Malayan Chinese should be 'cauterised' and taught a lesson. In conjunction with the terrifying military round-ups of suspected anti-Japanese elements, the Japanese Military Administration (JMA) forced the Chinese throughout Malaya to collect a $50 million gift of atonement to appease Imperial pique, and as proof of repentance for having financially supported Nationalist China and Chiang Kai-Shek's forces against Japan. It was nothing short of extortion!

Soon after the surrender of Singapore, most remaining Chinese community leaders were rounded up. Summoned before Lieut-General Yamashita and his staff, they were threatened with torture, severe punishment, or death if they did not cooperate immediately with the JMA and fully repent their previous actions. Those who had publicly expressed anti-Japanese sentiments were tortured and put to death. Others, released and allowed to go home, were later forced to form a Japanese-sponsored Overseas Chinese Association (OCA). At the association's first meeting, a Japanese official named Takasei bullied them, hammering on the table and shouting:

> 'You are my enemies, you know? You have been carrying out subversive activities against Japan the last few years. Now you know our strength, don't you? Your activities have deprived the Japanese of any standing here in recent years. You have helped the wicked to do greater evil. Now we have got you. We have a chance to have injustice done to us avenged. We shall have to kill you all.'[50]

The hapless community leaders in Singapore were put in an intolerable position in the wake of the thousands of arrests being made. At subsequent meetings with Takasei they were again threatened and insulted. In a desperate attempt to appease Yamashita's wrath, some of them tentatively agreed to make a monetary donation as a measure of goodwill. At their fourth meeting within a few days, shortly after the establishment of the Malaya Military Administration (MMA) on 2nd March 1942, about 50 OCA 'Liaison Officers' — as they were called by the Japanese — were summoned to the residence of the Chief Military Administrator, Colonel Watanabe, at Nassim Road. There they were told that the Chinese in Malaya were required to make a goodwill donation of M$50 million to the MMA before 20th April 1942. They were ordered to arrange the collection, which had then to be presented as a 'gift of atonement' for previous crimes against the Imperial forces of Japan. Their gift would be their pledge, a symbol of their willing support of Japan's war aims.

When this demand was made the total currency in circulation was only $220 million. The OCA committee met immediately after leaving Nassim Road to work out how much each State might be able to contribute. The allocations were as follows:

Singapore	$10,000,000
Selangor	10,000,000
Perak	8,000,000
Penang	7,000,000
Malacca	5,500,000
Johore	5,000,000
Negeri Sembilan	1,500,000
Kedah	1,100,000
Pahang	900,000
Kelantan	500,000
Trengganu	300,000
Perlis	200,000
Total	$50,000,000

Assets and properties exceeding a gross value of $3,000 were taxed at 8%, and collection campaigns were organised for each State. Subcommittees were set up to scrutinise submissions and prevent attempts to evade liability. A Hainan committee examined the Hokkien community's returns and a Teochew committee examined those of the Hainan community. All returns were compared with records held at the Land Office and the Income Tax Department. State OCAs cooperated with one another, examining each other's properties to determine what dues should be collected.

Despite setting up methods to counter-check returns, the contributions allocated to States caused considerable acrimony and recrimination. Singapore was accused of getting off lightly, while in Perak, Selangor and Penang the targets imposed grave hardship on the population. The Straits-born Chinese, who had not participated in any anti-Japanese activities, were particularly aggrieved with their China-born counterparts, considering it most unfair that they should also share in the hatred of the Japanese for the community as a whole. Straits-born Chinese had no prior dealings with Chungking. They considered themselves the 'King's Chinese', and proudly lived up to this. Discontent over the methods used to collect dues kindled long lasting grudges and ill-will. This was further exacerbated by rumours and some allegations of

> 'string-pulling and favouritism within the upper ranks of the Contribution Committees, and the frequent recourse to the use of brutal Japanese authority in fulfilling the designs of the Chinese Associations'.[51]

Collection of the $50 million gift — 'the biggest squeeze ever inflicted on the Chinese in Malaya'[52] — was made more difficult because at that time cash was not readily available. Banks had closed so that those who had money there were unable to get it out. Income from looted estates and mines had vanished. Business had virtually come to a standstill. General Yamashita's threat — 'to put every Chinese in Malaya to the sword for ingratitude to Japan'[53] — cast contribution committee members into hysterics.

In Perak, more than 100 of the State's wealthiest Chinese were thrown into police lock-ups and threatened that they would 'lose their heads if they valued money more than their lives'.[54] People panicked, desperately selling anything they could, including cars, houses, jewellery and rubber estates at rock bottom prices. Some rubber estates changed hands for as little as $45 per acre. A head tax was levied on every man, woman and child, and shop keepers had to pay a 10% tax on the assessed value of their total stocks.

Although people's problems in Penang were acute, they were considerably less than those experienced in Perak and Selangor, where many tin mines and rubber estates had been looted, in addition to the damage caused by retreating British forces implementing scorched earth policies. The Penang collection committee was sufficiently influential to negotiate loans with local banks for those needing help. Many resorted to selling their properties and family jewellery cheaply to make up their payments; small traders sold off their goods at give-away prices; others paid in instalments.

By the deadline on 20th April 1942 only $28 million of the $50 million had been collected. In Singapore only $3 million of the $10 million had been raised. Yamashita was incensed by this implied slight and further angered by requests for more time. Representatives of all state OCA committees were summoned to Singapore and severely reprimanded. However, respite was at hand. For some unexplained reason — possibly an attempt to save Japanese face — the Manager of the Yokohama Specie Bank offered a loan of $22 million at 6% interest, repayable within one year. The Chinese were saved! The loan was guaranteed by the collection committee of each state association. A beautiful casket was purchased in which to make the presentation, and a loyal address was prepared, to which Yamashita's staff ordered several amendments before it was approved:

> 'In the past we were running-dogs of British Imperialism. We wronged the Japanese and helped Chiang Kai-Shek in his criminal resistance to Japan. We now see the error of our ways and heartily repent. We pledge our support to the Military Administration. Of our own free will we offer the sum of 50 million dollars as token of sincerity.'[55]

Yamashita's acceptance speech lasted more than one hour. He declared that the gift had 'in no way redeemed the previous acts of the Malayan Chinese for having supported Britain and Chungking',[56] and went on to liken Europeans to monkeys. 'If there was war between Gods and Monkeys,' he said, 'even a fool could see who would win.'[57]

The Japanese made a mistake in forcing the Chinese to make the gift of atonement. It lost them an ideal opportunity at the outset of the occupation to win the Chinese over to their side. Although cruel use was made of the OCA to collect the money — causing considerable hardship — many people blamed OCA leaders for originating the scheme in the first instance to save their own skins. Community leaders were not at fault. Their position was made intolerable as there was no stopping the Japanese once the project had started and no option open to OCA officials but to help them with it.

The gift was regarded as a necessary evil. Many Chinese were of the opinion that if the Japanese wanted money, it was best to let them have it and be done with it. Both Chinese and Japanese knew the other to be insincere. The presentation can be seen in retrospect as little more than an expensive, shallow gesture embellished by platitudes. Some brave people refused to contribute and got away with it. The Yokohama Specie Bank harassed the Chinese for repayment of interest, but the principal loan of $22 million was never repaid.

Although most OCA community leaders attempted, at considerable personal risk, to protect the Chinese community from the unpredictable cruelties of the Japanese, they were regarded as collaborators by some members in the Chinese resistance movement. The communists in particular and the peasant classes distrusted the pre-war 'towkays', so much so that monied Chinese and those in prominent positions became marked men because of their association with the Japanese during the occupation. When Japan surrendered in August 1945, many OCA officers feared for their safety and went into hiding. They were labelled 'Japanese lackeys' and accused of supporting Japanese policies instead of ameliorating the sufferings of the Chinese community. They became prime targets for numerous acts of retaliation. Wee Twee Kim, a Taiwanese adviser and a hatchet-man for the OCA during the collection of the $50 million gift of atonement, was one of many who was sought out and summarily executed.

12:8 The Kaisha and Kumiai Scourge

In pre-war Malaya only opium was a government-controlled monopoly, placing constraint on the lives of opium addicts and smokers. Under the MMA's control everything from charcoal to nightsoil was monopolised in an attempt to mobilise all Malaya's resources for Japan's war effort, and for the needs of their armed forces. This was put before any consideration of the welfare of those under Japanese domination. Big business followed Japan's victorious armies and a total economic stranglehold gripped Malaya despite propaganda slogans heralding 'Co-Prosperity' and the 'Emanicaption of Asia', and reassurances about the equitable distribution of essential foodstuffs and commodities. It was not surprising, therefore, that hypocrisy such as this gave birth to resentment.

When the British surrendered, Singapore

> 'was filled to bursting with goods. All these supplies were immediately seized by the Japanese as part of the spoils of war',[58]

denying them to an island's population that had doubled during the preceding ten weeks. All large commercial enterprises ceased functioning and an immediate shortage of money ensued. Singapore and Malaya were not only dominated militarily, but also exploited economically by the Japanese army, air force and navy purchasing departments (butais), which were closely linked to big Japanese business concerns. Large and small Japanese companies took over most of the properties previously owned by British and other Allied countries' industrialists. The Chinese, however, suffered most. Those

> 'suspected of loyalty to the Chungking government had their properties ruthlessly confiscated, but most of the smaller producers, retail dealers, and suppliers were allowed to continue in these roles for Japanese firms',[59]

and in doing so they were compromised in one way or another.

The $50 million 'gift of atonement' by the Chinese was merely the tip of the iceberg in Japan's plundering of Malaya's resources, stripping the country and people to the bone. When the kaishas (big Japanese companies) arrived all major businesses and industries in the country — plantations, mines, foundries, banks, cinemas and food suppliers — came directly under Japanese control. Millions of dollars were given to the kaishas as overdrafts by Japanese banks, particularly by the Yokohama Specie Bank and the Nanpo Kaihatu Kindo, so that the market was flooded with money. Anything that could turn a profit was allocated to a kaisha — even ice factories.

The first arrivals were the Mitsubishi and Mitsui giants, to whom several important commodity monopolies were allocated, driving the Chinese involved in them out of business. The Mitsubishi Shoji Kabushiki Kaisha (MSKK) was given the rice monopoly and Mitsui Bussan Kabushiki Kaisha (MBKK) was given the monopoly over sugar and salt.

The best rubber plantations were handed over to the Syonan Gomu Kabushiki Kaisha (SGKK), which also purchased all grades of rubber at controlled prices and manufactured and distributed all latex to other processors. The best tin mines went to the Mitsui Kozan Kabushiki Kaisha (MKKK) and the Toyo Kojan Kabushiki Kaisha (TKKK). The former also controlled all coconut and oil palm estates, and distributed crude palm oil to other Japanese firms, who then made grease and lubrication oils. Marine transport was placed under the

Nampo Ungku Kabushiki Kaisha (NUKK), which was later supervised by the navy butais. In this way all industries essential to the production of war materials were brought firmly within the grip of the kaishas.

The land transport monopoly was placed with the Tokyo Kyuku Dentetsu Kabushiki Kaisha (TKDKK), which

> 'bought up local bus companies, using official pressure, and all types of lorries, trucks and motor-cars belonging to private owners. Later, with the authority of Government, it commandeered all privately-owned cars and lorries and paid miserable compensations for the seizures.'[60]

Previous owners of requisitioned vehicles had to apply to the TKDKK if they wanted to use their vehicles, and many owners were not compensated for their losses. In 1943 monthly hire rentals were between $1–2,000. By 1945 these had vastly increased, in addition to the exorbitant hand-outs demanded by kaisha officials and clerks.

Hydro-electric plants were controlled by the Nippon Hasoden Kabushiki Kaisha (NHKK), and the Taiwan Tokushoku Kabushiki Kaisha (TTKK) was given the monopoly for purchasing and distributing padi. They manipulated the movement of any excess stocks from one district to another, suiting their own purpose and pocket. Banks came under the Yokahama Specie bank, whose financial policy was determined by the Nanpo Kaihatu Kinko. In 1942 only Indian and Chinese banks were permitted to re-open for business, but they were not given any independent authority to make decisions on matters of financial importance. Even cinemas and 'third rate "talkies" in the Amusement Parks'[61] were controlled by the Eiga Haikyu Sha (Film Distribution Company).

In early 1944 some kaishas were amalgamated in an attempt to avoid clashes of interest and secure uniformity of effort. The Malai Manufacturers Association, Mining Association, Oil Council, Forestry Council, Malai Maritime Association and the Rubber Association were formed, bringing all important industries in Malaya directly under Japanese control.

The kaisha system was essential to the MMA and to Japan's war efforts. Kaishas were given massive financial backing and, with their monopolies, held a stranglehold over the availability and prices of many items. They were directly responsible for the fictitious shortages that occurred throughout the country and region, and for the accompanying scourge of inflation.

As Japan's war fortunes deteriorated, everything of value would have been shipped to Japan, and Malaya would have been entirely drained of her resources had it not been for the increasingly effective Allied blockade. Imports and exports, however, declined to such an extent that foodstuffs and other essentials became extremely scarce.

Kumiai were formed out of shoals of smaller civilian Japanese traders whose purpose was to absorb other commercial concerns. As such they became a curse and, as

> 'government-protected divisions of the "black market", were in fact mainly responsible for creating shortage of goods'.[62]

They were like syndicates or guilds. They were made into associations for smaller businesses (involved in similar functions or services), enabling them to amalgamate their resources, thus alleviating problems of supply and demand. They were also supposed to ensure a system of fair distribution of goods to the public. Kumiais and shokais received substantial government support and considerable overdraft facilities. Whatever their initial objectives, every kumiai in fact became

> 'nothing but a monopoly to fleece the public. As soon as a kumiai for any particular commodity was formed, that commodity soon disappeared from the markets and became difficult to get. As a result, prices soared.'[63]

Some unscrupulous, wealth-seeking elements, especially among the Chinese, also benefitted from this system.

Kumiais might have been a practical form of business in regimented Japan where rationing was accepted, but

> 'In Malaya, kumiais turned out to be a complete fiasco. They were a curse to the country. They did exactly the opposite of what they were expected to do. They became government-protected compartments of the Black Market.'[64]

The primary responsibility of kumiais was to supply army, navy and air force butais, along with those of the Provincial Governments (Seicho), the MPs and then Japanese civilians. When all of these had been satiated, any balance remaining was for the public. The majority of this ended up in the hands of manipulators and black marketeers who demanded hefty commissions. Kumiais caused hardship and misery as essential supplies vanished from the shops and markets, or could only be obtained at exorbitant prices.

Hypocritical press reporting hid the MMA's true intentions from the public. In August 1942 the *Penang Daily News* reported that numerous clerks would be employed in government offices to 'encourage trade between Penang and other countries in the Co-Prosperity Sphere'[65] and that they would issue passports and import/export permits to businessmen. In direct contradiction of this, on 15th May 2603 (1943) the Penang Bussi Haikyu Kumiai (Goods Distributing Association) was formed, exclusively through which all rice, sugar, salt and matches were distributed to the public. The alleged purpose of this kumiai was 'to prevent poor farmers and industrial labourers from being victimised by black market food operators'.[66] Interestingly, Japanese troops were always provided with the best fish and vegetables at nominal prices, and shortages were created and quickly exploited by unscrupulous dealers. The military commandeered all factories and oil mills, along with all machinery and wood in Penang, while other profitable businesses — bakeries, hotels and even fish-trapping — were requisitioned by kumiais without any possible redress. When the Japanese Governor of Penang was transferred to Selangor, he assured the Penang Chinese in his farewell speech that the Japanese were not there to take business away from them. Mr Hyder Tyebkhan — a Gujarati trader in Penang at that time — recalled the Governor's hypocrisy three decades later, confirming that

> 'there was no trade activity during the war. But like other traders, we bought whatever old stock was available and sold them on the five-foot way along Penang Road.'[67]

When butais — the Japanese army, air force and navy purchasing-departments — commenced their massive operations in Singapore and all major towns in Malaya they were supported by a flood of Japanese military script which was poured into the country. Enormous purchases were made by butai agents, who in turn demanded 10–15% handouts for their services from the businesses with which they dealt. Shop proprietors who cooperated were given more business and, despite payoffs to agents, were still able to secure substantial profits. Shop keepers and butai agents alike embarked on a 'strategy to fleece the Japanese'[68], and prices spiralled as butai agents hoodwinked their bosses and manipulated market shortages.

> 'By June 1942, prices of hardware in Singapore and Penang had risen 6 to 8 times above pre-war rates and by the end of 1942, prices had risen 12 to 15 times.'[69]

Massive inflation did not deter military butais from continuing to purchase what they wanted. Although butai officers paid little heed to prices, when they realised their own agents were taking advantage of them, obtaining large commissions for their services, they quickly followed suit, reaping similar benefits and obtaining a share of the bounty for themselves.

In Singapore and Penang dealers in engineering and electrical goods became rich by doing business with the butais. Privileged Japanese firms and kaishas mushroomed, acting as collection agencies for the military, and openly competing with each other to grasp whatever they could. The black market trade flourished. Brokers emerged as self-appointed buffers between buyers and sellers. Sought after goods were reserved in advance by labelling them with butai tags. Unsuspecting traders were expected to accept low prices — often slashed by half or more — and anyone declining to do so was accused of being un-cooperative and often publicly assaulted. Such treatment, with the attached public 'loss of face', forced many Chinese traders into hiding and made brokers even more indispensable to the Japanese.

Some of the large 'arm-chair' brokers were financiers and private speculators who operated with the aid of military-protection certificates. These fortunate few courted favour with kaisha and military executives, spending time and money on entertaining them. They used a well organised chain of command, employing their own commodity specialists who in turn controlled lower ranked field-brokers who did the leg work and hunted down deals. Field-brokers also made use of a pack of runners — the first link in a spiralling chain. Runners were rank and file operators, often ex-foundrymen or lorry drivers who hung around coffee-shops and lodging houses, or mingled with the crowds,

> 'drinking tea with ex-looters and their friends, gossiping with them, and eliciting information about so-and-so's motor, and so-and-so's diesel engine'.[70]

At each level of reporting, prices were increased.

The MMA's purchasing policies, supported by the attitudes of Japanese officials, nurtured this system. If something was wanted, price did not matter. In such an environment the dishonest and dishonourable thrived. Cost was immaterial — the efficiency of a broker was assessed by his speed in obtaining what was wanted. When the military wanted something, all other authorities, including the State governments (Seicho), had to wait. To ensure this, employees of military butais were provided with soldiers and transport to prevent police interference.

The system condoned graft. Self preservation became a way of life and the only principle to which many people clung. Despite numerous press statements threatening harsh retribution, bribery and corruption were rampant and became publicly accepted practices involving many Japanese officials in the administration — provincial governors, garrison commanders, high-ranking military and government officials, kaisha executives and heads of military government departments. The public had no option but to live with it. Exposure would have rocked the MMA's foundations. The decline in morality was daily more apparent and, as in Japan,

> 'Women . . . were relegated to a very inferior position and Malaya, that was never noted for its strict moral standards, became looser than ever . . . It is no exaggeration to say that three and a half years of Japanese rule put Malaya back, as far as the character of the people were concerned, at least half a century.'[71]

Military police and butais claimed autonomy over provincial and sectional garrison commanders and civil government departments, frequently encroaching on their reserves and privileges. This, combined with Japanese lust for prestige, resulted in no one being held responsible for anything.

Many Japanese officials were jealous of each other, demanding the best treatment at all times, which ran at cross-purposes to their instinctive fear of superiors and authority. Senior officers, sensitive to slight and loss of face, were quick-tempered, soft targets for ingenious face-saving alternatives. Their weakness for attractive women and stylish living made it relatively easy for calculating traders and opportunists to lavish expensive presents on them in exchange for favours.

Key men in government departments were frequently paid off. Japanese officials were largely dependent on their Asian clerks' knowledge of English and they in turn often interpreted regulations to their own advantage. The responsibility for stamping signed documents lay with heads of departments who were subject to regular transfer. This lack of continuity was exploited by the Chinese. As the seals of Japanese officers had to be stamped on all official documents, the Chinese adroitly introduced

> 'a pretty young girl as the private secretary to each important official. Thereafter it was a natural sequence for this private secretary to have control of the seal and it was a simple matter for a Chinese businessman to get any contract or official document duly chopped.'[72]

All levels of society suffered under the malign influence of extortion and corruption. Police and railway employees abetted smugglers, and many Japanese officials overlooked these activities when bribed with wine and women. Japanese executives cheated their own companies, and in most kaishas officials took large commissions by double billing and pocketing the difference. Executives who made large sums of money used it to purchase

> 'houses, bungalows and estates, in the names of their mistresses. They also bought gold, jewellery and British currency, and deposited them with those women or their relatives.'[73]

Black marketeers and smugglers frequently invited kaisha and kumiai executives and military police to dinners and rowdy parties where they were provided with as much alcohol and as many women as they could wish. Outdoor officers (ODOs) made such fortunes from importers and exporters when inspecting their goods at warehouses and railway sidings that Japanese station masters jealously refused to allow them to enter their station precincts, helping themselves to the pay-offs instead.

> 'Towards the end of 1944, to book a truck from Penang, Ipoh or Kuala Lumpur to Singapore, would cost an exporter from $10,000 to $15,000 besides giving dinners.'[74]

Police guarding road blocks on the outskirts of villages and towns were paid off by lorry drivers. Customs officers were bribed by importers and exporters, who had already paid handsomely for valid permits. Payment was always the easy way to circumvent inconvenience and to overcome the unpleasantness surrounding any official's loss of face. Those who fraternised with the military police were able to avoid the unwanted attentions of the civil police and their informers, while those in possession of any authorisation stamped with an MP's seal evaded both police and customs' road blocks. These organisations did not dare to interfere with any military police authorisation, or encroach on their protected rackets. Smugglers bribed transport officers in army and navy depots, enabling them to transfer goods from one state to another with relative ease, and even to Siam for barter trade. Respectable merchants seeking favours from government officials — to assist them in their business — often used dance hostesses when making their applications. Transport department clerks and transport kaisha officials took bribes from owners of vehicles previously requisitioned by the government. To obtain the use of a 'red label' car for a few hours during the day cost between $500 to $1,000. To get a 'black label' permit, which allowed an owner to use his vehicle at all times, cost much more. Transport company clerks demanded coffee money when allocating vehicles for journeys, and cross-country bus conductors demanded up to three times the normal cost of fares for a seat. Relatives of people in trouble with the police had to bribe informers and detectives to locate the correct official in charge of their relative's case. Relatives of prisoners paid guards on every prison visit for permission to give food or drinks, or even the barest of comforts. Bribes were paid even to talk to a prisoner. Without this, it was impossible to find out whether that person was dead or alive. Low ranked policemen on station duty became rich men, as did the sentries guarding prisoners in the cells. Even clerks at police stations expected tips, without which they ensured that inconvenience and delay surrounded any application for a marriage or funeral licence.

Abuse of power and official corruption knew no bounds. When the Kempeitai wanted to court-martial Colonel Koda — commanding officer of the Selangor garrison — for abuse of position and self-enrichment, they arrested his Italian mistress, Doris Van der Straaten, on a trumped up charge of spying. During brutal interrogation she slapped the Kempeitai inquisitor, Sergeant Murakami, and was thrown to her death from a second floor window of Kempeitai Headquarters in Kuala Lumpur. Her death was announced as suicide.

Government department employees constantly sought ways to increase their low wages. The bribe system was taken for granted. If people wanted a service, they had to pay for it! Some people in Malaya tolerated and publicly condoned both bribery and corruption. Weaker elements in society could do little else, but the quiet majority steadfastly remained decent, selling their possessions at give-away prices to survive, and refusing to succumb to the corrupt monster that the MMA's administration represented.

On 30th June 1945 the *Penang Shimbun* reported that the Foodstuffs Kumiai would cease to function, and 'from 5th July the control over daily commodities will be lifted'.[75] Free trading would be permitted, except in salt fish, which remained a controlled item. Free trading was encouraged only in appointed market places, and Syurei (State Order) No.12 regulated the formation of Market Associations. Traders had to form a market kumiai and were levied on a proportion of their wares by the government in lieu of paying rent. Eight markets within the Market Association in Penang were organised to operate without price controls, with stall holders allowed to charge as they pleased. All other hawkers and roadside stall operators were ordered to cease trading, and on 7th July the *Penang Shimbun* told the public to stop buying from them. In July 1945 the price of one kati of beef was $180, compared to only 32 cents in December 1941. Similarly, a kati of fish was $40, as opposed to the pre-war price of only 22 cents. Market Associations applied for the use of lorries previously requisitioned by the Fish Control Kumiai, and fishermen and vegetable growers were urged to bring their produce quickly to town for sale. This belated concern from the MMA over unreasonable prices and monopolistic practices was typically inconsistent and had been evident during the previous three and an half years.

When Japan's surrender was made public, kaisha, kumiai, butai and other government monopolies in Penang and other main towns sold off their hoarded stocks cheaply. For a while markets were flooded with items long denied to people. In a belated attempt to court favour, large wage increases and bonuses, plus generous food rations, were given to staff. This resulted in a dramatic decline in prices, which enabled poorer elements in the community to purchase basic necessities. Once again, however, it was too little and too late.

A later economic survey of Malaya by a prominent Japanese government official admitted that the MMA's administrative and financial policies had been a miserable failure. Administrators during the occupation had succumbed to massive corruption. Everyone, it appeared, at all levels of society, had wanted to get in on the act!

12:9 Decline in Health Standards

In pre-war Malaya health services and standards were well administered and maintained. During the occupation standards eroded and essential preventative measures against probable tropical diseases were neglected. This, combined with food shortages, caused a widespread increase in diet-deficiency related illnesses and the outbreak of various diseases.

Malaria and venereal disease (VD) levels escalated, closely followed by tuberculosis, typhoid and beri-beri — the last claiming the lives of thousands of people whose unbalanced diet consisted predominantly of sweet potatoes and tapioca. Countless skeletal-like beggars were commonplace, and most child beggars had bloated bellies and were covered with festering skin afflictions.

The Japanese strictly controlled most types of western medicines, including all antiseptics and quinine for the treatment of malaria. They overlooked Epsom Salts, seemingly unaware of its usefulness, and this continued to be available. Epsom salts cost 4 cents per pound in December 1941, rising to $150–180 per pound by August 1945. When made into a compress, it was a good cure for localised infected wounds.

Prostitution was legalised and pimping became an accepted form of employment. Thousands of young girls throughout the country were forced into prostitution in an insatiable sex market, and VD increased to become the third most prevalent disease. As more people sought treatment the cost also escalated. In December 1941 an NAB injection cost $1.50 but by August 1945, depending on the locality, it had spiralled to $700–1,000.

The west wing of the Adventist Hospital in Burma Road, Penang, built by the Japanese in 1943, was used as a VD centre. Both Japanese and Korean prostitutes were given treatment there and such was its intensive use for this purpose that it was nicknamed the 'Love Hospital'.

The MMA's health policy was inconsistent. Standards varied considerably between locations and were left very much to the whims and personality of those in charge. In Singapore,

> 'Buildings that had been bombed or shelled, or destroyed by fire, remained in ruins, and the greater part of the city was littered with debris. The drains everywhere, and the Rochor Canal, which ran through the city, were choked with filth. Public lavatories stank tens of yards away, and back lanes were heaped with rubbish and were repugnant with aggressive smells.'[76]

The MMA in Penang organised a series of intensive if intermittent clean-up campaigns, aimed at eradicating malaria and typhoid in the island, details of which were reported in various editions of the *Penang Shimbun* newspaper.

Three years later in Penang the authorities were still trying, without much success, to popularise 'Town Cleaning Week Campaigns'. In July 1945 people were urged to sweep out cobwebs, sun their bedding, clean their houses, drains and back lanes, and to change the water in fire buckets.

Ironically, a preventative instruction was published in Penang in July 1945, designed to contain the spread of an outbreak of Cholera.

By this time tens of thousands of hapless people throughout all Japanese held territories, including those in numerous POW and civilian internment camps, had been callously treated and allowed to die of cholera and other diseases, under conditions of abject misery and deprivation.

12:10 The Black Market's Malign Influence on Inflation

The traumatic changes that swept over the Malay Peninsula from mid-December 1941, culminating in Singapore in mid-February 1942, left the population bewildered and bereft of responsible leaders and administration. People were suddenly at the mercy of looters and other lawless elements.

Many who took advantage of the chaos and of others' misfortunes were unemployed and from the uneducated, poorer strata of society, such as bullock carters and rickshaw pullers. They, and others, realised quick profits would be made from exploiting the situation and resorted to the simple speculative ploy of hoarding. Looted stocks were sold slowly, creating a lucrative black market. A decree promulgated by the Japanese, threatening looters with summary execution, panicked speculators into indiscriminately ridding themselves of their enormous hoarded stocks. This caused massive wastage: rice and tinned foodstuffs were abandoned everywhere; in all major towns looters cluttered the streets, recklessly hawking their wide variety of booty at ridiculously cheap prices.

People who still had money and who could get it out of the banks hesitated to buy this abundance of goods, especially European products. They were afraid of advertising their wealth and being robbed, as others had been. Two weeks of this deceptive abundance was followed by a prolonged period of scarcity in all essential items.

Foolishness and greed established the black market. Inflation soared weekly, people were forced to go without, food supplies decreased, and profiteers manipulated events to keep markets empty and shops with nothing to sell. Shop keepers withheld the little they had to squeeze higher profits from the public. Town dwellers were trapped in a vicious circle. Within a few months following the surrender of Singapore, every essential item of foodstuff and all other basic requirements had fallen under the sinister influence of the black market, which became the dominant force governing everyone's way of life. In this climate anything could be obtained at the right price, and everything had a value. Even human excreta, used as a fertiliser, was traded or stolen. Nothing escaped from the black market's exploitation.

Few had sufficient scruples to avoid the black market. Respectable and prominent citizens hoarded foodstuffs, basic necessities — a 'thrifty' householder always kept a small stock of such essentials as Aspro and "M & B" pills in the house'[77] — luxuries and money, ignoring the appeals for help from people less fortunate than themselves. Many exploited others with a shrug of their shoulders, as people died of starvation on their doorsteps. Had the rich not become so utterly devoid of human feelings, many impoverished people might have fared a little better, and the black market might not have invoked the terrible havoc that it did. Inflation and shortages increased to dire levels in the closing stages of the war as the effectiveness of the Allied blockade intensified. The black market dominated everything. In an attempt to stave off starvation people sold off cheaply their jewellery, watches, fountain pens, furniture, clothing and any other possessions that they could. When they were left with nothing else to sell their morale rapidly crumbled. Hatred grew among the people, not only for the Japanese, but also for those fellow citizens who by their black market manipulations caused misery to others. Conscientious workers in public service were intimidated by others who thrived on bribery and corruption.

The urban Chinese in particular experienced terrible hardship. Many of them lived in fear of their lives. Self-preservation became paramount, an unending search to find something to sell to keep body and soul together in the face of runaway inflation. Unemployed ex-government servants, clerks and school teachers, as they had nothing of marketable value to bargain with other than their qualifications, were among some of the worst affected, especially if they had only modest savings.

The *Shimbun* newspapers to a large extent were the mouthpiece of the MMA's propaganda. Their pronouncements of social concern had a hollow ring. Many Japanese officers in licencing and purchasing departments, holding responsible positions with a commitment to the welfare of the people, were in fact the masterminds behind the corruption tainting every aspect of life.

A combination of factors contributed to snowballing inflation. These included: over-production and uncontrolled issue of Japanese military script; high prices paid by the Japanese military to racketeers for anything needed; un-coordinated competitiveness between army, navy and air force butais and various kaisha purchasing departments; price manipulation by speculators and brokers; exorbitant taxation and, despite enforced massive savings campaigns, the worthlessness of the 'Banana'-designed military script. Last but not least in importance was the pervasive mood of war jitters.

After the Japanese pumped military script into the country people tried to make quick profits by selling anything they could to them. For a short while an aura of temporary well-being accompanied the general rise in prices. The few who realised the folly of this policy were unable to take corrective action against it.

Strict food rationing was introduced. The prices of more than 800 items were supposedly fixed, and other harsh restrictions introduced on the movement, trading and distribution of basic necessities such as rice, sugar, salt, flour and matches. However massive inflation continued hand in hand with equally massive, unscrupulous black market activities, fuelled by scarcity and the continuous shrinking value of the 'Banana' currency.

Inflation rose by leaps and bounds between December 1942 and August 1945, despite the worthlessness of the 'Banana' currency and the contempt in which it was held. By March 1945 rubber estates, which pre-war had changed hands for $150–200 per acre, were being sold at $20–25,000 per acre. Shophouses had increased from about $5–6,000 to $160–255,000, depending on their location, and even 'shop-lots and building sites within town-limits fetched prices 50 to 60 times above pre-war quotations'.[78] In 1942 eggs had cost only 10 cents each. By August 1945 they were $35 each. Asprin tablets increased from 5 cents per pill to $8; normal-sized bicycle tyres from $6.50 each to $3,500 and a 60 watt electric light bulb from 70 cents to $210 each. A piano at Robinsons in Singapore costing $400 (Straits dollars) in December 1941 rose to $40,000, and a $25 Parker pen was $5,500. White rice, a basic necessity, cost only 6 cents per katty in December 1941, but by August 1945 had risen to $75 per katty![79] By the end of the war,

> 'A tin of State Express cigarettes cost $5,000, a bottle of Johnny Walker Whiskey about $12,000, a sheet of corrugated iron cost $1,300, a bag of cement $1,300, a yard of cloth between $300 and $400, woollens $1,500 a yard. A tin of butter would fetch $950, a case of powdered milk, $25,000.'[80]

Although regulations were promulgated to induce some form of control over inflation and the black market, they proved totally ineffective since the MMA made extensive use of the black market to satisfy the greed of both individual and official needs.

Initially the MMA passed a law designed to control the price of numerous goods at slightly higher prices than those prevailing before Singapore fell. Shopkeepers and retailers had to declare their stocks and all buyers had to obtain permission before anything could be purchased. Selected goods were withdrawn from the market and set aside for use by the Japanese only. The effectiveness of this law was short-lived, and between December 1941 and December 1942 the prices of most commonly used foodstuffs, medicines and hardware rose by anything between three to ten times.

In August 1943 anti-profiteering regulations were issued. 'The immediate result was that every essential commodity became more difficult to get, and prices soared still higher.'[81] Each intervention by the MMA worsened conditions and the black market secured more scope in which to function, especially as insufficient food was available to satisfy basic needs. Racketeers were not arrested and the corrupt activities of the Rice Policemen went unchecked.

Taxation was also drastically increased in another attempt to stem ever-rising inflation. In early 1944 the Acquisition of Immovable Properties Tax Enactment was introduced, which imposed

> 'a tax of 30 per cent, effective retrospectively from 1st January 1943 . . . on buyers of property. In spite of this Enactment, people loaded with money kept on buying.'[82]

The increase in taxation was also designed to absorb surplus money and to raise funds to promote various welfare activities. This was a ridiculous ploy which only served to aggravate inflation. Those affected by higher levels of taxation instantly passed their burden on to the public by increasing prices. Hawkers were required to pay tax increases of 300%, dentists 1,000%, waitresses and prostitutes 2,000%, and dog licences went up by 500%.

In addition to higher levels of taxation, corrupt officials who sold export and transit permits had to be bribed, and the cost of doing so was simply added to traders' overheads. The devious manipulations of many officials in the MMA-backed monopolies encouraged the black market to expand by creating inconveniences and shortages. Many of these people became black market 'barons'. The situation was fast reached when the innocent had no alternative but to turn to the black market or go without. In due course even newspapers, bus, railway and cinema tickets could only be obtained this way.

Savings campaigns, with banks encouraging people to save by offering them attractive prizes and interest rates, was one of the measures aimed at fighting inflation. Although millions of dollars were amassed in this manner, the effect on inflation was negative. Monthly lotteries were organised and gambling farms set up to raise revenue through licence fees and taxes. Although a source of diversion for some, many unfortunate people were financially ruined. Amid all this, people were still urged to make themselves self-sufficient by growing more food and alternatives to rice.

Through three years of soaring inflation the *Penang Shimbun* reiterated the government's determination to eradicate profiteering and control the cost of living. It labelled wartime speculators 'the enemy within' and urged their prosecution. The public were continually exhorted to make sacrifices so that Japan would be victorious and the Greater East Asia Co-Prosperity Sphere successful.

The Japanese were not good administrators. They had insufficient properly trained and experienced people for the task. Some officials in the MMA made an attempt to curb black market activities and inflation, but their efforts were invariably sabotaged by the military and by the widespread corruption existing at all levels of the MMA's administration.

12:11 Mythical Self-Sufficiency

Japan's economic policy for Malaya assumed the country could run on its own resources and would be self-sufficient. As food shortages worsened, especially rice, the MMA put pressure on people to increase food production, and to supplement rice with tapioca, maize and sweet potatoes. Self-sufficiency campaigns proliferated. Cooperative farming colonies were established in different parts of the country to reduce congested living conditions in Penang and Singapore. The Overseas Chinese Association, the Malay Welfare Association and the Indian Independence League were instructed to form committees to select suitable settlers for these schemes and to enthuse their respective communities with these concepts.

The MMA found two merits in the concept of self-sufficiency by August 1942. Firstly, it divested them of their moral obligation towards the population's welfare and, secondly, they saw in it good publicity for their efforts to control ever-rising prices. Malaya's delicately balanced pre-war economy had been totally disrupted by the enforced closure of tin mines and rubber estates, impoverishing many workers dependent on them. The Japanese had no one else to trade with for these commodities.

As the effectiveness of the Allied submarine offensive isolated Malaya, Japanese mercantile arrangements were so severely disrupted that trading routes for the movement of essential foodstuffs and commodities in and out of the country could not be sufficiently used. Consequently, a dire shortage of everything was imminent. 'Grow more food' campaigns were sponsored everywhere, and the growing of substitute foodstuffs to replace scarce, imported foods, and to make people less dependent on the black market.

Garden competitions, agricultural exhibitions, free technical advice, loans from the People's Bank and farming tips published in newspapers sought to promote people's interest. In different parts of the country thousands of acres of rubber and jungle were allotted to settlers and turned into agricultural colonies. Farmers were told to destroy rats, and prizes were awarded for their efforts. New strains of rice from Taiwan were introduced, with shorter maturity periods providing two crops annually. These were resisted by the Malay peasantry, who saw them as upsetting long-standing practices, interfering with irrigation systems and making pest control more difficult. Double-cropping affected their traditional annual patterns. The MMA also alienated them when they commandeered their rice.

> 'The forcible requisition of rice also destroyed rural self-sufficiency, compelling peasants to depend on government rationing. As a result of this economic suffering and social dislocation, they became increasingly aware of government administration, thus transforming them from a relatively tranquil and self-sufficient group to a discontented and disturbed one.'[83]

Despite every incentive the response of the public was poor, and all efforts to produce more food were unsuccessful. This annoyed the authorities and as shortages persisted, they resorted to a series of ration cuts to impose their wishes, using the conservation of existing stocks as an excuse for their actions.

By August 1943 allied submarine and sea route blockades made food distribution exceedingly difficult. Food was scarce throughout all Japanese held territories. Self-sufficiency therefore was made a priority by the MMA, especially in Singapore, with a population of over one million and insufficient land to grow food to feed them. 'Consequently the 7th Area Army headquarters ordered that at least 300,000 people be evacuated from Syonan.'[84] Thousands of acres of coconut and rubber plantations and jungle were destroyed and cleared for conversion into agricultural settlements under these schemes.

> 'The Authorities gave all sorts of enticements to intending settlers. They were given free rice and cloth rations; free vegetable-seeds and manures; free medicines and medical services; cheap agricultural implements; subsidies and loans. They were also promised travelling dispensaries, travelling cinemas and concert parties.'[85]

Approval was given to the OCA to establish a Chinese settlement, without Japanese involvement, at Endau in north east Johore. The Chinese were allowed to make their own arrangements and be responsible for maintaining law and order. The settlement was named 'New Syonan' and a construction committee was set up under the chairmanship of Dr Lim Boon Keng. By the end of 1943 'New Syonan' had a population of 12,000 people, many of whom, it was discovered after Japan's surrender, were active anti-Japanese guerrillas.

A non-self-governing settlement was set up at Bahau in Negeri Sembilan for Chinese Catholics and Eurasians, as part of the scheme to evacuate people from Singapore. Community leaders and the Roman Catholic Bishop of Singapore, Monsignor Devals, had to agree to the project, and an inspection team was sent to the area. Settlers were segregated into two groups, one for Eurasians including non-Catholics, and the other for Chinese Catholics. Many in both groups were reasonably well educated. No money was allotted to this project and many promises made by the Negeri Sembilan authorities were subsequently not carried out.

> 'There were several reasons why Bahau did not achieve the success of New Syonan. The soil was poor; there was not enough water. Malaria took the lives of many old people and children; the anti-malaria steps taken by the state authorities were inadequate. The Eurasians suffered most. Then the church bells tolled not to bring the faithful to worship but for the burial of yet another victim of malaria.'[86]

Less than 10% of the MMA's target of 300,000 were relocated in both these settlements.

Unavailability of land for food cultivation and congestion in the town areas of Penang caused considerable problems. In 1943, in an attempt to overcome this, committees were formed from the Overseas Chinese Association, the Malay Welfare Association and the Indian Independence League to recruit settlers for cooperative style farms to be formed in Province Wellesley. 8,000 acres were allocated and gradually thousands of acres of rubber and coconut estates, as well as jungle, were painstakingly cleared by hand.

The nearest settlement to Penang was on Bertam Estate in Province Wellesley. This scheme was allocated to Malays and Chinese. Potential settlers were lured by promises of food, medicines, entertainment and seeds. They were given about three acres of partially felled and cleared land per family unit, along with a free house, and cash loans of $500–3,000 were made available to them. The settlements were equipped with various basic amenities including food distribution centres, canteens and barber shops. The *Penang Shimbun* enticed potential settlers with reports of food available at farm settlements at prices considerably lower than they were in Penang at that time.

Much land was opened up in this manner under the MMA's directives. Some areas in traditionally restricted Malay Reserve lands were released to non-Malays and settled by Chinese. The urban drift of numerous Chinese to these agricultural settlements was viewed as a threat to the traditional position of Malay farmers, and altered the traditional division of labour with Malays as producers and Chinese as distributors, each dependent on the other. The Malays resented the Chinese squatting on lands previously reserved for them, and the friction arising from this was one of several causes for subsequent deterioration in race relations.

> 'The clustering of Chinese squatters outside the urban areas was a marked feature of the Japanese occupation, and they became an important source of food, supplies, and intelligence for the communist-led resistance movements.'[87]

These later were the focal point of the post-war squatter problem.

Settlement life, contrary to the glowing propaganda in newspapers, was monotonous and miserable. Numerous settlers died of a variety of illnesses, malaria and malnutrition being endemic. In the urban areas there were token attempts at private farming, usually growing the easiest crops, but these were equally unsuccessful. People were not interested in farming when there were easier ways to make money on the black market, and by speculation.

Some did enthusiastically grow more food for their families, and previously well kept badminton and tennis courts, as well as flower gardens, were planted with a variety of food crops. Food shortages affected rich and poor alike. Many housewives and unmarried girls became expert vegetable gardeners, using what limited space was available to them.

In December 1943 a Labour Service Corps was formed, with workers throughout the country conscripted into it. Those between the ages of 15 and 45 were eligible, and 20 out of every 250 within this age group were selected. Pengulus in rural areas, and the community control associations in towns, like the Overseas Chinese Association, the Malay Welfare Association and the Arab Welfare Association, were required to submit names for this. A Labour Corps for women was also formed, and each section was given land to cultivate where members worked for four hours every week. Large collective farms were also allocated to various Kaishas, who organised their own staff into labour corps. Even some Japanese officials turned their hand to tilling the soil. The Gunseikan (highest authority in the MMA) urged Sultans to set a good example to their people, and both the Sultans of Johore and Perak organised model farms in their states. In every town the Jeikaidan (Self Protection Corps) was allocated extensive areas of land and their members were ordered to work it by forming Kinroho-sitais (Voluntary Service Units). The authorities were never satisfied, for despite all threats and inducements, it was obvious that people were only going through the motions to keep themselves out of trouble.

The food situation had considerably worsened by 1944, following the ceding to Siam of Malaya's four northern states of Kedah, Kelantan, Trengganu and Perlis in October 1943, which were also the largest rice cultivating areas in the country. In Penang, the Nomu-Kacho (Agricultural Chief) warned that the importation of rice from Burma and elsewhere would no longer be possible, and made it mandatory for people to participate in the grow more food schemes. Other State Governors demanded immediate action and implemented aggressive measures against those whom they considered uncooperative. Government notification No 41, dated 25th November 2603 (1943), was published in the *Penang Shimbun*, instructing every family to start growing vegetables to achieve self-sufficiency within a month.

On 28th July 1945 the Governor of Penang, Lieut-General Shinohara, said more incentives must be offered to prospective settlers to overcome their waning enthusiasm for settlement life. A subcommittee was appointed by the Penang Sangikai (State Council) to collect contributions and to allot subsidies for new settler families. Community leaders Mr Heah Joo Seang and Dr M.K. Menon proposed that subsidies should be increased to $3,000 per family, with further increases up to $5,000 for larger families, on the basis of an extra $500 per person for families with over six members.

On 3rd August 1945 two articles appeared in the *Penang Shimbun*. One acknowledged the 'very serious problem of growing more food'. The other urged more Penang Chinese to 'forsake the comparatively unprofitable hustle and bustle of town life' and turn instead to the healthy life that awaited them on food-producing settlements. Here, they were told — at a time when the price of one katty of pork had risen to $280 and rice was $75 per katty — they could fell cartloads of firewood and earn up to $100 per day. Grossly undernourished people were urged to perform arduous manual labour under the blazing sun, at a time when most people realised through clandestine radio broadcasts that Japan was doomed to defeat.

On 7th August 1945 the *Penang Shimbun* again published an article in which community leaders appealed to people to grow more food. Heah Joo Seang mentioned the 'many special amenities' that awaited new settlers. N.K. Menon considered that 'rearing cattle and poultry' would give settlers a 'happy and contented life', while Mr A.M.Y. Izzudin stressed the importance of self-sufficiency to 'bolster up the war effort of our forces'.

It was ironic after Malaya was liberated that farming settlements were found to be the worst centres of disease and malnutrition. They were all areas needing particular attention by relief and medical workers under the British Military Administration (BMA).

Self-sufficiency and growing more food might have been beneficial programmes in themselves, but people were reluctant to cooperate with the Japanese. Many town dwellers joined settlement projects only to escape from being drafted, and many continued to believe, even in 1944 when economic circumstances and difficulties were at their worst, that the British would return in time to save them.

12:12 Fight for Survival

The real reasons behind the loss of Malaya were long concealed under very public and ill-informed criticism. The source of this criticism lay with those who could ill-afford any undermining of public confidence in their conduct of the war.

In reality many deserved high praise for their behaviour during the occupation, which visited 'a cruel and oppressive regime'[88] on

Malaya's multi-racial society, causing widespread destruction and death. Many civilians did succumb to the corrupting influences that circumscribed their existence, but thousands of others in every walk of life did not. It was they who

> 'sold all available gold and jewels and later their furniture and heirlooms, who overcame all hardships, lived on the barest necessities, and preferred an existence of hard toil and privations, rather than cooperate with the hated Japanese',[89]

refusing to become informers and exploit others, choosing instead to live a life of semi-starvation.

Many suffered indescribably cruel tortures at the hands of the Military Police (Kempeitai) but stoically refused to betray friends and neighbours. Condemnation of the few who did weaken under strain is easy, but the silent contribution of those who struggled every minute of the day and night to overcome the influence of evil should not be ignored.

> '. . . there were thousands of silent-sufferers, of all races, of all ranks and walks of life, who defied temptations, overcame hardships, and lived on the barest of necessities rather than eat out of the hands of the Japs. They were the redeeming feature of Malaya, for they fought a continuous moral war, and, although battle-scarred, were undefeated.'[90]

Considerable sacrifices were made. This silent suffering was a way of displaying loyalty to the cause of Britain and the Empire in the fight against the tyranny of Japan.

> 'At first the population was dazed by the rapidity of the Japanese success because the country had depended on British protection and this had been swept away.'[91]

Later, as imports dwindled under the MMA's ruthless regime, the

> 'great majority of the population was at starvation level because the Japanese had almost stopped the import of rice. Many others, Chinese especially, had been killed by the Japanese for giving assistance to the resistance groups in the jungle.'[92]

Conditions in towns were dismal. Shops opened late and closed early, having few goods to sell. Sanitation was neglected as thousands of labourers had been press-ganged into work on the 'death' railways in Siam and Burma. Streets, heaped with rubbish, were unswept and in disrepair. Markets were overcrowded with hawker stalls. Garbage was strewn everywhere, turning lanes and drains into foul breeding places for vermin and disease. Holes dug as makeshift air-raid shelters were filled with dirty, stagnant water, ideal breeding places for mosquitoes. Malaria soared. Fixed wage earners and the poorer classes suffered most from the rampant inflation, and even pre-war professionals, such as doctors, architects and lawyers, were reduced to eating at roadside stalls. People became increasingly shabby. Many chose deprivation and poverty, selling their possessions to survive rather than turning to the Japanese and becoming their paid lackeys.

Living conditions in Penang during the occupation were likened to 'a cauldron filled with burning oil . . . you could only jump from the frying pan into the fire'.[93]

Fanatics propounding half-baked theories and ill-conceived administrative measures terrorised people into submission. Cruelty was justified if there was 'one guilty person amongst 100 murdered victims'.[94]

12:13 The Importance of Rice

In 1941 Malaya imported sixty per cent of her rice from Burma, Thailand and elsewhere. Ample and easy means of transport were available enabling Malaya to import rice cheaply from both countries, where there were considerable surpluses. Burma and Thailand exported rice to pay for imports of Malaya's tin and rubber. It had not been necessary for Malaya to be self-sufficient in rice but more convenient and economical to import it. Imported rice was mostly used by non-Malay urban dwellers, as the Malay peasantry in rural areas were generally self-sufficient.

Following the setting up of the MMA, the Japanese initially prohibited the importation of rice from Thailand as they considered there would be a conflict of interests with the activities of the Mitsubishi Shoji Kabushiki Kaisha (MSKK), who had been allocated the monopoly over rice. This ruling was later relaxed and sufficient rice was obtained until the end of 1942, when the Thai rice exporters protested against the financial arrangements made by the Japanese, refusing to accept their 'banana' script and demanding instead to be paid with gold, diamonds, jewellery and machinery. This disrupted supply and, added to the increased effectiveness of Allied submarine activities severing sea links between Japan and her occupied regions, gave rise to massive food shortages throughout the whole area.

As Japan's war reversals increased, all imported foodstuffs, including rice, were in extremely short supply, bringing about a series of strict rationing measures. The production of rice in Malaya was disrupted and output declined, as buffaloes used to till the land were slaughtered to feed Japanese troops. With food shortages acute people were forced to eat sweet potatoes, which had been previously despised as nutritionally poor. However, they soon became an important food substitute.

In Singapore every family was issued with a Rice Card initially so that they could obtain the authorised monthly ration of eight katties of rice per adult. Children were allocated half this quantity. By early 1944 the rice ration was cut to six katties per person per month, the effect dramatically revealed in people's appearance. From 1st April 1945 monthly rice rations in towns were reduced to six katties for men, four for women and three for children. In rural areas only half these rates were permitted. The Penang Chief of Foodstuffs (Penang Shokunyokocco), Mr Nishizawa, was aware that this was insufficient but considered the hardship justified, as a reminder to those who had shirked changkol (spade) work, disregarding the government's policy to grow more food. In July 1945 the rice ration was again cut by half, and males living in towns were given only three katties per month. If the war had continued for another three to four months, tens of thousands of people throughout Malaya would have died from malnutrition.

The 'rice bowl' was the pivot of Malaya's existence. The country depended on labour, who in turn depended on rice. Rice not only sustained the body, it bolstered morale and controlled the destiny of the country. People needed rice despite Japanese dietitians' propaganda that substitutes were equally sustaining. The Chinese were utterly dependent on rice and had to obtain it at any cost. Prices of all other items were linked to it, and it became the nucleus of inflation levels. When shipments of smuggled rice arrived safely, prices on the black market dropped. When ships carrying rice were sunk by allied submarines, the prices of all commodities rapidly increased. The MMA's failure to supply sufficient rice to the population was the fundamental cause of all economic strife. Rice — the stable diet — became therefore an important political weapon and the Japanese were able to exploit any lack of it. They imposed cooperation by reducing rations. They bonded workers by increasing prices above their earning capacity. They recruited labour with promises of special rice allocations, especially to work in military factories and foundries. A promise of rice invited eventual submission. People worked for the Japanese as servants, many women became their mistresses, and the population in general was exploited by them in its need for rice, the unheralded king of the black market.

The MMA controlled all rice stocks and as the reality of starvation threatened they held the urban population in particular in a state of utter subjugation. Singapore was picked clean. Shops and warehouses were bare. Half-starved people squatted in long queues outside rice depots, patiently waiting for their meagre life sustaining ration, which was only obtained by bowing to the waist with muttered thanks to their Japanese masters.

Although rigid rationing was imposed, the shortages were fictitious and manipulated. There was plenty of rice in the country, held in military godowns and in Kaisha warehouses. The MMA's policy aimed at conserving existing rice stocks irregardless of people's needs, as they realised that Malaya would be eventually isolated from her pre-war traditional import sources. When Thai rice exporters refused to accept Japanese military script in payment for rice shipments, the MMA was thwarted from obtaining the large amounts of rice that were desperately needed, and was unable to live up to their Co-Prosperity Sphere boasts. Strict rationing ensured that rice went first to military garrisons and butais all over the country. Next were the thousands of government officials and the dozens of kaishas and kumaias. The people were the last priority! They were told to till the soil even as their rations were again reduced. Those who needed assistance most were instructed on the 'dignity of manual labour'[95] and continually harassed and thwarted in their efforts by interference from the military.

Most of the fertile areas, where foodstuffs were planted, were situated close to jungle fringes, where communist-led anti-Japanese elements were concentrated. Many innocent farmers were blamed and punished by the Japanese, following a shooting incident in the district, and numerous acts of recriminatory violence against innocent and guilty farmers alike occurred, with the unscrupulous using these incidents to settle private feuds.

> 'Without full evidence and without proper investigations the Military or the Police had been known to have destroyed hundreds of farmsteads and shot countless innocent people, merely on the grounds of suspicion.'[96]

Farmers were therefore caught in a vice. Those who refused to plant foodstuffs were accused of non-cooperation, and those who did plant were at risk of being implicated with the communists. The death of innocent people mattered little to the MMA.

In late 1944, when the economic woes of the MMA had worsened beyond reprieve, they attempted to improve their relations with the Chinese in Malaya.

> 'The Teochiu rice traders in Singapore and Penang played an important role in keeping open the rice supply from Thailand to Malaya. Initially this was done through smuggling and racketeering, in which Japanese officials were suitably bribed.'[97]

Through their links with other Teochiu rice traders in Thailand they managed to bring in 3,000 tons of rice every month, even though Japan's overland and sea routes to Malaya had been virtually paralysed.

12:14 Substitute Ingenuity

When Malaya became isolated from her traditional sources of supply, and goods previously imported were no longer obtainable, Chinese ingenuity went a long way to fill the void by finding substitutes, for which they deserve full credit. Numerous 'cottage-type' activities and industries mushroomed and functioned until either production costs became prohibitive, or raw materials were unavailable. An assortment of waste products such as stems of banana trees, pineapple-plant leaves, lallang, the pithy skins of durians and the burnt ashes of coconut shells were ingeniously used. At first many of these substitute items were crudely made using old-fashioned methods, but as techniques gradually improved, the end-products became both usable and acceptable as wartime substitutes. Numerous new inventions evolved to replace articles no longer obtainable. Other ideas formed the bases for new industries, spanning a wide range of goods including food and luxury items. Whiskey, cosmetics, household utensils, bicycle tyres, vitamins, a variety of foodstuffs, nails, ropes, sewing thread and cloth were but some of the things that Chinese ingenuity, fuelled by necessity, was able to produce locally.

Cars and lorries were converted to run on coal gas. Crude palm oil was used to replace lubricating oil and grease. A crude but not particularly successful form of petroleum — as it clogged up carburettors — was made from rubber. Large quantities of transformer oil was made from coconut oil.

Urban shortages in transport were cleverly alleviated in some towns by Chinese mechanics, who turned to making trishaws. These were registered for public hire, with fees of 10 cents per mile, a waiting charge of 10 cents for up to one hour and an additional 10 cents for every hour after that. Operators had to produce a price list when asked to do so, and the *Penang Shimbun* newspaper claimed that trishaw riders could earn between $2–10 daily. This would have meant either pedaling for one hundred miles daily, or charging waiting fees for 100 hours over a 24 hour period! This ubiquitous mode of transport was operated by impoverished teachers of English and clerks, who were forced into a career in pedalling as a means of earning a living, as well as out-of-work labourers and former jinrikshaw pullers.

As cars were used mostly by Japanese officials, except for the few with conspicuous red or black permits attached to their windscreens allowed for civilian use, the bicycle also became popular. Millionaires rode expensive models and women of all ages, and children, were familiar sights as they pillion-rode to market or went visiting their friends. By June 1943 Penang reportedly had 40,000 bicycles, and twenty police-approved cycle parks in the town area charged a daily parking rate of 5 cents per machine. The tax for bicycles was $3.50 per year, of which $1.50 was for a licence plate, which had to be prominently fixed to the machine. For most of the population, however, it was still a matter of going on foot.

Oil from rubber seeds was used to replace linseed oil in varnishes and paint. Rubber latex was coagulated successfully and cheaply using wood acid instead of the previously imported acetic or formic acid which were no longer available. Glycerine for medicinal purposes was obtained from coconut and vegetable oils and was also used for making explosives. Methylated spirits were derived from tapioca, and salt was extracted from sea water. Trades sprung up to recondition old electric light bulbs, and to make soap from coconut and oil palm residues.

Various new industries emerged, some of which were of economic importance. Between September 1944 and March 1945, pneumatic cycle tyres were in great demand and were also used as barter-exchange for Thai rice. Their performance was erratic, however, which led manufacturers to produce solid tyres for bicycles as well as for carts pulled by men and animals. A semi-pneumatic tyre was also developed and this became popular, as it was durable, more comfortable to ride on, and did not easily puncture.

Wire-nails of different sizes were made from strands of old barbed-wire and from old wire-ropes. Local foundry-men made thousands of frying pans out of scrap-iron. All sizes were made from 10-inch to 4-feet in diameter. Cast-iron was sought everywhere and increased in price from $7 per picul (56.7 kg) in December 1941 to $450 per picul in August 1945. A cottage-industry emerged making mosquito nets out of pineapple-leaf fibre threads. Students at Malay schools as well as inmates of mental asylums turned their hand to making a variety of rugs and mats out of pineapple-leaf fibre, coconut coir and banana-stem fibres.

Penang was described by Mr R. Robless of the Penang Shokoka (Commerce and Industry) as being a busy industrial centre during this period with a score of household and other personal items being made.

The manufacture of rope gave employment to numerous people. Women rolled coconut or pineapple-leaf fibres into strands, and men passed them through spinning machines which twisted them to the right size. Coconut fibres were turned into hair, coat and floor brushes. Paper was made from bamboo, pineapple or rubber leaves, and lallang.

During 1942 and 1943, with soap in great demand, many soap factories came into being all over the country. As foreign-made caustic soda was unobtainable, soap was made out of a variety of residues including coconut or durian-ash, salt, coconut-oil or palm-oil, and continued to be widely produced until 1944 when factories were forced to close down because basic ingredients were unobtainable. Toothpaste and tooth powders, cosmetics and hair cream, face creams and face powders were also made by many manufacturers in both Singapore and Penang. Cattle horns and bones were used to make an assortment of buttons and old tooth brushes were reconditioned into attractive new ones, using pig bristles. Tooth-picks were made from the ribs of coconut leaves, and numerous other useful articles, such as dusters out of pineapple leaves, were made out of leftover and waste materials. In Penang a variety of quality items, including rubber fountain pen sacks, brilliantine, face creams and baby dusting-powders, were made. Shoe and boot polish was manufactured, using lamp soot mixed with coconut oil and a colouring agent.

Some new industries produced food items. Coconut and sugar cane replaced sugar, and toddy sugar was used in cakes. Tapioca-flour was mixed with ragi, maize or rice-flour to make biscuits and cakes, instead of wheat-flour, and red palm oil replaced butter. Green-peas and soya-beans were also used to make bread. Shark liver oil was ingeniously substituted for cod liver oil by mixing shark oil with malt.

Luxury-goods were not ignored. Hundreds of cigarette and cigar factories sprang up, particularly in Perak and Selangor, and

> 'gave employment to tens of thousands of women, girls and boys whose nimble fingers were required for rolling, cutting and packing the cigarettes and cigars. Because of the great demand for tobacco-leaves, thousands of acres of semi-jungle land were cleared for tobacco-leaf cultivation. From $11 to $16 per picul (pre-war prices) locally-grown tobacco leaves rose to $15,000 per picul by April 1945!'[98]

The price of a comparable quality, pre-war cigarette was 1 cent, which in 1945 had risen to as much as $2 per stick. An assortment of liquors, wines, whiskies and brandies were made from ragi or toddy fermentations and a rice wine, of dubious purity, was produced, to which various flavourings were added.

New industries were started to manufacture agricultural implements in a bid to support the MMA's 'grow-more-food' campaigns. Scrap metal was turned into thousands of ploughs, shovels, rakes and changkols. Night soil was collected or stolen in every town and was either purchased by farmers or turned into fertilisers.

> 'A kerosene-tin-full of excreta, weighing approximately 50 katties, could be sold for $80 to $100 (say in June 1945).'[99]

Military-related industries made wooden vessels which were fitted with diesel or marine engines. Pig iron and bauxite foundries were operated by the Nippon Seitetsu Kabushiki Kaisha (NSKK) while the Tokio Gempi Juzai Tosei Kabushiki Kaisha (TGJTKK) took all raw hides from abattoirs, these subsequently being turned into boots among other things. Foundries were requisitioned throughout the country and shells, bombs, machine-parts, marine engines, bullets, gun-spares, gunpowder and a various assortment of other military stores were made. As the supply of raw materials became increasingly scarce, many of these military-related industries ceased to operate, and few survived the complete duration of the occupation.

Note: Much of the information contained in this section was found in *Malaya Upside Down*, ch.23, p.161–173, by Chin Kee Onn, to whom the author's appreciation is expressed.

12:15 Worthless Savings

During the occupation the military authorities issued their own currency with its decorative banana-pattern. Standards of printing and design visibly deteriorated as massive quantities of script were rushed into circulation in a bid to keep apace with the ever-spiralling inflation. The Japanese maintained no record of how much paper money was printed and issued as overworked presses continually rushed to satisfy the MMA's increasing demands. All safeguards were ignored. Initially, all notes carried serial letters and numbers, but after October 1942 numbers were discontinued and only the alphabetic headings remained. In early 1943 some issues even had no serial alphabetic letterings, so that keeping any record of what had been printed became impossible. The use of inferior paper affected cutting standards and made marginal spacings erratic and misaligned. Common irregularities, in conjunction with poor quality inks, caused print to fade so that forgeries could not be easily determined. The ink was not even allowed to dry properly on some issues before they were sent to banks for distribution.

When the circulation of surplus paper money was recognised as being instrumental in the rise of inflation, various saving campaigns were started to absorb some of the surplus, and establish an element of control. Saving schemes were advertised as 'one of the pre-requisites of quick victory'.[100] Postal savings schemes were sponsored by the Dai Nippon Government Post Office Savings Bank of Malai, and Fixed Bank Deposit Bonus Schemes were sponsored by the Malai Bankers Association, which was the financial department of the MMA.

In August 1943, to encourage more small savers to deposit funds in the Post Office Savings Bank, withdrawal regulations were altered, enabling a depositor to draw up to the limit of his account, provided he left in a token $1. Previously imposed limits of $2,000 and $5,000 were increased to $5,000 and $20,000 for ordinary and public joint accounts.

A series of Postal Savings Promotion-Weeks were arranged to encourage people to save. By 31st July 1945, 523,814 depositors throughout Malaya and Singapore had collected in excess of $33 million, and in Penang 84,308 depositors' total was $3,736,487.[101] The officials responsible for organising these campaigns were mistakenly gratified by this 'cooperation'. The truth, however, was that there was

> 'such an amount of worthless script floating around that "savings" meant nothing. People subscribed to these campaigns more to appease and to save their skins than to save money that was trash.'[102]

In February 1944 the first country-wide savings drive was launched by the Malai Bankers Association. Its object was to obtain $6 million, but by June this was exceeded, with $8 million being placed on

Fixed Deposits. A second savings drive having yielded more than $27 million, the Gunseikan, flushed with success, ordered a third savings drive in October 1944, with the mammoth target of $200 million. A quota was allocated to each State, to be obtained by the end of March 1945. A total of almost $271 million was saved and all States, except Penang and Negeri Sembilan, exceeded their quotas, Penang falling short of her quota by $4,026,000. By 31st March 1945, $486,290,000 had been put into fixed deposits in banks, of which Penang's total contribution was then $53,877,000.[103] A fourth drive, begun on 1st August 1945, was abruptly halted when Japan surrendered.

On 19th April 1945 the *Penang Shimbum* published an article entitled 'Save in Order to Win War', in which the Governor, Lieut-General Shinohara, emphasised the importance of savings to achieve a 'quick victory in the Greater East Asia War'. In Japan, he emphasised, everyone saved and gave their lives for their country. Recent war news had not been 'wholly satisfactory', but the situation was 'not really dangerous'.

These bland under-statements coincided with the USSR's refusal to renew their Non-Aggression Pact with Japan, with massive US bombing raids on Tokyo and the tide of the crucial Okinawa battle turning against Japan, none of which were factually reported in Penang. On 2nd June 1945 the *Penang Shimbun* published another article praising the merits of savings, entitled 'Savings and Stabilisation of Prices Essential'. Given the disastrous outcome of the Okinawa campaign, Hitler's suicide on 30th April 1945 and the continued massive B-29 bombing raids in May 1945, when 24,000 tons of bombs were dropped on Japan, the publication seemed even more incredible and devoid of reason. The Governor, thanking officers of the Penang Shu Savings Encouragement Committee, the Penang Banking Association, as well as the general public, claimed,

> '. . . a thrifty man is a credit to the community and as asset to his country. Besides, savings will also help the successful prosecution of the war. One of the surest ways of helping to provide more and more materials for the fighting forces to obtain freedom for the Asiatic nations for all times is to help in the stabilisation of our economic condition and prices. This is our duty as non-combatants on the home front.'[104]

This when white rice had risen to $36 per katty compared to only 6 cents in December 1941! Still planning for the future, the Governor expected Penang's savings to exceed $49,000,000 during 1945 as the MMA proposed to organise another two 'Fixed Deposit with Bonus Schemes' to absorb at least $500,000,000 throughout Malaya.

The Fourth Fixed Deposit with Bonus Savings Drive was supposed to be open to public participation from 1st to 31st August 1945. The Editorial headline of the *Penang Shimbun* on 4th August was 'Savings a Source of Power'. Everyone should save owing to the uncertainties of war and the Fourth Fixed Deposit with Bonus offered an 'excellent opportunity . . . for ensuring the future well-being of the whole population of Malai'.[105]

Peacetime extravagances had to be discarded, the paper declared, as they upset economic balance. Hypocrisy at this time was ludicrous. Under Co-Prosperity the price of white rice in August 1945 had risen to $75 per katty, more than double what it had been one month previously!

Lotteries were another means of encouraging savings. A country-wide monthly lottery, the Konan Saiken, was introduced in August 1943, for which tickets were sold through banks, government offices and community associations. It quickly became popular and offered a first prize of $50,000.

In 1945 the Overseas Chinese Association organised a state lottery (Shu-Saiken) in Penang. 100,000 tickets of $5 each were issued, and total prize money was initially set at $300,000. On 20th June 1945 the *Penang Shimbun* announced plans to increase the first prize to $200,000.

These lotteries were organised to relieve war induced distress, contribute towards grow more food campaigns, absorb surplus money and check inflation. The first prize was just sufficient to purchase four new lorry tyres in July 1945, but by August continued inflation had reduced this to less than three! Tickets sold rapidly and people thought nothing of buying them, as inflation made money of little value to them.

Money was the cheapest commodity during the occupation. It abounded, but became worthless as massive inflation put the most modest of requirements out of many people's reach. With every Axis defeat prices continued to soar. In 1944, when $100 bills were printed, they further aggravated inflation, but many people still spent freely, being convinced that this despised currency would vanish with Japan's eventual defeat.

Some who had amassed vast fortunes did not keep them but spent lavishly on gold, jewellery, diamonds, houses and estates. Others preferred the security of hoarded currency, hoping the Japanese government would eventually redeem it. On 9th September 1945 the *Straits Echo* suggested the best use for the currency – a bonfire!

12:16 Conscription

After August 1943 women were required to replace men in certain jobs, freeing them for essential war-related work. Women served, often out of economic necessity, in various menial or semi-skilled positions. Some became waitresses, clerks or telephone operators, or worked in factories and offices. Some did social work, while those with suitable qualifications taught. Women's Associations were formed in 1944 and through these women were exposed to social welfare and relief-related jobs with orphans and destitutes, first aid and auxiliary police welfare programmes, as well as cultivation programmes and propaganda activities.

Labour corps were formed throughout Malaya in December 1943 to impress workers for the benefit of Japan's declining war effort. Many workers evaded conscription as they feared being sent to Burma or Thailand. This resulted in a shortage of labour which, despite acute food scarcity, the Japanese tried to overcome by importing labour from Java and so more mouths to feed.

In December 1944 the Restriction of Male Employment Ordinance was introduced. This was to increase the availability of male settlers in various farming colonies set up under the MMA's self-sufficiency and grow-more-food campaigns. Women and girls were called on to replace men employed in non-essential jobs so that they could be conscripted into farm settlements. Others, so released, were drafted into other defence-associated projects, such as the Jeikaidan (Voluntary Vigilance Corps for Self-Preservation and Self-Protection), Heiho (Auxiliary Service), Giyu Gun (Volunteer Army), Giyu Tai

(Volunteer Corps) as well as the police preservation units, or military labour corps. Under the Restriction of Male Employment Ordinance, women took over jobs as telephone and elevator operators, waitresses, saleswomen, dhobis, attendants in amusement parks and theatres and also worked as tailors, cooks or hawkers.

In an article entitled 'All Males Must Change to Essential Work', published in the *Penang Shimbun* on 19th January 1945, it was explained that the ordinance, effective from 31st December 1944, required all males between the ages of 15 and 40 employed in non-essential jobs to leave them no later than 31st March 1945. A later press release implied that the change from non-essential to essential work — such as increasing food production, being employed in the Army or Navy, or joining the Giyu Gun, Giyu Tai or the Heiho — was in fact optional and enjoyable.

The conscription of labour, particularly after March 1944, brought about a deterioration in the living standards of Malays and Indians. Many able-bodied males were taken away to satisfy the demands on life imposed by the construction of the Kra and Burma-Thai railroads. Truckloads of unfortunates were spirited away to these projects, where the death toll was terrifyingly high. The Indian population throughout the country decreased from 14% to 10% between 1941 and 1945. This was directly linked to the MMA's labour conscription policies.

Indian workers — familiarly referred to as 'narlikis' (Romanised spelling for 'tomorrow' in Tamil) — were fondly regarded by most pre-war planters. Many remained faithful to their former employers as much as circumstances for survival permitted. Thousands were conscripted as slave labour in 1942 to the 'death railway' projects in Thailand, where some met, by chance, with their former employers, now in a similar plight. In many such reunions former masters and servants became genuine comrades, dressed similarly in loin cloths and doing the same work under the brutal yoke of the Japanese.

1. *Ma-Rai-Ee* by Chin Kee Onn, ch.8, p.81.
2. Ibid, ch.8, p.81.
3. Ibid, ch.8, p.82.
4. *History of the Second World War* by Sir Basil Liddel Hart, ch.23, p.358.
5. *The Jungle is Neutral* by F. Spencer Chapman, DSO, ch.4, p.68.

6. *Jungle Alliance — Japan and the INA* by Joyce C. Libra, ch.5, p.64.
7. Ibid.
8. *British Rule in Malaya 1942–1957* by Robert Heussler, ch.3, p.52.
9. *The Sara Saga* by M. Saravanamuthu, ch.9, p.114.
10. Ibid, p.115.
11. *Red Star over Malaya. Resistance and Social Conflict during and after the Japanese Occupation, 1941–1946* by Cheah Boon Kheng, ch.2, p.42.
12. Ibid, ch.2, p.25.
13. Ibid.
14. *Ma-Rai-Ee* by Chin Kee Onn, ch.13, p.143.
15. *The Straits Echo*, Wednesday 24th October 1973, 'The Kempetais and the Renegades', Bygone Kedah Series, by James F. Augustin.
16. *Red Star over Malaya. Resistance and Social Conflict during and after the Japanese Occupation, 1941–1946* by Cheah Boon Kheng, ch.2, p.36.
17. *British Rule in Malaya 1942–1957* by Robert Heussler, ch.3, p.58.
18. *Red Star over Malaya. Resistance and Social Conflict during and after the Japanese Occupation, 1941–1946* by Cheah Boon Kheng, ch.4, p.109. (Refers to FIR No.12, 12 August 1943.)
19. Ibid, ch.2, p.26.
20. *Penang Past and Present 1786–1963. A Historical Account of the City of George Town since 1786* published by the City Council of George Town, 1966, p.83.
21. *History of Malaya 1400–1959* by Joginder Singh Jessey, ch.19, p.298.
22. *Red Star over Malaya. Resistance and Social Conflict during and after the Japanese Occupation, 1941–1946* by Cheah Boon Kheng, ch.2, p.55.
23. *The Long Long War* by Richard Clutterbuck, ch.2, p.21.
24. *Syonan — My Story. The Japanese Occupation of Singapore* by Mamoru Shinozaki, ch.3, p.19.
25. *History of Malaya 1400–1959* by Jogindir Singh Jessy, ch.19, p.293.
26. *Red Star over Malaya. Resistance and Social Conflict during and after the Japanese Occupation, 1941–1946* by Cheah Boon Kheng, ch.2, p.19. (Refers to *Malay Mail* [KL], 10.12.1941.)
27. *The Masked Comrades. A Study of the Communist United Front in Malaya 1945–48* by Cheah Boon Kheng, ch.1, p.6.
28. Ibid, ch.1, p.6.
29. *Red Star over Malaya. Resistance & Social Conflict during and after the Japanese Occupation, 1941–1946* by Cheah Boon Kheng, ch.2, p.44.
30. Ibid, ch.2, p.41.
31. Ibid, ch.2, p.32.
32. *Straits Echo*, 17th October 1973. Article by J.A. Augustin.
33. *Red Star over Malaya. Resistance and Social Conflict during and after the Japanese Occupation, 1941–1946* by Cheah Boon Kheng, ch.2, p.43.
34. *The Masked Comrades. A Study of the Communist United Front in Malaya, 1945–48* by Cheah Boon Kheng, ch.1, p.7.
35. *British Rule in Malaya 1942–1957* by Robert Heussler, ch.3, p.60.
36. Ibid, ch.3, p.59.
37. *Red Star over Malaya. Resistance and Social Conflict during and after the Japanese Occupation, 1941–1946* by Cheah Boon Kheng, ch.2, p.21.

38. *Syonan — My Story. The Japanese Occupation of Singapore* by Mamoru Shinozaki, ch.3, p.21.
39. *When Singapore Was Syonan-To* by N.I. Low, ch.3, p.18.
40. *Ma-Rai-Ee* by Chin Kee Onn, ch.10, p.101.
41. *The Knights of Bushido. A Short History of Japanese War Crimes* by Lord Russell of Liverpool, ch.13, p.194.
42. *Shenton of Singapore. Governor and Prisoner of War* by Brian Montgomery, ch.8, p.161.
43. Ibid, ch.8, p.161.
44. *F. Kikan. Japanese Army Intelligence Operations in Southeast Asia during World War 2* by Lieut-General Fujiwara Iwaichi, translated by Akashi Yoji, ch.7, p.99.
45. *The Sara Saga* by M. Saravanamuthu, ch.8, p.108.
46. Ibid, ch.8, p.107.
47. Ibid, ch.9, p.113.
48. *Conflict and Violence in Singapore and Malaysia 1945–1983* by Richard Clutterbuck, ch.1, p.38.
49. *Ma-Rai-Ee* by Chin Kee Onn, ch.11, p.120.
50. *The Extortion by Japanese Military Administration of $50,000,000 from the Chinese in Malaya* by Tan Yeok Seong, pt.9, p.4. (Nanyang Book Co. Ltd, Singapore, 1947.)
51. *Malaya Upside Down* by Chin Kee Onn, ch.11, p.80.
52. *Ma-Rai-Ee* by Chin Kee Onn, ch.11, p.122.
53. Ibid, p.122.
54. Ibid, p.122.
55. *When Singapore Was Syonan-To* by N.I. Low, ch.9, p.54.
56. *Malaya Upside Down* by Chin Kee Onn, ch.11, p.81.
57. *When Singapore Was Syonan-To* by N.I. Low, ch.9, p.55.
58. Ibid, ch.10, p.57.
59. *Red Star over Malaya. Resistance and Social Conflict during and after the Japanese Occupation, 1941–1946* by Cheah Boon Kheng, ch.2 Economic Conditions, p.37. (Ref. OSS, 'Japanese Military Administration in Malaya', p.22.)
60. *Malaya Upside Down* by Chin Kee Onn, ch.12, p.84.
61. Ibid, ch.12, p.85.
62. *Red Star over Malaya. Resistance and Social Conflict during and after the Japanese Occupation, 1941–1946* by Cheah Boon Kheng, ch.2 Economic Conditions, p.37.
63. *Malaya Upside Down* by Chin Kee Onn, ch.12, p.86–87.
64. Ibid, ch.12, p.86.
65. *Penang Daily News*, Saturday, August 22, 2602 (1942). 'Army of Clerks Employed in Government Offices'.
66. *Penang Shimbun*, Wedneday, May 12, 2603 (1943). 'Steady Flow of Nippon Goods into Penang'.
67. *The Star*, Section 2, Wednesday, October 24, 1984. 'The Wealth of Khan' by Anna Cheah.
68. *Malaya Upside Down* by Chin Kee Onn, ch.7, p.39.
69. Ibid, ch.7, p.39.
70. Ibid, ch.7, p.41.
71. *The Sara Saga* by M. Saravanamuthu, ch.9, p.115.
72. Ibid, ch.8, p.109.
73. *Malaya Upside Down* by Chin Kee Onn, ch.10, p.68.
74. Ibid, ch.10, p.64.
75. *Penang Shimbun*, June 30, 2605 (1945).

76. *Ma-Rai-Ee* by Chin Kee Onn, ch.9, p.98–9.
77. *The Sara Saga* by M. Saravanamuthu, ch.9, p.113.
78. *Malaya Upside Down* by Chin Kee Onn, ch.7, p.43.
79. Ibid, Appendix C, Inflation Values. Selected prices taken from Ipoh Black Market figures.
80. *Syonan — My Story. The Japanese Occupation of Singapore* by Mamoru Shinozaki, ch.10, p.57.
81. *Malaya Upside Down* by Chin Kee Onn, ch.6, p.35.
82. Ibid, ch.7, p.43.
83. *The Japanese Occupation of Malaya. Interruption or Transformation?* by Yoki Akashi, p.73.
84. *Syonan — My Story* by Mamoru Shinozaki, ch.14, p.79.
85. *Malaya Upside Down* by Chin Kee Onn, ch.8, p.48.
86. *Syonan — My Story* by Mamoru Shinozaki, ch.15, p.89.
87. *Red Star over Malaya. Resistance and Social Conflict during and after the Japanese Occupation, 1941–1946* by Cheah Boon Kheng, ch.2, p.38.
88. *The Masked Comrades. A Study of the Communist United Front in Malaya 1945–1948* by Cheah Boon Kheng, ch.1, p.1.
89. *Malaya Upside Down* by Chin Kee Onn, ch.22, p.160.
90. *Ma-Rai-Ee* by Chin Kee Onn, ch.25 'Liberation', p.298.
91. *The Making of Modern Malaya* by N.J. Ryan, ch.15, p.206.
92. Ibid, ch.16, p.211.
93. *Straits Echo and Times of Malaya*, Penang, Thursday 12th September 1945. 'Terror, Torture, Tears. Penang during the Japanese Occupation', a Rotary talk by Heah Joo Seang.
94. Ibid.
95. *Malaya Upside Down* by Chin Kee Onn, ch.9, p.57.
96. Ibid, ch.9, p.58.
97. *Red Star over Malaya. Resistance and Social Conflict during and after the Japanese Occupation, 1941–1946* by Cheah Boon Kheng, ch.2, p.47.
98. *Malaya Upside Down* by Chin Kee Onn, ch.23, p.171.
99. Ibid, ch.23, p.172.
100. Ibid, ch.8, p.50.
101. Ibid, figures used from ch.8, p.51.
102. Ibid.
103. Ibid.
104. *Penang Shimbun*, 2nd June 2605 (1945).
105. Ibid, editorial, 4th August 2605 (1945).

Script for the enforced $50,000,000 Gift of Atonement presented by the Overseas Chinese Assocn to the Japanese.

Penang As Model Health Zone In Malaya

INTENSIVE CLEAN-UP CAMPAIGN BEGINS NEXT MONTH

Penang, August 20.

Penang is likely to become the model health zone of Malaya by the end of September, as the result of an intensive clean-up campaign launched by the local authorities.

Since the occupation of the island by the Japanese forces, wonders have been done in clearing the streets of mountains of accumulated rubbish and debris from fallen buildings.

The initial work in keeping at bay the dread pestilences which at all times threaten a war-torn city was done by the military. Their work had made Penang a clean island; it is now up to the public to co-operate with the local administration to make it still cleaner.

The present cleaning campaign is primarily aimed at eradicating malaria and typhoid, cases of which have occurred recently, but the broader purpose is to create conditions in which it would be impossible for harmful germs to breed.

GOVERNMENT'S JOB

From September 1, the whole personnel and labour force of the Health Department, numbering nearly 500 in the city alone, and using lorries and hand-carts, will be mobilized for sweeping, removing and burning all rubbish.

That is Government's job. The public's part will be to place rubbish in a position where it can be easily removed by coolies. To this end every householder or shop-owner must provide a dust-bin and all houses, shops and other buildings must be swept, and the drains in and around the buildings cleaned three times a day—morning, noon and evening.

Pedestrians are urged not to treat the streets as a sort of universal rubbish-bin, but to put litter in the proper place—that is, the roadside garbage tubs.

It is pointed out that these instructions apply not only to the city, but to the whole island.

With full public co-operation, it is expected that by the end of the month the clearing campaign will have secured the desired results.—Domei.

Penang Shimbun, 20.8.2602 (1942). 'Penang as Model Health Zone in Malaya'.

Town Cleaning In Full Swing

Public, Officials All Co-operating

At specially marked-off areas along all the streets in town, refuse from all houses was dumped to be carted away by coolies from the Eiseika, heralding the first day in the Town Cleaning Week, which began yesterday. The area bounded by Weld Quay, Prangin Road and Carnarvon Street through Chulia Street and Love Lane was thoroughly cleaned yesterday, thereby eliminating unhealthy places, which might prove potential breeding places for flies and mosquitoes.

Not only were streets and backlanes cleared of all rubbish, but houses in the area, which were marked off for cleaning yesterday, also received thorough clearing of dirt, cobwebs and the like. Bedding, including pillows and blankets were taken out for basking, members of the local police going round the places to see that no thieving of these articles occurred.

Led by the rimpohancho of each kumi, Sanitary Inspectors from the Eiseika went round to all houses to see that the rules laid down in town cleaning week were carried out by all householders. Empty tins or coconut shells, which might prove potential spots for the breeding of mosquitoes were cleared from backlanes. Open air shelters, which might be one of the most likely sources for the breeding of mosquitoes, when rain water was allowed to remain there were emptied. Enclosed shelters which often became the hide-out for mosquitoes were smoked.

Refuse tubs at the various lavatories were inspected and leakage in any of these tubs was notified to the Eiseika so that steps might be taken to have them replaced.

It is emphasised that the public would do themselves and their neighbours a good turn if they clean their back drains regularly. The regular cleaning of drains will eliminate the chance of flies collecting and the spreading of any contagious disease.

Today residents living in the area bounded by Sungei Pinang Bridge, Brick Kiln Road, Penang Road, Bridge Street and Maxwell Road will be required to carry out cleaning of their houses.

Penang Shimbun, 11.7.2605 (1945). 'Town Cleaning in Full Swing'.

Syurei (State Order)

(NO 13)

Preventive Measures Against Cholera

Preventive Measures against Cholera will be taken as follows:—

SHINOHARA SEIICHIRO,
Penang Shu Chokan,
6-7-05.

1. Any person, either coming direct from Thailand or passing through Thailand, who is not yet inoculated against Cholera, is strictly prohibited to enter the State of Penang.
2. All trading boats which come into the State of Penang either direct from Thailand or having previously called at Thailand must first be quarantined and subsequently carry out the instructions of the officials concerned.
3. Offenders under this Order are liable to severe punishment.
4. This Order takes effect from the date of publication.

Penang Shimbun, 11.7.2605 (1945). Syurei (State Order) No.13.

Government Notification

NO. 41.

GROW YOUR OWN FOOD CROPS AND VEGETABLES

1. In order to achieve self-sufficiency in the matter of food crops and vegetables, every family has to start its own home-garden which has to be opened up and established within one month from the date of the publication of this notice.

2. Families who are successful in the above purpose will be awarded prizes.

3. Those who fail to comply with this notification or leave their vacant lands unplanted will be punished.

NOTE: Those who need assistance and advice in the matter should consult Nomuka Penang or the Nomukakari in the districts.

ITAMI MASAKICHI,
Penang Shu Chokan.

25th November, 2603.

Penang Shimbun, 25.11.2603 (1943). Govt Notification No.41.

Penang Shimbun

"Labour With Changkol With Undaunted Will"

APPEAL TO YOUNG AND OLD TO EMIGRATE TO FARMS

"While Dai Toa's war is in progress and having had no self-sufficiency in foodstuffs in Malai, we are confronted with a very serious problem of growing more food. You are aware that the Government officers and the people have worked hard up to date in order to achieve this object," declared Mr. Niwa, the Sangyobucho at a press conference at the Sendenka this morning on the occasion of Emigration Propaganda Week, which begins today.

Penang Shimbun, 3.8.2605 (1945). 'Labour with Changkol with Undaunted Will'.

O.C.A. To Subsidise New Settlers

Mr. Joo Seang's Appeal To Penang Chinese

Many facilities, financial and otherwise, in addition to those already being enjoyed by present settlers, are being granted to those who are newly joining the food-producing settlements in Province Wellesley. Mr. Heah Joo Seang, in an appeal to Penang Chinese to forsake the comparatively unprofitable hustle and bustle of town life for the more healthy and financially paying occupation of food-growing, assures prospective settlers that, not only will they receive extra rations of six katties of rice each in addition to their usual rice rations, but that they will get substantial sums of money to help tide them over initial planting days.

SPECIAL RATIONS

The extra rice rations will be further supplemented by special rations of other foodstuffs which the Association will regularly distribute among Chinese settlers. This, it is expected, will solve the food problem for the newcomers.

Furthermore, the Association has devised a plan whereby it will be possible for a hard-working settler to earn money the very day that he lands in the farm. He can commence felling and for every cartload of firewood he chops up, the Association will pay $20 to $25. It is estimated that each settler can provide an average of four cartloads a day. While he receives payment for disposing of the wood, he is also speedily clearing up his own plot in readiness for planting.

Penang Shimbun, 3.8.2605 (1945). 'OCA to Subsidise New Settlers'.

Grow-More-Food Week

COMMUNITY LEADERS' APPEAL TO COMPATRIOTS

Mr. Heah Joo Seang

Many special amenities await the prospective settler in any one of the eight estates which the Penang Oversea Chinese Association has been allotted to open up for cultivation, Mr. Heah Joo Seang, chairman of the Association, points out in a statement on the occasion of grow-more-food week. Not only will new settlers receive additional rice and subsidies ranging from $3,000 to $5,000 to a family, but the Association will provide rations of beehoon, salt, pulot rice, beans.

Dr. N. K. Menon

"In addition to their farming activities the settlers have facilities for rearing cattle and poultry and many of them have taken advantage of these and on Batu Kawan Estate itself, which has always been an Indian colony, there is no lack of goats and the possibility of rearing goats there, with the abundant pasture available, is unlimited," declared Dr. N. K. Menon, Chairman of the Indian Independence League, Penang Branch, in an interview, revealing that good progress has been achieved during the past few months in the Indian Farm Colony at Batu Kawan Estate where the settlers are leading a happy and contented life.

Mr. A. M. Y. Izzudin

To bolster up the war effort of our forces is to make the country self-sufficient in foodstuffs was the view expressed by Mr. A. M. Y. Izzudin, Malai leader and chairman of the Malai Kosei Kyokai in a statement to the Penang Shimbun, appealing to members of his community to come forward and give their all out co-operation to the Government in its scheme to send more emigrants to the farm settlements in Province Wellesley.

"The supply of foodstuffs both on the battlefronts and the home fronts are essential factors to win the war. It is therefore of utmost importance that we must take to the land and do farming," Mr. Izzudin said.

Penang Shimbun, 7.8.2605 (1945). 'Community Leaders' Appeal to Compatriots'.

Japanese occupation currency, 'Banana Script', $10 and $1 notes.

$100, $5 and 50¢ notes.

"Save In Order To Win War," Urges Governor

SCHEME TO ACHIEVE ESTIMATED NETT SAVINGS FINDS SUPPORT

SPEAKING at a meeting of community leaders at the Post Office yesterday afternoon, the Governor, Lieut-Gen. Shinotiara, declared that savings constituted an important factor for the people of Dai Toa in achieving quick victory in the Greater East Asia War.

The meeting was called for the purpose of securing the views and opinions of the representatives of the various communities regarding the estimated nett monthly savings expected from the communities.

Commenting on the war news the Governor said that recent news had not been wholly satisfactory but though the situation appeared serious it was not really dangerous. But Nippon was confident of final victory.

Penang Shimbun, 19.4.2605 (1945). 'Save in Order to Win War' Urges Governor.

EDITORIAL

Savings A Source Of Power

IN view of the uncertainties of life, accentuated by the exigencies of war, it is of national as well as personal importance that every one who is in receipt of any kind of income should save. The fourth "Fixed Deposit with Bonus" campaign now in progress offers an excellent opportunity for members of the public, who have large funds at their disposal, to participate in this very important scheme for ensuring the future well-being of the whole population of Malai. There is no doubt that large sums of cash are now floating about, resulting in the cost of living taking an upward trend. If a substantial portion of these surplus funds were put aside for a stipulated period, there would be less money in circulation and consequently less extravagance.

Penang Shimbun, 4.8.2605 (1945). Editorial: 'Savings a Source of Power'.

Public Lottery

HUGE FIRST PRIZE OF $200,000

A public lottery to be called the Penang Saiken, offering a first prize of $200,000, will be on sale in Penang within a few days at the Penang Oversea Chinese Association, all the banks and the Goraku Koshi.

Each ticket is priced at $5. Issued by the Oversea Chinese Association, with the approval of the authorities, the tickets for each issue have been limited to 100,000. The first drawing will take place publicly at the Dai Toa Goraku Koshi at 9 p.m. on July 15. The drawing date for each issue is fixed on the 15th of the succeeding month of issue.

On production of the winning tickets cash will be paid by the Oversea Chinese Association within one month from the date of the announcement of the drawing. The prizes are:

1st prize -- $200,000.
2nd prize --- $50,000.
3rd prize $25,000.

25 consolation prizes $1,000 each.

Penang Shimbun, 20.6.2605 (1945). 'Public Lottery. Huge First Prize of $200,000'.

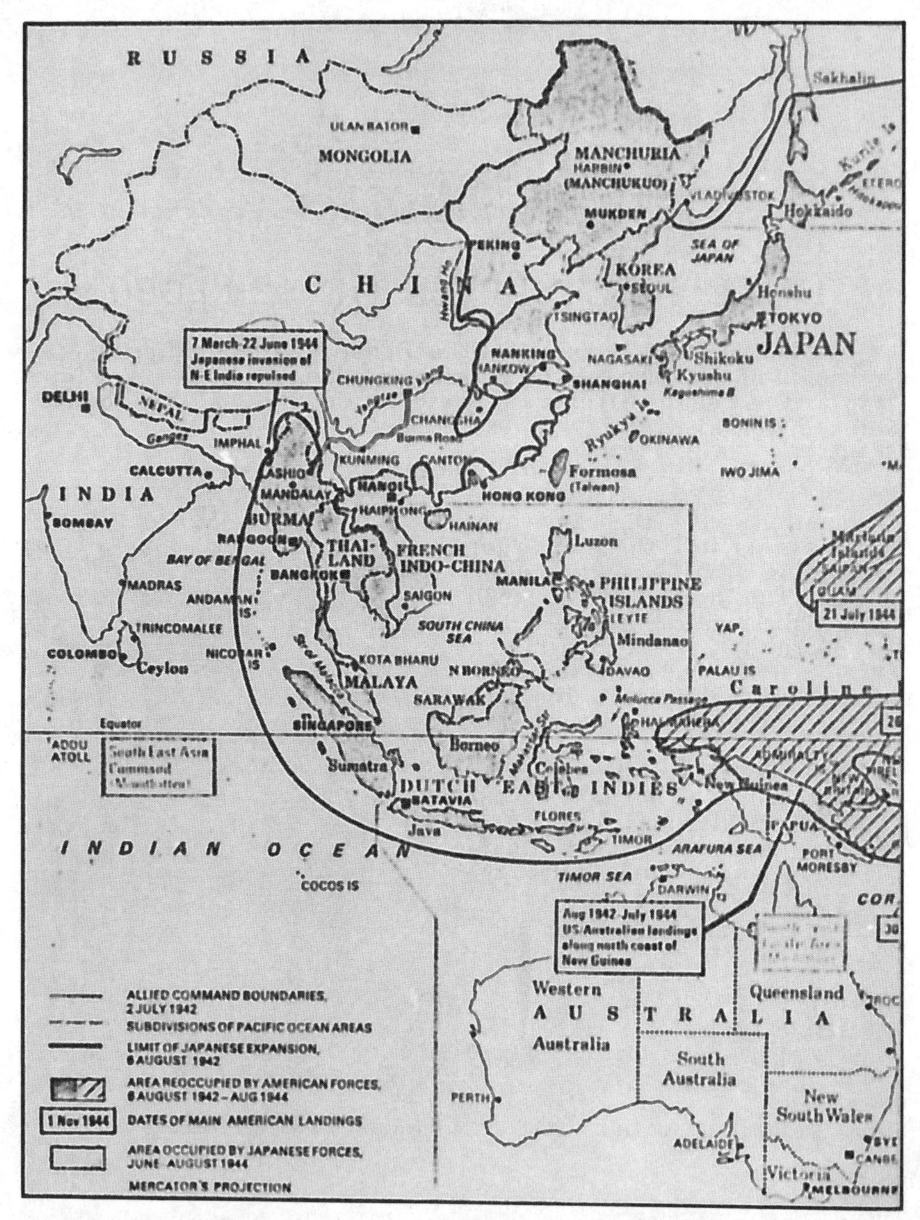

Area occupied by Japanese forces at June-August 1944, and area reoccupied by American forces from 6.8.42 to August '44. (Photo: *The Almanac of World War 2* ed. Brig. Peter Young, Hamlyn, Bison Books copyright, 1981.)

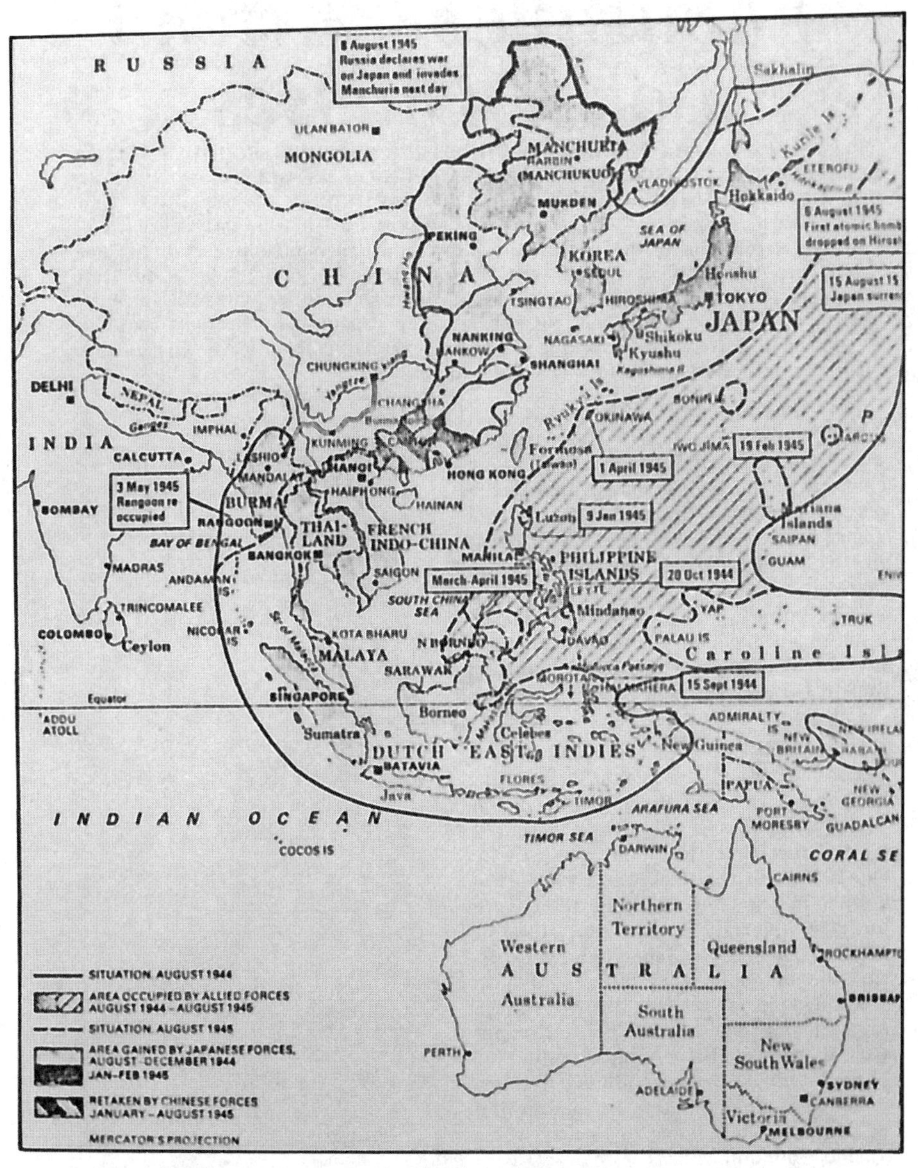

Situation at August 1944 and August 1945. (Photo: *Almanac of World War 2.*)

Thousands Attend Local Classes

EVERYWHERE IN PENANG—IN THE STREETS, SHOPS, SCHOOLS, OFFIC TELEPHONE EXCHANGE AND BUSES—NIPPON-GO IS BEING SPOKEN. TI USE OF THE LANGUAGE IS SPREADING RAPIDLY.

"Learn Nippon-Go" is one of the slogans used in the posters pasted u in the streets during the Nippon-Go Week campaign inaugurated early in June But even those who have not seen these posters are most anxious to lear Nippon-Go. In the Nippon-Go schools, many had to go away disappointe when applying for admission, but still a steady stream of applications continue to pour in daily. The enthusiasm of the general public to learn Nippon-Go i thus being demonstrated in a striking manner.

Is it that in order to keep pace with the prevailing fashion of the day that we desire to learn Nippon-Go? There exists a genuine enthusiasm among the people to learn Nippon-Go. Or is this desire actuated by the necessity of earning a livelihood? A knowledge of the language can no doubt be of some help in facilitating the earning of a livelihood, but the enthusiasm shown by the public to learn the language is not chiefly due to this, or because it is convenient for practical purposes.

Better Understanding

The purpose of the people in learning Nippon-Go is to gain some knowledge of the Nipponese, and is also actuated by the fact that the policy pursued by the British in the past was to keep the people in the dark, so that they were entirely ignorant of the real state of affairs. The people hope that by learning the language they will be able to take a step closer to the Nipponese and that as their knowledge of Nippon-Go increases their understanding of Nippon will be correspondingly greater. And by having a better understanding of Nippon they hope to rectify their various mistaken impressions of Nippon held by them in the past.

Penang Daily News, Saturday 15.8.2602 (1942). 'Thousands Attend Local Classes'.

New Feature

Six Months' Course In Nippon-Go

THE "*Penang Shimbun*" *introduces today a new feature "Six Months' Course in Nippon-go." Lessons will be published daily and it is the hope of the author that within six months readers will be able to acquire an elementary working knowledge of the language. The method introduced by the author is most scientific and the lessons are arranged in natural and logical order.*

As students of Nippon-go know, there is a sharp line of contrast between the colloquial and literary forms in the language. The written language is quite distinct from the spoken language, though there is a marked tendency for the spoken language to prevail. As a rule the difference between the two lies in the endings of the verbs, in the auxiliaries and in the post-positions.

The lessons here are confined mainly to the spoken form as used by the educated classes of Tokyo. There are various minor provincial dialects but the Tokyo accent is considered the standard, this having been adopted by the Department of Education as a model for the whole country.

LESSON I.

Writing And Pronunciation

In writing, the Japanese employ both ideographic and phonetic symbols. The ideographic consist of the "Kanji" while the phonetic consist of the "Hiragana" and "Katakana."

The "Kanji" or "Honji" consist of ideographs taken over from China. The "Katakana" (stiff-hand) and "Hiragana" (running hand) consist of approximately 75 letters devised for writing grammatical terminations. The whole language, not only tense endings and post-positions, can be written in "Hiragana" or "Katakana." Both of them can be used interchangeably. Foreign names, however, are transcribed in "Katakana" and never in "Hiragana."

We find that the Japanese language may be written with the ordinary English or Roman characters, without recourse to any other symbols, whether phonetic or ideographic. The comparative simplicity of Romaji will appeal to many who may find "Katakana" or "Hiragana" too difficult to start with; therefore throughout these lessons "Romaji" will be employed side by side with "Kana" (Katakana and Hiragana).

In Romaji the consonants are pronounced like those in English and each vowel has only one sound: "*a*"—as in pass; "*i*"—as in pin; "*u*"—as in bull; "*e*"—as in met; "*o*"—as in obey.

The following is a table of the Katakana with their pronunciation in Romaji:—

パ Pa	ダ Da	ガ Ga	ン N	ラ Ra	マ Ma	ナ Na	サ Sa	ア A
ピ Pi	ヂ Ji	ギ Gi		リ Ri	ミ Mi	ニ Ni	シ Shi	イ I
プ Pu	ヅ Zu dzu	グ Gu		ル Ru	ム Mu	ス Nu	ス Su	ウ U
ペ Pe	デ De	ゲ Ge		レ Re	メ Me	ネ Ne	セ Se	エ E
ポ Po	ド Do	ゴ Go		ロ Ro	モ Mo	ノ No	ソ So	オ O
	バ Ba	ザ Za		ワ Wa	ヤ Ya	ハ Ha	タ Ta	カ Ka
	ビ Bi	ジ Ji		ヰ I	イ I	ヒ Hi	チ Chi	キ Ki
	ブ Bu	ズ Zu		ウ U	ユ Yu	フ Fu	ツ Tsu	ク Ku
	ベ Be	ゼ Ze		ヱ (W)e	エ E	ヘ He	テ Te	ケ Ke
	ボ Bo	ゾ Zo		ヲ (W)o	ヨ Yo	ホ Ho	ト To	コ Ko

Penang Shimbun, 1.2.2603 (1943). 'Six Months' Course in Nippon-Go'.

Penang Shimbun

Relief Association Great Boon To Police Force

RIDDING MEN OF ANXIETY OF DAILY LIVELIHOOD

Pleased with the success of the formation of the Penang Shu Geachi-Jin Keisatsukan Koen Kai (Police Officers' Relief Association), the Governor, Lt.-Gen Shinohara, expressed his thanks to all those members of the public who had helped towards its establishment by their generous monetary contributions and congratulated the police authorities on their foresight.

The Governor pointed out this Association was different from all other associations in that its aim was primarily to relieve the living conditions of members of the police force who had very important duties to perform. "The elimination of their war-time livelihood will set the minds of the police force at rest, thereby enabling them to successfully carry out their duties not only as guardians of the law but also in the defence of the island," Lt.-Gen. Shinohara asserted.

Penang Shimbun, 2.8.2605 (1945). 'Relief Association Great Boon to Police Force'.

Jikeidan Soon To Be Formed In Penang

TO AID POLICE IN MAINTAINING PEACE AND ORDER

A MEETING was convened by the Keimubu of all local headmen and police inspectors in charge of the various town divisions at the Police Headquarters at 4.30 p.m. on Monday, to discuss the formation of a Jikeidan (Self-Protection Corp). In attendance were the Actiag Keimubu-cho (Mr. Fujinawa) and the Keimu-Shunin (Chief Inspector A. Rahman).

Addressing the headmen, the Acting Keimubu-cho stressed that the war was still on. Penang had in the past been enjoying law and order, but to maintain that peace continuously members of the public must give all possible aid to the Police Force. Mr. Fujinawa said that the formation of the Jikeidan was well under way and enlisted the help of the headmen in the formation of this Corp. He also thanked them for being able to spare their valuable time to attend the meeting.

The distribution of members of the Corp will be as follows:—Penang Road area 100 members, Central area 50, Simpang Anam area 50, Jelutong area 50, Dato Kramat area 50, Ayer Itam area 50, Pulau Tikus area 50, Beach Street area 30, Prangin area 30. Total 460 members.

In each area one headman and one assistant headman will be appointed to take charge of their respective district. The strength of this Corp, it is understood, will be increased. No uniforms will be provided yet, but members will be distinguished by their cloth badges. The members of the Corp, while on duty, will be armed with staves, and will be paid an allowance every time they go on duty. The work is entirely voluntary.

Penang Shimbun, 19.5.2603 (1943). 'Jikeidan Soon to be Formed in Penang'.

IN MAINTAINING PEACE

Should Also Have Faith In Prosecution Of War

Complimenting the Penang Jikeidan on the important contribution they are making in assisting the police to maintain peace and order in the Island the Governor, Lieut.-Gen. Shinohara at a meeting of all the Jikeidancho in Penang, at Police Headquarters yesterday, said: "The war situation is so acute that we must always be prepared to meet the enemy at any time."

He emphasised that we must defend Malai by all means and that the people of Malai must help in this defence. He hoped that the Jikeidan would play their role and assist faithfully in defending Malai.

Referring to the importance of growing more food, the Governor said that he had encouraged not only the growing of food but the importation of foodstuffs. It would be his duty to see that the people of Penang were not unprovided with food. He hoped that the people would continue to give their best efforts in the food-growing drive.

SUPPLY OF LABOUR

The supply of labour to the essential services, such as the Army and Navy, was also important and he hoped that as many men as possible would be sent when called upon.

We on the home front must look after the production of the implements of war and for this men would be required in the factories.

The Jikeidan should be air raid conscious, the Governor said, and be prepared for an emergency.

Penang Shimbun, 16.6.2605 (1945). 'In Maintaining Peace Should Also Have Faith in Prosecution of War'.

CHAPTER THIRTEEN: ENLIGHTENMENT AND NIPPON INDOCTRINATION

13:1 Education Policy

The Japanese made use of education as a tool to Nipponise Asians throughout the Greater Southeast Asia Co-Prosperity Sphere. Subjugated peoples were coerced into learning and using the Japanese language (Nippon-go) throughout the Empire, under the guise of uniting the cultures of individual nationalities to that of Japan. Their policies also aimed at eradicating Anglo-Saxon influence in Asia, and in particular to erase the last vestiges of British influence in Malaya. The teaching of English was banned, the screening of Anglo-American films was forbidden and statues of British personages, along with British coats of arms, were either removed or defaced.

All schools were initially closed, in a massive campaign to seek and destroy anti-Japanese literature. Schools that had previously offered instruction in Nippon-go in their curriculum, and had inculcated Nipponese cultures and ideals, were the first allowed to re-open. English schools were converted into Primary Common Public schools in which teaching the English language was banned. In all schools 'physical training was emphasised and every morning students sang the Japanese National Anthem and bowed in the direction of the Japanese Emperor'.[1] Through the medium of learning Nippon-go, priority was given to inculcating all students with the concepts of Nippon Seishin and to inject into them a burning desire to serve the Empire. Seishin imparted Japanese standards which required an iron discipline, absolute love of the Emperor (Tenno-Heika), total obedience and undying loyalty to him, and a willingness to die for His Imperial Majesty. Education was therefore used to develop the desire among subjugated 'liberated' people for unity with Japan's ideologies and acceptance of whatever hardships her incompetent administration chose to impart.

Primary schools in Singapore, along with Malay and Tamil schools in Malaya, were allowed to reopen in April 1942. At first these were half empty as parents were reluctant to allow their children to attend. As the teaching of English annoyed the military authorities, only Malay and Tamil were permitted to be taught in them. Pressure was put on children to learn Nippon-go, but as there were no books or teachers available, little could be initially achieved. In due course an Asian Institute (Koa Gakko En) was set up along with other teacher training schools (Syonan Shian Gakko) where the learning of Nippon-go was emphasised and encouraged. In October 1942 Chinese schools were permitted to reopen. Chinese schools were identified as having played a major part in the pre-war anti-Japanese campaigns and were prohibited from using or teaching Mandarin. In July 1943 this ban was relaxed and Mandarin was taught for three hours weekly. One year later, however, the ban was reimposed, and only instruction of Nippon-go was permitted.

The Japanese wanted to abolish completely the use of English, but they were forced to tolerate its continued official use in newspapers and in government offices where, without it, the administrative machinery would have slowed to a standstill. An Eurasian driving his car was threateningly questioned by a Japanese sentry who demanded of him, 'English Ka?' (Are you English?). Taking advantage of the man's obvious ignorance of the language, he replied, 'Wolseley Car!' Not wishing to display his lack of understanding, the sentry let him pass. All cinemas were banned from showing Anglo-American films, which had to be handed back to the authorities.

Under the Japanese system books in schools were given out free of charge, but later in the occupation fees were levied. High schools were barred from operating 'as they were considered politically undesirable'.[2] Instead, a number of marine, fishing, trade, technical, telecommunications and agricultural schools were established, along with other military sponsored institutions. Nippon-go classes were set up at every opportunity, in schools, clubs, commercial firms, government departments, guilds, community organisations and in kaisha departments.

Educational Nipponisation introduced radical social and political changes to the country. 'The older generations looked on helplessly with cynical composure. Theirs was an outward acceptance of everything.'[3] The Japanese concentrated on the younger generations, who in turn showed that they were capable of absorbing knowledge and propaganda at an amazing speed. Had the Japanese had more time to indoctrinate the young, they might have achieved their goal of establishing a Nippon-type imperialism that would subsequently have been most difficult to counteract.

School teachers' salaries were immediately reduced when schools were reopened. Those whose wages had previously been $300 or more per month were cut by more than half. Others earning less than $100 per month were not affected and continued to receive the full amount. As Nippon-go classes sprang up like mushrooms in all towns, teachers had to feign an outward show of willingness to learn it in order to survive. A smattering of the language proved most useful when passing the frequent road barricades, or in trying to win the goodwill of Japanese soldiers when they encroached into private homes. Learning it was no act of sincerity or love. For teachers it was a necessary evil and a means of scraping a livelihood.

In Singapore, arrangements were made for recognised teachers to be issued with passes which provided them with some immunity from molestations by sentries. Mamoru Shinozaki, the Director of Education at that time, wanted to employ as many teachers as possible, considering them able to inculcate the spirit of seishin and bushido into the youths who came into their charge. No one dared to criticise this ploy. The vast majority of teachers, however, remained passively pro-British, if not actually anti-Japanese, and not a single one among them was betrayed by his or her colleagues.

The teaching of Nippon-go was an integral part of Japan's education policy in Malaya. It was a compulsory subject in all schools, including technical, trade, medical and marine institutions, where English was disallowed as a teaching medium. In Singapore schools, Radio Taisho broadcast simple Nippon-go exercises to an accompaniment of music. The Huu Yu Seah Club (League of Helping Friends), initially registered in July 1914 to provide facilities to further the study of Chinese language and literature, was the first club in Penang to be taken over by the Japanese as a school for Nippon-go classes. Teachers and students were assembled every morning to bow to

Tenno-Heika and to sing the Kimigayu, for which the words 'Ubi Kayu' (Malay for 'tapioca') were frequently substituted. Classes were also organised in all commercial and government offices, compelling the population to learn. Bonuses plus accelerated promotion with salary increases were given to municipal and government servants as incentives for proficiency in Japanese. Evening classes were organised free of charge for the public and lessons were published in newspapers. Posters encouraging the use of Nippon-go were displayed at vantage points in towns. Defacing the caption 'Nippon-go' with 'British Come!' caused much popular amusement. Promising students were enrolled into specialist centres, and some were even sent to Tokyo to further their studies. Twenty-one year old Syed Mansor bin Syed Ahmat, an employee on the Governor's secretariat staff in Penang, was one of the students chosen by the Gunseikan for further studies, as was Mr E. Abdoolcadar, who undertook a three year course in Japan. Such people, on their return, were expected to become interpreters in the employ of the MMA. Abdoolcaadar was so proficient in the language that he was able to interpret the Governor's public speeches and to give Nippon-go lessons over the radio. However, despite all the pressure that people were subjected to, the end results were not enduring.

Promotion in government service depended largely on proficiency in Nippon-go. At first the Japanese enthusiastically encouraged people to learn and in the main towns Nippon-go promotion weeks were frequently organised during which debating, public speaking and essay writing competitions were held. Despite frenzied enthusiasm to make Nippon-go the main language in the country, the Japanese duly realised that English was still necessary and begrudgingly reverted to it.

Some success was achieved. Several common English colloquialisms, such as 'Good Morning', 'Thanks', 'Cheerio' and 'Okay' were replaced by their Japanese equivalents. Some people relished being seen in public with Japanese friends or officials and flaunted their prowess in Nippon-go. Some women became the mistresses of military policemen, either to further their own aims or to safeguard the welfare of their families. Japanese songs were sung at dinner parties, and at official functions speeches in Nippon-go became commonplace, accompanied by three vocal 'Banzais', with arms lifted skywards in mock adoration of Tenno-Heika.

Early in 1942 'it was decreed that all shops, restaurants, theatres, public buildings and places of amusement should display signboards in Katakana'.[4] Advertising in English was prohibited but romanised Chinese, Malay and Indian names were still allowed. Names of streets, towns and railway stations were also superscribed with Katakana. Penang was renamed Tojoto, but this never became popular.

The *Penang Daily News* reported on Saturday, 15th August 2602 (1942) the enthusiasm of the Penang public in learning Nippon-go.

Some people in Penang formed Speak Nippon-go Associations and members pledged to use the language at all times. The propaganda department arranged to publish cultural magazines with Japanese illustrations and also organised poster competitions, publicly displaying the winning entries. Essay and speech competitions on propaganda and related Japanese topics were frequently arranged. On 1st February 2603 (1943) the *Penang Shimbun* reported the commencement of a six month course in Nippon-go, in which the intricacies of the written language, as distinct from the spoken form, were explained as part of the first lesson.

Teachers who attended the Shihan Gakkos (normal schools for teachers) and became proficient in Nippon-go were rewarded with better appointments. Three year courses were also commenced at the Penang Government Trade School (Kogyo Gakko) where instruction was given in Nippon-go, and in general and electrical engineering. Applicants for these courses had to be between 15 to 20 years old, and to be eligible for enrolment, they were required to be physically fit and pass elementary tests in mathematics and general knowledge. The Penang Seicho Dobokuka (Technical Training School) took applicants of any nationality for a three month course of training to be mechanics, blacksmiths and carpenters. In April 1945 the *Penang Shimbun* was still advertising for enrolment into these courses.

A Culture and Research Institute was also formed, in which the culture section researched a wide variety of topics, including social systems, customs and habits, modes of dress, education, and the various preferences and dislikes of different races in the country. The economic section of this institute concentrated on banks and guilds, chambers of commerce and commercial systems. The purpose of these experiments was to try and improve inter-racial understanding, and to obtain a closer form of cooperation between people and government. Despite constant upsets by the military, some good came of this. After 1943 public slapping was reduced and the disgusting habit of urinating in public gradually disappeared.

The main festivals of the different races in the country were given some recognition and on these occasions, a holiday was declared to enable people to celebrate together.

Several Koa Kunrenjo (youth leadership training schools) were organised by the MMA, which specifically concentrated on physical and spiritual aspects of training, and indoctrinating students with Nippon Seishin. Cadets imbibed seishin and everything they did was dominated by its principles, which supposedly made them tough and fearless. Although students of all nationalities between the ages of 17 and 25 could be selected, preference was given to Malays. The six-month course entailed tough and vigorous training in various forms of martial arts, plus learning Nippon-go. At the end of the course, students were required to do a forty mile route march in the blazing heat of the day, dressed in full military gear.

Students who distinguished themselves on this course were selected to attend an Assistant Instructor's course and some were sent to Japan for three years further training at specially designed schools for foreign students, sponsored by the Japanese army.

Kao Kunrenjos were attended mostly by Malays and were one of the major devices used by the Japanese to further Malay interests and aspirations. About seventy per cent of the students graduated, and many were duly selected for high appointments. Training was more psychological than academic, and preference was given to spiritual indoctrination at the expense of academic learning. A post-mortem by former students on the benefits derived from these courses was mostly favourable, and many thought that the training they had been given was beneficial and had helped to develop self-discipline and perseverance. Some claimed that the courses had also assisted them to overcome previous bad habits and had prepared them to be of service to their country. Students were inculcated with theories of 'ganbaru-seishin' which required them never to give up, no matter how difficult a task became. Many felt that the course had taught them something about the true 'Nippon spirit' upholding the Kunrenjo's principles of loyalty, simplicity and diligence.

This Nipponisation of youth was orchestrated with machine-like efficiency and had considerable influence over children at primary school level. Some started to speak Nippon-go at home and the longstanding tradition of learning English nursery rhymes was either supplemented with or replaced by learning Japanese songs. Had the Japanese been given sufficient time, there is little doubt that their success in nipponising the youth and future citizens of the country would have been considerable. Forty years later the indelible impression left by Japan's occupational policies on some Malaysians is evident, when policy makers chose a 'Look East' philosophy, out of preference to long-established goodwill links with traditional friends and benefactors.

With the banning of Anglo-American films in 1942, the Bunka Eiga Gekijio (a government propaganda unit) started to screen fairly good Japanese newsreels and educational films. Their propaganda level was high and always emphasised the supremacy of Japanese family life and the social system which nurtured it. Japanese art and music were used to popularise Japanese culture and foster an appreciation of it. Japanese tunes were regularly broadcast and some tunes became popular with youngsters. In the larger towns, free concerts were performed, and at public functions as well as in private homes, Japanese music was played.

Nippon customs, mannerisms and greetings predominated. Bowing stiffly from the waist replaced shaking hands. In the morning and evening, office staff bowed to their superiors. In churches bowing replaced genuflection. Rival teams did it before and after any match. Everyone, everywhere, resorted to bowing. People bowed to each other in the streets, and most certainly they bowed low in deference on passing any Japanese sentry. Omission to do so was harshly punished as it was considered an intentional display of lack of respect.

Another aspect of nipponisation, which aimed at emphasising Japanese achievements, was the introduction and celebration of Japanese public holidays, which invariably paid direct and public homage to Tenno-Heika. Some of the more prominent celebrations were

Meiji-Setsu, the birthday of Meiji-Tenno, the grandfather of the Emperor; Tencho-Setsu, the Emperor's birthday; Kaigan-Setsu, Empire Day; as well as Heroes' Day, Harvest Day, and the respective Army, Navy and Airforce Days. During these events, mass meetings were organised and pledges to the Empire renewed. Community leaders praised the Japanese way of life in public speeches and articles designed to enlighten the populace were published in newspapers. Sports were organised, processions were held and dragon dances were allowed. The Hinomaru fluttered overhead from buildings as the subjugated demonstrated their loyalty.

The Japanese loved ceremonies. After the fall of Singapore, the first ceremony held was in commemoration of the Emperor's birthday on 29th April 1942. The Education Department hastily decided that school children should march through the city streets shouting 'Banzais' and singing patriotic songs. It did not seem to matter that very few children knew any patriotic Japanese songs or the national anthem, or that there were no copies of the anthem's music in Singapore. Some schools had just been reopened, having been re-equipped following the looting that had gone hand-in-hand with Singapore's fall.

Empire Day (Kaigan-Setsu) was celebrated in Penang. The Governor, Lieutenant-General Shotaro Katamaya, told a large crowd gathered at the Broadcasting Station ground that the Penang Fire Brigade would become more efficient if they learnt Japanese methods. On the first anniversary of the fall of Singapore, Penang was told to organise a large and colourful Chingay (a Chinese festival, usually celebrated with a flag-bearing procession and acrobatics), as well as an athletics meet. Kunrensho officers were inspected by the Governor on the Broadcasting Station ground and a horse racing meet was well attended at the Turf Club.

Despite the many restrictions imposed on the Chinese which officially prevented them from continuing with their studies, many parents encouraged their children to revise the school work previously completed in their former English-medium schools, and to privately continue with their studies of Chinese literature. Many people, convinced that one day the British would return to Malaya, wanted their children to be prepared for this.

13:2 Attitudes towards Others and Character Foibles

Japanese dislike and distrust of all things Western was concealed under a veneer of feigned politeness bordering on servitude in the presence of visiting white foreigners. Their bitter resentment of all things white veered towards a malicious hatred which distorted their reasoning. Their animosity towards the British and Americans was no greater than their true feelings for their Axis partners, Germany and Italy. German mannerisms jarred upon the nerves and sensitivities of most Japanese, and although they shared common warlike ambitions and sympathies, there was no real trust or cooperation, nor was Germany really taken into Japan's confidence prior to her declaration of war against Britain and the United States on 7th December 1941. Japan entered into the conflict at that point in time purely for self interest, not to assist Germany in the slightest respect. Japan's motivation was selfish aggrandisement. This brought the massive might of the United States actively into the fray, which was a disastrous blow to Germany. At no time was any offer or attempt made by Japan to relieve Hitler's battle-weary, beleaguered and starving troops on their fateful Russian front.

Before the war many of the Japanese who had worked and lived in Malaya and Singapore as brothel-house keepers, barbers and photographers were looked upon as social inferiors. Following the occupation of Penang and conquest of Singapore, with an outward display of superiority they immediately demanded obeisance and respect from the local population. The changing of Singapore's name, for example, to

> 'Syonan was indicative of Japan's arrogance as, drunk with initial victories, she disregarded the great principles of the Greater East Asia War, and pursued an intolerant policy following the example of the British Empire'.[5]

Many vain Japanese officers strutted through towns in thick tweed uniforms completely unsuitable for Malaya's hot, damp climate, with their overly long swords dragging behind them. Some behaved with a marked lack of respect towards Malay royalty. It had always been customary for British Advisors to stand in the presence of Malay

Rulers, but when the Sultan of Perak rebuked one Japanese officer for not doing so, he arrogantly displayed his annoyance and contempt by drawing his sword in the Ruler's presence.

Since Japan's attempt to conquer northern China in 1932 and annex Manchuria, the Japanese nurtured a vivid hatred and fear of communists. When communists actively participated in pre-war anti-Japanese riots in Malaya and then agitated for an anti-Japanese trade boycott, Japan anticipated the communists' potential for subsequent and determined resistance and this heightened their intense paranoia towards them. Drastic steps were taken immediately following the surrender of Singapore, to eliminate all communists and anti-Japanese elements within the Chinese society.

The Chinese were severely victimised (Ch 12:6) and subjected to considerable hardships. Thousands of them were massacred. The MMA's policy towards them was entirely different from that shown to other races, and while the Chinese were regarded as economically useful, they were also branded as politically undesirable. Only if they cooperated would they be able to retain their economic position. In addition to the 'atonement gift' of $50 million, other demands for donations were frequently made on the Chinese as a matter of Japanese policy towards them. Through the military and civilian administrations' ineptitude the Japanese lost an opportunity to be accepted as the 'liberators' of Asia. Instead, because of their brutality towards the Chinese, many flocked to swell the ranks of the anti-Japanese resistance movements in order to evade the MMA's sinister clutches.

Fear and hatred of communism was obsessive with the Japanese. Everyone ran the risk of being branded a communist, regardless of circumstance and in the absence of any substantiated evidence. People who criticised the Axis, who listened to a short wave radio, discussed the progress of the war with a pro-allied bias, complained about inflation or shortages, were critical of the MMA, ridiculed local news bulletins, referred to the worthlessness of Japanese military script, joked about Nippon-go, belittled the value of savings' campaigns, were sarcastic about Heiho, or laughed at the Indian National Army (INA), even those who did not appreciate Nippon music, all were considered likely communists! This phobia clouded Japanese reasoning and subjected countless innocent people to needless suffering, and denial of previously granted concessions. In pre-war Malaya the British had allowed the Chinese to display the China national flag during the Double Tenth celebration. This was stopped after senior staff officers in the Japanese 25th Army criticised this practice, although Indians were not prevented from displaying their national flag whenever they wanted. The ill will that already existed between the Chinese and the Japanese increased, and as more influential Chinese community leaders fled to safety overseas, many others from towns and villages flocked to join the predominantly Chinese, communist-backed, anti-Japanese forces.

Eurasians were distrusted with almost equal intensity, because of their racial connections and social aspirations towards the West. Only the Chinese suffered more than the Eurasians, many of whom died because of their courageous subversive activities and involvement with resistance movements.

The MMA's policy towards Malays and Indians was different from that to the Chinese and Eurasians. Instead of being automatically treated as enemies, Malays and Indians were cultivated as friends, within specific limitations. The occupation for Malays and Indians was a period of economic deprivation and hardship, rather than domination by hostility and brutality. Cooperative Indians in particular received special treatment and were less discriminated against, as Japan vied for their assistance in the planned invasion of their British-controlled homeland. The upsurge of Indian nationalism in Malaya was used to advantage by the Japanese to further their own designs. They encouraged the Indian Independence League (IIL), and the Indian National Army (INA) under the initial leadership of Rash Bahari Bose, an exiled Indian terrorist from Japan, and later of Subhas Chandra Bose, their Commander-in-Chief, who had been a previous President of the Indian National Congress (INC).

The MMA regarded Malays as politically malleable but economically less useful. In early 1942 Lieut-General Fujiwara Iwaichi wrote of the Malays' eco-social standing,

> '. . . that part of the responsibility for the Malays' inferior status could be attributed to their low political and cultural standards, their indolence and

> their weak physical condition, though British colonial policy was responsible for keeping Malays where they were . . .'[6]

Making use of Malay nationalistic aspirations, the Japanese hinted that some form of independence might become a possibility. This was in order to secure their cooperation in matters relating to defence and security.

The Malays therefore had less reason initially to dislike the Japanese. They were treated more favourably than the Chinese, and had no real incentive to join the predominantly Chinese-organised, anti-Japanese resistance movements. They did not escape, however, from being exploited, and by the end of 1943, when they were more affected by increasing economic hardship and the MMA had started to neglect their interests, a change of attitude occurred. As Malay disenchantment with the Japanese increased, so their relations with the Malayan Peoples Anti-Japanese Union (MPAJU) and the Malayan Peoples Anti-Japanese Army (MPAJA) became somewhat less strained.

Britain's pre-war, pro-Malay, segregationist policy had ensured relatively harmonious inter-community relations. The MMA's pro-Malay policy, however, in conjunction with the massacre of thousands of Chinese, soured each community's social and political sentiments for the other, and subsequently brought the Chinese and Malays into open conflict. The Chinese were discriminated against in government service, schools and businesses, whereas the Malays were encouraged to become involved in these, as well as in the police force and other local volunteer defence units. The large number of Malays enlisted into these was resented by the Chinese, who reciprocated by not cooperating with the Japanese. In late 1943 some attempt at conciliation was made by the Japanese to integrate Chinese into businesses and onto Advisory Councils. Too much damage had already been done, however, and this attempt failed to overcome both their hostility towards the Japanese and the build-up of resentment for the Malays.

Japanese policies created discord and social friction and resulted in vicious inter-racial conflict.

> 'There is, however, little evidence to show that the Japanese deliberately promoted racial animosity between Malays and Chinese as a matter of policy. It was the overall social tensions which their policies created, and the local interpretations of these policies by Malay and Chinese communities, which led to bitter inter-racial conflicts.'[7]

It has to be acknowledged that

> 'some of the civil and military officers were decent, solicitous men who tried to serve the public good and to curb the excesses of their fellows, even when this involved risk to themselves'.[8]

Mr Mamoru Shinozaki was one of these. Having lived in Malaya before the war, he was interned by the British in December 1941. During the occupation, as an Education Officer in Singapore, Shinozaki attempted to relate to the suffering of the people, and all races, including the British, spoke well of him, even after 1945. His sympathy for their plight and his attempts at decency made him unpopular with his own superiors, as well as a suspect of the Kempetai.

Some heads of departments behaved in a courteous manner, earning the respect of their employees, and did not become overly familiar. It was only a minority who did not consider it beneath their dignity to be polite to their subordinates. A total show of respect from all employees was mandatory in military, government and kaisha offices, where they were required to stand up on the arrival and departure of their superiors and bow to them when a command of 'Rei' was given. Those who behaved with consideration towards others refrained from slapping them in public, or outraging the modesty of women, and did not urinate in the streets. They were also generally gentle to children. Although rudeness was abhorred by the Japanese, and courtesy was considered a virtue, many were totally unpredictable. They would obey everything that they were instructed to do by their superiors, no matter how improbable or offensive the order might be.

Many small and large differences affect the life-styles of the British and Japanese. Basic ones, such as pushing or pulling a saw, or the method of gesturing to indicate 'come here', reach the foundation of a child's upbringing, as do methods of reading and writing, which the Japanese do vertically and in reverse order to the British and other Westerners. The British stand to attention with fists clenched and thumbs outstretched downwards, whereas the fingers of the Japanese remain outstretched. The Japanese language contains no obscenities that compare with the British four-lettered words. Instead they place emphasis on their vocal chords to shriek words such as 'Bakayaru', which simply means 'Fool'. Additional emphasis could be expeditiously conveyed with slaps, kicks, or blows with anything readily at hand.

Many of the Japanese who served in Malaya had some knowledge of English as they had been taught two foreign languages at secondary school. Many could read it, but only a few spoke with any degree of efficiency. The Japanese have always been impressed by scholastic expertise and

> 'were addicted to translating, and their translations were inspired by a laudable zeal for exactness. "We must take British war news with a pinch of salt", Japanised, became "We must read British war news and eat some salt".'[9]

Despite country-wide food and commodity shortages the Japanese in occupied Malaya lived well. The best bungalows and houses were commandeered by senior military and civil officers, and any damage caused by looters was promptly repaired. Sentries were posted at main entrances of houses occupied by senior officers. They appreciated good food and many liked European food and preferred foreign cigarettes. Some senior officials, who had previously experienced Western standards, employed Hainanese cooks and kept well set tables adorned with freshly-cut flowers and elegant crockery. Their prosperity made them conspicuous. They always got what they wanted in luxuries, good clothes and pleasure. Ordinary people had little entertainment or enjoyment. The main theatres and the better class bars and restaurants were reserved exclusively for Japanese soldiers. Had the public been allowed to frequent them, only very few could have afforded to do so.

The Japanese loved cars, which were a status symbol. The bigger the car, the more important the person. They liked being respected and addressed as 'Sir' or 'Tuan'; even 'Master' pleased them. Some

Japanese stationed in Penang took a liking to the Penang Hill Railway. The cable of the upper section was replaced in 1942, and in 1945 the railway was still being used and in a reasonable state of repair.

Sporting activities were encouraged and Japanese officials joined in to enhance their public image. Most of them were friendly on the sports field and baseball, tennis and golf were popular. Horse racing was patronised by Provincial Governors, Military Police Chiefs and Kaisha executives, and turf clubs were revived throughout the country. No Japanese, however, was allowed to enter the gambling farms.

Within the complex Japanese character there were diverse conflicting components. Their frenzied reaction to a frustrating situation could easily result in a fury of wanton killing. Their extreme sensitivity to ridicule was a character trait to beware, as was their sense of inferiority. Their irrational behaviour was imponderable as it frequently bordered on fanaticism, in which a potential for make-believe created reality out of illusions. Success through hard work gave rise to massive conceit, although some did have a good sense of humour. Foreigners were looked upon as unclean, and most Japanese anyway were 'utterly uninterested in foreigners; iron-willed; punctilious; enigmatic; paradoxical; ambiguous; deceptive; and insane'.[10] When Hugh Frazer and Brigadier Newbiggin wanted to meet senior Japanese officers to arrange for a truce in February 1942, they were delayed for more than one and a half hours as the first Japanese troops they met were more interested in having their photographs taken with them, and would not escort these officers to meet with their Japanese counterparts until the whole role of film had been completed.

These extremes in character were somewhat stabilised when they dealt with children. The same guard who offered a child a trinket, because she reminded him of his daughter, had moments before hit a woman in the mouth for wearing lipstick. Many Japanese slapped with an obvious show of enthusiasm. A variation on this routine, and one which provided an element of sinister amusement, was to insist that two Chinese should slap each other in public.

The disciplined Japanese soldier could never attune himself to

> 'the slovenly Chinese who seemed so inclined to greet an order with airy badinage and to brush it aside with a wave of the hand'.[11]

Any slovenly response to an instruction was deemed an Imperial affront, not a mere misdemeanour. The soldier expected to be punished as a matter of routine for the slightest infringement, but when he meted out similar punishment to any Chinese, he was affronted by the open resentment with which it was received.

Most Japanese applied themselves pertinaciously to work and detail and were professional in their approach. They had no sympathy for the inspired amateur, and gave no opportunity to them. Some favoured improvisation, showing contempt for well planned schemes. The fait accompli was ardently admired without caring much for the manner in which it was achieved.

Official visits by dignitaries were preceded by a spate of deceitful and elaborate preparations. To impress upon their visitors that the rural self-sufficiency policy was thriving, improvements would suddenly be made and benefits given, only to be withdrawn within one hour of the departure of the dignitary. Whether arrogance made them callous towards the plight of fellow human beings, or whether by some fantasy these deceits could be justified, remains a matter of grim conjecture. When they were later placed in similar circumstances, they certainly found ample voice to complain about the same living conditions that they had imposed on others for the past three and a half years.

The average Japanese soldier was unimpressed by majestic or historical surroundings, and places such as Raffles Hotel and the Singapore Cricket Club did not deter him from unashamedly

> 'discharging the minor obligations of nature with an easy grace — at the roadside . . . Like the Greek of classical times, he was not ashamed of his body and his concerns.'[12]

Some guards seemed to be scared of the dark and invariably carried oversized torches with them. Others, who had little to do as they rested under a tree and watched prisoners work in the mid-day heat, would start to knit. They were prepared to pay for any old woollen garments, either in money or with cigarettes, and would unravel these and knit them into other things. Others liked bicycles and would stop cyclists as they passed and take what they wanted.

The Chinese were invariably sent on their way with a couple of slaps, but Indians and Malays were not infrequently compensated for their loss by the payment of a nominal sum.

13:3 The Role of the Police

Ninety percent of the police force in pre-war Malaya and Singapore were Malays, many of whom abandoned their posts as the Japanese overran the country. After the capitulation of Singapore, all serving policemen were instructed to return to duty and report to their previous places of work. During the two months that Penang was occupied by Japanese troops, before Singapore fell, the void left by police desertions was filled mainly by responsible civilians of all nationalities, who manned police stations on the island and tried to maintain law and order as best they could. Recruits came from remnants of the Volunteer and local Defence Corps, from clerks, lawyers and teachers, as well as other civic-minded people who responded to the public need. Malay policemen recalled to duty had to obey their new masters as they had obeyed the old. It became a period of distinctive badges, caps and uniforms. The police were given semi-military training and issued with new uniforms and rubber-soled shoes. They 'donned semi-military caps with the Japanese star',[13] but were only permitted to be armed with a coil of rope.

The regular civil police force was assisted by the Jikeidan (Self Defence Corps) and the Tonarigumi (Neighbourhood Associations) from mid-1943, as the Japanese increased their use of the local population for internal security control. All organisations came under the ever-watchful, malign scrutiny of the Kempeitai. A police structure similar to the pre-war British colonial police organisation was adopted, and those officers who had previously served in the Special Branch were assigned to deal with political affairs, especially those concerning anti-Japanese activities. This political police force, known as the Tokkoka, made extensive use of agents and informers, many of whom were dubious characters who provided information only to settle personal grudges and further their own ends.

Each Province (State) was sub-divided into police districts, in which the officers-in-charge were allowed vast powers. Malays and non-Malays held the post of District police officers (Sho Cho) until the latter part of 1943, when they were replaced by Japanese.

> 'The Sho Cho were empowered to issue orders to shoot or behead anyone suspected of anti-Japanese activities, and even the DO, the local civilian administrator, was subordinate to him.'[14]

During the early stages of the occupation the Japanese had to make use of experienced people who had served under the former British police administration. In June 1943, however, they started to build up and train various para-military organisations, into which Malays predominantly were recruited. These were used to supplement their occupational forces against the Chinese-backed, anti-Japanese, guerrilla resistance movements. Malay and Sikh cooperation with the Japanese resulted in large numbers of them being recruited into the police force. Both races were used

> 'to attempt to suppress the Chinese resistance movement with the result that when the Japanese surrendered there was Chinese retaliation against the Police Force, and more indiscriminately against the Malay population at large'.[15]

A Police Officers' Relief Association (Shu Geachi-Jin Keisatsukan Koen Kai) was belatedly formed in Penang to relieve their difficult living conditions. It aimed to

> 'set the minds of the police force at rest, thereby enabling them to successfully carry out their duties not only as guardians of the law but also in the defence of the island'.[16]

13:4 Jikeidan and Tonarigumi

The Jikeidan (Self Defence Corps) was established because the 'Japanese authorities blamed the public for insincere cooperation'[17] and held them responsible for the nuisance caused by the communists. It formed part of the MMA's militarisation policy which strictly governed the whole area. As the war situation deteriorated Japan increasingly used local manpower for local defence and internal security.

The Jikeidan, along with the Tonarigumi (Neighbourhood Associations), were set up to assist with the policing of towns. By September 1943 Singapore boasted 80,000 Jikeidan recruits and by March 1944 sections had been organised for many other parts of the country, especially in Malacca, Penang, Perak and Selangor, where the problem of maintaining law and order had become more difficult.

The Jikeidan was supposedly a voluntary neighbourhood watch system. All able-bodied males between the ages of 16 and 40 had to carry out night patrols around the areas in which they lived, with a certain number of households made collectively responsible for their respective areas. Towns were divided into sectors and sub-sectors and patrol members were armed only with changkol-handles and whistles. They were required to register all families living in their sectors, report on suspicious happenings, restrain strangers and arrest petty offenders. Families wanting to move to another area had to inform the Jikeidan, and travellers from other provinces were required to give reasons for wanting to stay. The Jikeidan was used as an information bureau by the Japanese and assisted them to keep tabs on people's movements. A Good Neighbourhood Family Registration scheme and a rice rationing system enabled the Japanese to keep track of the movements of every man, woman and child in the urban areas. Conscripted labour for various war-related work was obtained in this way also.

The Jikeidan concept was similar to that of the ARP in England. It also assisted with community welfare projects including the distribution of food, clothes and other essentials to needy people. As the MMA did not agree to organise charitable institutions or welfare facilities for the aged and sick, some Jikeidan members also became involved with these civic-minded projects.

Although it was a meritorious system the Jikeidan failed to secure mass support on account of the widespread hatred for the Japanese. Consequently, it developed into a farce with people participating only to avoid the danger of seeming defiant. In some parts of the country Jikeidan members cooperated actively with communist elements by giving them both material and financial support.

In Penang the Jikeidan was actually formed on 18th March 1944, although as early as 19th May 1943 the *Penang Shimbun* had reported that it would be much sooner.

On 16th June 1945, in the *Penang Shimbun*, Lieut-General Shinohara complimented Penang's Jikeidan. He urged them, however, to be more air raid conscious!

Strict censorship denied people accurate war news throughout the occupied territories. No doubt the Governor, in referring to air raid consciousness, had in mind the recent massive B29 bombing of Japan, when 42,000 tons of bombs had been dropped. Also, by this time he would have realised that Japan's losses in the long-drawn-out and disastrous Okinawa campaign were irretrievably devastating. At the conclusion of this battle, on 22nd June 1945, 120,000 Japanese military forces and 42,000 civilians had been killed and 7,830 planes and 16 ships had been destroyed.

13:5 The KMM's Involvement with Para-Military Organisations

On 7th December 1941 Ibrahim Yaakob, the President of the dissident Kesatuan Melayu Muda (KMM) (Young Malay Union) was arrested. In the weeks that followed 110 other KMM members in different parts of the country were detained. Ibrahim, in particular, was known to be a pro-Japanese sympathiser who advocated an independent Malaya in political union with an independent Indonesia, and who had been financed to purchase the *Warta Malaya* newspaper in which propaganda articles had been published. Although British intelligence sources had allowed the KMM to function openly pre-war as a legal and authentic political entity, it was secretly

> 'allied to a Japanese-sponsored Fifth Column organisation called Kame (Japanese for "tortoise"), inspired and directed clandestinely by the Japanese Consulate-General in Singapore'.[18]

It was through this organisation that the funds to purchase the *Warta Malaya* were arranged and from the late 1930s the Japanese supported the KMM with the express aim of using the organisation to aid Japan in any future invasion of Malaya and Singapore.

During the flurry of arrests in December the KMM's Vice-President, Mustapha Hussein, along with members and other officials stationed in northern Malaya who had managed to escape the net, contacted Fujiwara Kikan to whom they offered their services as guides and interpreters during the early stages of the campaign. An elated Mustapha, in January 1942, after Japanese troops had seized Kuala Lumpur, sought the support of Japanese commanders to

> 'back a proclamation of Malay independence, citing Japan's promise to liberate Malaya from British rule'.[19]

His request was flatly rejected. He was told to examine why the Malays were inferior to other ethnic groups in the country, and instead of prematurely seeking independence, they should prove their usefulness by supporting a Japanese-sponsored propaganda campaign to enhance the mutual friendship of Malays with the Japanese. They could be of assistance to Japan by disrupting British military lines of communication and by collecting as many discarded weapons as possible. On the fall of Singapore Ibrahim and his associates were released from Changi prison and the KMM was reorganised, but no Japanese military assistance to promote its campaign for Malay independence was forthcoming. Iwaichi Fujiwara viewed any such proposal as being premature and one that excluded the Rulers, the elite ruling classes and the Chinese, would be contrary to Japan's philosophy for the Greater East Asia Co-Prosperity Sphere. On 17th February 1942 a free, wiser if somewhat despondent Ibrahim Yaacob declared,

> 'Comrades, Japan's victory is not our victory. Our struggle has still a long way to go . . .'[20]

Between February and June 1942, in a brief spate of popularity, the KMM acquired influence and power among the Malays.

> 'Its membership leapt spectacularly to about 10,000 . . . (and) members emerged as the new privileged political elite, whose prestige superseded that of the Malay aristocracy and the British-trained Malay bureaucratic

> elite. With easy access to Japanese officers, political influence, information, special food rations, and allowances, they could extend protection and help to the Malay peasants and so became their new patrons.'[21]

Throughout this period the Japanese relied on the KMM, both as a source of intelligence and for manpower. Also, through the KMM's activities and at their instigation, many among the Malay elite were arrested, and charged with being uncooperative, thereby souring relations between them. The KMM's period of influence was short-lived. Following the formation of the MMA, the KMM was banned and dissolved in June 1942, as the Japanese considered that any revival of Malay nationalism would be against their own immediate interests. Members were dispersed throughout the country and Ibrahim was given a post at the MMA's headquarters in the Internal Affairs Division, where he was kept under close surveillance. The aristocratic groups and the British-trained Malay elite administrators quickly reasserted themselves after the KMM's fall from grace and were depended on by the Japanese to assist them in running the administration. They also lost no time in exacting revenge on KMM members who had instigated their arrest. The KMM's dissolution was part and parcel of the MMA's policy to discourage local groups from participating in politics, and inevitably, the organisation slowly disintegrated as its members became increasingly pre-occupied with their own economic and material survival. In an attempt to offset KMM members' disappointment, the MMA openly adhered to a pro-Malay policy which, during the succeeding three years, contributed to uplifting the morale and political consciousness of the Malays.

Ibrahim's dismay when the KMM was banned, and subsequent disillusionment over the ceding of Malaya's four northern states to Thailand on 20th August 1943, was somewhat assuaged when he was told to organise Malay Pemuda (Youth) into both the Giyu Gun volunteer army and the Giyu Tai volunteer corps. The Giyu Gun was intended to be used as a fighting force to assist with the defence of Malaya if an Allied invasion was mounted, and similarly the Giyu Tai would be deployed for coastal defence operations and also for the preservation of public order. Both would be supplemented by the

Heiho (Auxiliary Servicemen), which was created in June 1943 to augment occupational Japanese forces by providing labour services.

It was originally intended that the ranks of the Giyu Gun and the Giyu Tai should be multi-racial, but mostly Malays were recruited. They had to be single, physically fit, of good conduct and, most of all, have a dedicated sense of responsibility, combined with an avid zeal to serve their country. They also had to swear allegiance to Tenno-Heika. Training was centralised at the Giyu Gun's headquarters at Johore Bahru and, in both the Giyu Gun and the Giyu Tai, recruits were given similar training to their counterparts in the Japanese army. The first intake commenced in December 1943, and by April 1944 six classes, each of 300 recruits, had been trained and graduated. They were given training in artillery methods, unarmed combat, and in 'Seishin' (Japanese spirit). They were taught to admire courage and strength and required to pledge to serve as front-line troops, subject to the Nippon code of military discipline.

> 'In March 1944 the Japanese tried to attract educated men to enlist by offering officer ranks to doctors, lawyers and teachers, but the appeal had limited success. Financial incentives were few and candidates were expected to be ideologically motivated. Salaries were quite low — soldiers' pay varied from $30 to $40 and officers' from $130 to $300 — and the only material incentives were free food and clothing.'[22]

Ibrahim was given the rank of Lieut-Colonel when he completed his training in June 1944, and the Giyu Gun commenced anti-guerrilla operations in south-east Johore, where 25 guerrillas were killed in skirmishes in the jungles around Kota Tinggi. When, during a subsequent operation near Ipoh in Perak, they made no contact with MPAJA forces, the Japanese became suspicious. The unit was withdrawn to Singapore, and its officers and men were dispersed among various Japanese army units. Although Ibrahim was promoted to Colonel, his authority was curtailed and his movements restricted. Henceforth he was only considered as an adviser.

The Heiho also recruited Malays mostly, although its ranks were open to all races. Recruits were trained in a similar manner to Japanese soldiers and attached to Japanese units, but unlike the Giyu

Gun they were not supposed to carry arms, nor were they considered regular forces. Heiho recruits were mostly used in transport sections or worked as guides. In the latter part of 1944 a Womens' Auxiliary Corps was formed, and school girls and women took part in parades and mass drills. The Japanese contributed towards the political awakening of women in Malaya by permitting them to participate in the Women's Auxiliary Corps. This became manifest in the years following the conclusion of the war.

Bidin bin Mat's experiences in the Heiho ran counter to the official aims of that organisation. Bidin — a labourer with the survey department at Grik — was forced to enlist into the Heiho. After serving ten months at Kuala Lumpur, he went to Singapore, then to Indonesia, from where he and 2,400 other members were sent to Papua New Guinea. Each man was given a rifle, 500 rounds of ammunition, a bayonet, a parang, and two hand grenades. Only 200 out of the original 2,400 returned from Papua New Guinea. When the Japanese surrendered in Malaya, Bidin and his friends reportedly set about the Japanese in their camp, killing 300 of them. For his part in this action Bidin was awarded the King George VI medal for bravery.

When Ibrahim was instructed to disband the Giyu Gun he initially turned to the MCP, with whom some important contacts had been made, and proposed that the KMM and the MCP should join forces under his command to fight first the Japanese and then the British, when they returned, in a war for national liberation. Ibrahim's offer was rejected. He viewed the rejection by the MCP as a betrayal made on account of the

> 'taint of Japanese collaboration attached to the KMM movement. Another was that the KMM was more interested in achieving Malayan independence through a union with an Independent Indonesia.'[23]

In early 1945 the MMA revised its policy towards the KMM and encouraged its revival. It was allowed to reform and, being a civilian left-wing party inspired by events in Java, its leaders revived their pan-Indonesian sympathies. They sought a Malaya that would be included within the concept of an Independent Indonesia. The party took a new name, the Kesatuan Rakyat Indonesia Semenanjung (KRIS) (Union of Special People), under the leadership of Ibrahim Yaacob, whose deputies were Dr Burhanuddin and Onan Haji Siraj. A plan was drawn up for a declaration of joint independence for Indonesia and Malaya. The sudden proclamation of Indonesia's independence, without prior notice, followed by Japan's equally precipitous surrender, dashed to pieces KRIS's own plans for a joint declaration. A congress was held nevertheless in Kuala Lumpur on 16th and 17th August, but to no avail.

On 18th August 1945 the Giyu Gun, Giyu Tai and Heiho were officially disbanded. Ibrahim, with his wife and brother-in-law, escaped to Jakarta in a military aircraft on the 19th, unaware of the vicious inter-racial clashes between his disbanded Giyu Gun forces, joined by other Malays, and the Chinese-controlled MPAJA forces. They used weapons obtained from the Japanese, who tacitly condoned the blood-letting. Ibrahim's hope, that the Giyu Gun might evolve as a bonding force in Malays' fight for independence against the returning British, failed to materialise. They had not been properly deployed in this role before the Japanese surrendered.

Ibrahim, now a wanted man, remained in Jakarta. In the confusion following his departure, the inhibited leadership of his second-in-command, Dr Burhanuddin, failed to regain control over the deteriorating circumstances. The KMM's hopes of leading the post-war struggle for independence were shattered. As Malay disillusionment increased, party members publicly exhibited their frustrated anger, and many of the returning 'Pemuda' were abused and even stoned when they arrived at their villages. The taint of collaboration spread throughout all levels of Malay society and KRIS's efforts to oppose Britain's return quickly collapsed with the arrest of many of their delegates and leaders.

The KMM was a revolutionary, pro-Japanese political organisation which re-emerged under the new name of KRIS as a political rival to the MCP. Both organisations aimed for Malaya's independence, but their interests were vastly different. The MCP demanded equality and justice for all the races in the country in a multiracial communist republic, whereas

> 'the KMM was for "Malaya Merdeka" (Independent Malaya), which was to be joined to an independent Indonesia in a political union to be called

Melayu Raya or Indonesia Raya (Greater Malaysia or Greater Indonesia). Such a merger would achieve for the Malays a majority in numbers over the combined total strength of Chinese, Indians, and other races in Malaya as well as secure Malay political dominance in government.'[24]

Malay left-wing sentiments were suppressed with the collapse of KRIS. It was the post-war political threat posed by the MCP, plus the fiasco of the Malayan Union proposals, which was to provide the catalyst that subsequently forced the Malays to close ranks.

1. *History of Malaya 1400–1959* by Joginder Singh Jessy, ch.19, p.297.
2. Ibid, ch.19, p.297.
3. *Malaya Upside Down* by Chin Kee Onn, ch.19, p.144.
4. Ibid, ch.19, p.138.
5. *F Kikan. Japanese Army Intelligence Operations in Southeast Asia During World War II* by Lieut-General Fujiwara Iwaichi, translated by Akashi Yoji, ch.14, p.238.
6. Ibid, ch.8, p.115.
7. *Red Star over Malaya. Resistance and Social Conflict during and after the Japanese Occupation, 1941–1946* by Cheah Boon Kheng, ch.2, p.41.
8. *British Rule in Malaya 1942–1957* by Robert Heussler, ch.3, p.57.
9. *When Singapore Was Syonan-to* by N.I. Low, ch.13, p.84.
10. *Japan Against the World 1941–2041. The 100–Year War for Supremacy* by Russell Braddon, ch.22, p.323.
11. *When Singapore Was Syonan-to* by N.I. Low, ch.1, p.5.
12. Ibid, ch.2, p.7,
13. *Ma-Rai-Ee* by Chin Kee Onn, ch.9, p.98.
14. *Red Star over Malaya. Resistance and Social Conflict during and after the Japanese Occupation, 1941–1946* by Cheah Boon Kheng, ch.2, p.34.
15. *The Masked Comrades. A Study of the Communist United Front in Malaya, 1945–48* by Cheah Boon Kheng, ch.1, p.7.
16. Penang *Shimbun*, 2nd August 1945.
17. *Malaya Upside Down* by Chin Kee Onn, ch.15, p.104.
18. *Red Star over Malaya. Resistance and Social Conflict during and after the Japanese Occupation, 1941–1946* by Cheah Boon Kheng, ch.4, p.102.
19. Ibid, ch.4, p.103.
20. Ibid, ch.4, p.103. (Refer to Agastya, *History and Struggle in Malaya*, p.46.)
21. Ibid, ch.4, p.104.
22. Ibid, ch.2, p.35.
23. *The Masked Comrades. A Study of the Communist United Front in Malaya, 1945–48* by Cheah Boon Kheng, ch.6, p.62.
24. *Red Star over Malaya. Resistance and Social Conflict during and after the Japanese Occupation, 1941–1946* by Cheah Boon Kheng, ch.4, p.101.

CHAPTER FOURTEEN: THE KEMPEITAI

14:1 Harsh Controls and Informants

The Kempeitai (Military Police) answered directly to the War Ministry in Japan. They had unlimited powers to arrest and investigate civilians and military personnel, and resorted extensively to using torture during interrogations. The Kempeitai were fully experienced in torture techniques, having practised these on people in China, since hostilities commenced there in 1931.

Kempeitai chiefs lived in seclusion under an aura of mystery and were greatly feared. Early in the Japanese occupation they seldom made public appearances, except to address crowds during a 'Sook Ching'. The lower ranks of Kempeitai were seemingly everywhere. Noted for their unpredictability and violence, they were dreaded and avoided by all.

Theoretically, candidates for military police training were selected because they had been well educated and were of sound character. They were well trained for their job, the emphasis being on sound discipline, and had to profess loyalty to Tenno-Heika. In practice, they vied for power and jealously safeguarded their own positions, ending up little more than a bunch of bullying, often murderous, louts.

The Kempeitai was supposed to maintain peace and order. They did so by arresting anyone suspected of being a spy, of harbouring anti-Japanese sentiments, and particularly anyone remotely suspected of being a communist. The Japanese feared and hated the communists, and one of the Kempeitai's primary objectives in Malaya was to eliminate them. Numerous arrests were made on the dubious evidence of hundreds of informers drawn from all races and walks of life in an attempt to cauterise the communists and their supporters. Reformed communists, ex-members of secret societies and ex-detectives were among those recruited as informers or intelligence agents, as were peddlars, hawkers, pimps, mistresses and cabaret girls, in a Japanese inspired system of 'using rogues to catch rogues'.[1] It was a system that encouraged arrest, irrespective of innocence or guilt. Many innocent people were tortured and maimed for life under this system. Evidence was disregarded, suspicion alone being sufficient for arrests to be made. Those with grudges made false accusations, while those taken into custody were invariably tortured. People lived in fear and did not know whom they could trust. Kempeitai and garrison commanders had the power of life and death over them. The Kempeitai was notorious for its terror tactics and especially for its intimidation of the Chinese, many of whom were tortured during interrogation, and subsequently killed. No-one knew whether

> 'the next knock would not arouse his household from its early morning sleep to provide another victim for the tortures of the Kempeitai. For it was by such melodramatic methods that the Japanese military police achieved the dread in which they were universally held in the occupied territories. The darkness of the night, the sudden swoop, the atmosphere of terror were their agents to impose submissiveness upon a reluctant people.'[2]

The Kempeitai watched everyone and everything, and answered only to their own chiefs. No-one escaped their scrutiny. The civil police were watched, as were detectives and the CID. All were fearful of the Kempeitai. The dregs of society were recruited as detectives into the CID. Informers increased. With inflation rising, honour was sometimes forfeited for the sake of food. Some tried to enlist in the Kempeitai for their own safety. Shrewd businessmen got distant male relatives employed in the investigation departments of the police, or the Kempeitai, just in case some future help might be needed. Police officers and magistrates were often openly abused, or slapped in public at the slightest provocation, and suspects were invariably treated as criminals. Kempeitai agents were everywhere, disguised as labourers or trishaw drivers, mingling with unsuspecting crowds at roadside stalls and coffee shops, listening to gossip and picking up snippets of information. Many resorted to blackmail, or brought false charges to satisfy personal grudges.

> 'Friends were betrayed by friends and parents by sons and daughters.'[3]

Many people were so scared of the Kempeitai that they burned all photographs of themselves in any kind of pre-war uniform, or any that might associate them with groups which had given financial assistance to the China Relief Fund.

The Kempeitai supplemented the strength of the special police force by enlisting

> 'hundreds of foolhardy, blustering youngsters — the hoodlums and scum among the Chinese, Malays and Indians. These flocked into the ranks, lured by the special privileges which gave them greater scope for perpetrating violence with impunity. They conceitedly imagined that they belonged to a hierarchy greater than the ordinary police . . . Daily these braggarts could be seen drilling in open spaces or dog-trotting four-abreast, stamping noisily through the streets, showing off their bare bodies, streaming with perspiration.'[4]

These ruffians displayed bravado, teasing girls or bullying the public at roadblocks. Their ego was flattered by receiving the bow of obeisance from all passers-by, similar to that given to Japanese sentries.

14:2 Torture and the Tortured

During 1942 to 1945 thousands of suspects were interrogated and tortured in Malaya and Singapore as the Japanese Military and Kempeitai tried to eliminate the Malayan People's Anti-Japanese Army (MPAJA), which was backed predominantly by Chinese and the Malayan Communist Party (MCP). Many unfortunate beings were scarred for the rest of their lives by the unspeakable horrors inflicted on them by the Kempeitai.

> 'Thousands of Allied prisoners of war, and still more civilians in the territories occupied by the Japanese experienced excruciating torture at the hands of the Kempeitai and many hundreds died as a result of it.'[5]

There was no redeeming feature in this debased and degenerative behaviour!

Bestial methods of torture, commonplace during interrogations, included flogging, kicking, punching, slapping, and judo and jujitsu throws. Using lighted cigarettes, cigars or candles, hot irons, scalding oil or water to burn hands and feet, as well as the sexual organs and female breasts, was also favoured. Boiling water was injected in rectums; finger and toe nails were pulled out; electric shocks were given; and suspects were forced to kneel on sharp objects or pebbles for long periods, and flogged if they flinched or moved. Equally painful were a variety of suspension techniques, administered in conjunction with flogging, in which victims were hung upside down, with their hands tied behind their backs, or were suspended by their neck, legs, arms or wrists so that joints were pulled out of their sockets. The water treatment was among the more sinister tortures. Water was forced by hose pipe through a bound victim's rectum, mouth or nostrils until the stomach or lungs were filled and bloated.

> 'When the stomach became bloated, someone jumped on it, and that caused water to squirt out through the ears, eyes, nose and mouth of the victim.'[6]

> 'In Penang also the Kempei Tai used some unusual methods of torture on hundreds of innocent citizens with the object of forcing a confession from the victim that he was a Communist, or a spy, or in unlawful possession of a radio set. Two women were tied by a rope to a motor-cycle and towed naked round the prison yard.'[7]

The knee spread was another intensely painful torture with bound victims made to kneel with a pole placed behind both knee joints to spread them apart when pressure was put against the thighs. Pliers were used to rip out finger and toe nails, and small bamboo chips were frequently forced under them. Fingers were also bandaged tightly together with sticks put between them. When pressure was applied the pain was extreme, with fingers often fracturing. The Kempeitai's barbarous methods seldom failed to achieve their intended result. Many brave people withstood pain until death, while others, unable to endure the pain, betrayed innocent families and friends. The Kempeitai sergeants and corporals, aided by local ruffians, mostly inflicted these vicious tortures, on behalf of their superiors. The Kempeitai chiefs did not directly torture people. Their role was one of instigation and condonation!

In comparison, people in Penang were ill-treated less than those in other Japanese occupied territories. However, atrocities were perpetrated. People were tortured and mistreated.

Twenty-five of Penang's municipal officers were interned and three of them died while they were prisoners of war. They were Mr A.G. McCrea, the Municipal Vetinary Surgeon, Mr H.G. Mulding, the Assistant Municipal Engineer and Mr H.J. Dodd, the Assistant Distribution Engineer. Others who survived had no option but to seek premature retirement for reasons of ill-health.

The municipality's junior staff and labourers also suffered. On record is the death of nine Health Department workers, killed during the bombing, and another thirty-one subsequently worked to death on the Siam 'death railway'. The fate of many sent there remains unknown.

Mr Yeap Hin Tat, a sanitary inspector, was tortured to death by the Kempeitai in 1943. Mr C.O. Lim, a pre-war shipping agent in Penang, was severely beaten in the Taiping prison where he was sent for telling the Japanese that the Allies would win the war. Mr Cheah Eng Keat, a pre-war *Straits Echo* reporter, was hung for helping British and Indian soldiers in the jungles around Balek Pulau. Many other villagers were also arrested on suspicion of helping these soldiers, and some were sentenced to several years imprisonment. Goh Jin Hooi died at the hands of Sergeant Muira Ichizo, the second-in-command of the Penang Kempeitai, who inflicted the water treatment on him. Similarly, Inspector Scully was killed in July 1945 by Kamada Kietsu of the Kempeitai, who continually thrashed him and submitted him to the water treatment. John Netto died on 28th July 1945, after being tortured by Ogawa Takashi of the Kempeitai. Two British soldiers, John Bennett and Samual Freer, and one Indian soldier were caught in the lallang infested hills of Sungei Pinang on the evidence of a Malay/Siamese buffalo cart driver from Batu Ferringi. Following ruthless interrogation and torture, the information extracted was sufficient to haul in another twenty-four people from Teluk Bahang and nine from Balek Pulau. Twenty of these were released by 26th July 1944, but nine were sent for trial. Of these Chew Moi was sentenced to death! The Indian soldier died during interrogation, and

Samuel Freer died of beri-beri and malnutrition in Penang gaol in April 1945.

Major H.W. Harvey, commanding the Penang Salvation Army, refused to be evacuated with other Europeans from Penang. After the Japanese took the island he was initially beaten following his arrest and handcuffed for five hours to the gates of the Light Street Convent, which was used by the Kempeitai as their headquarters. Major Harvey stayed for thirteen months in the Penang gaol and was allowed only one hour of exercise daily. He occasionally saw the editor of the *Straits Echo*, Mr M. Saravanamuthu, who was mostly in solitary confinement, and had to shave his beard with the lid of an old milk tin. (Commissioner H.W. Harvey died peacefully in England in December 1986, after a short illness.)

Jitt Singh, a pre-war cycling champion and a gaoler at the Penang prison, was arrested on 12th March 1945. He was accused of transmitting war news to the British, from whom he was supposed to have received $700 every month. Jitt Singh was taken to the Convent in Light Street, where he was thrown into a five by eight foot cell, and his turban and shoes were taken from him. He was forced to stand bare foot for eight hours daily in the sun without a break, and after several days of doing this without any food, he often collapsed, only to be goaded and kicked into standing up again. After ten days and nights of this treatment, often with interrogation at hourly intervals, a signed confession was forced from him. During his thirty-four days of confinement at the Light Street Convent, he was not allowed to wash or change his clothes, and when he was subsequently taken to the Dato Kramat police station, he was locked up again for another three days, and not given food or water for thirty hours. At his High Court trial he was made to stand turbanless and bare foot in full public view, and sentenced to five years imprisonment.

The Kempeitai prison at Outram Road in Singapore had a sinister reputation, as did many others in main towns throughout Malaya. Many people imprisoned in them were never seen again. Prison cells were small, filthy and invariably grossly overcrowded. The sexes were forced to mix with no privacy for toilet facilities given to men or women. The cells crawled with lice, bugs, cockroaches, mosquitoes and vermin, making sleep almost impossible. The foul atmosphere blended with the agonised cries of those being tortured throughout the night in adjoining cells. Strong naked lights were purposely left on all night, hurting the eyes and aggravating the helplessness of prisoners. The system intended to humiliate and degrade, and lost no opportunity to do so.

Prisoners were fed twice daily on smelly rice balls with coarse grains of salt, mixed with tasteless vegetables and a bowl of thin gruel. No bail or visitors were allowed and there was no system of appeal. The only power that could invoke leniency was the infrequent intervention of a more senior officer, or someone's mistress. Some innocent people were detained for more than a year, and if they were released, were told they were lucky to be alive and warned not to discredit the military police's good name. Under such a malevolent system many suspects rotted in military prisons, becoming mere non-entities!

Sikh prison guards in particular expected submissive bows from prisoners. They regarded themselves as superior, since they represented their new masters. Many police also delighted in being cruel, and used their new-found power and position for personal advantage. They took what they wanted in shops and markets, without consideration of others' plight. In 1943 a favoured Singapore police inspector gave his Japanese doctor a present of a loaf of bread. Most of the population by that time had not seen bread for more than a year!

The Kempeitai and police were hated. They lacked scruple and primarily looked after their own needs. Many enhanced their income through their involvement with the eight hundred gambling dens which sprang up in Singapore alone, oblivious of the misery these caused.

Hatred of the police stemmed from their apparent support of the Japanese. They answered to no regulations and their absolute power was corrupting.

> 'For instance, one cannot but feel that the Malay inspector who laid on his blows with a leather belt day after day on a Malay suspect until his victim died was a free agent, and not only a man carrying out orders. Nor can we conscientiously say that this was an exception. It was the rule, not the exception . . .'[8]

Circumstances forced many people to cooperate with the Japanese. On 16th November 1942 the Malayan Association passed a Quisling Resolution demanding that the British government, immediately on its reoccupation of Malaya, 'take action against all "quislings" by banishing them forever from Malaya'.[9] Tan Cheng Lock, the Straits Chinese leader who sought refuge in India during the occupation, considered this resolution unfair, as Asians had been left to their own fate whereas Europeans had been evacuated. He contended that

> '. . . half, if not all, of the population of Malaya, including the Sultans and their families, would have to be banished forever; for everyone there must be compelled somehow to work in order to live and thereby assist the Japanese whether directly or indirectly in the governance of the country'.[10]

The extent of collaboration differed from individual to individual. All races were affected. Those who reaped enormous benefits from collaboration deserve condemnation of their activities.

1. *Malaya Upside Down* by Chin Kee Onn, ch.16, p.112.
2. *The Knights of Bushido. A Short History of Japanese War Crimes* by Lord Russell of Liverpool, ch.9, p.158–9. (*War Crimes Trials Series*, edited by Colin Sleeman, B.A., and S.C. Silkin.)
3. *Malaya Upside Down* by Chin Kee Onn, ch.16, p.112.
4. *Ma-Rai-Ee* by Chin Kee Onn, ch.13, p.136.
5. *The Knights of Bushido. A Short History of Japanese War Crimes*, by Lord Russell of Liverpool, ch.14, p.217.
6. *Malaya Upside Down* by Chin Kee Onn, ch.17, p.117.
7. *The Knights of Bushido. A Short History of Japanese War Crimes*, by Lord Russell of Liverpool, ch.14, p.219.
8. *When Singapore Was Syonan-to* by N I Low, ch.16, p.110.
9. *The Masked Comrades. A Study of the Communist United Front in Malaya, 1945–48* by Cheah Boon Kheng, ch.1, p.8.
10. Ibid, ch.1, p.8 (Tan Cheng Lock, 'Malayan Problems', Singapore 1946, p.47).

CHAPTER FIFTEEN: INDIAN NATIONALISM – 'AZAD HIND'

15:1 The Japanese Connection

Discontent with the pre-war colonial system in India had been brewing over many years. There was also massive discontent among the ranks of the British Indian Army in Malaya, much of it stemming from long-endured prejudices present from its inception. Soldiers' wages were less in the British Indian Army and service conditions were much worse than those enjoyed by their British counterparts. Equal rank status had always been denied to officers and non-commissioned officers. The Japanese were fully aware of the extent of this discontent and cleverly resolved to use it fully to further their own ends. They offered, in a propaganda gesture that thousands of Indians were unable to resist, an independent India free of British rule. All the Japanese had to do was to initiate their schemes playing on the sentiments of bewildered and leaderless Indian prisoners of war, and on the politically ignorant Indian civilian masses. To ensure success the Japanese made full use of ardent, nationalistic and radical-thinking characters, who were eagerly waiting in the wings to commence their anti-British activities.

The stage was already set before the war. Co-Prosperity propaganda — 'Asia for Asians' — was the catalyst. Nationalistic fervour was the driving force during the occupation. The Indians were exploited. Only in 1947, and without Japan's help, did India gain independence. Decades later Indians in Malaya — independent Malaysia since 1957 — continue to be identified as the nation's impoverished sector, and still have scant political representation.

* * * * * *

Colonel Tamura Hiroshi spoke fluent English and was well trained in intelligence work. From 1939 to 1942 he was the chief military attaché in the Japanese Legation in Bangkok, and was instrumental in bonding Japanese-Thai relations, resulting in the Japan-Thailand Treaty of Alliance in December 1941. He also played a significant role, prior to the outbreak of hostilities in Southeast Asia, in developing friendly links with Indian nationalists and freedom fighters.

Japan's long-term planning was thorough. As early as September 1940, Major Fujiwara Iwaichi, the commander of a Japanese intelligence unit, the Fujiwara Kikan, was instructed to assist Colonel Tamura to liaise with Indian Independence League members who had formed an anti-British organisation dedicated to the liberation of India from British domination. Fujiwara was also instructed, in the event of war, to encourage and develop friendship and cooperation with the Malays and Chinese in Malaya, for the benefit of Japan's eventual military campaign. His mandate included

> 'the total Indian situation and to consider future Indo-Japanese relations from the standpoint of establishing the Greater East Asian Co-Prosperity Sphere'.[1]

In addition to the 'Indian Independence Movement' project, Fujiwara Kikan was also involved with the Malay Youth League, the Overseas Chinese Merchants, a Sumatran project, and the Harimao Project, using as contact a Japanese gangster chief who had lived for some time in Malaya and spoke fluent Malay. Fujiwara Kikan had to coordinate all these projects so they could be used to assist Japan's military offensive against Singapore.

Colonel Tamura held several secret meetings with Giani Pritam Singh, the Secretary General of the Indian Independence League (IIL) in Bangkok, who was working under Amar Singh, the IIL's benevolent leader. Tamura gained the impression from these meetings that the

> 'IIL was a secret political society determined to carry out anti-British independence activities in which it would not hesitate to use force, if necessary; secondly, that the IIL had a network of members in such places as Shanghai, Hong Kong, southern Thailand, Malaya, Indian and Berlin, . . . and thirdly, information about the political situation in India and military preparedness in Malaya could be obtained through the ILL network.'[2]

On 12th October 1941 Fujiwara, accompanied by Tamura, met Pritam Singh for the first time. Fujiwara was impressed by Pritam Singh's sincerity and enthusiasm for India's liberation, and realised this could be used for Japan's advantage. Fujiwara decided to work closely with Pritam Singh as the latter's

> 'organisation already had men scattered through south Thailand and north-east Malayan coastal cities . . . The Sikh and his cohorts were already distributing propaganda leaflets among Indian officers and men in the British Indian Army in the border states of Malaya. According to Pritam Singh, Indian soldiers in the British Indian Army harboured anti-British feelings.'[3]

After a series of discussion between Fujiwara and Pritam Singh, Colonel Tamura agreed in a memorandum that Japan and India should cooperate with each other to establish friendly relations as independent nations. An assurance was given by Colonel Tamura that Japan had no

> 'territorial, military, political, economic, or religious ambitions in India, nor does she demand anything from India in return for her assistance'.[4]

In return, the IIL agreed to cooperate fully with Japan and to use force if necessary to gain the complete independence of India. All Indians, irrespective of ethnic origin, political or religious differences, who wanted to fight against the British for independence would be welcomed into the ranks of the IIL. The IIL would also endeavour to promote friendship among the other races within Japan's intended area of military operation. If war was declared against Britain, Pritam Singh's followers would infiltrate British lines and through propaganda activities

> 'engage in operations to win over Indian masses and Indian soldiers from British Indian troops, by instigating an anti-British sentiment amongst them'.[5]

The IIL also agreed to form an Indian Independence Voluntary Army into which Indians from British Indian Army units would be recruited as well as Indian civilians resident in Malaya. The Japanese Army agreed to assist the IIL's efforts by recognising their independent control, and making Fujiwara Kikan responsible for promoting the IIL and liaising with them. Indian POWs and civilians would not be regarded as 'hostiles' by the Japanese, who would

> 'treat them with friendship and guarantee their lives, property, freedom and honour . . . The Japanese Army shall protect temples and prohibit use of temples by troops.'[6]

It was also agreed that broadcasting facilities in Tokyo, Bangkok and elsewhere (as other areas came under Japanese control) would be made available to the IIL to assist them extend their propaganda activities. Aeroplanes would be provided to distribute IIL propaganda leaflets, and to transport materials and funds. An assurance was given that the Japanese Army would

> 'not obstruct the IIL campaign to solicit materials and financial aid from local Indians in the war zone'.[7]

In subsequent discussions between Fujiwara and Pritam Singh (this in addition to the memorandum approved by Colonel Tamura) it was agreed that immediately after the outbreak of hostilities IIL agents would accompany Fujiwara Kikan into southern Thailand and northern Malaya. These IIL agents in the field would be provided with an identification card inscribed with the letter 'F', for 'Freedom, Friendship and Fujiwara'.

* * * * * *

In 1941 Mohan Singh, a 33 year old captain and second-in-command of a battalion in 15th Brigade of the 1/14th Punjab Regiment in the British Indian Army, was proud to hold a viceroy commission. He was, however, incensed by the racial prejudice prevalent in the British forces, and the unequal treatment of Indian officers by the British. The Japanese were well aware of Mohan Singh's sentiments.

Fujiwara first met Mohan Singh after his surrender at Alor Star. Fujiwara emphasised to Mohan Singh that freedom and world change would only be possible through the use of fighting soldiers, and could not be achieved through the endeavours of political and religious leaders alone. He asked Mohan Singh,

> 'And what are you going to do about it? You are a soldier, it is for you to choose. Your old master is dead. If you really want freedom for your country you must aspire to do something active. You must raise an Indian National Army.'[8]

A nationalist at heart, Mohan Singh was impressed by Fujiwara's enthusiastic persuasiveness. He was prepared to fight for India, providing that Indians would not be exploited. However, he would not condone the shedding of Indian blood for any cause other than their own. Such forthright sentiments convinced Fujiwara. He sought Mohan Singh's help in curtailing the confusion in Alor Star, and on 17th December 1941 Mohan Singh was taken to meet the Japanese commander-in-chief, who agreed that all Indian prisoners of war would be placed under his control.

The political vacuum left in Alor Star after the hasty British withdrawal led to scattered outbreaks of violence and looting. Chinese merchants, fearful of Japanese reprisals, closed their shop doors. The Malays and Indians misinterpreted this as an attempt to exploit them by raising prices, and vented their frustration by attacking and looting Chinese properties in broad daylight. Alor Star was temporarily in a state of chaos. Fujiwara entrusted the newly recruited Mohan Singh, with other recently surrendered Indian officers and men from the Punjabi battalion, to restore law and order to the town. Other dejected Indian stragglers from the Jitra defeat soon joined with those who had surrendered with Mohan Singh, realising the Japanese had extended to them an element of protection.

When law and order was restored discussions commenced between Fujiwara, Pritam Singh and Mohan Singh. Fujiwara again expressed his personal view that the Pacific war could become an ideal opportunity to further India's struggle to win freedom. Japan could help, for both Japan and India regarded Britain as their common enemy. The two countries had historical ties which originated in their mutual connection with the Buddhist faith. Although impressed by Fujiwara's statement, Mohan Singh remained unconvinced of Japan's sincerity, persisting in his opinion that 'Indian independence would never succeed without the support of the Indian Congress Party', for without its backing their efforts '... would be divorced from the mainstream of Indian politics'.[9]

* * * * * *

On 25th December 1941 an IIL meeting was organised in Penang and attended by 10,000 Indians. It was at this gathering that Fujiwara first met the lawyer N. Raghavan who represented the Indian community in Penang. His modest appearance was belied by his deep booming voice as he expressed gratitude to the Japanese for their assistance in India's pursuit of freedom. Pritam Singh explained to the meeting the objectives of the IIL, declaring his intention to form a volunteer Indian National Army in the near future. Both men were given a standing ovation amid a fluttering of Indian national flags.

Mohan Singh agreed to discuss the new developments with his officers and men. At a meeting with Fujiwara on 31st December 1941 he told him that, notwithstanding his own reservations, they had reached a unanimous decision to take up arms to liberate India from British rule. Provided the Japanese acceded to certain requests and conditions, he would organise an Indian National Army to work alongside Pritam Singh's Independence League to fight with the Japanese against the British. Mohan Singh asked for sole authority to organise an Indian People's Army, and for the full support of the Japanese Army. For the time being this army would cooperate with the IIL, but he alone should be recognised as the leader of all surrendered Indian personnel. Mohan Singh also wanted an assurance that those Indian captives wishing to join up would be liberated and treated as friends of the Japanese. His final demand, and one that became a major stumbling block, was that this Indian army should be considered an ally of Japan.

Discussions continued for two days and accord was reached on numerous points. The new revolutionary army was named the Indian

National army (INA), and Mohan Singh, as its commander-in-chief, insisted that it should fight only on the Indo-Burmese border, and nowhere else in Asia.

Lieut-General Yamashita's approval was obtained. He insisted that the IIL nationalists and the INA aspirants should work closely together so that Indian civilians in Malaya could be recruited along with defectors from the British Indian Army. However, he refused to acknowledge the concept of the INA as an ally of Japan, based on the unconvincing technicality that India was not officially at war with Britain. This remained a contentious issue for the duration of the Pacific war.

Mohan Singh was given charge of all Indian prisoners of war. He was instructed to organise them so that they could assist Yamashita's 25th Army. They were also to keep order in towns that had been overrun by the Japanese. Mohan Singh's most important task, however, was to persuade as many Indian soldiers as possible into renouncing their loyalty to Britain and defecting, as and when they were captured.

Fujiwara's objective in giving limited support to the IIL and INA was both political and military. Such an outward show of support was aimed at exploiting the IIL and other nationalist movements in Southeast Asia for the benefit of Japan. Fujiwara Kikan made use of the INA to develop an intelligence network to carry out anti-British propaganda on their behalf, and foster anti-British sentiments throughout the area, particularly within the rank and file of the British Indian Army in Malaya. The plan offered protection to those Indians caught up in and afflicted by the war, and sought under a veil of sincerity

> 'to induce them to participate voluntarily in IIL activities, and to expand IIL organisation all along the battlefield, and finally to reach Indians' [10]

in the British lines, where their actions could be turned into a major disruptive influence. Japan also anticipated that she would want the INA to help defend Burma and the other western borders of the intended Greater East Asian Co-Prosperity Sphere.

15:2 The Defectors

When General Yamashita's forces were over-running the Malay Peninsula, IIL members infiltrated British Indian Army lines, urging their countrymen through loud speakers

> 'not to fight their Japanese friends. There is no doubt that this had a considerable effect on the loyalty of the Indian troops.'[11]

These propaganda units cunningly targetted those Indian troops not commanded by British officers, anticipating they would be more easily subverted. Going behind British lines was dangerous, especially as they first had to pass through Japanese lines to reach their targets. In the early stages of the campaign Japanese commanders were still unconvinced of the importance of these missions. Suspicions increased when a Japanese command post was fired on after some IIL agents had crossed into British-held territory.

By mid-January 1942 an estimated 2,500 Indian soldiers had surrendered throughout Malaya in response to IIL/INA propaganda. Their large numbers made it necessary to concentrate them in a centralised location near Kuala Lumpur. Mohan Singh was confident of the loyalty of these defectors, and proposed that a number of them should be trained to form a more powerful propaganda unit to infiltrate other British lines, and induce even more Indians in the British Indian Army to join them. Such was his enthusiasm that he even envisaged Singapore being handed over without much of a fight.

Fujiwara Kikan's objectives and operations were initially viewed with scepticism by Japanese commanders in the field, but as more and more Indian soldiers defected, sometimes surrendering en masse, the reaction of the Japanese turned to one of utter amazement. Such behaviour was totally alien to their training and upbringing.

Fujiwara's success exceeded all expectations. As the 9th and 11th Divisions of the British Indian Army retreated chaotically southward, leaving vast quantities of equipment in their wake, the task of infiltration proved easier than Fujiwara had originally envisaged. The Kikan's activities were rapidly expanded to take full advantage of this. Fujiwara thought the British High Command had him on their wanted list, but judging from their disarray, breakdown in communication and inaccurate intelligence, it is doubtful that much, if any, attention was given at that time to the political aspirations of their disheartened Indian stragglers. In retrospect, however, Fujiwara Kikan's actions were regarded as having been very serious indeed.

Fujiwara fantasised that 350 million Indians in the world would rise up spontaneously in a fraternal gesture of revolution with Japan in her war against British imperialism. Indians would support Japan's ideal of Co-Prosperity, while Japan would support India's independence movement.

When Singapore capitulated on 15th February 1942, almost 60,000 Indian soldiers became prisoners of war. An immediate colour bar was introduced, segregating Indian officers and men, along with other Asian prisoners, from their British and Australian counterparts. The Indians were put into a special camp at the Farrer Park race course, where two days later on the 17th, a surrender ceremony was held.

Isolated in this manner, they were forced to listen to propaganda speeches by Mohan Singh, Pritam Singh and Fujiwara Iwaichi, urging them to discard their allegiance to Britain. They were told they should align themselves with the cause of Indian independence, join the new national army formed with Japan's consent, to fight for liberation from British rule. They were misinformed, told that the war was over and Britain defeated. The choice was theirs, either to dig latrines for the Japanese, or become soldiers once again to fight for Indian independence.

Fujiwara's speech was designed to highlight Japan's professed dedication to the cause of liberation for all people throughout Asia from the grasp of Western imperialism. The fall of Singapore was a momentous first step forward.

He explained to the bewildered, defeated masses that Japan's Co-Prosperity scheme was formulated on the principles of freedom, friendship and equality. Japan would aid their crusade for independence. The Japanese army would treat any joining the INA as friends, and not as prisoners-of-war. As he concluded,

> 'the whole Indian audience stood and shouted enthusiastically. Thousands of caps were tossed into the air.'[12]

Most of the prisoners were exhausted, confused and depressed. They had lost to a seemingly invincible force and deprived of other guidance, it was natural that many fell easy prey to such subtly delivered deception. This created for many a grave personal dilemma, with numerous officers and men flatly refusing to abandon their loyalty to the British Indian Army. Many among the initial 25,000 coerced into joining the INA subsequently deserted when they realised they were required to fight against their former comrades. Others who resisted joining the INA underwent a terrible ordeal. They were threatened with punishment, including starvation and torture, to induce them to change both their minds and their loyalty.

Many were tortured in the Bidadari concentration camp. Some were even beheaded for refusing to join the renegade army, and many more died of ill-treatment. It is to

> 'their undying credit that so many of them resisted all the efforts of the Japanese to sway them from allegiance to their King-Emperor'.[13]

Although 25,000 were recruited into the INA, 35,000 defied brutal efforts to make them change their minds, preferring the hardships of internment to breaking their oath of loyalty to the British crown. Many Indians passionately believed that those who went over to the enemy did so in 'an outburst of nationalist fervour'.[14] Most British soldiers condemned their actions as a betrayal of faith. Not a single Gurkha betrayed his oath of loyalty!

There were four main categories of Indians who did join the INA, and all of them were technically guilty of mutiny. A few joined to evade punishment and deprivation, fully intending to rejoin the British forces as soon as they could. The majority, left without leadership, were puzzled and misled into believing it to be an honourable choice and the only one open to them. Others were opportunists, and yet others were ardent nationalists. These four types encompassed men with mixed feelings and motives, many so thoroughly confused that they probably fell into all of the four categories.

Major Shah Nawaz Khan of the 1/14th Punjab Regiment was among the thousands of officers and men who refused to join the INA. He considered Mohan Singh politically incapable of dealing with the

Japanese, and he was also very suspicious of Japan's sincerity. He advised other officers and men against joining, and organised a group in the Nee Soon camp actively opposed to the formation of the INA.

Friction and violence broke out between volunteers and non-volunteers and led to many cases of indiscipline. Non-volunteers were segregated and kept isolated under separate guards as POWs, while those who agreed to join the INA were given improvements in pay, rations and accommodation. For many individuals it became a matter of saving one's hide in extremely adverse circumstances!

> 'Most of the INA officers, including Mohan Singh, felt a conflict of loyalty when first confronted with the prospect of fighting Britain for independence, in cooperation with the Japanese. These officers were all professional soldiers, many of them from families with traditions of long and loyal service to the British Indian Army. Training and experience could not be disavowed overnight. Once they resolved their personal conflicts, however, they fought doggedly for Indian independence, refusing in many cases to retreat when ordered to do so. At the opposite end of the spectrum there was also professionalism and even opportunism among some of the officers and men. The material inducements to volunteer for the INA were attractive, irresistible for many.'[15]

15:3 A Crisis Looms

In December 1912 the terrorist Rash Bahari Bose was involved in a bomb assassination attempt on Viceroy Lord Hardinge in New Delhi. Bose was pro-German and in 1914 was an active agent of the Indian Revolution Society. He was one of the first Indian revolutionaries to flee to Japan as an exile, having escaped from Calcutta in May 1915 under the pseudonym of T.S. Tagore. From his arrival in Japan as a political exile in 1916, he was recognised as the leader of the Indian community there. Rash Bahari Bose had been disillusioned for a long time with Gandhi's policy of non-violence to win independence for India, and with Nehru's leadership of the Indian Congress Party.

Bose frequently contacted other Indian revolutionaries in Tokyo, and was fortuitously placed

> 'under the protection of Tôyama Mitsuru, leader of the Black Dragon Society and friend of revolutionaries from all parts of Asia'.[16]

Toyama's influence with the government and police protected Bose and thwarted all British Embassy agitation for his extradition to India.

To ensure his permanent safety in Japan a plan was devised by Toyama for Bose to marry the daughter of Soma Aizo, the proprietor of the famous Nakamura-Ya restaurant in the Shinjuku district of Tokyo. Bose became a naturalised citizen of Japan in July 1923 and by the time his wife Toshiko died in 1925, their union had produced a son and a daughter. His son was subsequently killed in action, serving with the Imperial Japanese Army. Bose founded the Japanese branch of the IIL, which was still active in 1941, becoming its President in October 1937.

A considerable amount of friction existed between Indian revolutionaries who had sought refuge and taken up residence in Tokyo and those originating from Southeast Asia. The former looked upon the latter as having been loyal to British rule in India, and considered them merely amateur revolutionaries. The Indians who were exiles in Tokyo were, however, suspected of having been influenced by the Japanese, and had to a great extent lost their Indian identity and many of their Indian values. It is not surprising, therefore, that against such a background Indians throughout Southeast Asia, and particularly POWs from the British Indian army, regarded Bose with suspicion. His Japanese wife and his 27 year residence in Japan attached to him the nickname of 'Imitation Bose'. Many saw him as more Japanese than Indian. Although he was looked on as a convenient Japanese tool, he was chosen by delegates, along with other Indian nationalist intellectuals and lawyers from Malaya and Thailand, to be President of the Indian Conference, which began on 28th March 1942 at the Sanno Hotel in Tokyo, and which determined the provisional establishment of the IIL throughout Japanese-held Asia.

After the Sanno Conference some delegates from Malaya met Premier Tojo at the War Ministry. He assured them of the Japanese government's intention to help the Indian independence movement. Some delegates at this brief interview doubted Tojo's promises, considering them perfunctory. The Sanno Conference ended with differences of opinion, and hostilities between the Tokyo-led and the Southeast Asia factions were never satisfactorily resolved. To mend this breach and reduce the dissatisfaction arising from leadership of the organisation being in the hands of one man, it was decided that a Council of Action (C. of A.) should be created to function as a steering committee over IIL policy and its implementation. Mohan Singh was far from satisfied with Rash Bahari Bose's selection as their leader.

> 'To us he appeared to be quite a weak person and we thought the reigns [sic] of this movement should not be allowed to be entrusted to a single individual like him. We proposed that a Council of Action consisting of five members should be elected in a bigger conference to be held in Malaya . . . and the Council of Action should take the joint responsibility of running this movement. It appeared to us that Shri Rash Bahari Bose and his colleagues from Japan were not absolutely free in their actions.'[17]

The Sanno Conference in Tokyo affirmed the determination of Indians to fight for independence. It also agreed that another all-Asia conference should be held within two months in Bangkok. After meeting with Tojo some leaders of the Asian faction expected more to come out of the conference, while their Japanese counterparts looked upon it quite differently.

* * * * * *

In late March 1942 Fujiwara Kikan was reorganised, expanded and taken over by Colonel Iwakuro. Iwakuro — renowned as politically astute — was such a powerful military figure that some officers thought he had been sent to Malaya by Tojo to command a regiment in the Konoye Imperial Guards Division to get him away from the political scene in Tokyo. In May 1942 Iwakuro Kikan's headquarters was moved to Bangkok, by which time several branches had been opened, and were operating out of Penang, Singapore, Rangoon, Saigon and Hong Kong.

Within a few months the staff of Iwakuro Kikan had been increased to more than 500 people, allocated to six specialised departments, each with its own head and specific functions. The most important was the Political Section, which liaised with the IIL. Next were the Intelligence and Administrative Sections whose function was to co-ordinate all intelligence information concerning India. The Special Mission Section sent out agents either by submarine or parachute to gain access to India, and the Military Section was in charge of Indian POWs. Lastly, the Propaganda Section took charge of all propaganda distribution networks and radio broadcasting from Singapore, Rangoon and Saigon.

In May 1942 Rash Bahari Bose arrived in Malaya. He was a vibrant speaker and after he had addressed a series of mass meetings in Singapore, Kuala Lumpur, Ipoh and Penang, the membership of the IIL increased everywhere. Many Indians looked to the organisation as a heaven-sent opportunity to organise revolution against British rule in India, with Japan's support. Others continued to view with suspicion the close scrutiny maintained by the Japanese over the League's affairs. While Indian leaders made broadcasts from Tokyo, calling Indians to arms, the Domei news agency intensified its propaganda campaign to undermine British prestige. Funds and membership of the IIL continued to increase. Japanese Provincial Governors and military officers alike used their influence to stress that it was every Indian's duty to support the movement.

On 15th June 1942, as agreed at the Sanno Conference in Tokyo in March/April 1942, over 100 IIL delegates, representing two million Indians from all parts of Japanese-occupied Asia, assembled in Bangkok for the Bangkok Conference. They came from Malaya, Burma, Thailand, Java, Sumatra, Borneo, the Philippines, Hong Kong, Manchukuo, Nanking, Shanghai, Canton and Japan. Discussions continued for nine days, on organising and co-ordinating the independence movement throughout Japanese-occupied Asia, and on the best methods of cooperation with the Japanese. Although the Southeast Asian and Tokyo factions continued to be suspicious of each other, and Mohan Singh continued to have misgivings about the leadership capabilities and sincerity of Rash Bahari Bose, he still proposed Bose as presiding Chairman of the Conference, for Bose seemed the most likely candidate to have some influence over the Japanese. His appointment also recognised his many active years as a revolutionary and his previous cordial relationship with various Japanese leaders.

At the end of the Conference a resolution containing 34 articles setting out the IIL's policies in East Asia was unanimously adopted. The movement was officially proclaimed as the sole organisation in East Asia working towards Indian independence, and the INA was declared its military arm. Mohan Singh was made the INA's commander-in-chief. A Council of Action (C. of A.) was set up, and Rash Bahari Bose was elected its President. Four other members were elected to the Council. Mohan Singh was Army commander; Mr K.P.K. Menon was in charge of publicity and propaganda; Mr N. Raghavan, a Penang lawyer, was responsible for organisation; and Lieut-Colonel G.Q. Gilani was in control of military training.

The C. of A. was to function as a steering committee, becoming the IIL's ultimate authority if the INA was used in an act of war. INA members were required to swear allegiance to the League, which in turn would make all arrangements for recruiting for the INA, and raising money and materials for its support. The IIL would also liaise with the Japanese government in providing the INA with arms and equipment. The C. of A. was required to ensure, however, that its actions would accord with the views and intentions of the Indian National Congress.

Various articles in the Bangkok Resolution defined proposed areas of INA and Japanese Army cooperation. They are briefly summarised as follows:

1. Indian autonomy to be guaranteed in all activities of the independence movement.
2. An alliance to be formed between the Japanese military and government and the INA and IIL, based on mutual cooperation and equality.
3. Indian soldiers in all Japanese-occupied territories to be placed under Indian control.
4. The INA to be recognised as an allied army on an equal basis with the Japanese.
5. The INA to be used only to further the struggle of Indian independence.
6. Requests for finance made by the C. of A. to be treated by Japan as loans repayable to the Japanese government.
7. Provision of propaganda, communication and transport facilities to be given in areas under Japanese control.
8. Matters affecting the local administration of Indians to be decided in consultation with the nearest IIL branch.

9. The Japanese government to declare India's territorial integrity and to recognise her full sovereignty, free of foreign influence or control, immediately on India's severance from the British Empire.
10. Japan to exercise influence with other powers to assist recognition of India's national independence and sovereignty.
11. In areas no longer under British control, Japan to hand back to the C. of A. properties previously owned by Indians, to be held in trust for their rightful owners.
12. Indians residing in Japanese occupied territories not to be considered as enemy nationals, provided they did not indulge in any injurious actions.
13. Japan not to consider movable or immovable properties of Indians as enemy properties.
14. The Japanese government to use its good offices to enable Subhas Chandra Bose to come to East Asia.

The resolution's 34 points were meticulously drafted in full by N. Raghavan and K.P.K. Menon, two lawyers newly elected to the C. of A.

The resolution was handed by the C. of A. to Colonel Iwakuro, who forwarded it by telegram to Tokyo, where it was received with some dismay. There was uncertainty in Tokyo regarding the extent to which Japan should support the IIL. There were limits to Tojo's sympathy for the Indian liberation movement. Iwakuro, always politically astute and sensing the disquiet of some prominent people in Tokyo, sought to anticipate and exploit this mood in his telegram to Imperial General Headquarters (IGHQ):

> 'From here the contents of the resolution appear from the Japanese standpoint to be counting their chickens before they are hatched. . . . we must spur these people on for the broad objective of the anti-British independence movement. So, rather than worry about each individual item, I believe we should show an attitude of generally accepting their ideas.'[18]

Tokyo's reply, received only after ten days, was vague. The specific requests embodied in the Bangkok Resolution were simply ignored. This led to a surge of dissatisfaction among members of the

the C.of A., and increased the suspicions of Mohan Singh and other INA officers on the nature of Japan's true intentions. Acknowledgement of the equal status of the INA was never conceded by Japan.

The responsibility for Tokyo's attitude falls to a large extent on the shoulders of Iwakuro Kikan as this organisation

> 'failed to get the confidence of the IIL and lacked understanding of the peculiar characteristics of the Indians and the Indian national movement'.[19]

The lack of discretion and impatience displayed by Indians at this time was equally to blame.

* * * * * *

After the Bangkok Conference Mohan Singh returned wearing the badges of a general. He then concentrated in earnest on boosting INA recruitment. By the end of August 1942, 40,000 prisoners of war and civilians had signed their pledge to join. Three factors contributed towards the success of this campaign. First, many rank and file applicants pledged their loyalty direct to Mohan Singh and were reassured that they could be released from their pledge if things went wrong. Secondly,

> 'the INA offered personal liberty, comparative comfort and freedom from the labour gangs of the Pacific Islands, where several thousand Indian prisoners had already gone.'[20]

Thirdly, camp commanders used very harsh methods to increase recruitment. In the opinion of Mohan Singh their motive was one of personal enhancement. The threat of being sent to the Bidadari camp — a place of terror — was enough to convince all but the very strong-willed to volunteer. Mohan Singh was probably unaware of these harsh recruitment methods, although his arrogant high-handedness permitted no criticism. Defaulting officers were punished without remorse.

Mohan Singh's ultimate aim was to recruit 250,000 men into the INA. He considered this could be easily achieved in Malaya, where masses of civilians were volunteering their services. Such an increase, however, would conflict with

> 'the running-down of the Japanese forces in Malaya and the labour requirements of their vast new airfield programme. The INA at its present strength was quite enough for the depleted Japanese garrison in Malaya to handle in an emergency . . .'[21]

A serious dispute arose between Mohan Singh and Iwakuro Kikan over an estimated 25,000 Indian British Indian Army POWs in Singapore who flatly refused to have anything to do with the INA. Mohan Singh wanted to train them as reserve units for the INA. Iwakuro Kikan wanted them allocated to labour units for use in Japanese army projects.

Mohan Singh's leadership led to an impending crisis. Only a Captain when Singapore capitulated, he was junior to several other Indian officers. Some of these objected to his leadership, viewing his political acumen with misgiving. Others also strongly objected to making the oath of personal loyalty to him instead of directly to the INA. Some civilian members of the League and of the C. of A. considered that he dealt with the Japanese with cavalier disregard.

In September 1942 a climax was reached when Colonel Iwakuro told Mohan Singh that Japan did not wish the INA to expand further in Malaya, and that their first division was to be quickly transferred to Burma.

> 'They wanted the army and organisation just as a show-piece and as [a] convenient puppet of theirs but not a strong and powerful reality which may become a problem for them later on in thwarting their secret designs on India.'[22]

* * * * * *

In October and November 1942 the C. of A. met on several occasions. On 29th November, despite Bose's obvious hesitancy, a letter was handed to Iwakuro asking for clarification on various important outstanding matters. These included:

1. The Japanese government's attitude and response to the Bangkok Resolution.
2. Recognition of the C. of A. as the sole executive body of the Indian independence movement in East Asia.
3. Formal recognition of the INA, and facilities to expand it into a powerful army.
4. A binding declaration on any future Japanese government to recognise the absolute independence and sovereignty of India.

Mohan Singh and other Council members realised from Bose's attitude that he would do nothing to oppose Japanese wishes. He was simply a liaison tool between themselves and the Japanese, and was not the forceful president they required. Mohan Singh openly accused him of having become a Japanese puppet! The inevitable showdown loomed.

By late 1942 Japan's military and naval dominance were under severe stress. The Imperial Navy had lost the initiative at sea in early June 1942 with the Midway defeat, and Japan's land forces were engaged in a shattering campaign at Guadalcanal, where, by early 1943, 10,000 would have been killed. Supply lines to Chiang Kai-Shek's forces from India via Assam had been reopened, and with increasingly effective allied bombing in Burma, it was obvious that a counter-attack was being planned. The attention of the Imperial General HQ and that of Tokyo was therefore diverted from the INA, and they had no intention of providing a point by point answer to the repeated reminders sent concerning the Bangkok Resolution.

A report in late November 1942 on the mishandling of Indian property in Rangoon was the last straw. This, with other issues, brought matters to a head, and at subsequent discussions Japan's true attitudes were revealed. She refused to accept the Bangkok Resolution and declared that the C. of A. had no status. The crisis erupted when Mohan Singh and other members in the C. of A. realised that they were powerless to influence the course of events and had become subject to the ever-increasing control of the Kikan.

Mohan Singh resolutely opposed any proposal for major movement of INA forces to Burma until satisfactory assurances could be given. He was adamant that if Japan refused to concede, he would disband all INA forces under his command. The Japanese remained equally resolute.

> 'Japan recognised no obligation regarding the Bangkok Resolutions; there would be no further Government statement on India at present; all Indian soldiers would revert forthwith to Japanese control except for the Indian National Army Division. INA expansion . . . was a matter for the Japanese and they would not be hurried.'[23]

Another incident occurred which angered Mohan Singh and aggravated his already uneasy relationship with the Japanese. Colonel Gill, a senior INA officer, was arrested. Iwakuro suspected him of masterminding an espionage operation. Bose was simply told to get rid of him. Mohan Singh then decided to declare that he was no longer willing to work with the Japanese. On 29th December 1942 Mohan Singh was summoned to the Iwakuro Kikan office. He was arrested and stripped of his command by Bose. Having anticipated his likely dismissal, Mohan Singh accepted the decision with dignity. In earlier discussions with his officers, preparations had been made to dissolve the INA in the event of his arrest, and sealed instructions had been left with them to burn all INA documents. His orders were implemented as soon as his arrest was known. He and his adjutant, Rattan Singh, quietly disappeared into internment, firstly to a remote part of Singapore, and later to the small Saint John's Island, north-east of Singapore in the Johore Straits.

Senior INA officers wanted to revert to their previous POW status, but Iwakuro Kikan would not agree to this, or to the dissolution of the INA. For the next six weeks Bose made desperate attempts to salvage the IIL and restore some semblance of order in the INA.

N. Raghavan promptly returned to Penang. As President of the IIL movement in Malaya, he summoned a meeting of all Branch Presidents, at which it was unanimously agreed that the movement must still continue to function. Bose, however, would be asked to secure Tokyo's formal clarification on matters that were still in dispute. A lengthy 13-point memorandum was handed to Bose covering the following issues:

1. A formal declaration was required from the Japanese government clarifying its India policy.

2. Civilian and military factions of the movement must fully cooperate with each other and coordinate their various activities.
3. Civilian IIL members in the C. of A. must be consulted on matters concerning the INA's recognition and expansion.
4. Information and publicity activities should be left entirely in the IIL's charge, with only advice from Iwakuro Kikan.
5. Vacancies in the C. of A. should be expeditiously filled.
6. Only accredited League leaders were to be taken into the confidence of the Japanese for any work involving either India or Indians.
7. Japan was asked to provide further assistance to resolve local economic, developmental and educational problems.
8. The Iwakuro Kikan was expressly asked not to become involved in the affairs or organisation of the Indian Youth League, or to take action on behalf of the Indian community, unless they were specifically requested to do so by the League.
9. Indians found guilty of attempting to injure Indian unity or Indo-Japanese friendship would be severely dealt with.
10. The League wanted Japanese assistance to help collect donations from the Indian community.
11. Mutual confidence and understanding between Japanese and Indians should be developed and encouraged.
12. No further progress towards working together would be made unless the above conditions were agreed to; and
13. If a solution was not forthcoming, all branch presidents and territorial committees would resign.

Bose believed that Raghavan and others were trying to destroy the movement, and consequently forced Raghavan to resign. Raghavan remained in Penang and returned to practising law. He severed his connections with the movement, refusing to be involved with it while the Japanese continued to interfere.

In January 1943 Bose sent a questionnaire to all INA officers. Replies revealed that most of them still wanted to fight for India's independence, but many were reluctant to take up arms against the British. By mid-February Bose had managed to reorganise the INA, but his methods met with criticism and opposition, and only 8,000 officers and men rejoined, compared to the 45,000 who had volunteered at its inception. To avoid repetition of earlier IIL-INA rivalries, the military bureau director, Lieut-Colonel Bhonsle, and his staff were categorically placed under the IIL's authority.

Discouraged by the response to his reorganisation, Rash Bahari Bose called for a two-day conference in Singapore in April 1943, at which delegates repeatedly demanded that the Japanese should allow Subhas Chandra Bose to come to Singapore.

> 'The conference made other decisions also, empowering the president of the IIL to nominate his successor, to make laws or regulations as he deemed necessary for the independence movement, and forbidding Army members from participating in political activities. These were sweeping powers, with no checks except Bose's own assurances of benevolence.'[24]

In early June 1943 Bose left for discussions with Japanese officials in Tokyo. He had only just succeeded in keeping the dispirited IIL and INA movements together, and when he next returned to Singapore, Subhas Chandra Bose — the Netaji — was with him.

15:4 Subhas Chandra Bose — Flight to Japan

Subhas Chandra Bose — a Bengali revolutionary and a former rival of Pandit Nehru for the leadership of the Indian Congress Party — favoured

> 'the use of force as the only means to rid the motherland of the British imperial power'.[25]

He was arrested in Calcutta on 2nd July 1940, charged with sedition for his involvement in a demonstration against the Black Hole of Calcutta Memorial, which Indian nationalists claimed offended their sentiments. On 29th November, having threatened to fast until he died or was freed, Bose was permitted to return home under house arrest to await trial on 26th January 1941. However, before dawn on 17th January, Bose, disguised as a Muslim, escaped from Calcutta by car, and travelled westwards to a town 200 miles away, where he caught a train to Peshawar. Disguised now as a deaf/mute Pathan, he made his way by car and on foot to Kabul in Afghanistan, and then to Nazi Germany, arriving in Berlin on 28th March 1941.

Bose anticipated a welcome in Berlin, but this did not materialise, as the Nazis were reluctant to publicise the liberation of India as one of their war aims. Bose was subsequently allowed to use the broadcasting facilities in Berlin for a propaganda offensive against Britain, as the German High Command considered this would benefit them. He was also allowed to publish a monthly magazine, *Azad Hind*, which increased his popularity and usefulness to the Germans. Bose realised that

> 'something more was needed to fire the imagination of Indian patriots around the world. An army equipped, armed and trained to fight against the English for Indian freedom would strike an even bigger propaganda blow at the British. The Nazi High Command agreed, and the Indian Legion was born.'[26]

Chandra Bose's Berlin dream, of an Indian legion of liberated British-Indian Army prisoners of war freeing India from British rule side by side with the Nazis, crumbled in 1942 at Stalingrad and at El Alamein. Disillusioned by this, Bose turned to Japan for help, inspired by reports of Japanese assistance to captured Indian troops from the Malaya campaign, and the formation of the INA there.

Bose, accompanied by his secretary Hassan, stealthily left Nazi Germany in February 1943 aboard a German submarine. They rendezvoused southeast of Madagascar on 26th April with the *I 29*, a Japanese submarine out of Penang, which ferried them safely to tiny Sabang Island, off the northernmost tip of North Sumatra, where they met Colonel Yamamoto, an old friend of Bose from his Berlin days. They left Sabang together by plane for Tokyo, stopping briefly at Penang, Manila, Saigon, and Taiwan, and arrived in Tokyo on the morning of 16th May 1943.

Bose's arrival in Japan silenced many of his civilian critics. His authority and vitality, along with his international status, were a powerful inducement to Indians in East Asia to align themselves with him. On 10th June the first of two meetings between Bose and Premier Tojo were held. Bose was afforded official recognition, in vast contrast to the treatment previously extended to Mohan Singh. Bose's charisma reportedly enchanted Tojo and the other prominent persons he met, and this enhanced his personal image as well as his cause. On 16th June he was invited to attend an extraordinary session of the Diet, during which

> 'Tojo made an historic address on the Greater East Asia Co-Prosperity Sphere . . . [He] said, "India has been for centuries under England's cruel rule. We wish to express righteous indignation at their agony and sympathy for their aspirations for complete independence. We firmly resolve that Japan will do everything possible to help Indian independence."'[27]

On 19th June Bose held his first press conference in Japan. He expressed his gratitude to Tojo and reiterated his faith in an Axis victory. For the first time he met the older, and by now sickly, Rash Bahari Bose, who told him of the IIL's decision to make him the supreme commander of the INA.

After a successful and eventful month in Tokyo, highlighted by numerous official banquets and public statements, Bose left on 27th June for Singapore, where he arrived on 2nd July 1943, in the company of Rash Bahari Bose, to a tumultuous welcome. His old friend Colonel Yamamoto had recently taken over Iwakuro Kikan, which was renamed Hikari Kikan.

15:5 The Netaji — Birth of 'Azad Hind'

On 4th July 1943, at a general conference of the IIL at Cathay Hall in Singapore, Rash Bahari Bose introduced the vital and younger Subhas Chandra Bose to other IIL and INA leaders. The Presidency of the IIL, and supreme leadership of the INA, were formerly handed over to Subhas Chandra Bose. Many in the capacity crowd were overwhelmed by his presence and the legend surrounding him. In front of IIL representatives from all parts of Asia, Rash Bahari Bose spoke of the event as

> 'one of the happiest moments in my life. I have brought you one of the most outstanding personalities of our great Motherland to participate in our campaign.'[28]

In his acceptance speech Subhas Chandra Bose emotionally exhorted his audience 'to do or die in the cause of India's freedom'.[29] He told them that he planned to organise a Free India Provisional Government (FIPG) to lead an Indian revolution and prepare all Indians for total armed struggle.

On the following day, at a march past and review of 15,000 INA troops, in the presence of Premier Tojo, who was visiting Singapore at that time, INA's existence was announced to the world. Bose's slogan for the INA was 'Total mobilisation for war!' He lifted his audience to a frenzy with his speech, declaring:

> 'This is the proudest day of my life. This is the glorious day that I declare to the world the birth of Azad Hind Fauj [Free India Army] . . . This Army is not just an army to liberate India from the yoke of British colonialism, but it is the Army that is going to be the national army of free India when we have achieved independence.
>
> 'My dear comrades! My dear fellow soldiers! Your battle cry is "Chalo Delhi". I do not know how many of us will survive this war, but I am positive that we will win this war in the end.
>
> 'The Japanese Army drove through Malaya like a tidal wave in order to capture the fortress of Singapore. Its battle cry was "Chalo Singapore, Chalo Singapore." . . . Following the Japanese model, let us shout once more "Chalo Delhi, Chalo Delhi".'[30]

25,000 civilians and soldiers spontaneously took up the cry:

> '"Chalo Delhi, Chalo Delhi" and "Jai Hind Netaji Bose".'[31]

At another mass rally in Singapore on 9th July, Bose called for the total mobilisation of Indian manpower and finances throughout East Asia. He spoke for two hours, his entranced audience listening as they stood in pouring rain. His aim was to recruit 300,000 men under arms, financed by the three million Indians in East Asia who, he anticipated, would contribute $30 million. Bose also wanted to form an Indian women's unit, called the Rani of Jhansi Regiment, commemorating the 1857 mutiny heroine who had led troops against the British Raj. Many women responded to this call and were trained and equipped under the command of Captain Laxmi Swaminathan. Although proud to play their part towards Indian freedom, the Rani of Jhansi Regiment was little other than a nuisance to the Japanese.

The Japanese Army's recognition of the INA as an allied army was continuously opposed, particularly by Count Terauchi Hisaichi, the Japanese Supreme Commander of the Southern Army. It was argued that the INA was only the military arm of the IIL and did not represent any legally recognised government. Bose sought to remedy this by establishing 'a government which could deal diplomatically on an equal basis with the Axis powers'.[32]

On 21st October 1943, in the Cathay Cinema building in Singapore, the Free India Provisional Government (FIPG) was born. It knew it would be given recognition by Japan, 'in order to strengthen the propaganda offensive in its India policy'.[33] Bose was nominated as head of state. Most IIL leaders were scared of and openly subservient to the Japanese. Bose was the exception and stood up for what he believed. The achievement of his goal, to make the FIPG a truly free organisation, was in many instances clouded by his consuming hatred of the British.

N. Raghavan made no attempt to meet Bose when he first arrived in Singapore, and only did so subsequently at Bose's request. Bose explained to Raghavan that in the changed circumstances his services were indeed needed, whereupon he agreed to join the FIPG as its Minister of Finance.

Every Indian was expected to pledge his allegiance to the FIPG which was promising to free India from foreign rule, and establish a national government, in accordance with the will of the Indian people. Japan officially recognised the FIPG on 23rd October, immediately followed by the governments of Germany, Italy, Croatia, Manchukuo, Nanking, the Philippines, Siam and Burma. The President of the Irish Free State, Eamon de Valera, sent his personal congratulations to Bose. Recognition, as it later proved, was a far cry from legitimacy! On 24th October the 'Azad Hind' government declared war on Great Britain and the United States.

Before October 1943 the IIL was unable to prevent thousands of Tamil labourers being press-ganged for use on various Japanese works, including the Thai Burmese 'death' railway. With the formation and declaration of the FIPG, Bose had sufficient political influence

> 'to ameliorate the plight of the Indian population. Indians were allowed to serve the Indian National Army (INA) and other allied services of the Provisional Government, and about 20,000 men were recruited into the INA from the ex-Indian Army prisoners of war and 30,000 from among the Tamil labourers.'[34]

The poorer classes of Indians and estate workers were the main supporters of the IIL and INA. Tamil-speaking school teachers, estate *kanganis* (foremen) and the more educated younger workers on plantations were foremost among the lower ranks of its leadership. By early January 1944, when the FIPG and INA headquarters were transferred from Singapore to Rangoon, Indians lost much of their protection and were again exposed to abuse by the Japanese. Compulsory recruitment of Indian labour resumed, with local branches of the IIL unable to resist this.

Power was a corrupting influence on Bose's character, making him increasingly arrogant and intolerant. He refused to compromise. His declaration that he could not bear to see suffering contradicted the blood sacrifice he proposed all Indians should make to achieve their liberation, in the manner he had chosen. The intensity of his conviction could not, however, be doubted.

Bose always needed more money. This was obtained by persuading people as they listened to his speeches. Initially both rich and poor donated generously, but this waned as many were left with less to contribute, and were faced with ever-spiralling inflation. On 25th October 1943 Bose's bullying threats tarnished his image in an address to merchants:

> 'Legally speaking there is no private property when a country is in a state of war . . . If you think that your wealth and possessions are your own you are living in delusion . . . Your lives and your properties do not now belong to you; they belong to India and India alone . . . If you do not want to realise this simple truth then you have another path clearly chalked out for you . . .. the path taken by the Englishmen. . . .. you can go to the prisons and keep company with the Englishmen.'[35]

Bose went on to declare that the Provisional Government of Azad Hind had

> 'absolute rights over your lives and properties . . . Everyone who refuses to help our cause is . . . our enemy.'[36]

Soon afterwards he initiated the setting up of Boards of Management to raise funds. All Indians, regardless of status, were made to declare their assets, on which a levy of 10% to 25% was made and vigorously collected.

In early November 1943 Bose flew from Singapore to Tokyo, on the invitation of Tojo, to attend a Greater East Asia Conference. Pledges were made to fight for Asian solidarity, delegates swearing to 'push aside the artificial barriers which Western intruders had set up . . .'[37] between them. The Conference was held at the Diet building between 5–7th November. Bose participated as an observer only, as he was unable to commit India to the Co-Prosperity Sphere.

One of his reasons for going to Tokyo was to request the Japanese government to hand over to the FIPG the captured Andaman and Nicobar Islands in the Indian Ocean. Both islands were of symbolic importance to Indians, having been places of exile and penal servitude for political prisoners, and others accused by the British of conspiracy. The FIPG had no territory of its own and needed the islands so that the provisional government could be recognised by international law. On 6th November Tojo announced that Japan was

> 'ready shortly to place the Andaman and Nicobar Islands, now under the occupation of the Imperial Japanese forces, under the jurisdiction of the Provisional government of Azad Hind'.[38]

The transfer never materialised!

Delegates issued a Greater East Asia declaration on 7th November, condemning the United States' and Britain's aggressive exploitation of Asia. It called for the restoration of Asia to Asiatics, and denounced racial prejudice. Signatories pledged to defend those areas already liberated by the Japanese, and insisted that within them there should be free access to natural resources, communications, trade and culture.

> 'This Japanese-inspired appeal to Asian nationalist opinion against colonial rule was well calculated. It served Japan well repeatedly in Southeast Asia.'[39]

Japan never intended to cede the Andaman and Nicobar Islands to the FIPG. Only a gesture was made for propaganda purposes, and to mollify Bose's demands. In December 1943 Bose secretly visited the islands. A ceremonial transfer took place and the Indian national flag was hoisted. The islands were renamed Shahid (Martyr) and Swaraj (Independence) and Lieut-Colonel Loganadham was nominated chief commissioner in charge of civil administration. This was a nominal position only, and Loganadham was just an adviser to a Japanese civil government section which continued to have full authority over all civilians on the islands. Bose, dissatisfied with Japan's limited handover to the FIPG, continued to strive for their de facto control.

Japan's policy towards the IIL and INA was always one of duplicity. Ostensibly the FIPG was recognised, and the Andaman and Nicobar Islands were transferred to FIPG control — in name only. Japan deceived Bose and other Asian nationalists, creating the impression of willingly dealing with the Azad Hind provisional government as an independent entity, and extending due recognition to the INA as its military arm. In reality, Japan's actions were motivated by the one purpose of self-advancement.

In early January 1944, before Bose moved the FIPG and INA headquarters from Singapore to Rangoon, he was persuaded to meet the imprisoned Mohan Singh. At this meeting Mohan Singh tried to explain his motives and actions in 1942, but Bose was strangely unsympathetic. Mohan Singh volunteered to help Bose if a suitable post was vacant, but Bose did not agree to this. Neither did he concede that the INA was in any way indebted to Mohan Singh. He did not wish to condone the rift caused by Mohan Singh in late 1942, and had him moved to healthier surroundings in Sumatra, ostensibly on account of his poor health. There Mohan Singh stayed until the war ended.

15:6 Japanese Sponsored Spy Schools in Penang

Through the initial efforts of Fujiwara Kikan, and subsequently the enlarged Iwakuro Kikan,

> 'the major Japanese thrust was to encourage the proliferation of Indian intelligence activities throughout Southeast Asia. Under Fujiwara and still more under Iwakuro, training centres and liaison facilities were developed to expand propaganda and sabotage missions behind enemy lines.'[40]

The Penang branch of Iwakuro Kikan contained a special missions section headed by Captain Kaneko Noboru, an expert in intelligence and sabotage techniques. The purpose of this section was to monitor the training of agents, who were being prepared to infiltrate into India, Ceylon and Nepal. An important aspect of their work involved liaising with, and supervising the activities of the Swaraj Institute (Freedom Institute). In 1942 the Director of the Swaraj Institute was the ex-Madras Penang lawyer and community leader, N. Raghavan.

In addition to tuition in politics and culture, potential Indian agents also received training in espionage, propaganda and counter-intelligence assignments.

> 'The training course, supervised by Nakano Gakko graduates, included instruction in opening letters, tapping telephones, monitoring wireless, coding and decoding, developing secret ink, forging documents, making explosives, countering guerrilla warfare and camouflaging.'[41]

Instruction was also given on how to print training leaflets and produce training films. Field exercises incorporated techniques for infiltration operations, secret communications, as well as methods for disguise, ambush and escape. Training was intensive, designed to develop considerable ingenuity among trainees to enable them to put their experience to good use when sent on subsequent missions to India. A laboratory was set up at the Swaraj Institute by the Penang Kikan, to train recruits to manufacture and use incendiaries, explosives and poisons. Although unsuccessful in attempts to formulate and break codes, they were adept at producing

> 'secret ink, time bombs, hand grenades, carbide bombs, tear gas, bottled incendiary bombs and sulphur bombs. A speciality was concealing lethal materials in whiskey bottles, telephones, alarm-clocks, shaving cream and other innocuous-appearing objects.'[42]

Captain Kaneko arranged to send secretly by night the first two parties of ten Indian trainees. They left by Japanese submarine from Penang naval base, to carry out propaganda, terrorist and sabotage work in India. He did so without reference to the Swaraj Institute and without its Director's knowledge or consent. When Raghavan learnt of this the following morning, he was incensed and immediately resigned as principal of the institute. No suitable replacement was found for him, resulting in a serious breakdown of cooperation, and disrupting future work of the Penang Kikan branch.

Indian espionage attempts, sponsored by the Japanese during 1942 and in early 1943, were generally a failure. Agents taken from spy schools established in Penang, as well as other special service groups incorporated by Mohan Singh into the INA, all met with scant success. When Subhas Chandra Bose arrived, he demanded some form of direct wireless link with India as soon as possible, but his inspection of the spy training schools both in Penang and Rangoon left much to be desired.

The Penang Kikan also tried to train two small groups of Gurkhas for intended operations in Nepal, but met with considerable opposition, as they remained unswervingly loyal to the British. One of these groups was duly sent by submarine to Ceylon, where they rendezvoused at Trincomali and carried out some subversive activities.

The Osman Khan group was another small unit coordinated and trained in Penang. It was made up exclusively of Sikhs from the Punjab, many of whom had some previous revolutionary experience. The notorious Osman was in fact a soft-hearted giant who was fond of children. His talents impressed the Japanese, as did his awesome size compared with their diminutive stature.

Under the direction of Osman Khan, Captain Balwani Singh Sanga led and opened the Sanga Triad Spy Training School in Penang in January 1943. Little is known about the school or its students, and it probably closed in early December 1943. Sanga moved to another Bengali, Penang based, spy school where new students were given training in wireless operations.

Lieutenant-Colonel Gilani led a small spy group composed entirely of Indian Muslims. In April 1943 Gilani was suspected of pro-British sentiments, and was arrested with his whole group by the Japanese. They were charged with spying for the British army, and the Japanese supervisor of the unit committed suicide.

Another group in Penang with some potential was run by a Batu Pahat schoolmaster named S. N. Chopra. Bose made a direct proposal, accepted by the Japanese, to send a four-man submarine party to India under the command of Chopra. They were dispatched in December 1943, taking with them the equipment brought in by Swami from Germany. Bose claimed the success of this mission was due to his personal intervention and briefing during their training.

> 'Secret work must be related to the political situation in India: the essence was the right choice of men and right instruction, and only he could guarantee these.'[43]

This small group, active for only about two months, achieved no results. They were then arrested by the British authorities. The Japanese respected Bose for his dedication and courage, withdrawing their previous objections to his control of spy schools and their networks. In their view the INA would never be free of the taint of disloyalty, which they despised. Blissfully ignorant of these sentiments, Bose was allowed to send Swami to take control of the spy schools in Penang, and concentrated his own efforts on asserting his authority in Rangoon.

Captain Mahmood Khan Durrani, the officer in charge of the Sandicroft School in Penang, was

> 'simultaneously directing and sabotaging the training of agents who were to be landed in India by Japanese submarine'.[44]

In late February 1944 the *I-26* left Penang with 22 Indian Muslims, trained at the Sandicroft School, who were ostensibly INA sympathisers. Their mission was to land in India as agents for the Japanese, and to transmit information to Japanese listening posts established behind British lines in Burma. The first attempt to land near Pasni on 20th March failed, but a second attempt was successful some seven days later. The Japanese were unaware that these agents were hostile to the INA, and had been persuaded by Durrani (who had been responsible for their training) to hand themselves over to the British authorities immediately on landing. Durrani hoped they would provide the British Indian Army with information concerning INA activities in Malaya, and so thwart Iwakuro Kikan.

When news of the agents' surrender leaked out in a radio broadcast from Delhi, Subhas Chandra Bose went to Singapore in early June, determined to make his own enquiries. It was clear to him that their motivation had been to escape. The Japanese were equally suspicious of Durrani, who had been arrested and interrogated. Bose was convinced he was guilty and in a rage

> 'confronted him at a secret midnight arraignment in the Bidadari Concentration Camp. Durrani, who had suffered ten days of Japanese third degree, was weak and dazed. Bose would take no denial. "You should be grateful to me," he said, "that I have saved you from the Japanese firing squad, and that you will be shot by Indians. Of this such as you should be proud".'[45]

After Bose left, senior INA officers persisted in their efforts to extract a confession from Durrani. Long periods of interrogation gradually degenerated into torture. The hideous water treatment was inflicted on four occasions. Bose did not specifically sanction the use of torture, but could not 'escape responsibility for what happened to Captain Durrani'.[46] Durrani resisted all efforts to break him, and was still alive in prison when the Allies reoccupied Malaya in September 1945. In 1946 he was awarded the George Cross for his gallantry and counter-espionage work against the Indian Independence movement.

By early 1944 all spy schools in Penang were grouped under Indian control. Most agents were intimidated and did as they were told, but many deserted as soon as they could. Missions sent to India were invariably unsuccessful. They did not return, nor did they communicate with Iwakuro or Hikari Kikan. Many of them, on reaching India, either defected or allowed themselves to be arrested. Other minor training centres in Penang continued to operate during 1944 and 1945, but without much success. One week before the Japanese surrendered, all spy schools were disbanded and their students sworn to secrecy.

15:7 The INA and Imphal

Japan's sponsorship of the FIPG in Malaya and show of support for the INA impressed numerous Indians. The ploy of placing Sikhs to guard

British prisoners of war also boosted Asian stature and morale. However, although many Indians made a gesture of supporting the INA, when Indian volunteers were

> 'sent by the Japanese to stir up trouble in India [they] usually turned themselves in at the nearest British police post'.[47]

INA ranks were swelled by people from diverse backgrounds, many coerced into joining. Numerous rubber tappers, cooks, lorry drivers, labourers and coolies, having hastened to join, were given scant military training based on Japanese methods, which was viewed suspiciously by many of them. On active service the INA was always subordinate to Japanese discipline and command. By the end of 1943 the INA totalled an estimated 80,000 men. Much of their equipment was war booty and leftovers, and the majority of the rank and file were ill-equipped and dressed in torn and tattered uniforms.

The Japanese Army remained reluctant to let the INA become a large fighting force, even after Bose assumed personal command on 8th August 1943. The problem of equipping the INA was always given as the reason, but in fact the Japanese seriously doubted whether such a force could become a military asset to Japan if it was ever allowed to enter India.

The INA's participation in the proposed Imphal campaign had been discussed earlier with the Japanese, but Field Marshal Count Terauchi, the Commander in Southeast Asia, was reluctant to have them involved in any way. He considered INA soldiers

> 'had been demoralised by defeat in Malaya; they could not stand up to the rigours of a Japanese campaign, and would have an irresistible compulsion to cross over to their old friends and easier circumstances. He proposed that the Japanese army should do all that was necessary to liberate India, that Bose himself should assist by enlisting the goodwill and cooperation of the Indian population, that the main part of the I.N.A. should be left in Singapore, and that only espionage and propaganda groups should be used in the field.'[48]

Bose's arguments eventually prevailed. Terauchi consented to a trial deployment of three INA battalions in order to assess their standard.

A major task confronting Bose was to improve morale within the INA. His ill-equipped and poor-spirited troops were required to oppose a numerically larger and better equipped enemy. The INA

> 'was slack, idle and ill-disciplined. Desertion and pilfering were rife, there was disloyal talk.'[49]

Bose tried to overcome all this by threatening to dismiss the half-hearted. To those who remained he promised care for the wounded, rewards for bravery, and pensions for the families of men killed in action. By increasing pay levels and improving troop rations, he succeeded in arousing more interest in the INA among its non-commissioned officers.

In December 1943 a second INA Division was formed. Sufficient men were still coming forward to warrant the formation of a third division, but this never materialised. Recruitment centres festered with discontent, despite increasing numbers. In November 1943 a serious mutiny erupted among recruits in Singapore due to the harsh discipline. Unsuspecting recruits, already in poor health, found the unaccustomed discomforts inflicted on them unbearable.

Plans for a Burma-India offensive were being considered by the British and Japanese Chiefs of Staff in the spring of 1943. The British viewed Imphal a most suitable staging area in their plans to reconquer Burma, and the Japanese also selected it as a suitable take-off point to strike at British forces in northeast India.

The Japanese 15th Army was instructed to prepare for the campaign in September 1943, and their commander, Lieut-General Mutaguchi, ordered the Imphal operation to commence in March 1944. By this time the war situation in Burma was critical, and turmoil surrounded Britain's tenure in India, where 'anti-British political activities . . . had reached a state of ugly insurgency'.[50]

The Japanese offensive began on 8th March 1944. Its aim was to quickly destroy British forces at Imphal and Kohima. By 7th April the British 161st Brigade near Kohima had been encircled and the Japanese had seized the town's main waterworks. Supplies were being air dropped to the British to enable them, particularly in the Imphal garrison, to continue fighting. By 30th April 1944, with the battle prolonged, Japanese attacks were markedly less effective as their own food shortages became acute.

Japan wanted a quick advance into India. During March and April 1944 newspaper reports in Penang and other Japanese occupied territories heralded INA and Japanese successes, raising the hopes of Indians throughout Malaya, who interpreted them as a foretaste of Indian independence.

> 'The fence sitters came out into the open and gave enthusiastic support to League activities. INA Training Centres were filled to capacity, and recruiting centres were overworked. Only a minority of Indians kept a cool-head, and avoided joining the Movement.'[51]

On May 24th, however, disconcerting news reports vaguely referred to decisive battles on the Indian front. As June passed the initial enthusiasm of many began to flag. There was a feeling that something had gone terribly wrong.

On 22nd June the siege of Imphal was put down when advance units of the 2nd and 5th Indian Divisions met at Milestone 107 on the Imphal/Kohima road. By this time Japanese forces had been shattered. Their losses continued to increase, exacerbated by food shortages, illness and the virtual collapse of their supply system. One INA division had been almost obliterated!

Japan publicly abandoned the disastrous Imphal campaign on 26th July 1944, the same day that Premier Tojo resigned. August was a month filled with horror. The victorious British Indian Army, chasing up the Japanese retreat, were confronted with

> '"pitiful, starving and utterly demoralised INA soldiers, crawling up to our troops to point out others of their comrades too weak to move. With the hundreds of bodies of Japanese dead" were found many of the INA who had died of starvation.'[52]

Although more than half of the Japanese force was dead, the remainder were still a fighting formation. In contrast,

> 'the INA had little cohesion left and it was shown scant sympathy . . . Relations deteriorated fast. The Indians stole without scruple from Japanese stocks, and on at least one occasion the Japanese bayoneted to death INA

> soldiers as enemy spies. Nearly all were unfit when they started to withdraw: throughout the march disease and starvation took their daily toll.'[53]

Until this time the Japanese defeat at Imphal was the most significant in their military history, due to the large number of casualties. The Japanese 15th Army, at a conservative estimate, lost 30,000 men between mid March and mid June. On 10th July, when a general retreat was ordered, 'only shreds of their Army survived'.[54] Out of 85,000 troops brought by Japan into action for the Imphal campaign, more than 50,000 were lost in their prolonged offensive. This compared with 17,000 British losses. Three Japanese divisions had been deployed,

> 'plus a so-called division of Indian Nationalists, low in strength and poor in quality . . . the Japanese had forfeited their advantage in tactical skill by blind conformity to an unrealistic military tradition . . .'[55]

The INA's performance was a shattering disillusion to Subhas Chandra Bose. His exhortation of 'Chalo Delhi', which on 5th July 1943 had driven 15,000 INA troops into a frenzy of emotion, was dashed to pieces with their disastrous humiliation at Imphal. The IIL's aspirations of participating in the liberation of India were also destroyed. Bose had been unable to transform his men into heroes, while his expectation of shaking the loyalty of the British Indian Army had not materialised.

Imphal was a catalyst. It was of critical military importance to Japan. It determined Japan's strategy for subsequent cooperation with nascent independence movements in Southeast Asia. For the INA it represented the one real opportunity to overrun the India-Burma border and ignite the flames of Indian revolution from within.

> 'The battle of Imphal was . . . one of the most controversial Japanese campaigns of the entire Pacific war. A total of five Japanese generals-in-command and numerous staff officers were dismissed during and immediately following the action in an unprecedented attempt to fix blame for the fiasco.'[56]

* * * * * *

After sending a second INA division to Burma, the Japanese flatly refused Bose's request to commit additional INA troops there. With the increased effectiveness of Allied air offensive throughout South-east Asia, and the transport difficulties this imposed, the Japanese High Command decided they needed all existing INA forces to maintain defensive functions in areas already under their control and occupation.

By November 1944 the estimated strength of the INA was 47,650 — a far cry from the earlier vision of 300,000 men under arms. 16,900 were in Burma, 13,750 in Malaya and 2,000 were staff at various recruit training camps, where 15,000 were still under some form of training. The Japanese had agreed to pay and provide for only 35,000 INA forces under arms. Bose would have to raise the funds to provide for any more. He had no option but to agree that the INA's proposed third division — recruited from civilians and being trained in Johore — should remain in Malaya to defend it.

Throughout East Asia, with Allied victory seemingly imminent, recruitment was adversely affected. In Singapore, in May 1944, recruitment into the INA had peaked at 10,000, but by November — only six months later — it had dwindled to barely 560. The demoralising effect of the Imphal disaster increased the number of deserters in Malaya to more than 2,000. Every month about another 200 bolted from INA training camps. Fund raising in Malaya had dwindled by November 1944 to only $617,000. Seven months previously it had been in excess of $2 million. People now concealed their assets and delayed or evaded making payments. With an Allied victory becoming apparent, apathy set in.

On 16th December 1944 Bose toured Malaya in a frantic attempt to rally support among senior INA officers. He insisted that his demands on civilians were to be met, and emphasised this point by having a defaulter in Penang arrested as an example.

Many Indians in Malaya put to good personal use the protection offered by the INA and IIL. Only a minority, including former Indian army officers and soldiers, and some educated professionals, chose not to become involved. The INA in Malaya was never officially disbanded. It just ceased to exist at the end of August 1945. There were mixed feelings: pity for the thousands of recruits roaming aimlessly in tattered and torn hand-me-down uniforms; admiration for genuine believers in the cause, who had been willing to die to free their motherland from British rule; and violent contempt for those who had become involved, only to exploit the situation for their own ends. However,

> 'the general feeling was that the INA was a colossal waste of effort, money and men . . . from the beginning, it was felt that its ultimate failure was a foregone conclusion.'[57]

Indian involvement in the INA was regarded by many as a justifiable course of action in pursuit of India's liberation from British rule. The extent of collaboration with the Japanese did not prompt much localised hostility. After Japan's capitulation on 15th August 1945 the IIL was not viewed as a likely security menace. It was felt that the majority of Indians had joined the League from inherent feelings of patriotism.

Subhas Chandra Bose's magnetic personality had initially affected them, but as the war effort of Japan and the INA crumbled, particularly after Imphal, their fervour decisively waned. Towards the end of the war Bose's desire for personal gain obscured his originally stated ideals for the movement, and much of the funds collected in Malaya, from an already hard-pressed sector of the community, was being diverted into the pockets of grasping office bearers. However, the INA and IIL did contribute towards the transformation of Indian political and social awareness in Malaya. They also altered Indian attitude towards the returning British during the post-war years. The Malayan Communist Party (MCP) was able to take advantage of anti-British sentiments among the Indians, recruiting the more vocal among them as leaders in MCP controlled labour unions.

15:8 Death of Subhas Chandra Bose

Mystery surrounded the death of Subhas Chandra Bose on 19th August 1945. Newspapers in Malaya only published the story five days later on the 25th. The IIL organised formal memorial services for him in Penang, Kuala Lumpur and Singapore, but flags were not flown at half mast. Nor was there much press coverage. Gandhi expressed admiration for Bose's courage and patriotism, although he had no faith in his methods. He initially doubted the veracity of the reported Formosa plane crash.

Bose's death was not announced by the Japanese news agency, Domei, until 23rd August. Evidently, on the fateful 19th August, concern for safety evoked pre-flight discussions between the pilot and ground engineer, and the port engine was tested several times. Five minutes after take-off the propeller and engine fell from the left wing. The plane veered sharply, then crashed to the ground. Several torch-like figures staggered from the wreckage — one was Subhas Chandra Bose. He was rushed by truck to the Nanmon Military Hospital, south of Taihoku, where he died of third degree burns a few hours later.

Bose's remains were cremated. His ashes were flown to Tokyo and entrusted to Rama Murti, the President of the Tokyo IIL, who arranged for a memorial service on 14th September 1945. The only final resting place that could be found by Rama Murti for Bose's ashes was at the Renkoji Temple at Suginamiku in Tokyo, a temple of the militant nationalist Nichiren Buddhist sect.

Ambiguity surrounds Bose's final secret flight. The Japanese sponsored a simple 'disappearance' plan, whereby he would enter the Soviet Union, to evade British interrogation. Another possibility was that the crash had been pre-arranged so that, with his death, Bose could be erased from the Japanese conscience. The delay in announcing the crash invited much speculation and suspicion.

1. *Jungle Alliance. Japan and the INA* by Joyce C. Lebra, ch.1, p.3.
2. *F. Kikan. Japanese Army Intelligence Operations in Southeast Asia during World War II* by Lieut-General Fujiwara Iwaichi, translated by Akashi Yoji, ch.1, p.6.
3. *Jungle Alliance. Japan and the INA* by Joyce C. Lebra, ch.1, p.5.
4. *F. Kikan. Japanese Army Intelligence Operations in Southeast Asia during World War II* by Lieut-General Fujiwara Iwaichi, translated by Akashi Yoji, ch.3, p.45.
5. Ibid, ch.3, p.45.
6. Ibid, ch.3, p.46.
7. Ibid, ch.3, p.46.
8. *The Springing Tiger. Subhash Chandra Bose* by Hugh Toye, ch.1, p.3.
9. *Jungle Alliance. Japan and the INA* by Joyce C. Lebra, ch.2, p.21.
10. *F. Kikan. Japanese Army Intelligence Operations in Southeast Asia during World War II* by Lieut-General Fujiwara Iwaichi, translated by Akashi Yoji, ch.3, p.40.
11. *History of Malaya 1400–1959* by Joginder Singh Jessy, ch.19, p.292.
12. *Jungle Alliance. Japan and the INA* by Joyce C. Lebra, ch.3, p.38.
13. *The Knights of Bushido. A Short History of Japanese War Crimes* by Lord Russell of Liverpool, ch.9, p.141.
14. *The Springing Tiger. Subhash Chandra Bose* by Hugh Toye, Foreword, p.v.

15. *Jungle Alliance. Japan and the INA* by Joyce C. Lebra, ch.13, p.216–7.
16. Ibid, ch.4, p.49.
17. Ibid, ch.4, p.52.
18. Ibid, ch.6, p.80.
19. *F. Kikan. Japanese Army Intelligence Operations in Southeast Asia during World War II* by Lieut-General Fujiwara Iwaichi, translated by Akashi Yoji, ch.14, p.240.
20. *The Springing Tiger. Subhash Chandra Bose* by Hugh Toye, ch.1, p.9.
21. Ibid, ch.1, p.10.
22. *Jungle Alliance. Japan and the INA* by Joyce C. Lebra, ch.6, p.88.
23. *The Springing Tiger. Subhash Chandra Bose* by Hugh Toye, ch.1, p.11–12.
24. *Jungle Alliance. Japan and the INA* by Joyce C. Lebra, ch.6, p.100.
25. Ibid, Foreword, p.xii.
26. Ibid, ch.7, p.109.
27. Ibid, ch.7, p.116.
28. Ibid, ch.7, p.119.
29. Ibid, ch.7, p.119.
30. *F. Kikan. Japanese Army Intelligence Operations in Southeast Asia during World War II* by Lieut-General Fujiwara Iwaichi, translated by Akashi Yoji, ch.15, p.249–250.
31. Ibid, ch.15, p.250.
32. *Jungle Alliance. Japan and the INA* by Joyce C. Lebra, ch.8, p.128.
33. Ibid, ch.8, p.129.
34. *Red Star over Malaya. Resistance and Social Conflict during and after the Japanese Occupation, 1941–1946* by Cheah Boon Kheng, ch.2, p.48.
35. *The Springing Tiger. Subhash Chandra Bose* by Hugh Toye, ch.5, p.96.
36. Ibid, ch.5, p.97.
37. *Eagle Against the Sun. The American War with Japan* by Ronald H. Spector, ch.20, p.465.
38. *Jungle Alliance. Japan and the INA* by Joyce C. Lebra, ch.8, p.133.
39. Ibid, ch.8, p.132.
40. Ibid, ch.5, p.65.
41. Ibid, ch.5, p.71.
42. Ibid, ch.5, p.73.
43. *The Springing Tiger. Subhash Chandra Bose* by Hugh Toye, ch.6, p.106.
44. *The Penang Submarines* by Dennis Gunton, ch.1, p.8.
45. *The Springing Tiger. Subhash Chandra Bose* by Hugh Toye, ch.6, p.114.
46. Ibid, ch.6, p.115.
47. *British Rule in Malaya 1942–1957* by Robert Heussler, ch.3, p.58.
48. *The Springing Tiger. Subhash Chandra Bose* by Hugh Toye, ch.5, p.86.
49. Ibid, ch.5, p.87.
50. *F. Kikan. Japanese Army Intelligence Operations in Southeast Asia during World War II* by Lieut-General Fujiwara Iwaichi, translated by Akashi Yoji, ch.15, p.248.
51. *Malaya Upside Down* by Chin Kee Onn, ch.18, p.130.
52. *The Springing Tiger. Subhash Chandra Bose* by Hugh Toye, ch.6, p.120–1. (Refers to 14th Army report.)
53. Ibid, ch.7, p.126.
54. *Mountbatten* by Philip Ziegler, ch.21, p.276.
55. *History of the Second World War* by Liddle Hart, ch.29, p.544.
56. *Jungle Alliance. Japan and the INA* by Joyce C. Lebra, ch.9, p.149.
57. *Malaya Upside Down* by Chin Kee Onn, ch.18, p.135.

CHAPTER SIXTEEN: THE MALAYAN COMMUNIST PARTY (MCP) AND THE MALAYAN PEOPLE'S ANTI-JAPANESE ARMY (MPAJA)

16:1 MCP Growth in Malaya

The Kuomintang (KMT) evolved from the revolution in China in 1912 and was legal until 1925 in the Straits Settlements and Malaya, where it was registered under the Society's Ordinance. In 1925, under this legal cloak of convenience, the first communist group was formed within the Malayan branch of the KMT, and

> 'communist agents entered the country where they soon gained influence in schools and small trade unions.'[1]

In 1924, with the setting up of the Profintern (Communist Trade Union International), work within labour unions became one of the most important objectives of communists in Southeast Asia. The organisation of communist-controlled labour unions in Malaya became more formalised, and inciting disorder and creating martyrs became a general communist ploy. In this manner the communists organised the Nanyang General Labour Union in Singapore in 1926, which came under the direct control of the Chinese Communist Party (CCP). In 1927 a violent split severed ties between the KMT and the communists in China, and Chiang Kai-Shek dissolved their so-called alliance. This also severed the tenuous link between the two organisations in Malaya, denying the communists access to Kuomintang branches, which by this time had been forced into a discreetly illegal existence.

> '[The] blueprint for revolution in the colonial areas of Asia . . . was prepared at the Second Congress of the Communist International and given full form at the Sixth Congress held in 1928.'[2]

The policies evolved at this 'World' congress aimed at establishing some form of national unity, agrarian revolution and the development of trade union organisations, as well as securing equality of race and sex. These aims were more difficult to set in motion in Malaya as there was no single national political entity. This, along with the failure of the British Communist Party to nurture and develop revolutionary activity in Malaya, slowed down the growth of communism there.

When Sir Cecil Clementi became Governor of the Straits Settlements in 1929, he advocated continuing strong curbs on the KMT, demanding its dissolution in the colony. This forced the communists to stand alone once more and they duly set up their own forum in Southeast Asia — the Nan-yang kung-ch'an-tang (South Seas Communist Party) — which assumed responsibility for supervising all communist activities in the region. This was the first definite attempt to affiliate various Southeast Asian areas under a single party structure. The Nan-yang achieved only limited success and was dissolved by Comintern directive in the last week of April 1930. Hoping to wrest leadership of Malayan communists from China, the International Communist Organisation now decided that a Malayan Communist Party (MCP) should be set up in Singapore under the direct operational control of the Far Eastern Bureau of the Comintern, which had its regional headquarters in Hong Kong. From its outset the MCP competed with the KMT for membership and support among overseas Chinese in Malaya, who comprised 38% of the population.

On 1st June 1930 Joseph Ducroux (alias Serge Lefrance) was arrested in a brilliantly executed Special Branch coup in Singapore. Amazingly he confessed and gave away full details of the entire communist network in East and Southeast Asia, delivering a crippling blow to the communists in Malaya and casting them into a state of utter disarray. Fourteen leading communists were put behind bars. Outside financial assistance was disrupted, as was the much needed guidance from the Comintern. This police action caused serious disruption to the communist movement in the country. In Decroux's estimation,

> 'the Communist organisation in Malaya at the time of his arrest numbered the following; some 1,500 party members, about 10,000 members of

> Communist-led labour unions, 50 active women party workers and 200 members enrolled in the Anti-Imperialist League, a party-front organisation.'[3]

These arrests, plus the repatriation of other ringleaders to their countries of origin, helped to reduce the early menace of the MCP. As it began to slowly rebuild its revolutionary organisation, the MCP continued to be a disruptive influence before the war, causing serious unrest in plantations, mines and docks.

By 1933, with the re-establishment of the Far Eastern Bureau of the Comintern in Shanghai, much needed political advice and financial assistance became available once again to communist parties throughout Southeast Asia. First signs of communist activity in Malaya were noted in 1934, when the Comintern in Shanghai sent directives to the MCP ordering them to organise

> 'mass demonstrations, strikes, sabotage of the British naval installations at Singapore, transportation boycotts, demonstrations against increased taxation, and so forth'.[4]

Dire poverty, resulting from the world-wide economic depression, also assisted the resurgence of communism in Malaya. Many among the impoverished and jobless became even more receptive to communist propaganda, especially in Malaya where personal and national economic welfare were subject to the volatility of rubber and tin prices.

A campaign of 'Party Purification' was launched by the Malayan Communist Youth Corps (MCYC) in response to the Comintern's directive to cause as much disruption as possible. Less aggressive members were discarded and an all-out recruiting campaign was initiated to expand party membership and achieve the Party's long-term revolutionary goals. According to Wu Tien-wang, a communist writer,

> '[The] "party apparatus" was established in every State throughout Malaya during this period.'[5]

On 6th March 1934 the Central Committee of the MCP held its Sixth Plenary Session, at which the MCP's constitution was agreed. It laid down the foundations on which a strong party could develop and clarified various anomalies and problems concerning membership, organisation, duties, discipline and finances. It also set up a formal method of liaison with the Comintern. In May 1935 the Malayan General Labour Union (MGLU) demonstrated against the Silver Jubilee Celebrations. Anti-British slogans were displayed. In Penang, Kuala Lumpur and Singapore, the decorations at these celebrations became targets for arson attacks.

Over this period the police and Chinese-speaking members of the Malayan Civil Service (MCS) were aware that clandestine meetings were being held in Chinese youth clubs and Chinese schools. Featured topics for discussion at these meetings included ridding the country of the British and establishing a form of dictatorship to resolve various matters in dispute with China. The authorities also realised that the Chinese in Malaya were more sympathetic towards their country of origin, after Japan's attacks in 1931 and 1937. The Chinese in Malaya increasingly realised throughout this period that their continued survival in their adoptive country depended on retaining and protecting their separate identity as best they could.

16:2 MCP's Anti-Fascist and Anti-Imperialist Policies

The MCP evolved as a predominantly Chinese organisation because of its early and close relationship with the CCP. Only a few Chinese-educated intellectuals ranked among its pre-war leadership, which was mostly drawn from factory workers, shop assistants, barbers and even sailors. The better educated MCP leaders were either students, journalists or school teachers, and were predominantly Chinese-educated. They distrusted English-educated Chinese, believing them tainted by exposure to British cultural values, even though the English-educated were at that juncture the least politically conscious group, compared to the

> 'Chinese-educated and Malay-educated intellectuals [who] were already increasingly involved in political agitation against the British authorities'.[6]

The MCP's early attempts at organising Malay peasants and Indian workers into trade unions were severely hampered by the arrest and banishment of some of its capable labour leaders. Another of its initial aims in Malaya, to agitate for class unity for all races, was also unsuccessful. In 1936 an internal crisis in the Party's organisation forced them yet again into another policy change.

> '[A] weakened party attempted to direct all races into "anti-Japanese Fascist" and "anti-British Imperialist" struggles, while encouraging Malays, Chinese and Indians to pursue their own separate racial or national independence struggles.'[7]

Anti-Japanese feeling among the Chinese reached fever pitch after Japan invaded Manchuria in 1931. The communists quickly capitalised on people's fear and sentiment, setting up organisations which were both anti-imperialist and anti-Japanese. These were especially attractive to young and patriotic Chinese. The new organisations served the MCP's dual purpose of being a front for its subversive activities, and enabling it to openly expound militant nationalism. A strongly anti-Japanese union of overseas Chinese was set up in Singapore following Japan's occupation of Manchuria. This was promptly taken over by hard core communists, who reorganised it into a Party instrument for anti-imperialist and anti-Japanese propaganda, and called it the Malayan Anti-Imperialist League. Behind the anti-Japanese facade the MCP simply expanded its revolutionary and subversive work.

In 1937, when northern China was attacked and occupied by Japan, Chinese patriotism again served the communists well. The anti-Japanese movement united Nationalists and Communists in China against their common enemy.

> 'This re-alliance was extended to Malaya, where both parties began to cooperate in a joint anti-Japanese movement. They functioned for a while in an organisation known as the National Salvation Association, an organisation which later came under Leftist domination.'[8]

Many rushed to become involved with the National Salvation Movement, which emphasised external events as opposed to local conditions in Malaya. Young men from all over the country enthusiastically joined in various anti-Japanese activities to assist their motherland.

Clan and guild association officials – both China-born and educated, as well as Straits-born and English-educated – as leaders of the Chinese community, mobilised their followers to oppose the common enemy of their homeland.

> 'Chinese residents unanimously decided to cooperate with the British war effort. The authorities in Chungking told the British Ambassador that the Chinese Government was ready to instruct Chinese overseas to stage "an anti-Japanese movement in cooperation with Britain, if the British government found it necessary".'[9]

Communist popularity among Chinese in Malaya was revived by the Party's taking a leading role in encouraging anti-Japanese feelings. Emphasising Chinese nationalism from 1937 to 1940, the MCP managed to regain much of the influence lost among the Chinese community after the arrest of unionists. Many young Chinese were attracted to the communists because they believed the MCP represented a system that would oppose Japan and her imperialist expansionism. The anti-Japanese movement naturally attracted more support from the Chinese than other races, and automatically led to Chinese domination of MCP leadership.

By December 1941 the various anti-Japanese groups, which had grown hand in hand with the MCP, were all brought under the direction of the Overseas Chinese Anti-Japanese Mobilisation Federation (OCAJMF). This was outwardly a non-political organisation, but had really been set up as a propaganda tool and training school for prospective communist party members. The Federation boasted more than 2,000 active participants, and by the time Japan attacked Malaya the MCP had consolidated and increased its membership considerably.

16:3 MCP Militancy in Labour Unions

Throughout the 1930s the MCP concentrated on infiltrating trade unions and youth organisations, with some success in the second half of the decade. In the early 1930s attempts to infiltrate and coerce workers' unions were plagued by misfortune and misjudgement. Many experienced union officials and party agitators were either deported, or arrested and serving long terms in prison.

By 1934, with much of the Party's structure rebuilt, a gradual resurgence of communist-dominated labour activity became evident. This was considerably helped by the general economic unrest following the Depression. By 1935 the communists had made significant progress. To the grave concern of the government, labour agitation had reached alarming proportions, culminating in a strike at the Batu Arang coalmine in Selangor. The authorities considered the continuing smooth operation of this mine essential, as it supplied much of the fuel used by electric power plants and the railroad. In a surprise night raid 300 policemen were ordered to retake the mine, which they did after a brief clash with armed strikers. This armed intervention did not deter the MCP in its labour agitation efforts and Wu Tien-wang, a communist historian, considered 1936 as the 'high tide in party labour work'.[10]

One of the better MCP organised strikes in that year involved some 30,000 labourers in both the pineapple-canning and building industries. The MCP retaliated when its labour agitators were arrested during these strikes by

> 'calling out thousands of longshoremen, foundry mechanics, rubber tappers, and tin miners . . . under the guise of a so-called "sympathy walkout"'.[11]

MCP-orchestrated strikes continued unabated throughout 1937–1939, when the communists infiltrated numerous unions representing a large percentage of the workers in the country. It was estimated that during this period they recruited more than 37,000 supporters in Singapore and Malaya — mostly Chinese, with a high proportion of Hainanese — many of whom were 'deluded into believing that the MCP was struggling for their well-being'.[12]

The British authorities in Malaya took various repressive measures to curtail communist activities. The MCP was declared an illegal organisation, and 'active party members were therefore subject to arrest and imprisonment'.[13] In the late 1930s the Banishment Ordinance was frequently used to get rid of embarrassing and troublesome top party leaders. Under the Ordinance, any non-British subject could be declared an undesirable alien and deported. The Trade Union Enactment of 1940 was another effective legal tool to curtail the growth of communist activities in trade unions. The Enactment required the compulsory registration of all associations with trade union objectives. Union accounts had to be audited and the use of union funds for political purposes was prohibited. This Enactment provided genuine trade unions and their members with legal protection in their official activities, but it also restricted communist activity within the Malayan labour movement.

Although some progress was made by the MCP in labour agitation, grave 'internal difficulties'[14] divided the Party. A group of revolution-bent extremists urged more militancy and aggression against the British. Impatient with the tedious, devious path their bid for revolution was following, they openly challenged the leadership of the Central Committee to the extent of attracting the Comintern's attention. Ironically, it was a trouble-shooter named Lai Tek — a triple-agent cum Comintern liaison chief in Hong Kong — who was ordered to come to Malaya to resolve the dissension within the MCP. He did so, personally directing a

> 'purge, restoring "the ideological unity within the party" and wiping out "the last remnants of incorrect inclinations". And most important following this, Lai Tek "emerged the beloved leader of the party".'[15]

The MCP's influence and membership grew significantly under Lai Tek's competent leadership in the late 1930s, but it is doubtful whether its active ranks in Singapore and Malaya ever exceeded 10,000. Party organisation extended its influence to all States throughout the Malay Peninsula, with the main directives and control emanating from a Central Committee in Singapore. State Committees were set up in Penang, Malacca, Kuala Lumpur, Johore, Negeri Sembilan, Muar, Batu Pahat, Ipoh, Selangor and in Kuantan. Meetings were held once or twice yearly to discuss party policy and Comintern directives. Leadership was youthful and spontaneous, with Lai Tek only 33 years old at that time, and the average age of the policy-making, fiery-spirited Central Executive and Standing Committees, only 26.

With Great Britain and Germany locked in war, and Japan's military strength and territorial greed increasing, the MCP realised that war between Britain and Japan was more than a probability. In an apparent volte face, the communists hinted at cooperation on their terms with the local government in Malaya, but this evoked no response. The communist-sponsored Anti-Enemy Backing-Up Society therefore continued to issue anti-British literature until September 1940, when a CCP directive from Hong Kong instructed the MCP to suspend immediately all anti-British acts and industrial strikes. In future it had to consolidate its anti-Japanese front and support the National Salvation Movement in Malaya. The MCP was also instructed not to oppose any campaign promoted by the Chinese community in Malaya to support the British war effort. The MCP agreed to this change in the Party's role, responding wholeheartedly after Japan attacked.

16:4 MCP Policy Changes and Implications

During 1935 to 1939, with the rise of fascism in Italy and Germany, and the escalation of Japan's military might, the Soviet Union deviated from her militant Comintern approach, to counteract any threat in the Far East. The Soviets courted both the leaders and the masses in Southeast Asian countries, attempting to manoeuvre them into an alliance of convenience with the extreme left. The Soviet Union wanted total control over the Right-Left United Front, as this would enable her to discard at will any Right-Wing leaders, or other elements considered undesirable. This tactic, aimed at curbing the growth of fascist power, was also taken up as a policy by the MCP, and coincided with its ardent anti-Japanese movement. Having boosted the popularity of the MCP's so-called Popular Front, the Party resolved to struggle towards an eventual republic in Malaya.

After the Stalin-Hitler non-aggression pact was signed on 23rd August 1939, the MCP suddenly changed its earlier anti-imperialist and anti-fascist stance. Directives were sent out to cancel any strikes that might cut off or adversely affect the flow of strategic materials earmarked for fascist areas. Following the signing of the Tripartite Pact by Germany, Italy and Japan in September 1940, the MCP altered course once more, on orders from the Hong Kong branch of the

Communist Party. It discontinued all anti-British activity, and opposition to 'any campaign initiated by the Chinese community in Malaya to aid the British war effort'.[16]

When Nazi Germany invaded Russia in June 1941, and Russia became Britain's war-time ally, the MCP's party line and attitude altered once again. Its anti-fascist policy was vigorously renewed, noticeably excluding previous anti-imperialist aspects. The MCP still clandestinely adhered to its policy slogan — to 'Establish the Malayan Democratic Republic'.[17] This enabled the Party to retain a certain degree of flexibility with its own people. The Soviet Union, as an ally of Britain, had to be supported by the MCP, who offered in July 1941 to cooperate with the British, for local defence purposes in Malaya, in the event of a Japanese attack. This offer was conditional on democratic rights being granted to the people. The MCP would then suspend its anti-British policy and rally its forces behind Britain for any subsequent defence of the country.

Throughout the frequent changes in the MCP's party line between 1939 and 1941 it remained poised to take what advantage it could of any opportunity to expel Britain from Malaya. Its pro-British tack was, however, diametrically opposed to this and to the communists' long-term plans for struggle in the country.

16:5 MPAJA Origins — 101 STS

The MCP's exploratory overture in mid-1941 to cooperate with the British administration in Malaya was rebuffed out of hand. The British refused to compromise on their earlier stance to 'deal with the outlawed political factions in the Chinese community'.[18] This rejection arose from the view that employment of Asians in any defensive role at such a juncture would be an admission that enemy occupation of a British Colony was a possibility. It was considered this would have a demoralising effect on the people of Malaya.

On 8th December 1941, when Japan attacked northern Malaya, circumstances of the British and all Chinese — those within the MCP, supporters of the KMT, and others with no political leanings — were drastically altered. Ch'en Chia-keng, in charge of the MCP's anti-Japanese movement,

> 'recommended immediate armed resistance to the invader, exhorting his fellow-members to renew their pledges of assistance to the British authorities'.[19]

The Central Executive Committee of the MCP endorsed this proposal and the communists, along with other overseas Chinese organisations, volunteered their services and urged the government to allow the Chinese to form a military force to fight the Japanese.

In Singapore, 15 leading Chinese residents formed a non-political Anti-Japanese Mobilisation Committee under the chairmanship of industrialist Tan Kah-kee. They called for voluntary mobilisation of all overseas Chinese to form a Chinese militia force to assist the British in the defence of Singapore city. Tan Kah-kee — a prominent Chinese Nationalist Party member — agreed that all clique and party differences had to be cast aside. He worked closely with J.D. Dalley of the Malayan Police Special Branch to recruit Chinese volunteers into Dalforce, whose ranks included Kuomintang members, followers of other independent organisations, as well as the communists, who took an active role in the force. Dalforce members were untrained and ill-equipped. They fought bravely for four days in the mangrove swamps outside Singapore city, many of them armed only with staves, home-made clubs and kitchen cleavers. Many were killed, and after the surrender many more were summarily executed by the Japanese.

On 15th December 1941 the MCP's offer of assistance was accepted by the British and, as a measure of goodwill, leftist political prisoners and communist detainees were set free. The MCP publicly announced its support for the British authorities and, in concert with KMT supporters, both factions called on all Malayan Chinese to assist in defence activities. President Chiang Kai-Shek also appealed to all Chinese nationals in Malaya to rally behind Britain, and the Governor, Sir Shenton Thomas, lifted the ban previously outlawing the MCP and the KMT, as well as other Chinese associations.

On 18th December 1941, 'in a small upstairs room in a back street in Singapore',[20] a secret meeting was held between Lai Tek, the Secretary General of the MCP, a Chinese-speaking police officer (an authority on Chinese secret societies) and Major Spencer Chapman, the Deputy Commandant of the newly formed 101 Special Training School (101 STS) specialising in guerrilla warfare and sabotage.

An agreement was reached, with the MCP providing as many young Chinese as the 101 STS would accept for training, to fight as the British saw fit in European-led parties behind enemy lines. The subsequent calibre of these MCP-selected recruits was good, as was their enthusiasm and loyalty to the MCP, an aspect sorely underestimated by the British at that juncture.

Immediately after these negotiations, on 19th December 1941, the MCP formed its own sponsored Malayan Overseas Chinese Anti-Japanese Mobilisation Society (MOCAJMS), under the chairmanship of Ch'en Yang-ch'ing. Two days later, on the 21st, the MCP's Central Executive Committee gave formal approval to negotiations with the British. The MCP's underground efforts now concentrated on assisting the British to defend Malaya against the Japanese; arming all party members to wage an all-out war of resistance; wiping out all enemy agents, traitors and fifth columnists; and finally, resisting the Japanese occupation by means of planned terror activities and the formation of guerrilla groups.

Also on 21st December the first ten-day instruction course for 15 Chinese communists was hastily organised, and commenced at the 101 STS in Singapore. Lieut Colonel J.M. Gavin — a specialist in guerrilla warfare — commanded the school's instructional and operational departments, which had another 10 officers and 50 enlisted men on its staff, all specialists in various forms of para-military warfare. In the short time available, before 101 STS was closed down early in January 1942, 165 MCP-selected Chinese were hastily trained and graduated 'in the difficult art of guerrilla warfare'.[21] This nucleus of British-trained communists subsequently proved their worth, and many survived to form the hard core of the MPAJA, which grew to 7,000 during the three and a half years of Japanese occupation. They were joined by other guerrillas and by a few British and Australian soldiers left behind after Singapore surrendered. Many young Chinese — some only 19 years old — refused to be subject to the Japanese and joined the MPAJA.

The initial plan for European-led, Asian stay-behind parties was changed at the last minute. The speed of the Japanese advance demanded that as each class graduated, it had to be sent immediately into areas already occupied by the Japanese, to operate as an independent guerrilla resistance team. These guerrilla bands, often poorly equipped and left without any means of liaison with the British, were forced to resort to their own devices for survival. Many were bitter at having been left in this manner, and as the occupation progressed, they followed the dictates of the communists, as opposed to those of the British.

The first class of 15 men to graduate from 101 STS was sent near Kuala Lumpur. They were successful in causing limited disruption to Japanese lines of communication north of that area, and subsequently in the mountainous regions of northern Selangor. In March 1942, having liaised with the Central Committee of the MCP, they were formed officially into the First Independent Force of the MPAJA. The second class, totalling 35, was overrun by the Japanese as they reached Negeri Sembilan. They were then provided with additional weapons by the local British commander, but on 7th January were decisively routed while trying to raid police headquarters at Kuala Pilah. The MCP in mid-February designated this hapless band the Second Independent Force of the MPAJA, and despite continuous Japanese action against them, they recruited disgruntled union-minded labourers from tin mines in their area, increasing their strength to more than 160 during the first six months of the occupation. The third class of 60 graduates left Singapore on 20th January 1942. They operated in the mountainous jungle regions of north Johore and within a few months numbered some 360 men. They became the Third Independent Force of the MPAJA. The final classes of 101 STS infiltrated Japanese lines on 30th January 1942. They operated in the southern jungles of Johore, and within one year their numbers had increased to more than 250. They became the Fourth Independent Force of MPAJA.

The MCP's plans to go underground were finalised as British defences collapsed in Malaya. A policy of armed resistance throughout the occupation was declared by all top-ranking MCP members at a final meeting in Singapore in February 1942. This decision proved beneficial to the MCP's political and military advancement, as they were the only political organisation prepared to commit itself to a policy of active anti-Japanese insurgency. It gained for them large support among the Chinese in Malaya, who suffered most at the brutal hands of the Japanese.

16:6 Survival and Expansion

Japanese viciousness in imposing law and order, and especially their cruelty towards the Chinese during the 'Sook Chings', alienated the hearts of people. Many young Chinese, of both sexes, fled to live in the discomfort but relative safety of the jungle, where they endeavoured to keep out of the clutches of the Kempeitai, and to avenge the wrongs committed against them. Although MPAJA ranks were swelled by this untrained, vengeful tide, all units fared badly through the first one and a half years of the occupation, as people were too scared to help the guerrillas, and were often prevented from doing so by the tyranny of the Japanese. During this period an estimated one third were killed.

After the fall of Singapore resistance forces were cut off from any outside assistance. Their limited supply of motley weapons, equipment and ammunition had now to be used with added caution, as replacements were only obtainable by finding what had been discarded by retreating Allied forces, or in direct engagement with superior Japanese forces. The guerrillas' lack of training and experience added to their misfortune during initial raids on targets behind enemy lines, and following a brief period of offensive activity, these original MPAJA units became more defensive as they embarked on

> 'an all-out struggle for bare survival. In the first months of occupation, the jungle was an enemy as well as a protecting friend. Most of the Chinese guerrillas were ill-prepared, both mentally and physically, to live in the jungle, and the toll from disease, desertions, enemy attacks and insanity increased by the day.'[22]

Front-line battle-hardened Japanese troops were deployed early in the occupation in an all-out effort to eliminate them. At the end of 18 months, despite massive recruitment during the first few months, an estimated one-third of the entire guerrilla force was lost. Food shortages became critical and some units went for days without food except for what could be foraged from the jungle vegetation.

MPAJA guerrilla forces were drawn from the communists, KMT China-nationalists, outraged townsfolk and farmers, motivated by hatred and seeking revenge, and bandit elements, vagabonds and riff-raff, who enlisted only to get out of it what they could. The ranks of these assorted 'hill people', as they were familiarly called, were swelled by those whose homes had been ransacked by the Japanese, or whose wives, sisters and other female relatives had been raped. Some women also joined, especially those who had lost fathers, brothers, husbands, sons, or other family members. The rural Chinese hated the Japanese and were avid supporters of the guerrillas.

The average age of most guerrillas was between 18 and 22 years, while the officers, who were slightly better educated, were between 23 and 26. Only a few were older. They wore no specific uniforms and although some were in clean shirts and creased trousers, others were dressed like coolies. It was

> 'those who went out to the kampongs for food or on other work [who] dressed as smartly as possible, since at that time ragged Chinese were always suspected of being guerrillas. The girls wore the severe but attractive black Chinese blouse and trousers, had their hair bobbed, and used no make-up.'[23]

From mid-1942 MPAJA's Supreme Command was in the hands of a Central Military Committee of the MCP. The chairman was Liu Yao. Parallel with this initial arrangement, every State had its own Military Affairs Committee, and each regiment was allocated its own political commissar. The political commissars were normally second-in-command in MPAJA units, although they were invariably senior in the party hierarchy to the unit's military commander. They took direct charge of all political training and education, and also attended to all non-military problems. Guerrillas in jungle camps were given lectures on party politics, and educational courses including theories of communism, international affairs and MCP policies. They were also required to participate in 'self-criticism' sessions. The political commissars' approach to sensitive human and racial issues was one of indifference. MCP statements were always prepared in Chinese, as most of the guerrillas — 95% being Chinese — could not speak Malay.

Political commissars often exceeded their authority, encroaching upon military matters and thereby clashing with their military counterparts.

The initial chain-of-command was abolished by the end of 1942, after a disastrous Japanese ambush at Batu Caves in Selangor, in which more than half of the political commissars were killed. Thereafter the system of Party command was handed over to a three-man Central Military Committee: Lai Tek, the Secretary General of the MCP; Chin Peng, the Perak State Secretary; and Lau Yeh (Liu Yao), who was the Chairman. The location of the triumvirate's headquarters — 'The Plen' — was hidden somewhere in Pahang. Their extensive controls directed all subsequent MPAJA guerrilla activities in the jungle, as well as those of political workers and local urban party cells. After this any liaison between different MPAJA regiments in the jungle was forbidden, with every communication having to pass through the 'Plen'.

* * * * * *

Mystery surrounds the pre-war activities of Lai Tek, and the role he subsequently played did much to discredit the MCP and MPAJA. He was sent first to Singapore by the Comintern as its trusted agent, with instructions to deal with the rift in the leadership of the MCP. He was successful and purged the Party of its radical hard-liners, duly assuming leadership as Secretary General. Lai Tek was Vietnamese in origin and had lived for a while in China. Before the war he was also a triple agent, planted in the MCP by British Special Branch, having worked previously for both the Russians and the French in Indo-China. The French passed him over to the British, describing him as a very useful sort of fellow. By 1939 Lai Tek had organised an effective cell system throughout Malaya. He was then unanimously elected as Secretary General of the MCP, a post he held throughout the Japanese occupation, and until 1947.

Lai Tek's activities became suspect after his rumoured involvement in the Batu Caves disaster in Selangor. Some survivors believed that following his arrest in Singapore in April 1942 by Major Onishi of the Kempeitai,

> 'Lai Tek had actually concluded an informal "live and let live" agreement with local Japanese intelligence officers'[24]

and had agreed to work for them. In August 1942 he avoided arrest when the Japanese raided a full session of the Central Committee of the MCP, as he was late in arriving for the meeting. These arrests conveniently left Lai Tek as the sole important communist official in Singapore.

The Batu Caves killings on 1st September 1942 brought the political commissar problem within MPAJA to a head. Many of those killed had begun to query Lai Tek's policies, and contemplated opposing him. The events leading to the pre-dawn raid and betrayal are not clear, but subsequently some have thought that Lai Tek informed on the conference venue to the Japanese. This raid certainly helped Lai Tek to purge antagonistic elements in the Party, leaving the path open for him to act as he chose.

The communists were completely taken by surprise. Ninety-two of them were killed, 22 from the Central Executive Committee. Among those reportedly killed were half the political commissars, including

> 'Hsiao Chung, a member of the Central Committee; Chu Wei, political commissar of the Fourth Independent Force; Ho Fu, Commander of the Fourth Independent Force; Hsiao Cheng, member of the Selangor committee of the Malaya Communist Party; Ch'en Shu, political commissar of the Second Independent Force; Hsu Tu-piao, political commissar of the First Independent Force'.[25]

Many other influential party members were also killed, effectively curtailing subsequent activities of political commissars in the MPAJA.

There are conflicting opinions on who was to blame for this shattering set-back to the Party's hierarchy. There may have been inadequate secrecy in organising important meetings, weaknesses within MPAJA organisation, inadequate military training for the guerrillas, or an overall inability of MPAJA leaders to formulate sound military planning.

Suspicion about Lai Tek increased after the Batu Caves incident, but his betrayal of the location was not proven. He continued to disappear at will for long periods, during which his spies and informants kept him fully appraised of Party and MPAJA happenings, while he maintained his connections with Major Onishi. Lai Tek's actions weakened the MCP both organisationally and militarily. The Party's Central Committee became increasingly ineffective, with most decisions and powers diverted from them and concentrated in Lai Tek's hands. Such was his control in September 1945 that he emerged with the reputation of being the brilliant organiser who had held the Party together during the occupation, and the one responsible for its growth and prestige.

* * * * * *

MCP propaganda did not give the impression of being anti-British, although it still retained a definite anti-imperialist slant. Early in the occupation some guerrilla leaders showed more interest in planning the establishment of a Republic of Malaya than fighting the Japanese. Public speaking was the communist means of persuading thousands of predominantly Chinese peasants — but also some Malays — that oppressors should justifiably be murdered in the cause of vengeance. The ill-repute gained by the guerrillas could have been avoided had their speeches not concealed their deception and heartless disregard in pursuing their aims.

During 1942 the MPAJA had just over 70 Allied soldiers in its ranks. These were mainly stragglers bypassed in the retreat southwards, but also included some sent intentionally behind enemy lines, who had joined the small, Chinese, stay-behind guerrilla parties after Singapore had fallen. By the end of 1942 only ten of the original group of stay-behind British officers remained scattered over different parts of the peninsula with various guerrilla units, and they seemingly never took command. They were used to provide weapon training and to write training manuals. Invariably they were not informed of the guerrillas' activities outside their immediate areas, and some were held under protective watch which restricted their movements. Major Chapman met Chin Peng, the liaison officer between Perak headquarters and the outside, as early as March 1942. He was the 'first

English-speaking contact among the guerrillas at Tanjong Malim'.[26] He

> 'never met the unit commanders as such, but worked through secondary liaison officers, men who he continued to believe were, in fact, the real commanders. . . . he later wrote in his excellent narrative, *The Jungle is Neutral*, that attempts made by him to learn Chinese were deliberately frustrated: each daily lesson was given in a different dialect!'[27]

The Fifth Independent Force originated from an isolated band of Chinese who fled Japanese urban oppression in Perak during the British retreat. These 70 guerrillas, after a brief spate of successful action against the Japanese, contacted the Perak Military Affairs Committee of the MCP and came under communist influence and control. They originally operated from a mountain base called Chu-Mao Mountain, (named after Chu Teh and Mao Tse-tung, the Chinese communist leaders) and were established as the notorious Fifth Independent Force of MPAJA in December 1942. Their purpose was to kill traitors, whose numbers had increased alarmingly throughout the year. Independent killer squads of approximately ten men sought out suspects and dispatched them in a variety of ways. In due course similar squads were incorporated into all MPAJA units. In the latter part of the occupation the MPAJA's

> 'traitor-killing programme . . . more often than not took precedence over guerrilla action . . . against the Japanese'.[28]

Guerrilla killer squads from all units reportedly murdered 2,542 supposed traitors, a number equal to the Japanese killed or wounded during the war in Malaya. The Fifth Regiment did this on a larger scale than other regiments and in a more professional manner. They were credited with the assassination of numerous suspected traitors, among them Chinese community leaders who were heads of the Japanese-sponsored Overseas Chinese Association (OCA). They were regarded in particular by the guerrillas as arch-collaborators and traitors, and were prime targets for elimination.

By the Autumn of 1943 a larger, better trained and more experienced guerrilla organisation emerged, compared to the force that had originally taken on the might of the Japanese in the jungles in early 1942. By this time the Sixth Independent Force had been raised, and was predominantly involved in propaganda and political work, and training guerrilla cadres. The People's Academy in Pahang, which gave potential officer candidates a two-month course, came under the command of the Sixth Independent Force, and its commandant, Ch'en Kuang, a graduate of the 8th Route Army's Guerrilla School in Yenan, China. It patterned training programmes on tactics already used by communists in China. Platoon level officers were not well trained and many lacked initiative and incentive. This shortage of good officer material became more critical as the occupation progressed and became the 'weakest link in the guerrilla set-up'.[29]

By late 1943 many of the hardened front-line Japanese soldiers had been replaced by secondary occupational forces. These proved to be less successful in organising and executing large-scale counter-actions against the guerrillas. The MCP's political propaganda meanwhile made significant inroads among the people, in what was referred to by them as a 'period of political struggle'.[30] The masses were generally more sympathetic towards the MPAJA, who depended more on them for food, supplies and intelligence, as well as a source of potential recruits. This period of political enlightenment, which continued until the end of 1944, nurtured a four-fold increase in the ranks of MPAJA, with tens of thousands increasingly sympathetic to their activities and ambitions. At State level the Peoples' Anti-Japanese Federation was established to maintain a link between the guerrillas in the jungle, the underground party organisation and the people. In each State clandestine party committees worked tirelessly on behalf of the guerrillas, as did others at local and municipal levels. People's Representative Congresses at State level assisted with communications, intelligence and finance, and a Military Affairs Committee in each State concentrated on important functions such as recruitment, liaison and other connected activities.

The main link and support organisation backing MPAJA in the areas in which it operated was the Malayan People's Anti-Japanese Union (MPAJU). This was a strong if loosely organised collection of Chinese squatters and villagers, held together by varying degrees of anti-Japanese sentiment in villages and towns. Members were not necessarily communists, coming from a wide cross-section of the public. Once recruited, however, they were required by intermediaries in their respective areas to maintain contact with both the MCP and MPAJA.

MPAJU was of considerable assistance in raising funds, collecting food, fighting equipment and intelligence and their members also acted as guides to assist MPAJA patrols when they entered unfamiliar areas. The organisation also assisted by recruiting all races and classes of people, irrespective of religion and united only by their opposition to Japanese rule.

The communists

> 'operated an efficient intelligence network in the villages and towns, and usually picked their targets for elimination with accuracy'.[31]

Contact was made with policemen, government officials and local defence volunteer units to obtain information to assist the guerrillas. This was only a partial success, as these sources were constantly fearful of reprisals by the Japanese administration, and their terror tactics. Occasionally however, sufficient information was obtained about the activities of military and civil police, and other government and Kaisha department officials, assisting the guerrillas to organise ambushes and killings. Jungle news bulletins were also secretly brought into towns, aimed at correcting the false information constantly published in the Domei Agency controlled newspapers. Of necessity, the position of district officers, village chiefs and local government officials was compromised, as they did their best to keep aloof from both the MPAJA and the MPAJU. Many among them did become unpopular with Malays and non-Malays alike. The Malays looked on MPAJA as a Chinese-dominated organisation ostensibly used

> 'as a weapon of terror and intimidation resorted to by the local Chinese to avenge themselves against any abuses of authority or excesses of Japanese officials and their subordinate Malay staff'.[32]

MPAJA recruited manpower by organising volunteer units, Ho Pi Tui (Reserves) in every village, town and district. The majority of these were Chinese, with a few Indians and Malays. They were not required to leave their local areas unless they were called up. After a two-month course in the jungle, they were sent back to their villages and left under the control of village elders or other trusted community representatives to provide self-defence in the villages. Instead many degenerated into 'gangs of robbers and bandits, given to rape, looting and terrorism'.[33] Other roving gangs of bandits also formed resistance groups, arming themselves with discarded weapons, including

> 'Chinese criminal gangs or secret societies known variously as Samseng Tong, or Hong Mun, specialising in "protection" rackets. Some of these gangs were converted by the MPAJA and joined the Ho Pi Tui. However, most continued to exist on their own, claiming to be "Anti-Japanese Forces", MPAJA or KMT in whatever manner suited their best interests at the time.'[34]

16:7 Force 136 and the MPAJA

Force 136 was part of a Special Operations Executive. Its purpose was to disrupt enemy government activity in occupied territories. It was therefore essential to establish some form of direct contact with guerrillas or other resistance groups in areas targetted for liberation. In July 1942 the Malayan Country Section, or Group B of Force 136, was activated for this purpose in Malaya, under the leadership of Lieut-Colonel Basil Goodfellow.

When Malaya was overrun, some British guerrilla specialists on the instructional staff of 101 STS realised that if Singapore surrendered, the whole area would lose all intelligence communications. Instead of going into the jungle with other 101 STS staff and stay-behind groups, they set up an escape route. They acquired a small steamer which took them via Java to Ceylon, eventually arriving at Colombo in April 1942. Colonel Richard N. Broome of the Malayan Civil Service, and John L.W. Davis, a former officer in the FMS police — both Chinese speaking, and close friends — were among those who escaped in this manner. They duly became attached as advisers to the Malayan Country Section of Force 136.

This force initiated a detailed study of available expert information on Japanese occupied Malaya, as a precursor to an eventual Allied return. Progress was slow, frustrated by a lack of up-to-date information on current conditions. Eight months later, in October 1942, the first news of the ordeal and massacre of thousands of Chinese reached Force 136 headquarters. It was only then realised that the morale of the Chinese, despite cruel reprisals against them, had remained high. They had not been subjugated, retaining their resolve to resist the Japanese in any way possible.

> 'Even the Malays, who had bowed to the Japanese occupation, now saw the rottenness of their new overlords.'[35]

This information was verified during the interrogation of a Chinese, who had escaped from Singapore via Penang, and had then followed a dangerous overland route through Japanese occupied territory.

Force 136 recognised some subsequent agreement with MPAJA guerillas was possible to provide mutual active support. Contact had first to be made with them. Broome and Davis, familiar with the country and fluent in Chinese, were selected to be sent to Malaya to contact the guerrillas and gather whatever information was available from them. They were instructed to live in the jungle with the guerrillas, and to radio back any information. They were also instructed to contact the supposedly European-led, stay-behind parties, and to pave the way for agents, arms, medicines and other essential military requirements to be smuggled in or air dropped into the country in due course. They went first to Calcutta to find suitable Chinese recruits to accompany and assist them on their mission. Here they met Lim Bo Seng.

* * * * * *

Lim Bo Seng was a Straits-born Singapore Chinese businessman and an ardent KMT supporter. He was an agent for the Chinese Nationalist government in Chungking, and outspoken in his anti-Japanese opinions. He and his brother had been liaison officers in the Civil Defence office in Singapore, and had worked tirelessly during the six weeks before Singapore fell, to keep what labour there was at their place of work. Lim had previously been of immense assistance to British business interests when trouble broke out at Japanese-owned iron mines in north Malaya, and would certainly have been on their black list. Although he and his family could have evacuated, Lim Bo Seng chose to stay in Singapore, where he courageously served with the Dalforce volunteers. It was only on 1st February 1942, when administrative chaos overtook Singapore, that he and his family were given permission to leave. They did so on the 7th, and reached Sumatra safely.

Lim Bo Seng volunteered to join the Force 136 Malayan unit and offered to go to Chungking, to recruit ex-Malayan and Straits-born Chinese prepared to return to Malaya and have another crack at the Japanese. It was agreed that Force 136 would train any volunteers for two months as radio operators and interpreters, before dispatching them into Malaya as members of British-led liaison teams, where they would operate in areas occupied by the guerrillas.

In Chungking Lim Bo Seng obtained the consent of Chiang Kai-shek to provide the British with prospective trainees. The politically astute Chiang, however, arranged that those selected were all

> 'trusted members of the Kuomintang – men whom the British officers expected to use as key liaison personnel with the Communist guerrillas in the jungle'![36]

* * * * * *

An initial 'in-and-out' reconnaissance sortie was made by Davis (then Colonel) and five carefully selected and trained KMT agents. They landed on the west coast of Malaya from a Dutch submarine in the early hours of 24th May 1943. By June Davis was back in India, leaving the Chinese to settle in and make what arrangements they could for more Europeans to be received there. British planners were unaware that the

> 'so-called "united front" between the Communists and Nationalists . . . had long since reached the breaking point and Kuomintang men were received with hostility in Communist-dominated guerrilla regions'. [37]

In August, 'Gustavas 1', the first official landing, was made by a Force 136 liaison team led by Davis, accompanied this time by Broome, Lim Bo Seng and four other Chinese agents. They were dropped by submarine off the Perak coast and paddled ashore in folding canvas boats, landing near Tanjong Hantu (Ghost Point) just north of Pangkor Island. More landings were made in a similar manner in operations 'Gustavas' 2, 3 and 4, the last one being on 12th September 1943. It was only on 30th September, however, that first contact was made with Chin Peng, the Secretary of the MCP, and the second-ranking communist leader in Malaya at that time.

* * * * * *

In 1942 Chin Peng, alias Wong Ping or CTP, was a young Hokkien, and ardent admirer of Lai Tek. Chin Peng, Lee Fah, an intelligent English-speaking Chinese, and Itu were 'the three alleged leaders of the Perak guerrillas'.[38] In addition to his work as the Perak State Secretary of the MCP, Chin Peng was also responsible for liaison between Perak headquarters and the various camps within the state, and with general headquarters located somewhere in Selangor. As such, he was grossly overworked and invariably sickly.

* * * * * *

On Christmas day 1943, having lived for two difficult and dangerous years in the Malayan jungle, Spencer Chapman met Davis and Broome at the Blantan camp on the Perak/Pahang border. He was informed of Force 136's existence and purpose, and that some instructional staff from 101 STS had escaped and been absorbed into it. Little, however, could be accomplished by the British-led liaison teams until some form of binding agreement had been drawn up with the guerrillas.

On 30th December 1943, and on New Year's Day 1944, Davis and Chapman, representing Southeast Asia Command (SEAC) in Malaya, conferred cautiously with Lai Tek, Chin Peng and Chang Hung, all representing the supreme command of MPAJA. Lim Bo Seng was also present at these meetings as an interpreter. It was agreed that MPAJA guerrillas would cooperate with, and accept orders from, Force 136 liaison officers while the war against Japan lasted, and for any period after that during which a British military occupation of the country was in force. In return MPAJA would be supplied with 2,000 weapons, finances, medical supplies and other necessary equipment as soon as this could be arranged. If more than 2,000 weapons were needed to equip them fully, these would have to be obtained by raiding police stations and Japanese military posts. Training would also be given to the guerrillas to help them in their struggle. Financing would be 150 taels of gold monthly, equivalent to £3,000, not as wages, but as a provision for food and upkeep expenses. MPAJA's insignia – the three stars (*bintang tiga*) – would represent the three major races in the country.

It was also agreed that at the conclusion of hostilities, when Japan had been defeated, all weapons supplied by Force 136 would be promptly handed back, and all guerrillas would return to normal civilian life.

An important aspect of these discussions was a pledge that during this military liaison, 'no questions of post-war policy were to be discussed'.[39] This was a missed opportunity by the MCP, betraying a lack of understanding of communist policies outside the country. Arming guerrillas under British control was part of a policy to prepare them to assist in any future allied invasion of Malaya. However, this agreement did not deter the MCP from its earlier professed intention of turning Malaya into a communist republic state after the Japanese had been beaten.

Mutual trust had to be integral to these agreements and in all plans devised in deep jungle camps for any action taken prior to the return of the British. However, as most Chinese with Force 136 were Kuomintang members, the communists were wary, which contributed in part to their unwillingness to cooperate.

> 'In many cases, the liaison officers met with everything from mild toleration to open resentment on the part of the guerrillas. Intelligence gathering, one of the prime functions of Force 136 personnel, was kept at a minimum and only scanty information was supplied by the reluctant guerrillas.'[40]

From January until November 1944 wireless contact with Force 136 headquarters in Colombo or with SEAC in Calcutta was impossible. During this period the terms of the agreement could not be set in motion. Davis, Broome and Chapman were reduced to mere guests of the guerrillas, depending on them for their very existence. It was a humiliating period, but was accepted by most of the guerrillas. Colombo presumed that the three Europeans had been lost. At the end of March 1944 Lim Bo Seng was captured by the Japanese. He later died in prison, when he was only 37.

The year of inactivity was marked by boredom, frustration and illness. Medicines, especially quinine, were difficult to obtain, and scarcity of food caused considerable weight loss. Illness hampered the Europeans' attempts to gain the confidence of the guerrillas; inactivity brought with it a depressing feeling of impotence. Evasive tactics, rather than taunting the now weakened Japanese caretaker forces by acts of sabotage, became a distasteful if wise policy. It avoided brutal recriminations against innocent people in neighbourhoods where raids occurred. Some of the Chinese undoubtedly resented this decision and, not surprisingly, showed openly that they had 'lost every shred of faith in the British!'[41] They felt they were being let down and did not hesitate to say so.

There was a little friction among the Europeans; the difficult jungle camp conditions, illness, hunger and the frustration of being unable to assist the war effort were humiliating enough. Early morning tempers in camp were invariably edgy, especially after a cold, wet and uncomfortable night. Davis would not speak to anyone until after he had had his coffee. His forthright character was in contrast to Broome's delightful wit, but as party leader he was frustrated by the delays, and frequently annoyed by Broome's indolence. Broome would

> 'go off a suitable distance into the jungle and either play his home-made flute or sing Gilbert and Sullivan and other songs to himself . . . He had an excellent baritone voice and seemed to be able to remember both the words and tune of any song he had ever heard . . . Davis only knew two songs: "Nine Green Bottles" and "The Drunken Sailor" . . . and if he forgot the words there were plenty of prompters, as all the Chinese soon learned to sing them, though they had not the faintest idea of the meaning.'[42]

* * * * * *

The Chinese in Malaya, natural conspirators, wanted to oppose the Japanese in any way they could, provided no harm came to their families. Their capacity for subtle obstruction was cloaked by outward compliance. They appeared cooperative, but worked against the Japanese all the time. Even among the most disreputable and complicit elements of the Chinese community, there was probably no one who did not 'secretly hate and despise the "barbarian dwarf".'[43] Chinese ingenuity and resourcefulness were most destructive when applied to hindering authority. Ignorance of their language was turned into an effective tool. When generous, a Chinese was at his most dangerous, hospitality invariably implying eventual investment! They always attach importance to remembering a kindness, considering ingratitude a mortal sin. '. . . if a debt is not paid in this incarnation, it will have to be paid in a future one.'[44]

'Privacy was of little importance to the Chinese in guerilla camps, except when it involved public nudity. If someone hurt himself, they would laugh infuriatingly — even the victim, who might have shot himself in the foot, or gouged his knee with a parang! Monopoly was a popular game and they would shout and scream so loudly that it was quite impossible . . . to play any other game or even to read!'[45]

* * * * * *

In late 1944 the new Mark 4 Liberator bombers brought Malaya within flight range of India and Colombo. It then became possible to plan for air supply of men and stores. This continued for the duration of the war. Prior to this, only old Catalina flying boats were able to reach Malaya from bases in India, providing they flew in favourable weather conditions. Two Dutch submarines were also occasionally available, as both were normally deployed against Japanese ships. With such limited resources, entry into the shallow, mine-infested Malacca Straits was an extremely high-risk exercise.

On 20th December 1944 a British party was landed on the Johore coast. They were contacted by the British members of Force 136 and asked to send a radio message to Colombo, which was subsequently transmitted on 1st February 1945. After one year's silence, the broadcast was at first suspected of having been made under duress, but once its authenticity was clear, both Davis and Chapman were told that they had been awarded the Distinguished Service Order (DSO). Broome was required to prepare a full report of activities in Malaya, while Chapman was told to remain with the guerrillas and liaise with them further on behalf of the Allies. Davis was instructed to remain at the guerrillas' headquarters.

The first of many air drops began in December and between then and August 1945, these totalled more than 1,000. Five hundred and ten men and £1.5 million of equipment and supplies were parachuted into Malaya's mountainous jungle ranges, to prepare for the intended Allied invasion. Two pre-war MCS officers – Derek Headly and D.A. Sommerville – returned in this manner and others returned by submarine or flying boat. Fifty wireless sets were dropped to supply day and night information to SEAC HQs, and more than 3,500 Chinese were fully armed. Thousands of others lived and waited in reserve in the towns. Many other guerrillas, however, remained outside the sphere and influence of Force 136.

Among these were three groups of armed KMT guerrillas totalling approximately 400. They operated in the northern part of Malaya, in the Perak Hulu and Kelantan areas in a loosely organised Overseas Chinese Anti-Japanese Army (OCAJA), identified as the 'One Star Army'. Their leader was a gunman named Lee Foong Sam, and although none of these groups were armed by Force 136, they did receive some supplies from them. The MPAJA guerrillas looked on the KMT guerrillas as bandits

> 'who resorted to looting, extortion and intimidation of the local population; and the KMT guerrillas considered the MPAJA as communists to whom they were politically opposed'.[46]

Both equally distrusted the Malays!

To J.K. Creer, a pre-war District Officer at Kuala Trengganu and the only MCS member to stay in Malaya for the duration of the occupation, it was plain that

> 'the MCP were just as anti-British as they were anti-Japanese . . . To their KMT rivals they were at first seductive, and if this failed they became utterly ruthless, torturing captives and killing men, women and children in raids on the camps of any who dared to oppose them. The KMT were no less tough . . . But they were more human. They lacked the fanaticism of the MCP.'[47]

Creer tried to intervene in the MCP attacks against the KMT guerrillas. He arranged that both should sign an agreement committing them to a policy of peaceful cooperation. The KMT agreed to recognise the newly named AJUF's efforts to resist the Japanese throughout Malaya, except in Perak Hulu and Kelantan, where they wanted to retain their own influence. Colombo condoned Creer's proposed agreements, but to his utter dismay, refused to provide the KMT guerrillas with arms. The MCP signed the agreement, but obviously had no intention of abiding by its terms.

By February 1945 Force 136 had extended its activities and several British-led parties had been dropped into different parts of the country, with instructions to contact the various Chinese and Malay resistance groups. Only then was Force 136 made fully aware of the agreement made one year earlier between British officers and MPAJA.

In early April Major Jim Hannah — a good friend of Broome — led in a party in which Broome's pre-war house boy was a qualified wireless operator. A meeting was arranged with the guerrillas on 16th April 1945, at which previous cautious feelings were replaced by understanding and cordiality. It was obvious 'that the Plen had come from his headquarters with instructions to "get on with the war",'[48] and no bargaining or written agreements were needed to do this. Arrangements were speedily concluded to provide arms and training for 3,500 Chinese guerrillas, enabling them to take part in the Allied invasion of Malaya as soon as it started.

As regular air drops of men and supplies increased, British prestige was dramatically enhanced, as was the morale of the guerrillas in their jungle camps. In April Broome had to be ordered out of Malaya for health reasons, and Chapman accompanied him. Davis remained until Japan's sudden capitulation.

16:8 Malay Resistance and Force 136

Malays were harshly exploited by the Japanese during the occupation. As their economic and social difficulties mounted, many became disillusioned with Japan's policies and lack of morals. Some Malays joined resistance movements, and some later became notable political figures in the post-war, and pre-independence years.

Until May 1944 SEAC had no direct communication with Malays in the country. Only in the closing stages of the war, coinciding with heightened suspicion of the MCP's post-war political intent, did a change of heart occur among the British. They shelved their inherent distrust of the Malays sufficiently to help set up two Malay resistance groups — the Wataniah (Fatherland) in Pahang, and the Askar Melayu Setia (AMS) (Loyal Malay Army), located in north Perak. Both organisations were confined to collecting information rather than actual fighting, as their security arrangements were not considered adequate.

Lieut-Colonel Richardson was the Force 136 liaison officer of the Wataniah. Dato Yeop Mahyuddin, the commanding officer, and a platoon commander named Abdul Razak, later destined to become the second prime minister of Malaysia in 1969, were other Wataniah officers of note.

The first contact that Force 136 made with the AMS was in north Perak in December 1944, in an operation led by Major Dobree. He found them

> 'only too enthusiastic to take up arms against the Japanese and had to discourage many from joining him'.[49]

Ironically, it was only belatedly realised that the

> 'history of postwar Malaya would have been very different had the British created more Malay guerrilla forces . . . to fight the Japanese'.[50]

Two Malays who gave valuable service to SEAC during this period were Mohammed Suffian bin Hashim — destined to become Lord President — and twenty-two year old Lieutenant Ibrahim bin Ismail, who later became Tan Sri General, and the Chief of the Malaysian Armed Forces Staff. Force 136 officers reported obtaining good support from both organisations, but very few Malay guerrillas became involved in the predominantly Chinese MPAJA. At no time did the Malay guerrillas in MPAJA exceed 500.

It was indeed a breakthrough for the MCP that some Malays were recruited into MPAJA. This was largely due to oppressive conditions during the occupation, plus 'the fact that the British were supporting the communists, and the Malays were keen to identify themselves on the side of the Allies'.[51]

Many Malays resented MPAJA. Those in any position of authority were threatened by both the Japanese and the Chinese. Distrust increased communal tension, which became manifest during the last six months of the occupation when retributive action was brutally carried out against suspected Malay collaborators and informers, with a total disregard for Islamic ethics and values. When racial violence erupted in August and September 1945 many Malays left MPAJA and the MCP. The degeneration of the Interregnum into a 14 day period of terror was the determining factor that alienated them. In later years the MCP went out of its way — with some success — to win back the support of the Malays. By June 1948 when the Emergency was declared, they had recruited more than 1,000 of them.

16:9 Racial Conflict and Revenge Killings

MCP policy during the Japanese occupation initially advocated maintaining good relations with people in rural areas, considering it essential to their long term aims. They assisted villagers and jungle-fringe dwellers whenever they could, and made a point of paying for anything provided for them. At first MPAJA guerrillas lived near the numerous Chinese squatters on the jungle fringes, but when cruel Japanese reprisals during retaliatory raids inflicted increasing hardship and casualties on the squatters, the guerrillas gradually withdrew into the main jungle ranges. Many Chinese squatters followed them into the jungle, where they continued to eke out an existence.

The brutality of Japanese reprisal raids subdued many villagers, so cutting off the guerrillas' life-line support. This forced the guerrillas to retaliate against Japanese patrols and also those villagers intimidated against them. Remote villages and small towns suspected of collaborating with the Japanese were raided, the inhabitants brutally assaulted and ruthlessly killed. Malay villages were prime targets for these vengeance raids, with foodstuff forcibly taken from them as a form of retaliatory taxation.

Although small numbers of Malays were reluctantly accepted into MPAJA, from early 1942 the Chinese guerrillas started to distrust them in general when reports were circulated about Malay villagers betraying the locations of MPAJA camps to the Japanese. From then on

> 'the attitude of the MCP and the MPAJU/MPAJA leaders was that Malays were "unreliable", if not downright "treacherous" . . . In every reported Japanese raid on MPAJA hideouts, Japanese troops were led by Malay guides and informers (and, in some instances, by both Malay and Indian guides). These Malay guides and informers would often help the Japanese to execute or torture Chinese victims.'[52]

Malays as the majority race in the country were used by the Japanese in police and various volunteer forces. They were also purposely used to suppress MPAJA and other resistance forces and guerrillas. There were many incidents of abuse of authority and unwarranted bullying by Malay policemen in search parties on the outskirts of towns. They pilfered goods and indecently manhandled women during searches, molesting them further if they protested. Such behaviour exacerbated the general dislike of the police by the Chinese. The eventual retributive action of the guerillas against the police in general and numerous specific detectives was considered by many, therefore, to be justified.

By the end of 1943, when economic hardship had increased and the Japanese showed less interest in the welfare of Malays, some did attempt to foster a more cordial relationship with the MPAJU and MPAJA, with limited success. In contrast to this, relationships continued to deteriorate with District Officers (DOs) and other minor community leaders, as they were

> 'used to requisition labour for Japanese government and military projects, as well as to collect rice and other commodities in their areas for the Japanese army'.[53]

These later became a main target for MPAJA reprisals and recriminatory killings. Their lack of any real authority was despised, while their actions were interpreted as a betrayal of trust. To many Malays the war was a Japanese and MPAJA Chinese affair, with Malay villagers regrettably caught up in the middle. MPAJA guerrillas forced them to provide men, information, food and money out of the meagre resources of their already impoverished villages. The guerrillas imposed their will, in direct contrast to the unfortunate Malay officials who had no real power under the Japanese administration. MPAJA's interference with DOs' and their subordinates' dealings with people caused strong resentment. The Japanese allowed communal tension to develop. It was inevitable that racial clashes would be the final outcome.

The first clashes between Malays and Chinese erupted in February 1945 at Batu Pahat in Johore. Several Chinese were killed, and MPAJA guerrillas immediately retaliated by burning down some Malay villages and executing their headmen. The Malays in turn took their revenge on any Chinese in the vicinity. The Japanese at first stood aside, appearing to support the Malay killing of hundreds of Chinese and the destruction and looting of several hundred Chinese homes. After this inter-racial feelings deteriorated, with future lines of racial battle indelibly drawn. By 1945 the Chinese MPAJA guerrillas no longer wanted assistance from the Malays. Having managed so far without them, they felt they could do without them in the future! The MCP, however, continued to try to disguise the extent of racial bitterness, still advocating a policy of multi-racial unity.

MPAJA killer squads sought out and ruthlessly killed collaborators of all races. Any Chinese guerrilla taken prisoner by the Japanese and suspected of cooperating with them in the slightest degree was later hunted down and murdered by killer squads, as were those Chinese who had flocked to join the guerrillas initially, only to become disillusioned later and to turn informer. In many instances they were tortured before being finished off in prepared graves.

Japanese violence engendered an atmosphere of brutality which spread into all walks of life and tempted some to settle old arguments and grudges violently. The communist guerrillas meted out cruel punishments, similar to those inflicted by the Kempeitai, on proven or merely suspected informers and collaborators. A climate of fear and hatred spread throughout the country.

For the Malays it was a bitter experience.

> 'The psychological fermentation of mistrust, anger, and frustration of the Malays stemming from insults, scorn and arrogance thrown upon them, had to reach its saturation at a point in time.'[54]

The forcible imposition of taxes and extraction of information and supplies was part of the offensive behaviour of the Chinese guerillas. Young able-bodied men and women were abducted to work in guerrilla camp kitchens, and some Malay women were molested and kept as mistresses. There were rumours of pigs slaughtered in mosques and of Malays forced to eat them. Many Malay policemen, penghulus and government officials were cruelly tortured and killed without trial, on the slightest suspicion of collaboration. Even their wives and children were similarly butchered or executed.

The elite Malays who had collaborated with the Japanese were naturally fearful of MPAJA's harsh recriminatory measures. When Malays were murdered and mutilated in a manner contrary to Islamic precepts concerning the treatment of the dead, resentment spread rapidly, uniting all classes of Malays against the predominantly Chinese MPAJA.

> '... general distrust of Malays, their refusal to give Malays an equal role in the movement, and their failure to ensure that reprisals against Malay officials were carried out only by Malays were all construed as examples of Chinese chauvinism and Chinese political attempts aimed at dominating the Malays and their country.'[55]

Only a spark was now needed to provoke violent conflict between them. One

> 'special Traitor Killing Squad in the jungle near Ipoh ... was credited with killing over 1,000 people of all races, mainly by descending on the towns and villages and picking out its victims in houses, coffee shops or police posts. The killer-squad was never given away to the Japanese by witnesses.'[56]

Killing collaborators and traitors was always done by guerrillas from the jungle and not by their supporters in towns and villages, as these were too vulnerable to discovery.

Chinese headed the list of victims, closely followed by Sikhs, Malays, Japanese, and lastly, Tamils. The methods used were varied, inventive and always brutal. Various weapons were used, some of them makeshift — grenades to tommyguns, changkols to bare hands!

One member of a killer-squad was reputed to have 150 killings to his credit. He had been wounded three times, tortured twice, and captured by the Japanese on five separate occasions.

> 'His parents, wife and two children had all been killed by the Japs; of his six brothers and sisters, two had simply disappeared and the rest were in guerrilla camps in Pahang . . . he was not the least interested in the Communist's scheme for a Malayan Republic, as he thought the Chinese and Malays would never get on together without the help of the British.'[57]

An 'interregnum' followed Japan's capitulation on 15th August 1945, during which MPAJA guerrillas launched unprecedented terror throughout the country. Although there were only two reported cases of guerrillas attacking Japanese forces in strength during this period, there were numerous clashes with the Japanese-trained, and despised Malay police. This was undoubtedly fermented by the commanders of withdrawing Japanese troops as a final gesture to antagonise racial feelings in the country. Police stations were taken over, as were district offices. Guerrillas went on a rampage of murder and robbery in Malay villages. Gangs of bandits also took advantage of the chaos to embark on their own campaigns of terror, demanding protection money in exchange for worthless protection certificates.

One of these gangs operated in this manner in the Ampang district of Kuala Lumpur from late 1944. Their activities enraged the MPAJA whose name they used. Following Japan's surrender, this gang changed its name to the Kee Tong (in Hokkien meaning Public Service) guerrillas, and cunningly negotiated a settlement of cooperation with MPAJA. Under this pretence they pursued their illegal activities until they were later disbanded by the British police.

Sporadic outbreaks of fighting also occurred between MPAJA guerrillas and a few non-communist guerrilla units. Violent clashes were reported in north Perak and Kedah against the small Malay guerrilla force, the AMS, and also with the pro-KMT guerrillas operating along the Siam/Malaya border.

Communal violence reached alarming levels during this brief but bloody interregnum and continued unabated for several months. In August 1945, as MPAJA forces started to seize control in parts of the country, the Japanese provoked Malays to kill approximately 400 Chinese near the Johore coastal towns of Muar and Batu Pahat. In retaliation for this many Malays suspected of collaboration were killed by Chinese.

> 'Between September 1945 and the 1 April 1946, 600 murders were actually recorded by the police but there were undoubtedly many more.'[58]

As the news of the surrender spread, MPAJA guerrillas left their jungle camps and entered the towns, where they were initially welcomed as conquering heroes.

> 'In many places there were premature celebrations, sometimes in defiance of Japanese pleas that the open display of joy would cause an unbearable loss of face on their part.'[59]

Some guerrillas attacked Japanese sentries and isolated police posts to steal their weapons, and as Japanese troops vacated smaller towns and villages, the guerrillas replaced them in greater numbers.

The MCP and MPAJA continued to seize control of large parts of the country during the interregnum. As the Japanese were concentrated in the larger town areas, the guerrillas embarked on a brutal form of summary justice against random pro-Japanese elements, including civil and military police, profiteers, as well as Butai and Kempeitai agents. Suspected informers were hunted down, and others on MPAJA's black lists. Girls who had been mistresses of Japanese were arrested and either marched or dragged through the streets of towns to be dealt with in summary trials. The Japanese Club in Singapore was used by the guerrillas as their headquarters. It was there they prosecuted those they considered traitors.

Sikh policemen were prime targets for revenge as they had been ruthlessly efficient and loyal to the Japanese. Sikh and Malay police, left behind as the Japanese withdrew, became the first victims of reprisals. Lawlessness during the interregnum incited many to settle old grudges by taking the law into their own hands. Opportunists took advantage of hapless people's fear, realising their time for uncontrolled self gain was limited.

> 'Whether as gangsters or "guerrillas" or liaison men of this and that clique, they pursued a campaign of vengeance against "traitors and running-dogs of the Japs" to give their activities the countenance of patriotism. Policemen, detectives and inspectors who had been black-listed were hunted down.'[60]

The many public executions at this time

> 'outstripped the performance of the Japs for sheer barbarism. News of such executions terrorised the population.'[61]

Victims suspected of committing crimes against the people were abducted and dragged to public open trials, where they were forced to kneel with hands tied behind their backs as mobs screamed for the death sentence. This was often carried out with utter brutality, preceded by hideous forms of torture. Those who had enriched themselves during the occupation and failed to purchase their way to freedom by paying ransoms were publicly tried and summarily executed.

The Malays and the Chinese blamed each other for what happened. It was difficult to distinguish fact from myth. Many incidents were exaggerated from their origin in real events. Malay retaliation against the Chinese took on the form of a holy crusade or *Jihad*. Koranic verses invoked bravery, with the promise of paradise for any who fell in battle!

Many feigned acceptance of communist ideology. The MCP displayed posters in towns and villages calling on people to welcome the People's Anti-Japanese Army as liberators of the country. Although MPAJA guerrillas in many districts were initially lauded by the Chinese as heroes,

> 'their arrogant and ruthless behaviour also antagonised many people who sought protection from other groups such as the Chinese secret societies.'[62]

The MCP failed to perceive the consequences of allowing carte blanche to its rank and file and the effect of their acts of retribution. Many Malays left the MCP because of the excessive terror tactics and brutal killings of the MPAJA during this period. MCP leaders later became aware that communism would never become popular in the country without first establishing a solid basis for racial peace.

16:10 MPAJA's Actions against the Japanese

The value of the MPAJA to the Allied cause is debatable. The MCP's ultimate objective was to establish a communist republic in Malaya rather than just resisting the Japanese. MPAJA guerrillas nevertheless were a potential threat to the Japanese occupational forces, harassing their communications and forcing them to divert more troops to Malaya than originally intended.

Until December 1944 the guerrillas had been little or no match for the Japanese. They tantalised them, invariably disappearing into the depths of the jungle whenever the Japanese tried to engage them. They concentrated on ambushing Japanese patrols, attacking police stations and murdering informers. They also cut telegraph wires, dug up railway lines and ambushed ranking military officers and military police. The innocent always suffered, many living in those areas where attacks were organised being subsequently rounded up and viciously interrogated.

MPAJA claimed that they carried out 340 individual operations against the Japanese, of which 230 were classified as major efforts. They estimated that they had killed 5,500 Japanese troops and about 2,500 traitors, and that they had lost only about 1,000 of their own men. Japanese estimates are considered more accurate than those of MPAJA. The total number of Japanese killed and wounded in Malaya between December 1941 and August 1945 was approximately 2,300, with only about 600 of these reportedly at the hands of MPAJA. About 2,000 local police were casualties, however, in one way or another. The Japanese claimed that they inflicted 2,900 casualties on MPAJA guerrillas, excluding the thousands of men, women and children living along the jungle fringes below the hills who were brutally massacred in reprisal raids. Neither figure is significant considering that MPAJA fielded a force of 5,000 guerrillas. The higher estimate equates to just over four kills per day, the lower one to less than one kill every other day!

In his account *The Communist Struggle in Malaya* Hanrahan considered that

> 'The over-all contribution of the MPAJA to the cause of the Allies was, therefore, negligible. As it was . . . the total record of the MPAJA does not deserve the credit given it by pro-Communist writers.'[63]

He viewed their contribution in tying down the occupational forces and harassing their communication and supply lines as small, no more 'than a minor irritant and certainly no strategic threat . . .'[64] Be this as it may, the effect that MPAJA guerrillas had on the Japanese was sufficient irritant to make them so nervous that in early 1943 a decree was issued offering guerrillas a free pardon, if they would surrender and hand in their weapons, reject their communist ideals, and take an oath of allegiance to Dai Nippon.

1. *The Making of Modern Malaya* by N.J. Ryan, ch.16, p.218.
2. *The Communist Struggle in Malaya* by Gene Z. Hanrahan, ch.1, p.24.
3. Ibid, ch.2, p.43. (Refers to *Singapore: A Police Background* by R. Onraet, p.117.)
4. Ibid, ch.2, p.45. (Cited in *The Chinese in Southeast Asia* by Victor Purcell, p.363.)
5. Ibid, ch.2, p.45. (Refers to Wu Tien-wang, the Communist Party of Malaya. Unpublished ms, 1947, p.1.)
6. *The Masked Comrades. A Study of the Communist United Front in Malaya, 1945–48* by Cheah Boon Kheng, ch.5, p.58.
7. *Red Star over Malaya. Resistance and Social Conflict during and after the Japanese Occupation, 1941–1946* by Cheah Boon Kheng, ch.3, p.57.
8. *The Communist Struggle in Malaya* by Gene Z. Hanrahan, ch.2, p.50–1.
9. *The Knights of Bushido* by Lord Russell of Liverpool, ch.13, p.199.
10. *The Communist Struggle in Malaya* by Gene Z. Hanrahan, ch.2, p.53. (Refers to *The Communist Party of Malaya*, unpublished manuscript by Wu Tien-wang, p.2.)
11. Ibid, ch.2, p.53.
12. Ibid, ch.2, p.54.
13. Ibid, ch.2, p.57.
14. Ibid, ch.2, p.54.
15. Ibid, ch.2, p.55. (Refers to Wu Tien-wang, p.3.)
16. Ibid, ch.2, p.56. (Cited in *The Chinese in Southeast Asia* by Victor Purcell, p.365.)
17. *Red Star over Malaya. Resistance and Social Conflict during and after the Japanese Occupation, 1941–1946* by Cheah Boon Kheng, ch.3, p.57. (Refers to *Nan Tao Chih Ch'un [Spring in the Southern Islands]* by the Malayan Communist Party, p.22.)
18. *The Communist Struggle in Malaya* by Gene Z. Hanrahan, ch.3, p.61.
19. Ibid, ch.3, p.62.
20. *The Jungle Is Neutral* by F. Spencer Chapman DSO, ch.1, p.18.
21. *The Communist Struggle in Malaya* by Gene Z. Hanrahan, ch.3, p.64.
22. Ibid, ch.3, p.68.
23. *The Jungle Is Neutral* by F. Spencer Chapman DSO, ch.6, p.106.
24. *The Communist Struggle in Malaya* by Gene Z. Hanrahan, ch.3, p.75.
25. Ibid, ch.3, p.75.
26. *The Jungle Is Neutral* by F. Spencer Chapman DSO, ch.18, p.348.
27. *The Communist Struggle in Malaya* by Gene Z. Hanrahan, ch3, p.78.
28. Ibid, ch.3, p.84.
29. Ibid, ch.3, p.73. (Refers to *The Jungle is Neutral* by Spencer Chapman DSO, p.157–8.)
30. Ibid, ch.3, p.71.

31. *Red Star over Malaya. Resistance and Social Conflict during and after the Japanese Occupation, 1941–1946* by Cheah Boon Kheng, ch.2, p.33.
32. Ibid, ch.2, p.55.
33. Ibid, ch.3, p.81.
34. Ibid, ch.3, p.81. (Refers to WO 203/5642.)
35. *The Jungle Is Neutral* by F. Spencer Chapman DSO, ch.11, p.213.
36. *The Communist Struggle in Malaya* by Gene Z. Hanrahan, ch.3, p.80.
37. Ibid, ch.3, p.80.
38. *The Jungle Is Neutral* by F. Spencer Chapman DSO, ch.5, p.102.
39. *The Communist Struggle in Malaya* by Gene Z. Hanrahan, ch.3, p.81. (Refers to *The Jungle Is Neutral* by Spencer Chapman DSO, p.234.)
40. Ibid, ch.3, p.83.
41. *The Jungle Is Neutral* by F. Spencer Chapman DSO, ch.8, p.162.
42. Ibid, ch.16, p.311, 318 and 319.
43. *The Chinese in Malaya* by Victor Purcell, ch.7, p.256.
44. *When Singapore Was Syonan-To* by N.I. Low, ch.17, p.117.
45. *The Jungle Is Neutral* by F. Spencer Chapman DSO, ch.16, p.317.
46. *Red Star over Malaya. Resistance and Social Conflict during and after the Japanese Occupation, 1941–1946* by Cheah Boon Kheng, ch.3, p.78.
47. *British Rule in Malaya 1942–1957* by Robert Heussler, ch.6, p.151.
48. *The Jungle Is Neutral* by F. Spencer Chapman DSO, ch.17, p.343.
49. *Red Star over Malaya. Resistance and Social Conflict during and after the Japanese Occupation, 1941–1946* by Cheah Boon Kheng, ch.3, p.79.
50. Ibid, ch.3, p.80. (Refers to 'Nationalism in Malaya' by Aziz and Silcock, in *Asian Nationalism and the West*, ed. by William Holland.
51. *The Masked Comrades. A Study of the Communist United Front in Malaya 1945–1948* by Cheah Boon Kheng, ch.6, p.63.
52. *Red Star over Malaya. Resistance and Social Conflict during and after the Japanese Occupation, 1941–1946* by Cheah Boon Kheng, ch.3, p.70.
53. Ibid, ch.3, p.66.
54. Ibid, ch.8, p.197. (Refers to 'The 14 Days of Terror: Before, During and After' by Hamzah bin Mohamed, BA Hons Thesis, University of Malaya, 1969–70, p.29.)
55. Ibid, ch.2, p.45.
56. *Conflict and Violence in Singapore and Malaysia 1945–1983* by Richard Clutterbuck, ch.1, p.38.
57. *The Jungle Is Neutral* by F. Spencer Chapman DSO, ch.15, p.295.
58. *Conflict and Violence in Singapore and Malaysia 1945–1983* by Richard Clutterbuck, ch.1, p.40.
59. *British Rule in Malaya 1942–1957* by Robert Heussler, ch.4, p.79.
60. *Ma-Rai-Ee* by Chin Kee Onn, ch.25, p.295.
61. Ibid, ch.25, p.295.
62. *Red Star over Malaya. Resistance and Social Conflict during and after the Japanese Occupation, 1941–1946* by Cheah Boon Kheng, ch.7, p.173.
63. *The Communist Struggle in Malaya* by Gene Z. Hanrahan, ch.3, p.84.
64. Ibid, ch.3, p.84. (Refers to *Japanese Military Administration Documents: The Occupation of Malaya*, Section 1V-2.)

CHAPTER SEVENTEEN: V-J DAY

17:1 The Tide Turns

At the outset of war, even while fanatical militarist politicians and many others were still gloating over Japan's early ambitious victories, both Marquis Koicho Kido, Lord Keeper of the Privy Seal and a man of considerable influence in Emperor Hirohito's court, and Admiral Isorku Yamamoto, the Navy Minister, had serious misgivings about Japan's eventual success in any protracted war. These fears were not made public, but Kido urged Hirohito

> 'to grasp any opportunity to bring about the earliest possible termination of the war'.[1]

By the middle of 1942 peace-minded factions in Japan were locked in a dangerous rivalry of opinion with General Hideki Tojo's army-controlled government. They foresaw calamitous defeat unless a favourable settlement could be quickly negotiated, especially after the Battle of Midway had dealt a disastrous blow to Japan's short-lived naval supremacy, costing her the initiative at sea. Tojo's views also changed after Midway. He urged Japan to be 'prepared to fight for a hundred years until victory is won and our enemies are crushed'.[2]

By mid-September 1943 it was clear to Imperial GHQ that their forces were stretched far too thinly over too large an area. The Americans had by this time shaken off their early defeats, and now held a dominant position both in the air and at sea. Japan was forced to reduce the area that she could defend by consolidating in fewer positions. A new operational policy, based on the minimum area of defence essential to achieve Japan's war aims, was established. The so-called

> 'absolute national defence sphere . . . meant that most of New Guinea, and all the Bismarks (including Rabaul), the Solomons, the Gilberts and the Marshalls were now considered, and classed, as non-essential — although they were to be held for a further six months'.[3]

During the first 12 months of fighting 300,000 Japanese soldiers were killed. Before the madness was finished another two million would die!

While the army persisted with its policy of inevitable self-destruction, would-be peace-makers and protesters, recalling the spate of assassinations of moderates in 1936, lived in fear of the all-powerful Thought Police and Kempeitai. Hate-propaganda dominated people's lives and their devotion to Hirohito meant that any national debate on the progress of the war was impossible. By mid-1945 only the military's fanaticism and the population's deification of Hirohito kindled what in effect had already become a calamitous conflict for Japan.

* * * * * *

Japan's economy at the outset of the war seriously affected the productivity of essential industries, which in turn undermined the military's position. Insufficient aircraft were manufactured to meet the American challenge, and to protect Japan's life-supporting merchant fleet. There was too little emphasis on developing the all important aircraft-carrier force, and the planes needed to support this. The Japanese soon forgot that their early achievements in the war had been mostly due to air superiority, while the Allies had quickly learnt this lesson from bitter experience. The Japanese proved 'slower than their opponents to apply the lesson of their own great successes at the outset of the war'.[4]

The tide of events had clearly turned against Japan by June 1943, despite their protestations to the contrary. Food shortages became acute as Allied submarines increased their toll among the determinable clock-work routings of the Japanese mercantile marine in the Straits of Malacca. Food was particularly scarce in civilian internee camps in Java, where Japanese guards and even a camp commandant on occasion joined in to plant sweet potatoes and tapioca roots.

The disruption to Japanese shipping prevented rice and other foodstuffs being transported to Japan. Imports, so urgently needed for war industries and to supply various spread-out armies in Burma, Malaya and other distant areas, were almost completely brought to a standstill. On 3rd September 1943, to coincide with the announcement made in the United States that 2.539 million tons of Japanese shipping (more than a third of her estimated pre-war total) had been destroyed, Premier Tojo exhorted the Japanese to become self-sufficient in food!

By late September 1943 frogmen from the Royal Australian Navy, led by a British officer, Major Lyon of the Highland Light Infantry, had carried out a daring and successful raid in Keppel Harbour in Singapore, where they sank seven warships and merchant vessels, and extensively damaged others. The September toll of Japanese shipping sunk, mostly by US submarines, was 160,000 tons, reaching a new peak in November when 265,000 tons were sunk. By October 1944 Penang had been closed by RAF mines, and convoys to Penang through the Malacca Straits had to be abandoned by the Japanese.

> 'It was fitting that Allied airpower, to which the Japanese had no effective answer, should reach out over thousands of miles exactly three years later and close Penang as an aggressive port. The mining was not of formidable proportions, although the Japanese were unlikely to know how many mines were laid . . . A base that cannot be defended must be evacuated.'[5]

At the outset of war Japan's merchant fleet was almost 6 million tons. By November 1943, despite massive new construction works, this had been reduced to less than 5 million tons. The combined effect of submarine attacks and extensive mining carried out from the air was catastrophic for Japanese shipping. By the end of the war an estimated 4,800,000 tons had been sunk by submarines and another 2,250,000 tons destroyed by mines.

* * * * * *

Vice-Admiral Takijiro Onishi — a fanatical militarist and something of a cult figure among his staff — was the Commander of the Fifth Base Air Force at Luzon in the Philippines in October 1944. He was the initiator of the Kamikaze Special Attack Force, which was used as a desperate tactical alternative to conventional warfare due to the shortage of experienced pilots and effective combat aircraft.

During the summer of 1281 the Mongolian Emperor of China, Kublai Khan, having failed in earlier bids to obtain tribute from Japan, sent 140,000 troops to conquer the Japanese islands. A powerful typhoon smashed the Mongolian fleet and thousands of his warriors were drowned. Japan was saved and the people gave thanks to the gods for sending the Kamikaze (Divine Wind).

Suicide in Japan carried no stigma, and was if anything honoured for its purity. Every soldier, it was recognised, owed his life to his country and the Emperor. More than 2,000 young Japanese pilots, many of them with little training and experience, became devotees of Kamikaze missions between October 1944 and August 1945. Many who missed their targets and crashed into the sea, or were subsequently captured, felt so utterly disgraced by their failure that they could not bear the thought of returning home alive.

This appalling concept developed into a full-time defensive/ assault strategy during the invasion of Okinawa in April 1945, when the lightly armoured American aircraft carriers became favoured targets. Many Kamikazes failed, but those that did succeed invariably devastated their targets. During the 11–week Okinawa Battle, Kamikazes sank 32 US and British ships and damaged 216 others. Three British aircraft carriers, the *Illustrious, Victorious* and *Formidable,* also suffered some structural damage from Kamikaze attacks, but as their armoured decks were stronger than their counterparts in the US fleet (which had been built with cruiser hulls and streamlined for speed) none of the British flat-tops were sunk.

During the final ten months of the war the Special Attack Kamikaze squadrons used up more than 2,000 planes and 2,198 pilots. Many who flew the later, massed Kikisui (Floating Chrysanthemum) attacks were glory-seeking teenagers, who had barely learnt to fly, sent out on a one-way mission of possible glory and certain death. A desperate measure invoked in desperation by fanatics! Admiral Onishi died by his own hand, having taken it upon himself to assume responsibility for the failure of the Kamikazes to save Japan by total sacrifice.

* * * * * *

The principal Axis leaders all met their deaths within two days of each other in April 1945.

On the 28th Benito Mussolini, with his mistress Clara Petacci, and 12 other leading fascists were caught by Italian partisans as they attempted to escape from Italy into Switzerland. They were executed at Giulino di Mezzenegra, near Dongo, on Lake Como and publicly hung upside-down by their heels in a main square at Milan.

Hitler's marriage to Eva Braun on 29th April 1945 coincided with the surrender of German forces in Italy. They both committed suicide the next day. Hitler's death was only announced over Radio Hamburg on 1st May 1945, following which, on the same day, Dr Joseph Goebbles shot his wife and then committed suicide, having personally poisoned their six children. Martin Bormann disappeared. The war in Europe officially came to an end at midnight on 8th May 1945, and with this, the isolation of Japan was complete.

* * * * * *

By July 1945 Japan's potential to mount effective opposition or defence in the air was virtually non-existent. This had a demoralising effect on the civilian population in Tokyo and in other major Japanese cities, especially with the launching of an Allied propaganda campaign in which leaflets were dropped warning people of future targets to be bombed. The reaction to this was devastating, especially for Japan's war production industries, since more than 8,500,000 people fled the major towns and cities into the surrounding countryside. By this stage production levels in oil refining had already been reduced by 83%, with similar enormous declines in aircraft engine production by 75%, and in aircraft frame manufacture by 60%. The potential to supply electronic equipment had dropped by 70%, and in excess of 600 important wartime factories had been destroyed or were badly damaged in incessant bombing raids. It was at last brought home to the civilian population in Japan — by now desperately hungry and war weary — that they could no longer depend on the Imperial military forces for protection.

17:2 Behind the Scenes

General Hideki Tojo was summoned to power by Emperor Hirohito and became Prime Minister on 16th October 1941, after the resignation of the more moderate Prince Konoye. Tojo brought Japan into the war, and by dint of being Prime Minister, War Minister and Chief of the Army Staff, he was fully responsible for the conduct of the war until he resigned.

As Japan's military set-backs increased, Tojo's position became severely weakened and by the time he was forced to resign on 18th July 1944, the Marianas had been newly lost, with an estimated 27,000 Japanese dead. Earlier defeats undermining Tojo's position, particularly as aspirations for peace grew, included:

Date	**Battle**	**Losses**
February 1943	Guadalcanal	10,000 dead.
May 1943	Aleutians	2,350 dead.
November 1943	Gilbert Islands	Garrison annihilated.
January 1944	Marshalls	8,700 dead.
June 1944	Battle of the Philippine Seas	240 planes and 2 aircraft-carriers lost.

Most people in Japan were not aware of Tojo's forced resignation as Chief of the Army Staff and did not seem to care when later he was relieved of office. On the day that Tojo departed from public life and responsibility, the Imperial General Headquarters announced that Saipan had been captured along with the destruction of its substantial garrison.

> 'No one, . . . it seemed, was sorry to see the departure from public life of the humourless, merciless and hitherto omnipotent Razor.'[6]

Tojo attempted to commit suicide after Japan surrendered, but he survived and was one of the seven war criminals later tried and hung by the Allies.

On 22nd July 1944 Lieut-General Kuniaki Koiso formed a cabinet, its immediate concern being the defence of the Philippines, as the loss of these islands would fatally affect the fighting potential of Japanese forces by curtailing their oil supplies. Within one month Koiso had introduced conscription for all Japanese women between the ages of 12 and 40, requiring them to do war related work.

In the Koiso cabinet, and among several senior Japanese statesmen, there was a growing desire to end the war quickly. There was also mounting concern that this could only come about through an unfavourable peace settlement. Japan discreetly started to put out feelers towards peace in February 1945, seeking Russia's help as an intermediary. Neutral Russia ignored these attempts, deeming the proposals insufficiently definite to act on. No hint of these pleas was mentioned to the United States until three months later when Harry Hopkins, as President Truman's personal envoy, met Stalin in Moscow in May 1945. Even then it was only mentioned at their third meeting. It was impossible to publicise such peace-seeking efforts in Japan's militarily controlled state, so the government continued to maintain its strong outwardly warlike stance, hiding the efforts of its would-be negotiators for peace. This the Allies interpreted as a desire to continue with the carnage.

By February 1945 it was clear that Japan's situation was hopeless. The thought of an unconditional surrender was still regarded as a

> 'betrayal of the forces in the field, so willing to fight to the death; these forces, who still held the lives of thousands of near-starved Allied civilian and military prisoners in pawn, might refuse to obey a "cease fire" order if the terms were abjectly humiliating . . .'[7]

On 5th April 1945, however, as a 'bolt from the blue, shattering all . . . illusions',[8] the Japanese Ambassador in Moscow was told that Russia would not renew the Soviet-Japan Non-Aggression Pact of 1941. This major set-back, plus the American landings on Okinawa from 1st April onwards, precipitated the resignation of the Koiso cabinet. The respected and aged Admiral Kantaro Suzuki became Prime Minister on 5th April, and immediately formed a new cabinet with less military influence and more members already agreed that no reasonable offer of peace from the Allies should be disregarded. Despite this faction, the Suzuki government was again rebuffed in their approach to Russia to help mediate favourable peace terms for them, and on 8th June 1945 saw it fit to resolve at an Imperial conference to 'prosecute the war to the bitter end'.[9]

Emperor Hirohito intervened on 20th June 1945, summoning a conference at which the Inner Cabinet and the Supreme War Direction Council were told to consider ending the war as quickly as possible. Prince Fumimaro Konoye was dispatched to Moscow to lead a delegation seeking peace, which the Emperor had privately told him to secure at any price. The Russian response again was both chilly and negative, and Viachislav Molotov refused to meet Konoye. The elderly Suzuki had hoped that under the auspices of the Russians, Konoye would be able

> 'to persuade the Americans that a negotiated peace was preferable to the frightful losses they would suffer in pursuit of the unattainable goal of unconditional surrender'.[10]

He was unaware that Stalin had already been persuaded by President Truman to enter the war against Japan.

17:3 Devastating Conclusion

The unconditional surrender terms agreed by Churchill and Roosevelt at Casablanca in Morocco in January 1943 took

> 'no account of the fact that the so-called Restoration of Showa had rendered the Imperial Japanese Army psychologically, and legally, incapable of any kind of surrender'.[11]

Churchill belatedly acknowledged this, and at Yalta in February 1945 proposed to Roosevelt that some relaxation of the formula ought to be considered, if it might shorten the war. By this time many others also viewed its continued inclusion as a major obstacle to any early Japanese surrender. Unconditional surrender would exclude any safeguard for Emperor Hirohito and the Japanese Imperial system. Without some form of guarantee in this respect, the Japanese would more than likely continue to fight all the harder. People in Japan who had deified Hirohito were justifiably fearful for his future safety, as many American leaders and people throughout the United States, still enraged by the ignominious attack on Pearl Harbour, regarded him as a feared and hated symbol of Japanese militarism. A gallup poll taken in June 1945 revealed that 33% of all Americans wanted Hirohito to be executed as a war criminal. Another 11% wanted him imprisoned, and 9% wanted him exiled.

After the demise of Roosevelt on 12th April 1945 a committee was set up by the newly installed President Truman to prepare draft terms for surrender. The original version contained a clause stipulating that any post-war Japanese government

> 'may include a constitutional monarch under the present dynasty if it be shown to the complete satisfaction of the world that such a government shall never again aspire to aggression'.[12]

When Truman met Churchill and Stalin at Potsdam in July 1945, his newly appointed Secretary of State, James F. Byrnes – convinced that any relaxation of the unconditional requirement would have devastating political consequences – prevailed on Truman to reword the document so that when the Potsdam Declaration was issued on 26th July, no direct reference to the Emperor's position was contained in it. It simply referred to the establishment of a 'peacefully inclined and responsible government'[13] that had to be elected according to the freely expressed wishes of the Japanese people.

The meetings between Churchill, Stalin and Truman at Potsdam, between 17th July and 2nd August 1945, contained surprise revelations for all concerned. Stalin announced Russia's intent to declare war on Japan and confirmed that, in her 'neutral' state, she had chosen not to convey the earlier peace moves made to her by Japan. For the first time Truman and Churchill mentioned to Stalin the existence of a new and awesomely powerful weapon specifically developed for use against Japan. They did not, however, provide any explicit details. Churchill, also in the strictest secrecy, divulged to Admiral Lord Louis Mountbatten – the Supreme Allied Commander of Southeast Asia Command – that the United States had developed a prototype atomic bomb, and that they proposed to use it in August to force the Japanese to capitulate as soon as possible after that date. Such a drastic, short-cut measure might in retrospect have 'saved literally millions of lives, most of them Japanese',[14] for if it had been necessary for the Allies to invade Malaya, Singapore and then the Japanese home islands, countless casualties would certainly have occurred, and most likely all Allied prisoners of war and civilian internees in Japanese hands would have been massacred.

On 26th July 1945 the terms of the Potsdam Declaration were broadcast to Japan. An assurance was given that Japan would not be reduced to poverty, but no mention was made as to whether or not the Emperor would remain at the head of any subsequently formed government. By this stage it was impossible to prevent the news being divulged to the Japanese public, as all over the country Allied planes were continuing to drop thousands of leaflets with the peace terms translated into Japanese. With the Japanese cabinet clutching at the delicate and desperate final straw of hope that Russia might still agree to intercede on their behalf for more favourable surrender terms, no immediate response was made to the terms of the Declaration. The Cabinet, however, agreed that newspapers should publish only a censored version of the Declaration, and that the government should not make any official response to it, but instead would 'maintain a discrete silence'.[15]

On 27th July Domei, the Japanese News Agency, declared that unlike Germany, Japan was 'not on her knees' and was 'determined to battle tooth and nail for every inch of her sacred soil',[16] as not one single enemy soldier had yet set foot on the Japanese mainland. Things were further confused one day later when Prime Minister Suzuki was misquoted in the Tokyo press, having said that his government would 'treat it (the Declaration) with contempt'.[17]

The Allies chose to conclude that Japan had haughtily rejected the Declaration's terms. This was not the case, but Suzuki indeed proved inept, still trying to play for time, while inferring the Declaration to be 'of no great value'.[18] This was again misrepresented in the Japanese press, which reported that the cabinet had treated the Potsdam Declaration 'with silent contempt'.[19] Japan's apparent rejection could be used to justify Truman's terrible decision to resort to the use of the atom bomb.

* * * * * *

Throughout 1945 huge formations of B29 Superfortresses flew unimpeded over Japan, and bombed at will one city after another. From most of these cities 'the children had been evacuated to the country, where they lived harsh, hungry lives, awaiting the Allied invasion'.[20]

City dwellers with relatives in rural areas also fled, but the greater part of the urban population had no other choice but to stay where they were. Flight during a raid was futile, as the fire storms that swept through the cities could not be out-run, and these left behind a gruesome toll of charred and shrivelled bodies that littered the streets after every raid. Despite such dreadful casualties, the army's determination to continue with the war was blared through loud-speakers on every street and in many shops.

By late July 1945, in contrast to the devastation caused by these large formations of B29 Superfortresses, the Japanese had also become accustomed to seeing small formations of B29s, as they made practice runs over Japan from their base at Tinian in the Mariana Islands for several months. These had caused little damage, and people were not very apprehensive when they saw them.

On 5th August more than 400 Superfortress bombers and fighters, based on Okinawa, caused massive devastation to the port of Tarmuizu in south Kyushu, and the nearby town of Kungibaru was also severely damaged. Leaflets were dropped on more than 12 other Japanese towns, warning them of imminent heavy raids and telling civilians to evacuate them quickly. By early August, 31 towns had been warned in this manner and 10 of them had already been destroyed. In the preceding month B29s had unleashed almost 50,000 tons of bombs on Japan, and since the Potsdam Declaration 3,000,000 copies of the surrender ultimatum — signed by Churchill, Truman and General Chiang Kai-shek — had been dropped.

On 6th August, at 9 a.m., the first atomic bomb — a uranium fission weapon — was dropped on Hiroshima, the eighth largest city in Japan. The *Endola Gay*, a Superfortress bomber from the 509 Composite Group of the Twentieth Air Force, was used for this purpose and had been named by its pilot, Colonel Paul Tibbets, after his mother. William Parsons was in charge of the bomb and Major T.W. Ferebee was the bomb aimer. The great port of Hiroshima, located near the southern tip of Honshu, with its garrison town and accompanying red-light district, had a population of about 340,000. It was reduced to rubble. 4.1 square miles of its total area of 7 square miles were completely obliterated, and extensive additional damage was caused outside this area. A large part of Hiroshima dissolved into a vast cloud of dust, and 100,000 people were instantly killed as the area disappeared in a searing flash of heat and light. Many, many more were horribly burned.

On the evening of the 6th President Truman announced from the White House that an atomic bomb had been dropped on Hiroshima by an American plane. This awesome weapon, with a blast power 2,000 times more than the British 'Grand Slam', had the equivalent power of 22,000 tons of TNT, half the tonnage dropped on Berlin by the RAF in the whole duration of the European war.

There was immense consternation in Japan and an immediate cabinet meeting was held. Radio Tokyo announced that

> 'most of Hiroshima no longer exists. The impact of the bomb was so terrific that practically all living things, human and animal, were literally seared to death . . . Buildings were crushed or wiped out. Those outdoors were burned to death and those indoors were killed by an indescribable pressure and heat. The city is a disastrous ruin.'[21]

The Domei agency accused the United States of violating the laws of war and the Hague Convention.

Truman warned the Japanese people in a broadcast made from Washington that their continued non-acceptance of the Potsdam terms would give rise to a 'rain of ruin from the air the like of which has never been seen . . .'[22] or imagined before. Hirohito declared that the Hiroshima tragedy must not be repeated, but, typical of the army's stubbornness, they did not accept that such a dreadful weapon could have been manufactured. The Japanese nation was horrified but most people still remained ready to obey their leaders. Seishin signed the ultimate death warrant.

At noon on 8th August 1945 the second atomic bomb — a plutonium fission device — was dropped on the city of Nagasaki on the west coast of Kyushu. It was detonated at a pre-determined height above ground to maximise its blast effect against structures, and to disseminate its radio active products in the form of a cloud. The bomb that was dropped on the port of Nagasaki, with its population of

250,000 and its arms centre, was more powerful than the one dropped on Hiroshima. Approximately 40,000 people instantly perished. Accurate aerial reconnaissance was impossible for up to 48 hours after the blast, owing to a pall of deadly dust. When the damage was assessed it was estimated that

> 'one-third of Nagasaki had been wiped out, chiefly the industrial area, including the great Mitsubishi steel plant; . . . US airmen reported that Nagasaki "went up in a roar of smoke and flame" visible 250 miles away, that a great cloud of black smoke rose 10 miles until it blotted out targets which were being attacked by Superfortresses 50 miles away, and that Nagasaki looked like an "erupting volcano".'[23]

No mention of the second atomic attack was made over Tokyo Radio, but instead they declared that

> 'the American and Japanese people must get their leaders together to put an end to this senseless destruction'.[24]

In conjunction with the devastation of Nagasaki, B29s continued their own pounding raids on 8th August against various other cities, as well as industrial and military targets. The Soviet Union, after weeks of procrastination — not wanting to be denied any of the final spoils of war — added its own coup de grace by formally declaring war on Japan, citing as her reason for doing so Japan's failure to respond positively to the terms required by the Potsdam Declaration. At dawn on 9th August the Russians opened their attack along a 1,000 mile front in Manchuria, adding to Japan's dilemma. Conventional air attacks continued to be strongly forced home and included a raid by 80 Superfortresses that dropped nearly 500 tons of demolition bombs on an oil refinery and on oil storage tanks near Osaka. Coal mines and chemical works at Omuta were attacked by Liberators and Thunderbolts. For the first time since the 3rd US Fleet entered Japanese home waters Kamikaze planes were sent to intercept them, but to no avail.

B29s continued to drop leaflets all over Japan, stating:

> 'We are in possession of the most destructive weapon ever designed by man. A single one of our atomic bombs equals the explosive power carried by 2,000 Superfortresses. We have just begun to use this weapon. Before using

> it again to destroy every resource which your military leaders have to prolong this useless war, we ask that you now petition your Emperor to end the war.'[25]

At last Hirohito intervened, requiring the Japanese militarists to call a halt to the madness. Unconditional surrender was agreed to on 14th August 1945, and

> '. . . a bigoted and arrogant nation — a nation poisoned by the myth of invincibility poured down its throat by power-crazy militarists; . . . a nation founded on Seishin and finally led to its own destruction by Seishin',[26]

was brought to its knees.

* * * * * *

Japan's desperation to end the war conditionally was well known to the Americans. Even so,

> 'President Truman and most of his chief advisers . . . were now as intent on using the atomic bomb to accelerate Japan's collapse as Stalin was on entering the war against Japan before it ended, in order to gain an advantageous position in the Far East.'[27]

Japan's collapse was by now a certainty. With 90% of her

> 'shipping sunk or disabled, her air and sea forces crippled, her industries wrecked, and her people's food supplies shrinking fast,'[28]

the use of the atomic bomb was not really necessary to bring about the imminent surrender. If the United States had been willing to wait, they could have been starved into submission by the American naval blockade alone. Admiral William Leahy — an invaluable adviser to Truman in the last months of the war — realised that the Japanese had been defeated and were ready to surrender. He declared the bomb to be of 'no material assistance in our war against Japan'.[29] Why then was it used?

A few days after Nagasaki was bombed, Truman wrote:

> 'when you deal with a beast, you have to treat him as a beast . . .'[30]

The savage fanaticism of the Japanese invited such a terrible termination to the conflict which they had willfully begun with their surprise attack on Pearl Harbour and other Far Eastern locations. Throughout the war people in all Allied countries were disgusted and enraged by the atrocities encouraged and condoned in POW camps, and by the death-wish attitude of Kamikaze pilots.

In a note to Mr Eden, written a few days after his meeting with Truman on 18th July 1945, Churchill recorded that

> 'It is quite clear that the United States do not at the present time desire Russian participation in the war against Japan.'[31]

This was part of the political scenario which dictated the use of the atomic bomb, a powerful economic factor being the sum of more than US $2 billion already spent by the U.S. in the development of atomic weapons.

17:4 To Bear the Unbearable

The devastation of Hiroshima and Nagasaki was insufficient to induce the militarist representatives of the Supreme War Council to agree to ending the war as soon as possible, and in accordance with the terms of the Potsdam ultimatum as insisted on by the Allies. Prevarication persisted, and when the Allies refused to provide any assurance that Japan's national sovereignity would be preserved, with the prerogatives of the Emperor as ruler safeguarded, the cabinet meeting on 8th August ended in deadlock. Ministers argued vociferously for and against surrender in the presence of Hirohito. Foreign Minister Shigenori Togo, Admiral Mitsumasa Yonai and Prime Minister Kantaro Suzuki were in favour of accepting the terms. War Minister Admiral Anami and Admirals Yoshijiru Umezu and Soemu Toyoda were adamantly opposed. They insisted on trying to obtain further amendments to guarantee Japan's national identity, and pre-determine the size of any occupational force. They also wanted safeguards about proposed action against suspected war criminals, and demanded that Japanese troops should only be disarmed by Japanese officers.

Early on 10th August, at 2 a.m., Hirohito made it clear that he no longer had faith in the boasts of the militarists and had decided that the war should be ended.

> 'In these conditions, how can we prevail, even in the homeland? If the entire population is killed, we can hardly hope to perpetuate the nation! It is my opinion that we must end the war, although that is an unbearable thing . . . but the time has come to bear the unbearable.'[32]

The Allied ultimatum therefore would be accepted, provided it did not compromise the prerogative of the Emperor as sovereign ruler.

Later, on 10th August, Tokyo Radio announced that the Japanese government had requested the Swiss and Swedish governments to convey their earnest desire

> 'to bring about an early termination of hostilities with a view of saving mankind from the calamities to be imposed upon them by the further continuance of the war . . . [They were] ready to accept the terms enumerated in the joint declaration issued at Potsdam on the 26th July . . . with the understanding that . . . [it] does not comprise any demand which prejudices the prerogatives of His Majesty as a sovereign ruler.'[33]

The following day Mr James Byrnes, the US Secretary of State, handed the Allied reply to the Swiss Ligation in Washington. This firmly reiterated that

> 'from the moment of surrender the authority of the Emperor and the Japanese government to rule the State shall be subject to the Supreme Commander of the Allied Powers, who will take such steps as he deems proper to effectuate the surrender terms'.[34]

The immediate transport of all POWs and civilian internees to places of safety was ordered, and the ultimate form of government for Japan had to be established by the freely expressed will of the Japanese people. Until these and other conditions of the Potsdam Declaration had been completely satisfied, forces of Allied powers would remain in Japan to enforce them.

Australia's Minister of External Affairs, Dr Evatt, considered Japan's request that

> 'the prerogative of the Emperor should not be changed by unconditional surrender was entirely unacceptable to the Australian government . . . [which believed] that supreme authority over Japan after its surrender must be vested exclusively with the Allies. No one in Japan, of whatever rank or station, should be given immunity from proved responsibility for policies of aggression or for atrocities . . . Australians can never forget the outrageous cruelties inflicted on her Servicemen and prisoners of war by Japanese troops under the command of their militarists and the Emperor.'[35]

The militarists continued to argue for outright rejection of such humiliating terms, but Marquis Kido prevailed on the Emperor to call for another Imperial Conference. War Minister Anami was reprimanded for the Army's inflammatory reaction, when Suzuki, Togo and Kido were branded as traitors by 15 junior officers, and plans to occupy the Imperial Palace to protect Hirohito from further bad advice were thwarted. The thought of Hirohito's fate after the surrender depending on the whim of General Douglas MacArthur inflamed zealots' hatred and passions.

On the morning of 14th August, at a meeting of cabinet ministers at the Imperial Palace, Hirohito stunned his audience by insisting that they 'bow to my wishes and accept the Allied reply forthwith'.[36] The arguments of politicians were terminated. Hirohito ordered the war to be ended in accordance with the Potsdam ultimatum, and at 8.10 p.m. on the 14th, the official Japanese reply accepting the Allied surrender terms was handed over by the Japanese Minister in Berne to the Swiss Foreign Office. This was transmitted to the Swiss Legation in Washington, where it was passed to the US government, acting on behalf of the four Allied nations. Japan was at last forced to accept the demands clearly requiring 'Unconditional Surrender'. Instructions were issued to prepare an Imperial Rescript announcing Japan's ending of the war, and Hirohito recorded a radio message for release the next day to the Japanese people. A daring eleventh-hour attempt to steal this recording, a gesture of desperation, was foiled by palace guards on the night of the 14th. Attlee and Truman made joyous midnight announcements telling the world that Japan had unconditionally surrendered, and declared the next day, 15th August, as VJ Day.

In his midnight broadcast on 14th August, from London to the British people, Attlee declared:

> '"Japan has to-day surrendered. The last of our enemies is laid low".'[37]

He paid tribute to all those who had

> '"fought so well in the arduous campaign against Japan. Our gratitude goes out to all our splendid Allies and above all to the United States, without whose prodigious efforts the war in the East would still have many years to run. We also think especially at this time of the prisoners in Japanese hands, of our friends in Australia and New Zealand, in India, in Burma, and in those Colonial territories upon whom the brunt of the Japanese attack fell. We rejoice that their sufferings will soon be at an end, and that those territories will soon be purged of the Japanese invader . . . Peace has once again come to the world. Let us thank God for this great deliverance and his mercy. Long live the King".'[38]

President Truman, in Washington, announced to a press conference at the White House, that Japan's reply was

> '"a full acceptance of the Potsdam Declaration, which specifies the unconditional surrender of Japan . . . General MacArthur has been appointed Supreme Allied Commander to receive the Japanese surrender. Britain, Russia and China will be represented by high-ranking officers". . . . the President appeared in front of the White House in response to clamorous crowds and declared: "This is a great day, the day we have been waiting for since Pearl Harbour. This is the day when Fascism finally dies, as we always knew it would. This is a day for democracy — but our real task lies ahead".'[39]

On 15th August, while waiting for Hirohito's pre-recorded radio address to the nation, people knelt beneath loud speakers attached to lamp posts in every street, and all work in every factory, office and barrack came to a halt. Traffic stopped throughout the country as people knelt and waited. It was the first time that the masses had heard the Emperor's recorded voice. In very carefully chosen words, he said:

> '. . . We have decided to effect a settlement of the present situation by resorting to an extraordinary measure. We have ordered our Government to communicate with the Governments of the United States, Britain, China and the Soviet Union that our Empire accepts the provisions of their joint declaration . . . Indeed, we declared war on America and Britain out of our sincere desire to ensure Japan's self-preservation and the stabilisation of

> East Asia, it being far from our thoughts either to infringe upon the sovereignty of other nations or to embark upon territorial aggrandisement . . . the war situation has developed not necessarily to Japan's advantage, while the general trends of the world have all turned against her interests.
>
> 'The enemy, moreover, has begun to employ a new and most cruel bomb, the power of which to do damage is indeed incalculable, taking toll of many innocent lives. Should we continue to fight, it would not only result in the ultimate collapse and obliteration of the Japanese nation but would lead also to the total extinction of human civilisation . . . we have resolved to pave the way for peace for all generations to come by enduring the unavoidable and suffering what is insufferable.'[40]

He averted opposition to the ensuing occupation by implying that the Imperial State's structure would be maintained and the people were urged:

> 'Unite your total strength and devote it to rebuilding for your future. Cultivate the ways of rectitude; foster nobility of spirit; and work with resolution so that you may enhance the innate glory of the Imperial State and keep pace with the progress of the rest of the world.'[41]

Not once did Hirohito mention the word surrender, but instead he astutely laid down the guide-lines for Japan's subsequent spectacular future and effectively opened the door for the start of her industrial-winning marathon, a marathon that would achieve far more world-wide power than the previous decade's militarists could ever have conceived.

In Tokyo many people committed suicide, and this was repeated in all parts of Japan. Outside Hirohito's palace people knelt and wept, with their foreheads touching the ground, murmuring: 'Forgive us, oh Emperor, our efforts were not enough.'[42]

* * * * * *

In Burma, on 15th August, Lord Louis Mountbatten ordered

> 'the suspension of all offensive land, sea, and air operations in the SEAC theatre "so far as consistent with the safety of the Allied forces". In a broadcast to the troops under his command he said: "You have fought a great campaign under hardships and difficulties which have probably never

> been equalled. You have beaten a fanatical enemy from whose vocabulary the word 'surrender' is officially deleted and is replaced by the word 'suicide' in the last resort. . . . Our 'D Day' was just around the corner, but happily this operation is no longer necessary. We shall now be able to reoccupy peacefully the areas which, a week ago, we were preparing to liberate by force of arms".'[43]

Radio Tokyo, also on the 15th, announced the resignation of the Suzuki government. Admiral Anami had already committed ritual suicide. People were told to obey the Imperial Rescript and Japanese forces overseas were told:

> 'We have to remedy our shortcomings. We have lost, but this is temporary.'[44]

In a bid to boost home morale the broadcast continued:

> 'We have bowed to the enemy's material and scientific power . . . We did not lose the war spiritually. We are still fighting for the independence of East Asia. Our ideals are not wrong about that.'[45]

In Singapore's Changi prison, where 12,041 prisoners from all other camps on the island were concentrated, from 11th August onwards rumours abounded that surrender negotiations had started. Every prison guard who could be spared was taken to increase defences around the island and along the southern coast of Johore. Those who remained to guard prisoners became visibly more irritable and apprehensive. Field Marshall Count Terauchi, Commander-in-Chief of the Southern Army, who was ill at the time, did not want to surrender the island. He tried initially to disassociate himself from the order to stop fighting, being fully aware of the existence of plans to execute all prisoners if Singapore was invaded. General Itagaki, his stand-in, also revealed his abhorrence of the surrender by broadcasting from Singapore on 19th August that the

> 'Japanese armies in the Home Islands had "an unchallenged dignity . . ." and that "they are fully prepared to crush their foes"; whilst accepting surrender, he accused the USA of "inhuman treatment" and of "disregarding all the principles of humanity" by the use of the atomic bomb'.[46]

On the evening of 16th August, Tokyo Radio announced the unprecedented appointment of Prince Naruhiko Higashikumi as the new Prime Minister. Higashikumi — 58 years old and married to the daughter of Emperor Meiji (Hirohito's grandfather) — was also Hirohito's cousin. For the first time in Japanese history, the Emperor had personally appointed an imperial prince as Prime Minister, without the customary consultation with elder statesmen. In Higashikumi's first broadcast to the nation, on 17th August, he ordered the army to follow strictly the Imperial Rescript, urging the nation to

> 'work to recover from the ravages of war and reconstruct the country as soon as possible'.[47]

The following day Shigemitsu, the newly appointed Foreign Minister in Higashikumi's cabinet, openly admitted defeat in a broadcast to the nation. He cautioned people to change their way of thinking and not to be optimistic over the surrender terms.

> 'The sooner the Japanese people convince the Allied powers that the terms of the Potsdam Declaration have been carried into effect, the shorter will be the period of occupation.'[48]

Ten years elapsed before the Japanese openly admitted their armies had surrendered. Many believed during this period that the Emperor simply terminated the war. In David Bergamini's book, *Japan's Imperial Conspiracy*, he charged Hirohito with being personally responsible for the Pacific War, and for condoning the many atrocities committed. Hirohito personally denied these accusations in November 1971, insisting that throughout Japan's years of aggression he had acted 'as a constitutional monarch'[49] only.

Insistence, however, does not confer innocence.

17:5 The Official Conclusion

On 2nd September at 10.30 a.m. Tokyo time (2.30 a.m. British Standard Time) the war in the Pacific and World War II officially ended when the unconditional surrender of Japan was formally signed on board the American battleship *Missouri* in Tokyo Bay. General Douglas MacArthur, the Supreme Allied Commander, accompanied by some 50 Allied generals, admirals and other delegates empowered to sign on behalf of their respective countries, accepted the surrender on behalf of the Allies. Admiral Sir Bruce Frazer signed for Great Britain, and Fleet-Admiral Chester Nimitz signed for the United States. China was represented by General Hsu Yung-Chang. Lieut-General Arthur Percival — a prisoner of war in Manchuria since the surrender of Singapore — was especially flown in to be present at the surrender ceremony.

After the Japanese delegates had signed and withdrawn, MacArthur eulogised:

> 'To-day the guns are silent. A great tragedy has ended. A great victory has been won. The skies no longer rain death. The seas bear only commerce. Men everywhere walk upright in the sunlight. The entire world lives quietly at peace. The holy mission has been completed, and in reporting this to you, the people, I speak for thousands of silent lips for ever stilled among jungles and beaches and in the deep waters of the Pacific which marked the way. I speak for the unnamed brave millions who are homeward bound to take up the challenge of that future which they did so much to salvage from the brink of disaster.'[50]

Following this ceremony, President Truman — whose birth state was Missouri — declared 'VJ Day' to the world from the White House. He said:

> 'It was a long road to Tokyo — and a bloody one. We shall not forget Pearl Harbour. The Japanese militarists will not forget the *USS Missouri*. The evil done by the Japanese war lords can never be repaired or forgotten. But their power to destroy and kill has been taken from them. Their armies and what is left of their navy are now impotent. . . . it is the day which we Americans shall always remember as the day of retribution as we remember that other day, the day of infamy (the attack on Pearl Harbour). God's help has brought us to this day of victory . . . Our thoughts go out to our gallant Allies in this war: to those who resisted, to those who were not strong enough to hold out but nevertheless kept the fires of resistance alive within the souls of their people, to those who stood against great odds and held the line until the United Nations were able to supply the arms and men with which to overcome the forces of evil. This is a victory of more than arms alone. This is a victory of liberty over tyranny.'[51]

The surrender of Japanese forces in Malaya and in Southeast Asia was not officially concluded until 12th September 1945. It was accepted by Admiral Lord Louis Mountbatten, the Supreme Allied Commander SEAC, in the Council Chamber of the Municipal Building in Singapore. He was accompanied by Lieut-General Sir William Slim, Admiral Sir Arthur Power, and Air-Marshal Sir Keith Park. In addition to military representatives and witnesses from all Allied nations, the Sultan of Johore, the Maharaja of Cooch Behar, the Bishop of Singapore and representatives of the Chinese community, former internees and prisoners of war were also among those present.

On this commemorative day Mountbatten stated:

> 'The defeat of Japan is the first in history. For hundreds of years the Japanese have been ruled by a small set of imperialists, and have been told to look upon themselves as a superior race of divine origin. They have been taught to be arrogant to foreigners and to believe that the treachery they practised at Pearl Harbour is a virtue so long as it ends in Japanese victory. They are finding it very hard to accept the defeat or try to wriggle out of the terms of surrender.
>
> In the new territories you will be occupying the Japanese have not been beaten in battle. You may well find that these Japanese still fanatically believe in the divine superiority of their race. They may try to behave arrogantly. You have my support in taking the firmest measures against any Japanese obstinacy, impudence, or non-cooperation.'[52]

Sixty-one Allied warships were in Singapore harbour for the ceremony and Allied air squadrons droned overhead. General Itagaki led the Japanese plenipotentiaries, deputising for Field Marshal Count Terauchi, the Commander of Japanese forces in Malaya, Java and Sumatra, who had suffered a paralytic stroke. Other high ranking Japanese commanders from Siam, Burma, Malaya and Singapore were also required to be present to witness the concluding humiliation. Mountbatten accepted Terauchi's explanation of illness, but in doing so sternly warned him that his personal surrender was expected as soon as he was fit enough to do so.

At the time of the surrender, authorities in Washington estimated that Japan had committed more than 6.5 million men into the bitter fray, of whom at least 1.5 million had been killed or captured. In addition to these, over half a million civilian deaths had also occurred. When the hostilities ended 3.2 million of them were still serving in overseas locations and their repatriation in due course was a formidable task, especially as Japan's mercantile fleet had almost been wiped out. In Malaya and Singapore there were reportedly 86,000 Japanese when the war officially ended.

1. *Japan against the World 1941–2041. The 100–Year War for Supremacy* by Russell Braddon, ch.7, p.106.
2. Ibid, ch.7, p.107.
3. *History of the Second World War* by Sir Basil Liddell Hart, ch.29, p.530.
4. Ibid, ch.34, p.651.
5. *The Penang Submarines* by Dennis Gunton, ch.5, p.47.
6. *Japan against the World 1941–2041. The 100–Year War for Supremacy* by Russell Braddon, ch.7, p.120.
7. *History of the Second World War* by Sir Basil Liddell Hart, ch.39, p.724.
8. *Japan against the World 1941–2041. The 100–Year War for Supremacy* by Russell Braddon, ch.21, p.307.
9. *Eagle against the Sun. The American War with Japan* by Ronald H. Spector, ch.23, p.548.
10. *Japan against the World 1941–2041. The 100–Year War for Supremacy* by Russell Braddon, ch.10, p.153.
11. Ibid, ch.7, p.110.
12. *Eagle against the Sun. The American War with Japan* by Ronald H. Spector, ch.23, p.546.
13. Ibid, ch.23, p.546.
14. *Mountbatten* by Philip Ziegler, ch.23, p.300.
15. *Japan against the World 1941–2041. The 100–Year War for Supremacy* by Russell Braddon, ch.10, p.155.
16. *Keesing's Contemporary Archives. August 11–18, 1945*, p.7371.
17. *Japan against the World 1941–2041. The 100–Year War for Supremacy* by Russell Braddon, ch.10, p.155.
18. *Eagle against the Sun. The American War with Japan* by Ronald H. Spector, ch.23, p.549.
19. Ibid, ch.23, p.549.
20. *Japan against the World 1941–2041. The 100–Year War for Supremacy* by Russell Braddon, ch.10, p.151.
21. *Keesing's Contemporary Archives. August 4–11, 1945*, p.7366.
22. *Japan against the World 1941–2041. The 100–Year War for Supremacy* by Russell Braddon, ch.10, p.157.
23. *Keesing's Contemporary Archives. August 4–11, 1945*, p.7376.
24. Ibid, p.7367.
25. Ibid, p.7367.
26. *Malaya Upside Down* by Chin Kee Onn, ch.20, p.151.
27. *History of the Second World War* by Sir Basil Liddell Hart, ch.39, p.725.
28. Ibid, ch.39, p.727.
29. Ibid, ch.39, p.728.
30. *Eagle against the Sun. The American War with Japan* by Ronald H. Spector, ch.23, p.555.

31. *History of the Second World War* by Sir Basil Liddell Hart, ch.39, p.728. (Refers to *The Second World War*, vol.vi, p.553, by Churchill.)
32. *Japan against the World 1941–2041. The 100–Year War for Supremacy* by Russell Braddon, ch.10, p.161.
33. *Keesing's Contemporary Archives*, August 11–18, 1945, p.7371.
34. Ibid, p.7371.
35. Ibid, p.7371.
36. *Eagle against the Sun. The American War with Japan* by Ronald H. Spector, ch.23, p.557.
37. *Keesing's Contemporary Archives*, August 11–18, 1945, p.7371.
38. Ibid, p.7372.
39. Ibid, p.7372.
40. Ibid, p.7372.
41. *Japan against the World 1941–2041. The 100–Year War for Supremacy*, by Russell Braddon, ch.12, p.194.
42. Ibid, ch.13, p.197.
43. *Keesing's Contemporary Archives*, August 11–18, 1945, p.7378.
44. Ibid, p.7372.
45. Ibid, p.7372.
46. Ibid, August 18–25, 1945, p.7380.
47. Ibid, August 11–18, 1945, p.7373.
48. Ibid, August 18–25, 1945, p.7380.
49. *Japan against the World 1941–2041. The 100–Year War for Supremacy* by Russell Braddon, ch.15, p.218.
50. *Keesing's Contemporary Archives*, September 1–8, 1945, p.7403.
51. Ibid, p.7403.
52. Ibid, September 8–15, 1945, p.7423.

Penang Shimbun

VOL. IV. No. 201. PENANG, TUESDAY, AUGUST 21, 2605.

Supreme Commander's Message To People Of Malai

Dear People of Malai!

By the August Command of Tenno-Heika of Dai Nippon, we were ordered to cease hostilities as of August 14, 2605.

The occupation of Malai by the Nippon Army was based upon the ideal of establishing peace in Dai Toa, the co-prosperity of Dai Toa races and consequently for the peace and security of the whole world.

The Imperial Command to terminate hostilities is due to the limitless virtue of Tenno-Heika to avoid unnecessary casualties among human beings in this world. We were quite ready to fight to the last soul and were waiting for the enemy's attack prior to the receipt of the Imperial Command, which is absolute and irrevocable. Now and without hesitation, we shall obey the Imperial Command.

The visitation of peace to Malai, without the attending ravages of war, is due entirely to the solid defence of the Nippon Army as well as to your unreserved co-operation with the Army.

If the United States of America and Great Britain aim at the peace of the world, then the entire races of the world are to hereafter help and co-operate with each other as kinsmen, and we shall earnestly pray for such peace on your behalf.

We firmly believe that some day we will visit Malai, on a goodwill mission of peace and also as peace-time industrialists, and work hand in hand with you.

PROCLAMATION

August 21, 2605.

"Those who commit any of the following acts shall be severely punished.

1. Looting and destruction.
2. Any injury.
3. Spreading rumours based on unfounded facts."

COMMANDER,
Penang Navy H.Q.

Penang Shimbun, 21.8.2605 (1945). 'Supreme Commander's Message to People of Malai'.

Gay Throngs Welcome British Back To Penang

UNFORGETTABLE SCENES OF JOY

"THE BRITISH HAVE COME! THE BRITISH HAVE COME!"

From Weld Quay to Penang Road, from Carnarvon Street through the Chinese quarters of the town, the joyous cry was rapidly taken up yesterday morning as the crowd on the waterfront caught sight of two British transports steaming into Penang harbour and passed the word round. Faster than a telephone message, the news of the arrival of British troops—an arrival eagerly and impatiently awaited since the declaration of peace was announced—spread through the whole town.

The result was a general movement of pedestrians, cyclists, men, women and children towards the waterfront. Shopkeepers deserted their work, mothers hurriedly caught up their infants to make their way to Swettenham Pier. Already crowding the vicinity of the disembarkation point were thousands of people of all nationalities waiting to greet the arrival of the first British troops to set foot in Penang after three years.

A reception committee and a band headed the crowd. Outside the pier spectators clambered up drain pipes, climbed the tops of air raid shelters, stood on precarious footholds against walls to gain a glimpse, above a sea of heads, of the scene as the troops on disembarkation mounted Army lorries and were speedily driven to their new quarters in town.

Straits Echo and Penang Gazette, 4.9.1945. 'Gay Throngs Welcome British Back to Penang'.

EDITORIAL

NON NOBIS

One thousand three hundred and fifty-four days—that was the exact duration of the hideous nightmare of Japanese rule that Penang had to endure. The relief and joy of the people of this island was amply manifested in the spontaneity and magnitude of the demonstration with which the British and Allied forces that landed shortly after midday yesterday were greeted. Nothing could crush the enthusiasm of the Penang public, and although barricades were put to the approaches to the waterfront, thousands managed to slip through the corden of sentries placed by the Japanese. But once the British Marines had landed scant respect was shown to the Japanese sentries and crowds surged forward to welcome and cheer the lorry loads of troops that passed through on their way to their billets. It is, therefore, somewhat redundant for us to state that the people of Penang to a man, woman and child, down to the newest-born babe, are glad and happy that the Japanese have been turned out and that British rule has returned, as we knew it eventually would, in the pretty little island of ours. We do so only because it is proper that the fact should be placed on record.

This publication of our old newspapers can be taken as an indication that the old order is being restored and take this opportunity to appeal to the public of Penang to assist in every way to the restoration of that order. Some there are among us who have suffered more than the rest; some have even lost loved ones not only as a result of war but through unjust oppression. We share their sorrow and extend our sympathy to them. But we beg that no personal rancour or petty revenge be allowed to mar the peace that has come to Penang, Malaya and the world. It is a stupendous thing and should overshadow all else.

In the midst of our rejoicing we also must be pardoned if we strike a sober note. The Allies have won this war. We would have found it hard to believe in a benign Providence if that had not been the final result. So let us not forget that through all the trials and hardships it was the hand of that same benign Providence that guided events and brought them to this happy consummation. We were one of the thousands who underwent incarceration during the Japanese occupation of Penang but it gave us an opportunity for reflection and meditation, deriving much comfort from the virile sentiments expressed by the Psalmist. On this occasion we would, therefore, refer our readers to Psalm 115 and urge them say with the Psalmist with heart and voice: "Non Nobis."

Editorial. 'Non Nobis'.

115 To you alone, O LORD, to
you alone,
and not to us, must glory be
given
because of your constant love
and faithfulness.

Why should the nations ask us,
"Where is your God?"
Our God is in heaven;
he does whatever he wishes.
Their gods are made of silver and
gold,
formed by human hands.
They have mouths, but cannot
speak,
and eyes, but cannot see.
They have ears, but cannot hear,
and noses, but cannot smell.
They have hands, but cannot feel,
and feet, but cannot walk;
they cannot make a sound.
May all who made them and who
trust in them
become[p] like the idols they
have made.

Heaven belongs to the LORD
alone,
but he gave the earth to man.
The LORD is not praised by the
dead,
by any who go down to the
land of silence.[q]
But we, the living, will give
thanks to him
now and forever.

Praise the LORD!

Psalm 115, verses 1–8 and 16–18.

INSTRUMENT OF SURRENDER OF JAPANESE FORCES UNDER THE COMMAND OR CONTROL OF THE SUPREME COMMANDER, JAPANESE EXPEDITIONARY FORCES, SOUTHERN REGIONS, WITHIN THE OPERATIONAL THEATRE OF THE SUPREME ALLIED COMMANDER, SOUTH EAST ASIA.

1. In pursuance of and in compliance with :

   (a) the Instrument of Surrender signed by the Japanese plenipotentiaries by command and on behalf of the Emperor of Japan, the Japanese Government, and the Japanese Imperial General Headquarters at Tokyo on 2 September, 1945 ;

   (b) General Order No. 1, promulgated at the same place and on the same date ;

   (c) the Local Agreement made by the Supreme Commander, Japanese Expeditionary Forces, Southern Regions, with the Supreme Allied Commander, South East Asia at Rangoon on 27 August, 1945 ;

to all of which Instrument of Surrender, General Order and Local Agreement this present Instrument is complementary and which it in no way supersedes, the Supreme Commander, Japanese Expeditionary Forces, Southern Regions (Field Marshal Count Terauchi) does hereby surrender unconditionally to the Supreme Allied Commander, South East Asia (Admiral The Lord Louis Mountbatten) himself and all Japanese sea, ground, air and auxiliary forces under his command or control and within the operational theatre of the Supreme Allied Commander, South East Asia.

2. The Supreme Commander, Japanese Expeditionary Forces, Southern Regions, undertakes to ensure that all orders and instructions that may be issued from time to time by the Supreme Allied Commander, South East Asia, or by any of his subordinate Naval, Military or Air-Force Commanders of whatever rank acting in his name, are scrupulously and promptly obeyed by all Japanese sea, ground, air and auxiliary forces under the command or control of the Supreme Commander, Japanese Expeditionary Forces, Southern Regions, and within the operational theatre of the Supreme Allied Commander, South East Asia.

3. Any disobedience of, or delay or failure to comply with, orders or instructions issued by the Supreme Allied Commander, South East Asia, or issued on his behalf by any of his subordinate Naval, Military or Air Force Commanders of whatever rank, and any action which the Supreme Allied Commander, South East Asia, or his subordinate Commanders, acting on his behalf, may determine to be detrimental to the Allied Powers, will be dealt with as the Supreme Allied Commander, South East Asia may decide.

4. This Instrument takes effect from the time and date of signing.

5. This Instrument is drawn up in the English language, which is the only authentic version. In any case of doubt as to intention or meaning, the decision of the Supreme Allied Commander, South East Asia is final. It is the responsibility of the Supreme Commander, Japanese Expeditionary Forces, Southern Regions, to make such translation into Japanese as he may require.

Signed at Singapore at 0341 hours (G.M.T.) on 12 September, 1945.

陸軍大将板垣征四郎	Louis Mountbatten
SUPREME COMMANDER JAPANESE EXPEDITIONARY FORCES, SOUTHERN REGIONS.	SUPREME ALLIED COMMANDER, SOUTH EAST ASIA.

SACSEA Instrument of Surrender of Japanese Forces in S E Asia, signed by Lord Louis Mountbatten, dated 12th September 1945.

Japanese officers arrive on board the British battleship *HMS Nelson*, flagship of Vice Admiral H.T.C. Walker. One is carrying a chart and in the centre is Captain Shinsaku Hidaka, Senior Japanese Naval Officer at Penang. (By courtesy of Imperial War Museum, London.)

HMS Nelson. Surrender and re-occupation negotiations. Rear Admiral Uzuni and the Japanese Governor of Penang signed for the Japanese, after which the documents of agreement were signed by Vice Admiral H.T.C. Walker at 2115 hrs on 1.9.45. (By courtesy of the Imperial War Museum, London.)

3.9.45. Ceremony on quayside at Swettenham Pier as the Union Jack flew once again over Penang after three years and eight months of Japanese occupation. In front is Capt. T.J.N. Hilken DSO, RN, Naval Officer in Charge, Penang. (By courtesy of the Imperial War Museum, London.)

3.9.45. Japanese soldiers holding back Penang's cheering crowds as they welcomed the Royal Marines. (By courtesy of the Imperial War Museum, London.)

4.9.45. Japanese sailors pushing their equipment to the jetty. They were removed from Penang to the mainland of Malaya, many of them still carrying loot which they had acquired during the occupation. (By courtesy of the Imperial War Museum, London.)

12.9.45, Municipal Building, Singapore. Adm. Lord Louis Mountbatten leading cheers for H.M. the King after Japanese surrender.
(By courtesy of the Imperial War Museum, London.)

Outside view of some of the classrooms of the Light Street Convent in Penang that were used as cells to hold prisoners of war by the Japanese navy.

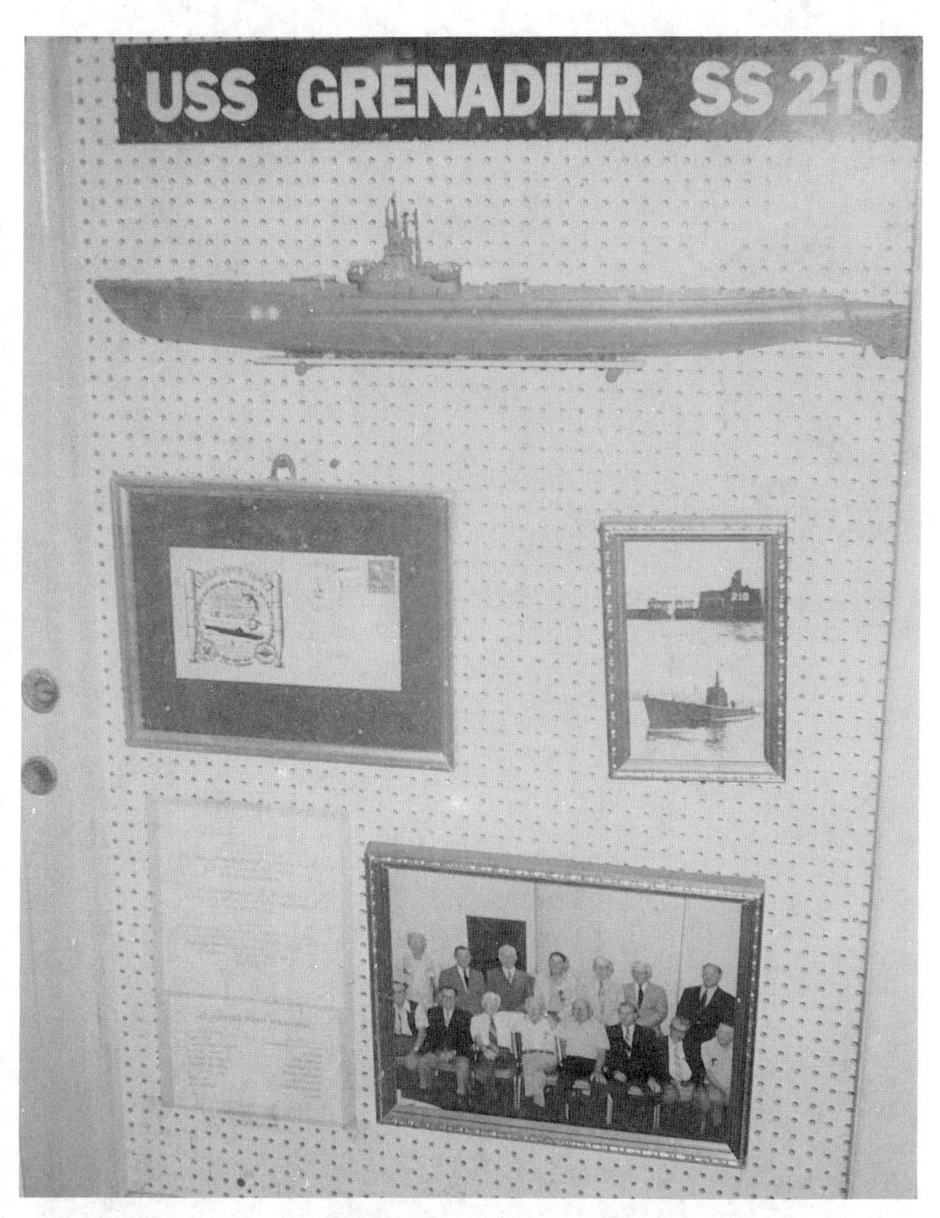

USS Grenadier (SS210), commanded by Lieut-Commander J.A. Fitzgerald, was damaged, bombed and forcibly abandoned on 22.4.43. Two Japanese vessels picked up the crew and took them to Penang for interrogation and imprisonment.

Scratched names of Commander and crew of *USS Grenadier* on wall of classroom in Light Street Convent in Penang which was used as a cell. The POWs were moved from Penang to Seletar in Singapore and thence to Japan. Four did not survive internment.

War memorial at junction of Ayer Hitam and Penang Hill Railway roads in memory of Penang Chinese killed in Sook Chings during the Japanese occupation, from 19.12.41 to 3.9.45.

On Penang War Memorial.

PART FOUR: AFTERMATH

CHAPTER EIGHTEEN: THE REOCCUPATION

18:1 Loss of Face

Britain's policy throughout the various parts of her Empire during the first two decades of the 20th century was not based on military might alone but on upholding individual and national prestige. This prestige was a hallmark of British power. A befitting life style was expected of and nurtured by most of the numerous colonial officials who made up the administrative and commercial system. Many among them considered that socially isolated standards of conduct and living enhanced their status in the eyes of those over whom they held command. It was part and parcel of a system designed to preserve their prestige and hence their power. If life styles were not suitably upheld, respect for them would diminish and this in turn, they considered, would lead to the unavoidable loss of status and effective governmental control.

British prestige — that greatly cherished pre-war entity — therefore suffered an irreversible humiliating blow with the loss of Singapore to the Asiatic conquerors, and by the manner in which 160,000 civilian internees and prisoners of war were subsequently treated by their Japanese captors. It was little surprise that after such a débâcle, many Chinese relegated Britain's standing to that of a 'paper tiger', referring to 1941 as '. . . the time when the red-headed ones (Europeans) ran . . .'[1] away. The military defeat was undeniably the cause of considerable personal suffering for many Europeans living in Malaya at that time. Retrospectively, many in the POW camps must have had serious misgivings about the significance of their treasured prestige, and wondered if it had been for too long only imaginary. Very few Asians lifted a finger to resist the Japanese invasion. One Indian in the pre-war Malayan Civil Service (MCS) later conceded that although

> '. . . his reason utterly rebelled against it, . . . his sympathies instinctively ranged themselves with the Japanese in their fight against the Anglo Saxons'.[2]

Critics of the disaster later sought some explanation for this, and pointed to the life-style of Europeans, which some saw as decadent by nature. Indeed the system did glorify status; Europeans certainly did remain aloof, failing to mix socially with Asians, and this must have rankled in the hearts and minds of many. Had this not been so, the outcome might have been different.

Throughout Southeast Asia a lasting impression of British failure was indelibly imprinted on the Asian mind by Japan's sweeping victories in 1941 and 1942. Despite Co-Prosperity propaganda, however, the new masters of Malaya treated the indigenous people very badly and with 'no dram of mercy'.[3] The 45 months of occupation degenerated into a nightmare with long-lasting and catastrophic consequences that undermined Britain's future prestige in the area, and any confidence in her capability to provide protection in the future. It was inevitable that after the war the indigenous people would strive for and anticipate independence.

In 1945 therefore, when the British returned to govern Malaya, although they received a rapturous welcome from all sections of the population, they also had to redeem their godlike pre-war image which had been shattered in early 1942. Many British officials realised they would never be regarded again as invincible, although people were genuinely relieved by their return, and many Chinese '"literally wept with joy" when the first British soldiers reappeared',[4] such was their relief that the terror of the hated Japanese occupation was over. Britain's defeat and humiliation in 1942 had had a massive

> 'impact on the local population but, . . . its effect was less than was later assumed to be the case: "The first reaction of the population was one of overwhelming joy that the Japanese occupation was over and that the people they knew and had previously trusted had come back to help them recover from the damage done by the war, because that was the first priority — to repair power stations and water supplies, to get food in . . ., and to get the economy going again."'[5]

The occupation had shred the country bare. In towns there was an acute shortage of food, and health care and other services had deteriorated alarmingly. All races saw the end of the war as a liberation from tyranny and the start of better political, economic and social circumstances. Mahathir bin Mohamad — author of *The Malay Dilemma* in 1970 and Prime Minister of Malaysia since 1981 — wrote in 1945, as editor of his school magazine:

> 'Nearly four years have passed, weary years full of trials and hardships, of cruelty and evil deeds, of murder and torture. The War seemed interminable. It was wearisome. It wearied the soldier in the frontline, the mother at home, and the schoolboy in his school. It taxed one's strength, one's endurance, one's stolidity, and left one broken and shattered.
>
> But Peace with all that the word implies, has come. God be praised for the Peace that we have now. It could be another "Peace" in which the Powers of Evil triumph. But it is not. It is a Peace worth living through; for have not the Powers of Right and Justice won? Though in some corners of the world there is still some fighting, yet it is only the natural aftermath of a great upheaval and it too will die down. And may Almighty God prolong the Peace till Doomsday.
>
> Humanity is on the threshold of the greatest Age of all — the Age of Atomic Energy, and we, as members of the human race pray and hope that this revolutionary energy will be turned to peaceful usage. We hope that this marvellous discovery will enhance the progress of mankind, raise the standard of living, and maintain Peace even as it stopped War.'[6]

Some Malays, and particularly the Straits-born Chinese, had deep affection for the British before the war. When the liberation forces at last arrived, both communities welcomed them with wild joy and deep gratitude.

> '"The villagers came running out, carrying baskets of fruit for the troops and kissing their hands. No doubt the reason for that was the Malayan memory of the quality of the pre-war British administration."'[7]

Acceptance of British rule for an undetermined period in 1945 was essential, but this should have been drawn up from the outset along new lines perceptibly slanted towards the granting of eventual self rule to the country. The only question was when. Having failed to deliver the pre-war protection that Britain's treaties guaranteed, the post-war policy should have aimed at healing wounds that our failure had caused. At least the views of the people should have been considered. Instead, altered treaties were thrust on bewildered Sultans, some of whom initially accepted them in good faith. Whitehall's rushed and ill-conceived Malayan Union 'purification' process showed a remarkable lack of concern for the people in Malaya. Confusion and disbelief were soon to emerge as a powerful catalyst for a national consensus among the Malays, the like of which had never existed before.

18:2 Operation 'Zipper' Negated

Repeated rumour invites distortion of the truth, the outcome of which is mass confusion. Such was the dilemma facing people in Malaya as the war drew to a close.

By 11th August 1945, although rumours of the Japanese being on the verge of surrender were wildly circulating in Penang and other towns throughout the country, many people remained sceptical. It seemed too good to be true. The Japanese continued to aggressively deny all such rumours, threatening anyone suspected of spreading them with severe punishment. Rumour mongers were arrested, and on 15th August the *Syonan Shimbun* ordered everyone to keep quiet on the subject.

> 'No one has any sympathy for those who deliberately repeat idle rumours and get themselves into trouble over it. But for the sake of the good citizens, it is desirable that all foolish rumours should be stifled and those who are given to gossip warned of the serious harm which indulgence in what might seem harmless gossip might lead to. The insensible type of gossiper has had enough time and warning. If they persist in their foolish ways, they must be taught a severe lesson.'[8]

The Malays who, unlike the Chinese, had not played a significant role in opposing the Japanese were particularly influenced by the rumours during this uncertain period, especially as they felt their standing in the country threatened. Some rumours were purposely ill-founded and no doubt encouraged by the Japanese themselves as a means of stirring up racial friction. One rumour in particular led the Malays to believe that the Chinese Nationalist Army of Chiang Kai-shek would soon arrive in Malaya and Singapore as the reoccupying force, not the British they had anticipated. This would have been utterly abhorrent to them, as would have been the fear of their country coming completely under some form of Chinese domination.

The Japanese kept their surrender secret until 18/19th August, and only then did posters start to appear in market places in towns. Then it was confirmed that the nightmare regime had really come to an end. It was not, however, until 21st August that the Imperial Rescript dated 14th August was announced in the *Penang Shimbun*, along with a message from the Supreme Commander of the Dai-Nippon Army in Malaya, Lieut-General Teizo Ishiguro. In this article no mention of surrender was made.

Although the war of aggression might have been lost, Japan's industrial assault on the world's markets had already been conceived in the Rescript, and would come gradually into effect during the ensuing 50 years.

* * * * * *

Britain's loss of prestige with the ignominious fall of Malaya and Singapore made it important that she obtain an honourable share in the final defeat of Japan. With over 160,000 British prisoners of war and civilian internees incarcerated for three and a half years by the Japanese, there was much loss of face to be redeemed.

A major amphibious invasion — Operation 'Zipper' — was planned to recapture Malaya and Singapore, and was designed to be the zenith of Mountbatten's tenure as Supremo of SEAC. Originally set for November 1945, it was brought forward to August to enable Mountbatten to capture Singapore before the end of the year. During the planning stage of Operation Zipper the Americans voiced serious doubts as to whether such large numbers of forces could be spared for the operation, still having reservations about SEAC's set up, which some had already maliciously nicknamed 'Save England's Asian Colonies'! Political manoeuverings on the home front threatened the operation's existence even before plans got under way. Without prior consultation, Mountbatten was deprived of some 32,300 officers and men — many of them his most skilled troops in SEAC. Their period of service was suddenly shortened by four months to three years and four months, as a vote-catching political ploy to get them home in time for the approaching elections.

As it turned out Japan's sudden capitulation on 15th August caught everyone by surprise, invalidating Operation Zipper, which was carried out later but only as a peaceful reoccupation exercise.

Speed was essential to re-establish law and order in Malaya, and the original plan envisaged the reoccupation of Penang on 21st August. General Douglas MacArthur however, added to the already increasing tension in the country when, on 19 August, he forbade allied forces from landing in any territories occupied by Japanese troops until the formal surrender of the Japanese had been signed in Tokyo Bay, on 2nd September 1945.

MacArthur had cause to be cautious, considering the volatile nature of the Japanese, and especially in view of Field Marshall Count Terauchi's reaction on 22nd August. Penang was a defensive bastion, garrisoned by 5,000 Japanese, mostly navy personnel, and destruction contingency plans had been secretly formulated to counteract any allied landings. Had these occurred, many thousands of people would have perished, and George Town would have been razed. A list of Penang's 1,000 most prominent citizens — including lawyers, doctors, teachers and many others suspected of pro-British sympathies — had been compiled. In the event of an invasion these people were to be summarily executed. As surrender drew apparently closer, people on this list were all registered and photographed so that they could be quickly and easily rounded up.

By 19th August almost all the East Indies fleet, commanded by Vice Admiral H.T.C. Walker, were en route to the Malay Peninsula, their first mission being to reoccupy Penang. It was essential to have an advanced base, from where mine sweepers would be able to clear the final approaches to Singapore.

The delay imposed by MacArthur upset carefully conceived plans, resulting in a temporary but serious supply problem. To overcome this the fleet was anchored for shelter and refuelling in the lee of the Nicobar islands. Of more importance was the delay in the arrival of reoccupying forces in Malaya, causing a period of uncertainty, violence and widespread lawlessness.

18:3 The Interregnum

The sudden termination of hostilities in mid-August 1945 caught both Force 136 officers in Malaya and the MPAJA guerrillas 'completely by surprise'.[9] Neither had formulated any clearly defined immediate post-war plans, and when the reoccupying forces were delayed, there was a period during which no recognised military or civil authority was effectively in control. The MCP and MPAJA conspicuously failed 'to take advantage of this singular opportunity',[10] particularly as, during the first few weeks after the Japanese capitulation, they were the only organised and real power throughout the land. MPAJA tried for a short period to gain some control, especially in remote inland areas, but concentrated on vengeance killings of known or suspected collaborators. They also took advantage of the mounting chaos to add to their arsenal of weapons, disarming isolated Japanese posts, and attacking police stations. Chaos soon engulfed the country, and the 6–7,000 strong guerrilla force was able to operate 'almost unimposed in the liberated regions'.[11] Having no clearly thought out plan, however, they were unable to capitalise on this to their long-term advantage.

On 11th August 1945 Colonel John Davis, Chief of SEAC's Force 136 in Malaya, was instructed to inform the MPAJA guerrillas (now referred to as the Anti-Japanese United Forces — AJUF) that their contribution towards the imminent victory was appreciated and recognised as important to the Allied cause. On 17th August Force 136 personnel were ordered to cease fire. Davis instructed guerrillas within Force 136's influence to stay out of any main towns and districts still occupied in numbers by the Japanese. He was also to tell them to avoid unnecessary bloodshed and conflict with the Japanese, as SEAC was aware that any unwarranted and premature action might set back the reoccupation plans. In remote districts from which the Japanese had already withdrawn, MPAJA guerrillas were instructed to take temporary, limited charge in conjunction with the Force 136 officers attached to them, until British reoccupying forces arrived. The guerrillas were expected to enter these remote areas and assume responsibility for the maintenance of law and order.

These instructions — given to a scattered 350 strong advance party and small group of Force 136 officers — were sensitive in nature and difficult to put into effect, as anti-British sentiments among the communists were still as strong as ever. Many guerrillas, especially those with whom Force 136 had had no previous contact, were difficult to control. Force 136's minority position also meant that they were no challenge to the 7,000 strong MPAJA forces. Had the few British officers already in MPAJA camps persisted, they could easily have been detained.

Colonel Davis, perturbed by the implications of the orders, telegrammed Force 136 headquarters on 19th August:

> 'Your recent telegrams are disturbing. . . . Controlled AJUF are soldiers under command of SACSEA. They expect . . . specific orders and not vague directives. . . . they will obey such orders provided they are reasonable. Orders for them to remain half starved in the hills, while the Allies leisurely take over the administration from the Japs will not be reasonable.'[12]

He emphasised that the AJUF should be given a full share of the honours of victory. He thought that an outward display of good treatment of guerrillas under the influence of Force 136 personnel might have a beneficial effect on others outside their control, many of whom might be absorbed in due course. Davis further reiterated:

> 'The alternative to all this is chaos and anarchy which may take decades to eradicate. The matter is very urgent. There is serious risk of a disastrous anticlimax.'[13]

Realising the seriousness of the situation SEAC cancelled their instructions of 15th and 17th August. On the 22nd they authorised Force 136 controlled personnel to move into areas vacated by the Japanese, and in doing this endorsed MPAJA headquarters' orders of that date for its eight regiments to take over all towns in the country. In some of the areas where guerrillas had already attacked individuals on sentry duty, police stations and small isolated Japanese posts, confusion was already evident. This was further aggravated by bandit gangs taking advantage of the chaos to resort to similar action and falsely claiming to be MPAJA forces.

From 23rd August, when the Japanese started to withdraw from outlying districts and towns, chaos and racial tensions replaced any previous facade of law and order. Although MPAJA guerrillas were delighted by the Japanese defeat, many among them did not want the British to return.

> 'Local communist publications had been appearing supporting opposition to the British. There had been advances to the Japanese to sell their arms; and there were indications that Force 136 officers had difficulty in controlling guerrilla groups not in contact with them.'[14]

These factions attempted to spread turmoil and usurp authority in areas prematurely vacated by the Japanese. Although MPAJA headquarters gave no indication of sanctioning their actions, they were not rebuked for their attempts.

Unrest also broke out in the ranks of MPAJA and was exacerbated by delay and uncertainties. The MCP in Johore suggested that all Force 136 officers with MPAJA units should be killed, and the British on their return should be presented with a fait accompli.

> 'Neither of these ideas was taken up by the MCP leaders, who also failed to endorse the guerrilla takeovers by declaring independence and establishing a national government. Instead, the policy statement of 27 August called on cadres and guerrillas to cooperate with the returning British and to adopt a constitutional line of struggle.'[15]

* * * * * *

However much their policies were disliked, and whatever hatred was engendered for the Japanese as individuals and as a race, their ingrained sense of discipline was admired. Japanese garrisons in major towns, including Penang, during the weeks immediately following the surrender did help to prevent a complete state of pandemonium. This was not the case in remote districts where lawlessness became widespread.

After his initial dismay and disbelief, General Seishiro Itagaki, commander of the Seventh Area Army in Singapore, declared:

> 'Now that the Emperor has accepted the Potsdam Declaration, we must lay down our arms. Obeying the Emperor's order, we shall not fight. We must keep peace and order and we shall not make any trouble.'[16]

Some of his staff officers committed suicide. Others attempted to flee to Sumatra, or even defect to the Chinese guerrillas — thinking that all communists would be automatically anti-British. The majority, however, stoically accepted the discipline required of them.

Japanese troops were concentrated into specific areas from where they attempted to maintain firm control of the larger towns and communication centres such as Ipoh, Kluang, Kuala Lumpur and Taiping. State governors and garrison commanders issued proclamations to deter civil disturbances, but avoided any mention of the communists, who were obliquely referred to as troublesome elements, bandits and robbers. After the surrender many Japanese behaved with an outward and commendable show of calm. Civilians in commerce wound up their businesses and government officials made preparations to hand over to the incoming British.

At Jurong in Singapore the Japanese even built a concentration camp for themselves. In Penang, before the surrender was officially publicised, all liquor dealers were instructed to stop selling alcohol to Japanese soldiers in case it exacerbated violent reaction to news of the defeat and capitulation. In Singapore particularly the public was urged not to aggravate the tense situation by rash behaviour. They were told to wait patiently until Allied forces arrived. There were some incidents of recriminatory behaviour, when hastily hoisted Chinese national flags were torn down by armed and angry Japanese soldiers, many still prepared to fight if provoked or told to do so. The military, trying to maintain order in larger towns, inevitably clashed with roving gangs of looters and marauders, but did not provoke any incidents in Penang. They kept order there as best they could from the announcement of surrender to the arrival of British forces.

On 21st August 1945 the Penang naval commander issued a proclamation that rumour-mongers, looters, or anyone caught damaging property or causing injury to other people would be severely punished. On the following day the Kempeitai chief in Penang urged everyone to keep the peace. He expressed his personal regret for any trouble caused by his military policemen in the performance of their duty. He stated that maintaining law and order was still the responsibility of Nippon forces, and they intended to hand over everything in good order to the British. Ironic after three and a half years of government-induced fear and brutality! People were expressly warned against rioting, arson, murder, looting and assault, and by 24th August martial law was declared in Penang. Any offenders were threatened with death. Despite such threats the mood of elation was not dampened and people continued to celebrate the surrender in the streets. The police and Jikeidan were instructed to carry out their duties as calmly as possible. Editorials in newspapers urged all responsible citizens to uphold the law and act as self-appointed policemen. Had it not been for such stringent measures, outbreaks of violence and revenge killings in larger towns would have been considerably worse than they were.

In outlying areas and villages things were vastly different. The predominantly Chinese guerrillas — the military arm of the MCP — imposed their will and in several places disturbances broke out. Japanese troops were withdrawn from public sight and confined to barracks to reduce tension and prevent provocation. This had, however, the opposite effect as the balance of power was handed ostensibly to MPAJA, whose ranks included few Malays. It invited an appalling and violent lapse of law and order since it left a void which was filled by the guerrillas' lust for violence and retribution.

Hard core elements of MPAJA were communist. At the time of the surrender it was anticipated that they would cause disturbances and try to wrest control of the country. In parts of Pahang some guerrilla leaders were hostile and openly ignored Force 136 instructions, choosing to act as they saw fit. By 24th August the guerrilla situation had so deteriorated that Colin Mackenzie, a commander in Force 136, urged the British government to disclose relevant details concerning the impending Malayan Union proposal, which he considered might help to alleviate two of the AJUF's major grievances: the inferior citizenship status of domiciled Chinese, and the pre-war concept of the Communist Party as an illegal association under constant police scrutiny. The new government policy, he hoped, would resolve these grievances.

On 25 August broadcasts from SEAC headquarters authorised the resistance movements under the influence of Force 136 personnel to occupy those areas vacated by the Japanese.

> 'Their first duty would be to keep order, to prevent looting, burning and stealing, and to guard roads, railways, bridges, and other important places from attack by bandits or by collaborators "who want to stir trouble, so that they will be able to disappear in the confusion that follows".'[17]

Guerrillas were told they would be under the control of local British commanders when these arrived, but in the meantime it was their responsibility to ensure peace and stability. The broadcast also advised them that when the BMA was formed, it would provide them with assistance and financial help to enable them and their families to resume their place within the framework of Malayan society. Training for work in various occupations would also be found for them. SEAC headquarters was fully aware that the bulk of MPAJA guerrillas were Chinese. Despite instructions that these important broadcasts must be clearly understood by the Chinese, they were made in Malay and English only. This serious misjudgement, although supposedly corrected in a newsletter, did not resolve the problem as the message was directed at all resistance movements, not just MPAJA. The broadcast and later written instructions fell far short of Colonel Davis' expectations. Neither clearly imparted the view that MPAJA forces were looked on as SEAC troops. By the time this was acknowledged on 4th September, a breakdown of law and order had already occurred in many parts of the country, with guerrillas taking matters into their own hands.

The extent to which MPAJA guerrillas gained control in Malaya is disputed. One source claims that 70% of small towns and villages came under communist control, and the state of Johore, excluding the town of Johore Bahru. Another report implies that the guerrillas had virtually complete control of the whole country, although the area in which they were effective was difficult to define accurately. In Penang, the concentration of 5,000 predominantly Japanese naval forces at the naval garrison curtailed the takeover activities and influence of guerrillas on the island.

* * * * * *

Racial unrest broke out before 15th August. When the British landed in Penang on 3rd September there was abundant evidence of communal strife in various parts of the country. News of Japan's surrender was withheld by the MMA for one week and during this time, following previously made arrangements with British officers in Force 136, MPAJA guerrillas came out of their jungle hideouts to occupy police stations. Policemen were disarmed and collaborators of all races were rounded up for trial and execution. Incidents of lawlessness, caused by pent-up bitterness suppressed during the years of occupation, erupted during this time of confusion. The MCP tried to gain political control, assisted by its MPAJA guerrillas who tended to take the law into their own hands. The methods they used were reminiscent of Japanese terror tactics and served only to denigrate their cause, resulting in their loss of popularity.

MPAJA guerrillas were told to establish a People's Committee in every State, to take over responsibility for security, the rescue of refugees and the re-establishment of communications. MPAJA and MPAJU branches were instructed jointly to convene a State People's Representative Congress. When this happened SEAC HQ was left with no choice but to cancel their instructions of 15th and 17th August 1945, and endorse MPAJA HQ's orders of 22nd and 23rd August.

A demonstration of communist power emerged as the MCP and its guerrilla arm took advantage of a high degree of mass support. Many thousands of people were sympathetic towards them, giving them credit for Allied efforts. Uniformed MPAJA guerrillas entered areas vacated by the Japanese and were greeted excitedly by large crowds of Chinese. They attacked and overran isolated posts sparsely manned by soldiers or police, and in other places where the Japanese were still deployed in strength, they carried out minor acts of sabotage and looted military stores. As the Japanese withdrawal accelerated so the scale of these attacks increased. Police posts were invariably among the first places to be overrun and many were ransacked and burnt down. Many Malay and Sikh policemen either ran away when the Japanese pulled out, or tried to barricade themselves inside their posts. In doing so they became the first victims of the guerrillas' revenge against collaborators.

> 'They were often fair game, the first victims of revenge meted out by guerrillas to collaborators. If the policemen did not surrender, their police stations would be attacked. If they gave themselves up without a fight, they would be disarmed, victimised, or killed.'[18]

In many places decorative arches, constructed over main streets and bridges in towns to welcome the British, and adorned with

American, British, Chinese and Russian flags, and inscriptions welcoming the 'Victorious Allied Forces', were redecorated with Soviet, Kuomintang and Three Star Flags. Inscriptions were painted over, giving credit for victory to MPAJA's forces. Property previously owned by Japanese was seized. Labour unions were hastily set up to represent every trade and occupation in the country. Communist prestige increased, as did their ranks, due to a mixture of bravado tactics supported by subtle propaganda. In the chaos many credited them with the liberation of the country; many more were too frightened to resist them. By the time the reoccupying British forces arrived, village and rural districts, including masses of squatters along jungle fringes, had come under local communist control.

> 'They had sown the seeds of a hydra-headed chaos which must engulf the whole of Malaya. We could see that they would propagate their doctrines and poison the masses with Marxism. We could hear them talking of Stalin as the "Father of the Proletariats". We could see that they would not rest satisfied until they had secured domination over the populace.'[19]

Communists naively assumed that 'Malaya would be reoccupied by a Chinese army'.[20] When this rumour was found to be incorrect the party leadership still continued to act with an indecision which led to an internal rift within the party organisation as to what post-war policy they should adopt. One side favoured immediate civil struggle; the other advocated a policy of labour infiltration and agitation similar to that carried out before the war. The so-called Moderate Soviet policy prevailed and 'was established as the correct tactical line'.[21]

In 1945 there was no real danger of the MCP switching its role from clandestine leader of a guerrilla movement to promoters of a revolutionary war against the returning and victorious Allied forces. These — earmarked for Operation Zipper — were far too strong for the MCP to take on at this point, and with the attitude of the British government gradually changing, by the time the war ended the communists had emerged as the natural enemies of the future. The tension this created manifested itself in some racial clashes, especially between the Chinese and Malays. For the most part however, after nearly four years of hated Japanese oppression the majority of people welcomed the British reoccupation.

* * * * * *

In pre-war Malaya British authority had curtailed racial conflict among the three different communities. The Malays, Indians and Chinese, without necessarily liking each other, had led their separate lives with relative social harmony and without any apparent confrontation. Separatism, among Malays and Chinese in particular, intensified throughout the occupation, stemming largely from the contrasting attitude of the two races towards the Japanese, and the concomitant treatment that they received. Some Malays were actively pro-Japanese; the remainder, if not actively sympathetic to them, nevertheless welcomed their 'new masters', seeing their administration as a means of stemming the economical and political encroachment of the Chinese.

> 'The Chinese were naturally discriminated against by the Japanese, while the Indians identified themselves with the struggle to liberate India.'[22]

Patterns changed drastically as the war drew to a close. The Malays were increasingly ignored by the Japanese as their usefulness to them declined, whereas mounting numbers of Chinese collaborated with them in order to gain favour. The distinction between the two races increased with growing mutual antagonism.

The period was especially stressful for the Chinese, as their age-old social structure cast aside some traditional concepts. Many of the more influential and older Chinese — who had not fled the country — were discredited, having been coerced initially into cooperating with the Japanese, and were now despised for doing so. The 'towkays' lost their prestige, being identified as spokesmen and apologists for the Japanese and their inept administration. Their communalistic influence was superseded by that of the young Chinese communists in whom the experience of the occupation invoked a greater awareness of Chinese nationalism and ethnic identity. During the closing stages of the occupation, the credibility of many OCA 'towkays' and leaders was completely destroyed by their continuing cooperation with the Japanese, and they were sought out as collaborators for elimination by the MPAJA guerrillas. By the time the British returned, Sino/Malay relations had broken down. Bloody clashes erupted as the mostly Chinese communists sought to establish their political influence in each state.

The brutal behaviour of the Japanese, their policies and discriminatory attitude towards the various races were instrumental in exacerbating these tensions which culminated in racial conflict between the Malays and Chinese. Retaliatory raids by Chinese guerrillas on Malays were directed not only against suspected spies for the Japanese, collaborators, government officials and the police but also the Malay population in general. Advantage was taken of the chaos to even old personal scores and there were many instances of abduction and murder. Unruly elements and secret societies thrived in the horrific interlude of lawlessness and anarchy which followed. A wave of crime and terror on a scale never seen before exploded throughout the country. Guerrilla reprisals and looting were rife. Helpless people of all races were vindictively murdered, occasionally with the assistance of the Kempeitai, who were looking to save their own skins. Even mistresses of the Japanese were shown no mercy and

> 'many of those arrested by the guerrillas were marched or dragged through the streets and given a "people's court" trial'.[23]

The conflict revealed the Malays' hatred of communism. It ignited both Islamic fervour and a spirit of nationalism which determined 'to prevent Chinese domination of their country'.[24]

Pro-Japanese people and associations lived in fear of retribution and quickly turned to acts of charity, hoping in this manner to atone for their previous actions. They outwardly supported the communists, and

> 'displayed their new-born allegiance by flying the "Three-Star Flag" and the Soviet Flag on their car radiator and at the front of their house'.[25]

Many district officers, penghulus and kampong ketuas were caught and summarily executed, and policemen in small stations vanished overnight. In the vigorous manhunt for informers, guerrilla reprisals were cruel and violent. Ordinary policemen did not escape this and as a result the police were completely demoralised, and disintegrated as an organised force. A later enquiry conducted by the British Military Administration (BMA) showed that the police force was

> 'the only public service of Government which had completely fallen down as a result of their activities under the Japanese rule'.[26]

Chinese guerrilla reprisals were directly aimed against the police, many of whom were either killed or kidnapped. The force was completely discredited in the eyes of the public, with most policemen

> 'afraid to show themselves outside stations or barracks, and police work and duties generally were non-existent'.[27]

A Malay ex-police sergeant who had served under the Japanese recalled:

> 'It was a world gone mad, a world turned upside down. Suddenly, people seemed to remember every little wrong I did, even when I did not do them. There was a lot of anger and hatred about, and this resulted in people being abducted, beaten and murdered. Initially, before the violence became racial, even some of our Malay kinsmen believed that the police force was the tali barut (lackey) of the Japanese and had discredited themselves. But they came to our help later when they could not bear some of the things done to the Malay policemen, such as their bodies were mutilated and their eyes gouged out. . . . These actions which the people seeking revenge did were no different from the Japanese troops against whom they railed. They had degenerated to the same level of barbarism . . .'[28]

The communists' cruelty caused Malays to retaliate equally violently, particularly in Negeri Sembilan where many Chinese were massacred. On 21st August the first racial clashes between Malays and Chinese broke out in Muar and Batu Pahat, closely followed by others at Kluang and Mersing.

* * * * * *

In Penang civil disruption and a breakdown of law and order started only a few days before 3rd September 1945, when communist guerrillas, along with other armed Chinese ruffians and gangsters, crossed over from the mainland and rampaged throughout the island at will, dealing out rough justice against policemen, suspected profiteers and traitors and anyone even remotely thought to be an informer. A Chinese restaurant was used as the communist headquarters. The response of those living on the island to the arrival of the guerrillas varied according to whether they had collaborated with the Japanese, or suffered at their hands. To those who had enjoyed the luxury of non-involvement it was akin to a day of judgement.

> 'Many people were abducted or taken from their homes because they had been informers and henchmen of the hated Kempeitai. They were never seen again. The communists carried out most of these summary executions. They had a very good spy network and as far as the Chinese population on this island was concerned, they were regarded as heroes, dedicated and fearless fighters against the Japanese and their lackeys. . . . I believe that some of the people who were killed deserved their fate, especially the evil-doers and the informers.'[29]

Communal friction started in Penang on 4th September, when several minor outbreaks of rioting occurred between Hindu and Muslim Indians. One Chinese policeman was denounced as a 'quisling' and was murdered. Throughout the following day and night the same factions continued looting and rioting, purportedly over the foodstuffs from various storage dumps left behind by the Japanese. The *Straits Echo*'s editorial on 6th September denounced with disgust the communal unrest as 'A Blot on Penang's Fair Name'. Three days of liberation, following 1,354 days of Japanese occupation, had appeared to undermine people's resolve to live in harmony.

The clashes between Hindu and Muslim Indians were the outcome of stringent rationing imposed during the occupation. Agitators had purposely panicked people into behaving in this manner. The Muslims were the first to act aggressively, but in subsequent clashes on 6th September both factions were equally to blame. Shortage of transport made it impossible to redistribute the large stocks hoarded by the Japanese and knowledge of this made matters worse.

On the surface these disturbances were caused by food shortages. In reality tensions were heightened by the political divisions among the main protagonists. Muslim Indians in Penang had suffered during the occupation at the hands of the Hindu supporters of Subhas Chandra Bose because they had remained loyal to the British. They had a long-standing score to settle.

18:4 Reoccupation by Allies

On 28th August 1945 the *Penang Shimbun* published a proclamation issued by the Imperial Japanese Naval Headquarters in Penang advising the public that British vessels would soon be carrying out mine sweeping operations in the waters around the island. On the same day Vice Admiral H.T.C. Walker, in the battleship *HMS Nelson*, and the main body of the Allied fleet reached Penang. *HMS* Nelson took on board some Japanese naval envoys sent from Singapore. They had been instructed to provide charts of Japanese minefields in the area, to assist with their clearance, and to provide the relieving fleet with a safe passage through the Malacca Straits. On 30th August mine sweeping operations in the waters around Penang were still being carried out. The delay caused by these precautions heightened the frustration of people in Penang as they waited for an end to their hateful subjugation by the Japanese. This temporary set-back however did not dampen enthusiasm for organising celebrations on a grand scale for the imminent arrival of the relieving forces, scheduled on 3rd September. By that date the tops of many buildings in the town were bedecked with an assortment of Allied flags and bunting, and liquor shops were fully restocked for the occasion.

By 1st September speculation over the landing date had intensified. There was frustration and disappointment over the delay in the arrival of the British forces, especially as Churchill, Stalin and Chiang Kai Chek were heroes in the eyes of Malayans at that time.

Admiral Sir Arthur Power, C-in-C East Indies Fleet, arrived at Penang on 1st September in the cruiser *HMS Cleopatra*. He held prolonged discussions that night on board *HMS Nelson*. On the following day Rear Admiral Uzumi — decorated during the 1914–18 war with a DSC and an Allied Victory Medal — was summoned on board *HMS Nelson* to lead the Japanese delegation in signing the surrender terms with Vice Admiral Walker, and the terms for the reoccupation of Penang Island. On Monday morning the 3rd of September shortly after 8.30 a.m. Force Roma, the first Allied reoccupation forces comprising 480 Royal Marines commanded by Lieut-Colonel R.N. Grant and a Royal Navy contingent commanded by Captain T.J. Hilken RN DSO, set foot on Weld Quay without incident. Huge cheering crowds greeted Force Roma at the quayside. In a brief ceremony the 'Union Jack' was raised and the 'Rising Sun' was lowered. The quickly reformed Penang Service Committee lined up in welcome on the quayside. One company of Royal Marines then ceremonially marched off towards the Eastern and Oriental (E & O) Hotel.

> 'The thunderous ovation the masses accorded the marines as they landed was symbolic of Malaya's full-hearted welcome and jubilation. Penang went into hysterics of joy. People in inland towns were jealous of Penang.'[30]

Jubilant cheering crowds lined the streets. Armed Japanese soldiers restrained an estimated excited crowd of 10,000 men, women and children of all races, who had been waiting for hours from surging forward into the path of each lorry as it passed.

On the 3rd evening between 6.30 and 8.30 p.m. Captain Hilken, as the Acting Military Governor of the island, made a brief broadcast in English, translated into Malay, Chinese and Tamil for the benefit of all people living on the island. The headlines of the first post war issue of the *Straits Echo and Penang Gazette* dated 4th September 1945, captured the prevailing emotion: 'Gay Throngs Welcome British Back to Penang. Unforgettable Scenes of Joy. The British have come. The British have come.' Crowds on the waterfront rapidly took up this cry when they saw two British transports steaming into Penang harbour. Shop keepers shut their shops, and in the Chinese part of the town Union Jacks, Stars and Stripes, Soviet Union flags and Chinese National flags intermingled with each other, fluttering from shop windows and the tops of buildings. Hidden throughout the occupation, under threat of death if discovered, they were now raised in final defiance of Japanese imperialism and tyranny. Fire crackers staccatoed through the air. Church bells everywhere, led by those of the

Church of Assumption, peeled out their welcome to the final ending of the years of ordeal. An editorial on 4th September – entitled '*Non Nobis*' – declared the 1,354 days of Japanese rule in Penang a hideous nightmare!

At 10.30 a.m. on 4th September a deputation of prominent local community leaders was received by Vice Admiral Walker on board *HMS Princess Beatrix*. The deputation, led by Mr M. Saravamuttu, included Mr Khoo Sian Ewe OBE (Chinese Town Hall), who presented to Vice Admiral Walker the original Union Jack which had flown over the Residency in December 1941, and had been hidden at considerable risk throughout the occupation. Also present were: Mr Lim Lean Theng (Chinese Chamber of Commerce), Dr Lim Chwee Leong (Straits Chinese British Association), Mr H.H. Abdoolcadar CBE (Indian Community), Dr Kamil Md Ariff and Mr C.M. Hashim (Malay Community), Dr E.W. D'Cruz (Eurasian Association), The Very Reverend Brother James OBE (Visitor, St Zaviers Institution), Mr Heah Joo Seang and Mr A. M.Y. Izzudin. Reports of many atrocities perpertrated in the early part of the occupation were recounted at this meeting, and Captain Hilken was asked to obtain details so that the guilty could be brought to justice. Mr Khoo hailed the termination of the war with relief and heartfelt thanks. Mr Abdoolcadar welcomed back with unbounded joy 'our old rulers'[31], and Dr Kamil Md Ariff said that the first thing that came to his mind on learning of Japan's unconditional surrender was to give thanks to Almighty God. The mental anguish and physical suffering of the last 43 months was now a thing of the past.

On 6th September Vice Admiral Walker, standing at the entrance of the old town hall, took the salute at a victory parade and march through the streets of the town. Three bands and 19 platoons, two each from *HMS Nelson, Ceylon, Nigeria, Antar, Tattar, Vollage, Penn, Redoubt* and from the RIN sloop *Kistna*, took part in the parade, joined by the hurriedly resurrected Penang town band and members of the Penang Service Committee, along with representatives of the local Defence Services, Rovers and Boy Scouts. Mr Khoo Sian Ewe organised a large party for the occasion, ceremoniously digging up a bottle of champagne buried in his garden since December 1941.

* * * * * *

Following the completion of mine sweeping in the Malacca Straits, *HMS Cleopatra* left Penang and made her way to Singapore where she rejoined the other ships in the reoccupation fleet. She arrived there on 3rd September in time for the arrival of *HMS Sussex* on the following day, bringing Rear Admiral Holland and Lieut-General A.F.P. Christison — the representatives of Lord Louis Mountbatten at the reoccupation arrangements for Singapore. On 5th September at 11.30 a.m. British, Indian and Gurkha troops went ashore to be greeted by wildly cheering crowds. General Itagaki and other Japanese officers were present on the quayside to receive them, and Lieut-General Christison — commanding the 5th Indian Division which formed the spearhead force for the reoccupation — signed an agreement with Itagaki on behalf of Mountbatten for the reoccupation of Singapore by the British. They encountered no difficulty on landing. At Collier Quay British Indian Army troops destroyed in disgust an INA troop memorial that had been erected there, cheered on by the watching crowds — the very same who not long before this had cheered with the same enthusiasm as the memorial had been built.

Upon resuming control over Radio Singapore, the first message to be broadcast was one prepared by His Majesty King George VI. He expressed his deepest gratitude that people in Britain's Far Eastern territories had at last been liberated from the oppression of the Japanese. Japanese laws and regulations were promptly rescinded, Tokyo time was abolished and an estimated 85,000 Japanese civilians were rounded up and concentrated in camps located in southern Johore and elsewhere, while disarmed Japanese troops were made to fill in trenches and start clearing up bomb damage in and around the dock areas.

At the formal surrender ceremony for Singapore, on 12th September, Mountbatten insisted that all senior Japanese officers should be required to relinquish their swords in front of their men. The swords were duly distributed among selected officers and dignitaries.

> 'Mr Lee Kuan Yew described the "final humiliation of these little warriors" as "one of the greatest moments of the history of South East Asia".'[32]

Mountbatten later commented on these events in his diary:

> 'I have never seen six more villainous, depraved or brutal faces in my life, ... I shudder to think what it would have been like to be in their power. When they got off their chairs and shambled out, they looked like a bunch of gorillas with great baggy breaches and knuckles almost trailing to the ground.'[33]

* * * * * *

Meanwhile in Penang the large food storage dumps set up by the Japanese were taken over by the British so that food could be distributed to those in need. The reoccupying forces also recovered a considerable amount of war booty, including 12,000 tons of rubber and 1,000 tons of tin. When the BMA set up the Malayan Rubber Produce and Buying Unit, it was empowered to ship these essential raw products to Great Britain and the United States.

The Japanese used indentured labour and prisoners of war to excavate tunnels near the lily ponds on the boundary of the Penang Botanical Gardens. These were intended as makeshift air-raid shelters, but were mostly used to store large quantities of ammunition during their occupation of the island. An ammunition works, complete with railway tracks along which heavy items could be moved, was also set up in this part of the gardens, masked from the sky and from prying eyes by the foliage of the trees. Numerous torpedoes were assembled here. Immediately after the reoccupation large quantities of abandoned war materials, as well as 1,226 twenty-eight inch torpedoes, were found in various parts of the Botanical Gardens, as well as two large artillery guns. Time has obliterated most of this evidence of war time activity, except for some overgrown remnants of rusty metal rail tracks and the haphazardly sealed entrances of former excavations.

On the remote south-west corner of Penang island, overlooking the coast at Gertak Sangul, the Japanese forced prisoners of war and some civilians to dig well concealed tunnels totalling almost one kilometer in length into the hillside. The exits to these tunnels overlooked the sea and were manned by anti-aircraft guns. They were also used as sentry posts and storehouses for ammunition, explosives and a variety of other supplies.

* * * * * *

On 12th September thanksgiving services were held in many churches, temples and mosques throughout the island, and a victory day parade and Chingay were organised. The first post-war Hari Raya occurred on Thursday and Friday, 29th and 30th September 1945. The celebrations were relatively subdued, and there were few if any candles or lubricants to burn. The Raya sermons in the major mosques for the first time were read in Malay, and not in Arabic.

The 34th anniversary of the foundation of the Chinese Republic on 10th October 1911 — the Double Tenth — was resoundingly celebrated in Penang in 1945. The Chinese, including those from the MCP, were joined by many Indians in their procession which stretched for over one and a half miles. A tea party and stage performance were attended by representatives of all communities on the island.

Penang's festive mood continued through the first Christmas after the liberation. Midnight services, night shows and carols, dancing and music in the streets abounded. A joyous yet solemn Christmas eve was celebrated and for the first time in four years fears of oppression did not dampen the seasonal cheer. Hotels, cafes, cabarets and theatres did a roaring trade, and at midnight, the joyous solemnity of the occasion was tolled out as Christians again participated in their midnight masses and services with an appropriate background of resounding church bells.

Gusto and revelry greeted 1st January 1946, despite the town being drunk dry. In a new year message Brigadier L.E.C.M. Perowne CBE, the Sub-Area Commander, wished

> 'all people of Penang and Province Wellesley security, sufficiency and contentment in 1946. The miseries of war do not wholly and suddenly disappear, nor does the role of the army cease abruptly when the cease-fire sounds.'[34]

Citizens were reminded that their first duty was to assist in restoring the country, and Penang in particular, to its former happy state of prosperity. In his New Year message, Captain G.A. Harrison, the Naval Officer-in-charge, said:

> 'You have withstood oppression, cruelty and indignities under the Japanese rule and have come through unflinchingly, determined to rebuild and

return to decent ways of living. The war was hard and you fought it in a spirit of self-sacrifice and tenacity.'[35]

18:5 Internment and Release

When the surrender was made known among rank and file Japanese troops, many tried to flee by one means or another and some officials and officers committed suicide. The majority however decided that life with ignominy was better than heroic death, and proceeded to make hurried arrangements for the welfare of their occupational wives and the children of such unions, as well as to safeguard their ill-gotten wealth. An immediate change came over many of the Japanese after the surrender. Gone was their arrogance and with typical thoroughness they even adopted a most impressive form of humility for having lost the war. If a Japanese 'has to eat humble-pie, he eats it with such a grace as to make even his worst enemy relent'.[36]

In Penang on 4th September Japanese soldiers were relieved of their duties by Royal Marines and interned at Glugor. By 3.30 on the afternoon of 5th September all Japanese civilian and naval personnel, totalling about 4,000, had been despatched from the island to Bedong on the mainland in south Kedah, where another concentration camp had been set up. Admiral Uzumi, the former naval commander of Penang garrison, was among those sent to Bedong, and it was not until one month later, on Saturday 6th October, that the official surrender ceremony for this assortment of internees took place.

The ceremony was held at the Sungei Patani aerodrome, where Brigadier J.C.W. Cargill OBE, the officer commanding the 74th Indian Infantry Brigade, was officially handed the Japanese naval commander's sword. Captain Hidaka, a naval officer previously attached to the Penang garrison, and one other senior Japanese officer both fainted during the ceremony. Five work forces of internees, each equivalent to a battalion in strength, were used in land clearing and drainage works in Province Wellesley. The area, totalling 800 acres, was destined to be flooded for planting paddy.

All civilian Japanese in Singapore or southern Malaya at the time of the surrender were promptly rounded up and concentrated at

Jurong. Some of these, who had lived in Singapore for a long time, owned property there and had amassed considerable fortunes, which were immediately confiscated and placed under the control of the British Custodian of Enemy Property. In the end all

> 'the Japanese had to show for their years in Singapore and Malaya were bundles of Japanese script, banana money . . . [which] they were told to burn . . . because it was now worthless'.[37]

In Singapore Japanese prisoners of war were allocated to labour units used for cleaning and rehabilitation work in and around the city. Many were put to clear bomb damage at Keppel Harbour, and to work at Bukit Timah and Paya Lebar airports. The construction works at Paya Lebar had been started by Allied prisoners of war on their return to Changi prison after surviving the ordeal on the Siamese 'death' railway. Now Japanese prisoners were required to continue the construction of this airport. The roles had been reversed! Various camps were prepared to cater for about 40,000 Japanese prisoners in Upper Changi Road, Seletar, Nee Soon, Keppel Harbour as well as on the hillside adjoining Clementi Road. They remained there — and some died in these camps as prisoners of war — until mid-1947. At the western corner of the Japanese cemetery in Chuan Hoe Avenue, a memorial of three tombstones bears the inscription:

> 'In memory of the souls of the Labour Force comprising Army and Navy personnel who died in Singapore between September 1945 and April 1947.'[38]

Behind the memorial the ashes of those who died were put into a hole which was sealed over with concrete. A small concrete pillar marks the spot where the ashes of 135 Japanese war criminals executed at Changi prison were buried. Another one marks the burial spot of 79 convicted war criminals executed in different parts of Malaya.

28,000 Japanese civilians surrendered in Malaya. Of these, 9,000 were employed in the civil government, another 8,000 were used to clear jungle for growing rice and maize for the civil population. The military employed approximately 10,000 civil internees, 8,000 of whom were used for engineering works. Without using these Japanese the intensive rebuilding programmes required in Singapore and Malaya would have been considerably slower. By December 1946 most of the Japanese had been repatriated to Japan and only the minimal essential numbers were retained to carry on with important reconstruction works.

An awesome rehabilitation programme was needed with the ending of conflict. Extensive clearing and cleaning up was urgently required, along with a complete overhaul of the administrative machinery to govern daily life. Everyone's cooperation and assistance was required.

Some Japanese internees complained bitterly about their working conditions and accommodation during their period of internment. They disregarded the fact that the same huts they used, which they referred to as pig sties, had previously been inhabited by Allied prisoners of war.

* * * * * *

In Penang the transfer of sick, tortured and brutalised prisoners from gaol to hospital was a priority. The General Hospital was taken over by Surgeon Lieut-Commander Foster. By 4th September all persons who had not committed offences against British law were released, and the relatives of others still waiting to be set free were told to be patient while release procedures were finalised. In due course a total of 54 prisoners, including 15 women, were set free from the Penang gaol, where they had been incarcerated by the Japanese for political reasons. Some had been conveniently branded as communists — this, in the opinion of the Japanese, justifying their brutalisation and torture. Court decisions dictated by the Japanese were reviewed, and action was taken against those directly responsible for ordering and carrying out the torture of prisoners, suspects and those who had been falsely accused.

By late October 1945 it was possible to repatriate to Penang the first large group of conscripted 'comfort girls' from brothels and vice dens in different parts of the Dutch East Indies. Most of these women had been forced into this degrading service, explicitly reserved for the use of Japanese military personnel. These 80 Chinese women and girls, mainly previous residents of Penang, were found in different parts of Sumatra. On being returned to Penang in three aircraft, they were initially quarantined on Pulau Jerejak, where during the occupation the Japanese had conscripted almost 300 Javanese youths into various forms of forced labour. The girls were a mixed bunch. Some of them had been dance hostesses before the war; others had been seamstresses, amahs or factory workers. For almost one month before they were repatriated, they were temporarily sheltered on the tiny spice island of Sabang at the northern tip of Sumatra, where they were given food and medicine by both the British and Chinese Red Cross organisations. For many of the women the joy of coming home was tainted with the harsh memory of what they had been forced into, and the shame cast on their families. Many were in dire need of sympathy and moral support, and for some this was not forthcoming.

One of the classrooms of the Penang Convent in Light Street was used as a makeshift small and stuffy cell in which both European and American prisoners of war were incarcerated for several months. Included among them were 70 American submariners from the *USS Grenadier*, commanded by Lt-Commander J.A. Fitzgerald. This was scuttled after being severely damaged in the waters of Lem Voalen Gulf on April 22nd, 1943. Survivors were picked up by two Japanese vessels and taken to Penang to be imprisoned initially, then interrogated and in some cases tortured by the Kempeitai at the Light Street Convent. They were kept there for just over three months, before being sent to separate camps. The names and initials of these prisoners were scratched on the classroom walls, along with improvised calendars and dates of their incarceration. Scratchings indicated that some prisoners were still being held there until late 1944, and vividly portrayed the extent of the suffering and ill-treatment they experienced in this hell-hole hidden in the middle of a busy township.

* * * * * *

Prisoners of war from the Far East were in need of considerable help, both physical and mental, in order to repatriate and ease them into some form of useful civilian employment. Often regarded by the higher military command in Britain as military undesirables, many did not even receive a friendly welcome on return to their country, a sad contrast to the rapturous reception received by their Australian counterparts, particularly women internees. In England the Home Office even went to the extent of telling relatives and friends not to meet ships when they docked, and no formal press coverage was given to these victims of the war. The authorities maintained a silent shamefaced public attitude towards the returning internees' ordeal. The only official recognition granted to them, other than additional petrol and clothing coupons, was a standardised letter signed by King George VI sent to each survivor. Those in dire financial difficulties obtained little or no assistance, as no central relief fund had been set up by the government for this purpose. Even the extra clothing coupons made available were more often than not received with suspicious scorn by shopkeepers, often with queries as to their authenticity. It was only through a chance newspaper advertisement that ex-internees learned they could make a claim at the Colonial Office, but these were processed slowly, some taking a year from the time a claim was made, until standard amounts of only £35 were handed out.

By mid-1942 prisoners of war in the Singapore and Malayan campaigns were forgotten entities. Few people in Britain realised the extent of the brutality they had endured. It was only in 1944 when Mr Anthony Eden (later Lord Avon) made a grave statement to this effect in the House of Commons that the extent of their suffering was appreciated. The euphoria of peace brought with it many urgent demands on the country's over-extended and denuded finances and resources, and the sufferings of ex-POWs soon faded once again to a forgotten entity. The British POW Association did massive background work to assist in restoring the self-respect of prisoners when they returned, and much was done by this organisation to salvage both bodies and minds and make them fit again for a role in civilian life and employment. An assortment of associations grew from this and became the Federation of Far East Prisoners of War, under the leadership of the number one FEPOW, Lieut-General A.E. Percival.

Percival had been interned mostly in Manchuria, but on 2nd of September 1945 was flown to Tokyo Bay to witness the final surrender of the Japanese. When he attended an investiture at Buckingham Palace to receive a decoration awarded to him earlier in the war, King George VI spoke privately to him with the greatest understanding and sympathy. In contrast, both the Chiefs of Staff and the British government maintained an icy silence towards him right up to his death on 31st January, 1966. He was required to retire soon after returning to England, without being promoted to the substantive rank of Lieut-General, which would have helped to increase his pension. Percival was 58 years old when the war ended and although painfully thin, he was still in a remarkably good mental and physical condition. His immediate concern was the plight of those British prisoners of war who had returned to England from his Malayan command. The time he spent as President of the Federation of Far East POWs were years of unending endeavour and unselfishness, and among the noblest years of his life.

* * * * * *

Rubber planters gradually filtered back to Malaya to take up where they had left off in December 1941. Major T.W.T. (Bill) Bangs arrived in Penang on 26th May 1946, bringing with him 940 displaced persons, who like him had been sent to work by the Japanese on the infamous Siamese railway. He said on his return, 'The Malays were good to me on the railway and I will be returning to Kuantan.'[39] Three other planters — Perky Perkins, Richard G. Bower (Haji, as he later became and was familiarly known because of his initials 'RG'), and Hugh Watts — were all volunteers at the outset of war, and were among the many planters who managed to survive the Siamese death railway. Hugh Watts returned to his beloved Sungie Ara Estate on Penang Island, and brought with him his workers' balance of wages for December 1941. His first thought was for their welfare.

On 17th March 1946 the *Sunday Gazette* announced the return to Penang of Dr L.W. Evans CBE, who had been Chief Medical Officer at the Penang General Hospital in December 1941. Dr Evans — who had only come to Penang in 1941 to assume the post — was one of the few Europeans, with Major F.W. Harvey of the Salvation Army in Penang, who had flatly refused to evacuate from the island, willingly staying behind to continue helping and treating the sick and those wounded during the bombing raids. On his return Dr Evans was greeted by more than 100 members of the St John's Ambulance Brigade and Nursing Unit, then called the Medical Auxillary Services.

1. *British Rule in Malaya 1942–1957* by Robert Heussler, ch.7, p.190.
2. *Allies of a Kind. The US and Britain and the War against Japan 1942–5* by Christopher Thorne, p.727.
3. *No Dram of Mercy* by Sybil Kathigasu.
4. *Conflict and Violence in Singapore and Malaysia 1945–1983* by Richard Clutterbuck, ch.1, p.41. (Refers to F. Spencer Chapman, *The Jungle is Neutral*, London 1949, p.419.)
5. *Tales from the South China Seas. Images of the British in South-East Asia in the Twentieth Century* edited by Charles Allen, Epilogue — 'Staying On', p.288. (Bill Goode's quotation.)
6. *The Straits Echo*, Wednesday, 28 November 1973. (Quote by Dr Mahathir bin Mohamad.)
7. *A History of Malaya* by R.O. Winstedt, ch.15, p.254. (Mr Driberg's description to the House.)
8. *Red Star over Malaya. Resistance and Social Conflict during and after the Japanese Occupation, 1941–1946* by Cheah Boon Kheng, ch.5, p.127–8. (Refers: *Syonan Shimbun*, 15 August 1945.)
9. *The Communist Struggle in Malaya* by Gene Z. Hanrahan, ch.4, p.87.
10. Ibid, ch.4, p.87.
11. Ibid, ch.4, p.87.
12. *Red Star over Malaya. Resistance and Social Conflict during and after the Japanese Occupation, 1941–1946* by Cheah Boon Kheng, ch.6, p.161. (Message of Colonel John Davis, attached to Memorandum of Commander, Force 136 H.P.D., 'Force 136 Policy — Malaya', 19 August 1945, in WO 203/5642.)
13. Ibid, ch.6, p.161.
14. Ibid, ch.6, p.148–9. ('Memorandum on the Force 136 Organisation in Malaya' by Lt-Col D.G. Gill-Davies, 13 September 1945, p.3 in B.M.A. PSD/39.)
15. Ibid, ch.6, p.149.
16. Ibid, ch.5, p.130. (Refers to Mamoru Shinosaki, *Syonan — My Story*, Singapore 1975, p.94–5.)
17. Ibid, ch.6, p.165. (SACSEA to Rear SACSEA, 'Special talk for resistance movements in Malaya to be used in Malay, Chinese and English', 25 August 1945, in WO 172/1778.)
18. Ibid, ch.7, p.178.
19. *Ma-Rai-Ee* by Chin Kee Onn, ch.25, p.296.
20. Ibid, ch.4, p.88. (Refers to Purcell, *The Chinese in Malaya*, London, Oxford University Press 1948, p.264–6.)
21. Ibid, ch.4, p.88.
22. *The Malay Dilemma* by Mahathir bin Mohamad, ch.2, p.6.
23. *Red Star over Malaya. Resistance and Social Conflict during and after the Japanese Occupation, 1941–1946* by Cheah Boon Kheng, ch.5, p.133. (Shinosaki, op. cit., p.97.)
24. *The Masked Comrades. A Study of the Communist United Front in Malaya 1945–48* by Cheah Boon Kheng, ch.2, p.17.
25. *Malaya Upside Down* by Chin Kee Onn, ch.25, p.182.
26. *Red Star over Malaya. Resistance and Social Conflict during and after the Japanese Occupation, 1941–1946* by Cheah Boon Kheng, ch.10, p.272. (Refers to DCCAO's Report on the

Military Government of the Malay Peninsula for the period 12–30 September 1945 in MU Secret C/1/4.)

27. Ibid, ch.10, p.272.
28. Ibid, ch.5, p.134. (Cheah Boon Kheng interview with informant in Kuala Lumpur in November 1976.)
29. Ibid, ch.5, p.144. (Refers to Cheah Boon Kheng interview with Mr Khor Cheang Kee, former Penang bureau news editor of *New Straits Times*, Penang 11 January 1977.)
30. *Malaya Upside Down* by Chin Kee Onn, ch.25, p.186–7.
31. *The Straits Echo and Times of Malaya*, Tuesday 4 September 1945, 'Local Leaders' Sentiments of Joy and Happiness'.
32. *Mountbatten* by Phillip Ziegler, ch.23, p.303. (Refers to 'Life and Times', Post-production script, Programme 8, Reel 1, p.4.)
33. Ibid, ch.23, p.303.
34. *Straits Echo and Times of Malaya*, Tuesday 1 January 1946, 'New Year Message to the People of Penang and Province'.
35. Ibid.
36. *When Singapore was Syonan-To* by N.I. Low, ch.18, p.127.
37. *Syonan — My Story. The Japanese Occupation of Singapore* by Mamoru Shinozaki, ch.20, p.120.
38. Ibid, ch.20, p.122.
39. *Straits Echo and Times of Malaya*, 30 May 1946.

CHAPTER NINETEEN: INHERITED PROBLEMS

19:1 The British Military Administration (BMA)

The Japanese occupation changed the values and aspirations of people in Malaya, as it did in the various other countries under their control. Nationalist movements had sprung up in these countries, and in the wake of their liberation these aspirations were renewed. The formation and maintenance of a stable government in these areas was desirable therefore in the aftermath of war, and even though these South-east Asian territories were not yet ready for full independence, Mountbatten was one who firmly believed that the aspirations of the people should not be ignored, but that they should be allowed where possible to control their own destiny. He also realised that the pre-war status quo in these areas would never be reasserted. This left him open to the criticism that he was too willing to listen to upstart leaders representing emergent liberation forces. In Malaya Mountbatten's political philosophy did err. Although he never condoned communism, or had the remotest sympathy for it, his sense of fairness and an over-willingness to assume the best of others led him to underestimate the threat that communism posed.

The political situation in Malaya was different in 1945 from what it had been in 1941, and this was only slowly appreciated by the returning British after the reoccupation. They were duly made aware of the altered circumstances at work in 1945, and that the political atmosphere in the country had undergone an entire volte face during the preceding four years. The post-war political scene was dominated by two factors. The first was the MCP's predominant position, and the second was the resurgence of Malay nationalism.

Proposals under consideration before the war now needed amendment to uphold Sir Shenton Thomas' recognition in December 1941 of Chinese political factions, including the Kuomintang and MCP, both not previously registered by law. Also the activities of various resistance forces during the occupation had to be recognised, especiallly following the agreement made by the British with MPAJA in January 1944. This had greatly altered opinions on both sides. Similarly the Colonial Office's complete reversal of decision in allowing amendment to the Society's Law — thereby permitting greater freedom of speech, press and association — would become the cause for subsequent repercussion and further dissension.

Of utmost concern was the drastic deterioration in racial relations between Malays and Chinese during the last stages of the occupation, which to a great extent had been deliberately fostered by Japanese policies. This required urgent consideration and conciliatory mediation at the very first opportunity. The resurgence of Malay nationalism also arose partially out of what the Malays endured during the occupation, as well as their overall concern about the MCP's post-war intentions in their homeland.

Now that peace had been restored, the BMA was an unwelcome form of government in a country that had already endured three and a half years of enemy occupation. This was however the only type of government available under the circumstances, in the rapidly changing events following the dropping of the atomic bombs. There was no time to find the people needed to establish a civil form of government. The Allies had thought they would return to Malaya only after a bitterly fought military campaign to defeat the Japanese, as had happened in Burma, and the BMA was installed as part of the original plan for this.

Any military administration is of necessity a rather rough and ready method of government, and many of its officers had little knowledge of the diverse social and economic problems that prevailed in Malaya. Penang and Singapore, along with all the other states in the country, came under the BMA's control from 3rd September 1945 until 31st March 1946. Initially, attention was concentrated on the restoration of essential services, food supplies, health facilities, inflation control, communications and education, all of which had suffered considerably during the period of occupation. One of the BMA's priorities was to attempt to re-establish some semblance of law and order and to re-open the law courts. High courts were given powers to pass the death sentence, and District courts to award punishments of up to three years. Looting, because of its intensity and despicable nature given the depressed conditions in the early reoccupation, carried the death penalty.

BMA control was in the form of an unified administrative system identical to what had been set up by the Japanese during the occupation. Although martial law was not officially declared, in many respects

> 'the BMA operated in much the same fashion as if this had been done. All legislative, executive and Sultans' state councils were suspended. The Sultans could not function until civil government was reintroduced'[1]

in 1946, and their various rights, acquired properties, records and activities during the Japanese tenure were thoroughly checked out by Brigadier H.C. Willan, the Deputy Chief Civil Affairs Officer (DCCAO) Malaya, much to the annoyance and consternation of the Sultans in question, and the Malay populace in general.

From the autumn of 1944, selected officers for eventual service with the BMA underwent training courses organised by the Civil Affairs Staff Centre at Wimbledon in Surrey, England. Several MCS men who had managed to evade capture by the Japanese, some Indian Army officers — interested in taking up regular appointments — as well as a few men who worked and lived in Malaya before the war, either in commerce or in another capacity, were commissioned into the BMA, the latter on account of their local knowledge of the country. Force 136 officers who were already in Malaya, and some of those destined to be parachuted in, also made up the eventual BMA staff which included John Davis, Richard Broome, F. Spencer Chapman, D.A. Sommerville and Derek Headly. Some, but not all of them, were old MCA hands. J.K. Creer — the District Officer in Kuala Trengannu in 1941 — was the only member of the pre-war MCS who stayed in Malaya throughout the whole Japanese occupation. He lived for long periods with the KMT and communist Chinese guerrillas in Kelantan, as well as in other places, and by the

> 'war's end no other Britisher was as knowledgeable as he on relationships among competing Chinese groups and on their respective encounters with the Malays and the Japanese'.[2]

Most of the MCS members who survived their internment ordeal first went home on recuperation leave before returning to Malaya to take up their pre-war positions. For a while therefore the country had to be administered by

> 'new cadres specially assembled and trained for the purpose. As always with conquered territory, a bureaucratic organisation would be needed to administer the cities, towns and rural areas and to keep public services going while the military got on with its own task of disarming and repatriating the enemy, garrisoning strong points and restoring order.'[3]

The progress that Malaya made under the BMA's tenure is debatable and in some instances not particularly satisfactory.

> '. . . civil administrators all held military ranks and the palpable mistakes they made led to them being dubbed "Banana Colonels" and "Banana Majors" etc., a reference to the worthless currency circulated by the Japanese. . .'[4]

Serious friction also occurred within the BMA between pre-war MCS members who had been interned and the new arrivals. The former were critical of the new administrators who, they felt, made serious errors in judgement on account of their unfamiliarity with local conditions and people. Several of the new BMA officers, who had no previous service experience in the Far East, were even the cause of embarrassment to Asian members of their staff by resorting to back-slapping familiarities. Many people still felt that the British had let them down in 1942, but had subsequently had their faith in Britain restored

> 'by the cruelty of the Japanese and the stoicism of British internees and prisoners. Now, under the BMA, the pendulum was swinging back again. "We Chinese never realized that there were Europeans like them."'[5]

Some of the officers who served in the BMA lacked integrity and a sense of responsibility. Some were exceedingly good, but others were openly guilty of corrupt practices. Following the sentencing of a colonel at Butterworth to twelve months in gaol on a charge of corruption, the BMA was subsequently referred to as the 'Black Market Association'.

Despite criticism from various sources it was not possible for the BMA to function exactly in the same manner as the pre-war government and administration had done. Not only was the job an entirely different one, but it required an expeditious entry into the country, where they had to take over from a defeated and cruel administration. Many BMA officials were army officers and had little if any experience in civil government functioning and administration. They were also confronted with numerous immediate and enormous problems, with essential stocks of most items, particularly food and medicines, almost exhausted. Public morale had been low for a long period. What little transport there was was in a state of chaos, and race relations were strained. When problems such as these are taken into consideration it was surprising that the BMA was able to function as well as it did. No authority, however suitably equipped, could have made the task of hauling Malaya back on its feet again in 1945 an easy one, especially when many of the people required were new to such specialised work.

E.M. Glover, the author of *In Seventy Days*, was an adamant critic of the BMA. During the months that the BMA functioned, Glover focused a barrage of criticism on their activities. This included allegations of a mix-up over rice allocations; anomalies concerning back pay for Civil Defence and ARP members; a scandal over the rate set as a cost of living allowance; the non-payment of dues under the Compulsory War Risks Insurance Scheme and other war claims, the settlement of which was constantly delayed and aggravated by procrastinations of government officials. He complained that businesses were held in a stranglehold because of the delay in lifting a moratorium on prices, and this was further exacerbated by the untimely introduction of income tax, before any war claims had been settled. The new hurriedly invoked constitution leading to the Malayan Union was anathema to many people, and certainly to all Malays, throughout the country. These and many other criticisms were voiced and later published by Glover and others, but to little avail as the BMA, without consideration for personal feeling or consequence, attempted to plough its way through all opposition. After the war the rice ration in Malaya was less than five ounces per person per day. In defeated Japan at this time it was eleven ounces. Interned European government servants were paid in full for their three and a half year period of incarceration, minus any sum already paid to their dependents. Asiatic government servants however did not receive similar treatment. There was much to criticise.

Further criticisms of the BMA were published in the Chinese press following the trial, retrial and conviction of the MPAJU leader Soong Kwong and other General Labour Union (GLU) officials in January 1946, on charges of extortion and sedition respectively. Criticisms were also voiced at various meetings, accusing the BMA of failing

> 'to consider the welfare of the people, its refusal to implement promises made under the United Nations Charter, its interference with freedom of speech and assembly, the ruthless behaviour of British troops towards the local populace, and "imperialistic determination" of the British to impose the reactionary conditions of former colonial rule. Accusations were even made that conditions were worse than they had been under the Japanese.'[6]

In response the BMA suspended the publication of six leftist newspapers.

The imposition of the BMA, fully backed by armed forces, did prevent racial clashes from deteriorating into full-scale racial conflagration. The clashes reached a peak in December 1945, but by March 1946 the attacks by Malays and Chinese on each other were suddenly halted and calm was gradually restored. A combination of influences enabled the British to bring about this welcome change. The Sultans assisted in restraining their subjects, and the MCP added their support to those of the Chinese Chamber of Commerce, both appealing to the Chinese for restraint. By this time many among the communists were frustrated with their own leadership's indecisiveness and failure to seize power. The Malays on the other hand had unsuspectingly welcomed the British back, assuming that relationships would revert to their pre-war paternalistic state.

By the time a civil government came into effect on 1st April 1946, despite the improvement of conditions throughout the country, many

Malays who had survived the occupation were looking forward to the post-war era, firmly resolved to carve out improvements for both the country and themselves. They were vexed by the controversial demands for constitutional change which the Malayan Union was endeavouring to impose and the shabby treatment of the Rulers. This untimely action united the Malays as never before. They were unanimously diverted into the alternative cause of anti-Malayan Unionism.

19:2 Food and Related Problems

In August 1945 the most up-to-date available population figures for Malaya and Singapore had been compiled 14 years previously in 1931. When these were taken the official population had stood at 4,877,678, but by 1945 this figure was hopelessly out-dated. The number of ration cards in circulation then was over 5,965,500.

By the time the war ended the Japanese were forced to admit that stocks of rice in the occupied countries were so depleted that they had 'no idea how they could have fed the subject population if the war had continued any longer'.[7] Not only had their inefficient and corrupt administration caused massive suffering in rice producing and exporting countries under their control, but the agricultural standards in these places had also been neglected. In Malaya, conscription and enforced movement of the population disrupted the supply and cycle of labour traditionally employed in the cultivation of rice.

From 14th August onwards surrender rumours escalated food prices by the hour. Crowds stampeded for food — wanting to get rid of the Japanese script which they foresaw would be valueless when the British returned. This forced prices up further. Many rushed to change their 'banana' notes for Straits Settlement notes or got rid of them by frantically buying anything still available. The exchange rate for Straits Settlement notes rose sharply overnight from 12 to 1 to 30 to 1, and gold peaked at $110,000 a tahil. (One tahil equals 1.33332 oz or 37.799 gms; thus gold reached M$2,910 per gram.) The Japanese also sought to exploit this chaos and decided to release stockpiles previously held back by both military and civilian authorities at prices far below those currently prevailing. This only prompted a further frenzy of panic buying. Rice reached $7,500 a picul (equivalent to M$132.27 per kilogram), and the poor were driven to breaking point. The belated exhortations of Japanese governors, government officials, judges and community leaders, that people should show restraint and refrain from feverish buying fell on deaf ears. Tradesmen also took the opportunity to accrue sudden, exorbitant profits, and even previously belligerent policemen were known to throw away their uniforms and obligingly pay whatever price was demanded. When the Japanese started to burn their 'banana' script, and Straits notes and gold were released, fortunes were made or lost. The Japanese joined in, buying through syndicates and other operators, among whom were notorious collaborators. Some later committed suicide, but many lived on to enjoy their ill-gotten gain, and some in due course were even looked on as honourable citizens.

Such was the panic by 25th August that Mr. Nishizawa, the Chief of the Foodstuffs Department in Penang, in a belated attempt to gain some control, magnanimously announced that people had suffered enough and that rations for rice, sugar, salt and matches would be immediately trebled. This was not done. A free handout of rice was however made to 4,254 Jikeidan members in Penang. Others with guilty consciences — those who justifiably had cause to fear recrimination — turned to charitable deeds to court favour and sudden popularity. Even Captain Shinsaku Hidaka, the Naval Chief of Staff in Penang and head of the Japanese Anti-Espionage Organisation, donated 200 bags of rice to the lepers on Pulau Jeregak. The orphanages at the Christian Brothers and Sisters, the destitutes at St Joseph's Novitiate and the Convent at Pulau Tikus, as well as the blind at St Nicholas Home for the Blind were suddenly included among those given handouts.

While the Japanese were in control in Penang and throughout Malaya, morality had lapsed to a great extent. Their repressive and unjust administration invited abuse and supported a system in which a few became exceedingly rich on the sufferings of the many who were driven to corrupt practices in order to survive. The black market was so generally accepted that it took a long time to be eradicated. However, by 30th August the price of white rice and sugar had fallen to $50 and $30 per kati respectively. The price of rice was the barometer for the cost of living in the country and as it declined so other prices followed suit.

* * * * * *

A Currency Declaration by the BMA on 4th September 1945 made Japanese script worth less than the inferior quality paper on which it was printed. Only Government of the Straits Settlements currency notes above $1 and less than $1,000 in value, and Malayan currency notes issued by the Board of Commissioners of $1 and above, and all coins less that $1 in value issued by them were recognised and permitted for use as legal tender. The *Straits Echo* it its editorial the next day reported that the Declaration had caused considerable confusion and alarm, and that a large percentage of the population had been hard hit by it. Rumour mongers and speculators had added to the confusion, as had Japanese firms, purposely subscribing to undermine stability by selling off a lot of their goods in exchange for their own worthless script, which they burned in secret to give the public a false impression of its value.

The Declaration caused widespread indignation and alarm. A shortage of legal tender suddenly curtailed people's purchasing power, and the poor and those who had hoarded Japanese script were left without any means of obtaining basic needs. Shops refused to open and lightermen in Penang stayed away from work, refusing to unload the ships in the harbour. In an effort to alleviate some of the hardship of poorer elements in the community, the Penang Service Committee asked for donations of rice and other foodstuffs from merchants, and also set up six food kitchens in various densely populated parts of the island. Each day for one month, at 11 a.m., these kitchens provided one free meal of rice and vegetables to an average of 10,000 poor and needy people. Colonel J.A. Harvey, the BMA's Senior Civil Affairs officer in Penang, contrived with some members of the Penang Service Committee to obtain substantial donations of rice, red beans, jagong (corn), ragi (millet) and salt fish from suspected collaborators, and such was the success of this ploy that when the food kitchens were closed down, large surpluses of jagong and ragi were sold off to race horse owners to feed their horses.

By 6th September some respite was at hand to alleviate the plight of the poor. An emergency short term amendment was made to the Currency Declaration allowing Japanese notes of $5 and below to be used to pay for government services and dues, and for the payment of relief supplies. An exchange rate of 100 to 1 was set. Later, $10 Japanese notes were also included at the same exchange rate, but the Acting Governor, Captain T.J. Hilken DSO RN, resisted numerous pleas to relax the Declaration in respect of higher denominations. After the BMA paid an advance of one month's salary to all government servants in September 1945 a lot of official Malayan currency was put back into circulation, easing that segment of the populace's difficulties, and ending the exigency of allowing further use of the low value 'banana' script. The BMA's decision not to recognise the occupational Japanese currency came as a shock to the MCP and was a cause for much of their early post-war financial difficulties. Although not substantiated, it was thought that

> 'the BMA suspected that the MPAJA had amassed a large sum of Japanese Occupation money, and was afraid that this would be used to finance communist activities in the post-war era'.[8]

On 18th September five banks in Penang reopened for business. The Overseas Chinese Banking Corporation (OCBC), the Bank of China, the Indian Bank Ltd., Ban Hin Lee Banking Corporation and the Indian Overseas Bank were allowed to operate new accounts and to negotiate loans to private and public commercial concerns, but only in the officially recognised Malayan currency. Accounts held at the Penang Post Office with the British Postal Savings Bank were also honoured, provided these had not been withdrawn in 1941, and all accrued interest was guaranteed. Japanese postal savings accounts however were closed and any deposit made into them was disregarded and forfeited.

* * * * *

Many food dumps left by the Japanese were scattered over Penang island, and guarding these was a major difficulty because of widespread looting. One of these, discovered at the top of Penang Hill in seven summer houses previously owned by European residents, comprised almost 600 tons of food as well as petrol and other stores. These once elegantly furnished houses had been converted into miniature warehouses, with foodstuff stacked literally to the ceiling. The Japanese had reportedly transported these supplies up the hill by railway over a period of eight months, as part of their contingency plans to make a last ditch stand up there. One officer and 32 men of the RAF Regiment mounted a 24 hour guard over this booty until arrangements were made to send it all down the hill again by train. Lieut-Colonel J.N. Gibbons, commanding the 41 Northern Supply Headquarters, arranged for its distribution.

In October 1945, in a bid to reduce the cost of living, the ration level for rice, sugar, salt and oil was increased to three times the level last authourised by the Japanese. Prices per kati (1 kati = 1.25 lbs) were fixed at 15 cents for rice, 16 cents for white sugar, 12 cents for salt and 20 cents for coconut oil. Price control enabled the poor to buy essential food items at reasonable cost. Food retailers were ordered to cooperate with the authorities and ensure that foodstuff reached the markets at correct prices. They were warned that controlled prices would only be abolished on condition that prices remained at a reasonable level. While the public were urged to grow more food to reduce prices, and various food controllers and economic advisers were warning of an imminent food crisis, it was surprising that a considerable amount of food was being wasted. Rice and half eaten cakes were discarded in dustbins and could be seen strewn in the streets. In a bid to discourage this and curb wastage, the rice ration was reduced on 20th May 1946 to 1 kati a week for each man, woman and child. By this time the official price had come down to 8 cents per kati.

19:3 Housing and Health

The extensive damage to buildings in George Town during the bombing raids in December 1941 was mainly ignored by the Japanese, and not cleared up during the three years and eight months that they ruled Penang. In addition they mismanaged the undamaged parts of the town, as their standards of maintenance and administration were low. At the time of the liberation the Secretariat was in a state of chaos over debenture stocks and rates of pay. Drains, roads and buildings had been neglected, the electricity supply was on the point of collapse, and because of a major housing shortage hundreds of attap squatter hovels had been allowed to mushroom in a haphazard insanitary manner, without any municipal planning or consideration for health standards, with the result that they obstructed traffic and caused severe fire risk.

In an area bounded by Penang Road, Brick Kiln Road and the sea, over 400 of these attap hovels and stalls had been indiscriminately erected. Back lanes were blocked with uncollected debris, the municipal workshops were in a state of disrepair, and a general run-down appearance replaced the pre-war grandeur previously enjoyed by Penang. As population levels had also increased in Penang during the occupation a massive rehabilitation of slum areas and an immediate reconstruction task confronted the BMA. Even in 1947 nearly 190,000 people were still crammed into the small George Town area. The reconstruction of Penang took another four difficult years.

No construction work was carried out in Penang between 1941 and 1945. With 1,100 buildings destroyed in bombing raids, in conjunction with widespread looting, there was much to be attended to. The population increase, with hundreds of squatters crammed into unsightly and insanitary hovels which were difficult to remove, made the remaining houses far more overcrowded than ever before. Between 1931 and 1947 records show that the number of occupied houses increased from 16,000 to 18,000 only. But during this same period the average number of persons in each house soared from 9.3 to 19.4 persons per unit. Within the municipal limits there were on average only 33 people per acre, but in the town area there were 150 people per acre, and in the small area bordered by Chulia, Campbell and Kimberly Streets there were 263 people per acre. By 1947 33.7% of the total population of the island were living in only 7.5% of the space available.

In direct contrast to the mismanagement and neglect of the Japanese occupational administration, some Japanese individuals behaved with scrupulous care during their stay in Penang. Several

British officers and executives on their return to the country were surprised and relieved to find that their homes and belongings had been well looked after and were still in perfect condition. In some instances everything had been inventoried, even items of cutlery and single ashtrays. Mr E.A. Stains, on his return to Penang after internment in Singapore, found that very little material damage had been done to his house in Bagan Jermal Road. His kind Chinese neighbours and pre-war servants had faithfully looked after his house and furniture during his absence.

Landlords were instructed by the BMA to restrict rent to 1941 levels. During September and October 1945 house owners and landlords could charge only 50% of the 1941 rate, and this gave rise to grave discontent. Owners complained that there were insufficient houses available for returning evacuees, and that incumbent tenants were making small fortunes by sub-letting. Such tenants were also refusing to move out when pre-war owners came back to their houses, unless they were amply rewarded for doing so. House rentals, they complained, were the only item on which there had been no inflation.

Although in early 1946 the municipality still assessed rates based on 1941 levels, and landlords were expected to charge rents on a similar basis, 'coffee money' was demanded by tenants. For a small shophouse in China Street, with a monthly rent of only $55, $4,000 was being demanded and paid for a change of tenancy, and for sub-letting a single room, a perk up to $500 was expected.

In September 1945 the bronze statue of Francis Light — founder of Penang in 1786 — was discovered behind a house the Japanese had used as a naval store. The statue's bronze sword and scabbard were missing and wooden replacements were made. On 11th August 1946 in a simple ceremony in front of the Supreme Court Building to commemorate the 160th anniversary of the foundation of Penang, the statue was once again unveiled. In 1939 in the original impressive unveiling ceremony the statue had stood proud on its pedestal in front of Fort Cornwallis. (Its present resting place is to one side of the entrance of the Penang State Musuem.)

* * * * * *

At the end of three and a half years of Japanese occupation, Malaya was sick. Malaria, scabies, yaws, typhoid, syphilis and particularly tuberculosis had all increased. In Singapore during the first three weeks after the liberation, tuberculosis caused the death of 94 people out of the 140 cases that were reported, and during the first year after the war ended, one death in ten throughout the whole country was due to TB. Smallpox was only just contained at the border area of Kedah and Siam, and a cholera threat in Kelantan was held at bay by an intensive inoculation programme of 144,000 people. In the whole country in 1945 there were only 20,000 hospital beds available.

The Japanese had neglected health precautions in Penang. George Town was swarming with mosquitoes that bred without restraint in open, wet spaces such as slit trenches and air raid shelters. Streets in the town were in an appalling state, dirty and neglected and heaped with litter and decaying vegetables. Many drains were choked with grass and bomb damage rubble, rats scurried at will from one festering garbage heap to the next, arrangements to collect night soil had collapsed, street lighting had broken down, and the unabated breeding of flies was yet another grave danger to health. Public health facilities such as maternity and child welfare had been completely disregarded.

In 1941 24 lorries by day and 16 by night had been used for scavenging and for doing the rounds for night soil collection. By September 1945, due to lack of maintenance, only two lorries were in running order and available to carry out all health work. Hand carts were put into use, as were any other available alternative means of transport, but night work was hindered by a lack of torches and street lighting.

Dr W.H. Brodie, the Municipal Health Officer in Penang, advised the public to take precautions against smallpox, and to be re-vaccinated if they had been given vaccinations by the Japanese during the occupation, as he considered these not successful.

The BMA immediately closed a Pauper Hospital established by the Japanese in Penang, and sent all patients for free treatment to the General Hospital. The Penang Overseas Chinese Association (OCA) started a free treatment clinic for destitutes at Swatow Lane.

19:4 Control of Crime

Rumours of a breakdown in law and order spread like wildfire and a state of virtual anarchy swept through many villages and towns as Japanese forces were withdrawn and the police remained indoors out of public view. Incidences of lawlessness increased in both daring and frequency as organised gangs attacked outlying places and looted many Japanese-owned estates, factories and mines.

> 'Abduction, murder, robbery, looting and seizure of property on the slightest pretext increased. Armed plunderers, who claimed to belong to this and that unit of this and that "regiment", went about extorting money from people. Those who lived on the outskirts of towns became panicky. The very mention of the word "Communist" struck fear in them.'[9]

Each day cases of pillage, murder and general disorder were reported in the *Shimbun* papers throughout the country, increasing public apprehension, especially when these reports were corroborated by people who had travelled into these districts on matters of urgent business. People had previously feared the Japanese, but as their moment of final liberation came, it was the communists and other law breakers that they feared the most.

Penang was not spared its share of a spate of rioting, looting, recriminatory killings and general lawlessness. With the establishment of the BMA a gangster myth, circulated by a gang of robbers who had been terrorising Penang that they belonged to some patriotic society, was quickly exposed. People were told that only the military and the police could legitimately investigate unlawful acts. Even with this assurance the public remained apprehensive of reprisals by 'patriotic societies' and did not report many of the crimes being committed. In eight night raids on hotels in Penang on 1st November 1945 only 40 suspects were arrested, much less than hoped for, due to the public's lack of cooperation with the authorities.

On 5th November two murders occurred in Penang. The first was the killing of a Chinese detective in Lebuh Tye Sin, and the other just six hours later, was the death of a boat owner in a gang fight. A night purge on many known gangster hangouts netted 43 suspects and Captain W.G. Street of the civil police warned that from then on the town would be made as 'hot as hell' for gangsters and murderers. Night raids were carried out on hotels, private houses and coffee shops, for firearms and people suspected of being responsible for the 5th November killings as well as a series of other murders and robberies. A reward of $1,000 was offered for any information that might lead to arrests, especially as in the first few months since the re-occupation three civil policemen had been murdered by gangsters disguised as visitors, who had infiltrated the island from the mainland.

Roundups of suspects continued throughout November 1945. By the end of the month these were extended to daily raids on gambling haunts in the districts of Penang Street, Jalan Kuantan and near the main market in Penang Road to rid the town of gambling racketeers. Inspector G.S. Windsor, the officer in charge of Beach Street police station, made several arrests, and gambling promoters were fined between $150–200 each time they were caught.

In early December 1945 a set-back to the little progress made to reimpose law and order in Penang occurred, when a former Civil Affairs officer for Butterworth and Province Wellesley was charged on two counts of criminal breach and was sentenced by Lieut-Colonel A.W. Bellamy to 12 months imprisonment. Lapses of this nature earned the BMA its 'Black Market Association' pseudonym, although for the most part this was unwarranted.

By January 1946 the public's ongoing fear of reprisals from criminals continued to handicap the police's efforts as many people still declined to come forward to report serious crimes. In that month alone, five murders, eleven armed robberies and four armed gang robberies were recorded in Penang. Certainly more did occur, but only the victims and the criminals were aware of them. The crime wave continued unabated, and on 14th April a 'Rival Gang Shoot Out' was reported in the *Sunday Gazette*. Seven gang members had fought a gun dual near Jelutong in Sungei Pinang, and one Chinese had been killed and two others seriously wounded.

In May 1946 flying squads – army trucks fitted with two-way wireless telephones and manned by military and civil police – were introduced. These patrolled and operated in the town and suburbs both by day and night, and had a marked effect on curtailing crime levels. By early July these radio cars, and launch patrols, led to a decline in lawlessness in Penang, although there was little improvement in other parts of the country. In Singapore the crime wave reached new peaks. As urban crime in Penang declined, with fewer firearms used in robberies, the police were able to give more attention to criminals who had sought refuge in hilly areas of the island, where their inaccessibility still posed a problem.

19:5 Revival of Trade

London in 1945 faced political unease and dire economic dilemmas. In the immediate post-war years, when balance of payment difficulties were at their most acute, there was cause for concern that the United States of America might want to impose her will on Britain's colonial territories, and especially on Malaya, which was seen by Britain's leaders as one of the country's greatest sources of dollar earnings. Two basic factors were in interplay. The Americans wanted cheap rubber and Britain wanted reasonable prices for her commodities. Without these the colonial government would be deprived of those physical resources necessary for recovery, both within the colonial areas and in the British Isles. Despite such reasoning, America held the upper hand since she had ample capacity to mass produce alternative forms of synthetic rubber at about ten pence per pound. The Secretary of State for the Colonies, Mr G. Hall, was therefore forced to advise rubber producers in Malaya not to strive for inflated prices, as America had given an undertaking to purchase as much rubber as the Joint Rubber Committee in Washington would allow from Malaya, the Dutch East Indies and French Indo China, at a price not less than 14 pence per pound.

Both rubber estates and tin mines had been seriously damaged during the war. None of the country's 120 tin dredges were in operation in 1945 and a lot of rubber processing machinery had been smashed in 1941 to prevent its being used by the Japanese. During the occupation, little attempt to revive these mainstay industries had been made, despite the fact that, ironically, Japan's principal reason for wanting to occupy Malaya had been her large and readily available supply of tin and rubber. Plantations and mines were inoperative in

1945 and many months elapsed before production could begin on a large scale. The importance of the tin industry to Malaya's post-war recovery was recognised by the colonial government who authorised loans totalling M$1.529 million to Chinese miners to assist them with rehabilitation work.

In 1945 British commerce blithely returned to Malaya and to its pre-war practices. Massive government reconstruction contracts were handed out to old and new British firms. These were deeply resented by local Chinese businessmen who were also lured by the prospect of making vast profits. Although Chinese financial and economic involvement in pre-war Malaya was almost equal to that of the British, the more lucrative contracts were still unavailable to them as long as the British ruled the country.

Despite the disparity in awarding large contracts the post-war business rehabilitation of the Chinese was rapid. The disruption of the occupation, with its ever increasing scarcity of goods, massive inflation and suppressive monopolistic practices of the Japanese, took its toll on them, but under the BMA impoverished Chinese traders were able to take full advantage of the situation to re-establish their old businesses, aided by a multitude of small to medium-sized contracts made with the BMA. There was also an alarming increase in black market deals.

Chinese business revolved essentially around the family, an extremely important entity in Chinese society, supplying the solid foundation on which a business was built, especially during the lifetime of the founder. Outside the immediate family, the Chinese were united by a combination of clans, provinces of origin, race and dialect. These in turn formed important means of communication in conducting business, but less so than the family. Loyalty to the family took precedence. The Chinese did not normally like or tolerate the participation of other races in their business ventures. Guilds and chambers of commerce were other important controlling factors able to minimise competition within particular trades, and reduce overheads by providing members with facilities paid for by subscription. Guilds also collected a percentage of the value traded and part of these dues were used to operate cheap lodging houses for members and their employees when they travelled on business. The guild also acted as a block to non-members, preventing them from obtaining retail trade benefits. Retailers being almost exclusively Chinese, and the guild a racial organisation, the combined effects of their liaison was to exclude other races from participating in and benefiting from selected forms of business.

* * * * * *

Penang had enjoyed a 'free port' status from its outset as a British possession. From 1914 onwards the port had been a particularly active and bustling one. This continued throughout the 1930s, under the paternal eye of the Penang Harbour Board. Traders in general viewed the free port status of Penang as an essential element in the island's prosperity, so much so that during the first six months of 1941 it had been possible to generate a monthly trade volume of $32 million, and Swettenham Pier could boast an alongside water depth of 32 feet.

Penang lost its free port status under the BMA, much to the chagrin of traders and various trade chambers. From 1st January 1946 taxes were imposed on both imports and exports, based on the 1941 tariff rates of the Federated Malay States. The Chinese Chamber of Commerce in particular was dismayed by this premature decision, expressing the view that taxes had been introduced too early, and that this should not have been done until at least some form of civil government had been resumed. A petition by representatives of both the Chinese and Indian Chambers of Commerce, to lobby the Secretary of State for the Colonies, Mr Creech-Jones in London, argued that the imposition of taxes was likely to reduce Penang's status to that of a fishing village, and give rise to trade disparities with neighbouring countries. At this meeting it was intimated that by 18th March 1946 Penang would revert to being a free port, but another two and a half months elapsed before anything was done, and by April the monthly total trade volume passing through Penang had dropped to $15,435,000, a mere 48.2% of what it had been during the second half of 1941. Mr Norman Grice, the Resident Commissioner in Penang, attempted to placate disgruntled businessmen by linking the timing for the transition to a date when the municipality would be established and customs officials could be suitably accommodated at

Butterworth. By Thursday 9th May 1946 no official notification had yet been received from Kuala Lumpur concerning this.

When civil government was reintroduced on 1st April 1946 Penang was placed under a Customs Union. This again was a prevarication over the issue of restoring its free port status. An initial plan was proposed to convert just the city into a customs free area from 1st June, but this decision failed to envisage the numerous problems entailed. It meant that only George Town would be customs free, and that custom checkpoints would have to be established at numerous points along the city limits. Only after considerable debate and argument did the authorities realise this was unworkable, and agreed to return Penang to its free port status from 1st June 1946.

* * * * * *

A rubber buying unit had been set up under the BMA. This ceased to function from 3rd May 1946, when the crude rubber (Prohibition of Sales) Penang Order became effective. Under this order, all traders, manufacturers, producers, commission agents, clearing and forwarding agents and auctioneers had to declare their total stocks of crude rubber from all sources in the island within four days, to the Controller of Customs and Excise, without whose permission no sale could be made.

On 27th May, under a Malayan Union gazette notification, the import duties on all intoxicating liquors and tobacco were doubled. The price of a quart bottle of whisky rose from $7 to $9.50 and the retail price for a packet of ten cigarettes increased by 5 cents.

On 1st June Penang regained its free port status. From this date all items exported from Penang island did not attract duty, except rubber, on which an excise duty of 4 cents per pound was still imposed. Only imports of liquor, tobacco and petroleum into the island would still be dutiable. If duty on these had already been paid on entry into Penang, it would not be re-levied when they entered the mainland. All other dutiable goods entering the mainland from Penang would incur duty, whether or not duty had already been paid in Penang.

* * * * * *

The first post-war four-page edition of the *Straits Echo* appeared in Penang on 4th September 1945. It sold out as soon as it hit the streets, as people were hungry for authentic news after three years and eight months of *Shimbun* propaganda. Such was the interest in the lead article — '*Non Nobis*' — that this edition was resold at a premium by anyone who had a copy of it.

From 14th September telegrams in English or Malay could be sent to addresses in Kedah, Province Wellesley and North Perak at 6 cents a word, and two weeks later it was possible to send letters to destinations anywhere in the world. Initially this was free of charge, providing that one ounce of weight was not exceeded. Free postage facilities in and from Penang were discontinued on Thursday 18th October, 1945.

At the time of the reoccupation, none of the trolley buses in George Town were operating. Two had been destroyed during the bombing in December 1941, but the remainder had been used until they broke down due to lack of spare parts and maintenance. Trolley buses were run on improvised tyres during the occupation, and this further aggravated the problems of upkeep, especially as many of the municipal workshops had fallen into a state of disarray. As an initial measure, Mr J.A.C. Sharp, the Municipal Engineer, rounded up an assortment of 85 miscellaneous vehicles, 25 of which were military lorries, some fitted up for use as public buses.

From 26th September free daily train services for civilian use were organised between Prai and Ipoh. Prior to this only military personnel were permitted to make use of the limited train services that had been put back into operation. The ferry service — with two free trips each day for civilians — was restarted on 20th September.

The Penang Swimming Club reopened on 29th September. On 23rd October a new short wave transmitter was commissioned in an equally new studio near the Esplanade, enabling broadcasts from Penang to reach the whole of Malaya, as well as Ceylon, Rangoon and, under good weather conditions, even Australia. Unemployed ex-1941 employees of Frazer and Neave Ltd, Penang, were told to report to the company's office in Hutton Lane before 20th November, and by 1st December the Borneo Motors showroom was ready for the sale of Austin, Morris and Bedford vehicles.

* * * * * *

By early September 1946 the Chairman of the Penang Harbour board, Mr H.B. Basten, was able to report that Penang was the first port in South-East Asia to quickly rehabilitate much of its pre-war capacity. In November 1945 levels in the harbour had deteriorated to 18–26 feet, but these had since been deepened to 31 feet in most places. Nowhere was now less than 30 feet in depth. The pre-war godown capacity of 178,173 square feet had been reduced to half of this by the bombing, but with extensive rebuilding after the Japanese surrendered, the capacity increased to 137,200 square feet and soon reached its pre-war level. The port had had 88 lighters in use in 1941, and had been able to handle 36,000 tons of cargo each month. In September 1945 all lighters except one had been lost. The Board immediately ordered 25 new lighters. These arrived in July 1946, and were added to 18 left-over poorly conditioned Japanese lighters. Another 33 were under construction at Bagan Dalam, and in August 1946 it had been possible for the harbour to reach the 35,000 ton level once again.

* * * * * *

No summary of Penang's commercial and economic post-war revival would be complete without a tribute to the 'grand old benefactor and gentleman of agriculture' of Sungei Ara Estate. Hugh Watts first arrived in Penang in September 1921, as a 24 year old veteran of World War I. Following a difference of opinion over planting techniques with his manager, he set off for Perak in 1925, where he joined the Malay States Volunteer regiment, and at a party in the Ipoh Club, he met Mary Culleton — his future wife. During the great slump, like many planters, Hugh's contract was not renewed, but undeterred he returned to Malaya and joined Messrs. Katyz Brothers in June 1933, and managed the South division of the 4,000 acre Glugor Estate owned by the Brown family.

During mobilisation on 1st December 1941 Hugh reported to the headquarters of the 3rd Battalion of the Straits Settlement Volunteer Forces (SSVF) in Peel Avenue, where he was made a Company Sergeant Major of B Company — the Machine Gun Company. After the fall of Singapore he was interned and sent to the dreadful Siam railway. Fortunately Mary and her daughter were evacuated with other women and children from Singapore to Australia and eventually back to England. Hugh only learned of this three and a half years later when he reached Singapore after the Japanese surrender.

His first thought on returning to Penang in October 1945 was for the estate. With no transport available he set out on foot, arriving at the estate office, much to the surprise and relief of the estate staff and the District Officer of Balek Pulau, who promptly handed over to him again. Hugh brought $2,000 sent by the Brown family from England, and paid the workers their wages for December 1941 in October 1945. By January 1946 rubber production had begun although several years were needed to rehabilitate the estate and undo the damage done by the Japanese.

Hugh and Mary continued to live on the remaining portion of Sungei Ara Estate, much of which has since been converted into housing land, from which his long-standing and loyal employees have benefitted. Tennis on Saturday afternoons — with delicate cucumber sandwiches served on a silver platter — was a most delightful social engagement, and Hugh's yacht still continues to adorn the idyllic cove on which the Penang Swimming Club is located, in lingering memory of them.

19:6 Disbandment of Malayan People's Anti-Japanese Army (MPAJA)

The promise made by the MCP in January 1944 (and reiterated in their policy statement on 27th August 1945) that guerrillas would cooperate with the returning reoccupation forces to re-establish British rule in Malaya turned out to be an embarrassment to the MCP's central committee. There were elements within the party that wished to oppose the British by force on their return and to discontinue any semblance of cooperation between them as soon as possible.

Colonel John Davis of Force 136 determined in long and hard negotiations with the MPAJA's supreme command when and under what terms the guerrillas would hand in their weapons. He did not meet with much success in this, although an initial disbandment date of 1st November 1945 was set. As that date drew closer all talks relating to gratuity payments ground to a standstill and no agreement was yet finalised. Those guerrillas who had come under Force 136's influence, and to a lesser extent under their control, were regarded as being in a different category from the others who had operated more independently, although several of these latter factions were perfectly genuine. In particular the Kuomintang guerrillas, who had operated in the remoter parts of Kelantan and along the Perak Siam border, and the smaller Malay Wataniah force were among those outside Force 136's influence. Following an invitation to them and others to join forces with MPAJA, more than 1,000 of them did so, bringing their weapons with them. The remainder could not be easily contacted in time and so were excluded from the agreement. Such independent guerrilla forces should not be confused with the ruffian gangs of roving bandits who disrupted various parts of the country for their own gain, and who only pretended to belong to the resistance forces.

Regardless of which faction guerrillas had operated under, the British required all of them to hand in their weapons and to disband. It was however with some reluctance that many communists subsequently agreed to hand in the weapons previously provided to them. December 1st 1945 was the date set, although the Kuomintang guerrilla forces were officially disbanded only seven months later in July 1946.

Japanese brutality, aimed mostly at the Chinese, was the main impetus in the growth of MPAJA. From an estimated strength of 3,000 guerrillas in 1944, MPAJA's strength increased by various means to an estimated 7,000 by August 1945 when they emerged from the jungles. Many Chinese who were non-communists, but who had feared for their lives or who were simply discontented with their lot in the towns, had fled into the jungles and had joined up with MPAJA. Although many of these did not become directly involved in fighting the Japanese, all were exposed to communist ideology and were gradually indoctrinated. MPAJA's three star emblem — designed to represent the three major races in the country — could not alter the reality of an organisation that was in essence a Chinese movement, effectively controlled by the MCP, and within it were hard-core elements intent on turning the country into a communist run state.

The increase in MPAJA strength, particularly throughout the early and middle parts of 1945, made the British suspicious that the

MCP had intended to form a secret army comprising trusted and long-tested members. This was partly the result of an MCP directive issued after April 1945 at a time when MPAJA guerrillas were being equipped with new weapons by SEAC. Secret units were indeed formed and these remained incognito in the jungles, not only to fight against the Japanese but also to gather as many weapons as possible, so that the force could be used to continue

> 'an armed struggle against the British "if a Peoples' Republic was not set up after the war to the liking of the MCP"'.[10]

In effect, therefore, it was only those known units of MPAJA who had been in contact with Force 136, and who had been armed by them for the purpose of assisting in any Allied landings, who agreed to be openly disbanded.

Lai Tek, the Secretary General of the MCP, seemed openly to favour the scheduled disbandment of MPAJA, reasoning that defiance could only invoke confrontation and more would be achieved through deceit. His opinions were strongly resisted by the rest of the Executive Committee. However, on 1st December 1945 Lau Yew, the Chairman of the Central Military Committee, begrudgingly ordered the official de-activation of MPAJA. This gave rise to considerable bitterness among the hard line element within its ranks. Lau Yew was far from happy, lamenting that

> 'no rewards were offered to the resistance patriots but given to the traitors and puppets who collaborated with the enemy'.[11]

The demobilisation proceeded smoothly except for some places in Kelantan and later with the Kuomintang guerrillas on the Perak-Siam border, where they terrorised the Malays in the countryside. It was carried out with at least the appearance of good faith by Chin Peng. 5,497 weapons were handed in by the 6,800 guerrillas who came forward for demobilisation at ceremonial parades at various MPAJA headquarters in the country. This was more than the 4,765 weapons originally issued by the British. According to Force 136 records most of the weapons that had been air-dropped into the country were eventually returned, but this did not take into account the thousands of weapons and the ammunition discarded during the British retreat in 1941–2, or the weapons secured by the guerrillas when police armouries and troop positions were abandoned and over-run. The Chinese guerrillas had simply helped themselves at will, and many secret caches of arms were established by the MCP in jungle hide-outs for use at some future time.

Each man on demobilisation was paid a gratuity of M$350 in two instalments — $250 on disbandment and $100 three months later — (equivalent to £42) for his services during the occupation. In addition to this, a salary of $30 per month for the period they remained in the service of SEAC was given, plus one bag of rice, issued to each man in January 1946. Some guerrillas and their commanders were decorated, but no political concessions were granted, and any approach that the MCP made to convert MPAJA into a permanent military force within the Malayan defence establishment was rejected. Each guerrilla was given a choice. He could either enter civilian employment or take up a post with the police, the volunteers, or the Malay regiment. Tributes were made with much ceremony for the guerrillas' services, but rumours spread that only a portion of their forces had disbanded. British intelligence also realised that their main forces

> 'would remain in the jungles or continue operating under the guise of clubs and similar organisations'.[12]

It was noticeable that only the older types of weapons had been handed in.

At Alor Star the commander of the 8th Independent Army in Kedah took the final salute. The Malays in general welcomed the demobilisation of both MPAJA and the KMT guerrillas, even though a few Malay guerrilla units, such as the Wataniah, were also involved. The Chinese disapproved, especially as the estimated ratio of Chinese to Malay guerrillas was about twenty to one. MPAJA Supreme Headquarters, although unhappy, went along with the decision.

The Chinese guerrillas in MPAJA were officially released with parades held in their honour.

> 'Release of the Malay personnel of Force 136 was not properly carried out. At no time did they ask for or even talk of reward in dollars, cents or land, but were satisfied with having served their country in time of need. But shamefully and except for the few who were decorated, their services, sacrifices and brave deeds were not fairly recognised by Government or public and they were soon forgotten.'[13]

Discharged without pomp or ceremony, they went home to their villages and were then ignored by the BMA who had their hands full in

> 'dealing with the rising opposition of the Malays against the enforced imposition of the Malayan Union'.[14]

* * * * * *

Although MPAJA was officially disbanded, the party structure of the MCP and its branch organisation remained intact in villages and towns. The uniformed guerrillas only surrendered their weapons, but many of the more trusted veterans afterwards registered their names with the Malayan Peoples Anti-Japanese Ex-Service Comrades Association (MPAJASCA) that was established in every town in the country. Lai Tek favoured the formation of this organisation. Its professed purpose was to look after the welfare of the ex-guerrillas and keep a record of them. The organisation's concealed and real aim was to keep alive the essence of the communist regiments, with their affiliation to criminal activities, so they would be ready to take up arms again when called upon to do so. Secret members within the Association did not register, neither did they relinquish their weapons. The Association became part of a 'People's' democratic movement, promulgating a subsequent campaign of anti-imperialist propaganda and also ensuring that the MCP organisation at village level, especially among the numerous Chinese squatters, was maintained. Through such an organisation the MCP would easily be able to reactivate, when the time came for renewed armed struggle, those units previously demobilised.

On 31st October 1945 the general public had been ordered to surrender all arms. After MPAJA's demobilisation on 1st December this order was made mandatory for the entire population and on 1st February 1946, in view of an alarming increase in armed robberies and murders, the British introduced the death penalty for anyone found in illegal possession of arms. Despite instructions and threats to invoke British control, the extent of the guerrillas' resourcefulness had been underestimated. It was claimed that 20% of the arms parachuted into the country by Force 136 were not located on arrival, and never received by the guerrillas. These were never subsequently turned in.

> 'Furthermore, weapons taken from disarmed Japanese troops and those picked up during the first stages of the war were also kept concealed.'[15]

Had the British anticipated this, and had they offered larger monetary incentives for handing back all these weapons, the final additional cost could have been considerably less than the eventual cost of the 12 year 'Emergency' which erupted in mid-1948.

19:7 Suspended Sentences

Records reveal that the Indian population in Malaya and Singapore decreased by 6.3% between 1931 and 1947. This was mainly due to the ravages wrought by the Japanese occupation on this segment of the country's population. Considerable loss of life occurred among the many thousands who were either conscripted into the INA, or one or other forms of labour battalions. This especially applied to those sent in their thousands to slave and perish on the hideous 'death' railway projects in both Siam and Burma. Despite such terrible ordeals suffered by so many Indians, Japan cunningly continued to make use of Indians' deep-rooted, fervent feelings of nationalism and their desire to see India freed from colonial rule. Japan intentionally fueled a revival of this passion for her own gain and benefit. This ploy was nothing short of a grandiose bluff. In addition to the grave depletion of their numbers the Indians also suffered from economic and social setbacks, which would continue for decades to come.

> 'Many Malaysians (including members of the Indian middle class) look down of the Indian working class because the workers are poor, drink excessively and do not conduct themselves with self confidence and a sense of dignity . . . When the poor are eventually accorded the respect they deserve, it will not be because rich Indians have become richer, or because

> Indian professionals have become cleverer. It will be because the Indian poor themselves have rediscovered their sense of self-worth and recovered their self-respect, and have begun working together towards solving their problems.'[16]

Before the events of early 1942 Indians domiciled in Malaya had shown scant interest in the local politics of the country. The Japanese occupation, the political implications arising from this, and the war in general did much to alter this attitude. Be that as it may, by 1945 most Indians in Malaya faced the problem of reconciling their Indian nationalism with a new requirement of loyalty towards their adopted homeland, Malaya.

After the war ended in mid-August 1945 and Japanese troops were abruptly withdrawn into low-profile peace preservation roles, INA troops were told basically to look to their own safety. Their local commanders were left very much on their own to decide on the means of surrender for the men under their control. Some time before 26th August instructions were given to cease all acts of hostility and to hand over all the arms and stores still under INA control to the returning British authorities. The long-planned Allied proposal to invade and retake Malaya had been disrupted by the sudden cessation of hostilities, and this was now to be converted as quickly as possible into a cautious, peaceful if openly victorious form of liberation and reoccupation. As it turned out, such a sudden change of plan was impossible, and the delay which occurred had long term effects.

Before Allied troops were able to return to take charge and restore law and order, the Japanese were provided with adequate time to ensure that the seeds of potential political unrest and distrust were sown among the various races domiciled in the country. Proof of such manoeuvring became increasingly apparent in the years to come, with various forms of social and political unrest emerging in all of Japan's war-time occupied territories. In Malaya, the first country to be reoccupied in any strength, a large number of Indians were arrested on the return of the British for their activities in supporting the INA. The general breakdown of law and order throughout Malaya and the unfortunate effects of the alarming three-week period of MCP-sponsored anarchy necessitated large occupational forces in the country for many years before any return to the former state of social and political tranquillity could be achieved.

In terms of both military and international law, those who joined the INA were guilty of committing a serious offence and could have been tried by court martial for desertion and mutiny. The legal punishment for this was death. Any attempt, however, to invoke the full force of the law on so great a number of people – over 20,000 were implicated – would have certainly invited considerable political problems.

Pandit Jawaharlal Nehru quickly seized upon the dilemma confronting the British authorities over this issue and deftly disavowed his earlier antagonism towards Subhas Chandra Bose's proposed armed invasion of India. In a smartly executed volte face, he publicly lauded the actions of the returning INA masses, which promptly transformed them into the heroes of the motherland. As early as 20th August 1945, Nehru declared:

> '. . . a very large number of officers and soldiers of the INA . . . are prisoners and some of them at least have been executed. At any time it would have been wrong to treat them too harshly, but at this time – when it is said big changes are impending in India, it would be a very grave mistake leading to far-reaching consequences if they were treated just as ordinary rebels. The punishment given them would be in effect be a punishment on all India and all Indians, and a deep wound would be created in millions of hearts.'[17]

It was impossible to execute all or any of those now being acclaimed as heroes by the majority of Indians. Their actions could not however be ignored for the sake of political convenience, especially as so many of the forces in the British Indian army had remained stoically loyal to the Allied cause.

An uncomfortable attempt at compromise was thought up by the inexperienced people selected to interrogate the INA masses, and this was duly accepted by the Secretary of State in London. It was decided that the men interrogated would be slotted into one of three categories according to their involvement with the INA, and in consideration of their likely post-war political leanings.

The 'Blacks' were to be those so imbued with enemy propaganda as to be still definitely hostile towards the post-war form of government in India. Their release was considered a real danger to the reliability of other serving members in the army and to the re-establishment of peace and good order in the country. The 'Blacks' were considered

> 'well aware of what they were doing and among them the Blackest were those who had previously been in positions of trust and responsibility and those who had tortured, flogged or killed their comrades, either to make them join the I.N.A. or after they joined to punish them for attempted desertion'.[18]

The 'Greys' were to be those misled into cooperating with the Japanese, but not active leaders on their behalf. Nevertheless, their exposure to enemy propaganda was thought sufficient to render them unreliable.

The 'Whites' were those able to offer some form of proof that their basic beliefs had not been tainted either by Japanese or German propaganda, and that they were still fundamentally loyal to the British Army.

The 'Blackest of the Blacks' were to be court martialled and executed. Other 'Blacks' would have the death penalty commuted to varying terms of imprisonment and would also be dismissed from the service. 'Greys' would be tried but then released and dismissed with forty days leave pay. The 'Whites' were the only ones restored to their former positions in the British Indian Army and accorded all previous privileges. By adopting such measures only a few officers in effect would need to be court martialled.

> 'This decision was felt by many Englishmen to be a betrayal, not only of the thirty-five thousand prisoners who had stood firm but also of the victorious Indian Army. And in a sense it was a betrayal. It shook the Indian Army; it disturbed the villages to which I.N.A. men went back; and it played a part in the naval mutinies of February 1946.'[19]

The intent of the British in September 1945 to convey an impression of compassion and leniency backfired as the All-India Congress Committee, highly critical of the proposals, urged that all those involved in the INA should be released.

Such was the situation a few weeks after Japan surrendered. No one anticipated how rapidly events and feelings would change. Had this been foreseen, faster action could have been taken to bring the 'blackest' minority to justice, rather than delaying their trials for a few weeks and then trying to keep them secret until they had been concluded. National emotion acclaimed all INA soldiers as heroes. They had fought for India's freedom. Any leader who valued his political future was prepared personally to defend the 'martyrs'. An INA Defence Fund was set up. INA Flag Days were spontaneously and generously subscribed to. Anyone who dared believe any rumours against the accused was labelled a traitor. The extent of the public outcry perturbed not only the British but also the Indian Congress Party, especially as India was close to gaining independence. It was surely

> '. . . incongruous to punish men for casting off an allegiance which the state was in any case on the point of relinquishing'.[20]

The British erred in judgement, attempting to proceed with the trials in the face of widespread public opposition. This was grasped by both Mohandas Karamchand Ghandi — the Mahatma (great soul) — and Nehru, and other leaders in the Indian Congress Party, and was promptly used to further fan the flames of anti-British opinion. These court martials were a miscalculated godsend for the aspirants and upholders of the Indian Independence movement, and Congress cleverly baited their trap by demanding an open trial. The British suddenly and embarrassingly found themselves enmeshed.

On 14th September all officers and men who had been placed on trial were publicly declared as heroes. Anti-British agitation and mass protests spread like wildfire as the first court martials proceeded. When, on 30th December, they at last came to an end, the sentences were not officially announced for fear of massive repercussions. Instead, on 3rd January 1946, General Claude Auchinleck (later Field Marshall Sir) commander-in-chief of the British forces in India — aware how critical the situation had become — diplomatically announced that the sentences would be suspended.

Any post mortem concerning INA wartime activities attracts various opinions. Were members of the INA the hapless tools of men of destiny? Or were they the convenient puppets of Japanese guile and greed? Would the INA have been formed and supported with such intensity without the support and guidance of the Fujiwara Kikan? In mid October 1945, Iwaichi Fujiwara appeared as a witness at the trial of INA officers. He was the only Japanese officer after the war with sufficient moral courage to assume some responsibility for his Kikan activities. Others evaded their connections with it.

The INA was certainly not united in their efforts. Many among their ranks had been coerced and bullied into following a path that, during a period of hopelessness, promised them some form of respite, with an element of glory. When Mountbatten met Nehru and his daughter Indira in Malaya in early 1946, Nehru gave scant thought to the leaderless and stranded thousands of INA followers, who were being treated as disloyal outcasts by the British and the public in general.

It was only on the eve of the trials of specific Azad Hind Fauj officers in New Delhi that Nehru decided publicly in their favour. Some critics of the INA argued that the organisation did not play any crucial part in furthering the cause of Indian Independence, because in 1945 the British were tired of war, and their mood under the benign Labour government would never have sanctioned any use of military force to repress Indian nationalism. This was perhaps the most singularly important stepping stone that led Britain towards granting India her independence.

19:8 Influence of Japanese Occupation

The political attitudes of the Malays were divided before the war. The educated had presented the British with little firm opposition to their rule, gently agitating for a share in it, while a socialist left-wing element made up of numerous

> 'poor Malays and disgruntled Malay school teachers, . . . attacked the Malay upper classes for their support of the British, and . . . urged for their immediate independence'.[21]

The whirlwind defeat of the British in 1942 and the subsequent occupation had a profound effect on both the Malays and their environment. It destroyed the British myth of invincibility. The Malays, confronted with unfamiliar hardships, had to discard their previous complacent reliance on others to survive. Many of them had to struggle for the first time in their lives. Thousands of Malays who had been in secure government employment in urban areas before the war were uncaringly retrenched, so that overnight

> '. . . it became necessary for these white-collar workers to involve themselves in hawking and peddling in order to keep body and soul together'.[22]

Necessity had thrust the hectic life of petty traders on many Malays, but they had apparently little ambition to overcome the dominance and monopoly of the Chinese in this field. Lassitude and non-determination suddenly forced Malays throughout the country to realise, as other more highly educated Malays had cautioned, that their economic dilemma would reach an irretrievably hopeless condition. They wanted to return to the enjoyable pre-war security of employment, to their humdrum lifestyle, hoping that this enforced transition, thrust on them between 1942 and 1945, would be of a temporary nature and duration. Even with such change imminent, there was still for many Malays

> '. . . a comfortable feeling that everything would be all right again once the British returned. But they were in for a rude awakening. The British came back but not in the role the Malays had cast for them. They came back not as the protectors of the Malays they used to be, but showed instead every intention to wrest everything away from the Malays'[23]

in their own land. When reality did strike, a transformation in Malay character occurred. Their docility evaporated and with remarkable speed and initiative they sought salvation in politics. Leaders appeared from nowhere. Suddenly Malays became organised and political issues — previously the reserve of the elite — were discussed openly and aggressively at all levels of society.

Japan's conquest of Southeast Asia did not create nationalism in the region, but her short-lived victory did prompt and hasten its further growth in those countries that came under Japan's occupational domination. As the white man's legendary supremacy crumbled, many astute Asians were quick to realise that the political status quo of pre-1941 days would never again return, so when the 'white tuan' did come back, the mystique on which his pre-war influence had depended did not accompany him.

The Japanese invasion terminated European political control in Southeast Asia. While stimulating the political consciousness of the Malays it also provided the communists with experience in guerrilla warfare. Conservative parochial Malay nationalists wanted the country to return to the pre-war 1941 treaties, with each Malay State accepting British advice on all matters other than Islamic affairs and Malay customs. However, a new element of nationalism, in which the early freedom fighters opposed British political and commercial domination, had already evolved. Britain's easy concession of Malaya and Singapore to the Japanese and the incarceration of thousands of British prisoners of war in Asian hands diminished the Englishman's status to less than that of a coolie.

The Japanese occupation proved a bitter experience from which much was learned. Through its depravity came a greater appreciation of justice and a greater desire for good government and freedom. Through its political manipulations all major races in the country grew in political awareness and sensitivity. By 1945 most people deplored Japan's cruelty and the poverty to which they had been reduced, and were happy to see the British return. However, many others wondered whether they wanted the British to return as subsequent administrators as well as liberators.

A very limited taste of self-government had been experienced under the Japanese concept of Co-Prosperity. Many Malays in particular had been given some form of military training by their Nippon masters. Many in the end used this training against Japan's usurpation and rule of their homeland, but this did not necessarily infer they were content to lay down their political aspirations along with their arms for the convenience of their pre-war rulers. When the war ended only the conservative Malay nationalists, the Chinese nationalists and the MCP held any immediate political sway in the country. The Malays generally feared that the Chinese nationalists might turn the country into a 19th Province of China, or that the MCP would make it into a communist state. Although there was little doubt that most people wanted the Japanese to go, the Chinese communist leaders certainly hoped that

> '. . . their forces could take over from the Japanese or failing that, could displace the British afterwards, by force if necessary. Many Malays and others spoke of Britain's return as a reoccupation rather than a liberation, and large numbers of Indians had mixed feelings.'[24]

While the Japanese may have taught many in Malaya to appreciate the British more, the conservative Malay nationalists – mainly from the Malay ruling classes, who were pre-war loyal supporters of the British – were to be quickly antagonised by the ill-founded proposals for the Malayan Union scheme and the offensive manner of the British government.

1. *Red Star over Malaya. Resistance and Social Conflict during and after the Japanese Occupation, 1941–1946* by Cheah Boon Kheng, ch.10, p.266.
2. *British Rule in Malaya 1942–1957* by Robert Heussler, ch.6, p.147. (Refers to footnote on p.180.)
3. Ibid, ch.4, p.81.
4. *The Sara Saga* by M. Saravanamuthu, ch.10, p.132.
5. *British Rule in Malaya 1942–1957* by Robert Heussler, ch.4, p.85. (Refers to A. Gilmour, 'My Role in the Rehabilitation of Singapore, 1946–1953', Singapore Institute of Southeast Asian Studies, Oral History Pilot Study No.2, April 1973, p.6.)
6. *Red Star over Malaya. Resistance and Social Conflict during and after the Japanese Occupation, 1941–1946* by Cheah Boon Kheng, ch.9, p.261. (Refers to MU 395/46.)
7. *War against Japan* by Major-General S. Woodburn Kirby, vol.4, ch.22, p.239.
8. *The Masked Comrades. A Study of the Communist United Front in Malaya, 1945–1948* by Cheah Boon Kheng, ch.4, p.47. (Refers to Gene Z. Hanrahan, *The Communist Struggle in Malaya*, reprint, Kuala Lumpur, 1971, p.97–98.)
9. *Ma-Rai-Ee* by Chin Kee Onn, ch.25, p.294.
10. *Red Star over Malaya. Resistance and Social Conflict during and after the Japanese Occupation, 1941–1946* by Cheah Boon Kheng, ch.3, p.62. (Refers to Yap Hong Kuan, 'Perak under the Japanese', BA Hons thesis, University of Malaya, 1957, p.45, 52–53; and Harry Miller, *Prince and Premier*, London, 1959, p.48.)
11. *The Communist Struggle in Malaya* by Gene Z. Hanrahan, ch.4, p.90. (This final order appears in full in Hai Shang-on, 'Ma-lai-ya jen-min k'ang-jik chun', Singapore, 1945, p.56–57.)
12. *Red Star over Malaya. Resistance and Social Conflict during and after the Japanese Occupation, 1941–1946* by Cheah Boon Kheng, ch.9, p.259.
13. *Have You Met Mariam?* by General Tan Sri Ibrahim bin Ismail, ch.11, p.136.
14. Ibid, ch.11, p.136.
15. *The Communist Struggle in Malaya* by Gene Z. Hanrahan, ch.4, p.91.

16. *Sucked Oranges. The Indian Poor in Malaysia* by INSAN and Authors, 1989, ch.4, 'Solutions?', p.39.
17. *Jungle Alliance. Japan and the INA* by Joyce C. Lebra, ch.12, p.200.
18. *Subhash Chandra Bose. The Springing Tiger* by Hugh Toye, Foreword, by Philip Mason, p.viii.
19. Ibid, Foreword, p.x.
20. Ibid, Foreword, p.ix.
21. *A History of Modern Malaya* by K.G. Tregonning, ch.13, p.280.
22. *The Malay Dilemma* by Mahathir bin Mohamed, ch.3, p.37.
23. Ibid, ch.3, p.30.
24. *British Rule in Malaya 1942–1957* by Robert Heussler, ch.4, p.79.

CHAPTER TWENTY: ATROCITIES AND WAR CRIMES

20:1 A Formula for Atrocity

The 'essence of Bushido' existed in Japan from the thirteenth century and was integrated and regulated within her traditional ways of life. Tradition was an essential element of Bushido. Newer aspects emerged during the eighteenth century, at the time of the Meiji Restoration, and were only formulated by law as late as 1890. Before 1931 and the rise of militarist fanaticism, even a Samurai could have surrendered in accordance with Bushido laws.

The Geneva International Convention was signed by 47 states, including Japan, on 27th July 1929. It was an international agreement aiming to govern the treatment of prisoners of war, but by December 1941 it had still not been ratified by Japan. It was during this twelve-year period in particular that the fanaticism of the power-crazed militarists brainwashed millions of Japanese males into believing that death was preferable to the humiliation of defeat and surrender. The Bushido code, which had elevated martial conduct to a religious state, became polluted in a most vicious and ominous manner. Millions of Japanese were inculcated with the conviction that dying for Japan was a religious duty. Surrender was disgraceful and forbidden under the Japanese military code. Those who surrendered automatically waived their right to further existence. Such an upbringing makes it less difficult to comprehend how

> 'the Japanese were prone to kill their own wounded in battle rather than allow them to fall alive into Allied hands. Their rationale was two-fold, to save their comrades from disgrace and to safeguard their information.'[1]

A soldier should never surrender. He was required to go away to war, to fight for the honour of Tenno Heika (Lord Son of Heaven), and to die. This doctrine was frequently affirmed by the Japanese public's apparent lack of care and negative reaction to news of the killing of numerous soldiers, or the suicide of many civilians. The only honourable conduct for a soldier was to fight to the death. If he was taken prisoner, even if grievously wounded, his family name would be held in contempt and be forever disgraced. Bushido pre-determined the actions of even seriously wounded Japanese soldiers, many of whom chose to kill themselves rather than be captured or delay the progress of their comrades.

Of the few Japanese captured many took on different names and never enquired of each-other's military or family background. They lived in dread of meeting anyone who knew them previously, and even those who had been desperately wounded on capture realised as 'non-persons' that for them, their families, honour and homeland no longer existed. There is no doubt that such a harsh upbringing, brainwashing and training induced in the minds of Japanese soldiers

> 'a feeling of utter contempt for those who surrendered to the Japanese forces. They had forfeited all right to any consideration. . . . This attitude of mind does much to explain, though it does not excuse the Japanese Army and Navy's treatment of Allied prisoners of war.'[2]

Prisoners of war were therefore regarded as disgraced, cowardly criminals — 'sub-humans'. Such was the dishonour attached to guarding them that alcoholics, misfits and even the insane were allotted this task. Japan claimed to abide by the Geneva Convention regulations, but in practice few of the rules were followed. International Red Cross inspection teams were barred from visiting prisoner of war camps and few formal records of Allied prisoners of war were kept. Even in the post-war years any reference to their treatment as 'non-beings' invited an impenetrable obliqueness.

The fanaticism of Japanese soldiers and their seeming indifference to death made them loathed by many Allied soldiers. Their planned death either by suicide or the hand of another was seen as a grotesque form of self gratification. It was an attitude that invited loathing and the feeling that to beat them, they had to be killed. Spectacular proof of their fanatical spirit, fierce patriotism and willingness to sacrifice their lives in unorthodox attacks and in suicide squads was provided on many occasions, and especially in the latter part of the war by their Kamikaze attacks.

Only 2,400 Japanese forces were captured or surrendered in all the major battles of the war, and in no single battle did this exceed 5% of the forces engaged, and usually it was as low as 1%. They withstood a stupefying intensity of air and sea bombardment on numerous occasions before fighting even began, which in comparison made the raids on Penang and Singapore seem minor. At Iwo Jima, despite American superiority in every respect, their fanatical stubbornness prolonged the battle for three months of bitter ferocious fighting before they were wiped out. Even so, the militarists continued to yell defiance and to control the home front, exhorting every man and woman to sacrifice all for His Imperial Majesty.

Despite all this, at the end of the war the Japanese soldier returning to his homeland did so in abject shame. A direct contrast to the rapturous welcome that returning Allied soldiers received. It was little wonder that each side found the other so hard to comprehend and easy to loathe.

Some infrequent but astonishing quirks of Japanese character were portrayed by a minority, mostly during the early stages of the war. When the battleships *Prince of Wales* and *Repulse* were sunk the loss of life could have been considerably higher if not

> '. . . for once – Bushido! As the British destroyers, *Vampire* and *Electra*, closed in to pick up the survivors in the water . . . Japanese planes overhead signalled to the ships, "We have completed our task. You may carry on".'[3]

This made it possible to save almost 800 survivors from the two ships out of the total complement of 1,300 officers and men. Just over two months later when Singapore surrendered, according to Tokyo's Domei News Agency, General Tomoyuki Yamashita accepted

> 'full responsibility for the lives of the British and Australian troops, as well as the British women and children remaining in Singapore. He declared "Rely on Japanese Bushido". Bushido is the ancient Japanese code of chivalry inculcating courage, loyalty, courtesy and self-control.'[4]

In fanatical hands Bushido became the password for the most debased cruelties exacted on prisoners of war and civilian internees alike throughout all areas that fell under Japanese control. The casualties in Japanese gaols as a result of this code of chivalry were far higher than on the battlefield.

* * * * * *

The Japanese both preached and practised the belief that Seishin to a large extent controlled mind and body, and thereby any action taken by them. Success was lauded as a result of Seishin. The essence of Seishin was a combination of loyalty, obedience, total love and a willingness to die for Tenno Heika. The Emperor — deified as a direct descendent of the Sun Goddess and the incarnation of God on earth — represented the divinity that had ruled the Nippon Empire for thousands of years, and his infallibility was never questioned. The educational system in Japan inseminated this doctrine into all children's upbringing, making them believe that their greatest duty and honour was to serve and die for Emperor and country. By doing this they would be regarded as national heroes, entitled to be enshrined in the Temple of Yasukuni.

Patriotism is a noble sentiment and Seishin inculcated this admirably. When it was misused however by powerful, lustful militarists who imposed their wills through it, turning militarism and patriotic duty to the Emperor into one and the same entity, it was transformed into a sickening and malignant excuse for national hysteria. Seishin was supposed to make people tough and fearless. There was no escape from it. Without Seishin people were nothing. Breaking minor rules — even satisfying one's hunger — was looked upon as a weakness and an unforgivable crime against Seishin.

The manner in which a Japanese private soldier took his punishment at the hands of a senior officer was impressionable.

> '. . . pity the poor one-star private who had displeased his superior, he was not "put on a charge" — oh dear no — it was smash, bang, wallop and a bloody nose if nothing worse.'[5]

Discipline in the Japanese army was merciless, veering towards the senseless. In addition to worshipping the Emperor, the Japanese soldier also revered everyone senior to himself, even another private soldier with only one day longer service. At roll call every evening they were ordered to turn eastwards and to worship the Imperial Palace while respectfully reciting the 'Five Imperial Doctrines'. These invoked a destiny of patriotism (many sought death in preference to living); observance of the rules of etiquette (applicable when committing rape, murder and torture); respect for martial courage (this could never be denied); truth; and austerity.

The essence of Seishin finally led to Japan's defeat. Power-crazed militarists poisoned the minds of the people of the nation by declaring that Japan was the 'Liberator of Asia'. They preached universal brotherhood, but also indulged in the barbarism and atrocities that arose out of their warped spirit of Bushido. By misuse of Bushido and Seishin, the nation became corrupted with egotism and self-delusion.

20:2 Unlimited and Condoned Atrocities

Japan was one of the signatories to the Hague Convention in 1907 which set out specific rules regarding the treatment of prisoners of war. Notwithstanding these regulations, some instances of ill-treatment by the Germans during the 1914–1918 war made it clear that there were still some serious shortcomings in this respect and on 27th July 1929, 47 states put their signatures to the Geneva International Convention, in a bid to strengthen the regulations governing the treatment of prisoners of war, and to make them more binding on any signatory parties. Japan was a willing signatory to this Convention in 1929 and despite her non-ratification of it by December 1941, she gave a formal assurance through her Foreign Minister, Shigenori Togo, that although not bound to comply with the Convention's provisions she would apply them,

> '*mutatis mutandis*, to all American, Australian, British, Canadian and New Zealand prisoners of war. By this specific undertaking, Japan became morally bound to comply with the provisions of the Convention . . .'[6]

However she conveniently interpreted her non-ratification of the Convention by following the rules only when it suited her. The Convention clearly stated that prisoners of war were not to repair weapons. When General Percival refused to allow his men to do so, he was viciously punished and confined in a small cell without food or water for three days. This was followed by another 14 days in solitary confinement, but he stuck stoically to his argument.

The assurance provided by Foreign Minister Togo proved nothing more than diplomatic verbiage, as most of the provisions of the Convention were blatantly

> '. . . contravened time and time again. They [POWs] were murdered, they were bayoneted, they were tortured, they were beaten. They were robbed of their possessions. They were worked night and day in appalling conditions and on prohibited tasks. They were kept in filth and squalor and many of them were starved to death or reduced to living skeletons.'[7]

The dogmas of Bushido resulted in utterly disgraceful ill-treatment of prisoners of war and the so-called 'knights' of the order of the Rising Sun became famous for murder and executions — not at sunset but at sunrise.

From the outset of hostilities,

> 'the generally accepted Regulations concerning the custody of prisoners of war and civilian internees were flagrantly disregarded. Prisoners of war were murdered by shooting, decapitation, drowning, and other methods. They died during death marches . . . In the prison camps the conditions were appalling . . . Prisoners were systematically beaten and subjected to a variety of tortures in attempts to extract information from them, or for minor disciplinary offences committed by them in the camps. Prisoners of war, recaptured after escaping, were shot and captured aviators were beheaded . . .'[8]

The Japanese conveniently amended war regulations governing prisoners so that an escapee on recapture, or anyone caught attempting to escape, could be punished in the same manner as a deserter. In almost every instance this meant the death penalty. Collective punishment was also imposed on prisoners on more than one occasion at the Havelock Road Camp in Singapore, where they were forced to run bare foot over broken glass while being beaten by guards with rifle butts.

Allied prisoners of war and senior officials were constantly humiliated and insulted, especially in front of Asians, and made objects of public ridicule. The Governor of Hong Kong, Sir Mark Young, the Governor of Singapore and the Straits Settlements and High Commissioner for the Malay States, Sir Shenton Thomas, Lieut-General Sir Lewis Heath, Lieut-General Arthur E. Percival, Major-General Jonathan Wainwright and three American Colonels all over the age of 60, were made to tend herds of goats. When the first batch of prisoners from Malaya arrived in Korea, they were in such poor physical condition through neglect, ill-treatment and malnutrition that when forced to march through the streets of Seoul and Fusan before enormous crowds of Koreans and Japanese, their condition was an undisguised invitation to contempt from all who saw them. British and Australian prisoners of war were often transformed into half-naked scavengers. They were stared at, made objects of ridicule, harshly punished and at times spat upon. Many among them must have

> 'cursed the day they surrendered. These wretched prisoners of war were paying the penalty of an Imperial tragedy.'[9]

The death penalty, or imprisonment for more than ten years, became the recognised sentence for captured Allied airmen. It was applied retrospectively following the Colonel Doolittle raid on various targets in Japan on 18th April 1942. It was also applied to airmen captured previously and already held prisoner in China. Totally ignoring Japan's previous attacks on civilian targets, in violation of wartime international law, in China, Penang, Malaya, Singapore, Hong Kong and the Philippines — all designed to terrorise the civilian population — this order initiated a policy of putting captured Allied airmen to death.

> 'It was the common practice to starve and torture these prisoners for a considerable period before they were tried, more often than not trial was dispensed with, and even if a trial was held it was nothing but a hollow sham.'[10]

For three years and nine months of war wherever Japanese forces went they left in their wake a dreadful toll of massacre, murder, rape, torture and other barbarous atrocities. These occurred in all theatres of war and on such a vast scale of similar pattern that they must have been secretly ordered and wilfully condoned by the Japanese government. Known offenders responsible for such terrible actions were not sufficiently punished. They acted without remorse, assuming eventual victory and that no questions would be asked. General Percival was very badly beaten because of an alleged speck of dirt under one of his finger nails. Similarly, General Sir Lewis Heath, whose arm was slightly withered so that he was unable to keep it straight down by his side, was so brutally beaten by a Japanese soldier for not doing so, that he nearly lost his eyesight. A protest was made, but only a mockery of an apology in Japanese was obtained in response to this disgraceful and brutal assault. On 20th August 1945 when Japan's imminent defeat was at hand, a signal was sent to all commands ordering the destruction of unfavourable documents, and condoning the transfer or even the flight of those who had ill-treated prisoners of war or civilian internees.

In Malaya alone during the first six months of Japanese rule more bloodshed occurred than in the preceding 100 years of British rule. Records of ill-treatment were compiled and these are shocking proof of Japan's barbarity and guilt. Only 4% or 9,348 of the 235,473 British and American prisoners in German and Italian hands died in captivity. In the Pacific theatres, however, no less that 26% of the 99,134 prisoners died, and this percentage is more than doubled if the Dutch, Indian, Indonesian and Filipino casualties are also included.

The Japanese army continually withheld the truth, despite Hirohito's admonition that the ill-treatment of prisoners was 'a serious breach of duty that reflected shame on the Army'.[11] Little notice was taken of this by the army. Many prisoners were wilfully and intentionally allowed to die either on death marches, as targets for bayonet practices, or in a variety of other appalling ways.

It was not until early 1944 that newspapers in America were allowed to publish a report prepared by William E. Dyess. This told of the horrors he had witnessed and survived on death marches, and how these prisoners were forced to march without food, rest or water over long distances. Those who fell behind, or who were sick and wounded, were beaten, tortured and brutally murdered. The consternation of the American people at this revelation was such that the immediate demand was made to bomb Japan out of existence and also to hang Hirohito as a war criminal at the end of the war.

* * * * * *

When Changi Prison was built on the eastern side of Singapore island by the British government in 1936, it was designed to accommodate 600 criminals. At the time of the liberation in September 1945, 12,041 prisoners of war were confined within its walls. Approximately 5,000 of these had been squashed into various cell blocks, with the remainder overflowing into the courtyards, and concentrated alongside the prison walls in an assortment of huts that previously had housed prison employees. The cell blocks were suffocatingly hot and claustrophobic, and only one square metre of space was allowed for each prisoner. Originally each cell had been built to accommodate one person only but throughout its use by the Japanese, to hold Allied prisoners of war, each cell invariably held four.

Despite such extreme overcrowding the initial routines at Changi enabled a considerable element of freedom of movement within the camp, and outside news was relatively easy to obtain. This initial laxity was short-lived, however, and from 30th August 1942 onwards discipline was tightened up, following the refusal of prisoners to submit to instructions issued by Major-General Fukuye requiring all prisoners to sign an undertaking that they would not attempt to escape. On 2nd September recriminatory action was taken and senior camp commanders were made to witness the execution of four recaptured prisoners. All prisoners, then totalling almost 15,400, were herded together and relocated at the Selarang Barracks, where they were crammed into an area that had been constructed to cater for 900 troops under peace-time conditions. While they continued to refuse to sign the demanded undertaking no food or sanitary facilities were provided and there were only two water taps for all of them. On 5th September an epidemic of dysentery and dyptheria broke out and Fukuye threatened to return the sick and dying prisoners to the camp. Only then under duress was the undertaking signed. This incident at

Selarang was not forgotten and Fuyuke for his part in it was executed as a war criminal in April 1946.

By the end of October 1942 instructions were issued to all prisoner of war camp commandants to cut food rations to 420 grams per day. In March 1944 the 'no work, no food' regulation was issued, irrespective of grave evidence by that time of widespread deficiency-related diseases. Prisoners of war and civilian internees alike were forced to cultivate prison compounds in a bid to supplement their already near-starvation rations, and in Changi, after an Allied air attack on the Singapore docks on 24th February 1945, the prisoners' almost invisible 310 grams of daily rations — of which 200 grams was rice — was further drastically reduced.

Prolonged periods of under-nourishment had various and severe ill-effects on prisoners. For many their eyesight deteriorated and loss of memory — medically known as Changi memory — became notorious. Teeth loosened or fell out, tongues swelled, skin became blotched with fierce burning patches, and quite often bowel movements and lower leg muscles became difficult to control. Physical illness was common and was invariably accompanied by a series of deep festering sores which spread viciously and refused to heal. Red Cross supplies were frequently confiscated and used for the benefit of the Japanese, who, by denying adequate medical supplies in all prisoner of war camps, caused the deaths of many thousands of prisoners and internees. During a period of just over three and a half years the average food parcel and Red Cross parcel actually received by prisoners of war was only one fortieth of one parcel on three separate occasions. To protest was useless. Protest invariably brought about the reply,

> 'Remember your status as prisoners of war. You have no rights. International law and the Geneva Convention are dead.'[12]

Moving large numbers of prisoners revealed the Japanese at their cruellest. Power altered some of them into monsters. Many of the journeys made by prisoners were scarred and degraded by barbarities which reached an all-time low in the treatment of human beings, and even the Japanese War Ministry recognised this as proceeding from a form of hysteria. In December 1942 an Army Asia Secret Order

Number 1504 was issued which gave recognition to the ill-treatment of prisoners of war during transportation. It acknowledged that many prisoners had been taken ill or died during the journeys, and worse still that they were unable to work on arriving at their various destinations. With typical Japanese euphemism the order referred to the treatment of prisoners of war on journeys as being 'at times . . . inadequate'.[13]

Far East Prisoners of War (FEPOWs) will never relate stories of 'jolly Japs'. Their bleak-hearted cruelty was always too readily evident, in the casual way many of them could either kick or bayonet a dog or cat to death, or could leave human beings to wither and die with a total lack of remorse. Prisoners were herded together, starved, beaten, deprived of medical facilities and sometimes literally worked to death in various camps. The anger of FEPOWs lingers, spanning the years and the scant publicity their sacrifices received. Their bitterness towards their previous captors also lingers, although their protest now is more or less confined to a refusal to purchase any Japanese car.

All prisoners in Changi

> '. . . suffered from hunger and hardship, loneliness and depression, as well as humiliation and insults from camp guards and sentries . . . Men or women who did not bow deeply enough to a sentry were kicked or beaten, or were locked up for 48 hours without food or water.'[14]

Many who survived captivity will continue to live with the marks of their ordeal for the duration of their lives, while the life-span of many ex-prisoners of war was considerably shortened. It was religion and a sense of humour that enabled many prisoners to withstand their terrible plight. As Lieut-General A.E. Percival wrote,

> 'In Malaya very soon churches began to appear. In some cases the ruined remains of existing buildings were adapted for this purpose; in others new buildings were erected with such materials as could be found . . . In those dark days, when news of the outside world was scarce, and when most of what there was came from enemy sources, there could be in those prison camps little of that national fervour which impels the people of belligerent countries in times of stress. Something else was needed to take its place. It

> was found in the development of an implicit faith in the ultimate triumph of right over the forces of evil which were threatening the very existence of peace-loving and God-fearing people . . . Inspired by faith, the British soldiers in these camps displayed some of the finest qualities of their race.'[15]

Every Sunday makeshift churches were filled to capacity and if no chaplain was available, services were conducted by the prisoners themselves in the open air. Faith inspired fine qualities and many prisoners suffered cheerfully and with dignity. All the evil efforts of the Japanese to break the spirits of many of them failed.

During the delay between the cessation of fighting on 15th August 1945 until the official surrender in Tokyo on 2nd September, the plight of thousands of Allied prisoners of war

> 'in the last stages of malnutrition and in fear of their lives from vengeful guards',[16]

was still an awful reality. Although nothing could be officially done prior to 2nd September, aid was parachuted in to many of the camps. On 13th September, large numbers of prisoners of war were released in Malaya.

> '. . . it was found that they also had been subjected to the greatest barbarities and ill-treatment. Many of the prisoners were scarred for life, others suffering from grave malnutrition and various diseases, while many had died before liberation. Indiscriminate thrashings, humiliations, and indignities, together with medieval forms of tortures such as the "water treatment" were carried out as a routine in POW camps of which Changi, on Singapore island, was the largest. . .'[17]

Admiral Lord Louis Mountbatten as the Supreme Allied Commander in Southeast Asia Command, accompanied by Edwina, his wife,

> 'visited the notorious Changi jail only a few hours after liberation. The impatient prisoners awaiting the invasion, had christened him "Linger-Longer Louis". He arrived, as one prisoner Russell Braddon remembered "in his tropical whites, and never did a man look more glittering, glamorous and splendidly handsome". He stepped on to his traditional soap-box. "I'm sorry I didn't get here sooner," he began.'[18]

20:3 Death Railway

The death rate on the Siamese railway was horrendous! Of the 3,663 prisoners who left Singapore in April 1943, 1,060 never returned. These, already reduced like many others to skin and bone through under-nourishment – with many suffering from various tropical skin diseases and deficiency sores – were certainly unfit to perform the arduous work required, to hand-chop a railway track through granite mountains and dense vegetation. It was little wonder that up to 65% of some of the later groups sent on this project perished before one year had elapsed.

Those who did survive and return to Singapore after the railway was completed were in a pitiable state, suffering from beri-beri, malaria, tropical ulcers and debility. The average loss in weight per person was 70 pounds, and 80 out of every 100 who got back had to be admitted to hospital. The treatment of the 150,000 Burmese, Tamil, Javanese, Malayan and Chinese conscripted coolies – who had no officers to make representations on their behalf – was even worse. Mostly from the poorer classes, they were driven north in a never-ending stream. Old men, women carrying babies and children were treated pitilessly by their 'mentors'. They had to labour under the complete indifference of the Japanese 'to their sufferings and a callous disregard for their lives'.[19] At least 60,000 out of the 150,000, lured there under false pretences, died. They were repeatedly beaten and subjected to extreme forms of violence. They were stripped naked and then left exposed in the sun and rain for up to three days. On occasions these hapless, innocent people were forced to hoist either a heavy log or stone above their heads. There was no respite even for women and children. They were similarly treated, and both sexes were

> 'subjected to obscene brutalities . . . in order to gratify the perverted sadism of their captors'.[20]

It was by this means the Japanese Imperial General Staff got their railway. Out of the 46,000 Allied prisoners of war sent to work there, a horrendous total of 16,000 were worked to death and effectively murdered. The number of conscripted Asians who died without a dram of mercy shown to them was far in excess of this.

20:4 Cannibalism

Mutilation of living and dead bodies was a common occurrence, and cannibalism was practised to the extent that the Japanese army deemed it necessary to issue orders about it. Towards the end of the war some Japanese army and navy personnel reportedly ate the bodies of murdered Allied prisoners of war. However most private soldiers — who had been left to starve to death — chose to die rather than resort to such a disgusting alternative.

On 10th December 1944 the 18th Army headquarters issued an order permitting troops to eat the flesh of any Allied dead. They were however forbidden to eat their own comrades. A disciplinary memorandum stated,

> '... although it is not prescribed in the criminal code, those who eat human flesh (except that of the enemy), knowing it to be so, shall be sentenced to death as the worst kind of criminal against mankind.'[21]

Eating the flesh of the enemy was not considered a crime. Sometimes it was done on festive occasions at officers' messes, and even some generals and admirals were known to have participated in this. Cannibalism in many instances was resorted to from choice rather than necessity.

> 'About half an hour from the time of the forced landing, the Kempei Tai beheaded the pilot. I saw this from behind a tree and watched some of the Japanese cut flesh from his arms, legs, hips and buttocks and carry it off to their quarters. I was so shocked at the scene and followed the Japanese just to find out what they would do with the flesh.
>
> They cut it into small pieces and fried it.
>
> Later that evening a senior Japanese officer, of the rank of major-general, addressed a large number of officers. At the conclusion of his speech a piece of fried flesh was given to all present who ate it on the spot.'[22]

20:5 Murder At Sea

Although the London Naval Treaty of 1930 between the United States of America, Great Britain, France, Italy and Japan expired on 31st December 1936, the provisions contained in Article 22 of the Treaty remained binding on all the parties who had been signatories to it by dint of Article 23 which specified that the section appertaining to submarines would remain in force without any time limit. Even without this Article, Japan was still committed to observe these provisions as she was party to, and a signatory of, a Protocol in London dated 6th November 1936, along with the other original signatories of the 1930 Treaty. However, the Japanese navy constantly ignored all such provisions during 1943 and 1944, and survivors, whether they were passengers or crews of torpedoed merchant ships, were murdered in large numbers. This dishonourable action by the Japanese navy followed talks held on 3rd January 1942 between the Japanese Ambassador to Germany, Oshima, and Adolf Hitler.

> 'U-Boat commanders were instructed not merely to abstain from rescuing crews but to exterminate them.'[23]

In a subsequent order issued by the commander of the Japanese Submarine Force at Truk on 20th March 1943, Japanese submarine commanders were also ordered

> '. . . [not to] stop at the sinking of enemy ships and cargoes. At the same time carry out the complete destruction of the crews of the enemy's ships; if possible seize part of the crew and endeavour to secure information about the enemy.'[24]

These orders were executed by Japanese submarine commanders. Having taken either the Master or a few passengers and crew for interrogation, they proceeded to destroy all life boats and rafts and to murder all survivors.

A few examples will illustrate the enormity of crimes committed:

When the 2,000 ton submarine *I 8* returned to base in Penang in early 1944, it was under the command of a new captain, Commander

Tatsunosuke Ariizumi. His command of this submarine was a period of infamy. He sank unarmed Dutch and American merchant vessels, and massacred their crews.

There were originally 98 survivors from the Dutch merchant ship *Tzisalak*. All of these were butchered. When the American ship *Jean-Nicolet* was torpedoed on 2nd July 1944, 96 survivors were picked up from the sea. With their hands bound behind them they were questioned by Ariizumi and then were forced to run the gauntlet between a line of laughing Japanese sailors armed with clubs, swords and bayonets, who hit, hacked and stabbed them. Only 35 remained when Ariizumi suddenly ordered the submarine to dive. Out of these, only 23 somehow survived by freeing themselves from their bonds and them clinging to floating wreckage. In August 1945, just after the war had ended, Ariizumi shot himself as he entered the harbour of Yokosuka, rather than face certain trial as a war criminal.

When prisoners of war were transported by sea, the cruelty inflicted on them was if anything even worse than that inflicted on their counterparts in various prison camps. Packed into holds and coal bunkers without adequate sanitation and ventilation, many of them half-starved at the start of the voyage, they were denied any form of medical attention. They were mostly kept below decks in dank, foul darkness throughout the voyage, and because of the meagre rations and shortage of drinking water, their health deteriorated considerably. To make matters worse, the ships in which they were forced to travel

> 'were unmarked and were thus subjected to Allied attacks from sea and air in which many of the prisoners on board perished'.[25]

The 1,700 ton *Tachibana Maru* — a so-called Japanese hospital ship clearly marked with a red cross — was found, on being boarded just ten days before Japan's capitulation, to be transporting 1,500 Japanese soldiers, all allegedly in need of hospitalisation. When the bandages of these soldiers were removed a large number of them were found to have no wounds. Crates marked with a red cross and labelled as medical stores were found to contain 38 machine-guns, artillery shells and other ammunition.

20:6 Rape

Rape was a scourge in Japanese occupied Malaya, although there is little documented evidence. There were alleged cases of rape by retreating Allied stragglers, prior to the British surrender in February 1942, and most certainly armed gangs of roving robbers from all races took advantage of the chaotic situation in the country at that time, combining their plundering activities with attacks on helpless women and girls.

The Japanese — the self-professed saviours of Asia — were the ones who committed rape at will and murder wherever they went. Indian women were sometimes, but not always, unmolested. Any attempt to resist was useless, and if menfolk tried to protect their women they were murdered in cold blood. Fleeing women were routed out and outraged inside and outside their own homes, often in full view of husbands and children, who were forced to watch and cruelly beaten if any objection was made. Frequently husbands, fathers, brothers and sons were bound and forced to look on helplessly while their women were violated and they themselves were then murdered.

To a large extent the degree of brutality depended on the sort of Japanese officer placed in charge of a town. Some, being disciplinarians, tried to enforce law and order. The opposite could apply when the rape-lust of the officers exceeded that of their men. This was the case in Johore where the highest levels of rape were reported. Eurasian and Chinese women were the main targets; for some reason European women were virtually immune and escaped lightly in this regard (despite the occasions when British women internees were intentionally humiliated by being stripped naked and put on public display in shop windows for days at a time.)

There are numerous verbal accounts of women experiencing very narrow escapes. Many families tried to keep on the move to avoid trouble and remain out of the way of Japanese search parties hunting for women. The cries of sick and hungry babies resulted sometimes in hiding places being discovered. Many women were hidden in underground rooms, large chests, dug-outs in back yards, in chicken coops, tool sheds, garages, bathrooms, under the stairs and even in latrines.

Some women tried to make themselves look ugly in a desperate bid to avoid unwanted attention that could culminate in rape.

Some Japanese committed gang rape — sometimes publicly. On such occasions even elderly women were not spared, and when young girls screamed in terror and agony they were brutally pinned down by the throat and invariably left bleeding and mutilated, or dead.

Some people attempted to ingratiate themselves with the Japanese by pointing out beautiful girls to them, while others assisted by joining the ranks of Japanese search parties. Protection certificates did help some families, unless the issuing officers proved as lustful as their men, when rape became generalised.

In large towns women and girls of varied backgrounds were rounded up and tagged for military use in army sponsored brothels — the more attractive ones being allocated to officers and the others for use by the rank and file. Brothels were organised in all garrison towns, but even here in a few instances Japanese soldiers were disciplined for rape and a few junior officers were actually executed. The incidence of rape in Malaya and Singapore could have been far worse had it not been for an attempt by some people to curtail it.

20:7 Terror Tactics

For most people the Japanese occupation of Malaya is remembered as a nightmare period of brutality. Right from the outset it was obvious that the guides accompanying the initial Japanese on their advance down the peninsula had not done so of their own free will, but were being bullied and beaten to do so.

> '. . . there was no question of the Chinese or Malays collaborating, but both were obviously frightened to death, and it was clear that the Japs were completely ruthless and would have no compunction in cutting off their heads.'[26]

Malays who refused to cooperate were invariably thrashed and often left tied to trees at the mercy of thirst, hunger, and the ants.

The Japanese were experts in 'tommy-gun' tactics which they used effectively to terrorise the inhabitants of villages and towns, to subdue into control. There was much looting by advance parties of

Japanese forces, who searched everyone when they overran villages. They forced entry into houses, foraging for supplies, and took away anything they wanted, especially wrist watches, rings, and fountain pens, mattresses, mosquito nets and any serviceable clothing. Shirts on occasion were even removed from people's backs. No one dared to protest, and no one dared to put up any resistance. When cars were requisitioned, owners simply had to hand over the ignition keys with a show of outward grace.

When the main body of Japanese forces arrived some element of order was restored and ultimately harsh punishments were meted out to looters and suspected looters alike — but not the Japanese soldiers who had previously rampaged and stolen on an unlimited scale. Public executions were summarily carried out, with the heads of the decapitated displayed on top of poles at cross roads, on bridges and in market places, as a grim deterrent and reminder of what Japanese justice entailed.

The Chinese in Malaya were the most severely persecuted community during the Japanese occupation, then the Eurasians, who attracted Japanese animosity because of their western heredity. Numerous Chinese were imprisoned and horribly treated. Thousands were executed and many tortured in a prolonged and sadistic manner.

Unfit labourers were conscripted from all races and walks of life to work for the 'glory' of the Greater East Asia Co-Prosperity Sphere. Many were inhumanly massacred on the slightest pretext and without remorse, and frightful accounts of these massacres have been documented in various sources.

In one instance some bored Japanese soldiers poured petrol over an elderly Chinaman's pigtailed head, then set it on fire and gave him a bucket of boiling water with which to put it out.

At Titi in Negeri Sembilan, thousands of Chinese men, women and children were brutally massacred for being suspected supporters of MPAJA guerrillas. Malays in contrast were beaten if it was thought that they had offered assistance to the guerrillas, with a few sometimes killed as an example to others in the village.

In a guerrilla camp in Kerling, F. Spencer Chapman, author of *The Jungle is Neutral*, met six men who had escaped from a Kempetai gaol in Kuala Lumpur. He recalls that he saw 'the scars where the Japs had pushed needles beneath their finger-nails and burned the flesh of their faces and chests with cigarette ends and hot irons. The chief outside worker of this camp had been permanently crippled because the Japs had made him kneel down and had then jumped on the back on his calves. When that failed to make him speak, they had put poles across his shins and, with a man standing on top, had rolled them from knee to ankle.'[27]

In some of the most savage organised massacres against the rural Chinese, who lived in villages along the fringes of the jungle, the killing was carried out with demonic and clinical intent.

'Each morning two or three two-engined planes would circle low round and round the area between the main road and the edge of the jungle. At the same time a cordon of trucks . . . would be placed every fifty yards along a section of road to shoot anybody attempting to break out. The cordon would close in. Young able-bodied men were taken away and seen no more . . . Girls, even children of twelve or thirteen years, were often raped at once or taken away to fill the military brothels. An enormous number of Chinese were tommy-gunned or bayoneted. Others were driven into attap houses and burned alive.'[28]

In a determined campaign to exterminate anti-Japanese elements and communists, the Japanese condoned such actions as justified if even one guilty person was discovered among one hundred victims.

* * * * * *

The sick and wounded seemed candidates for massacre to the Japanese mind. Ambulances, hospitals, medical staff and patients were prime targets. In January 1942 in north-west Johore,

'an ambulance convoy containing a number of sick and wounded Allied soldiers was captured by the Japanese. The patients, and the RAMC personnel and drivers were all removed from their ambulances and killed by shooting, bayoneting, and burning alive after being saturated with petrol.'[29]

At the Tyersall Indian Hospital located north-west of Singapore city, the dry attap-roofed huts were all clearly identified by red crosses. Having been hurriedly built, the hospital was a fire trap and when the Japanese medium bombers pushed home their attack,

> 'stretcher patients were roasted to death in their beds. Those who could walk attempted to escape but often could not force their way through flames up to thirty feet high . . . The smell of burning flesh made scores of helpers vomit as they worked. The screams of the trapped overshadowed every other noise — even the staccato rattle of machine-gun fire, for now Japanese fighters swooped low over the furnace, machine-gunning the rescuers and those wounded who had been got out and laid on the grass away from the huts . . . Over two hundred patients died.'[30]

In the Alexandra Hospital massacre, no one was spared. On the first floor, medical officers, orderlies and patients were bayoneted. This included one soldier undergoing an operation, plus the anaesthetist and the surgeon. On the second floor and from other parts of the building, patients and nurses were removed and two hundred of them were crammed into a bungalow overnight. In the name of Bushido they were taken out at sunrise on the following morning, made to queue up, and shot.

20:8 Details of Torture Used

The torture of prisoners of war and civilians was indiscriminately practised by the Japanese in all occupied areas, and in such a similar manner

> 'that there can be no doubt that it was the result of a definite policy adopted by the armed forces with the knowledge and approval of the Imperial Government'.[31]

The army and the navy used the same techniques as the Kempeitai, who were the undisputed peers in inflicting pain on other human beings. A captured copy of a Japanese Army training manual entitled 'Notes for the Interrogation of POWs' provides indisputable evidence that torture was both condoned and advocated. Interrogators were cautioned that torture could result in a person telling lies, thereby making them look foolish. A list was provided of potential threats which would cause acute mental and physical discomfort. These included the threat of murder, starvation, solitary confinement, deprivation of sleep and an assortment of other possibilities.

Interrogations were conducted at all hours of the day and night. Prisoners were dragged from their cells and beaten unconsciousness with

> 'metal bars, sticks, bamboos, wet knotted ropes, belts with buckles, or revolver butts, all over the body. While these beatings were being inflicted, the victims were sometimes suspended by their wrists from a rope passed over a beam. Sometimes their hands were tied behind their backs and they were forced to kneel while sharp-edged pieces of wood or metal were placed behind their knees so as to cut into the flesh as they knelt. A guard would then jump on their thighs or on the projecting ends of the bars behind their knees.'[32]

Prisoners were often forced to remain in these positions for long periods, frequently for up to ten hours, during which the interrogation continued without respite.

Suspension from trees, rafters and window frame beams with the victim's feet just off the ground was common, as was an upside-down position, causing intense pain as blood rushed to the head and eventual loss of consciousness. In all positions the thrashing invariably continued without mercy.

Prisoners were often stripped naked and burnt with lighted paper, cigarettes or cigars anywhere on their bodies, but particularly on the more sensitive private areas such as armpits, ears, navel, nostrils, between the toes, on the scrotum and penis. Women were always burnt on their breasts. Hot irons, scalding oil and water were also used to inflict burns, and several

> '. . . Asiatics had petrol poured on their bellies and ignited, and another Asiatic had his hands tied together and immersed in a bowl of methelated spirits which was then ignited'.[33]

The water treatment was a particularly barbaric form of torture carried out in various ways, depending on the props available to the interrogators. All systems required the full distension of the victim's stomach, on which a Japanese would either stand or jump, forcing water out of the victim's ears, mouth, nose and even through the eye sockets. Unconsciousness only brought a momentary respite, but by this time the victim would have been almost drowned. Victims were either trussed up and immersed in stone tubs in the squatting position, or a hose pipe was thrust into their months and nostrils and a tap opened, or they were forced to lie down in a monsoon drain which was then flooded by opening a hydrant. They were filled up with water until their stomachs were fully distended, or until they became unconscious. Their oppressors either sat on their heads or stood on their backs, or planks were put over their extended stomachs so that their interrogators or prison guards could jump up and down on them to force the water out. The purpose was always to extract a confession and the torture was often repeated until the victim succumbed.

Torture by electric shock was another method employed. Electrodes or the bare ends of wires were connected to the extremities of a victim's body, either to the hands, feet or nostrils, or to other sensitive parts and then the current was turned on. Excruciating agony and disorientation were the end results.

It was common practice to deny prisoners food and sleep and to expose them for hours at a time to the tropical mid-day sun. On many occasions after prisoners had been severely tortured, they were made to stand through a whole night. Other nasty forms of torture entailed the twisting of joints or repeated punching of the same place until the limbs and joints became permanently dislocated. Victims were also forced to kneel for hours on sharp objects and were flogged for the slightest movement. Pliers or nails were frequently used to pull or dig out finger and toe nails, and bamboo slivers were hammered under the quicks. The victims of interrogation were often made to believe that they were being taken out to their execution, then at the last minute, a change of decision was made, causing them to faint out of sheer fright. Threats against family members were a common ploy, and were the cause of great mental hardship to anyone already interned and being tortured.

Women were forced to share cells with men without facilities for privacy.

> 'They were subjected to insults and obscene gestures by Japanese prisoners in the same cell, who, with the assent of the guards, tried to compel them to perform the most sordid tasks.'[34]

There were numerous occasions when women prisoners were brutally assaulted by probing sticks into their bodies and when pregnant women were viciously kicked or punched in the stomach. In the Penang prison there were several reports of naked women being dragged around the prison yard behind a motorcycle or car, until they were rubbed raw and bleeding and limbs were broken. Sticking needles into women's nipples and breasts, and even cutting them off, was indulged in by a few of the most evil of Kempeitai interrogators.

Sybil Kathigasu was accused of assisting the resistance guerrillas in 1943. Over a prolonged period of time she suffered a varied combination of brutal tortures. She survived her ordeal and lived to give evidence by affidavit — she was too ill to be present in person — at a war crime trial in Ipoh in February 1946 of the head of the Kempeitai in Ipoh, a sergeant Ekio Yoshimura, who had brutally ill-treated and tortured her as well as suspending her seven year old daughter, Dawn, from a tree above a blazing fire, while he continued to beat Sybil viciously with a stick. Her daughter's pleadings to her mother to be brave fortified her resolve through her dreadful ordeal and, as if God had answered her prayers, a Japanese officer, on seeing their plight, ordered Yoshimura to release the child and send her home. Yoshimura was duly sentenced to death by hanging for his crimes against Sybil Kathigasu and for those against many other people in Ipoh whom he had tortured and brutally ill-treated.

All these tortures were deliberate. They can never be looked on as arising from the occasional outburst of sadistic passion. They were used routinely to obtain information. They were used wantonly, without regard for the age, sex, or physical condition of the victim. Those who committed them justly deserved punishment, as did the superiors who authorised them, and as did the one in whose name all actions and crimes were perpetrated — Tenno Heika.

20:9 Investigation of Collaborators

Suspected collaborators were rounded up and carefully investigated following the re-occupation of Penang. Many were duly charged in court. All Japanese subjects and troops were interned, as well as 50 Taiwanese who had been employed by the Kempeitai as interpreters. The Taiwanese in particular were intensely disliked by people in Penang, as they had capitalised on their knowledge of Nippon-go just to don uniforms to oppress and victimise people.

On Friday 5th October 1945 Squadron Leader C.M. Sheridan, the Penang Legal Adviser, was quoted in the *Straits Echo* as saying that those collaborators and war criminals currently under arrest in Penang would be dealt with by special military courts. Among these would be about 30 people who had been influential in the community during the course of the Japanese occupation, and who had recently been caught in different places on the mainland. They were being held for various war crimes, or for collaborating with the Japanese. An assurance was given by Major-General H.R. Hone MC, the Chief Civil Affairs Officer, that all 'quislings' and collaborators would be dismissed from their jobs in the public service.

On 6th October 1945 the *Straits Echo*, in its readers' forum column, published a list of 21 ways in which a collaborator could be identified. The tone of the article was resentful and bitter, and it urged the public to denounce them. This was to include anyone who had worked for the Japanese administration, or participated in slogan, essay writing, singing and drawing competitions. Girl hunters, those who had fêted or entertained Japanese officials, people with high-handed attitudes, those who had used their influence to enrich themselves, or worn office badges after working hours were all among those suspected. Equally suspect were those who had lectured or sung for the Japanese in public, or imitated them by wearing a white collar over a coloured shirt, or grown moustaches, shaved their heads, studied Nippon-go, or had been allowed to carry firearms, been seen in public with the Japanese, or anyone who believed that Japan was the saviour of Asia. All such people were to be considered as collaborators and 'quislings'.

Restriction notices requiring them not to leave home without informing the authorities were served on 300 people in Penang. In the first round-up 100 people were detained, two-thirds of them being subsequently released after investigation. Thirty-two people were kept in custody to await trial. Among those under suspicion and initially arrested were those Penang community leaders who, during the occupation, had been forced to act as buffers between the Japanese and the public, sometimes at considerable personal risk. Included among these were Heah Joo Seang, the Penang community leader who was President of the local Overseas Chinese Association (OCA) and Vice-President of the OCA of Malaya, Dr N.K. Menon, the Chairman of the Penang Indian Independence League (IIL), and N. Raghavan, a local barrister who had also been a member of Subhas Chandra Bose's Provisional Government of India. Three Chinese women and 90 Taiwanese were also taken into custody.

On 21st November 1945 a special court was opened to hear complaints against suspected collaborators and to examine witnesses. Mr G.H. Conaghan — a well known Penang lawyer — was appointed as a special magistrate for this purpose, and those with complaints or information regarding collaborators were required to bring their case before him for hearing. Complaints by this time had already been made against 800 people, but a lot of these upon detailed questioning were found to be without foundation. Doctor Menon was released, along with 13 other people, and by 20th February 1946 the charges against seven others had been dismissed. Heah Joo Seang was cleared of all allegations at a special court hearing presided over by Major T.M. Bishop on 16th March 1946.

Ten people in due course were brought to the Penang Police Court under heavy armed guard on charges of alleged collaboration. The main accused — Yuen Chee Wan, aged 26 and previously a Chinese school mistress — was charged with assisting the enemy, by informing on 42 Chinese people in April 1942, many of whom were subsequently interrogated, tortured and murdered by the Kempeitai. Another accused was Ng Yan Poey — a detective police inspector under the Japanese — who was charged on six counts of voluntarily causing hurt. Baug Singh — a gaoler at Penang Prison — was charged with assisting the enemy, by informing on loyal British subjects and British protected persons, and Ahmad bin Che Teck — a sub-warden of Penang Prison — was charged with two counts of murder, five of attempted murder and on ten counts of causing voluntary hurt. The remaining accused were charged with an assortment of crimes ranging from causing hurt to assisting the enemy.

Yuen Chee Wan was committed for trial on 16th October 1946. One of the 42 people who had been arrested by the Kempeitai at 3 a.m. on 6th April 1942 was Kuah Kok San. When Kuah and his uncle, along with ten others, were taken away by lorry to the Penang gaol, he had recognised the accused, dressed in men's clothing with a felt hat pulled down to cover part of her face. She had threatened them with death if the teachers and pupils among them of the Chung Ling High School did not reveal their identity. Yoshida Tamekeichi, another witness who had been a Japanese interpreter attached to the Kempeitai, also identified Yuen as being the same person who had occasionally brought information to the Kempeitai's office. Another witness — a 17 year old girl named Yip Lai Peng — was put in the line up in an identification parade when Yuen denounced many of them to the Kempeitai as being either teachers or pupils at the Chung Ling High School. The Chinese character 'Chung' was written on these people's backs and the character 'Kong' was marked on the backs of those suspected of being communists. Yip Lai Peng had never known Yuen before she was arrested on 6th April, and had never spoken to her, but on Yuen's information she had been kept in prison for more than five months and then had been charged with being a communist. She had been beaten and tortured by the Kempeitai and sentenced to 15 years imprisonment.

Another witness, Carlyle Da Silva — a sub-inspector during the occupation and a right-hand man of Hashimoto the 'Tiger' of Penang, who was then serving a five year sentence of rigorous imprisonment in the Penang gaol for assisting the enemy and causing voluntary hurt during the occupation — also identified Yuen as having gone to the Kempeitai headquarters on many occasions. Lim Ah Heng, who had been a detective at the end of February 1942, also identified Yuen as one of the three people who had pointed out suspects to the Kempeitai during the April 6th round-up. He had recognised her when she removed the hood covering her face, along with other informers in a room at the Kempeitai headquarters.

Yuen Chee Wan appeared in the crowded Penang Assizes before Mr. Justice C.W.W. Carey on Thursday 14th November 1946 when the charge of assisting the enemy was withdrawn, in order to make an application to amend it to another more serious charge under Section 121 of the Penal Code. Subsequently Yuen was charged with attempting to wage war against the King in Penang during the Japanese occupation. She was remanded in custody until 26th November 1946, when her case came up for trial. She was subsequently found guilty and sentenced to eight years imprisonment.

20:10 In Memoriam and Tributes

A war memorial, in memory of more than 1,600 Penang Chinese brutally killed during the occupation in three 'Sook Chings', stands at the roundabout junction of the Ayer Hitam and Penang Hill Railway roads. Half a century after these murders were committed this granite monolith is still a grim reminder of those days and of the scourge caused by the 'hooded terror' used by the Japanese, despite their self-nominated role as the 'Saviours of Asia' and the authors of Asian 'Co-Prosperity'. In Malacca, and in other major towns in Malaya and Singapore, similar monuments also pay tribute to those who were murdered during the Japanese occupation.

Many of the dead honoured by the Penang memorial were killed in rural areas, their bodies invariably dumped for burial in common graves in different parts of the island. This prompted the Penang Branch of the China Relief Fund Committee to seek permission to make a search for them and have them exhumed and re-interred in a more suitable location.

At a meeting of the Penang Branch of the China Distress Relief Fund on 17th September 1946 at the Hui Ang Association in Magazine Road, the government's approval for the exhumation of the corpses of Chinese war victims in Penang, and their re-interment at other suitable locations was confirmed. Diggings were subsequently made in various places, including the Rifle Range burial ground, near the reservoir at Batu Ferringhi, on some vacant ground near Magazine

Circus, at a location in Tye Sin Street and at Bukit Dumbar where the skulls and remains of 250 people were found in a ten foot deep trench.

* * * * * *

In February 1944 a Malay lumberjack spotted two British soldiers — Jack Bennett and Samuel Freer — who had been hiding for just over two and a half years in the hills of Balek Pulau. He reported this to the police who passed the information to the Kempeitai. Bennett and Freer were caught, tortured and subsequently died. Some brave Chinese at Balek Pulau, who had helped to harbour and feed them during their long period in hiding, were subsequently arrested, tortured and sentenced to death. Cheah Eng Keat — a correspondent on the *Straits Echo* newspaper was one of them. He was hanged.

On 8th June 1946, to commemorate King George VI's birthday, a Victory Day honours' ceremony was held on Victoria Green in Burma Road at which eight Chinese women, thirty Chinese men and two Indian men were honoured with testimonials signed by Admiral Lord Louis Mountbatten and presented by the Governor General, Mr Malcolm MacDonald. All these civilians had risked their lives and some had been tortured and had died for their kindness in hiding and feeding Allied soldiers. The first to receive this certificate of gratitude was the widow of Cheah Eng Keat, followed by Leong Look Moi, the widow of Ah Pitt Leong, who accepted it on behalf of her husband.

Doctor L.W. Evans, who had refused to evacuate from Penang, was awarded a CBE, and Dr R. Apparajoo received an OBE. Dr Apparajoo came to Penang as an assistant surgeon in 1934, and in December 1941 was left as surgeon in charge of the General Hospital. Many people owed their lives to his skill and patience during those difficult occupation years. Captain Yeoh Teik Ee — a former school boy at the Old Free School in Penang — was awarded an MBE in recognition of his daring reconnaissance exploits during the occupation when he landed by submarine at Telok Bahang and also at Lumut in Perak.

At another ceremony on Friday September 13th 1946, at the Chinese Recreational Club, 54 residents of Penang, Perak and Kedah received similar awards from the Governor General. Major K.H.G.

Milne (KRRC) of No. 6 War Crime Investigation Team addressed the gathering and explained that at the earlier presentation on 8th June 1946 it was realised that many more people had helped Allied troops during the occupation and the presentations now being given were a token of appreciation and gratitude for this. Some had come from Kedah, Perak, and Penang and some were there as representatives of whole villages, who had magnificently assisted soldiers in distress at grave risk to their own lives. A scathing reference was made to the relatively few collaborators who had enhanced their own wealth and position by cooperating with the enemy. It was apt that tokens of gratitude were presented at this time when those Japanese and Taiwanese charged with committing war crimes and atrocities were on trial. Madam Tay Hooi Eng from Taiping was the first person honoured for her help in harbouring Allied troops in Penang.

On Sunday 10th November 1946 the Governor General paid tribute to the war dead of two world wars at a Remembrance Day ceremony. As the roll of the drums faded into a two minute silence the Union Jack fluttered briskly on a flagpole at the Penang Cenotaph, and several hundred people stood in silence until reveille sounded. Ex-servicemen and women, and men of the 2nd Battalion of the West Yorkshire Regiment, with a detachment of the RAF Regiment, formed the guard of honour.

20:11 War Crimes Trials

Lord Maugham initiated a debate in the House of Commons on 7th October 1942 on the question of establishing an International Criminal Court to try war criminals after the war had ended. A War Crimes Commission began regular sittings in 1944 and in August 1945 the Chinese Ambassador, as Chairman of the Far East Sub-Committee at the United Nations War Crimes Commission (UNWCC), recommended that an International Military Tribunal should be set up to try those Japanese responsible for committing criminal activities. It was further recommended that a central War Crimes agency should be established in Japan to collect evidence, register war criminals, and make the necessary arrangements to surrender war criminals to the various countries wishing to charge them.

A blithe statement in late 1945 by Premier Morihiro Higashakumi, that

> 'Japan has already tried her war criminals — and it may be taken for granted that their punishment has already taken place,'[35]

totally outraged General MacArthur when he was advised that only two Japanese officers had been sent to prison despite all the savage crimes committed against those who had worked and died on the death railways in Thailand and Burma.

By special proclamation on 19th January 1946 MacArthur approved the establishment of the International Military Tribunal for the Far East, on which 11 nations would be represented. Twenty-eight accused were brought before this Tribunal, which opened in Tokyo on 3rd June 1946. The prosecution opened its case on 3rd June 1946. Responsibility for the brutal and wholesale slaughter of more than 100,000 people in Southeast Asia was firmly laid at the door of Prime Minister Hideki Tojo and his wartime government. The prosecution further recounted that one in every four British prisoners of war in Japanese hands had either been killed, or had died in captivity, and that the sadism of the Japanese in Malaya, Singapore, Burma, Hong Kong, Indo-china and Thailand had stemmed directly from the government's and military's policies, and had not originated with individual Japanese commanders. Indescribably cruel tortures and innumerable atrocities had been committed in the name of Bushido, with the Japanese reign of terror in Southeast Asia leading to the widescale massacre of innocent children, women and men. In Singapore alone well over 6,000 helpless Chinese had been killed.

The case proved a marathon, the prosecution concluding its evidence only on 24th January 1948. Evidence for the defence took a further 11 months, and the trial was not concluded until 12th November 1948, when death sentences were handed down.

Death by hanging was pronounced on seven of the 28 accused. Another 16 were imprisoned for life and two got lesser terms. Two of the accused died during the course of these lengthy trials, and one was declared unfit to stand trial. Among those receiving the death sentence were:

General Dohihera — a specialist on China — who had withheld food and medicines from prisoners of war and had condoned their appalling living conditions.

Hirota — a former Foreign Minister and Prime Minister — who had not stopped atrocities against the Chinese.

Itagaki — an army officer and Minister for War in 1938 — who from April 1945, as Commander-in-Chief of Japanese forces in Java, Sumatra, Malaya, Borneo and the Andeman and Nicobar islands, had been responsible for the deaths of thousands through malnutrition and deficiency diseases.

Kimura — a Vice-Minister of War in April 1941 — who had allowed prisoners of war to do prohibited work under terrible conditions resulting in the deaths of thousands (i.e., on the Burma-Siam Railway).

General Matsui (retired) — recalled in 1937 to command the Shanghai Expeditionary Force — who was responsible for the long and horrible spate of atrocities following the capture of Nanking from 13th December 1937 to February 1938.

Muto — Chief-of-Staff in the Philippines in 1945 — who was responsible for his troops' atrocities in Northern Sumatra.

Hideki Tojo — the most blameworthy of all the accused, having been in office as Prime Minister for almost three years from October 1941. He was responsible for Japan's criminal attacks on her neighbours, and the barbarous treatment of prisoners and internees, of which he was fully aware.

Over a period of time approximately 7,000 suspected war criminals were arrested, and many were punished severely. Lieut-General Tomoyuki Yamashita — the Tiger of Malaya — was born in 1885. As commander of the Twenty-fifth Army, he had overrun Malaya and Singapore in 70 days in a campaign without fault. In Penang, Yamashita had insisted that looters and rapists from one of his divisions must be summarily punished, but later in the campaign a bitter conflict of opinion between him and Lieut-Colonel Masanobu Tsuji arose about authorising the Alexandra Hospital massacre. Tsuji maintained that he had only authorised it to make Yamashita's demands for the Allied surrender more effective. Immediately after Japan surrendered, Yamashita was arrested, and in December 1945 a US Military Commission condemned him to death for condoning the behaviour of the forces under his command which had resulted in the mis-treatment of prisoners of war, especially on an infamous death march in 1942. Yamashita was hung in February 1946.

By 1948 British military courts had tried 931 Japanese war criminals, and at the infamous Changi Prison about 135 Japanese officers and men were executed for war crimes by hanging, from a gallows set up at the east corner of the prison. In other parts of Malaya another 70 were executed.

At the War Crimes trials in Singapore, which began in March 1946, the misdeeds of the Kempeitai were described by the prosecuting officer as

> 'actions which plumb the very depths of human depravity and degradation. The keynote of the whole of this case can be epitomized by two words, unspeakable horror.'[36]

Lieut-General Shinpei Fukuye, who had been in command of prisoners of war in 1942, was one of the first war criminals to be tried in Singapore. He was sentenced to be shot, and photographs of this were published in the Singapore newspapers. The execution was carried out in April 1946, on the very same spot on Changi beach where Fukuye had ordered the shooting of British and Australian prisoners of war four years previously. Vice-Admiral T. Hara, who commanded the Andaman and Nicobar islands, was found guilty with five of his men of having murdered nine Burmese in July 1945. They were hanged on 19th June 1946.

The war crime trials of the large number of Japanese officers responsible for the 'Double Tenth' massacre of Chinese civilians in Singapore on 10th October 1943 began on 10th March 1947 and ended on 2nd April 1947. Colonel Ichiji Sugita — a staff officer in the 25th Army who had escorted Yamashita at the British surrender of Singapore — and Mamoru Shinozaki were both called as witnesses in these trials. The most senior of the accused was Lieut-General Takuma Nishimura, former commander of the Imperial Guards Division, Lieut-General Saburo Kawamura of Defence HQ, Lieut-Colonels Masayuki Oishi, M. Yokota, and T. Jyo, Major S. Onishi and Captain Hisamatsu, all Kempeitai officers. The presiding judge was Lieut-Colonel Forsythe. He was assisted by four assessors. Prosecuting was Major Fulcher, assisted by Major Ward, and a Japanese, Mr Kurose, was the defence lawyer.

Sugita in evidence told of the Army's decision to clean up Singapore, and to maintain peace and order by rounding up all suspected communists, ex-volunteers and anti-Japanese elements. He estimated that not less than 5,000 Chinese from the city area were victims of this campaign, plus another 1,000 from the sector east of the city. Shinozaki said that as the only official in the Japanese Foreign Ministry in Singapore at that time, he had issued a considerable number of protection passes, with Kawamura's approval, to the Chinese, including some to bus loads of Catholics from the Upper Serangoon and Katong areas, as well as to some Italian, German, Siamese and Swiss nationals. Several thousand protection cards had been printed and signed by him and he issued them freely to any who asked for them. Hundreds of them had also been given to community leaders to distribute as they saw fit.

On 14th March 1947 a sole survivor of the Tanah Merah massacres told the court how victims had been machine-gunned to death having been forced chest high into the sea. Another witness told of the hundreds of Chinese towed out to sea in boats and then machine-gunned to death off the island of Belakang Mati. Death totals during the occupation in Singapore had been a closely guarded secret, but after the war, a study of Kempeitai reports and other evidence indicated a probable 6,000 people were killed, in addition to the 9,000 who died during the initial bombing raids. One hundred and forty-seven people had been executed by the Japanese at the Outram Road prison and another 1,470 civilians internees had died there from a variety of causes. Approximately 17,000 Chinese were thought to have died in Singapore as a direct outcome of the Japanese occupation.

When the war crimes trials in Singapore ended on 2nd April 1947, Kawamura, Oishi, Sumida and other Kempeitai officers were sentenced to death by hanging. Nishimura was sentenced to life imprisonment, but subsequently was taken to Australia to answer charges of having murdered 150 Australian and 35 Indian soldiers who had surrendered to him near Batu Pahat in Johore. He was found guilty of these crimes and was hanged on 22nd June 1950.

* * * * * *

When Vice-Admiral H.T.C. Walker was told about the atrocities which had occurred in Penang during the early stages of the occupation, he arranged to obtain the information to bring war criminals to trial. A Penang Chinese Victims' Committee was formed to gather as much information as possible about the several round-ups of Chinese in Penang, and also to assist the Number 6 War Crimes Investigation Team headed by Lieut-Colonel H.S.I. Haynes in obtaining evidence about the Kempeitai's many acts of oppressive brutality.

The first to stand trial were those responsible for torturing and murdering hundreds of victims in Penang Prison and at the Penang Kempeitai headquarters. For this purpose, four Japanese involved in the atrocities in Penang were returned from Japan. One of these was Major Yoshinobu Higashikawa, the Penang Kempeitai chief from March 1942 until February 1943, who was arrested in Tokyo. Among the others were Takeharu Hashimoto — referred to as the 'Tiger of Penang' — who had been the Japanese Special Branch chief from 1942 until the surrender, and Okinowa Sakae and Imaizumi Kunata, both superintendents at Penang Prison. T. Ando — a pre-war shoe maker and a Penang resident — who was made Penang's first Chief Police Officer during the occupation, was brought back from Bangkok, along with Sergeant Major Katsuno and Yasusabono Nakamura who had worked as an interpreter for the Kempeitai. The whereabouts of Lieutenant Gonichi Ueno, the first Kempeitai Chief in Penang, remained unknown after he was sent to Burma in 1943, but immediately following Japan's surrender Captain Isamu Terata — the 'Terror of Penang' and the Kempeitai chief at that time — was traced and arrested on the mainland and brought back to Penang Prison, along with 150 other suspected Kempeitai officers and other ranks. Many of the torture experts however had managed to flee from Penang island before the British forces arrived.

On the morning of 3rd July 1946, 33 Japanese and eight Taiwanese were paraded at Penang Prison before 20 witnesses, four of whom were Chinese women who had been imprisoned and tortured by some of the suspects. The identification parade was held up for 15 minutes when three of the Chinese women cursed Yeoh Chew Bok — a Taiwanese and a former Penang resident and band master during the occupation — and one woman struck him with her umbrella, cursing him for his part in taking her son away in March 1942. Many of the witnesses showed no hesitation, identifying many of those in the line-up before them. At another identification parade on 27th July, 25 witnesses — again many of them women victims of Kempeitai torture — had paraded before them another 48 Japanese and Taiwanese prisoners suspected of committing war crimes. Both Higashigawa and Terata were in this line up.

From these identification parades and from a display of alleged war criminals at the Penang information centre which was visited by 12,400 people, Lieut-Colonel Haynes, the Officer-in-Charge of the Number 6 War Crimes Investigation Team, was able to record the statements of 75 potential witnesses.

Although the Penang War Crimes trials were originally scheduled to start in July 1946, they only did so on 30th August, when 35 alleged war criminals were charged. The presiding officer at these trials was Lieut-Colonel H.E.R. Smith (Royal Artillery), assisted by four assessors: Major S.B. Sahay IPC BA BL, Captain A.R. Doyle-Davidson 15th Punjub, Captain R.D. Kohli 2nd Punjub and Lieut. C.H. Mohd Sadiq of the 4/15th PR. Majors P.M. Thomas and A.P. Southall were the prosecuting officers and two Japanese, Dr Kaichiro Tokiwa and Mr Kawamura Jozo, were the councils for the defence. Mr Muto Yoshizo and Mr Fank Hyoo Horichi were interpreters on behalf of the Japanese.

The 35 accused arrived at the High Court buildings in eight vehicles and under heavy armed guard by troops of the West Yorkshire Regiment. Having been paraded in full view of the public in front of the statue of Francis Light, they were escorted inside the packed court-house and seated in four rows. They were identified by numbers 1 to 35 pinned on their chests, and most of them sat immobile in the dock, staring fixedly before them. Major Higashigawa, accused No.1, sat with his head down for most of the time, while Captain Terata, accused No.2, closed his eyes and appeared to be dozing. At times Terata gave the impression that he might be praying.

All the accused were charged with crimes committed either in Penang island or Butterworth between 1st March 1942 and 3rd September 1945. In his opening submission the prosecutor likened life in Penang during that period to a

> 'reign of terror and promiscuous slaughter involving liberal use of torture against individuals and groups of citizens in the most brutal and sadistic manner that the mind could evolve'.[37]

In addition to the many vicious beatings, burnings and exposure to the terrible water and electric shock tortures, he cited pregnant women being kicked in the stomach and other women being dragged naked behind cars and motor cycles around the prison courtyards until their flesh was torn and bleeding and their bones were broken.

He outlined the Kempeitai's duties, which had been aimed at eliminating all anti-Japanese elements through a system of informers who were extensively used against both individuals and groups. At mass round-ups the 'hooded terrors' denounced hundreds of innocent people. Suspects were arrested and taken to the Kempeitai's headquarters in Burma Road for interrogation. Some were forced to sign confessions prepared in advance, without knowing the contents, and were summarily tried and sentenced. Others were tortured into implicating innocent people. Many gave in to such terror tactics, and in many instances people were executed because of these extracted confessions. Those who did not break at the Kempeitai headquarters were then taken to Penang Prison where interrogations were continued in a most sadistic and brutal manner, involving prolonged periods of torture.

Many witnesses were now dead and those who had survived had been kept in such a state of pain and fear that it was not always possible for them to identify individual criminals with certainty. There was however more than sufficient evidence to incriminate the accused.

Major Higashigawa (No.1) was responsible for the actions of his subordinates from March 1942 until February 1943, and had taken part in administering the water treatment torture. Captain Terata (No.2) had publicly admitted his responsibility for his subordinates' misconduct in April 1945, but had also indulged in witnessing hideous tortures. Kietsu Kamada (No.3) – one of the most brutal of the accused – had teamed up with Washio (No.13) to drag naked women behind motor-cycles, and by repeatedly torturing an Inspector Scully, had caused his death in July 1945. Ichizo Muira (No.4) was sometimes Terata's second-in-command and caused the death of Goh Jin Kooi by repeatedly subjecting him to the water treatment. Saburo Wakui (No.5), as Terata's senior warrant officer, had been frequently seen burning, flogging and torturing prisoners by electric shock. Takashi Ogawa (No.6) had been fully involved in causing the death of John Netto, plus committing a variety of other atrocities, and had beaten and tortured by the water treatment both Simon Sooza and Nawab Din, who had been arrested in Taiping in July 1944. Sadao Shimuzu (No.9) – described as one of the most zealous and ruthless of the accused – had on one occasion strangled an Indian prisoner with his bare hands, and frequently used a leather belt with a brass buckle to flog prisoners. Imai (No.10) repeatedly refused the prison doctor's requests to move very sick prisoners to hospital, and Toyoki Murakami (No.12) – the expert in electric shock torture – used this system daily to inflict pain and to extract confessions. Imai also tortured Choon Keat by electric shock, and he died from the injuries he received. Compared to the others Joji Washio (No.13) was the most bestial and vicious. He caused the deaths of Low Siong Siew and two women, Ong Chin Huat and Hwa Lun, and specialised particularly in interrogating and torturing female prisoners in a most sordid manner. Khor Kee Siang (No.33), Kwek Tiong Hin (No.31), Yeoh Chew Bok (No.34) and Motosugi (No.35) were all civilian interpreters attached to the Kempeitai. Not only did they help as interpreters but they actively tormented prisoners and found delight in brutalising them. Khor helped Washio to torture women and assisted him to drag two naked female prisoners behind a motorcycle. Kwek and Yeoh also helped Washio to torture Low Siong Siew, who died within half an hour of being subjected to the water treatment. Kwek was seen on one occasion to force a hose pipe into a prisoner's mouth and then stand on a bench on top of the victim's extended belly to force the water out. The remaining 20 accused had all been involved to various extents in committing acts of brutality and torture.

* * * * * *

Only a summarised extract of some of the more poignant and disturbing aspects of evidence presented by witnesses at the Penang trials is related below, but these provide more than sufficient proof of the guilt of the principal accused.

On Saturday 31st August 1946 Kassim Ali told the packed court that one part of his duties at Penang Prison had been to escort prisoners back to their cells after they had been interrogated. They were invariably in a state of undress and their bodies were covered with bruises and open, bleeding wounds and their wrists were lacerated and badly swollen. Some of them had insufficient strength to stand unsupported.

Another witness, Hashim — a sub-warden at Penang Prison — said that he had seen men being judoed and made to lie face downwards in a tub of water. Also, hoses had been turned on and forced into their mouths, and planks had been placed across their extended bellies so that a guard could stand or sit on them to squeeze the water out. He identified Washio (No.13), who had interrogated and flogged a naked Malay women with a stick. Others looked on as Washio poked the stick inside her several times before dragging her, still naked, behind a motorcycle around the prison yard. Although prisoners were beaten regularly, and were in terrible pain requiring medical aid, he was told, 'Let them die. Never mind about them.'[38] On one occasion he had been instructed to remove the dead bodies of nine Chinese who had been shot in their cells.

When the trial resumed on Monday 2nd September Terata, Higashikawa and all the other accused were brought in handcuffed in pairs. Witness Jitt Singh — a clerk at Penang Prison from April 1943 to September 1944, and then an assistant gaoler until March 12th 1945 — had been arrested by Nishigawa (No.24), and had been kept for 35 days at the Military Police Naval Headquarters at the Light Street Convent, where he had been intensively interrogated and two confessions extracted. He recognised Kamada (No.3), Wakui (No.5), Shimuzu (No.9), Yokomi (No.11), Washio (No.13), Ito (No.19), Kaku (No.32), Khor Kee Siang alias Hoki (No.33), and Yeoh Chew Bok (No.34). Although clerks were not allowed into the interrogation rooms, he had seen what went on there. He had seen prisoners suspended by ropes or wires from beams and beaten with sticks and iron rods. Their hands were tied either behind their bodies or in front, and they stayed suspended until they confessed. He saw Yamada (No.7), Wakui (No.5), and Yokomi (No.11) occasionally do this to people, but Washio (No.13) did it very frequently. The beatings were savage, with rotans, iron rods and even chair legs, all over the victims' bodies until a confession was obtained. Prisoners were invariably unconscious when they were eventually cut down, and their wrists were deeply scarred and lacerated where the ropes had cut into them. Jitt Singh saw Washio burn a suspended prisoner on his feet, and he also remembered seeing Yamada apply the water treatment torture to Ong Huck Lim. He also saw Murakami (No.12) using electric shock torture twice, and on each occasion it lasted for more than one hour. Shimitsu (No.9) had beaten a prisoner named Naidu on the head, legs and back with a stick and after five days and nights of interrogation he had confessed. Washio also used to bring a vicious monkey to the prison to bite prisoners.

On Tuesday 3rd September it was the turn of Dr Letchumanasamy to give evidence. He told the court that from early 1942 until the end of 1943 he visited Penang Prison almost every other day. In 1944 he was told to reduce his visits to twice a week. He remembered that he had treated Jasuan Singh, who had cut his throat and also eaten powdered glass causing internal bleeding, preferring to die rather than suffer further torture. A special ward was set aside at the General Hospital for prisoners of the police and Kempeitai and most of these arrived with marks all over their bodies and in a very poor physical state. The medical staff were forbidden to be present when prisoners were visited by the Kempeitai, but it was clear that after such visits both their physical and mental condition had worsened. Patients were not given time to recuperate. Katier Singh was forcibly discharged with a fractured forearm, and Geh Lye Onn had severe unhealed burns on his feet when he was discharged. Many of the injuries that required treatment had been, in his opinion, caused by violent assaults. Some patients had paralysed arms from being suspended, others had very deep cuts in their wrists, and some women had bad bruises and burns on their breasts and around their sexual organs. There were many deaths in 1942, and throughout that year the prison held about 1,200 people. From March 1944 alone, Dr Letchumanasamy said that he had been required to certify 217 deaths due mostly to beri-beri, dysentry and pulmonary tuberculosis.

On Wednesday, the following day, the statement of R. Naidu was read out at the trial. Naidu could not be present in person as he was in India, still recuperating from the injuries inflicted on him when he was tortured in Penang Prison. Naidu's statement had been made to the War Crimes Investigation Team on 11th March 1946, and in this he confirmed that he had landed by submarine at Penang on 29th August 1943. He had worked in Penang until March 1944, when he joined the crew of a Japanese tanker carrying gasoline. He was arrested in Siam and sent to Taiping Prison where he was handed over to the Kempeitai. After one week in Taiping he was transferred to Penang Prison. Naidu stated that he had been beaten unconscious with bamboo canes by Yamashita (No.8), Hashimoto (No.22), Shimizu (No.9) and Egusa (No.23). They had also burnt him with cigarettes and suspended him by the wrists. They made him stand for six days in the sun and rain, compelling him to watch as they tortured other prisoners. Out of extreme hunger he had eaten grass to keep from starving. He also identified Isamu Terata as the one who had interrogated him three times, and who on one occasion brutally beat him with a stick. Shimizu had also interrogated and tortured him twice. He had witnessed Jack Bennett being tortured by three men who inflicted the water treatment on him.

Another witness, Bhag Singh, had been a corporal in the prison guards in 1942. He said that only 120 people had been initially released out of the 1,000 who had been brought in. All of those remaining had been interrogated and tortured, and each morning up to ten people were found dead in their cells. Out of that original 1,000, about 600 had died. Washio (No.13) beat prisoners until their backs dripped red with blood. He also saw him burn one man and strip one girl naked before dragging her behind a motorcycle. Yamada (No.7) also viciously beat prisoners who were subsequently found dead in their cells. Saheki (No.21) had killed one man by dropping him down a well. Terata (No.2), Wakui (No.5), Miura (No.4), Shimizu (No.9), Murakami (No.12), Washio (No.13), Nagata (No.17) and Nishigawa (No.24) had all taken turns to torture Naidu, and Washio had killed one prisoner who had been burnt from the waist downwards. Kamisako (No.28), just before Japan surrendered, had bound and blindfolded one prisoner who was never seen again.

Miss Cecilia Wong — the matron in the women's ward of Penang Prison from 1st June 1942 until the surrender — identified Washio (No.13) and the Taiwanese Kempeitai interpreters Kwek Tiong Hin (No.31), Yeoh Chew Bok (No.34) and Khor Kee Siang (No.33). Washio had assaulted Wong Kung Fong, a Chinese woman, by tying her hands behind her, stripping her naked and probing her with a stick one and a half inches in diameter. She had been interrogated from October 1943, but had only died on 19th August 1945. Washio also assaulted Wha Lan — a pregnant, married woman — who after interrogation was unable to walk. She died in hospital one week later. Washio was the normal interrogator of women. He tortured some by squeezing shut their nostrils and then forcing smoke into their mouths. Many were given the water treatment, and in 1944 many of the women that he assaulted had subsequently died.

On 9th September 1946 Major D. Hayhurst, the second-in-command of the War Crimes Investigation Team, told of the grave exhumations undertaken at Bukit Dumbar on 26th August. Following up on a driver's testimony that he had taken many bodies for burial there, a trench 50 yards long and two and a half feet wide had been opened and revealed no less than 250 skulls after digging only to a depth of seven feet. To corroborate these findings, Hassan bin Nawi, Mohamad Esa bin Darus and Low Cheng Keat told how they had been employed as lorry drivers and had taken up to four bodies for burial daily to the Bukit Dumbar and the Rifle Range burial grounds. Go Teng Eong — a grave digger at the Rifle Range burial ground — confirmed that in 1942 he had buried 800 people there, another 200 in 1943, 300 in 1944 and another 300 up to the surrender in 1945. Many of the bodies were badly bruised or had been decapitated.

Witness Yeoh Cheng Lee had worked at the headquarters of the Kempeitai in Burma Road from December 1942 until the surrender. He had seen many of the accused torturing prisoners during that period. Another witness — Tan Wye Hin, a barber at Ayer Hitam at the time of the second 'round-up' — had been arrested because he had two tattoos on his left upper arm. At least 1,000 people were rounded up on that occasion by the Kempeitai, assisted by a Taiwanese interpreter and a detective named Boey Chee Yuen. They were herded into groups of 30 in the prison yard and two 'hooded' informers walked up and down selecting some from among them. Tan was imprisoned and tortured for 94 days.

Kolanda Vellu, another witness, said that he had been used by the Kempeitai first as a dispatch rider and then as an interpreter. Higashikawa was invariably drunk, and on one occasion he had seen him physically throw six Chinese, suspected of being communists, down a staircase. Kamada (No.3) had cut a man's head with his bayonet and then had deliberately struck him with his rifle butt. Wakui (No.5) seemed to enjoy burning prisoners with cigarettes and crushing their fingers between pieces of wood. He had seen Washio (No.13) and Hashimoto (No.22) burn one Chinese man's hair and another's nose. Tonishi (No.27) had stripped one woman naked, and subjected her for two hours to the water treatment. He had also burnt her cheeks, nose and breasts with a lighted cigarette. Tonishi had also praised his sword for its good work — 'Joto Na' — after beheading two Chinese youths aged only 12 and 13.

Yeong Leng Moi said that she was only 17 years old when she was arrested at Balek Pulau on 29th October 1943. Washio (No.13) had forced her to watch him beat her half-naked grandmother with a brass tube. He had also burnt her grandmother on her knees and legs before dragging her behind a motorcycle. She had later died in Penang Prison.

Abdul Rahman — who was an inspector attached to the Japanese garrison police at Butterworth — said that in May 1943 he saw Tonishi

(No.27) cut off the heads of two young Indian boys, aged about 10 and 13. A hole had been dug and the two of them were forced to kneel in front of it. One of them was crying.

When 17 year old Ang Ah Thong was arrested by Kwek Tiong Hin (No.31) and Washio (No.13) in 1942, Kwek had cut him on both arms with his sword. He remembered seeing one desperate young girl from the Fukien Girls School, whom Kwek had mutilated by sticking pins into her breasts to make them bleed. He then cut one of them off. He also saw him probe her vagina with a thick patrol stick used by the Jikeidan. Both Washio and Kwek also heated pieces of iron and placed them on women's breasts.

After similar evidence was given by more witnesses, each recounting additional horrendous acts, the case for the prosecution was wound up by Major Thomas and Southall reading sworn prepared statements made by the 35 accused.

Major Higashigawa's sworn statement, made previously to Lieut-Colonel Haynes, revealed that he had preferred serving in the Kempeitai as he did not like to kill people. He had arrived in Penang on 15th March 1942, and took over from Lieut. Gonichi Ueno who had a bad reputation for extortion. He remained in Penang until he handed over to Captain Terata in early February 1943. During his period in Penang he had never been aware that prisoners were being ill-treated, and when he visited Penang Prison on four occasions, he had not seen any signs of this. His second-in-command, Kamada (No.3), had been fully responsible for happenings in the prison and had never told him that anyone had died there.

Captain Terata's prepared statement under oath confirmed that he arrived in Penang from Singapore on 21st January 1943, and that he took over the command of the Penang Kempeitai from Captain Shigawa, who was sent back to Japan. Initially he received orders from Kempeitai headquarters in Singapore, until this was relocated to Taiping. His commanding officer at Taiping was originally Lieut-Colonel Oishi, and later Major-General Kojima. The Kempeitai was required to maintain peace and order, to safeguard military secrets — such as troop movements — and to arrest spies, anti-Japanese elements and suspected communists. His policies aimed at promoting his subordinates' cooperation with the public to enhance the image of the Kempeitai. He was aware that some of his men deserved the bad name that was attached to them. His subordinates were instructed to keep a record of all arrests and investigations made and were told not to force suspects to make statements. Terata denied knowing Naidu, although he did recollect that an alleged Indian spy had been arrested in Siam. As there was insufficient evidence against him, he was released on 15th August 1945. Terata recalled Goh Jin Kooi. He thought Goh had died because of poor health and not under interrogation, as he did not notice any revealing marks on his body. Muira (No.4), as his second-in-command, was the person responsible for interrogation methods, but as the Kempeitai chief, he had full responsibility if any of his subordinates failed to abide by his instructions. Terata claimed that he had known only three out of the twenty informers that his subordinates had used. In the early stages of the occupation informers had been paid $400 a month, but this was increased to $2,000 as the value of currency depreciated. They had also been paid by various other means in lieu of cash. Terata considered that Wakui (No.5), Sasajo (No.25), Washio (No.13) and Shimuzu (No.9) were all of sound character and all of them had worked efficiently.

In his sworn statement Yokomi (No.11) said that Yap Hin Tat, a sanitary inspector, had confessed to listening to radio broadcasts by the Allies and when a search of his house was carried out British currency was found there. Yokomi was told that Yap committed suicide after he confessed.

The statement of Yamashita (No.8) confirmed that he and Kamisako (No.28) had been ordered to take a blindfolded Jack Bennett to the ferry to be sent to Singapore. Bennett however became ill on arrival in Butterworth, so they were instructed by Sasajo (No.25) to take him back to the Leith Street headquarters. A few days later he took a box containing Bennett's body from the convent in Light Street, to a Japanese burial ground in Perak Road, where it was drenched with kerosene and set on fire.

Kamada (No.3) in his sworn statement said that he could remember three mass 'round-ups' but denied all knowledge of beating or violence to prisoners. Wakui (No.5) admitted that some of the Kempeitai did raise their hands to prisoners, but claimed that he had never done so. Murakami (No.12) said that prisoners were occasionally beaten and Washio (No.13) admitted to having done so. He confirmed that some prisoners had died of malnutrition.

The sworn statement of Kwek Tiong Hin — a Formosan interpreter with the Kempeitai — described the method of carrying out the mass 'round-ups' and also gave the names of some of the informers and 'hooded terrors'. Potential informers were firstly arrested on charges of being communist and then were coerced into informing on others. Kwek gave the names of four police officers used in this manner by the Kempeitai: Detective Inspector Chong Chee Wan, and Detectives Ah Tsai, Teng Son Toh and Lee Yap, all attached to Kempeitai headquarters in Penang Road. Most of the other informers had been students between the ages of 15 and 23, and one was a Chinese newspaper reporter named Ng Kai Chong. As some of these people had already been sentenced to death on suspicion of being communists, they tried to save their lives by claiming to know others who also had communistic leanings, or who were anti-Japanese. These informers accompanied the Kempeitai during mass round-up operations all over the island, wearing hoods to conceal their identities. It was mostly the Chinese who were arrested and tortured to obtain confessions. In early 1942, there had been many deaths in the prison as a result of torture, close confinement and malnutrition. Kwek admitted that he had assisted some of the Kempeitai to torture prisoners, and that he had been forced to suspend victims and assist with giving the water treatment. He denied however beating anyone on his own accord. Kwek admitted that he had joined Washio (No.13) and Yeoh Chew Bok (No.34) in interrogating female prisoners, to compel them into confessing that they were communist supporters.

* * * * * *

When Dr Kaichiro Tokiwa, the defence counsel, opened the case for the defence on Thursday 19th September 1946, he admitted that the military administration of Penang had been coercive and oppressive, and peaceful residents had lived 'in a dark age of terror'.[39] He also said that he sincerely regretted the very drastic measures the Kempeitai had taken to impose their form of law and order, and apologised to all those who had been ill-treated and suffered permanent physical injuries, and especially to the families of those killed.

The first witness called by Dr Tokiwa was 45 year old Major Higashigawa, who related that the second round-ups, carried out on 2nd, 6th and 7th April 1942, had been on the orders of Lieut-Colonel Oishi. It was Higashigawa's opinion that a bomb explosion on 11th February was the reason for organising this second round-up, and a third was subsequently carried out six months later in October 1942. Mainly Chinese males were arrested in the April round-ups, but Higashigawa categorically denied any knowledge that his Kempeitai officers or men had used any force on these suspects, neither was he aware of any deaths occurring in Penang Prison. He did confirm however that the aim of round-ups was to liquidate all suspected communists.

In his defence Captain Terata claimed that the Kempeitai in Penang were the best in Malaya. In 1942 only 110 people had been arrested, declining to 60 in 1944, and merely 30 in 1945. Although he required his subordinates to maintain discipline, he also wanted them to be gentle and fair-minded. He considered the physical condition of Jack Bennett at the time of his arrest by the police, and when he was handed over to the Kempeitai, was very poor. Later, when he was being sent to Singapore, something went wrong and Bennett died at the Navy Headquarters at the convent within 30 minutes of being given an injection. Terata praised the actions of Ito (No.19) and Mitsui (No.14) who had helped to save lives during an Allied bombing raid of Penang. On another occasion Watanabe (No.18) and Katto (No.30) had helped to rescue many passengers when two ships had collided in the harbour. Terata claimed that on the surrender he gave strict orders to his Kempeitai subordinates to guard Penang until the British arrived. Those three weeks were difficult as many unruly elements tried to infiltrate the island intent on instigating trouble. Mrs Van Sanden — a housekeeper at the Kempeitai headquarters — said in evidence that Terata had on several occasions admonished his subordinates for ill-treating suspects. By contrast, Terata's own efforts to try and save his subordinates at his own expense compared favourably with the self-survival attitude of Major Higashigawa.

In response to the accusation that he had decapitated two young boys, Tonishi (No.27), a short barrel-chested 30-year old, claimed that he had refused to do so. Suzuki (No.15), a very evil character, had threatened both him and Hasagewa (No.26), and only after that had Hasagewa carried out the order.

Kamada (No.3) was warned by the president of the War Crimes Court, Lieut-Colonel Smith, that he should not attack the character of any of the prosecution witnesses when he gave evidence as this would entitle the prosecution to use such evidence in a personal attack on his own character. Kamada's attitude was negative. He claimed that witnesses had lied and the military court had no jurisdiction over him. He considered it unnecessary to defend himself. He was instructed that the prosecution had already established proof of their charges against him, and without any reliable witnesses to refute this evidence, his denial was no defence. Kamada reaffirmed that he had no witnesses to produce. The first round-up on 11th February 1942, he claimed, was to arrest suspected communists who had been terrorising the island. One senior Japanese officer had been murdered and several civil affairs officers had been attacked. People cooperating with the Japanese had also been killed, and police stations had been raided. Kamada denied that he had interrogated females, and stated that Tonishi's previous statements about 600 people having been arrested and tortured in April 1942 was a matter of incorrect translation, as was the evidence of Kwek Tiong Hin (No.31) concerning his part in torturing prisoners.

Following this, Shimizu (No.9) admitted he had beaten Naidu with a ruler but denied suspending him or giving him the water treatment. Under cross examination Shimizu admitted that Dr Letchumanasamy had probably seen him beating Naidu. Wakui (No.5) said he was in Penang only from 20th January until 30th November 1943. He denied beating Scully and burning a suspect's cheeks or crushing his fingers between pieces of wood. The witness Kolanda Vellu had a grudge against him.

Miura (No.4), with hands in pockets while giving evidence, denied torturing people despite the evidence of several witnesses.

Similarly, Murakami (No.12) denied using electric shock treatments on prisoners, although eight witnesses had said that he was the electric torture 'expert'. The only explanation he could offer was that they must have disliked him intensely. Washio (No.13) barked out his replies. He denied stripping women or dragging them naked behind a motorcycle. He denied hitting any women, despite Sergeant Saheki's (No.21) statement that it was a known fact. Washio insisted that suspects' hands were only tied behind them when they were in the cells to prevent them from committing suicide. He denied all the evidence given by 19 independent witnesses that he had stripped women naked and probed their bodies with sticks.

In his closing defence address Dr Tokiwa separated the overall responsibility for the supervision of activities in Penang Prison from the individual circumstances surrounding the various accused. In Penang, in addition to the Kempeitai, there had also been the occupational Military Administration, as well as the Japanese Navy and Army. Each had its respective headquarters and worked in parallel with the others. The role of the Kempeitai was, he claimed, subsidiary to the others and more for liaison purposes. The Japanese garrison commander had ordered the round-ups, and supervision of the prison came under the Military Administration, not the Kempeitai. It was acknowledged that many deaths had occurred in the prison, but most of these were from acts of suicide, or were legal executions, or due to various diseases, malnutrition, and insufficient medical facilities, or from natural causes.

Terata and Higashigawa both pleaded for clemency on behalf of their subordinates before the court retired. In a loud, firm voice Terata said,

> 'I do not care a bit what happens to me. I only ask the Court to be lenient for my men.'[40]

He admitted that some of them had done wrong, but the real fault stemmed from the Japanese military system. He sincerely regretted the ill-treatment of civilians in Penang caused by his own carelessness. The strict discipline in the Japanese army had perverted his subordinates. Higashigawa pleaded on behalf of his subordinates' many relatives in Japan. He said that their families would be grateful if a lenient sentence was passed.

* * * * * *

The Penang War Crime trials invoked massive local interest and lasted almost one month. Throughout the proceedings the High Court was invariably packed, especially when sentences were announced. A verdict was handed down on 28th September 1946, and 20 of the accused were sentenced to death by hanging, one was sentenced to be shot, with a recommendation for mercy, and another 11 were sentenced to varying terms of imprisonment. Only three were acquitted.

The following accused were sentenced to death by hanging:

No.1 Major Higashigawa
No.3 Kamada
No.4 Miura
No.5 Wakui
No.6 Ogawa
No.7 Yamada
No.9 Shimizu
No.10 Imai
No.11 Yokomi
No.12 Murakami
No.13 Washio
No.17 Nagata
No.18 Watanabi
No.21 Saheki
No.22 Hashimoto
No.23 Egusa
No.27 Tonishi
No.31 Kwek Tiong Hin
No.33 Khor Kee Siang
No.34 Yeoh Chew Bok

When sentence was handed down in respect of Captain Terata (No.2), Lieut-Colonel Smith said,

> 'Captain Terata — death by shooting, with a recommendation to mercy on the grounds that although you were directly responsible for the acts of your subordinates, it has been given in evidence that since you assumed command of the Penang Kempeitai, conditions were improved through your personal efforts.'[41]

When this was translated Terata seemed unable to believe what he had heard.

On 18th December 1946 the *Straits Echo and Times of Malaya* headlines read: 'Twenty Kempeis Hanged; Life Term for Terata'. The recommendation for mercy for Isamu Terata had been upheld and the sentence of execution by shooting was commuted to one of life imprisonment. The other 20 war criminals were hung on 17th December at Penang Prison under conditions of strict secrecy. Before their execution, a Japanese priest from Kedah performed the last Shinto rites, and several of the condemned went to the gallows singing Japanese military songs and shouting 'Banzai'.

* * * * * *

Many derived grim consolation from the various War Crime Trials as they endeavoured to forget and somehow forgive the evils of the Japanese occupation, and cope with the after effects of the war. By 31st December 1946, 199 Japanese war criminals had been sentenced to death in Malaya and Singapore, and 109 had been executed. In addition to these, another 246 had been sentenced to varying terms of imprisonment. The reaction of the public in general however was one of dismay over what they considered to be Britain's leniency in the aftermath of so much suffering.

Japan's guilt for war crimes committed in the Far East continues unabated and spans more than half a century, evoking another recent apology proffered in Singapore by Prime Minister Toshiki Kaifu in mid-1991.

* * * * * *

'Have you forgotten yet? . . .
For the world's events have rumbled on since those gagged days,
Like traffic checked awhile at the crossing of city ways:
And the haunted gap in your mind has filled with thoughts that flow
Like clouds in the lit heaven of life; and you're a man reprieved to go,
Taking your peaceful share of Time, with joy to spare.
But the past is just the same — and War's a bloody game . . .
Have you forgotten yet? . . .
Look down, and swear by the slain of the War that you'll never forget.'[42]

1. *Shenton of Singapore. Governor and Prisoner of War* by Brian Montgomery, ch.9, p.178.
2. *The Knights of Bushido. A Short History of Japanese War Crimes* by Lord Russell of Liverpool, ch.3, p.55.
3. *The Fall of Singapore* by Frank Owen, ch.4, p.57–8.
4. Ibid, ch.1, p.11.
5. *The Way It Was* by Alex L. Archer, ch.13, p.109.
6. *The Knights of Bushido. A Short History of Japanese War Crimes* by Lord Russell of Liverpool, ch.3, p.53–4.
7. Ibid, ch.3, p.54.
8. Ibid, ch.3, p.55–6.
9. *Ma-Rai-Ee* by Chin Kee Onn, ch.9, p.99.
10. *The Knights of Bushido. A Short History of Japanese War Crimes* by Lord Russell of Liverpool, ch.3, p.66.
11. *Japan Against the World 1941–2041. The 100–Year War for Supremacy* by Russell Braddon, ch.9, p.140.
12. *The Knights of Bushido. A Short History of Japanese War Crimes* by Lord Russell of Liverpool, ch.9, p.127.
13. *Women Beyond the Wire* by Lavinia Warner and John Sandilands, ch.14, p.232.
14. *Shenton of Singapore. Governor and Prisoner of War* by Brian Montgomery, ch.8, p.151.
15. *The Knights of Bushido. A Short History of Japanese War Crimes* by Lord Russell of Liverpool, ch.9, p.164.
16. *Mountbatten* by Philip Ziegler, ch.23, p.301.
17. *Keesing's Contemporary Archives*, September 8–15, 1945, p.7423.
18. *Mountbatten* by Philip Ziegler, ch.23, p.302.
19. *The Knights of Bushido. A Short History of Japanese War Crimes* by Lord Russell of Liverpool, ch.5, p.81.
20. Ibid, ch.5, p.82.
21. Ibid, ch.12, p.191.
22. Ibid, ch.12, p.188.
23. Ibid, ch.11, p.172. (Refers to *The Scourge of the Swastika*, ch.3.)
24. Ibid, ch.11, p.173.
25. Ibid, ch.7, p.101.
26. *The Jungle Is Neutral* by F. Spencer Chapman DSO, ch.2, p.31.

27. Ibid, ch.10, p.207–8.
28. Ibid, ch.14, p.282.
29. *The Knights of Bushido. A Short History of Japanese War Crimes* by Lord Russell of Liverpool, ch.6, p.87.
30. *Sinister Twilight* by Noel Barber, ch.8, p.161.
31. *The Knights of Bushido. A Short History of Japanese War Crimes* by Lord Russell of Liverpool, ch.14, p.216.
32. *Shenton of Singapore. Governor and Prisoner of War* by Brian Montgomery, ch.8, p.152.
33. Ibid, ch.8, p.153.
34. Ibid, ch.8, p.154.
35. *Japan Against the World 1941–2041. The 100–Year War for Supremacy* by Russell Braddon, ch.21, p.308.
36. *Women Beyond the Wire* by Lavinia Warner and John Sandilands, ch.10, p.161.
37. *Straits Echo and Times of Malaya*, Saturday 31 August 1946. Article entitled 'Kempeitai's Reign of Terror. Slaughter Recalled at War Crimes Trials'.
38. *Sunday Gazette*, Penang, 1 September 1946.
39. *Straits Echo and Times of Malaya*, Friday 20 September 1946.
40. *Sunday Gazette*, Penang, 29 September 1946.
41. *Sunday Gazette*, Penang, 29 September 1946. Article entitled 'Crowded Court Hears Sentence on Kempei. Hundreds Jammed the Gallery of the Penang War Crimes Court'.
42. 'Aftermath'. The first verse of the poem by Siegfried Sassoon, 1886–1967. 'My Subject is War and the Pity of War'. *The Lives and Writings of the 1914–18 War Poets* by Robert Giddings, p.181.

Bibliography

Kathigasu, Sybil — *No Dram of Mercy*. Oxford University Press, Singapore, 1983.

Kennedy, J. — *A History of Malaya. AD 1400–1959*. Macmillan, London, 1967.

Kirby, Woodburn S. Maj-Gen, CB, CMG, CIE, OBE, MC — *The War Against Japan*. Vols 1 & 5. 'Singapore – The Chain of Disaster.' H.M.S.O., 1957.

Lebra, Joyce C. — *Jungle Alliance — Japan & the Indian National Army*. Asia Pacific Press, Singapore, 1971.

Lindsay, Oliver — *At the Going Down of the Sun. 1941–45 Hong Kong and South East Asia*. Sphere Books, London, 1982.

Low, N.I. — *When Singapore Was Syonan-to*. Eastern Universities Press, Singapore, 1981.

Lucas, Laddie — *Wings of War*. Hutchinson, London, 1983.

Mackensie, Compton — *Eastern Epic*. Chatto & Windus, 1951.

Mahathir, b. Mohamad — *The Malay Dilemma*. Federal Publications, Malaysia, 1982.

Mars, Alastair — *British Submarines at War 1939–45*. Kimber, London, 1971.

Maxwell, Sir George, KBE, CMG — *The Civil Defence of Malaya*. Hutchinson, London, 1944.

Montgomery, Brian — *Shenton of Singapore; Governor & Prisoner of War*. Times Books International, Singapore, 1953.

Moran, Jack W.G. — *Spearhead in Malaya*. Peter Davies, London, 1959.

Owen, Frank — *The Fall of Singapore*. Michael Joseph, London, 1960.

Packard, Jerrold M. — *Sons of Heaven. A Portrait of the Japanese Monarchy*. MacDonald, London, 1988.

Percival, A.E. Lt-Gen. — *The War in Malaya*. Eyre & Spottiswoode, London, 1949.

Purcell, V., CMG, PhD. — *Malaysia*. Walker, New York, 1965.
The Chinese in Malaya. Oxford University Press, Kuala Lumpur, 1967.

Rahman, Tungku Abdul, Putra al-Haj — *Looking Back: Monday Musings and Memories*. Pustaka Antara, Kuala Lumpur, 1977.

Rivett, Rohan D. — *Behind Bamboo*. Angus & Robertson, 1950.

Robertson, Eric — *The Japanese File. Pre-war Japanese Penetration in Southeast Asia*. Heinemann (Asia), Hong Kong, 1979.

Roff, W.R. — *The Origins of Malay Nationalism*. University of Malaya Press, Kuala Lumpur, 1980.

Rose, Angus — *Who Dies Fighting*. Cape, 1944.

Roskill, Capt S.W., DSC — *The War at Sea*. Vol.4, Part 2. H.M.S.O., 1956.

Russell, E.F.L., Lord of Liverpool — *The Knights of Bushido. A Short History of Japanese War Crimes.* Corgi Books, England, 1980.

Ryan, N.J. — *The Makings of Modern Malaysia. A Study from Earliest Times to 1966.* Oxford University Press, 1968.

Saravanamuthu, M. — *The Sara Saga.* Penang, Malaya, 1951.

Searle, R. — *Forty Drawings.* Cambridge University Press, 1946.

Shinozaki, Mamoru — *Syonan — My Story. (The Japanese Occupation of Singapore).* Times Books International, Singapore, 1982.

Simson, Ivan — *Singapore. Too Little Too Late.* Leo Cooper, 1970.

Smyth, Sir John G.,VC — *Percival & the Tragedy of Singapore.* MacDonald, London, 1971.

Spector, Ronald H. — *Eagle against the Sun: The American War with Japan.* New York, 1984.

Tan, Yeok Seong — *The Extortion by Japanese Military Administration of M$50,000,000 from the Chinese in Malaya.* Nanyang Book Co., Singapore, 1947.

Thorne, Christopher G. — *Allies of a Kind: The United States, Great Britain and the War against Japan 1941–1945.* Oxford University Press, 1979.
The Far Eastern War, States and Societies 1941–45. Counterpoint, London, 1986.

Tierney, Jane — *Tobo: One Woman's Escape.* Piatakus, London, 1985.

Toye, Hugh — *Subhash Chandra Bose (The Springing Tiger). A Study of Revolution.* Jaico Publishing House, Bombay, 1978.

Traill, H.F. O'Brien — *Some Shape of Beauty.* The Incorporated Society of Planters, Kuala Lumpur, 1986.

Tregonning, K. Gordon — *A History of Modern Malaya.* Eastern Universities Press, 1964.
Malaysia. Donald Moore, Singapore, for the Australian Institute of International Affairs, 1965.

Warner, L. and Sandilands, J. — *Women Behind the Wire. A Story of Prisoners of the Japanese, 1942–1945.* Michael Joseph, London, 1982.

Weller, George — *Singapore Is Silent.* Harcourt Brace, New York, 1943.

Winstedt, R.O., KBE, CMG, FBA, D.Lit, LL.D — *A History of Malaya.* Marican & Sons (Malaya), Kuala Lumpur, 1988.
Malaya and Its History. Hutchinson, London, 1953.

Young, Peter, Brig. (Edited by) — *The Almanac of World War 2.* Hamlyn, Bison Books, 1981.

Ziegler, Philip — *Mountbatten. The Official Biography.* Fontana Paperbacks, 1985.

Other Sources

Penang Past & Present; Historical Account of the City of George Town since 1786. Published by City Council of George Town, 1966.

Malaysia in History — Focus on Penang, December 1978.

Penang Shimbun Publications. 2602–4 and 2605.

Articles from *Straits Echo & Times of Malaya* and *Sunday Gazette* by Augustin, J.A. and Cheah, C.L.

Malayan Gazette editorial, Friday 16th December 1941 (Penang State Museum).

Straits Echo & Times of Malaya and *Sunday Gazette*, Tuesday 14th September, 1945.

Articles from *The Star* newspaper (various dates).

Chronology and Index of 2nd World War. Newspaper Archives Development Ltd.

Encyclopaedia Britannica, Vols 12, 14 & 23. (William Benton, 1966.)

Keesings Contemporary Archives seen at Worthing Library, West Sussex, England in 1985.

Unpublished References
Public Record Office, Kew, London

WO 172/1784 — Captain T.J. Hilken DSO, Diary Report of the Proceedings at Penang, 25th September 1945.

PREM 3/161/1 — Malayan Civil Defence.

PREM 3/363/3 — Publicity concerning Japanese Treatment of British Prisoners of War and Civilian Internees, dated 24th January 1944.

PREM 3/161/1 — Duff Cooper to the Rt Hon. Winston S. Churchill, dated 18th September 1941.

Duff Cooper to the Rt Hon. Winston S. Churchill, dated 20th September 1941.

Telegram from Governor Sir Shenton Thomas to the Secretary of State for the Colonies, dated 3rd January 1942.

Extract from telegram from Duff Cooper to the Secretary of State, dated 3rd January 1942.

From Lord Moyne, Colonial Office to the Prime Minister, dated 6th January 1942.

T.O.O. 1500R/12. From the Prime Minister to the Colonial Secretary.

PREM 4 — Selection from Confidential Papers, 1939–1946.

CAB 69 — Selection from War Cabinet Defence Committee (Operations), 1940–1945.

CO 717 — Selection from Federated Malay States Original Correspondence, 1920–1951.

Other Unpublished Sources and Personal Letters to the Author

Childs, Jack — Series of letters, November 1984 – August 1989. Mr Childs was in the 2nd East Surreys and Leicester Regiment and was taken prisoner in Penang in December 1941.

Harvey, F.W. (Comm.) — Salvation Army, Penang. Comm. Harvey refused to evacuate when Penang was overrun by the Japanese.

James, C.H. (Col. Rt) — Letter dated 22nd November 1984. Col. James was a Dental Officer at Glugor in 1940–41.

Laird, R. — Letters dated 30th October, 23rd November and 31st December 1984. Mr Laird was in Penang from October to December 1941.

Lewis, S.D. — Mr Lewis was at the RAF station at Butterworth in November 1941.

McLeod, Capt. A.L. — Personal experiences between 1939 and 1942.

Molesworth, E.W. — Letter dated 3rd January 1985. Mr Molesworth was in Penang from 1936 to 1941 and served in the 3rd Bn SSVF.

Pettitt, S.R. — Hon. Secretary, London FEPOW Assocn.

Pitcher, G.R. — Letters dated 25th November 1984, 18th February and 23rd October 1985. Mr Pitcher was in the 11th Division Royal Corps of Signals at Sungei Patani in 1941.

Skinner, R.M. — Letter dated 24th July 1984.

Watts, R. Hugh (dec.) — Personal Memoirs, 1981.

Interviews

6th June 1984, Penang. Sister Xaverine, Convent of the Infant Jesus, concerning pre-war conditions in Penang.

29th June 1984, Penang. Dr Arnold Warltier of Middlesex, England, who was a Lieut. in the Royal Marines in Force Roma on 3rd September 1945.

2nd July 1984. Mr Hugh Watts, proprietor/manager of Sungei Ara Estate, Glugor, Penang, who was a pre-war planter and in the 3rd Bn SSVF and thence a prisoner of war after the fall of Singapore.

14th July 1984. Mr Pothera Sreedharan of Sungei Ara Estate, Glugor, who was a pre-war planter in Penang.

5th August 1984. Mr Law Joo Keun AMN, PKT, PJK, the Hon. Secretary of the Senior Citizens Assocn in Penang, who was born in Penang.

25th August 1984. Mrs Lily Cordea De Seira at her home in Penang, on life in occupied Penang for a young mother.

16th December 1984. The Very Reverend Father I.I. Aloysius (Vicar General) at the Church of Saint Francis Xavier, Penang Rd, on his recollections of Penang before and after the Japanese occupation.

4th February 1985. Brother Anthony McNamara, Superior of the Community of Saint Xaviers in Penang, regarding pre-war living conditions in Penang and the after effects of the occupation.

5th June 1985. Mr Heah Hock Khoon JSM, eldest son of the late Mr Heah Joo Seang, Penang Chinese community leader during 1942–45, regarding the difficulties that his father faced during that period.